TEACHING ADOLESCENTS
IN SECONDARY SCHOOLS

TEXTBOOKS IN EDUCATION

William H. Burton, *Consulting Editor*

An Approach to Guidance, by Edna Dorothy Baxter.

Growth and Development of the Preadolescent, by Arthur Witt Blair and William H. Burton.

The Diagnosis and Treatment of Learning Difficulties, by Leo J. Brueckner and Guy L. Bond.

Student Teaching in the Elementary School, 2nd ed., by James R. Burr, Lowry W. Harding, and Leland B. Jacobs.

Guidebook for Elementary Student Teachers, by Isabel Miller, George E. Dickson, and Loren R. Tomlinson.

The Guidance of Learning Activities, 2nd ed., by William H. Burton.

Supervision, 3rd ed., by William H. Burton and Leo J. Brueckner.

Education for Effective Thinking, by William H. Burton, Roland B. Kimball, and Richard L. Wing.

Education and Morals, by John L. Childs.

Public Education in America, 2nd ed., by George R. Cressman and Harold W. Benda.

The Third Curriculum, by Robert W. Frederick.

Educational Psychology, by Karl C. Garrison and J. Stanley Gray. Also accompanying *Workbook,* by Karl C. Garrison, Ira E. Aaron, and Joseph C. Bledsoe.

Introduction to Educational Research, by Carter V. Good.

Methods of Research, by Carter V. Good and Douglas E. Scates.

Human Relations in School Administration, by Daniel E. Griffiths.

Guidance in Democratic Living, by Arthur Hollingshead.

The Guidance Function in Education, by Percival W. Hutson.

Early Elementary Education, by Myrtle M. Imhoff.

The Child and His Curriculum, 3rd ed., by J. Murray Lee and Dorris May Lee.

The Child and His Development, by J. Murray Lee and Dorris May Lee.

The Preadolescent, by Mary Jane Loomis.

Changing the Curriculum, by Alice Miel.

Teaching Adolescents in Secondary Schools, 2nd ed., by Harry N. Rivlin.

The American Secondary School, by L. O. Taylor, Don R. McMahill, and Bob L. Taylor.

Education and the Democratic Faith, by Ephraim Vern Sayers and Ward Madden.

Statistical Methods in Educational and Psychological Research, by James E. Wert, Charles O. Neidt, and J. Stanley Ahmann.

HARRY N. RIVLIN

Dean of Teacher Education
The City University of New York

TEACHING ADOLESCENTS

in Secondary Schools

THE PRINCIPLES OF EFFECTIVE TEACHING IN JUNIOR AND SENIOR HIGH SCHOOLS

Second Edition

New York: APPLETON-CENTURY-CROFTS, Inc.

PRINTED IN THE UNITED STATES OF AMERICA
E-74396

To My Wife

EUGÉNIE GRACIANY RIVLIN

with even more gratitude and affection

PREFACE

FEW EXPERIENCES are the equivalent of the process of revising a book after a decade has elapsed. Rereading what one wrote a little more than ten years earlier focuses attention on the changes in thinking and in practices that have occurred, changes that are sometimes unnoticed as they go on from day to day.

During the past decade, secondary school teachers have seen the reappraisal of the curriculum by both educators and laymen, the development of new proposals for changes in the organization of secondary education and in curricular practices, increased concern for the education of bright adolescents, and growing recognition of the impact which population movements have had on the secondary school.

These four factors are reflected in this edition but not to the exclusion of other major questions that are also important for secondary school teachers. Schools must adjust to changes in the society they serve, but they must be more than weather vanes which change direction with each breeze.

At no other period has secondary education been the topic of so much public discussion. Unfortunately, much of the criticism of secondary education has been emotional rather than rational, and the factual basis for the criticism has sometimes been less than convincing. Yet, educators themselves have raised significantly pointed questions. Without becoming defensive or panicky, educators have been re-examining school practices in order to see whether secondary education can be improved, and how. This revaluation is bound to help secondary education, for the teacher's level of aspiration affects the quality of learning just as surely as the student's level of aspiration does.

The secondary school teacher must be capable of examining the various proposals for change that have been advanced not only to evaluate their desirability but also to see whether they can be improved by modification. For example, the key question today is not whether team teaching is good or bad or whether teaching machines are effective or ineffective. More important, the teacher must help determine when team teaching and teaching machines are better than existing procedures and such a book as this must help him to see how, or whether, they can be employed to improve the education of boys and girls.

The protests of the life-adjustment advocates that secondary schools are underestimating the needs of adolescents who are not preparing for college have been all but drowned out by the criticism that the bright students are being neglected. Here, too, the criticism is not entirely justified. The question it raises, however, is one which concerns the secondary school teacher more and more. It has led to numerous ways of enriching the quality of education for all youth and to improving the opportunities available to the gifted. For example, the high school curriculum now includes the study of areas of mathematics which were only recently reserved for colleges. Similarly, the procedures described in this book must be stimulating enough for our ablest students.

Probably the most dramatic change in the secondary schools has come about as a result of a vast population movement. Throughout the country millions of people have left the big cities for the suburbs, and one-time rural communities and small towns have had to cope with the problems attendant upon the sudden increase in the junior and senior high school population, without adequate school facilities or staff for absorbing it.

The vacuum created in the larger cities by the flight to the suburbs was soon filled by the return to the cities of some ex-suburbanites and by a sizeable population movement from the southern states and Puerto Rico, a movement which was well under way even before there was a vacuum. Many of these new in-migrants were poorly prepared for secondary school work and had little motivation for succeeding in a program that seemed so remote from their background and interests. Simultaneously, there was a population movement westward that was numerically many times larger than the Westward Migration we studied in our high school history classes.

This concern with the effects of population movements illustrates the increased attention that educators are now giving to the social factors in learning. To be sure, the adolescent's intellectual and physical development affects his ability to learn. But how he learns and, even more important, what he learns, are also influenced greatly by the family and the peer group of which he is a part and by the values of the community in which he lives. This edition, therefore, treats more fully than did the first one the role that social factors play in influencing the adolescents' learning. There is also more attention to the ways in which the teacher can apply in the classroom some of the principles and procedures that have evolved from the studies of group dynamics.

More than ever before, secondary school teachers must be experts rather than merely intelligent amateurs. The increased complexity and importance of secondary education underline the significance of some of the attributes that have always characterized good junior and senior high school teachers: they must be masters of their subject matter; they must understand adolescents; and they must be adept at guiding and stimulating learning. New teachers must be ready to serve in the wide variety of secondary schools we have today but they must also be able to help these schools become the kind we shall need tomorrow.

For this reason, this book tries not only to give the new teacher the help he needs in solving his most pressing problems but also to develop a point of view toward teaching and toward his students that should help him to solve the countless other problems that have not been discussed. Because the development of this point of view plays so important a part in determining the teacher's success, I have addressed the last chapter to the teacher as a person. I hope no teacher will be surprised by anything he finds there, for if the book has been effective, by the time the reader comes to that chapter, he should have arrived at much the same conclusions as I.

It is encouraging to find when one rereads a book that much which was sound a decade ago is still sound and is referred to by students and their teachers as being of considerable help. It is equally encouraging to see that there have been so many new developments in some areas of secondary education that new sections had to be added to the book. And, of course, it has been necessary throughout the book to bring all the material up to date. The illustrations in this book of the ways in which the principles of effective teaching are applied have been chosen from the wide array of junior and senior high school activities, but most of them have been selected from areas that are most likely to be familiar to all teachers. In deciding which parts of the first edition were to be retained in the second edition, I found the reactions of teachers and students who used the first edition to offer invaluable guide lines, but I alone must take the responsibility for deciding what was kept, what was discarded, what was revised, and what was added.

In the questions suggested for discussion at the end of each chapter, there is little reason for stressing those that ask for nothing more than the repetition of material presented in the body of the chapter. Instead, they should apply to new situations which illustrate the principles discussed in the chapter, indicate the difficulties which arise as these principles are applied, or challenge the premises on which these principles rest. Because the question is often the most effective method of teaching, some of the most important material has been presented in the questions at the end of the chapter rather than in the textual content. So much use has been made of these questions at various colleges that new questions have been added and those that have been found to be most worthwhile in the earlier edition have been brought up-to-date when necessary.

One of the satisfactions in the preparation of the second edition came from the opportunity of seeing once more how eagerly school systems participate in the preparation of prospective teachers and in the in-service education of their present teachers. Boards of education and school superintendents, despite the pressure of all of their other duties, have been most helpful in pointing to some of the promising practices going on in their schools, as well as to the problems they face. I appreciate their graciousness, for example, in making available to me their files of pictures.

I feel especially indebted to Superintendent Samuel Miller Brownell of Detroit, Michigan; Superintendent Frederick J. Gillis of Boston, Massachusetts; Superintendent Calvin E. Gross of Pittsburgh, Pennsylvania; Superintendent Ellis A. Jarvis of Los Angeles, California; Superintendent Joseph Manch of Buffalo, New York; Superintendent Mark C. Schinnerer of Cleveland, Ohio; Superintendent John J. Theobald of New York, New York; Superintendent Harold S. Vincent of Milwaukee, Wisconsin; Superintendent Allen H. Wetter of Philadelphia, Pennsylvania; Superintendent Benjamin C. Willis of Chicago, Illinois; and to the National Education Association and other groups that granted permission to reproduce pictures. In all instances, of course, the appropriate acknowledgment of the source appears under the illustration.

As I reread the manuscript, I realized repeatedly how fortunate I was to have received so many helpful suggestions from those who were generous enough to read the earlier drafts. Only I know how much I gained from having them read by Dr. William H. Burton, Dr. Deborah Elkins, Dr. Milton Gold, Dr. Dorothy Gray, Dr. Herbert Schueler, Dr. Helen Storen, Dr. Samuel Streicher, and my wife, Eugénie G. Rivlin. The manuscript would never have become a book had it not been for the intelligent assistance of my secretary, Mrs. Adele F. Larschan.

I wish there were some way of acknowledging my indebtedness to all of the secondary school teachers and prospective teachers who have strengthened my conviction that the effectiveness of secondary school education depends so largely upon the quality of the individual secondary school teacher.

H. N. R.

CONTENTS

TEACHING ADOLESCENTS
IN SECONDARY SCHOOLS

CHAPTER 1

Secondary School Teaching Today

»»»»»»»»»»

THOSE WHO ARE about to become secondary school teachers have the great satisfaction of knowing that they are wanted and that the role which awaits them is intellectually and emotionally rewarding. It feels good to be wanted, especially when what has to be done is important and stimulating.

In our culture, a secondary education is no longer a luxury for the few; it is now a necessity for virtually all, whether we think only of earning a living or of the larger responsibilities of citizenship. The first casualties of automation are the unskilled workers. We do not need so many hewers of wood and drawers of water, but we need more people who can design our machines and operate them. In a democracy, moreover, where issues of national import are decided at the polls, our citizens need an understanding of world problems without which intelligent decisions cannot be made. When San Francisco Bay was discovered, it was six months away from Madrid; today we measure distance by the clock instead of the calendar. Our citizens must know more about their own country and about the other nations of the world than ever before, and more important, they must know how to keep on learning even after they have been graduated from school.

It has been said that the Battle of Waterloo was won on the playing fields of Eton. It is not melodramatic to say that the future of our country is being determined in its junior and senior high schools. Our secondary school teachers have the awesome responsibility of helping to shape the country's future by influencing the development of those who will be the leaders and the followers in the next generation. What will they know? What will they be able to do? What sense of values

1

will they have? With what attitudes and habits of work will they approach their tasks?

Teaching is a succession of rigorous intellectual challenges. To be sure, it is difficult for a teacher to help a secondary school student to understand the mathematics of probability but it may be even more difficult to stimulate the will to learn it. It is when the teacher tries to communicate his knowledge to others that he realizes how complete his own understanding must be before he can concentrate on the formidable task of developing understanding in his students.

Secondary school teaching is more than a succession of challenges and triumphs; it also has its annoyances, frustrations, and drudgery. Teachers have their own context for understanding the complaint: There is so much to do and so little time in which to do it. They, too, are fighting the current American problem of keeping their heads above the engulfing tide of paper work. Teachers know the thrill of seeing a student's eyes light up in a flash of insight but they also experience the frustration of being unable to strike any kind of spark in a student who seems to be encased in an impenetrable cloak of indifference.

Teaching has been called an inspiring profession and a dull job. Fortunately, each teacher has an important voice in deciding which it will be for him, since so much depends upon his grasp of his subject matter, his understanding of the students he teaches, and his insight into the teaching process. Though no teacher ever eliminates all of the annoyance and frustration, the better his command is of the teaching process the greater is the likelihood of being able to reduce the annoyances and frustrations as he goes on to enjoy the satisfactions and rewards that make teaching worthwhile.

THE TEACHER AS AN EXPERT

The teacher has always been expected to be a scholar, but today he must also be an expert in stimulating and guiding learning, in building the curriculum, and in understanding and working with people. Moreover, he has to understand the community of which the school is so important a part. The days are gone when any well-intentioned adult who knew his subject more or less well could do all that was expected of a secondary school teacher. Teaching is no longer for amateurs and one of the secondary schools' basic problems is that it is sometimes difficult to recruit and to retain teachers with the needed degree of expertness.

The Teacher as a Scholar

As a member of the community of scholars, the teacher is deeply concerned with the preservation of scholarly values and with the expansion of understanding and knowledge. To be sure, few science teachers will make an original contribution to what we know about science. Yet, in his own life, the scholar is ever expanding his own knowledge and understanding in the area he has chosen as his intellectual home.

It is not enough for the teacher to know the specific point he is trying to clarify for his students; he must know its background and its implications, and he must be informed about recent developments lest he teach a point that has been disproved and disowned by scholars. To say that a teacher must know his subject is to stress the obvious, for clearly no one can teach what he himself does not know. Yet, to say that a teacher must know his subject is also to suggest an almost unattainable ideal, for no one can ever know all about an important subject.

Requiring the teacher to have devoted a considerable portion of his collegiate and university years to the study of his special field is only a first step toward the development of the teacher's scholarship. Such a requirement may even interfere with the teacher's scholarship if it suggests that at any given point, wherever it may be determined by counting college credits, he has achieved final mastery of his subject. No scholar ever achieves such final mastery, but it is the joy of working toward that ideal which is the source of much of the scholar's satisfaction. If a school wants its teachers to be scholars, it must not only examine its requirements for appointment to the faculty but also provide the stimulation and the resources that encourage the faculty to continue studying. Whether or not the teacher will continue his studies, however, depends ultimately on his own intellectual drives.

The Teacher as an Expert in Stimulating and Guiding Learning

As the symbol of learning, the teacher wants his students to develop a love of learning. If he is to be successful, he must know how boys and girls learn and he has to be adept at stimulating and guiding learning.

It is not enough for the teacher to present his material and to give low grades to those who do not learn it. He must know how to teach those who want to learn, and he must have the spark that will light the fire in those who are indifferent to learning. He has to know how to diagnose the causes of inadequate and ineffective learning and he must know how to work alone and with others in the improvement of learning. Since the adolescent's attitude toward education is affected by the peer group of which he is a member and by the community in which he lives, the teacher must understand the social as well as the individual factors that influence learning.

Secondary education now aims at so many goals that the teacher must master various techniques in order to achieve these outcomes.

Thus, he must know how to stimulate independent thinking and he must be able to get adolescents to work together. He must be able to stir students to ask penetrating questions and he must know how to sustain interest as students drill on material that has to be mastered. The gifted adolescent with a flair for creative writing may have to be taught how to edit and revise what he has written, while another student in the same grade is still trying to master the ability to read so that he can understand what is written in his textbooks.

The Teacher as an Expert in Building the Curriculum

The teacher plays an important part in building the curriculum because of his influence on the learning activities in his class. Though the science teachers in the school may decide as a group which topics should be allocated to the various grades, each teacher must know how to select the materials, the illustrations, and the applications that will mean most for his students. The English teacher must be so thoroughly familiar with literature that he knows what is appropriate not only for his class as a whole but also for each of the students in it.

The imaginative teacher finds in this freedom to build the curriculum the means of making teaching more stimulating. For the beginner, however, this very flexibility creates additional difficulties and makes adequate preparation for teaching more important.

Contrary to what some ill-informed critics think, modern secondary school education makes heavier rather than lighter demands on the teacher's scholarship than did the secondary school of a generation or two ago. The mathematics teacher who knows no more than how to get the correct answers to the textbook problems is incapable of helping his students to develop an understanding of mathematical concepts. Similarly, the science teacher who is limited to the textbook cannot help his students to understand the methods and the findings of scientific studies, and the social studies teacher who does not have a rich background on which to draw may develop misconceptions rather than insight into social problems.

It takes more than knowledge of subject matter, however, to arouse in students the desire to learn what the teacher wants to teach. There are some would-be teachers who walk into the classroom, filled to the brim with knowledge of their subject, and walk slowly so that they will not spill anything. They walk out just as slowly—nothing has spilled. Teaching is an art and a skill which few people master without study and practice—and which some do not master even after much study and practice. Our schools should not have to choose between men of learning and those who are skilled in the technics of teaching, for our students need teachers who are both wise and skillful.

The Teacher as an Expert in Understanding and Working with People

That the secondary school teacher is expected to be an expert in understanding and working with people, especially with adolescents, is a reflection of our growing awareness of the importance of emotional adjustment. Intellectual ability is, to be sure, as important as it ever was, but we now recognize that intellectual ability alone, even highly trained intellectual ability, does not lead to achievement if the individual is seriously handicapped by emotional difficulties. Every college has students who drop out or are dropped from the college during the freshman year regardless of how high the intellectual and academic requirements for admission are set or how carefully the prospective students are selected [9]*. These failures arise largely from problems of poor adjustment. Similarly, in every junior and senior high school there are students who do not perform at the highest level of achievement of which they are capable and who need more than the nagging reminder to get to work if they are to reach that level.

When we speak of the teacher as an expert in understanding and working with people, we are not thinking of him as a clinician who is helping a disturbed child to better adjustment. In fact, we are not referring to disturbed children at all. The teacher can make a notable contribution if he confines his attention to the wide range of personality patterns included within the range of normality. The teacher has the responsibility for creating a wholesome classroom atmosphere that is conducive to achievement. He must understand why boys and girls act as they do if he is to have any lasting influence on their behavior. He needs insight into the motives underlying adolescent behavior if he is to encourage the learning he knows to be so important.

Developing insight into adolescent behavior is difficult, but it is in some respects even more difficult for the teacher to develop insight into his own behavior. Yet, it is important that he do so, for the teacher is himself an important factor in the classroom interpersonal relationships. The teacher who is tied up in emotional knots is likely to interpret classroom situations in terms of his own emotional needs instead of being free to think of his students' development. Thus, the teacher who feels a desperate need to be loved by his class may be unwilling or unable to do anything that may endanger his popularity. Similarly, the teacher who regards classroom misconduct as a personal affront and as a public demonstration of his own incompetence is handicapped in his attempts to improve classroom discipline. The teacher must understand adolescents and be able to live with them, but he must also understand himself and be able to live with himself.

* Throughout this book, the numbers enclosed within brackets refer to bibliographic references that are listed at the end of the chapter.

THE TEACHER AND THE COMMUNITY

In the United States, it is the people who ultimately decide what is to be taught in the schools and who will teach it. It is significant that the board of education, which appoints the superintendents and the teachers, is composed of lay people and not of professional educators. If the school is to fulfill its role in the contemporary scene, the teachers must understand the community that supports—and controls—the school.

The Community's Impact on Adolescents

There may be thirty-four students in the teacher's class but he must deal with more than thirty-four as he teaches because each of his students reflects the influence of parents, friends, and neighbors. The teacher who is unaware of these influences may never know why some of his most carefully prepared plans just did not materialize.

By both tangible and intangible means, the community often has a marked influence on the student's motivation for learning and on his ability to profit from his experiences at school. An adolescent living in a community which respects learning will obviously approach his school work with a different attitude from that of another youth whose community regards scholastic honors as being unattainable and unnecessary. Students coming from a community where good books are plentiful and good music is frequent have a richer background for learning than have those coming from culturally impoverished communities.

Though there are decisions which each family must make for itself, many of those choices are dictated by community pressures. For example, in most cases a married woman is free to decide whether she should seek employment now that her children are older, whether she should throw herself wholeheartedly into community organization work, or whether she should keep her home obligations uppermost in her mind. Yet, communities do vary in the way mothers spend their time, and what mothers do affects their children. Freed from adult supervision when school is out, some adolescents quickly become dependably self-reliant while others suffer from the lack of parental guidance and supervision. Similarly, the quality of family life, which is influenced by community standards and practice, will affect what adolescents do, not only outside of school but also within it.

One of the least noticed changes in the adolescent's world is the decline in his importance to adults. A century ago, the adolescent did an adult's work and helped support his family. A generation ago, he was kept off the labor market by child labor laws, but the family had many important jobs for him to do. Today, a largely urbanized and suburbanized America seemingly has little need for anything an adolescent can do—and nobody likes to feel unneeded.

There are communities where the only concern with the adolescent is to get him off their lawns or away from their street corners. Other communities think they are doing well by their adolescents when recreation centers are provided. It is the fortunate, and rare, adolescent who lives in a community where he gets the impression that he is needed right now, that there are important jobs for him to do—for example, helping bring books from the bookmobile to the bedridden patients at a hospital—and that he has more to do than merely wait till he has grown up.

Clearly, the adolescent who knows that he is a respected and important member of his community is a different kind of student from the one who feels hostile toward a hostile world.

Understanding Community Values

What makes it so difficult for the teacher to understand the community is that the community is not an abstraction; it is people—many kinds of people. Community values, moreover, are not an average of all the values held by the various people. Each of the groups in the community may have its own set of values and insist on the school's accepting it as setting the goals and determining the practices in the school, while every other group is equally insistent that its values must prevail.

The overwhelming majority of American parents are sincerely interested in helping their children to rise to a level the parents never achieved. Parents differ among themselves not so much in their devotion to their children as in the ways in which they express this devotion and in the direction which their ambitions for their children take. A father who sees the executive positions in his firm going to the men who know how to get along well with others prefers to have his son become a leader in the school's club and athletic program instead of earning pocket money by holding inconsequential part-time jobs after school. Another parent, by contrast, vividly aware of the family's poverty in his own childhood and of his later difficulties in earning enough to support his wife and children may think it more important for his sons and daughters to learn how to get a job and hold it than to fritter time away in club meetings.

Nor are parents the only ones in the community interested in what the schools do. Oddly enough, it is the faith that our citizens have in the school's power to influence students, regardless of what other forces are at work in the community, that is responsible for the school's being blamed for many of the problems that face us today, for the delinquency and the reckless driving of some youth, for the materialistic values in our culture, and for the difficulties which America faces in its technological race with the communist world.

Communities, or groups within the communities, are taking a lively interest in secondary education and are expressing that interest in many ways. Some of them, determined that their adolescents get the best education available, seek to achieve this goal by voting the increased taxes and approving the bond issues that mean higher salaries for teachers and newer school buildings, as though money alone can solve all educational problems. Others, equally sincere in their concern, believe that secondary education must return to the curriculum practices of generations ago, drop all "new-fangled frills," and reduce costs. Still others argue for concentration on that phase of the curriculum they deem most important in today's world; for example, they stress the teaching of science and mathematics even if it becomes necessary to lessen the amount of time devoted to other areas like art and music, or they urge that schools devote more time to the fine arts so that we may become what they consider a truly cultured society. No wonder some teachers wish the community would stop pushing the school in different directions.

Differences Among Communities

Despite the unifying influence of a common language and excellent transportation and communication systems, local communities vary considerably among themselves and expect their schools to reflect these differences.

The middle-class family which moves to a one-family home in the suburbs is often eager to have its children continue the social climb. These families usually provide music lessons, dancing schools, and dramatics instruction for their teen-agers so that sons and daughters will not be deprived of any of the experiences shared by their classmates. Because the high school record may determine whether or not the student will be admitted to the college favored by their neighbors, and therefore by them, the parents become active workers in every effort to improve the high school's reputation, while they exert pressure on their children to do well at school.

By contrast, there are other communities that offer their children little that nurtures the ambition to do well at school. Even affectionate parents can be so sensitive about their own lack of formal education and their poor clothing that they rarely attend parent association meetings and cannot conceive of ever speaking at one. Grimly aware of the struggle to earn enough to support a family, the parents may not appreciate the vistas which education can open to their boys and girls.

Communities differ, too, in their interpretations of democracy. Whereas one community has clearly defined social groups, members of another community may be so free in their social relationships among themselves that they cannot understand all this talk about class and caste in American society.

Yet, each community, viewing education in terms of its own values, expects the school to reflect them. The teacher must understand the community if boys and girls are to get the education they need. Such understanding, however, does not imply passive acceptance. The teacher need not and should not accept community whims and prejudices as unchangeable laws of nature. He can work toward changing them, but he cannot afford merely to ignore them.

Changes Within the Community

The teacher's understanding of the community is hindered by the fact that it may be changing in composition, in values, and in practices. Sometimes the change may be so gradual that teachers are unaware of it. For example, many an experienced teacher in a stable community does not realize how many more mothers are going to work now than was the case when the teacher was first appointed. Unaware of this change, he assumes that the family supervision of the adolescent's leisure time activities which characterized the community a generation ago is still prevalent.

At other times, the change in the community may be so rapid that he can almost see it happen. Of course, there are the resort towns where the school population surges upward as the visitors arrive in the winter or in the spring. Then, there are the schools in communities which employ migrant workers and have an almost constantly changing school population. More profound in its influence on the school are the great population movements which move thousands to the West Coast and other rapidly growing areas, more thousands from cities across the nation to the suburbs, and still other thousands from Puerto Rico, Mexico, and the southern states into the big cities in the north.

The In-migrants

For many of these children and their parents, the move to the big northern city is a giant step upward, but for the secondary school teachers accustomed to dealing with college-bound sons and daughters of striving middle-class parents, the new population creates problems and a threat to familiar standards of scholastic and social behavior.

To some teachers, the changing population of the big city makes secondary school teaching both more difficult and less pleasant. They are, apparently, interested in teaching only those students who are like what they believe themselves to have been as adolescents. They do not know how, and they sometimes are not eager to learn how, to deal with teen-agers who have no family tradition of going on to complete the high school education as preparation for going to college. That many of the new arrivals live in overcrowded homes and under conditions most teachers could not endure does not make teaching, or learning, any easier.

Learning how to teach culturally deprived adolescents takes insight and skill, but should not interfere with the teacher's ability to work with other teen-agers. If anything, the teacher should be better able to deal with his other students as a result of the attitudes, the understanding, and the skills he develops as he works with the culturally deprived. As he learns to appreciate the social and the psychological factors which affect learning, he will be better able to deal with the slow learners and the reluctant learners he will encounter in any secondary school, regardless of the source of its student body. His ability to fire the ambition of a culturally deprived group will stand him in good stead as he works with other secondary school students.

The Nation as the Community

Ours is such a mobile population that no teacher can think of secondary education as being adequate if it prepares its students only for life in that community. His students must be ready to live elsewhere in the country, and many of his students will change residence many times in a lifetime. While it is intriguing to think of a community school, our secondary schools must also be national schools. The study of vocational opportunities, for example, is inadequate and unrealistic if limited to local occupations.

National trends affect all schools. The effects of war and of peace or of recessions and of booms touch all students, albeit in varying ways, regardless of the local community pattern. Similarly, a Supreme Court decision and state or national legislation have an impact that transcends the local community. Less easily seen because the change is less sudden, the effect of changes in values and in ways of living also may come to the community from outside sources. For example, the changes in family life can be understood better when seen in the larger setting as well as in the local one.

While the secondary school curriculum reflects local community values, it must also reflect the values and the needs of the nation.

The World as the Community

With the United States a world power and with the improvement of world-wide transportation and communication, it is essential that our secondary schools see the implications of international education. The social studies courses of a generation ago are clearly inadequate today, for they usually stressed only American and European history. Too few of our citizens understand what is happening in Africa and Asia, or even in the Latin American countries nearer to us. The citizens of a world power are ill prepared for their responsibilities if they have nothing more than outworn stereotypes as a basis for judgment.

Nor is history the only subject affected by what is happening elsewhere in the world. Can we understand our economy if we ignore international interrelationships? Should our students in science classes be unaware of the progress in science being achieved in other nations? Does the study of foreign languages merit a new and more important place in the secondary schools of a world power? How can our students learn to appreciate their American heritage and to appreciate, too, America's present role in world affairs? These are typical of the questions our schools must answer as they seek to meet their responsibilities to the broader definition of the community.

Even the problems which a teacher faces in his own school can be understood better by those who recognize the similarities and the differences between American secondary education and secondary education in other countries. For this reason, we are including in the Appendix a copy of *Recommendation No. 50 to the Ministries of Education Concerning the Preparation and Issuing of General Secondary School Curricula* as adopted at the Twenty-third International Conference on Education by the representatives of sixty-six nations. By reading this resolution, American secondary school teachers can see the basic similarity in the questions which confront educators throughout the world. The teacher may also be interested in the contrasts between secondary education in a country such as ours, which considers all adolescents to be entitled to secondary education, and the conditions which prevail in countries which are so far from achieving universal elementary education that they see little prospect of developing a system of secondary education for all youth. There are, moreover, the differences to be found between the practices of countries which have a highly centralized ministry of education and the educational practices in countries which favor local control.

THE COMMUNITY'S QUESTIONS ABOUT SECONDARY EDUCATION

While secondary school teachers have been studying the community, the community has been studying the secondary schools. In neither case is the evaluation always favorable.

School people used to be concerned with public apathy toward education. Now that there is so much public discussion, school people are disturbed because the discussion, unfortunately, is often so highly charged with emotion. People seem to be dividing themselves into two camps: the attackers of secondary education, who see almost nothing good in anything that is being done, and the defenders of secondary education, who feel compelled to come to the immediate defense of any school which is being criticized.

In some respects, the criticisms of secondary education parallel those which are leveled at contemporary American culture. Thus, we hear that the schools are anti-intellectual and we also hear that America is a non-intellectual nation. We are told that high school students attach more importance to learning how to drive a car than to mastering the intricacies of a foreign language, but we are also told that families spend more money on new refrigerators than on new books. There are critics who say that America is becoming a soft nation, more concerned with extending the coffee break and shortening the work week than with improving the quality of the product. In almost the same breath, some critics add that the secondary school curriculum has grown so soft as to be limp.

Such generalizations as these are always difficult to prove or to disprove. To the extent, however, that they are true, they need correction and need it at once. However rich and powerful our nation may be, it cannot maintain either its wealth or its strength once we become complacent about our values or allow our practices to fall short of the ideals we profess. Have some secondary schools reflected all too well the current values and the inadequate practices of society?

Secondary school teachers may not be in a position to change American life, but they can certainly affect the lives of the students enrolled in school. A teacher who condones shoddy work is being untrue to the ideals of scholarship and to his responsibilities as a citizen in a democracy. It is difficult for the citizens of an established and prosperous country to maintain the enthusiasm and the morale of the citizens of a new country which is fighting for its existence. For this very reason, the American secondary school must help our adolescents to understand their importance in the world and the responsibility that only they can assume for their contribution to the continued development of our country.

Such an objective is not to be achieved merely by hardening the curriculum or by lengthening the school day. What the teacher must sense, and then help students to understand, is that education is life and that the important values in life are also important in the school. He must convince his students that although a high school diploma may be important for opening the door to job opportunities that would otherwise be closed, high school education is more important than the diploma which is awarded at graduation. He must help them to see the importance of the standards and the values they develop while at school.

The thought that schools are getting along fairly well is as unsatisfying as is the thought that the nation is getting along fairly well. We cannot afford to glorify the nonexistent value of getting along fairly well when the temper of the times demands more. No teacher, aware as he is of the importance and the power of education, should ever condone inefficient or ineffective education. On the other hand, no intelligent citizen can blind himself to basic contemporary social problems by blaming all of our national difficulties on the secondary school curriculum. We must examine both our schools and our culture, rejoicing in the progress that has been made and removing the obstacles which stand in the way of further improvement.

There are some very real problems confronting the secondary school and there are basic questions that demand careful thought. Yet, our attempt to define the purposes of the secondary school and to evaluate the success with which the schools are achieving these goals has been hampered by emotional appeals and by the intrusion of irrelevant considerations.

The Increased Competition for the Tax Dollar

The American people demand more and better services from the government: they want hospitals, parks, police, schools, and much more—and they want them in quantity and in quality. Unfortunately for the secondary schools, the period of great increase in the size of the secondary school population has come at a time of rising government budgets and mounting public resistance to higher taxes.

When schools do not get the money they need, there are overcrowded schools, over-sized classes, over-worked teachers, and in all too many cases, temporary and only partly prepared teachers. Communities which want first-rate schools are getting second-rate ones, even though their school tax has gone up.

There is a popular fallacy that there is no problem in education that money cannot solve. But a bad chef can spoil even the choicest cut of beef. Nevertheless, poverty does not improve either teaching or cooking. When schools are so pinched for money that they do not have the funds for books, for equipment, or for adequate housing, even good teachers become less effective. How can one teach science without a laboratory and a library?

Since the costs of education are ordinarily the largest single item in the local budget, they are an obvious target for criticism. Can our secondary schools be run for less money? Are they worth what they cost? These are the thoughts in people's minds as they ask questions which seem to concern themselves with the goals of secondary education and the procedures used in the schools.

Inexpert Execution of Educational Plans

Sometimes criticism of secondary schools arises not because the educational objectives or procedures are unwise but rather because they are imperfectly executed. A sound program badly conducted by inexpert people is hardly likely to arouse enthusiasm. Many a parent, after leaving a PTA meeting where he heard an inspiring talk about the newer procedures in secondary education, feels enthusiastic about the description of what the secondary school is doing for its students until the jarring thought comes to mind, "But that isn't the kind of teacher my Charlie has."

There is no gainsaying the thesis set forth earlier in this chapter that modern secondary education demands expert teachers. What does the "newer mathematics," with its attempt to develop insight into mathematical relationships, mean to a teacher whose knowledge of mathematics is so limited that he feels completely lost if you take his set of geometry propositions away from him? No wonder students are confused. The remedy is to be found not in discarding the new mathematics but in getting expert mathematics teachers.

At times, public pressure compels the school, or at least school administrators think the school is being compelled, to adopt procedures it considers unwise or which it is not prepared to adopt. Thus, some schools admit students to a college preparatory program, one for which these children are not suited, because the principal does not have the courage to tell the students and their parents that these youths are not college material. Communities want the best for their children and, when they hear that the "new mathematics" is being taught elsewhere, they want it taught in their schools, even when they have no teacher who understands the new mathematics or knows how to teach it.

There is as much variation of ability among secondary school administrators as there is among secondary school teachers. Though educational research provides an increasingly valid source of data upon which to base a decision, making the decision calls for judgment. Thus, a study which demonstrates that an experimental program worked well under one set of circumstances does not prove that it will be equally successful under other circumstances. Jumping onto the bandwagon is always easier and more popular than trying to see where the parade is going. As a result, we have seen fads sweeping education, accompanied by wide swings of the pendulum. Usually, it is in the schools in which the leadership is least courageous and least wise that the swings are widest.

Here, too, we have an instance in which people who think they have found serious weaknesses in the school's objectives and curriculum should be attacking the causes which made the curriculum an ineffective way of attaining these objectives.

The Basic Question about Secondary Education Today

We cannot dismiss the questions that communities are asking about the purposes and procedures of secondary education merely because extraneous issues are also being raised. Answering these questions is difficult because there are such wide differences among schools.

In one city, for example, there is a public high school from which almost 85 per cent of the graduates go on to higher education, and another public high school, only a short bus ride away, in which 60 per cent of the student body drop out before graduation and fewer than 15 per cent go on to any form of higher education. Yet, both schools are called high schools. We can make contradictory statements about high schools and be correct both times, for among the more than 21,000 schools classified by the United States Office of Education as secondary schools, one can find instances to support almost any statement, whether it be most laudatory or devastatingly critical.

Americans have a right to be proud of their achievement in making secondary education almost as universal as is elementary school education. Are we paying too great a price for the extension of secondary education?

Are Our High School Students as Well Educated as They Used to Be?

Fortunately, this is a question that can be answered by looking at the facts. For example, one of the most widely used test batteries are the tests that comprise the General Educational Development Tests of the United States Armed Forces Institute. Comparing the results when this battery was administered to high school seniors in 1955 with the results of a similar testing program in 1943, Bloom summarized the findings as follows:

In each of the GED tests the performance of the 1955 sample of Seniors is higher than the performance of the 1943 sample. These consistent results give evidence that today's students are achieving to a greater extent the objectives measured by this battery of achievement tests than were the students of 1943. The greatest change is in mathematics, while the least change appears in the social studies. One way of expressing the change is to note that in mathematics the average Senior tested in 1955 exceeds 58 per cent of the students tested in 1943. In the natural sciences, literary materials, and English, the median Senior tested in 1955 exceeds approximately 54 per cent of the 1943 students, while in the social studies, the median 1955 Senior exceeds approximately 52 per cent of the Seniors tested in 1943. These differences are not attributable to chance variation in test results.

In general, the differences are such that the entire distribution of scores has shifted up by about 5 percentile points. Assuming comparability of tests, test conditions, and samples of students, these test results indicate that the high schools are doing a significantly better job of education in 1955 than they were doing in 1943.*

We should be justified if we were dissatisfied with these test results because we want our high school seniors to be even better than they are today, but there is no support in these test results, or in any other large-scale objective testing program reported in the literature, for being alarmed by the supposed steady deterioration of the high school.

Are the Secondary Schools Too Heterogeneous to Be Effective?

At first glance, there appears to be a simple way out of our problems in secondary education: Why not limit secondary school attendance to students who are prepared for it and eager to come? Why not separate the academic students from the nonacademic students for instructional purposes while they mingle freely in such activities as take place, for example, in the auditorium or the gymnasium?

In any school system, we can select a varying percentage of students—say, ten per cent in some schools and twenty-five per cent in others—who are top students and who need and should get a strongly academic secondary school education. We can also identify fairly accurately another percentage of students—say, ten per cent in some schools and twenty-five per cent in other schools—who will profit little from an academic secondary school education. There is a large group of students, however, who have intellectual ability that should be nurtured and among whom there are some potentially really able people whose promise must not be snuffed out prematurely.

European countries which have had long experience with a two-class system of education can give eloquent testimony of the tension and often the tragedy that result when the day of sorting the sheep from the goats approaches [13, 15]. The United States, too, has had a taste of these conditions. Which school has not met the ambitious parent who, in order to have his child admitted to a special program, takes the youngster to psychologist after psychologist in the search for a higher IQ score, alternately coaxes and threatens his child to get him to raise his school grades, and then argues with the principal to get the teacher's ratings

* Reprinted by permission from B. S. Bloom, "The 1955 Normative Study of the Tests of General Educational Development," *School Review*, Vol. LXIV, No. 3 (March, 1956), p. 113.

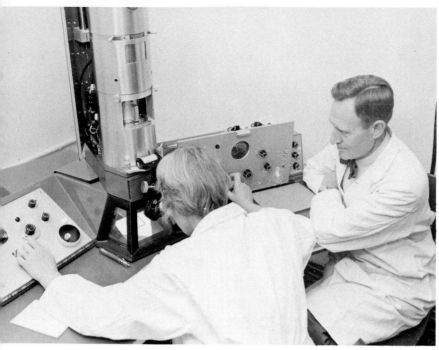

The teacher is a scholar
and is expert in stimulating and guiding learning.

The teacher understands adolesce

nd knows how to work with them.

*Teachers select appropriate
materials for their own classes.*

The teacher is skilled in organizing materials for learning.

*Curriculum committees help
shape the school program.*

changed? Is this the pattern that points the way to better secondary education?

The American tradition of democracy in education is too deeply rooted in our national life to offer much support to any plan which aims at dividing the population into an intellectual elite and ordinary folk.

There is, however, a difference between equality of educational opportunity and identical educational treatment. All school systems have to face up to differences in abilities, in interests, and in ambitions. These adjustments may take the form of special schools for different groups of students, of special programs for the varied student body in a cosmopolitan high school, of special classes for the ablest students and for the least competent, or of differentiated assignments even within a single class.

With students of secondary school age, there is no point at which we can make the kind of rigid classification suggested by some of the critics of heterogeneity. While many school systems have been most successful in conducting special schools and special programs for their ablest students, the soundest programs are those which are sufficiently fluid in their grouping that students can move from one to another as necessary and which avoid stigmatizing students in any of the groups.

New York City has provided an eloquent answer to those who see little purpose in secondary education for relatively unpromising students [20]. Taking one of the most difficult of its junior high schools, a school with a low median IQ and a high incidence of school failure, truancy, and delinquency, the board of education provided adequate and appropriate educational services. The project, which started at this junior high school and was later extended to the high school to which its graduates went, included extensive testing, guidance and counseling services, and enriched school programs designed to detect and develop the full potential of each child.

Special help, such as remedial classes in reading and mathematics, was provided both during and after school hours for those pupils who needed it. To broaden the cultural horizons of the pupils, field trips were arranged to operas, concerts, theaters, art galleries, and college campuses. The school strengthened its relationship with the parents in order to get them to encourage their children in their educational careers.

The results were dramatic. School attendance went up and the incidence of delinquency went down. School achievement improved; for example, in two and a half years, the average pupil showed a growth in reading of four years. Even the scores on intelligence tests were affected. The improvement in achievement, behavior, and attitudes continued when these junior high school students went on to the high school. Thus, from the group which formerly supplied most of the disciplinary problems in the high school, not a single disciplinary case was referred to the office for treatment. When these students were graduating from the high school, there was an increase in the percentage planning to go on to higher education as compared with the educational ambitions of earlier senior classes in the same school.

We have erred, not in admitting children of varied abilities to the secondary schools, but in failing to provide adequately the personnel and the facilities needed for dealing with a heterogeneous student body. When schools are overcrowded, teachers are overworked, and the curriculum is rigid, the educational program is hardly adequate or appropriate for any group of students. The New York City experiments and those which are being conducted in schools across the country show how much the school can do even for unpromising students when it has the will and the wherewithal. Given the resources that are needed, the schools can take care of these students as well as of the average and the superior ones.

The challenge which American secondary schools face is to provide educational programs appropriate for all of the groups they enroll but not at the expense of any one of them.

Are the Secondary Schools Today Anti-intellectual?

To some extent, the charge of anti-intellectualism results from too narrow a definition of intellectualism. Some people apparently believe that the only way in which we learn to think is by considering abstract problems that are far removed from the students. These critics still cling to faculty psychology with its doctrine that some subjects develop reasoning, others improve memory, and so on.

The evidence is clear that no subject is exclusively appropriate for developing the ability to think, even though school subjects do differ in the opportunities they afford for intellectual stimulation. A class in philosophy does little to help a student think for himself when it is taught by a person who has no insight into, and no respect for, any school of philosophy other than the one he accepts and who sees his mission to be that of getting students to memorize his own formulation of life's values. On the other hand, a class in so practical a subject as industrial arts, if taught appropriately, may be rich in its opportunities for helping a class to formulate a problem, to marshal the evidence in support of various solutions, to evaluate the evidence, to formulate a tentative answer, and then to judge the adequacy of the answer. If we are interested in teaching students how to think, it is important that we give them an opportunity to think about problems that merit thought.

The nature of the problems discussed in class is important, but the way in which these problems are treated is also important.

In the hands of a skillful teacher, the discussion of a major problem that cuts across subject lines has almost infinite opportunities for encouraging sound scholarship. Thus, a high school class that is studying the town's housing situation sees the reason for digging into history, economics, sociology, and political science and often conducts its research and discussion on such a high level as to make the old-time high school recitations seem superficial and nonintellectual. The teacher has the responsibility of making certain that, despite his eagerness to stimulate widespread participation in classroom discussion, he does not fail to stress the importance of accurate and sufficient knowledge as the basis for informed opinions.

When the schools appoint only well prepared teachers who are thoroughly grounded in the scholarship of the areas in which they are to teach, we need not worry about anti-intellectualism, for it is as difficult for a scholar to be anti-intellectual as for a deeply religious person to encourage atheism. When, however, we appoint only superficially prepared teachers, or teachers whose concept of scholarship is limited to university studies and does not include material within the compass of adolescent minds, or teachers who are prepared in one subject matter field and then are expected to teach subject matter with which they themselves have only superficial contacts, the schools will not encourage intellectual growth.

Has the Curriculum Been "Watered Down"?

The charge is frequently heard that the secondary school curriculum has been watered down so much that it is soft and mushy, that courses like driver education are increasing and courses in mathematics, science, and foreign languages are decreasing. This is a charge that is difficult to deny because it appears to be supported factually—if only some of the facts are considered. Even worse, there are schools among the more than 21,000 American secondary schools that should be criticized on this score. Nevertheless, when we consider all the relevant evidence and look at all our schools, it is inaccurate to say that the secondary school curriculum has been diluted.

It is true that, under the pressure of the tremendous numbers with which the schools have had to deal, curricular guidance is sometimes slighted and able students are allowed to elect courses far less strenuous than they can tackle. Left to his own devices, many a high school junior would rather spend his time in a social dancing class with his arms around a girl than in a science class wrestling with a physics problem. In good schools, however, students are counselled to follow a total program which provides for both maximum intellectual stimulation and growth in social maturity.

It is true, too, that there are public secondary schools which do not offer a full program in science, mathematics, and foreign languages, but these are most often small schools with small enrollments and small faculties. When educators urge that these small schools be consolidated into larger schools that can offer an adequate program, their efforts are sometimes put to naught by local pride and political pressure.

It is also true that the percentage of high school students enrolled in mathematics, science, and foreign language courses is lower than it was at the beginning of the century. Here, part of the explanation of the change is to be found in the composition of the secondary school population, for the students who are not enrolled in these courses are the prototypes of the boys and girls who did not come to the secondary school at all in earlier years. We cannot afford to forget that in 1889-90, only 6.7 per cent of the population aged 14-17 were enrolled in Grades 9-12 in the public and private high schools while in 1953-4, 80.4 per cent of the population in this age range were enrolled in Grades 9-12 [17, p. 161]. If we count the total population from 14 to 17 years of age rather than the number of secondary school students, we find that the percentage enrolled in science and mathematics courses has gone up from 7 per cent in 1900 to 35 per cent in 1950 [17, p. 162].

The schools, however, are not entirely blameless for some of the decline in the percentage of secondary school students enrolled in science, mathematics, and foreign languages. When investigators demonstrated that the study of mathematics did not necessarily help students learn how to think and that the study of a foreign language did not always improve the student's ability to write English correctly, some schools were ready to reduce the importance of these subjects in the secondary school curriculum as though there were no other reason for studying mathematics and foreign languages.

Mastery of mathematics and foreign languages is so important for a number of reasons that such subjects as these must be part of the education of those students who have the mental ability for pursuing them. Unless these subjects are included in the elementary and secondary school curriculum, we shall not educate the specialists we need in these areas nor shall we build international understanding or the mathematical competence needed by every member of our society. To be sure, some secondary school students do not have the ability needed for success in such subjects and can gain much more from their secondary school education if they concentrate their efforts on other studies. However, we are not justified in using the limitations of some students as the reason for dropping these subjects from the curriculum of the abler students.

Throughout the country there is evidence that the secondary school curriculum is becoming increasingly rigorous. In some instances the apparent improvement in standards is spurious because all that has been done is that the assignments have been made longer rather than more demanding. In most secondary schools, however, subject matter that was formerly reserved for college level students is now being included in the high school program. For example, calculus has become almost a standard part of the high school mathematics program and student experimentation in science has gone far beyond the routine laboratory experiments of a generation ago. Similarly, more students now have an opportunity to study a foreign language long enough to be able to master it.

Is Modern Secondary Education the Product of Sentimental Psychology and Soft Pedagogy?

Secondary education has made significant progress in accepting and applying the lessons learned from mental hygiene. The schools have learned that frustration, for the sake of frustration, is unwholesome and ineffective. They know that average students cannot be nagged or shamed into becoming brilliant. They know, too, that substandard students, with little ability or interest in a college preparatory course, should have more to show for their years at school than the feeling that they are failures and incompetents. Schools have demonstrated that they know how effective are a feeling of self-respect and the satisfaction of having succeeded as incentives for further progress.

We take these gains so much for granted these days that we easily forget some of the earlier secondary school practices that were unnecessarily harsh and wasteful. When we admitted all elementary school graduates to the academic high school and compelled them to enroll in courses in which they did not have the ability to do work of passing quality, when we gave them courses of little meaning or purpose to them and then failed them term after term until they dropped out of school, that was not hard pedagogy and realistic psychology; it was bad pedagogy and bad psychology—and an egregious waste of school resources and of years out of the young people's lives.

We do nothing to disparage this remarkable revolution in school practices when we admit that there are teachers who have misinterpreted the teaching of mental hygiene. Indeed there are some teachers who are so fearful of endangering adolescents' emotional adjustment that they underestimate their students. Adolescents are made of sterner stuff than some adults realize. They do not fall to pieces at the first sign of failure. They can stand frustration, provided that they do not lose their self-respect and their confidence in themselves. The teacher who thinks he is being a superb psychologist when he praises everything his students do, however weak and unacceptable it may be, is not helping his students or even pleasing them. A self-respecting adolescent rebels against the wishy-washy teacher who beams beatifically and indiscriminately whenever any student makes any remark in class.

When adolescents are at work on something they regard as important, they sometimes set much higher standards for themselves than adults dare set for them. A group of boys constructing their own stereophonic record player or operating a ham radio will keep on improving and improving their equipment and performance long after their parents think perfection has been attained.

What adolescents need more than a series of easy successes is the feeling of self-respect and self-confidence, and the sense that what they are doing is worth doing. Teen-agers do not expect their teachers to abandon standards. In fact, they demonstrate repeatedly how much they respect the teacher who knows what he is doing and regards it so highly that he wants his students to come up to his standards of performance—and helps them to do so.

Those schools that abandon standards and set no goals worth attaining reveal their misunderstanding of modern education and mental hygiene. We should judge modern education by the overwhelming numbers of secondary school teachers today who respect their students and their subjects and, in turn, have students who respect themselves, their teachers, and their work.

It is clear that such questions as we have just been discussing often cannot be answered by a categorical affirmative or negative reply for all of our thousands of secondary schools. This is not a trial to be ended by a verdict of *guilty* or *not guilty*. The questions serve a more useful purpose when they are regarded as cautions of which all teachers and administrators must be fully aware. Despite the difficult conditions with which many secondary school teachers have had to contend in recent years, they have achieved much that they and their communities can regard with pride.

CONANT'S STUDIES OF SECONDARY EDUCATION

One of the more significant contributions in the wave of reappraisals came as a result of the program called *A Study of the American High School* which began in 1957. James B. Conant, former President of Harvard University, Ambassador to Germany, and member of the Educational Policies Commission, was commissioned by the Carnegie Corporation of New York to study the comprehensive high school in the United States. Conant made personal visits to a number of high schools identified as among the best in the country and expressed his confidence in the general pattern of the comprehensive high school. He made, moreover, a number of specific recommendations [5a], some of which support newer practices and policies and some of which seek a return to older patterns. Conant subscribes to the principle of providing a varied program of education to meet the needs of all youth of high school age. To do so properly, he advised strengthening of counseling services. He also urged a pattern of homogeneous grouping more rigorous than that employed in the large majority of American school systems.

For many years Conant had been concerned with providing more adequate programs for the academically talented student. In his report he defined this group as the top 15 per cent of the school population, with the top 3 per cent representing a still more exceptional group. For this 15 per cent he outlined a relatively heavy program of academic subjects closely prescribed, a special diploma, and a deemphasis on competitive ranking of students which often causes bright youngsters to take only those subjects where they may expect "A's." He argued that these students should be grouped separately from others in all classes except senior social studies and the homeroom. To insure their working up to capacity, he set a homework load of three hours a day. Prerequisites were to be set up for advanced academic courses in order to maintain selectivity. At least three years of a foreign language were recommended, and more science than is now typical. To make this possible, a seven-period day was suggested.

For the average and for slower students, Conant recommended greater emphasis on developing marketable skills and a recognition that high level vocational skills require students of high ability. He called for remedial reading, ability grouping, and individual programming. Individual programming is recommended by most educators because of greater adaptability to individual needs and interests. At the opposite pole are selection of a four- or three-year course at the ninth or tenth grade and the requirement that the student stay within the academic, general, commercial, or vocational framework throughout his career. Woe betide the girl in the academic course who wants home economics or the boy in the commercial curriculum who seeks to enroll in college preparatory mathematics. Conant urged individual programming to prevent these weaknesses of group planning.

While there was much support for a number of Conant's recommendations, much criticism was expressed, too. One objection was to the definition of high school education in terms of a series of courses— the counting of credits as in college—rather than in terms of behavioral goals. May this kind of definition lead to confusion of means and ends? Another criticism was that the program was defined in terms of a preconceived pattern of education rather than in terms of individual and social needs and interests. The tacit acceptance of courses as they profess to be did not imply an effort to examine what actually is done or ought to be done in any of them, with the exception of the recommendations of a developmental reading program and greater emphasis on composition in English.

The static view of high school education, since Conant suggested little that was different for the bright youngster from programs of many years ago, did not prove especially attractive to critics experienced with newer programs. Current thinking on programs for gifted youth puts emphasis on developing creativity, and this element was not conspicuous in the Conant proposals. The seven-period day could mean a return to the forty-five minute period in those schools which have established the hour-long period because the longer period gives more time for creative endeavor, for discussion, for directed study, for research, and for committee activities.

A basic assumption of the Conant report was the belief that the time-honored college preparatory program represents the best preparation for college. This assumption is contradicted by research findings of investigations which discovered more value in motivation, interest, and application than in a specific pattern of courses [1]. The recommendation of intensive academic work for the top 15 per cent may constitute a multiple threat. In some cases, school boards may attempt to show that they are really taking the proposals seriously by strait-jacketing a large percentage of the students into such a program. In others, limiting the program to the suggested proportion may exclude many students who should be given a chance to show their mettle. In any case, the selective factor generally causes parental pressure upon their children and upon the schools for admission into a program that carries special prestige value.

On the other hand, many of the people criticizing the Conant proposals in this manner were frank to express approval of other recommendations. Generally accepted by all educators were recommendations dealing with consolidation of small high schools, improvement of guidance services, individual programming, programs of developmental reading, and recognition of the limited proportion of students for whom the strictly academic program is appropriate.

In his study of junior high school education [5b], Conant stressed the importance of basic required subjects for all students, with adequate emphasis on the development of such skills as reading. In the junior high school, too, he favored a seven-period day in order to reduce the necessity of forcing students to have to choose between taking courses in mathematics or science or a modern foreign language, and to facilitate scheduling of remedial help for pupils who need it.

In order to provide for a smooth transition from the elementary to the secondary school, he approved of organizing seventh grade instruction in large blocks of time, but without necessarily endorsing core teaching. Referring to the lack of articulation between instruction on one school level with that on another as being one of the most serious problems of many school systems, he urged that there be careful co-ordination in each one of the subject areas in grades K-12.

With Conant's concern that instruction should be intellectually challenging for all junior high school students, it is only natural that he should ask both for remedial reading when needed, and for the study of the newer mathematics and foreign languages when appropriate. He suggested flexible scheduling and some form of homogeneous grouping as other aids to the adjustment of instruction to individual differences. Conant urged the maintenance of high standards, with a policy of non-promotion that would be applied judiciously.

In order to enable the junior high school to reach the goals he outlined, Conant stressed the importance of having a sufficiently large and competent professional staff as well as adequate facilities. Thus, he recommended that there be a full time guidance and testing specialist for every 250-300 students; that most teachers should not be asked to teach more than five periods a day or more than 125-150 students—and that English teachers should not have more than 100 pupils; and that there be enough clerks and assistant principals to enable the teachers to teach and the principal to function as an educational leader.

WHAT LIES AHEAD?

The secondary school has changed a great deal in the past generation and is probably on the threshold of even greater change. Which direction will this change take?

As we shall see in the next chapter, the secondary school curriculum is undergoing careful scrutiny and is the subject of considerable research and experimentation. How will the schools teach adolescents all they need to know? Will the content of existing courses be modernized or will new courses be developed? How will secondary schools provide for the academically talented, for those whose academic potentiality is not yet discovered, and for those whose abilities are in other areas than academic learning? What will the secondary schools in the big cities do for their inmigrant adolescents? No new teacher need fear that all has been discovered and that no problem awaits those with insight and imagination.

How will the status of the teacher differ in the immediate future? Will the demand for secondary school teachers lead to improved salary and working conditions that will enable schools to recruit and retain good teachers, to classes that are of manageable and teachable size, to adequate school equipment and supplies, and to relief from the nonteaching duties that consume so much of the teacher's time? Or will communities take the short view and lower the standards for teaching so that they can get "bodies" into the classroom?

Will educational television expand the horizon so that every school can offer its students a richer program than is now available? Or will schools think that television makes qualified classroom teachers unnecessary, to be replaced by monitors who can take attendance and tune in the proper channel at the right time?

Will the secondary school teacher work more intensively with fewer students, as for example in the core program we shall be discussing later, or will he become a member of a team as described by Trump [19], including a master teacher, one or more certified teachers, some part-time teachers, a secretary or teacher-aide, and an intern? Will schools that try team teaching think of the team as consisting of a superb master teacher assisted by qualified associates or will they see it as an economy measure whereby they need have only one average teacher whose teammates will be of less than average ability?

Will the school session be lengthened as suggested by Hechinger [11] and others because the school "faces a tougher task and therefore needs much more time—and much more money"? Or will we find ways of utilizing our time and resources more efficiently than we now do?

One thing is certain. Regardless of the changes that may be introduced, the teacher will continue to be the key person in secondary education. If he is incompetent or indifferent, educational plans come to naught, no matter how skillful are the plans made by the administrator or how inspiring are the prefaces to the school's curriculum guides.

Secondary school teaching is undoubtedly more complex and more important than ever before. It is with full awareness of its difficulty and its significance that we turn to the question which will concern us for the rest of this book: How do we teach adolescents in secondary schools?

QUESTIONS FOR STUDY AND DISCUSSION

1. At a professional meeting of school superintendents and principals, a newly-elected superintendent argued that secondary education would be much more efficient if the schools applied the principle of division of labor the way industry did. Instead of expecting his teachers to be experts in adolescent psychology, in the psychology of learning, and in curriculum building, all he wanted of his teachers is that they know their subject matter and be able to teach it. If his schools needed psychologists and curriculum builders, he added, he would see that his school board appointed specialists in school psychology and curriculum building instead of expecting his teachers to be specialists in these areas.

    a. Assuming that the superintendent is capable and his school board is co-operative, what values is he likely to realize by following the policies he advocates?

    b. What are the fallacies in his argument?

    c. How would you like to accept an appointment as a teacher in that school system?

2. For nine years, Mr. M. has been a successful and respected teacher in a suburban senior high school. At a PTA meeting which he attended on the

topic of The Future Our Children Face, the discussion veered toward the values held by the modern high school generation. Parent after parent described their sons and daughters as being superficial in their thinking, as never reading anything more profound than the current best seller, as being conformists who dressed like and thought like everybody else, as materialists who thought more of clothes and cars than of ethical values, and as egotists who thought only of their own convenience and comfort and paid little heed to social needs.

As Mr. M. listened to the discussion, the thought came to mind that everything the parents said was an accurate description of the parents themselves. It seemed odd, he thought, that parents should criticize their children for imitating their parents.

It was at this point that the chairman called on Mr. M. for his opinion.

   a. What should he say?

   b. What responsibility does a teacher have for influencing the attitudes of his students' parents?

3. A superintendent of schools has had such great difficulty in getting good teachers for secondary schools which enroll large numbers of culturally handicapped adolescents that he resorts to several stratagems, none of which succeed in attracting many teachers.

As a prospective teacher, what would you want the superintendent to do in order to get you to accept an appointment to a school with a heavy enrollment of culturally handicapped students?

4. Gideonse, in his article, On the Educational Statesmanship of a Free Society [8, pp. 9, 10], writes:

> On the higher levels of education, American schools could benefit greatly from earlier discrimination between children who have an aptitude for academic achievement, and those who should continue in general or vocational studies. We should not confuse the American ideal that all children should have "equality of opportunity" with the egalitarian notion that all children have equal endowments, and we should not permit our able students to use the excesses of our elective system to evade the full development of their intellectual potential. European experience underlines the warning, however, that some methods of eliminating the existing variety of standards in American local school systems might expose us to the great danger of closing the doors of educational opportunity to large numbers of pupils with great potential ability, and no matter how careful our testing and examination procedures, there is always the question concerning the so-called "late bloomer." *

   a. Assuming that you accept the point of view presented in this excerpt, what should you do if the parents of one of the students in your junior high school class insist that their son enroll in the college preparatory program at the high school to which he will go next September and you know that his past work does not augur well for his success in that program?

   b. One of your bright high school juniors, in planning his program for his senior year, includes none of the "hard subjects" that will challenge him and includes, as electives, courses intended for average or below-average students.

   When you try to interest him in pursuing a program that is more appropriate for his abilities, he explains that his chances of being admitted to college will be better if he gets high grades in easy subjects than low grades in difficult subjects.

   What should you say to him?

* Reprinted by permission from H. D. Gideonse, On the Educational Statesmanship of a Free Society (New York, The Woodrow Wilson Foundation, 1959), pp. 9, 10.

    c. What can be done to keep the doors of educational opportunity open to "late bloomers" whose early school achievements paint too dim a picture of their true potentialities?

    5. Dr. Conant reported that more than half of the country's high schools are too small to offer effective and defensible programs and recommended that their number be reduced from 21,000 to 9,000 in order to insure minimum graduating classes of at least 100 students.

    In keeping with this recommendation, a group of citizens in a small town are trying to have their high school closed, with the students being merged with those in a neighboring town.

    The parents object to having the school closed and present the following arguments:

    a. If our sons and daughters have to attend school in another town, the parents will not be able to supervise their children as closely as they now do, and "you know how wild boys and girls can be when parents can't keep an eye on them."

    b. It is local interest and local pride that makes a school good. Our town is small enough to care about its schools. What will we gain if our children go to a big, impersonal school?

    c. Ours is a good school. We went to it and we loved it. What's wrong with it? Why do we have to close it?

    What would you say if you, as a graduate of that high school and now a graduate of a college, are called upon for your opinion?

    6. As a young teacher, what advantages do you see for yourself in the possibility of being appointed to be a member of a teaching team as described by Trump?

    What disadvantages do you see in such an appointment?

    Considering both sides of the question, would you rather accept such an appointment or go to a school where you would be assigned to teach your own classes?

    7. If the secondary schools adopt a longer school day and a lengthened school year, are there any changes in current school programs that should be modified because of the time extension?

    Many secondary school teachers feel overworked under the present time schedules. What can be done to prevent crushing teachers under impossible work loads if the school day is lengthened and the school year extended?

BIBLIOGRAPHY

1. AIKIN, Wilford M., *The Story of the Eight Year Study* (New York, Harper and Brothers, 1942).
2. BLOOM, B. S., "The 1955 Normative Study of the Tests of General Educational Development," *School Review,* Vol. 64, No. 3 (March 1956), pp. 110-124.
3. CANTOR, Nathaniel F., *The Teaching-Learning Process* (New York, Holt, Rinehart and Winston, Inc., 1953).
4. CASWELL, Hollis L., ed., *The American High School,* Eighth Yearbook of the John Dewey Society (New York, Harper and Brothers, 1946).
5. (*a*) CONANT, James B., *The American High School Today* (New York, McGraw-Hill Book Co., Inc., 1959).
    (*b*) CONANT, James B., *Education in the Junior High School Years* (Princeton, N.J., Educational Testing Service, 1960).

6. Educational Policies Commission, *Public Education and the Future of America* (Washington, D. C., National Education Association, 1955).

7. FRENCH, William M., *Education for All* (New York, The Odyssey Press, 1955).

8. GIDEONSE, Harry D., *On the Educational Statesmanship of a Free Society* (New York, The Woodrow Wilson Foundation, 1959).

9. GILMORE, John V., "A New Venture in the Testing of Motivation," *The College Board Review* (November, 1951), pp. 221-226.

10. HANDLIN, Oscar, *The Newcomers* (Cambridge, Mass., Harvard University Press, 1959).

11. HECHINGER, Fred M., "Education in Review," *The New York Times* (November 29, 1959), Sect. 4, p. 11.

12. HOLLINSHEAD, Byron S., "Education in America," *The Educational Record,* Vol. 40, No. 3 (July, 1959), pp. 212-217.

13. KING, Edmund J., *Other Schools and Ours* (New York, Holt, Rinehart and Winston, Inc., 1958).

14. National Education Association, *Will Your Child Get a Quality Education?* (Washington, D. C., the Association, 1959).

15. NIBLETT, William R., *Education—The Lost Dimension* (New York, W. Sloane Associates, 1955).

16. Report of the Committee for the White House Conference on Education (Washington, D. C., U.S. Government Printing Office, 1956).

17. Research Division of the National Education Association, "Ten Criticisms of Public Education," *The NEA Research Bulletin,* Vol. XXXV, No. 4 (December 1957).

18. Rockefeller Brothers Fund, *Pursuit of Excellence: Education and the Future of America* (New York, the Fund, 1958).

19. TRUMP, J. Lloyd, *Images of the Future* (Urbana, Illinois, The Commission on the Experimental Study of the Utilization of the Staff in the Secondary School, 1959).

20. WRIGHTSTONE, J. Wayne, "Discovering and Stimulating Culturally Deprived Talented Youth," *Teachers College Record,* Vol. 60, No. 1 (October, 1958), pp. 23-27.

21. YOUNG, Michael D., *The Rise of the Meritocracy* (New York, Random House, Inc., 1959).

CHAPTER 2

Achieving the Goals of Secondary Education

»»»»»»»»»»

THE AMERICAN SYSTEM of secondary education rests upon three assumptions: first, that our civilization is so complex that an elementary school education is not sufficient as preparation for the responsibilities of adulthood; second, that our country is rich enough to be able to afford to send its adolescents to school instead of to work; and third, that our citizens see education as a principal means of social and economic advancement. Secondary education runs into trouble when these assumptions are invalid, for example, when parents of environmentally deprived children do not see education as a means of advancement and, therefore, do not nurture the educational ambitions of their children.

In terms of these assumptions, the goals of secondary education are relatively simple. We want to make the years the adolescents spend in secondary schools so productive, so stimulating, and so rewarding that adolescents will be better off while they are adolescents for being in school, and that our young people will be better adults for having had a secondary school education. We are all agreed that the secondary schools should teach the student what he has to know, and help him to become what he should be. Where we differ is in our answers to what it is he has to learn, what it is he should be, and what role the school should play in helping him. We shall, therefore, look at the objectives and at some of the patterns of curriculum organization through which schools try to achieve these objectives. We shall also observe a teacher as he works to meet these goals.

Educators have been attempting to formulate the goals of education ever since the first teacher met with the first student, and the professional literature is rich in its helpful and stimulating statements of educational objectives [4, 6, 9, 11, 14, 25]. In order to indicate the role which teachers must play in achieving the purposes of modern secondary education, we shall use only one of these formulations as the basis for discussion, even though such a decision means that we shall not give as much attention to other statements of educational goals as they deserve.

THE PURPOSES OF EDUCATION IN AMERICAN DEMOCRACY

There are several reasons for basing the present discussion on *The Purposes of Education in American Democracy* as formulated by the Educational Policies Commission [11]. Since it was issued by a commission representing the National Education Association and the American Association of School Administrators, it comes closer to representing the beliefs of American educators than does a statement prepared by an individual or a small group. Moreover, by dealing with the total educational process, *The Purposes of Education in American Democracy* compels the secondary school teacher to view secondary education as part of a larger program rather than as an isolated part of a school system. This statement also reflects modern educational thinking in its concern with both the individual student's development and the social implications of education.

The Educational Policies Commission groups the goals of education as the objectives of self-realization, the objectives of human relationship, the objectives of economic efficiency, and the objectives of civic responsibility. These major objectives are further defined as follows: *

THE OBJECTIVES OF SELF-REALIZATION (11, p. 50)

The Inquiring Mind. The educated person has an appetite for learning.
Speech. The educated person can speak the mother tongue clearly.
Reading. The educated person reads the mother tongue efficiently.
Writing. The educated person writes the mother tongue effectively.
Number. The educated person solves his problems of counting and calculating.
Sight and Hearing. The educated person is skilled in listening and observing.
Health Knowledge. The educated person understands the basic facts concerning health and disease.
Health Habits. The educated person protects his own health and that of his dependents.
Public Health. The educated person works to improve the health of the community.

* These statements of the objectives of education are reprinted by permission of the National Education Association from *The Purposes of Education in American Democracy* (Washington, D. C., National Education Association, 1938).

Recreation. The educated person is participant and spectator in many sports and other pastimes.

Intellectual Interests. The educated person has mental resources for the use of leisure.

Esthetic Interests. The educated person appreciates beauty.

Character. The educated person gives responsible direction to his own life.

THE OBJECTIVES OF HUMAN RELATIONSHIP (11, p. 72)

Respect for Humanity. The educated person puts human relationships first.

Friendships. The educated person enjoys a rich, sincere, and varied social life.

Co-operation. The educated person can work and play with others.

Courtesy. The educated person observes the amenities of social behavior.

Appreciation of the Home. The educated person appreciates the family as a social institution.

Conservation of the Home. The educated person conserves family ideals.

Homemaking. The educated person is skilled in homemaking.

Democracy in the Home. The educated person maintains democratic family relationships.

THE OBJECTIVES OF ECONOMIC EFFICIENCY (11, p. 90)

Work. The educated producer knows the satisfaction of good workmanship.

Occupational Information. The educated producer understands the requirements and opportunities for various jobs.

Occupational Choice. The educated producer has selected his occupation.

Occupational Efficiency. The educated producer succeeds in his chosen vocation.

Occupational Adjustment. The educated producer maintains and improves his efficiency.

Occupational Appreciation. The educated producer appreciates the social value of his work.

Personal Economics. The educated consumer plans the economics of his own life.

Consumer Judgment. The educated consumer develops standards for guiding his expenditures.

Efficiency in Buying. The educated consumer is an informed and skillful buyer.

Consumer Protection. The educated consumer takes appropriate measures to safeguard his interests.

THE OBJECTIVES OF CIVIC RESPONSIBILITY (11, p. 108)

Social Justice. The educated citizen is sensitve to the disparities of human circumstances.

Social Activity. The educated citizen acts to correct unsatisfactory conditions.

Social Understanding. The educated citizen seeks to understand social structures and social processes.

Critical Judgment. The educated citizen has defenses against propaganda.

Tolerance. The educated citizen respects honest differences of opinion.

Conservation. The educated citizen has a regard for the nation's resources.

Social Applications of Science. The educated citizen measures scientific advance by its contribution to the general welfare.

World Citizenship. The educated citizen is a co-operating member of the world community.

Law Observance. The educated citizen respects the law.

Economic Literacy. The educated citizen is economically literate.

Political Citizenship. The educated citizen accepts his civic duties.

Devotion to Democracy. The educated citizen acts upon an unswerving loyalty to democratic ideals.

These objectives reflect the trend of current educational thought because they focus attention on the boys and girls in our schools as people rather than only as students. They emphasize the changes that should occur in boys and girls, and consider the curriculum as a means of helping young people to mature into responsible members of the community.

Making the Goals Specific

When we speak of the goals of education, we sometimes succumb to the temptation of thinking only in terms of vague generalities. Thus, many a commencement speaker refers to the need for developing good citizens and is applauded for saying so; yet every member of the audience may have his own interpretation of what is meant by being a good citizen. Even when we think we are being specific, all we sometimes do is to substitute many generalities for a single one. For example, we can say that a good citizen is loyal to the traditions of his country, that he helps make democracy work, that he is a responsible member of his community, that he. . . . Yet, we are still not being overly specific because we have not defined what we mean by the many words we have substituted for the one expression *being a good citizen.* What do we mean by *helps make democracy work* or *is a responsible member of his community?* Unless we can do better than merely rephrase generalizations, statements of goals are almost certain to remain merely parts of the forewords to curriculum guides and topics for discussion in commencement addresses.

If we are to achieve the goals of education, and it is important that we do so or schooling becomes purposeless, we must translate these goals into action. What should students do? What should teachers do?

The Educational Policies Commission statement helps meet part of the problem by presenting a number of subsidiary statements referring to what people *do.* For example, it speaks not only of *civic responsibility,* or even of objectives like *social justice* and *social activity,* but it also defines them in terms of behavior.* Reread the sentences under *The Objectives of Civic Responsibility* and note how much they do to clarify the meaning of the objectives to which they refer.

---

* See pp. 314-316 for a further explanation of behavioral definitions.

Relating Objectives to Desired Growth in the Student

Further refinement is needed before we can use these objectives as a basis for secondary school teaching. What do we expect boys and girls to do to reach these objectives? How do they behave when they have reached them? What kinds of behavior indicate that they are far from the goal? How can we evaluate the progress they are making in reaching the goal?

Education should lead to desirable changes in the ways in which people behave. The educated man has greater knowledge than the uneducated one, but if his increased knowledge does not lead to deeper insight and greater understanding, he is little more than a pedant. His education should broaden his interests and develop new ones, but interests that do not modify his ways of living hardly merit being called interests. Similarly, education modifies one's attitude and sense of values, but here, too, these modifications should be reflected in what one does.

One of the fallacies in popular thinking is the assumption that knowledge leads inevitably to virtue. Yet, we all know that a student may memorize answers to questions about the organization of our government and be far from being the ideal citizen. It is equally fallacious, of course, to assume that we improve citizenship by keeping our students ignorant of the ways in which our government is organized. If we want the study of history and civics to lead to good citizenship, we must define what we mean by good citizenship in terms of what good citizens know, what they believe, and, above all, what they do. Our teaching can then be oriented toward what adolescents do as they work toward the goal of being good citizens—and as they live as good citizens while they are yet boys and girls.

French and his associates [13] have presented just such an analysis of the Educational Policies Commission statement of *The Purposes of Education in American Democracy*. What they have attempted to do is "to discover and publish a statement of the general consensus of what high school graduates should be able to do—how they may be expected to think and feel and act—as a result of the general education element of their high school program."

The nature of their analysis is indicated by the developmental equivalents for *Evidencing Intelligent Appreciation and Support of Democratic Goals and Principles and of American Cultural, Social, and Political Traditions*, which, for younger and less mature students, lists the following, among many others:

Is beginning to learn skills in handling controversy through persuasion and legitimate compromise, rather than through force.

Knows that there are several major political parties which stand on somewhat different platforms.

Questions any statement which purports to attribute special vices or virtues to a specific national, racial, or religious group. Asks for the evidence on which such statements are made.*

A major question still remains unanswered: How can we effect these changes in behavior so that we attain our educational goals?

THE SECONDARY SCHOOL AND OTHER SOCIAL AGENCIES

Meeting these goals is too great a task for the secondary school alone. No secondary school can take the place of the home, the church, the recreational agency, the health department, the mental hygiene clinic, the welfare department, the stationery store, the savings bank, and all the other agencies which our society has developed for life in a complex culture. At times, the secondary school has been so keenly aware of adolescent needs and of the inadequacy of other social agencies that the school assumed one additional responsibility after another, without getting the additional personnel needed for discharging these new responsibilities adequately while continuing the basic educational program.

It is difficult to draw the boundary line between the school's responsibilities and those of other agencies. To be sure, the art teacher is no dentist, but the art teacher cannot develop a sense of the beautiful when a girl has a toothache and no money with which to pay for a visit to a dentist. On the other hand, should the school divert school funds and facilities to operate a dental clinic, even in an underprivileged area, if other agencies can do it better and with greater appropriateness?

Basically, all teachers are vitally interested in the educational development of their students and see all of the other responsibilities sometimes assumed by the school as distracting it from achieving its major function. Yet, schools are so concerned with the boys and girls they teach that teachers and administrators feel compelled to do something when they see great gaps in the community's provision for its young people. Thus, a school in a community which offers little opportunity for wholesome recreation and much temptation for unwholesome activities thinks it necessary to conduct a week-end recreational program, which should not be part of the school's business at all.

Ideally, the school should be able to focus its attention on the intellectual development of its students and on providing a wholesome emotional climate in which this development occurs. It best discharges its share of the responsibilities which the community must shoulder by being the leader in the mobilization and co-ordination of community services for youth. When the school has to assume obligations because other agen-

* Reprinted by permission from Will French and associates, *Behavorial Goals of General Education in High School* (New York, Russell Sage Foundation, 1957), p. 184.

cies have defaulted, it must see these supplementary services as being only a means to an end, namely, better education, and should be eager to divest itself of responsibility for conducting them as soon as another agency can assume it.

ORGANIZING THE CURRICULUM TO ATTAIN THE GOALS OF SECONDARY EDUCATION

Once we know what we want our schools to achieve, it seems as though it should be a simple matter for the secondary schools to organize the curriculum so as to attain these goals, but nothing in education is simple. When we speak of the curriculum, we are thinking not only of the outlines of the various courses taught in the schools but of all the planned experiences which are part of the school program. The auditorium programs and the school's club activities, for example, should be oriented toward the attainment of the desired educational goals or what is accomplished in the classroom can be counteracted by what goes on outside it.

The revaluation of our educational goals and the changing composition of the secondary school student body have led to widespread changes in curricular practices. While secondary schools have varied markedly in the degree to which they modified their curriculum, it is nevertheless true that the past twenty-five years have seen more changes in secondary school curricular practices than probably any other similar period of time in American educational history. There have been changes in both the content of instruction and the organization of the curriculum.

What are the major changes that have taken place? What do these changes seek to accomplish? How desirable are these changes? How do they affect the teachers as they work with adolescents?

Changes in Subject Matter Content

Even though the title of the course may have remained unchanged, there are few subjects taught in our secondary schools today that are as they were in past days. *English I* may still be called *English I* but in some schools it will include instruction in reading that was formerly reserved for the elementary school and in other schools it will include extensive reading rather than the intensive study of one novel, one play, and one collection of poems.

Some of these changes in content result from our expanding body of knowledge. Certainly the science courses must include studies of atomic physics that were little known up to recently. Other changes result from changes in our goals. Thus, a foreign language teacher who wants his students to speak the language teaches a different course from that taught by teachers who are concerned largely with the ability to read and write the language. As we modify our concept of the scope of the course, of necessity the content of the course will change. Thus, the school reflects no lessening of its pride in the American heritage when it believes that a student needs more than a study of American history if he is to understand what is happening in the world and includes world history and international problems in its social studies program. In some instances, the subject itself has changed. For example, the new mathematics, with its concern with symbolic logic, is a far cry from plane geometry with its list of axioms and propositions.

While the familiar subjects have been changing, entirely new ones have been added, largely because of the broader population base that now constitutes the secondary school population and the broader purposes that the secondary schools try to serve. Secondary schools now offer a wide array of elective courses, from household mechanics to experimental research projects in science, in an attempt to satisfy the variety of interests and needs to be found in a heterogeneous student body. According to a count reported by the United States Office of Education in 1950, 274 different high school courses were being offered.

Probably the most widely used and the most hotly debated new course is Driver Education. One group of citizens hails the effectiveness of driver education in reducing the automobile accident rate and points to the fact that insurance companies reduce the accident liability premiums for young drivers who have had such training in school. Critics of driver education do not dispute the effectiveness of the course but question whether driver education should be included in the high school curriculum as the intellectual equivalent of a course in mathematics or foreign language. In many secondary schools, therefore, driver education is included in a student's program as an additional subject rather than as a substitute for a course required for graduation.

Even though the constant modernization of the content of the various subjects included in the secondary school curriculum is important and though it is inevitable that some subjects will be added and others dropped as changes occur in our ways of thinking, we need more than subject matter changes if we are to achieve the goals of secondary education. We must have a plan of curricular organization that is conducive to achieving these goals and we must have the kind of teaching which is pointed toward attaining them.

Building a Program of General Education

When we adjust the curriculum to a changing student body merely by adding new courses and letting students choose which ones they will study, we have a curriculum which is not a planned curriculum at all. Rather, we have a collection of courses without any central purpose, satisfying no one who is concerned with the totality of secondary education and with the effect that secondary schools should have on youth. Though the elective system makes it possible to prepare a custom-made curriculum for a student, it may also lead to ineffectiveness and chaos. Secondary schools have become increasingly concerned, therefore, with the need for planning a program of general education that will assure every student's developing the basic skills and acquiring the knowledge needed for effective living today.

Are schools losing sight of the common purposes of education as they adjust to the almost infinite variation of individual differences in the adolescent population? This conflict between meeting individual needs and meeting common needs is reflected in the attempt of secondary schools to move in two different directions at once. On the one hand, they try to adjust to individual differences by use of the elective system and by providing for individual differences even among those in the same course. On the other hand, they are developing new patterns of curricular organization that stress the importance of general education, of a common background that all students need.

General education in the secondary school. The outstanding contribution of the public school to American culture has been its service in creating *e pluribus unum*—out of many, one. In days when few students went to high school, general education was the primary task of elementary education. Now, when practically all boys and girls attend secondary schools, our junior and senior high schools have an opportunity to develop the sense of common values and goals at a more profound level. Today, there is general agreement on the goal, but considerable debate on the means toward that goal. The *seven liberal arts,* which were the common culture of educated man in the Middle Ages and Renaissance, no longer fulfill this function by themselves. The *constants* of the curriculum in the first quarter of the twentieth century also fall short in terms of applicability to the contemporary scene and suitability to a near-universal school population.

One of the significant facts of life today is its diversity. In American industrial society we find extreme specialization of function: not just the butcher, the baker, and the candlestick maker, but more than 20,000 different job classifications as defined by the United States Department of Labor. The *common* schools (kindergarten through senior high school) bring all students together with their diverse vocational destinies—and are expected both to give them what they all need in common and to start them on the path toward differentiation.

In our social life we find the age-old differences from family to family and the distinctions in socio-economic background which the sociologist categorizes as class differences, even in democratic America. In addition to differences based on income, distinctions are found among the multitude of social organizations to which we belong as a nation of "joiners." While there is much overlapping of membership in many organizations, there are others where sharp demarcations separate the "in-group" from the outsiders [21].

The United States population comes from many ethnic backgrounds. Forebears of students in any one classroom may come from as many countries as there are students. The students in our schools represent all races, all national backgrounds, and all religions. They or their ancestors have known all kinds of governments and ideologies.

The diversity of our geography adds color to the kaleidoscope. Our population is not only urban and rural; it is coastal, mountain, and mid-continent; it is metropolitan, suburban, small town, and farm; it is large farm and small, commercial ranch and subsistence farm. Politically it is reactionary, conservative, middle-of-the-road, liberal, radical, and "lunatic fringe" at either end of the rainbow—but all may send their children to the public school.

More than our population and environment are diverse; the knowledge of man is perplexingly complex. The encyclopedists of the eighteenth century dreamed of encompassing all of the knowledge of man. No longer is this a realizable ideal. Today a biologist, for example, has no hope of complete mastery of the entire field of biology alone, to say nothing of all the natural sciences, even less the arts, sciences, and humanities. The growth and diversification of knowledge have had tremendous impact upon our graduate schools, only slightly less effect upon our colleges, and even considerable influence upon our secondary schools, too. The elective system was not devised simply to provide "easy ways out" for slower students; its real rationale was the development of so many different disciplines that a student had to elect, that is, he had to specialize, in order to make any dent upon the mountain of knowledge now available to mankind.

Attempts to Establish Unity in Diversity

For all these reasons a search has been under way for the past quarter-century to identify a common ground for understanding and co-operation in our highly differentiated culture. This common ground for all students is usually referred to as *general education*.

This search for a program of general education appropriate for our times helps explain much of the curricular experimentation which is still in process. It represents no attempt at watering down existing curricula or at making education easy, either for the student or the teacher. Nor can we end this period of experimentation merely by returning to the secondary education curriculum of past generations, when conditions in the world and in the school were so different from what they are today. The secondary school is now a permanent part of our common school system and has a responsibility it cannot abdicate for developing a sound and effective program of general education.

Required subjects as general education. Different approaches have been employed in seeking to define the content of general education. One point of view stresses the heritage that has been developed out of the long experience of education in the western world. In this perspective, the *required subjects* constitute the general program which should be common to all young persons growing up in our culture. General education is then defined in such terms as three years of English, two years of social studies, one year of science, and one year of mathematics—the minimum requirements in most states—with some states adding physical education, home economics, industrial arts, more English, more social studies, more mathematics, or more science. These prescribed subjects are sometimes referred to as the core of the school's program or the core program of that school.

Social processes as general education. A second approach to the problem sees the content of education as geared directly to man's personal and social functions in life. In the middle of the nineteenth century, Herbert Spencer was inspired to seek the substance of an effective education not in tradition but in the process of meeting the demands that life in a given culture places upon an individual. He asked the question, "What Knowledge Is of Most Worth?" and wrote an epoch-making essay in reply [25]. Implicit was the assumption that education must make a direct and functional contribution to the individual as he lives his life. This assumption is also fundamental in the Seven Cardinal Principles enunciated in 1918 by the National Education Association Commission on Reorganization of Secondary Education [6], in the statement of The Purposes of Education in American Democracy [11] by the Educational Policies Commission, and in the Commission's definition of the Ten Imperative Needs of Youth in 1944 [9].

This second method of defining general education bases its hypothesis on a type of analysis which seeks to identify those functions, activities, skills, attitudes, understandings, and aspects of knowledge which a young person should develop if he is to live a personally rewarding and socially effective life in our culture. The educational needs which apply to all individuals then become the substance of the general education or *common learnings* program. The various subject disciplines in this case are taught not as subjects whose importance is inherent only in their content, but as resources which make an important contribution to the functions of a human being, a citizen, a family member, a producer, and a consumer in our times.

The approach through social functions has particular validity in terms of current psychological orientation. Individual personality is viewed as an entity which is dynamic and unitary. The individual is not passive. He reacts to a situation not only in terms of the immediate factors encountered but also in terms of his experience and outlook. The individual does not merely add new experiences to his background but he absorbs, interprets, and refashions experiences so that his present outlook represents a fresh integration of the new experiences with the old outlook. Dewey called this process the reconstruction or restructuring of experience [7].

This conception of experience and personality leads to the search for school programs which will mean more than acquisition of facts, important though knowledge is as a major concern of education. It implies a basic concern for development of personality, for individual growth, for what the learner does with the content he learns. Accordingly, some efforts have been made in recent years to organize functional programs of education, programs that will contribute directly to the major modes of life activity: self-realization, citizenship, family membership, vocation, recreation. To help the adolescent integrate his new learnings into a fresh synthesis, some educators have tried to develop "unified" programs, believing that the process of integration would be easier for the student if he were working with related rather than unrelated learnings in school—with a learning content that seems to have a direct bearing on present and future life problems.

As a result, the second definition of general education looks to a kind of curriculum organization different from the first. Instead of simply requiring specified courses, the new approach takes the required courses and tries to reorient them with two objects in mind: to develop relationships within the common body of learnings, and to work on relationships that make so significant a contribution to personal development that they enhance the process of integration. It is important to note that it is not the teacher or the curriculum that "integrates." Just as we cannot *learn* anything for anybody, we cannot *integrate* anything for him. Instead, the school and the teacher help the individual himself to effect his new integration.

The teacher's responsibility for general education. To the new teacher, certain points should be clear. First, schools in America have an obligation to help develop common backgrounds upon which the necessary specialization of modern life may later be built. Second, every subject in the secondary school should be examined in terms of its general contribution as well as of the preparation it offers for vocational and avocational specialties. The general contribution is the role of the subject in educating adolescents as future citizens of the United States, as family members, as workers, and as individuals with distinct personalities. Third, schools emphasize learning of specific subject matter, but they are also concerned with personality as expressed in individual and group behavior. Fourth, this concern with personality development underscores the role of guidance in the school and its function in the general education of boys and girls.

It is indeed proper for the teacher as a scholar to be enthusiastic about his subject in and of itself. As a teacher he must in addition constantly be seeking ways of planning learning experiences so that his subject may make a contribution both to the student with a special interest in that subject and to the student who takes the subject as preparation for a better life as a citizen, a family member, a worker, and an individual.

The Revolt Against Compartmentalization

Secondary school teachers have become increasingly dissatisfied with the fragmentation of the secondary school curriculum into narrowly departmentalized courses and with the school bell schedule which divides the school day into segments that are too small to enable the teacher and class to carry on major activities without interruption. Although departmentalized teaching assures students of teachers who are conversant with at least one area of knowledge, it erects artificial barriers between school subjects. To understand a single important bill being debated in Congress, the student may have to understand constitutional law as well as economics, American history as well as international relations, statistical fallacies as well as current labor problems, and the meaning of specific words as well as the principles of logical thinking. Can students understand all of the issues and all of the implications of the bill if it is analyzed piecemeal in half a dozen classes?

The school day is divided into numerous brief periods, each begun and ended by a bell. An uninitiated visitor is unprepared for the suddenness with which sentences are cut short by the bell, never to be finished, and for the haste with which students rush out of class as soon as the bell rings. He would be a naïve visitor indeed if he interpreted the hasty departure as arising out of eagerness to get to the next class, for students leave the next class with just as great dispatch. Even though we grant that students have to leave class promptly to get to their next class on time, is there not something lacking in a class discussion that students drop eagerly and completely as soon as the bell rings?

The bell that begins the period is just as peremptory. With the bell, classroom conversation is expected to stop as the teacher steps forward to start the lesson. As a rule, he does not pay much attention to the varied activities in which his students participated during the preceding period nor to the many directions in which they will go next period. Out of all the eternity of time, he is concerned only with these forty, fifty, or fifty-five minutes. Life, however, is not made up of discrete experiences and a school day may be filled with five or six lessons, each good in itself, and yet be lacking in the total effect which is desired.

Objection has been raised to the sharp cleavage between class activities and the cocurricular activities conducted after school. In many schools the cocurricular activities offer students their only opportunity to do the work they consider important. Producing plays, publishing newspapers, discussing current events, seeing foreign films, playing in an orchestra, these are all activities that have such great educational value that they should properly be part of the school day rather than an appendage.

When we speak of the attempts of secondary school teachers to overcome the barriers created by departmental lines, we must not give the impression that teachers have arisen throughout the country to smash subject lines in a kind of educational Bastille Day. There are thousands of teachers throughout the country who have kept right on teaching English, or typewriting, or art, or electrical wiring as they have always been doing or with only minor changes in the content of these subjects. In a steadily increasing number of schools, however, particularly on the junior high school level, the old subject lines have been fading as teachers organized instructional materials in large blocks that transcended departmental lines.

Correlation

Once attention is focused on the functional aspects of subject matter rather than on a prearranged body of content, it is almost inevitable that teachers of related subjects should seek to co-ordinate their efforts. How can we justify the practice of having the social studies teacher discuss ideas and of having the English teacher discuss how one expresses ideas? Why should the teaching of mathematics be divorced from the application of mathematics to the solution of problems in physics and chemistry?

Correlation is sometimes almost casual, as when each teacher tries to help his students to apply to other classes what they have learned in his. The mathematics teacher, for example, uses a science situation as the basis for problems in mathematics, and the English teacher uses assignments written for other teachers as proper material for a lesson in composition. At other times, correlation is achieved by having two teachers, working together as a team, teach a joint course or by having one person teach two related courses. A popular combination has been that of social studies and English; combined mathematics and science courses are less frequently found.

Whether team teaching is effective depends largely upon the background, the educational philosophy, and the personality of the teachers involved. If the two teachers are more firmly convinced of the values of their own subjects than of correlation, the social studies teacher will continue to teach social studies and the English teacher will continue to teach English, even though both share the same desk and the same class. If one teacher is aggressive and the other timid, the students may find that they are having a double social studies class and omitting English rather than getting a correlated social studies–English course. Some schools, however, have been successful in using correlation of subject matter and team teaching as an important means of curricular progress.

Fusion

Correlation can be carried to such an extent that the former subject matter lines disappear and a new subject is born. For the sometimes haphazard correlation that is achieved when subject barriers are preserved, fusion substitutes a planned unification of related areas. Fusion places more emphasis on important problems, generalizations, and themes and thus suggests a criterion in terms of which the content of the component subjects can be selected. Since fusion gives rise to new subjects, it is possible to plan the sequence in which the various topics are to be studied in successive semesters.

If a general science course, for example, is well-organized and well-taught, the student does not get miniature independent courses in physics, chemistry, and biology. Instead, he develops concepts that cut across the departmental lines. Similarly, social studies or citizenship courses are more than courses in history, economics, civics, and geography taught by the same teacher. Social studies courses, by stressing the interrelationships among the component disciplines, can deal with important problems in their many aspects and enable students to see how geography has helped shape history and how economics and civics are intertwined.

Fusion is not without its difficulties. If it is to be more than just a new name for an old course, it needs careful planning and competent teaching. Some attempts at fusion have fallen short of expectations because the subject matter specialists, unable or unwilling to accept the challenge of building a new course, seek, instead, to retain every topic and every detail of the old courses which were supposedly superseded.

These broader courses call for teachers who have an adequate background for guiding learning effectively. Unfortunately, many teachers who are competent in one area of knowledge are only slightly better informed than laymen in other areas, even in areas that should be considered closely related to their field of special interest. Coming from colleges and universities where they considered themselves "majors" in a single subject, they have much background and interest in history and relatively little in economics, geography, and civics, or they are at home in chemistry but inadequately familiar with physics and biology.

Like most other curricular reforms, the extent to which fusion is successful depends largely on the extent to which classroom teachers accept and understand the demands of fusion and are adequately prepared to teach their new subject. We shall continue to have difficulty in finding teachers who know enough to be able to teach these fused courses as long as the colleges, from which these secondary school teachers come, continue to focus their attention on preparing undergraduate students for graduate work in a specialized field rather than on giving prospective secondary school teachers the broader background they need for teaching.

THE CORE CURRICULUM

A more fundamental approach to the program of the secondary school is that of the core curriculum, which combines changes in both administrative and instructional structures. The core curriculum stems from the idea that a program of general education for all students can be devised and that such a program should be the basic part of secondary education.

The use of the expression *core curriculum* differs markedly from the way in which *core* was used in the discussion of general education. As used earlier, the core referred to the areas of knowledge and types of skills which the school regards as being the heart or the core of its program. As used in the present context, the *core program* or *core curriculum* is a way of organizing the curriculum in terms of a large block of subject matter, frequently including content taken from a number of school subjects, with which the teacher and students may deal for a period of weeks, with the class in session for more than one class period at a time, and with considerable freedom for teacher and class to choose the kinds of learning activities which will be conducted.

Widely different secondary schools refer to their *core*, even though one school is organized in terms of prescribed subjects that are taught most conventionally while another school uses the expressions *core curriculum* or *core program* to refer to the kind of reorganization of curriculum and teaching procedures we are discussing here. It is unnecessarily confusing to have the word *core* used in such different ways, even though the advocates of the core curriculum will be quick to add that there is no confusion, since the core curriculum does deal with what they regard as being the core of the curriculum. At any rate, for the rest of this book we shall be using the *core curriculum* as referring to the organization of the curriculum into large blocks of subject matter selected and taught in terms of students' needs and interests.

Changes in Organization and Content

Teaching in the core program has required changes both in organization and content. Significant is the extension of time so that the core program can be scheduled as a two- or three-period block of time which students spend with one teacher. The longer period gives teachers more of an opportunity to observe and to study students so that guidance can be better informed and more effective. For the student, it means reducing the number of teachers to whom he must adjust each semester.

Schools do not organize the entire curriculum in terms of the core program. The usual procedure is to have students meet with their core teacher for two or three periods a day and then to take separate courses in such subjects as science, foreign language, mathematics, health education, and the fine arts.

The core teacher sees the block of time as improving the effectiveness of teaching, since each extension of a period reduces the number of pupil contacts by 25 or 30. The teacher with an average class size of 25 students meets 125 students in 5 periods—more compositions to read, more personalities to fathom, more students to attend to individually than can be done conscientiously. The teacher with two double core periods and one subject class meets only 75 students daily, with the result that an important part of his work is cut almost in half quantitatively and the qualitative aspect may be improved. When the class average is 30 or 35, the need for reducing pupil contacts becomes even more pressing and the argument for the larger block of time more convincing.

The extended session makes possible significant differences in content and method, too. First, it facilitates dealing with problems that are of genuine concern to the students and to the community although they are too broad to confine within the dimensions of a single subject. Sometimes the problems are as broad as the "developmental tasks of youth" [15] —those problems which young people necessarily face in growing up in our society. These center about the adolescent's concern with his bodily development, defining his role as a man- or woman-to-be in our society, developing relationship with his peers, achieving emotional and economic independence from parents, and building a set of values. Sometimes these problems are social, such as the conservation of natural resources, which involves not only the study of the resources themselves, but questions of public policy and history (social studies) as well as the skills of reading and communication (English). Sometimes at issue is the broader understanding of topics dealt with more narrowly in separate subjects: the historical and social framework of New England's golden literary era prior to the Civil War, for example—an intriguing topic for combination of literature and history.

The advantages of organizing the curriculum in larger blocks of subject matter and of planning the school day in longer units of time appeals to many teachers, regardless of whether or not the school uses the core program as its basic pattern. As a result, many secondary schools now use longer periods for daily instruction and arrange to have their teachers, especially in junior high schools, meet their classes for more than the conventional one period a day.

Not only is informational content affected, but basic skills are also seen in a different light. The lengthened class period makes it possible to combine the skills of expression with content in any of several fields. The combined period, as indicated, reduces the number of students to whom the teacher must give personal attention—needed by the bright and average as well as the slow learner—in reading, and oral and written expression. Also, it ensures a functional context for practice in communication skills. To some extent, possibilities open up in science and mathematics skills as well, particularly in the junior high school.

The longer block of time also facilitates use of less conventional learning resources. Learning that is circumscribed by the four walls of the classroom may be a rather meager fare. Human relations, industrial processes, relationships in production, governmental activities, utilization of natural and human resources—to name just a few—may be mere verbalisms when viewed only through the perspective of the textbook, the teacher's presentation, and perhaps a motion picture or film-strip. Field trips, the educational use of resources in the community, actual observation of and perhaps participation in industrial processes or governmental services make learning more real, make the experience more vivid, and therefore better remembered. The extended period makes such activities possible without disrupting other parts of the school program.

The familiar recitation pattern is inappropriate for the core curriculum, and schools have departed from the practice of having the teacher give an assignment and then spend most of the next day's class session testing student mastery of the assignment. Instead, the boys and girls are analyzing problems into questions that must be answered. They are planning procedures to be used in finding the answers. They are working both as individuals and as committees to find the answers which their class needs. They are evaluating the adequacy of the answers they have found and they are planning the use they can make of the material reported to them. The teacher is there to guide and to help, to point to implications that might otherwise be overlooked, to raise pertinent questions that no one else has thought of, and to help students discover a way of overcoming what looked like an insuperable obstacle. In short, the teacher is there not as taskmaster and policeman, but as a guide who makes available to the class the fruits of his maturity and learning.

Incorporating Guidance Within the Normal Program of Learning

The block of time, the integration of subject matter, and the incorporation of skill development are three important aspects of the core. A fourth, guidance, is closely related. While specialized guidance services and specially trained personnel are essential in a school, it is the classroom teacher who has daily contact with youngsters and is therefore better able to serve as a guide to students. By contrast, the short period which focuses on the mastery of a specified body of content leaves little time for this kind of assistance.

Both individual and group guidance are normally part of the curriculum of the core. The teacher is able to help the class work through the personal, vocational, and educational problems that they have in common. In addition, the core teacher, seeing his students over a longer period of time and observing them as they work together in group situations, can often give help to individuals in problems of personal adjustment. Both through the content of the curriculum and through individual relationships with students, the guidance process is enhanced. Problems of serious maladjustment, of course, are referred to specialized personnel.

Student Participation in Planning

The longer period and the nature of the core objectives provide a framework where students have more face-to-face contact with others as they work on problems of common concern. The impersonality of our increasingly urban civilization is partially compensated for when students have time to work together in this way. The school can help youth feel a sense of belonging to a group so that they may learn respect for the values of the group. If we wish young people to learn the values of our culture, we must help them build a sense of group membership and develop loyalty to the group as well as an understanding of the dynamics of group action which will help them to be more effective both as individuals and as group members.

One of the avenues through which group endeavors are directed is co-operative planning. A core content which utilizes problems that are of concern to young people lends itself to student participation in the planning of learning experiences. Current psychological theory emphasizes the role of purpose in learning. We know that people will persist in the most arduous of tasks when the goal is real to them. Through co-operative planning, students share with the teacher in setting their goals. Students who have a share in establishing objectives feel a sense of commitment, of responsibility toward the learning task. The goals seem important to them and are accepted by them. Continuing participation in planning helps students to feel involved in what is going on, helps them to know why certain steps are being taken and to see what the next step will be. Moreover, co-operative planning contributes to competence in group membership, since it is always a group activity and generally leads to study in large and small groups. Committees assume various parts of a job, and students are stimulated by interaction with their classmates as they work on problems that are of mutual concern.

Illustrations of Core Curricula

A survey of the themes which have been used as the basis for core units reflects this concern with both personal adjustment and contemporary social problems.

In a metropolitan high school situated in a slum area with a high delinquency rate, an outbreak of interracial violence led to the question of what could be done to improve conditions in the neighborhood. The students analyzed their community, evaluated its needs and its assets, studied the causes of crime, suggested needed community improvements, and went about trying to effect the more urgent changes.

As they studied the pressing problems of their own community, problems that were more real to them than were the problems prepared by textbook writers, they learned more civics and more economics than they would have learned in separate courses. Working on the talks they were going to give before various community groups, on the written materials they were planning to distribute among their neighbors, and on the letters they were sending to government officials, community workers, or to the press, they learned far more about effective speaking and writing than they would have in a term devoted to conventional oral or written English. Other subjects, too, were learned; art classes, for example, offered opportunities for working on some of the phases of the larger problems instead of being only a minor subject that everybody had to take.

How can we classify all that they learned as they studied the national origins of their neighbors and the cultural contributions these varied people could make to their community and their country? To which subject shall we attribute the learnings that came as these students led the community movement that brought about the erection of a federally-subsidized housing development, the formation of committees of adults on which neighbors of different nationalities learned to know each other better by working together on the solution of a common problem, and the opening of adequate recreational facilities for children, for youths, and for adults? Reread the list of objectives as stated by the Educational Policies Commission and note how easy it is to achieve these objectives when the curriculum is as vital and the students are as active as they were in this school.

In remote rural communities, secondary schools that have taken the students' problems to be the school's problems have studied community needs, have explored ways of raising the standards of living in the community, and have helped to build the community improvements that were so desperately needed even when the people living there did not realize their needs.

Problems Involved in Using a Core Curriculum

There is no denying the challenge that the building of a core curriculum presents to teachers nor its stimulus to effective learning and continued growth for both teachers and students. There is no denying, too, the serious obstacles to the general adoption of the core curriculum in all of the country's junior and senior high schools.

It is much easier to administer a school when the principal and the teachers know what each class in the school will be studying each semester. It is much easier to plan the curriculum for a six-year secondary school program if we know what will be taught in each subject each semester. It is much easier to teach if we know which assignment we shall give tomorrow or next week. It is much easier to stock the school library if there are separate subjects with prepared lists of books for supplementary or collateral reading. It is much easier to have high school graduates admitted to college when the students have taken a series of conventionally defined subjects. It is much easier to select teachers if we know which topics they will have to teach.

There are other difficulties. Before the core curriculum is suitable for general use, we must find acceptable answers to such questions as: How can schools best select the themes to be included in the curriculum? How can the core topics be planned for the entire secondary school course and yet be sufficiently flexible to meet the needs of a specific group of boys and girls at any given time?

Although the students undoubtedly do grow intellectually, their growth during a single semester or even during a school year may not be measurable by standardized achievement tests or state-wide examinations that are based on the semester by semester allocation of subject matter.

The core curriculum is expensive. This type of program cannot be conducted with classes that are as large as are found in large cities and in rapidly expanding communities. It requires teachers of higher caliber than are tempted by the inadequate salaries many communities pay. To be successful, it needs competent administrators and adequate school facilities.

Not all of those who criticize the core curriculum base their objection on the difficulties which teachers and administrators must solve if the core curriculum is to be successful. Some of these critics object to the apparent disregard for long established segments of the cultural heritage when they do not happen to fit in with the themes being studied.

There are other critics who concede that conventional secondary school courses of study contain much that is outdated but who argue that more will be gained by reorganizing the content of the present courses than by scrapping what we have learned about the present curriculum and embarking on a wholly new kind of curriculum. Still other critics, pointing to the fact that schools ordinarily supplement the core curriculum by systematic instruction in such subjects as mathematics and foreign languages, ask whether the core curriculum provides the organized background that students need in the subjects ordinarily included in the core, such as social studies, English, art, and music.

It is these critics who see the core curriculum as making for serious gaps in student background, gaps that are not compensated for by duplication of topics in succeeding semesters, and they believe that unintentional omission of some topics and unnecessary repetition of others are inevitable in a curriculum that is not planned in detail in terms of the students' total needs and resources over the full six years of secondary education. These critics characterize the products of the core curriculum as glib dilettantes who have never had the intellectual discipline of pursuing a topic beyond the immediate needs of the moment. Some opponents of the core curriculum admit that they are intrigued by the reports of the projects carried on by students in schools using a core curriculum, but they regard these instances as happy accidents. After all, they say, schools ordinarily do not describe projects that do not reach a successful culmination.

Using the Core Program in Secondary Schools

There is no ready answer to the question of whether the core curriculum is the solution to our curricular problems. Certain it is that some secondary schools have used it as a means of building a curriculum that is vital and stimulating. It is equally certain, however, that few secondary schools have exhausted the possibilities of vitalizing the departmentalized curriculum by examining their curricular content in the light of educational research findings and by encouraging departments to work together more closely than they usually do.

Fortunately, secondary schools are not forced to make the choice between accepting the core curriculum as the sole basis of curricular organization or rejecting it entirely. First, it is important to recognize the fact that core represents only a fraction of the school day in junior and senior high schools. Specialized learning continues to take place in separate classes in mathematics, science (although general science is sometimes included in the junior high school core), home economics, industrial arts, physical education, foreign languages, commercial subjects, and so on. Second, many secondary schools have modified cores, utilizing only those features which appeal to them most. What most frequently passes for core teaching is a double period in the junior high school in which the teacher deals separately with the usual English and social studies material. The advantage here lies in the larger block of time which the teacher has with his students, the reduced number of student contacts during the day, the improved potential for guidance, and a framework which may stimulate experimentation. In many school systems this constitutes the initiation to core programs, since it is the least marked deviation from familiar practice.

THE EIGHT YEAR STUDY

Throughout much of the current discussion of the secondary school curriculum, it is often assumed that the academic curriculum, being basically college preparatory, is appropriate for the boys and girls who are planning to enter college. That college entrance requirements color the thinking of the secondary school principals and teachers is apparent to all who know how secondary schools operate.

Can a high school that is freed from the domination of college entrance requirements evolve a new curriculum that will be closer to the needs of adolescents and yet graduate young men and women who are ready for college? [1]

In an attempt to answer this question, the Progressive Education Association conducted a carefully planned investigation that is a good illustration of co-operative research, even though it did not convince all educators that it had found the final answer to the basic question.

Thirty secondary schools which participated in the investigation were given the freedom to develop the kind of curriculum each thought most appropriate for its student body, with the comforting assurance that many of the nation's colleges agreed to waive their entrance requirements to admit graduates from these experimental programs solely on the high school principal's certification that he thought this boy or girl was ready for college. These schools were of many types: publicly supported schools and private schools, schools that were a part of a large school system and schools that were independently organized and administered, schools that were radical in their educational philosophy and schools that saw little need for basic changes in secondary education.

To assist the schools in rebuilding their curricula, the services of curriculum consultants were made available by the directing committee. An evaluation staff helped to appraise the results of the experiment and devised special measurement procedures to evaluate both the tangible and the intangible outcomes of education.

The study was designed to run for eight years so that a group of students might be followed all the way through high school and college. When these students entered college, each was paired, for purposes of evaluation, with another student who had entered from a nonparticipating high school by meeting the usual admission requirements. The members of the pair were alike in age and sex, and, as nearly as could be measured, they were comparable in intelligence, scholastic aptitude, family background, and other factors that might affect college success.

The experimental pattern was clear. Take two groups of college freshmen who are equal in ability and potentiality, save that one group has had a traditional secondary school background dominated by college entrance requirements while the other group has had a secondary education directed by a faculty that is free to think more of adolescents' needs than of college entrance requirements. Follow these groups through college and see which is the more successful.

The Findings of the Study

From the published results, even the most skeptical observer had to admit that those who had come from the thirty schools were at least as successful as were those who had met traditional entrance requirements.

As those who had conducted the inquiry summarized the results:

In the comparison of the 1475 matched pairs, the College Follow-up Staff found that the graduates of the Thirty Schools:

1. earned a slightly higher total grade average;
2. earned higher grade averages in all subject fields except foreign language;
3. specialized in the same academic fields as did the comparison students;
4. did not differ from the comparison group in the number of times they were placed on probation;
5. received slightly more academic honors in each year;
6. were more often judged to possess a high degree of intellectual curiosity and drive;
7. were more often judged to be precise, systematic, and objective in their thinking;
8. were more often judged to have developed clear or well-formulated ideas concerning the meaning of education—especially in the first two years in college;
9. more often demonstrated a high degree of resourcefulness in meeting new situations;
10. did not differ from the comparison group in ability to plan their time effectively;
11. had about the same problems of adjustment as the comparison group, but approached their solution with greater effectiveness;

12. participated somewhat more frequently, and more often enjoyed appreciative experiences, in the arts;
13. participated more in all organized student groups except religious and "service" activities;
14. earned in each college year a higher percentage of nonacademic honors (officership in organizations, election to managerial societies, athletic insignia, leading roles in dramatic and musical presentation);
15. did not differ from the comparison group in the quality of adjustment to their contemporaries;
16. differed only slightly from the comparison group in the kinds of judgment about their schooling;
17. had a somewhat better orientation toward the choice of a vocation;
18. demonstrated a more active concern for what was going on in the world.

The College Follow-up Staff had this to say about these findings:

Some of these differences were not large, but wherever reported, they were consistent for each class. It is apparent that when one finds even small margins of difference for a number of large groups, the probability greatly increases that the difference cannot be due to chance alone.

It is quite obvious from these data that the Thirty School graduates, as a group, have done a somewhat better job than the comparison group whether success is judged by college standards, by the students' contemporaries, or by the individual students.[*]

Critics of the Eight Year Study Respond

Critics challenged these conclusions from many angles. There were those who said that these two groups of students, equated though they might be statistically, really were not equal in ability since one group was admitted to college on the principal's certification while the second group was admitted on the basis largely of their high school grades and the scores of the College Entrance Board Examinations. All that the study proved, said these critics, is that the subjective judgment of competent principals and teachers is a better basis for predicting college success than is the average of a student's high school grades or his marks on a test.

Other critics argued that the superiority of the graduates of the thirty schools did not demonstrate that the educational program of these schools was superior to that of other schools. These critics attributed the difference in student achievement to the fact that the teachers in the thirty schools knew they were participating in a major educational experiment. They had curriculum consultants and evaluation experts to call on for help. They attended special workshops and felt they were among the elite of American teachers. Were heightened teacher morale and greater professional competence rather than the changed curriculum

[*] Reprinted by permission of the publisher, from Wilford Merton Aikin, *The Story of the Eight Year Study* (New York, Harper & Brothers, 1942), pp. 111-112.

responsible for the good showing made by the graduates of the thirty schools?

There were other criticisms, too. Some pointed out that in some of the thirty schools the curriculum differed little from that of all other American schools. Others attacked the statistical procedures and challenged the tests used.

The major finding of the Eight Year Study, however, has withstood challenge and criticism: It is possible for adolescent boys and girls to attend a school which is not dominated by college entrance requirements and then to become successful college students.

The Eight Year Study was possible only at a time when educators were questioning the effectiveness of college entrance procedures and the influence of these procedures on the high school curriculum. Whether it was the result of these doubts or the findings of the Eight Year Study we shall probably never know, but colleges did tend to relax the rigidity of their entrance requirements and high schools did feel freer to modify the curriculum for the college-bound students as well as for the others.

THE CLASSROOM TEACHER'S ROLE IN ACHIEVING THE OBJECTIVES OF SECONDARY EDUCATION

As we discuss the many developments in the secondary school curriculum, we must never forget that the classroom teacher is a key person in education and that it is he who often determines how successful any school will be in attaining the objectives it seeks, regardless of the curriculum pattern it follows. To be sure, some secondary school teachers may have a decisive voice in determining the organization of the school's curriculum. For the most part, however, the teacher's influence is limited to his own classroom, but it is of tremendous significance.

What can an individual secondary school teacher do to help realize the objectives of secondary education? In order to answer this question, we shall examine what can be done by a French teacher in a high school which requires its students to study a foreign language for three years. Such an examination could be made for every teacher of every subject in every type of secondary school, but that process would be most time-consuming and also repetitious. Instead, we shall look at what one teacher does and expect other teachers to examine the objectives of education for themselves in order to formulate their own patterns of teaching.

The French teacher is chosen as the illustration to be discussed here because he has a definite course to offer and has less apparent freedom to wander from prescribed subject matter than do teachers of English or social studies. French, moreover, is usually regarded as a subject difficult to teach, with subject matter that is not too close to the students' immediate interests. As we see what the French teacher can do to help educate his students, we may be in a better position to appreciate how much more can be done by other teachers whose subject matter is not so rigidly defined.

Even selecting the teaching of French as the illustration to be discussed is not sufficiently specific, for teachers vary, schools vary, and students vary. The teacher we shall be discussing is a young woman in her early twenties who has been teaching in this school for two years. The school is a smoothly-run conventional high school where uniform examinations are administered every term. The French department has seven teachers. Because our teacher is relatively inexperienced, she has been assigned to first- and third-term classes. Her classes consist of boys and girls coming from all the social and economic groups in the community and ranging in age from thirteen to seventeen and in IQ from 85 to 143. About two-thirds of her students plan to go to college, but data recently compiled by the school administrators indicate that only about a quarter of her students will actually enter college and that about a fifth will drop out of high school without being graduated. Under these circumstances what can she do to achieve the basic purposes of American education?

The Objectives of Self-realization

The Inquiring Mind. The educated person has an appetite for learning. Addressing herself first to the goal of self-realization, she resolves that she will try to develop inquiring minds and that her students will develop an appetite for learning. This objective she accepts wholeheartedly because she is herself intellectually alert. Fortunately she knows French well and enjoys both the language and the culture. Even more fortunately, she knows adolescents as well as French and enjoys them as much as she does French.

Instead of presenting French as a series of rules of grammar arbitrarily set down, she helps her students to use in simple conversation and dramatization the little French they know and she helps them to arrive at the principles of grammar inductively. Drill they need, as both teachers and students readily admit, but it is purposeful, motivated drill they get, drills that are short enough to stop before tension or a sense of drudgery sets in.

Because she understands adolescents, she knows how sensitive they are, and how much they want social approval; she is careful, therefore, never to embarrass any student publicly and she does not mistake a misplaced accent for a disciplinary offense. She knows there are other sentences to be used when verbs are conjugated than "I am not in my

uncle's garden," and she can anticipate the students' smiles as they con-
jugate "I am not his fiancée." She is not averse to using material for
reading practice that does not appear in the textbook and is ready to
have her class enjoy reading cartoons and jokes that appear in French
newspapers, or reading and even writing comic strips in French. Her
tests are frequent and fair, so that all students can see the progress made.

Her students do not know whether it is because of the teacher's personality, the content, or the teaching, that they enjoy studying French,
and they plan to continue studying the language as long as they can.
They read eagerly newspaper articles relating to topics mentioned in
class and they are happy when they can find an item to contribute to
the bulletin board or an article bearing the exciting label "Made in
France" that they can put on the exhibit shelf. There is no restraining
their excitement as they tell the teacher they actually understood the
French sentence in the popular movie being shown in town. To these
students, French is more than a foreign language; it is a culture, a world
fascinatingly different from their own.

Speech. The educated person can speak the mother tongue clearly.

Writing. The educated person writes the mother tongue effectively.
Although this teacher is interested in her students' ability to speak and
write in French, she knows that English is their mother tongue and that
educated men and women express themselves clearly and effectively
in their mother tongue. Her own speech and writing are good enough to
serve as models, and she seeks to develop similar standards in her students. Not in this class are stilted word-for-word translations accepted.
Instead, she helps her students to see translation as a way of expressing
an idea in language that is clear and idiomatically correct. She lets no
serious error go unnoticed but she is careful not to embarrass a student
by the way she corrects a serious mispronunciation or a grievous lapse
from accepted usage.

Explaining the ways in which the choice of words changes the meaning of the sentence, she can get her class to understand the importance
of careful diction and, possibly, to be a little less impatient when the
English teacher distinguishes between being *eager* and being *anxious*,
between *implying* and *inferring*, or between *permitting* students to smoke
and *allowing* them to smoke.

Because the teacher is interested in two languages, she will use
French as a means of enriching her students' English vocabulary, not
only by teaching such expressions as *tête-à-tête*, but also by explaining
the French origin of such words as *harbinger* and *cliché* which have become part of English. The very fact that the teacher is interested in
their use of English may lead students to use habitually the language
they apparently reserve for English classes and for other occasions on

which they expect an affirmative answer to the question, "Does punctuation count?"

Reading. The educated man reads the mother tongue efficiently. Although the French teacher is interested in developing her students' ability to read French, there is much that she will want her class to read in English. Much of the research work they do in connection with the preparation of individual or committee reports is in English. She will be encouraging them to read magazine and newspaper articles about France today, and she will interest them in reading novels about France, as well as some of the good translations of French classics. Although some language teachers frown on English translations, this teacher believes that the more her students know about France and French literature the greater will be their desire to increase their mastery of French and the richer will be their background for understanding what is discussed in class.

As she guides their reading and helps them to find what they are looking for, she gives them useful practice in reading and may open new areas of reading they can explore after they have left her class. The French teacher surely can teach her students not only how to read, but to read.

Number. The educated person solves his problems of counting and calculating. No French teacher tries to pre-empt the place of the mathematics teacher, but no French teacher who presents her subject effectively can avoid enriching the mathematical background of her students. How can she get students to visualize the relative size of France except by comparing it with the area and population of their own state and of the United States? How can she get them to understand certain French problems without having them understand the graph depicting the population growth in France? When students learn about the system of measurements used in France, are they to be allowed to infer that the French measure weight in kilograms and length in meters only because of a proud refusal to accept our system of weights and measures? Can the students understand the reference in the story to the liter of wine if they do not know whether the liter is approximately a gill, a quart, or a gallon?

Sight and Hearing. The educated person is skilled in listening and observing. Because the students are learning a language that is strange to them, careful listening is far more important in a French class than in most other high school classes. How can the students get the correct sound of *r* in *Parlez-vous français?* except by careful listening and imitation? In the French class, careful listening is an essential skill, even though we may question whether this habit of careful listening will be carried over to other situations or even to other classes.

Health Knowledge. The educated person understands the basic facts concerning health and disease.

Health Habits. The educated person protects his own health and that of his dependents.

Public Health. The educated person works to improve the health of the community. As the class studies French life and customs, there is much the students can learn about health habits, especially if the teacher does not feel compelled to gloss over any defect, however minor, in the country which is being studied or in her own country. Differences between French food habits and American food habits are often useful starting points for a discussion of important health topics. Differences between French and American customs may lead to understanding the differences between health superstitions and health knowledge. The French teacher is obviously too busy with her own prescribed content to have time to spare for extended discussions of health information and health habits, but these topics are properly included in the discussion when they are relevant to the material being considered.

In common with all other teachers, the French teacher should be vitally concerned with her students' health. A sick student who can describe his pains in fluent French is hardly the product the teacher hopes to graduate. The French teacher is, therefore, properly interested in the lighting, heating, and ventilation of the classroom, and she is careful that her home study assignments are not so burdensome as to eliminate the possibility of satisfying the adolescents' need for outdoor play.

Interpreting good health to include good emotional health, she will attempt to create a wholesome emotional atmosphere in the classroom and will avoid the tension, the exaggerated emphasis on competition and rivalry, and the frustrations not uncommonly found in American secondary school classrooms.

Recreation. The educated person is participant and spectator in many sports and other pastimes.

Intellectual Interests. The educated person has mental resources for the use of leisure. There is much that an interesting French teacher can do to encourage rich use of leisure time even though the nature of her contacts with adolescents does not encourage them particularly to be participants or spectators in sports. In their own way, the activities in which French classes engage may lead to the development of interests which may become leisure time activities. These classes listen to French music, sing songs in French, study French art, see French motion pictures, learn about French lace making and other applied arts, learn about French writers and of their contributions to world literature, and, in cosmopolitan cities, visit French restaurants and attend French theaters. All of these activities interest adolescents and all of them suggest leisure activities, provided that they are participated in as fun rather than as burdensome details of a prescribed curriculum. If the French teacher helps her class to enjoy these activities, her influence on her students should be almost as noticeable during the summer vacation months as it is during the school year.

Esthetic Interests. The educated person appreciates beauty. It is impossible to teach French properly without developing the students' appreciation of beauty, for what makes the label "Made in France" so desirable if not the beauty we have learned to take for granted in French products? One could not expect less of a people who, poor though they were, took generations to build churches and cathedrals that are among the outstanding beauties of the civilized world. By making appropriate visits with the class and by encouraging the students to bring to class such French objects of art as they may have at home, the teacher can help boys and girls to appreciate the beauty of French lace, of Gobelin tapestry, of dresses designed in Paris, of French china and glass, of French furniture patterned after that of Louis XIV and Louis XV, and of the French language itself.

Character. The educated person gives responsible direction to his own life. The French teacher, no less than other teachers, has her opportunity to influence the character development of growing adolescents. Her own traits influence those of her students whether she wills it or not. The standards she sets for her class and the qualities she approves, either verbally or by actions, help determine the kind of people her students will become. Whether she stresses the need for continuous self-improvement or complacent satisfaction with low standards—whatever she stresses will become part of her students to the extent that they accept her leadership, for the prestige of a popular teacher has greater weight than many people suspect.

Character education does not proceed in a vacuum or by means of lectures and sermons. It is shaped by the activities through which growing people develop. Since teachers influence the planning of the school's activities, which consume so large a part of the adolescent's day, it is inevitable that teachers should have so important an influence on adolescent character formation. Even the teacher who is indifferent to character development is, by that very indifference, leaving her stamp on her students.

In addition to the opportunities for character education which she has in common with all other teachers, the French teacher through discussion of another culture and other customs enables students to see their own culture and customs more clearly. The literary selections studied in her class are used not only for linguistic purposes but also as a basis for the study of character development and ethical values. The attitudes she expresses and those she conveys without words leave their impress on boys and girls.

The Objectives of Human Relationship

The detailed explanation of the procedures by which the French teacher can help achieve the objectives comprising self-realization by taking advantage of the fact that she is teaching both adolescents and French, suggests the ways in which she can achieve the other objectives as well, particularly the objectives of human relationship. By her own relationships with students and by the tone she sets for their relationship with each other, she can develop respect for the rights and feelings of others.

As boys and girls co-operate in the preparation of committee reports and group projects, they learn to work together. Both by her teachings and by her example she can show them how to criticize others and how to react to suggestions. In a modern classroom, students are not merely individual rivals competing for the teacher's favor and grades; they are members of a group working toward a common goal. In this atmosphere they learn effective behavior as members of a group through the many contacts they have with their classmates. The opportunities which the French teacher has for attaining the objectives of human relationship are those which are available to all other teachers who are interested in exploiting the opportunities presented in class.

Whether boys and girls will be better adjusted in their home life depends partly on the extent to which they are able to transfer to their homes the attitudes developed in class. To be sure, adolescents who learn how to get along with their classmates and teachers should be better adjusted at home than are other boys and girls who are tense, irritated, and frustrated when they leave school at the end of the day. Wholesome adjustment at school, however, does not assure wholesome adjustments at home, for so much depends on the other factors at home.

Parents who are themselves tense or disturbed, who do not understand adolescent boys and girls, who are overworked, or who are beset by personal worries, may create so unwholesome a home atmosphere that young people who seem ideally adjusted at school manifest entirely different personality traits at home. The home adjustments of youth depend, therefore, not only on their education, but also on that of their parents.

The French teacher, in common with all her colleagues, should take full advantage of every opportunity for co-operation between the home and the school and for parent education. Realizing that the general educational level of American citizenry is rising and that the difference between the cultural level of parents and teachers is far less than many teachers take for granted, our French teacher will resist the temptation to talk to parents in the patronizing or condescending manner assumed by some teachers. To her, parents are more than biological necessities;

they are partners in the co-operative undertaking of helping boys and girls to live so as to become the kind of men and women their country needs. Her reports to parents are more than just a series of numbers and her conferences with them rise above the level of mere "tattling."

Aware of the need for closer relationships between home and school, she takes advantage of every opportunity to meet with parents, either individually or in groups. Open School Week and Parent-Teacher Association meetings she does not regard as annoying concessions to the unpleasant circumstance that boys and girls generally have parents. If she is invited to address a parents' meeting, she avoids lecturing, and tries instead to stimulate a forum discussion on adolescent needs and on the ways in which parents and teachers can work together to satisfy these needs.

The Objectives of Economic Efficiency

It is not for lack of appreciation of the need for economic efficiency that the French teacher acknowledges she can make little direct contribution to the realization of the objectives subsumed under the heading of economic efficiency. She admits readily that few high school students ever learn enough French to put their knowledge to vocational use. Except for those few students whose unusual interest and ability indicate that they may continue language study long enough to make vocational use of French, the teacher is properly concerned with its present contribution to their personal and social development.

The personality and character traits which the good teaching of French or the good teaching of any secondary school subject seeks to develop should play a noticeable part in helping boys and girls to become men and women who can make satisfactory economic adjustments. Habits of careful planning and of persistence until the plan is successfully consummated are important outcomes of school instruction. A reasonable confidence in one's ability can stem from a sense of achievement as a result of hard work. Good teaching should help students to distinguish between what is genuine and what is shoddy, between the cheap imitation and the carefully wrought work of a craftsman proud of his skill. Even though high school students never use a single French word in adult life, they should be better producers and more discriminating consumers because of the guidance and the experiences they had in their high school French classes.

The Objectives of Civic Responsibility

French teachers can do far more to achieve the objectives of civic responsibility than is generally done, for French is a social study as well as a linguistic study; it is concerned with the culture of the French people as well as with their language. The study of a foreign language and culture is an excellent medium for teaching the difficult lesson that "different from" does not necessarily mean either "better than" or "worse than," a lesson that has not been learned by bigots. Instead of encouraging the condescending attitude that so often characterizes those who are merely tolerant of others who differ from them, the study of French should develop a fuller understanding of other peoples and a readier acceptance of their right to be different.

The more the student learns about France and the French people, the more clearly will he see that the typical Frenchman depicted on the motion picture screen is but a caricature and that there is as great variation among Frenchmen as there is among Americans. If this leads him to be skeptical of other stereotypes so prevalent in current propaganda, so much the more valuable has the study of French been for him.

To learn about the frugality of the French and to see how intensively they cultivate their soil should shame us for the extravagance that is so characteristically American. The French teacher can help her class to understand the importance of France's contribution to the development of the concepts of liberty and equality. To study the history of France in the last hundred years is to grasp the futility and the costliness of war and the need for working for world citizenship so that nations can differ without being enemies.

The high school French student should be able to understand and to appreciate the brilliant first chapter of Reves' *The Anatomy of Peace* [23], in which the author presents the history of the world between World War I and World War II as it would be told by an American, an Englishman, a Frenchman, a German, and a Russian. Each of these accounts is perfectly plausible if read through the eyes of the citizens of that country. We should all be better off if we studied world history not only from our own standpoint but also from that of other nations.

To see the world from the point of view of another people should not diminish our love of our own country nor our respect for our achievements, but it should enlarge our horizon till we grasp the interrelationships among the people of the world and we respect others' accomplishments and needs as well as our own.

ARE THESE OBJECTIVES ATTAINABLE IN OUR SECONDARY SCHOOLS?

At this point one may well ask whether the high school French teacher about whom we have been speaking is free, in practice, to teach her subject as has been suggested above. Will her students learn enough French to be able to do the work of succeeding semesters. Will they be able to pass in the uniform examinations administered at the end of the semester?

If we re-examine the implications of the kind of French teaching that has been discussed above, it is clear that broad objectives are attainable even where specific content demands are heavy. Her students should learn more rather than less French because she teaches her subject in a vital, stimulating way. They learn more about French culture, too, because she defines culture in terms of problems that are alive and important instead of in terms of such trivial, detailed bits of locational geography and literary and political history as the name of the river on which a certain city is situated or the town in which some king's body is buried.

Lest the reader conclude that the French teacher is in a particularly enviable position to apply the statement by the Educational Policies Commission of the purposes of education, he should be reminded that this list of objectives was not designed specifically for secondary school French teachers nor even particularly for high schools. The objectives we have been discussing have been proposed for American education in general. They seem made-to-order for the French teacher only because she studied them and then adapted them to meet her needs. They are equally appropriate for any teacher who will make the necessary modifications in the statement of objectives to fit a specific school situation.

Teachers are prone to exaggerate the confining restrictions of school requirements. "If only I were free to teach the way I want to!" is often a comforting rationalization for those who would make only inconsequential modifications no matter how free they were, and who lack the imagination, the ingenuity, and the industry to take full advantage of the opportunities they now have. Visit any moderately large secondary school and you are likely to find two teachers who have the same grade and subject assignments, whose classroom doors are separated by only an eight-foot corridor, but whose classes reflect a difference of fifty years in educational thinking.

This French teacher of whom we have been speaking never lost sight of the fact that she wanted her students to learn French and she did help them to learn French. These subject matter goals should never disappear or be slighted, even though they vary from subject to subject, from grade to grade, from school to school, and even from one student to another. A class in metal shop, for example, is conducted differently in a junior high school from the way it is operated in a vocational high school. For this reason, each teacher must supplement his study of the aims of secondary education as a whole by gaining insight into the specific goals he hopes to achieve in his own area of special competence.

If the objectives of education are to be achieved, it will be because teachers are willing and make themselves able to achieve them.

QUESTIONS FOR STUDY AND DISCUSSION

1. In this chapter we discussed the way in which a high school French teacher sought to attain the objectives of education as formulated by the Educational Policies Commission. As you think of the teaching position you now hold, or the one you hope to have soon, what can you do to achieve these objectives of education?

2. Assuming that you accept the objectives of education as formulated by the Educational Policies Commission, what can you do to achieve these objectives if you are appointed as a junior high school mathematics teacher and are evaluated by the principal solely in terms of the percentage of your students who pass in the annual examinations administered by the superintendent?

3. The Educational Policies Commission statement that was analyzed in this chapter is only one of the many formulations of educational goals that have been advanced in recent years. For many reasons, some teachers prefer these other statements of goals.

Examine the statement of educational purposes as listed in your state or city syllabus or read the other formulations of goals as given in the books listed below this set of questions.

What can you do, as an individual secondary school teacher, to achieve the educational goals listed in the statement you have read?

4. What can you do to develop the students' appetite for learning if you are teaching your subject to a class of dull over-age high school students who are in school only because they do not meet the minimum age requirement for leaving school to go to work and who are taking an academic course in high school because no other curriculum is offered in your school?

5. An English teacher, believing that "the educated citizen respects honest differences of opinion," interpreted this as meaning that students had the right to say anything they believed during a classroom discussion. For this reason she said nothing one day when, while discussing the writing of a letter of application for a job, one of the students indicated how the telling of a white lie in a letter of application improved the chances of getting a job.

The next afternoon the father of one of these students visited the teacher after school and indicated in forthright language his disapproval of any teacher who encouraged young people to cheat and to lie.

How should the teacher answer the parent's complaint?

6. A group of teachers in a vocational high school objected that the Purposes of Education in American Democracy were formulated by educators who were thinking only of the academic schools and not at all of the vocational high schools. Which of these objectives of education do not apply to vocational high schools?

7. Taking the secondary school subject you plan to teach, indicate the extent to which a teacher can achieve the objectives of modern education by revising the content of that subject without interfering with the customary organization of the school into separate departments.

8. Taking the secondary school subject with which you are most familiar, indicate specifically how you can correlate the work in that subject with the work students are doing in other subject classes during the same semester.

9. As a subject matter teacher in a traditional junior or senior high school who has to follow a fixed course of study, what can you do to achieve some of the values of the core curriculum?

10. Under the leadership of an energetic new principal, the faculty of a senior high school spent a year evaluating their curriculum and analyzing their students' needs. They then went on to reconstruct their curricular procedures till they evolved a curricular pattern they regarded as being much more appropriate than the one they had been following for years.

One of the serious mistakes they made was that they neglected to bring the parents into the discussions or even to keep them fully informed of the nature of the changes which were to take place. From time to time, the principal did tell the parents at the regular evening meetings that the teachers were re-examining the curriculum in order to assure the students of an up-to-date high school education. He was gratified to note that the parents usually received these announcements with obvious pleasure at having a conscientious and alert faculty that was willing to keep the school progressive and modern.

Neither the principal nor the teachers were prepared for the stormy protests that came at the annual Parents Meeting in May when the chairman of the Faculty Curriculum Committee described the program that was to go into effect in September. The parents, many of whom were graduates of this school, the only high school in the city, could not conceive of a high school curriculum that was so different from the one with which they were familiar. They were not convinced by the explanations they heard from the principal or the teachers.

What disturbed the principal and the teachers most was that the protests were both heated and unexpected. They got little comfort from the thought that they had almost completed their plans for introducing the new program in September, even to the extent of ordering a considerable number of new books and additional equipment, some of which had already arrived.

What should the principal and the teachers do now?

BIBLIOGRAPHY

1. AIKIN, Wilford M., *The Story of the Eight Year Study* (New York, Harper and Brothers, 1942).
2. ALBERTY, Harold B., *Reorganizing the High School Curriculum,* rev. ed. (New York, The Macmillan Company, 1953), Chs. 1, 5.
3. Association for Supervision and Curriculum Development, *What Shall the High Schools Teach?* 1956 Yearbook (Washington, D.C., the Association, 1956), Chs. 1, 2, 3, 5, 6.
4. BROUDY, Harry S., *Building a Philosophy of Education* (Englewood Cliffs, N.J., Prentice-Hall, Inc., 1954).
5. Commission on the Reorganization of Secondary Education, *The Cardinal Principles of Secondary Education,* Bulletin No. 35 (Washington, D.C., U.S. Office of Education, 1918).
6. CONANT, James B., *The American High School Today* (New York, McGraw-Hill Book Co., Inc., 1959), §§ 2, 3, 4.
7. DEWEY, John, *Democracy and Education* (New York, The Macmillan Company, 1916), Chs. 2, 3, 4, 6, 10, 11, 14, 15.
8. ———, *Experience and Education* (New York, The Macmillan Company, 1938).
9. Educational Policies Commission, *Education for All American Youth* (Washington, D.C., National Education Association, 1944).
10. ———, *Education for All American Youth—A Further Look* (Washington, D.C., National Education Association, 1952).

11. ———, *The Purposes of Education in American Democracy* (Washington, D.C., National Education Association, 1938).
12. Faunce, Roland C., and Bossing, Nelson L., *Developing the Core Curriculum*, 2nd ed. (Englewood Cliffs, N.J., Prentice-Hall, Inc., 1958).
13. French, Will, and associates, *Behavioral Goals of General Education in High School* (New York, The Russell Sage Foundation, 1957).
14. Harvard Committee, *General Education in a Free Society* (Cambridge, Mass., Harvard University Press, 1945).
15. Havighurst, Robert J., *Human Development and Education* (New York, Longmans, Green & Co., Inc., 1953).
16. Lurry, Lucile L., and Alberty, Elsie J., *Developing a High School Core Program* (New York, The Macmillan Company, 1957), Chs. 1, 2 3, 6.
17. National Manpower Council, *A Policy for Skilled Manpower* (New York, Columbia University Press, 1953).
18. National Society for the Study of Education, *Adapting the Secondary School Program to the Needs of Youth,* Fifty-second Yearbook, Part I (Chicago, University of Chicago Press, 1953).
19. ———, *The Integration of Educational Experiences,* Fifty-seventh Yearbook, Part III (Chicago, University of Chicago Press, 1958), Chs. 1, 6, 10, 12.
20. New York City Board of Education, *Developing a Core Program in the Junior High School Grades,* Curriculum Bulletin 1957-1958 Series, No. 12 (New York, the Board, 1958).
21. Packard, Vance, *The Status Seekers* (New York, David McKay Co., 1959).
22. Raths, Louis E., *An Application to Education of the Needs Theory* (Bronxville, N.Y., Modern Education Service, 1949).
23. Reves, Emery, *The Anatomy of Peace* (New York, Harper and Brothers, 1946).
24. Smith, B. Othanel, Stanley, William O., and Shores, J. Harland, *Fundamentals of Curriculum Development,* rev. ed. (Yonkers, N.Y., World Book Company, 1957), Part 3.
25. Spencer, Herbert, *Education* (New York, D. Appleton & Co., 1861).
26. Storen, Helen, "Personal Problems and Social Values as Core Content," *The Educational Forum,* Vol. XXI, No. 4 (May, 1957), pp. 397-407.
27. Stratemeyer, Florence B., and others, *Developing a Curriculum for Modern Living,* 2nd ed. (New York, Bureau of Publications, Teachers College, Columbia University, 1957), Chs. 4, 5, 6.
28. Taba, Hilda, and Elkins, Deborah, *With Focus on Human Relations* (Washington, D.C., American Council on Education, 1950).
29. Wright, Grace S., *Block-time Classes and the Core Program in the Junior High School,* Bulletin No. 6 (Washington, D.C., U.S. Office of Education, 1958).
30. ———, *Core Curriculum Development, Problems and Practice,* Bulletin No. 5 (Washington, D.C., U.S. Office of Education, 1952).

CHAPTER 3

Applying the Principles of Effective

Teaching and Learning

»»»»»»»»»»»

ALL OF US have had some teachers who were so effective that they have had a lasting influence; some, whose influence has been negligible; and possibly, even some whose effect has been far different from what they had intended it to be. Why do teachers vary so much in their effectiveness? Are there any principles which are basic to effective teachings, regardless of the school in which one teaches, the students one has in class, or the title of the course?

Few people realize how wonderful it is that anyone can ever teach anything to anyone else, that an idea can be conveyed from one person to another by means of words. Teaching consists largely of setting the stage so that students can learn. The important aspect of a lesson is not what the teacher says, but what the students hear; not what the instructor means to convey, but the impressions that students receive. Learning can take place without a teacher, but never without learners.

The naïve assumption is commonly made that if the teacher is efficient, learning is inevitable unless the students stubbornly refuse to profit. Many a teacher whose class has been unresponsive to his attempts to develop a complex concept interrupts his presentation to tell his students to put their feet flat on the floor and to face the front of the room, almost as though a student's IQ increases when both his feet touch the floor or the student's intellectual interests widen as he faces front till what formerly seemed difficult and remote becomes comprehensible and vital.

The young teacher is usually eager for rules that will assure successful teaching and is disappointed to learn that there are no such rules. If he were dealing with inert materials, he could be given specific directions. It is possible, for example, to follow the instructions in a cookbook and bake a cake that is edible, but there are no rules for making people eat that cake with zest. Similarly, the greater the recognition of the student's role in the learning process, the more difficult it is to formulate rules which, when followed literally, will assure desirable educational outcomes.

The teacher gains more from his understanding of the learning process and from his insight into adolescent psychology than from any attempt to memorize or to apply a rule of thumb procedure for teaching. The art teacher who is dismayed at the lack of imagination boys and girls display when they are given a box of water colors and a piece of paper will find no pat devices for stimulating their awareness of the colorful world about them.

Much that psychologists have discovered about learning is rich in its implications for teaching. The teacher who looks at educational psychology from a very practical point of view is constantly asking, "How can I apply this to my classroom?" The studies of the relative effectiveness of spaced versus unspaced learning, for example, suggest that the teacher provide for periodic reviews of the material studied in class rather than interpret the course syllabus as consisting of isolated topics, each of which is completed in its turn, never to be referred to again until the final examination is administered. The teacher's understanding of adolescent psychology enables him to gain insight into the reasons for some of the puzzling aspects of adolescent behavior. The teacher must use his knowledge of psychology not only as a source of suggestions for teaching procedures but also as a basis for evaluating the procedures he is using and the learning procedures his students employ.

The experiences of teachers and the insight into teaching that comes from the evaluation of many kinds of teachers and many kinds of teaching suggest that there are principles of teaching which can help guide the young teacher. These are principles, rather than rules. They must be understood rather than merely committed to memory; they must be adapted to meet specific situations rather than followed mechanically as though they were "tricks of the trade." In short, they are guides rather than directives, and they are most helpful to the teacher who understands the nature of the problems he must solve as he teaches boys and girls.

THE GOOD TEACHER UNDERSTANDS AND RESPECTS HIS STUDENTS

Because teaching depends so much upon the relationship between teacher and student, and between student and student, it cannot be effective unless there is mutual respect. For the relationship to be effective, the teacher must respect his students as individuals and not just as members of a group that teachers are expected to treat courteously. Boys and girls are quick to sense the difference between the professional smiles some teachers affect when they greet their students, and the facial expression that betokens "I *am* glad to see you." One of the serious but unrecognized drawbacks of large secondary schools with oversized classes is that teachers rarely get to know all their students as individuals and are sometimes hardly able even to recognize some of them when they meet on the street.

Affection cannot be commanded and we cannot ask the teacher to like every boy or girl in his class simply because the mechanics of school registration bring them together. When the teacher reaches the point, however, where he does not even respect them, much of his value for his class is lost. The teacher has to accept the fact that his students are less mature and that they may not know as much about some things as he does; if there were not these differences between them, they would not need him as a teacher. Their interests are naturally different from his, and he would no more care to spend every Saturday evening the way they do than they would care to spend every Saturday evening the way he does.

The respect which a teacher has for his students manifests itself in many ways. He treats his students with the courtesy and consideration he shows in his relations with his friends and colleagues. He corrects their errors without humiliating them, and he acknowledges the progress, however small, any student makes.

What can the teacher do with the occasional boy or girl he dislikes intensely despite all of his own good intentions? In most instances, it is helpful for the teacher to get to know the student better in order to know why this young person arouses dislike. If the teacher's interest in the student helps to uncover and to correct the source of the difficulty, the teacher can do a great deal to improve this student's ability to get along with others. Adolescents can be annoying because of emotional difficulties of which others are unaware. The young show-off, for example, whose loud voice, boisterous laughter, sophisticated clothing, and constant boasting about his dates are so irritating, may be acting that way in a pathetic attempt to keep from feeling shut out by the others. Fortunately, there are few adolescents who are so obnoxious that one cannot get to like them at least a little if one knows them better. In any event, the teacher must be careful to keep his personal dislikes under control, leaning over backward if necessary, to make certain that his emotional reaction to the student does not affect his treatment of him.

The teacher who is prejudiced against his students because of their race, religion, nationality, or social status is clearly unfit to be a teacher in schools which seek to prepare their students for life in a democracy. Though he may try to conceal his biases, adolescents are keen enough to distinguish between hypocrisy and a genuine regard for the many peoples who have helped build our country and shape its culture.

The teacher must respect his students. In turn, he must be the kind of person boys and girls can respect. They want him to be fair and to treat them without favor or prejudice. They want a warm person who likes them and whom they can like. They expect him to be wiser than they, but they also expect him to be clear and interesting when he tries to share his wisdom. They appreciate his sense of humor and his interest in the activities that fill their out-of-school time. Although students do not use the expression, they want a person who is himself emotionally well adjusted and who does not use his classroom position as a means of releasing the tensions within him.

THE GOOD TEACHER UNDERSTANDS AND RESPECTS THE MATERIAL HE TEACHES

The teacher must understand and respect not only the young people with whom he is working but also the content of instruction. The poorly prepared teacher who knows little more than is contained in the textbook or, worse still, in that part of the text which was assigned for the day, is clearly inadequate. But the teacher with an excellent command of his subject from the scholar's point of view may be similarly unprepared if he is unable to see the problem from the students' point of view and cannot develop his material so that it is readily understood.

If the teacher does not think the material being studied is vital, what attitude are his students likely to develop? The cynical, disillusioned, frustrated English teacher is hardly the one to stimulate young people to enjoy poetry, and the disappointed young man who regards his appointment as a science teacher to be a barely acceptable way of filling in the year until he can apply again to the medical school that rejected him last year is not likely to be interested in using a general science course as a means of introducing his students to a fascinating new world.

The school which is bound by custom to an unvarying body of fixed subject matter for each term's work is bound to have teachers who are not convinced of the value of some of the topics they must present. Do all English teachers thrill to the same poems, the same novels, the same plays? Because the teacher, to say nothing of the class, has no voice in selecting the material to be discussed, he often finds he must feign an enthusiasm he doesn't have. Alert boys and girls do not take long to penetrate the sham of the English teacher who turns the pages of the poetry anthology with the tell-tale smile which reveals the thought, "Now, which poem am I supposed to be enthusiastic about this morning?"

There is something to be said in favor of the superintendent who employed as English teachers only those who had strong preferences. Of course, it is possible for such intense feelings to cause overemphasis in some areas and neglect of others. Schools, however, can make more use of teachers with a contagious enthusiasm that begets converts instead of insisting on the dull level of never disliking anything in the prescribed course, even at the expense of getting teachers who never like anything very much either.

Most secondary school teachers have turned to teaching because of their interest in their special subjects. For the most part, they are teaching the subjects in which they majored at college. However adequate this background may have seemed when they began to teach, it is bound to be insufficient as the years go by unless the teachers have continued to be students in their field.

The best physics major at the best college ten years ago is unfit to teach science in a secondary school today if all he knows is what he studied ten or more years ago, even if he forgot absolutely nothing. Similarly, developments in all of the other areas of learning make it imperative that secondary school teachers continue their advanced study and their independent reading as an essential phase of their professional development. In addition to enriching their background of knowledge and subject matter skills, such continued study is likely to keep fresh the teacher's interest in the field in which he is working. In a very real sense, he is learning as he teaches and is less likely to rely on a constantly shrinking intellectual capital.

There are secondary schools, however, which do little to stimulate the teacher's intellectual growth and sometimes have even a deleterious effect. The overworked teacher has little energy for further study; the underpaid teacher has little time for study if he must rush off to a second job in order to earn enough money to support his family; and the demoralized teacher sees no reason to do more than the minimum that is required of him.

If we want to have secondary schools which develop in their students an appetite for learning, we must have teachers who continue to whet, and satisfy, their own appetite.

THE METHODS OF TEACHING MUST BE APPROPRIATE TO THE STUDENTS, THE SUBJECT MATTER, AND THE TEACHER

Everyone knows the difference between a dinner prepared at his home and the typical dinner he can get at an ordinary restaurant. At home, the food is seasoned and cooked in the way this particular family likes it, regardless of whether or not the family next door or the one two miles away prefers to have it done differently. The restaurant chef, on the other hand, has to be careful not to offend the tastes of any of the people who are likely to be patrons. Instead of catering to the tastes of individual people, he prepares food that is acceptable to most people, even though it is likely to inspire enthusiasm in few. The family chef knows, moreover, when the dinner is likely to be eaten and can plan the cooking schedule so that every course will be eaten at its peak of flavor. The restaurant chef, on the other hand, has to be prepared to serve dinner at any time over a four- or five-hour stretch and, sometimes, has to serve food that has been kept warm for too long.

The teacher should resemble the family cook rather than the less personal restaurant chef. The teacher must plan his classroom activities in terms of the specific needs of particular boys and girls instead of those of American youth in general. He cannot teach the same lesson in the same way to all classes, for a lesson that was excellent when taught to the class for which it was planned may be lifeless when repeated six months later to another class. He must take advantage of whatever opportunity he has to adjust the content of instruction, as well as the procedure, to meet the needs of his students.

It is impossible, for example, to think of a way of teaching *Hamlet* that is perfect for all situations. One class may be more mature than another. The differing backgrounds of students suggest different illustrations that can be used to help them see that *Hamlet* was written almost as though Shakespeare had been thinking specifically of them. Some students are barely able to understand the basic plot, while others are quick to grasp the psychological implications of the play. The teacher who follows too literally a lesson plan printed in a methods textbook or who imitates too closely a lesson he has observed taught by another teacher may be teaching in a routine, restaurant chef sort of way. He may not offend his students and he may even be fairly well pleased with the results, but he is not taking advantage of the opportunity to plan the kind of classroom activity that makes students impatient for more.

The methods of teaching must also be appropriate to the subject matter and to the desired educational outcomes. Two poems being studied by the same class may be presented and developed in entirely different ways. A light humorous poem with so definite a rhythm that boys and girls can hardly keep from tapping the rhythmic pattern with their feet does not need the detailed analysis appropriate for a second poem that presents a thought which invites class discussion. Not only should different poems be treated differently, but the same poem may be taught differently according to the educational outcomes desired. A class that is engaged in writing original poetry will be interested in the poet's craftsmanship. Another group, more interested in the study of social conditions, may interpret the poem largely in terms of the light it throws on the attitudes of people in the days of which the poet wrote.

The methods a teacher uses should also take advantage of his own particular strengths and minimize his weaknesses. It would be ideal if every teacher could do everything perfectly. Since he cannot, each teacher should take full advantage of what he does do well. The fact that some teachers have the happy ability of being able to create in a ten-minute talk the atmosphere that invites reading aloud *The Idylls of the King* does not mean that all teachers should introduce poetry by a ten-minute lecture. One teacher with a flair for the dramatic may step to the front of his room, wait for his class to quiet down, stand there for a full minute of absolute silence, and then in a soft, rich voice read aloud:

> These be
> Three silent things:
> The falling snow . . . the hour
> Before the dawn . . . the mouth of one
> just dead.*

Another teacher cannot get the same effect by waiting in an awkward silence before beginning to speak. One teacher can stimulate a love of poetry by the sheer artistry of his oral reading; another, by his gift for getting students to read their own interpretations into the poem; a third, by his singing of ballads; a fourth, by his understanding of the literary and social trends which led to the writing of the poem; a fifth, by his ability to stir the imagination so that it can grasp and appreciate the poet's vivid imagery.

Provided that monotonous repetition of the same procedure is avoided, and that teachers do not become complacent about their limitations, teachers are more effective when they try to develop procedures that exploit their own special abilities while being appropriate for their students and for the subject matter.

LEARNING IS AN ACTIVE PROCESS

All people have had the experience of spending an evening with friends while the conversation drifts to the telling of anecdotes. As the group is convulsed with laughter at the collection of stories that the prize raconteur tells, one can almost hear the members of the group resolve that here is a story they must remember. Yet, the next time these people have the opportunity to tell a story, each one of them tells the same stories he has always told and he remembers few of those he heard so recently. Why don't people remember the stories they thoroughly enjoyed? They remember the stories they themselves tell, but they remember few of the stories for which they serve only as auditors.

* Reprinted from *Verse* by Adelaide Crapsey, by permission of Alfred A. Knopf, Inc. Copyright 1915, 1922 by Algernon S. Crapsey, Copyright 1934 by Adelaide T. Crapsey.

This principle applies equally well to classroom situations. If we ask a student to summarize a heated classroom discussion in which he was one of many participants, the chances are that he will give a better and fuller account of his own contribution than of what the others said. The distortion need not be attributed to his conceit. The explanation is a simpler one; he remembers some ideas better because he played an active part in helping to express them.

Psychology plays no favorites. Learning is an active process whether the school be radical or conventional. Regardless of the kind of curriculum that is used, students who have a vital part in discovering a generalization, in phrasing it to their satisfaction, and in applying it, will understand it more fully and remember it better than they do a principle that the teacher has phrased, explained, and illustrated.

If the study of mathematics is to increase the student's understanding of the world in which he lives, we must not confine his school use of mathematics to the recitation of propositions in geometry. If we hope that from his work in social studies the adolescent will learn the obligations and the opportunities of citizenship so that he will be a citizen in the fullest sense of the word, he must do more than memorize the factual details enumerated in his civics book. In every subject there are important facts that students have to memorize, but whether these facts will be retained as a lasting part of the student's background depends largely upon the extent to which he plays an active part in learning this information and in using it.

Guiding student activities is relatively simple when the school is concerned only with mastery of facts or the development of subject matter skills. As the scope of the modern secondary school is broadened to include a more comprehensive definition of what the adolescent needs to learn, there is need for a wider variety of activities than were traditionally conducted in classrooms. For this reason, units of work include many different types of student activities and even the daily lesson is less likely to consist only of drill exercises or of questions on the textbook material.

Providing for Adequate Student Activity in Various Types of Classroom Situations

The inexperienced teacher is likely to confuse pupil activity with physical activity and to assume that learning occurs whenever students are doing something. Yet a student may do dozens of mathematics examples almost mechanically, with a minimum of mental activity. Similarly, the art student may follow his teacher's instructions and design several book jackets without thinking about the principles he is applying. On the other hand, there may be considerable pupil activity while the class is attending to a radio or television program that has been prepared for carefully and is presented well.

The degree of learning and of retention is influenced by the quality and the extent of the students' mental activity; it is affected only little by the amount of meaningless manipulation that is done. Even a lecture need not lead to passive listening, if questions asked at the beginning of the lecture prepare the students for what is to follow, if the content of the lecture is arranged logically so that students can follow the lecturer's trend of thought, and if the lecturer allows sufficient time for students to ask questions.

Pupil activity is not to be regarded as a separate part of the period which must be added if the lesson is to be a success. It is rather the mainstay of the entire lesson. The lesson must be planned in terms of the contribution the students make to the progress of the class. They must do as much of the actual thinking and planning as possible. In the art class it is they who paint the scene as they see it and in the science class it is they who must try to formulate the principle illustrated by the problems they have been solving.

The demonstration in a science class need not be an academic magic show in which the teacher changes red liquids into green ones or makes sparks fly by bringing two wires together. Nor need it be a monologue during which the teacher asks himself a question which he takes the rest of the period to answer.

There should be a preliminary discussion period as part of the demonstration so that students understand the purpose of the demonstration. Time should be taken during the demonstration to give students an opportunity to attempt to explain the causes of the phenomenon they have seen and to see what questions the demonstration raises in their minds. After the demonstration has been completed, there should be further discussion of the questions the demonstration attempted to answer, of the applications of the principles that have just been demonstrated, and of the unanswered questions the demonstration suggests.

The use of audio-visual aids sometimes provides only interesting interludes because there is little the student is expected to do while he looks at the slide or the film. The student may sit through a film and profit little more than he does from going to the movies on Saturday. The preliminary discussion which suggests questions that may be answered by the film, the key questions which are brought to the fore by the film, and the discussion that follows the presentation, can make the showing of the film a stimulating classroom experience.

Even though a discussion period seems to be the type of lesson in which pupil activity is greatest, the extent and the quality of the pupil activity may be disappointingly less than they are assumed to be. In many a classroom discussion in which there is lively give-and-take among the students and in which the major contributions come from the class and not from the teacher, a careful observer will note that only a minority of the students are participating while the others are as inactive as they would be during some lectures. When we examine the classroom discussion more fully, we shall see how the teacher can be effective in stimulating widespread pupil activity.

Understanding, Rather than Activity, as the Goal

Whether there is any mental as well as physical activity in a laboratory period depends largely upon how well the students understand what they are doing. Many a student has a full year of chemistry laboratory work without learning much beyond how to clean a laboratory sink and how to pack his laboratory drawer without breaking more than fifty cents' worth of glass at a time. Understanding is more important than the routine following of directions as if the laboratory manual were a cookbook. What does the student learn from adding 2 cc. of this to 4 cc. of that, holding the test tube over a Bunsen burner till the contents boil, looking at the muddy solution, and then writing "green precipitate" in his notes because that is what the textbook said he should have seen? The group discussion before any individual experiments have been completed can do much to stimulate genuine participation in the laboratory period.

Laboratory periods are not confined to classes in the natural sciences but are becoming important in the learning of almost all other school subjects. Social studies classes have their laboratory periods in which students spend their time in individual or group study. In addition, they may be using "laboratory practices in citizenship" which center about problems of active citizenship in the school or neighboring community. Language laboratories are being established in many schools in order to give students practice in listening to tape recordings of the foreign language being studied and in recording and appraising their own speech. The various vocational subjects have their shop periods during which students work on their projects. Remedial reading classes spend time practicing the skills they are acquiring. In all of these variations of the science laboratory class, it is important that students know what they are doing and why they are doing it, lest their activities degenerate to the level of the routine application of routine procedures.

That students may appear to be busily working during a practice period offers no certainty that they are as active mentally as they are physically. Whether a practice period is one in which much learning takes place, or merely a time during which students are busy writing unthinkingly, depends upon whether they accept the necessity for the practice period, whether they understand what they are doing, and whether they are actually doing what the teacher thinks they are doing. An algebra class that has just learned the binomial theorem and is supposedly gaining practice in applying it to various situations may be getting the correct answers by applying the same formula over and over again without recognizing that each problem presents a new situation and without gaining in ability to solve certain types of problems when they are not reminded to use the binomial theorem. Practice periods, if they are to be helpful, need more than the instruction: "Do the five problems at the top of page 143."

In short, the teacher cannot assume that his choice of the type of classroom procedure in which the class engages will assure the degree and quality of pupil activity without which learning is impossible. Because it is the pupil who should do the learning, it is the pupil who must be active if he is to learn. It is the teacher's function to stimulate and to guide this activity, not to make it unnecessary or impossible.

TO LEARN EFFECTIVELY THE STUDENT MUST SEE PURPOSE IN HIS ACTIVITY

If we agree that learning is an active process, we can appreciate the impossibility of effective teaching when students see no purpose in the learning activity the teacher is trying to conduct. This concern with students' needs and sense of purpose has done much to vitalize secondary school instruction, but it has also been responsible for some of the abuses in contemporary schools.

Much of the confusion arises from the way in which "student needs" are interpreted. Some schools and some teachers proceed as though they believe that nothing should be taught unless and until the students themselves want it to be taught. Teaching may be restricted to the surface aspects of a topic if important activities which were undertaken with great enthusiasm are dropped whenever the students lose interest in it or are distracted by something else that is, for the moment, more interesting or more exciting.

Such a superficial attitude toward student needs ignores the important role that teachers should play in developing new interests and in helping young people to become aware of needs they did not know existed. The function of the school is not simply to help students fulfill purposes they already perceive but also to help them establish new and more important purposes in life. There is much that students have to learn even when they are not aware of the need. The high school student who plans to become an engineer, for example, may have to study much more mathematics than he would otherwise elect. Similarly, a young bigot may be unaware of his prejudices and may see no need for examining his sense of values or his practices until someone stimulates him to ask questions.

That secondary education cannot consist wholly of elective subjects and that subjects cannot be limited to the material that students voluntarily offer to study does not mean that the teacher has to present his material to the student on a "Take it or leave it" basis—and they had better take it, or else. . . . What is more desirable and more effective is that the teacher should relate this material to the students' present needs or help his class to see why it is being studied.

Social and Emotional Factors in Learning

While students have intellectual and educational needs that are basic to education, they also have important emotional needs that affect learning. Adolescents, like everybody else, want to feel accepted by the group, to believe they are doing something that is important, and to experience a sense of satisfaction in what they are achieving. Recognizing these emotional needs helps us to understand the dynamics of behavior and makes it a little easier for us to see why people act the way they do.

In school, learning always takes place in a social setting. The teacher is necessarily concerned with the educational progress of every student as an individual, but he has to take cognizance also of the social nature of the classroom as a potentially important aid or obstacle. Robert and Ruth come to class not by themselves but in the company of twenty-five or thirty other adolescents. Moreover, they bring with them the background of their families and the community as well as neighborhood and national attitudes toward school and scholastic achievement.

In the school and in each classroom, students become part of a social microcosm, a small community. Adolescents are very much aware of each other. They are deeply concerned about the reaction of others to themselves and about the role they play in the many social groupings found in every school. These groups are not only small friendship cliques; they also include each class as a unit, the home room, clubs, teams, and the constellation of social relationships in each of these groups. Depending upon the nature of the group, consciously or unconsciously, the members develop common purposes, attitudes, and modes of behavior. Robert and Ruth act in different ways in their English class, their mathematics class, the journalism club, and the senior class meeting.

The attitudes that groups develop are an important factor in learning because these attitudes constitute the reinforcement that the group gives to each of its members. In the class that regards poetry as "sissy," Miss Jones will have a difficult job interesting Robert in "Lochinvar" or "Gunga Din," let alone in the "Ode to a Nightingale," because Robert will reflect the group attitude and be troubled if anything he does weakens his standing with his friends. On the other hand, in the senior class that is working hard to ensure admission to college, Ruth will be proud of her strenuous efforts to comprehend theories of atomic structure, for membership in a group which seeks high performance goals is most effective motivation for the individual.

Effective teaching depends upon understanding students as individual boys and girls, but it also stems from recognition of the influence of the classroom group upon each individual.

The Relationship Between Motivation and Students' Needs

When we think of *motivation* in terms of the motives people have for their action, we are using motivation in a much more profound way than when a teacher calls it motivation every time he tells a joke or poses a mathematical riddle in order to interest the class in a new process he is about to explain. Thinking of motivation as a reflection of the student's emotional and intellectual needs enables us to plan in larger terms than that of a single class period. Once the student feels that going to school helps him to fulfill purposes which are important to him, it is easier to stimulate him to learn than when we try to prod him into action every time the bell rings for a new class period by resorting to some stratagem or other.

A medical school student who wants to be a good physician will listen to a brilliant clinician delivering a dull lecture that violates every known principle of psychology and education—and he will listen attentively because he wants to learn everything he can from so distinguished a physician. To be sure, he would listen just as attentively and probably learn much more if the clinician also knew something about the arts of teaching, but the student's drive to learn is so great that it makes up for some of the clinician's lack of teaching skill.

It would be most unrealistic if we were to aspire to developing so great a desire to learn in all of our secondary school students, and yet there is a lesson for teachers in this medical school incident. This student learns from the lecture because attending to the lecturer is part of a larger pattern that makes sense to the future physician. In a similar manner, an adolescent will participate in even a most unexciting classroom activity if being in that class and being in that school make sense to the student.

Motivation should not be thought of entirely in terms of separate class periods when we should be thinking instead of the motivation for going to school. The student who sees the secondary school as one way of achieving his life's goal has better reasons for working than does another adolescent who sees the school as the obstacle that stands in the way of his earning the money he wants in order to buy a secondhand car. Similarly, it will take more than a joke a day, or even a joke a period, to sharpen the intellectual appetite of the adolescent who feels that the

Our students come from spacious homes
and from crowded tenements.

Their interests and talen

d in different directions.

Chicago Board of Education

Our students range in ability from
those whose writings are good enough for publication
to those who can profit from special instruction in reading.

Dr. Albert J. Harris (Queens College, N. Y.)

teachers do not care in the slightest what happens to him so long as he does not disturb the even tenor of the classroom.

Let students feel that they are really accepted in the school, let them feel the thrill of success, let them accept the basic purposes the school is trying to serve, let them see the worthwhileness of what is being done in a specific class, and we have a sounder basis for effective motivation for learning than is possible in any array of temporary shot-in-the-arm stimulants. These goals are not easy to achieve. At times they may even be impossible to achieve either because of the student's own problems or because of the limitations of the school program. Yet, every teacher we remember as a great one from our own school and college days was one who did achieve these goals and did not settle for less.

Developing Interest When Sense of Need Is Remote

However adequately the outline of a course may reflect the needs of students in general, it always contains topics that do not seem to be of pressing importance to some of the boys and girls in a particular class.

Is there anything else a teacher can do when he has to teach a specific topic to a specific class besides feeling sorry for himself or his students? In most instances, fortunately, the situation is not hopeless, for the topic must have been considered important or it would not have been included in the syllabus. It is the teacher's responsibility to bring the topic and his students closer together.

In practice, much motivation is *extrinsic*, arising outside the situation, rather than *intrinsic*, constituting an inherent part of the learning activity. Marks and grades are a common form of extrinsic motivation. Students know that they will be rewarded with a good mark if they co-operate and that they will get a low mark if they do not do the required work. Tests are used as other spurs to learning and teachers are not reluctant to remark, "This is one topic that is always included on the final examination." The teacher's sense of humor, another extrinsic factor, makes class activities less unpleasant, but a witty remark does not make the material more significant or timely. The teacher's anecdotes may even get the class to seem to enjoy the term's work, but it is the teacher rather than the topic that is the focus of the student's attention, and more than one student remembers the anecdote and forgets the point it was intended to illustrate.

Extrinsic motivation is sometimes a practical answer to the teacher's immediate problem—it certainly is better than teaching that offers no incentive at all to learning—but it is seldom the best answer. Extrinsic motivation deprives students of the satisfaction of working with material they recognize as important. It is so obvious and so simple a procedure that the teacher does not see the need for delving deeper into the topic and for studying his students more closely to find a more effective incentive.

Relating the Content of Instruction

Let's see what the teacher can do to make the material vital to his students. As an illustration, we shall look at a second-year high school lesson on the oil controversy between the United States and Mexico and a third-year high school home economics lesson on types of furniture.

In preparing to teach the topic, the teacher must use his students rather than the usual outline of subject matter as his point of departure. He must think not of students in general, but of the boys and girls in his class. It is sometimes helpful to think of one particular student and to approach the topic with a very clear picture in mind of that student's backgrounds and needs: for example, "If I were Bill Thompson, what would I want to know about that oil controversy with Mexico?"

There is only one Bill Thompson in the class. Is the teacher ignoring the rest of the class when he focuses his attention so closely on this one boy? By giving so much attention to analyzing the needs of one individual, he may come closer to meeting the needs of his other students than if he had thought of his class in the abstract, just as the Spanish dancer, who mentally selects one person in the audience and dances for him, makes everyone in the audience feel that he is the one to whom the dance is addressed. The problems Bill faces in his life are closer to the problems his classmates face than are most of the problems that appear in school textbooks, unless this boy is so atypical that he should not have been used in the teacher's preparation of the lesson. The teacher can, moreover, improve his preparation by thinking of the ways in which the other students, too, can use the material they are studying.

The social studies teacher who had to discuss the Mexican oil situation had to begin by thinking of his students rather than of Mexico. To them, Mexico is remote, and the oil controversy is hardly something to concern them. If you were a sixteen-year-old boy, what difference would it make to you whether Mexican oil wells were owned by Americans or not? Actually, sixteen-year-old boys would be closely involved if the United States did go to war with Mexico or with any other country. By waging an unequal war with Mexico, we would soon gain possession of her oil, but would we not lose much more if the other Pan-American countries regarded us as a potential enemy? If we were Mexicans, how would we like to have our country referred to as the poor nation whose wealth goes to foreigners? Can two nations, each believing its side of the dispute to be correct, settle their quarrel by diplomatic adjudication instead of war? Does the Mexican oil controversy help us to understand the Iranian question that almost wrecked the United Nations as soon as that organization was born?

The teacher used the oil controversy between Mexico and the United States as an opportunity for helping his students to understand world problems that are so important as to determine whether or not these boys and girls will be able to live the kind of life they hope to lead in the kind of world that is worth living in.

The home economics teacher who had to discuss types of furniture began, not with a series of charts headed Early American, Contemporary, and the like, but with a class of girls between sixteen and eighteen years of age. Since she had conversed with the girls and their parents on numerous occasions, she knew their social and economic background and the kind of homes in which they lived. She knew, too, that these girls were at the age when they become dissatisfied with the furniture their parents had bought some twenty-odd years before. Some of them were beginning to think of marriage and of homes they would like to have. The teacher knew, too, the mistakes that young people so often make when they purchase their first articles of furniture.

She introduced the study of styles of furniture by discussing with them why young women like to have attractive homes to which they can invite friends and in which they can have parties. They went on to talk of the ways in which one can improve the general impression that a home creates without discarding furniture that is still usable. They spoke of the little things that can be added, of odd chairs, lamps, draperies, and of all the other little touches that do so much without ruining the family purse. The teacher soon pointed out that what is added must be in harmony with the rest of the room. She showed them a picture of a living room and asked which of the two mirrors she showed them fitted in better. After some preliminary discussion, the class nodded agreement with the girl who said that one of the mirrors looked too delicate to harmonize with the rest of the room.

They looked at advertisements in newspapers and magazines and saw that there were various styles, some of which could be combined attractively and others which just did not go together. Before long, they were recognizing and using such words as *Early American* and *Contemporary* as a convenient way of avoiding such circumlocutions as "You know, a wide chair with legs like this."

The teacher stressed the point that furniture is made to be used rather than just looked at and that it must be appropriate to the use to be made of it. Once the point was mentioned, they saw it clearly and one student illustrated it by explaining that a chair she'd like to have in her own room would be out of place in the living room of a family with many small children. They looked at pictures of early American furniture and tried to recreate in their imaginations the homes for which it was intended, and they understood how it is modified for use in modern homes. In the same way they studied other furniture styles, learning much more than names and distinguishing characteristics.

Beginning at the Point of Application in the Students' Lives

Although both teachers used different approaches to their topics, there was one characteristic they had in common. The teachers began by thinking of their students and by trying to find that phase of the topic that came closest to their students' lives. It was this point of contact that the teacher used in introducing his class to the topic he had to teach.

There is such a marked difference between the kind of teaching we have just been discussing and the much less exciting lessons that we remember as we think of our own secondary school days that it is easy to conclude either that these were exceptional teachers or that the topics chosen for illustration were unusually well adapted to this kind of approach. To be sure, these were superior teachers, but their superiority suggests a pattern of thinking that may help other teachers, too, to become superior.

Similarly, the topics we have discussed lend themselves to the student-centered approach, but so do all other topics in the various courses of study, unless they are so clearly outdated or so inappropriately allocated to a specific grade that they do not deserve to take up the time of either teacher or students. The stenography teacher, the printing teacher, the home nursing teacher—all teachers, regardless of their subject or of the grade they teach—become more effective as they develop the habit of planning classroom activities in terms of the needs of their students.

The Maturity of Scholarly Interests

In our eagerness to relate classroom activities to students' needs, we must be careful not to concentrate our attention so completely on the student's life outside of school that we ignore the needs that arise from the nature of the subjects being studied, or that we concern ourselves so completely with the student's present interests that we ignore the opportunity to develop new interests and to get him to sense the importance of problems he had not noticed by himself. As the student's intellectual horizon widens, there is much that he will learn even though it has no immediate application to his daily life. To limit the scope of classroom activities to problems which students confront daily is to encourage the teacher to pose artificial, pseudo-realistic problems to develop the skill and knowledge basic to organized study. A chemistry student, for example, has to learn how to balance equations; the student who is learning Spanish must understand the principles which determine when he is to use *ser* and *estar;* and students who had never used clay before may find it to be a satisfying art medium.

Though the need arises in a school rather than in an out-of-school situation, topics do not have to be presented and taught in an authoritarian manner. The chemistry class that has learned that aluminum reacts with hydrogen chloride to yield aluminum chloride and hydrogen is ready to learn how one determines the amount of hydrogen chloride necessary for a given amount of aluminum and how the chemist can predict how much hydrogen will be liberated. Having learned that substances reacting in chemical change do so in definite proportions, adolescents can understand why no chemist uses more aluminum than is necessary for the amount of hydrogen chloride he is going to use or for the amount of hydrogen he wants to liberate. Like all other people, chemists must live within their means and no chemist can afford to use unlimited quantities of reagents either in an experiment or in industry. Students are ready to learn how to balance equations in chemistry when they understand why balancing equations is important.

Relating learning to students' needs contributes not only to more effective teaching but also to more effective learning, for as Anatole France said, "In order that knowledge be properly digested, it must have been swallowed with a good appetite."

EVERY LEARNING ACTIVITY SHOULD BE POINTED TOWARD DEFINITE AIMS

Every classroom activity should have an immediate and an ultimate purpose. If we know the specific objective of a class activity, we know what the group plans to do that day; but it is only by knowing the ultimate purpose that we can understand why the group is conducting that activity.

Thus, the specific aim in a mathematics class may be to help the students understand the concept of sets; in a social studies class, it may be to clarify students' understanding of the differences between totalitarianism and democracy; and in a typewriting class, it may be to develop speed with a particular combination of letters.

The ultimate purpose is sometimes obvious, as when the stenography teacher helps students to learn grammalogs so that they can take dictation faster by using a single symbol for an entire expression. At other times the underlying purpose may be lost sight of as, for example, when a speech teacher stresses the physiology of speech as though it were more important for the student to know how the sound of t is pronounced than it is for him to be able to speak effectively.

Unless teacher and class understand and accept both the specific objectives and the ultimate purposes to be served by the activity, little that is of value may be accomplished. Classroom discussions without a specific aim may be only idle talk, and a purposeless review lesson may contribute nothing to enrich students' understanding. Clear formulation of the ulti-

mate goal is equally important, for whether a forum discussion of socialized medicine is to be only an interesting way of spending a class session
or a means of introducing students to a new approach to the study of contemporary social problems depends largely on the clarity with which the
teacher and students recognize the basic purposes to be served by the discussion and on the skill with which the teacher sees that these goals are
achieved.

Although classroom activities cannot be conducted effectively if students and teacher work at cross-purposes, it is nevertheless true that the
teacher and the students may see the purpose of an activity from different
points of view. A junor high school class, for example, which is rehearsing a play that will be presented at a school assembly may not see any goal
beyond presenting the play so well that it will win the applause of the rest
of the school. The teacher, however, may be more concerned with the contribution which the presentation of the play can make to his pupils' development. The teacher is alert, therefore, to ways in which some of the less
forward members of his class can participate and is reluctant to restrict
the cast to the best performers in the group. As the teacher thinks of the
purposes of an activity, he must be aware of the ultimate and the immediate purposes, and he must recognize, too, the differences between his aim
and his students' aims [3, pp. 106-110].

Planning Classroom Activities in Terms of the Aims

Unfortunately the general aim of a course is sometimes not reflected
in the activities conducted in class. A general science course that purports
to help students to appreciate the scientific aspects of their environment
sometimes proves in practice to be just a summary of basic information in
science. The English teacher who says he is—or at least the course outline
says he is—most interested in developing an abiding love of poetry proceeds no differently from the way he did when he was, theoretically at
least, trying to trace the development of American literature from Cotton
Mather to today.

In some social studies classes, for example, one of the major aims is
that of helping students to understand how their community operates and
to see both the opportunities and the responsibilities of citizenship. This
aim is so important as to give direction to much that the students do for an
entire term. If this is the theme for the term's work, it is the teacher's responsibility to see that this theme is in the forefront of his mind and the
student's mind so that almost everything done in class contributes to the
attainment of this goal. To explain the goal eloquently during the first
meeting of the class and then to initiate a series of independent lessons not
explicitly directed toward the attainment of the goal is inadequate, even

though the teacher, if challenged, could prove that logically these lessons are related to the central theme.

The relationship of separate lessons to the major goal must be as clear to the student as it should be to the teacher. Instead of being one of a series of discrete lessons on the organization and function of the police department, health department, and so on, each lesson should suggest additional answers to the question: "Why should I be concerned with our local government?" A visit to a police station is of questionable value if it consists only of a morbid inspection of the lock-up. There must be follow-up discussions in order to clarify the relation of crime to other social problems and to see what the community can do to reduce popular indifference to the way police operate. The class should visit the police station not to get a new source of composition topics and two-minute speeches but to see in detail one more instance of the opportunities and the responsibilities of citizenship.

Though the teacher must plan classroom activities so that they contribute to the achievement of important outcomes, it is equally important that students recognize and accept these aims. Many students obediently answer the teacher's questions and follow his specific directions without understanding what it is they are trying to achieve by these questions and these directions.

Some teachers bluntly tell their students the aim for the day's work: "Today we shall study how. . . ." Although such a manner of beginning is abrupt, it does have the virtue of being brief and to the point and it suggests a criterion in terms of which teacher and students can judge what is pertinent and what is irrelevant. Other teachers prefer a more subtle approach and then let the students infer what the immediate objective is. Still other teachers begin with a problem so that students, aware of their inability to solve the problem with their present knowledge and skill, can see how the new processes and the additional information they are learning are applied to the solution of the problem that seemed insoluble just a few minutes earlier. Though teachers vary in the way in which they apprise students of the specific objective and the basic goal, the effective teacher must plan in terms of both types of purposes and be certain that his students are aware of them.

Co-operative Planning

While the teacher has the inescapable responsibility for planning class activities in order to achieve the objectives of the course and of the secondary school program as a whole, this planning will be more effective if it is done co-operatively rather than by the teacher working alone at his desk. Of course the teacher must plan his work in terms of what other teachers are doing; otherwise the content and the activities may repeat the work of a previous semester or omit important segments which no other teacher is including. What is sometimes less obvious is that the students themselves can gain from participating in the planning and that the activities will be better because of the students' participation. Selecting and formulating the questions to be studied and finding ways of getting answers are stimulating intellectual experiences, just as learning the answer is. Why should adolescents be denied this challenge?

Valuable though co-operative student planning may be if used well, it may be worthless and even detrimental if used unwisely. Clearly the extent of co-operative planning varies with the maturity and ability of the class—a twelfth-grade class can co-operate in planning on a far different level than a seventh-grade class can. The limits of co-operative planning are also influenced by the nature of the class activity—there is wider leeway for co-operative planning of the activities of a home room guidance program than of those in a class in high school physics. At each level and in each subject area, however, the quality of learning is likely to be improved if there is as much co-operative planning as is appropriate.

The extent to which co-operative planning is useful depends upon the teacher as well as upon the class and the subject area. Before the teacher can share the responsibilities of planning with his class, he must be sufficiently at home with his material and his group to be able to use the students' suggestions without feeling threatened by them. The inexperienced teacher may find himself unable to control the planning at all as the students assume the direction of the discussion as a direct result of his own weakness and insecurity. He may find, too, that because of his inability or ineptness, he has failed to establish the purposes of the course or to clarify the students' understanding of the goals. Under these circumstances, what began as co-operative planning of part of a course may turn out to be the planning of activities completely unrelated to what the class should be seeking to achieve.

Co-operative planning need not be thought of in terms of all or none. As we discuss in later chapters the planning of units of work, of daily lessons, and of other teaching and learning situations, we shall see some of the many degrees and varied forms that co-operative planning takes. The gradation of co-operative planning ranges from so minor a choice as having students select which of the three poems they have read they will discuss in class all the way to having the class select the specific topics they are to study and choose one of several ways in which these will be studied. As students mature and as they learn to select and to plan their learning experiences, they should have more and more opportunity to participate in co-operative planning.

At no time, however, does the teacher abdicate his responsibility for planning classroom activities. A student who is beginning a new course cannot appreciate its possibilities and is in no position to select the topics to be studied or the sequence in which they should be developed. Teacher planning is basic to successful co-operative planning. The teacher who enters the classroom with only a hazy notion of what should be done is not ready to guide co-operative planning. He must assume his full share of responsibility for initiating the discussion, for setting limits to the discussion, and for seeing that it moves forward. It is he who establishes the common ground on which they are to operate. Because there are limitations to the freedom with which most classes can operate, he must be careful not to violate the integrity of his students, or his own, by encouraging them to make suggestions which he ignores later as he builds the curriculum for his class. If he knows what the class must do and the way in which it must be done, there is no excuse for his going through the motions of pretending that the class is free to make major decisions concerning the content or the procedure.

Co-operative planning can contribute so much to developing an appetite for learning and to effective participation in learning that it is most regrettable when premature and ill-conceived attempts at co-operative planning lead to ineffective utilization of good intentions.

LEARNING ACTIVITIES SHOULD BE PLANNED IN A GRADUATED SEQUENCE

Although most laymen are convinced that teachers have an easy job, the father who has been trying to teach his son or daughter how to drive an automobile has greater respect for any teacher who is ever able to teach adolescents anything. This father's exasperation with his child's apparent inability to learn points to an important principle of teaching: learning activities should be planned in a graduated sequence.

To most experienced drivers, driving a car has been reduced to habit. Without paying any attention to what they are doing with their hands and feet, they can concentrate on trying to guess whether or not the man standing at the curb holding the child's hand will cross the street. The experienced driver does not realize that handling the automatic transmission or shifting gears is a major problem for a learner, and that the novice who has finally managed to get the car moving may not notice that the traffic light has turned red in the meantime.

The father will be more successful in teaching his son or daughter to drive if he teaches one skill at a time and if he does not try to convey the fine points of driving at a time when the new driver is still puzzled by fundamentals. To the experienced driver, all of driving is so simple that he does not realize how important it is that the learning situation should present only one difficulty at a time.

Teachers, too, sometimes take too much for granted, especially when they present a topic they know so thoroughly that it seems as obvious to them as driving a car does to an experienced chauffeur. To a mathematics teacher, for example, the computation of interest is so straightforward a process that once the basic formula is understood, students should be able to do all types of problems. For students, however, every variation from the original problem studied in class presents a new difficulty and they are confused if two or three such variations are presented at the same time. When a new mathematical process is introduced, the numbers should be kept simple so that the students can concentrate on the process without worrying about computational difficulties.

Much of the difficulty that students experience in such subjects as mathematics, science, and foreign language arises from the teacher's failure to provide a suitable gradation in terms of the learner. A topic such as interest should be presented in the simplest situations. It is better to introduce it as illustrated by a bond that pays 4 per cent simple interest than through a savings bank account that pays compound interest. It is preferable to begin with a situation in which the money is invested for one year than for three years. When the teacher introduces variations in the original situation, only one variation should be introduced at a time. If the rate of interest is different, the length of time should remain unchanged; and if the length of time is to be different, the rate of interest should be the familiar one.

As each variation is introduced, the student should have enough practice with it before another complexity is introduced. The teacher must not interpret the students' ability to follow his explanation as indicating their ability to solve these problems themselves. Thus, the teacher who presents a simple illustration of interest and then a more difficult one and then a still more difficult one until he has covered the many types of situations in which interest problems arise, may find that although his students seemed to follow his presentation as he solved the problems at the chalkboard, they are confused when they try to solve even the simplest problems. Students go farther and faster when mathematics is presented as a series of short steps, with opportunity to practice each phase before proceeding to the next one, than if mathematics is an unending series of steep stairs.

The teacher must be careful not to use too many arithmetic short cuts when he is explaining a new process, for what is obvious to the expert may be far from obvious to the novice. To the teacher, once a student knows how to compute interest at 3 per cent, the question of how much interest one gets on $100 deposited for a half-year at an institution paying interest at the rate of 3½ per cent is easily translated into the equation:

$$\text{Interest} = \$100. \times \frac{7}{200} \times \frac{1}{2}$$

The student, however, does not see how the teacher got the fraction 7/200, since up to this point the fraction representing the rate of interest always had a denominator of 100, as in 2/100, 3/100, 4/100, and so on. The teacher will be much clearer if he includes each of the separate steps in the computation even though they will be merged later as students gain in facility. He will be clearer, therefore, if he includes the steps:

$$\text{Interest} = \text{P.R.T.}$$

$$\text{Interest} = 100 \times \frac{3½}{100} \times \frac{1}{2}$$

$$\text{Interest} = 100 \times \frac{7}{200} \times \frac{1}{2}$$

The secondary school teacher need not analyze learning into any detailed series of artificial units. It is important, however, that the learning situations be so arranged that only one new difficulty is presented at a time and that each new skill is mastered before a more advanced skill is introduced.

This principle of stressing only one difficulty at a time can do much to improve the effectiveness of instruction in all subjects. Some English teachers, for example, conscientiously indicate all of the errors students make in their writing. As a result, the teacher may return a student's theme with notations referring to as many as fifteen different errors of eight or nine different types. Even though the student may correct every one of the errors to which his attention has been called, he is not likely to make the correct use habitual if he is trying to correct so many different errors at once. His very next theme may contain exactly the same types of errors.

It is much more effective to focus the student's attention on one major error at a time and to concentrate on the correction of that error, even at the expense of ignoring temporarily other errors that may be equally serious. The student who habitually uses sentence fragments or run-on sentences should be made so keenly aware of this error that he learns to edit everything he writes with a view to correcting his sentence structure. After this type of error has been corrected, teacher and student can work together to correct other errors, such as failure to have subject and predicate agree in person and number.

THINGS BEFORE IDEAS, AND IDEAS BEFORE WORDS

We are sometimes so impressed with the rapidity with which we think education has progressed that we do not realize how much we have to do to apply the principles propounded by educational philosophers of bygone centuries. It was more than three centuries ago that Comenius enunciated the principle, "Things—Ideas—Words," by which he meant that children must have firsthand experience with what is being taught before they can develop the concept, and it is only after they have the concept that they are ready to have it formalized into words. The sequence of first the experience, then the concept, and only last the verbal definition is as valid today as when Comenius first preached it. To violate this principle is to invite students to preoccupy themselves with words instead of ideas.

Who has not met the high school student whose only contact with modern art has been verbal, who can recite glibly the six outstanding qualities of modern art and name five modern artists with the title of one work by each one, and yet has never seen a real work of modern art and would not recognize one if he did see it?

The school is full of words, of words which students hear and which they later repeat verbatim and seriatim lest they be given a low mark by the teacher. They tell you glibly, "The legislature makes the laws, the judiciary interprets the laws, and the executive carries them out." What do they understand when they say, "The judiciary interprets the laws"? Does the expression help them to understand the role played by the judge who tells the traffic law violator, "Ten dollars or two days"? Does this expression enrich their concept of the role that an independent judiciary plays in the protection of human rights and civil liberties?

Firsthand Contacts as the Basis for the Development of Concepts

If we wish boys and girls to develop a new concept or a sounder sense of values, we must give them the firsthand contacts that are the raw materials out of which concepts are built. It is only when they express their ideas in their own words, crudely perhaps but certainly honestly, that we can get them to understand the definitions and the judgments expressed more precisely by others.

If we want them to understand the characteristics of modern art, we must first let them see modern art. The teacher, out of his greater experience and understanding, may help them to understand why the artist selected a given subject, what it was he was trying to convey by that picture, and therefore why he painted it as he did. It is only after they have had much contact with modern art that they can arrive at a list of characteristics of modern art. Only after they have made their own judgment of modern art are they ready to learn how art critics characterize modern art. To present an authoritative list of the six characteristics of modern art before the students have attempted their own description, is to teach them to accept ready-made judgments instead of learning to judge for themselves. To present this list even earlier, before they have seen any modern art, is to give them a set of meaningless generalizations.

This overemphasis on words rather than on understanding is not confined to the so-called academic subjects but can be found in every subject in the curriculum, even in those subjects that seem most concerned with the practical rather than the theoretical. Students can be as fluent and as ignorant when they speak of "sales resistance" in a merchandising class as when they speak of "harmonizing colors" in a home economics class.

Defining the terms that are used is an important step in understanding, but parroting a definition that has been memorized by rote is little more than a waste of time. Teachers often list the difficult terms or the unfamiliar words contained in the assignment and ask students to look them up in the dictionary and to learn the definition. But even students who have dutifully consulted the dictionary may not understand these words if used in another context and they may not be able to give a single illustration of a term they defined so accurately.

Oddly enough, verbal definitions are sometimes overemphasized in classes for duller students, who are least capable of grasping the abstractions they repeat. In schools with an undifferentiated course of study for each subject, the teacher of a class of slow learners usually has difficulty getting them to understand the concepts that are so far beyond them. Although these are the very boys and girls who need a rich background of experience if they are to grasp these ideas at all, the teacher often feels so overwhelmed by the mass of material he must present and by the amount of time it takes him to convey even a simple idea that he resorts to drill on definitions which students are required to memorize.

The modern teacher is fortunately in a much better position than his predecessors were to follow the sequence of Things—Ideas—Words. The trends in curriculum building, with their emphasis on students' needs and students' experiences, invite him to begin with realities instead of abstractions. The use of audio–visual aids enhances the opportunities for bringing students in contact with the experiences on which they can build generalizations. Modern transportation and communication facilities expand the range of experiences students can have and share. Under these circumstances, how can we defend any kind of teaching which does not proceed from experience to concept to words?

THE DEVELOPMENT OF ATTITUDES AND INTERESTS MUST BE PLANNED AS CAREFULLY AS IS GROWTH IN KNOWLEDGE AND SKILL

In every learning activity, usually two kinds of learning occur. There is, first, the learning of the specific skill or knowledge with which teacher and students seem to be most directly concerned at the moment. In the lessons to which we referred earlier, the teacher and class were developing the ability to recognize different furniture styles and increasing their knowledge of American history by studying the Mexican oil controversy.

Though teachers and students thought these were their principal concerns, other things, too, were being learned. Some students were learning to look at furniture as more than something to sit on or eat from and to appreciate the beauty of a graceful chair and the charm of an appropriately furnished room. Some students may have formed the attitude that Mexicans, like all other foreigners who were not wise enough to have been born in our country, are too lazy to work and spend their time trying to get all they can from the United States; other students were beginning to think that the only way nations will ever learn to get along without war is to have the people of one country learn what people who live in other countries are like and to understand the hopes and the aspirations, the problems and the worries of people all over the world.

We cannot ignore the attitudes that students form in class, for these attitudes persist long after students have forgotten the more detailed facts and skills on which they were concentrating. Few adults, for example, remember the names of the composers and the compositions studied in their secondary school music classes, but the attitudes formed in these classes do much to determine whether they are the people who make certain that their community does hear some good music.

Other attitudes, too, are being affected. In some classes, students will learn to respect the opinions and the sensitivities of their classmates while in others they will be concerned only with how much attention they can get for themselves. Similarly, there is much that happens in class that will affect the student's sense of values. Unfortunately, some of this influence is exerted by default rather than by design, for teachers are sometimes so busy with minutiae that it is easy to neglect some of the basic goals of education.

The development and modification of attitudes have been the subject of considerable psychological research recently, especially by those working in the field of social psychology. We have learned much from the studies already conducted and those that are still under way promise to add considerably to our understanding. It is no longer defensible to plan classroom activities solely in terms of subject matter, leaving to chance the development of attitudes and interests.

Sometimes teachers use procedures to develop attitudes which they would never think of using in teaching facts and skills. Some English teachers, for example, tell their students that poetry is beautiful and wonder why students are not convinced. They give students ready-made esthetic judgments: that Shakespeare is immortal, that E. A. Robinson wrote great poetry, and that Edgar A. Guest's work is trash. Small wonder it is that students copy all these statements in their notebooks and dutifully repeat them on examinations as unemotionally as they write that a kilogram is equivalent to 2.2 pounds.

There are times when the way in which the subject matter is treated in class actually interferes with the development of the very attitudes which the teacher is trying to encourage. Thus, one of the reasons for including the study of American history as a major part of the social studies program is to develop an appreciation of the American heritage and an understanding of the factors which helped make the United States a world power. Yet, our social studies classes often stress the problems and pay too little attention to the solutions. This overemphasis on what Henry Steele Commager refers to as the "Headache Theory" that history is just one "problem after another" deprives the student of the inspiration to be found in the study of history. To be sure, we have had our rogues as well as our heroes, and many of our heroes, moreover, had some serious imperfections. Untrue though it would be to teach American history as an unending series of triumphs won by saintly men and women, the like of whom are not to be found in any other country in the world, it is equally fallacious to ignore or to belittle the achievements of the men and women who made them possible.

Planning to Develop a Specific Attitude

The learning activity must be organized with a view to the development of the attitude the teacher seeks to develop. The learning of attitudes is as active a learning process as is every other type of learning. It is the teacher's task to see that the poetry, for example, is presented in such a way and under such circumstances that it is the student who decides poetry is worthwhile. Though the teacher's love of good poetry is contagious, it is not enough for the teacher to keep telling the class how good the poem is. Little is accomplished if the teacher makes all the esthetic judgments and leaves the pupil only the passive role of acceptance.

If the teacher is interested in developing an abiding interest in poetry, poems should be selected that are on the students' level of interest. They should be read in an atmosphere that is so pleasant that the students will have pleasant associations with poetry. Marks, for example, have little place in a poetry lesson. If the teacher cannot read poetry aloud so well that his students hear the music created by the poetry, he can play some of the excellent recordings of poetry that are now available. The students themselves should have the key role of interpreting the poem and applying the poet's thoughts and sentiments, and the teacher must be more concerned with what the poem means to them than with explaining all of the poet's allusions. The teacher must not become a barrier separating the class from the poem, talking so much about the poem and the poet that there is little opportunity for students to read and hear the poem.

When students are encouraged to react to the poetry they read, the teacher must respect their judgments even when they differ from his. They should be encouraged to develop their individual preferences, even though they may not share the teacher's enthusiasm for Dylan Thomas. Once students realize that they do not have to accept poetry on an all-or-none basis and that all people have their preferences for types of poetry and even for specific poems, they have made a notable step forward in their attitude toward poetry.

The Sense of Personal Involvement

Much of the teacher's skill in developing love of poetry is reflected in his choice of the poems he selects for class reading. Some teachers are so respectful of literary judgment that they confine class attention to poems that are classics, even though their boys and girls may not be mature enough to understand them. The teacher can do more to stimulate eagerness to read more poetry and to read and reread the classics, if he begins with poetry that may be less sublime but which means more to his students at the present stage of their literary maturity.

The students should do more with poetry than merely nod their heads respectfully when the teacher asks, "Isn't it beautiful?" They can tell of situations in their lives to which the poem applies and they can tell of people they know for whom the poem is most appropriate. They can read it aloud, alone or through choral reading. Some will want to hear or to sing poems that have been set to music. Others may draw pictures on themes suggested by the poem. They may want to know more about the poet or to read more poems of the same type or on a similar theme. They should have the satisfaction of discovering poems they think should be read to the others. They should see the poetry in life and perhaps try their hand at expressing it in words. The more they do with poetry, the closer some of them will come to respecting those who do appreciate poetry.

The procedures by which boys and girls can be helped to develop a truer appreciation of poetry suggests how teachers encourage the growth of other interests and attitudes. The shop teacher who is eager to develop pride in good workmanship, the social studies teacher who wishes to increase his students' understanding of other peoples, the teacher of commercial subjects who seeks to develop a concept of business ethics for today's world—all can gain by analyzing the procedures that are useful for developing love of poetry.

Attitudes and interests are not developed in response to the teacher's commands. They grow only as students participate actively in experiences which lead them to develop these attitudes and interests. That the teacher's influence is exerted indirectly as he guides these experiences is bound to make greater demands on the teacher's professional skill and on his insight into adolescent psychology than if he could develop these points of view by more didactic methods. Moralizing is a poor substitute for teaching, especially when one is dealing with such intangibles as a sense of right, an understanding of other men, and pride in good workmanship.

THE TEACHER MUST HELP PROVIDE FOR INDIVIDUAL DIFFERENCES IN ABILITIES AND INTERESTS

Meeting the range of ability and diversity of interests among secondary school students necessitates changes in the organization of secondary schools, but it also affects the ways in which teachers work with their students.

Schools have introduced many changes in order to deal with the increasing heterogeneity of secondary school students. New courses and new programs have been offered, even when at times there were not enough students or adequate faculty resources for so varied a program. Multiple track programs have been instituted so that gifted students could be stimulated to work at their level of ability while other students pursued programs more appropriate for them. Special classes have been arranged for slower students—even remedial reading is included in the secondary school curriculum; work-study programs are organized for those who will be going to work either directly after graduation or even without waiting for a diploma; and advanced classes are conducted which enable the superior students to enter college with advanced standing.

The secondary school is far more flexible in its procedures than it used to be. Thus, there are experiments in promotion and in grouping so that students may be with sophomores in one class and with seniors in another. One hears more and more of the need for a longer school day and a longer school year. And even more experiments will undoubtedly be conducted in the very near future in order to help develop a secondary school program that will be appropriate for the varied student body now enrolled.

Classroom Provision for Individual Differences

Administrative changes, however, cannot provide adequately for individual differences. Homogeneous grouping, for example, rarely creates a homogeneous group. If students are grouped according to ability, they may vary considerably in interest. Thus, the chemistry teacher of a bright class may find that some of his students plan to be physicians, others expect to be lawyers, two think they will be accountants, and so on through the rest of the class. So far as the chemistry teacher is concerned, this is far from a homogeneous class. Similarly, students who are grouped according to interests vary widely in ability.

It is the teacher, therefore, who always has the major responsibility for adjusting instruction to meet individual needs. He is handicapped, however, if he believes that he has to treat the class as a unit and consequently seeks to find a level of instruction that comes closest to meeting the needs of most students—a level that does not meet the needs of many students unless the teacher supplements class instruction with other procedures. As one experienced science teacher summarized the situation half-humorously, after years of experimentation he had discovered the level of presentation that bored his brighter students at the same time that it bewildered his duller students.

Grouping Students Within the Classroom

It is to avoid this type of solution that some teachers use group teaching as a practicable procedure. Realizing the difficulty of individualizing instruction when teachers have many classes each day and many students in each class, these teachers divide their class into several groups, ordinarily no more than five, and then try to meet the needs of the various groups as units. The chemistry teacher, for example, may divide his class into a group consisting of students who are planning careers in which they will have to study advanced science courses in college, a group of students who are planning careers that will take them to college where they may have some elementary science courses but probably no advanced courses, and the group consisting of students who will probably have no additional organized course in science after they leave his class. In recognition of the differing needs of these groups, he arranges for them to work on different assignments so that they may get the kind of course that is most likely to be of value to them.

Teachers of other subjects, too, find it helpful to use group teaching. The English teacher may group his students during a writing period so that one group consists of students who write so well that they are allowed considerable freedom in their choice of topic and procedure; a second group includes those who are working on the correction of some specific weakness of style that has been singled out for immediate attention; and the third group is composed of students who, despite their age and grade, are still trying to master the rudiments of correct usage. By seating the members of each group together, the teacher can call group conferences without distracting the rest of the class and can help them to get the kind of assistance they need.

Not all grouping is done on a basis of ability levels. Differences in ability are sometimes handled more effectively when small groups are formed on a basis of interest—when committees are organized around chosen topics, for example—and a wide spectrum of ability is found in each group. In a smaller circle like this, the slower students are more likely to see contributions which they can make and take inspiration from the more rapid learners. At any rate, grouping within a class should be quite flexible, changing the basis for selection from ability to interest as the particular learning task may suggest.

Group teaching is more difficult and more time consuming than is teaching the whole class, as a unit, but teachers who use group procedure point to the gains made by students during the term and to the improved discipline and class morale when students are working at their level of ability. When grouping is handled tactfully, say these teachers, no student need feel humiliated, since the teachers avoid labeling the groups publicly and never use the grouping as the basis for censure or praise. The teacher makes sure that all groups are represented when their written work is read aloud and that improvement in the "Mechanics of English" group receives as much recognition and praise as does the originality of the story written by a member of the "Free Writing" group. In his relations with students, the teacher must reflect the respect he has for each one, and he should treat them as individuals rather than as members of one group or another. Moreover, all of the students should be seated as members of a single large group whenever anything of common concern is being discussed and they can all work together on many class units. It is less humiliating for a weak student to be a member of a group that is getting extra help from a tactful teacher than to have his low marks commented on publicly in the undifferentiated class of a less understanding teacher.

Meeting Differences in Other Ways

There are other means, too, by which the teacher can provide for individual differences. When, for example, we discuss the preparation of the assignment as part of the teacher's preparation of a lesson, we shall see ways in which the teacher can use the assignment as a means of adjusting instruction to the individual.

One of the most obvious places where the teacher should adjust instruction to individual needs is in the conduct of practice periods. Many classroom drill periods are ineffective because all students perform the same remedial exercises even though their weaknesses may be varied. By administering diagnostic tests and by using other means of diagnosing the students' individual weaknesses, the teacher can assure each student the kind of help he needs.

Of all the basic methods of teaching, it is the unit plan that recognizes most fully that each student has individual needs that must be met and individual interests that must be respected. It is partly for this reason that students who are working on units participate more actively than they do when other procedures are used.

In any system of mass instruction it is inevitable that a pattern is created to which the individual student is expected to adjust himself. Adjustment, however, is a two-way process, and the school must do its share, too, in adjusting the pattern to individual students. To see that the adjustment is adequate and satisfactory is one of the many responsibilities of the modern teacher.

Teaching the Bright Student

The importance of devising appropriate education for our gifted students has been expressed forcefully by Lerner.

...the real educational revolution will come not through reaching the masses by TV but through shaping those whom I have called the carriers of promise. Only through the creation of a democratic intellectual elite can the true miracle of a democracy be achieved. That the idea of a creative intellectual minority is not incompatible with the idea of a democratic society seems to me almost too clear to be argued. I am convinced that the educational revolution which began in the early nineteenth century in terms of the mass must now be completed in terms of a spearhead society.*

It is deplorably true that overcrowded schools, oversized classes, and overworked teachers often combine to deprive superior students of the guidance and the stimulation they need. It is also true that we have in our schools many students whose level of performance is far below that of their capabilities. Some of these adolescents are satisfied with average performance when they should be stirred to doing brilliant and original work. Rather than attract the envy or the ridicule of their peers, they elect easy subjects along with the other students and settle for mediocrity instead of gaining distinction.

Whether or not we group bright students into special classes is not

* Reprinted by permission of the publisher from Max Lerner, "The Fabulous Country and the Underground River," *Saturday Review,* Vol. 42 (December 5, 1959), p. 14.

the pivotal question. What we do with them, grouped or ungrouped, is much more important. They need keen, competent, and inspiring teachers who have the materials they need and the time to use them. Bright students can work on a level of quality several years in advance of their school grade. Secondary school students have studied such subjects as anthropology and comparative literature; they have conducted original research; and they have done creative work of outstanding quality.

The teacher has to create a climate that stimulates intellectual growth and that makes distinguished achievement a matter of praise rather than ridicule. When Witty and Bloom studied the high schools which had distinguished themselves in such respects as winning a high frequency of awards in the Science Talent Search, they observed in each case "the far-reaching effects of a well-prepared, enthusiastic teacher" [12, p. 54.]. Achievement depends on motivation as well as intellect, and teachers are in a key position to stimulate the bright student to take full advantage of his ability.

It is important that the bright student be encouraged to do original thinking and original research. Developing the desire to ask questions and to try to find the answers is an important part of their education. We have to take advantage of the imagination and the creativity of those with brilliant minds before they are channeled into fixed ways of thinking. Many of the major discoveries in physics, for example, have been made by relatively young men, with the ages 25 to 35 apparently being the most productive period.

Conant's survey of the high schools argued persuasively for effective counseling that identifies the bright high school students and then sees that they follow a secondary school program that is up to their ability and will prepare them for the higher education from which they will profit. The various manpower studies point to the need for including girls as well as boys in every program for the gifted, for our country cannot afford to ignore the social waste that ensues when superior girls and their families blandly assume that college is not for them. Similarly, we must identify and encourage the gifted adolescents who come from culturally handicapped families whose level of aspiration does not include higher education.

Even though bright high school students are likely to be superior in many traits as well as in mentality, they still are adolescents with all of the problems of teen-agers. They, too, want to have dates, to be independent, to get along well with family and friends, and to select a career wisely. It is difficult to decide what to do when one is good in everything and every teacher urges you to enter his field. Because they set their sights so high, they may be beset by feelings of inferiority despite the popular belief that the gifted adolescent is insufferably conceited. Bright students need the guidance and psychological services that other adolescents need. It is tragic for both the individual and society when a brilliant person cannot use his brilliance because of his inability to face his emotional problems.

A wise and sympathetic teacher can often help the adolescent whose ambitious parents are so solicitous of his intellectual ability or special talent that they leave him little time for developing other interests, too. Here, the teacher will tread carefully, for he may be running the risk of helping to turn a possibly brilliant mathematician into a mediocre tennis player.

The "underachievers." Working with a bright student is one of the special joys that come to a teacher, but he should not be oblivious to the even greater satisfaction of discovering a gifted child who has been an "underachiever." We used to think of the brilliant child as being puny and maladjusted. Now we tend to think of him as shining in school. Both stereotypes may be wrong. Some gifted children have been considered as lazy or dull because they never had the incentive to exert themselves. They feel far more comfortable when they slow down to the pace of the average student or when they find their satisfaction in out-of-school activities.

There are many causes of underachieving and some can be brought to light only after prolonged psychological and pychiatric study. At other times, the explanation is to be found in the more prosaic circumstance that the gifted young person has simply never had the stimulation either at home or at school that might sharpen his appetite for achievement. The teacher should always follow up any student whose intelligence test score is considerably higher than that suggested by the quality of his work. The teacher should also be alert to the student who unexpectedly turns in a piece of work that is far above his usual standard, who asks a surprisingly good question, or who answers one exceedingly well. The teacher should come to expect superior performance on occasion from every boy and girl. Even if the child proves not to be gifted, he will be the better for the interest the teacher is showing in him.

There is no one plan, no one formula, for solving the problem of the education of the gifted. To educate our talented and gifted students, we must educate all children in the best way we know, with sound curricula, adequate schools, sufficient facilities, and capable teachers. We may even find that when we have applied the principles of good teaching to all children that there are few principles that apply only to the gifted. We must be aware of the danger of treating the gifted—or for that matter the slow learners or the physically handicapped or the talented in music—as a race apart from all other children. The important task confronting teachers is to make adequate provision for differentiation among learners, with due respect to the factors that make them similar to others as well as to those which make them different.

Democracy in education does not mean the same education for all students, but it does mean equally appropriate opportunities for all. We cannot dismiss the less-than-gifted with substandard education because from the ranks of these children will come not only the great mass of the population but also some of those who will later distinguish themselves by their achievements if they have the necessary education and the stimulation. History is replete with illustrations of supposedly mediocre children who later distinguished themselves by their achievements. We cannot afford to ignore any of our students.

The principles we have been discussing indicate how teachers work with their students, but they do not exhaust the help that new teachers can gain from the experiences of other teachers. Some of these principles are understood better in a situational context than in isolation and are, therefore, discussed elsewhere in this book as they relate to the specific topics being treated.

How helpful the knowledge of these principles of teaching is, depends largely upon the skill with which the teacher relates them to his own procedures. Though merely understanding and accepting these principles do not guarantee effective teaching, the habitual violation of the basic principles underlying good teaching is bound to reduce the effectiveness of even a well-intentioned and conscientious teacher.

It is with these principles in mind that we are now ready to examine the ways in which we can achieve the aims of secondary education today.

QUESTIONS FOR STUDY AND DISCUSSION

1. McKinley High School is on the "wrong side of the tracks" in an industrial city. Miss Brown is convinced that some of her brightest students will never realize their potential because the community in which they live does not attach much importance to schooling and academic achievement. She knows she has to do something to affect the value pattern of these bright students.

What can she do to develop more positive attitudes toward school?

2. A mathematics teacher has a freshman class, a sophomore class, and three junior classes. To conserve his time, he tries to keep his three junior classes progressing at the same rate so that he need prepare only three different lessons each day.

Under these circumstances, how can he make his methods of teaching "appropriate for the students, the subject matter, and the teacher"?

3. A health education teacher made a survey of his students' ways of living in order to relate the hygiene instruction to students' needs. After summarizing his results, he found that the most obvious need was for improved food habits. They drank too little milk and too much bottled soda. They ate too much fried food and too much pastry, but too little green vegetables.

When the teacher presented the results of the survey, he was surprised to see how indifferent the students were. Like adolescents everywhere, they were so full of energy that they could not understand why anyone should worry about their health.

How can this teacher relate personal hygiene lessons to students' needs without having his students become neurotics who are worried about the state of their health?

4. How can the sequence *Things—Ideas—Words* be applied to the teaching of such a rule as that when two positive or two negative numbers are multiplied the product is positive and that when a positive and a negative number are multiplied the product is negative?

5. How can the sequence *Things—Ideas—Words* be applied to the teaching of such concepts as democracy or freedom of speech?

6. How can a teacher encourage the development of attitudes and interests? For example, how can a science teacher develop the willingness to weigh the evidence on both sides of a question before arriving at a conclusion? How can a language teacher develop an appreciation of the culture of another people?

7. A music teacher at a combined junior-senior high school found that only a small minority of her students had ever learned to play a musical instrument. Determined to teach them that making music was more fun than just listening, she volunteered to teach any student who was willing to learn. In order to give the teacher the additional time she needed, the principal released her from home room and study hall assignments. So many students came for instruction that even though she taught them in small groups rather than individually, she was busy all through the day and long after her colleagues had gone home.

Because she did not have the time to decide which piece each student should play next, she ordered a well-known series of graded musical selections. The students soon lost interest in these lessons and began to drop out of the groups. Upon inquiry, she discovered that they objected to the kind of pieces they had to play, since the series apparently was intended for children rather than for adolescents.

The teacher stopped using this series and shifted, instead, to popular music these students heard on the air, intending later to shift gradually to music of a higher quality. The music lessons became popular again, but the enthusiasm waned just as quickly when the students found how difficult it was to play this music without a background of years of instruction.

From the point of view of gradation, what was wrong with each of these two approaches?

How should the teacher plan the gradation of instruction?

8. Hilgard, after examining theories of learning, presents a summary of principles of learning he regards as acceptable to psychologists. How can you apply these principles in a class you are teaching or are likely to be teaching in the future?

Here are a few statements upon which I would expect a majority of learning theorists to agree. It would be too much to ask for perfect agreement, for some statements require many qualifications, and there are always a few theorists who are sticklers for wording.

1. In deciding who should learn what, the capacities of the learner are very important. Brighter people can learn things less bright ones cannot learn; in general, older children can learn more readily than younger ones; the decline of ability with age, in the adult years, depends upon what it is that is being learned.

2. A motivated learner acquires what he learns more readily than one who is not motivated. The relevant motives include both general and specific ones, for example, desire to learn, need for achievement (general), desire for a certain reward or to avoid a threatened punishment (specific).

3. Motivation that is too intense (especially pain, fear, anxiety) may be accompanied by distracting emotional states, so that excessive motivation may be less effec-

tive than moderate motivation for learning some kinds of tasks, especially those involving difficult discriminations.

4. Learning under the control of reward is usually preferable to learning under the control of punishment. Correspondingly, learning motivated by success is preferable to learning motivated by failure. Even though the theoretical issue is still unresolved, the practical outcome must take into account the social by-products, which tend to be more favorable under reward than under punishment.

5. Learning under intrinsic motivation is preferable to learning under extrinsic motivation.

6. Tolerance for failure is best taught through providing a backlog of success that compensates for experienced failure.

7. Individuals need practice in setting realistic goals for themselves, goals neither so low as to elicit little effort nor so high as to foreordain to failure. Realistic goal-setting leads to more satisfactory improvement than unrealistic goal-setting.

8. The personal history of the individual, for example, his reaction to authority, may hamper or enhance his ability to learn from a given teacher.

9. Active participation by a learner is preferable to passive reception when learning, for example, from a lecture or a motion picture.

10. Meaningful materials and meaningful tasks are learned more readily than nonsense materials and more readily than tasks not understood by the learner.

11. There is no substitute for repetitive practice in the overlearning of skills (for instance, the performance of a concert pianist), or in the memorization of un-related facts that have to be automatized.

12. Information about the nature of a good performance, knowledge of his own mistakes, and knowledge of successful results, aid learning.

13. Transfer to new tasks will be better if, in learning, the learner can discover relationships for himself, and if he has experience during learning of applying the principles within a variety of tasks.

14. Spaced or distributed recalls are advantageous in fixing material that is to be long retained. *

BIBLIOGRAPHY

1. Association for Supervision and Curriculum Development, *Learning and the Teacher*, 1959 Yearbook (Washington, D.C., the Association, 1959), Chs. 2-6.

2. BULLOCK, Harrison, *Helping the Non-Reading Pupil in the Secondary School* (New York, Bureau of Publications, Teachers College, Columbia University, 1956).

3. BURTON, William H., *The Guidance of Learning Activities*, 2nd ed. (New York, Appleton-Century-Crofts, Inc., 1952).

4. CANTOR, Nathaniel, *The Teaching–Learning Process* (New York, Holt, Rinehart and Winston, Inc., 1953).

5. COMBS, Arthur W., and SNYGG, Donald, *Individual Behavior: A Perceptual Approach to Behavior*, rev. ed. (New York, Harper and Brothers, 1959).

6. CUNNINGHAM, Ruth, and associates, *Understanding the Group Behavior of Boys and Girls* (New York, Bureau of Publications, Teachers College, Columbia University, 1951), Chs. 1-4.

7. FAUNCE, Roland C., and BOSSING, Nelson L., *Developing the Core Curriculum*, 2nd ed. (Englewood Cliffs, N.J., Prentice-Hall, Inc., 1958), Ch. 5.

8. FRENCH, Joseph L., *Educating the Gifted: A Book of Readings* (New York, Holt, Rinehart and Winston, Inc., 1959), Sects. 5, 6, 7, 8.

* Reprinted by permission from Ernest R. Hilgard, *Theories of Learning*, 2nd ed. (New York, Appleton-Century-Crofts, Inc., 1956), pp. 485-487.

9. HAVIGHURST, Robert J., *Human Development and Education* (New York, Longmans, Green & Co., Inc., 1953), Chs. 1, 9-15.
10. HILGARD, Ernest R., *Theories of Learning*, 2nd ed. (New York, Appleton-Century-Crofts, Inc., 1956).
11. JONES, Marshall R., ed., *Nebraska Symposium on Motivation* (Lincoln, Neb., University of Nebraska Press, 1953 and succeeding years).
12. National Society for the Study of Education, *Education for the Gifted*, 57th Yearbook, Part II (Chicago, University of Chicago Press, 1958), Chs. 5, 12.
13. ———, *The Integration of Educational Experiences*, 57th Yearbook, Part III (Chicago, University of Chicago Press, 1958).
14. ———, *Learning and Instruction*, 49th Yearbook, Part I (Chicago, University of Chicago Press, 1950), Chs. 1, 2, 9, 12.
15. SCHEIFELE, Marian, *The Gifted Child in the Regular Classroom* (New York, Bureau of Publications, Teachers College, Columbia University, 1953).
16. SMITH, Marion F., *Teaching the Slow Learning Child* (New York, Harper and Brothers, 1954).
17. TROW, William C., *The Learning Process: What Research Says to the Teacher*, No. 6 (Washington, D.C., National Education Association, 1954).
18. WATSON, Goodwin, "What Psychology Can We Feel Sure About?" *The Teachers College Record*, Vol. 61, No. 5 (February, 1960), pp. 253-257.
19. WITTY, Paul, ed., *The Gifted Child*, American Association for Gifted Children (Boston, D. C. Heath and Company, 1951).

CHAPTER 4

Teaching a Unit

»»»»»»»»»

WHEN WE WERE DISCUSSING the ways in which cur-
ricular procedures can help achieve the aims of secondary education,
several references were made to the desirability of organizing the curriculum in terms of large blocks of subject matter. While teachers may
grant that it makes better sense to plan the semester's work according
to major topics rather than by daily fragments, many questions arise
when class work is organized in large blocks. Accordingly, we begin
our detailed analysis of instructional procedures by examining the unit
plan of teaching.

WHAT ARE THE CHARACTERISTICS OF UNITS OF WORK?

One of the basic characteristics of the unit plan of teaching is that
it organizes learning in terms of relatively large areas of knowledge or
comprehensive topics. The justification for using this kind of organization
rather than the smaller daily lesson procedure arises from the hope that
the unit plan of teaching makes it more likely that the student will incorporate as an integral part of himself what it is that he is studying.
The unit plan thus affects the choice and organization of subject matter, the way it is taught and learned, and the objectives.

The procedures employed when instruction is organized in terms
of units are sufficiently flexible that they can be used in almost all secondary schools. Many teachers work in situations where the curriculum
is predetermined, where there is little opportunity for student selection
of topics to be studied. Even so, the teacher can gain many of the advantages of the unit approach by organizing the year's work into broad
blocks of content, each focused on an important topic, using a variety of

procedures, materials, and assignments within each unit [6]. He can vary instructional techniques from day to day to fit the stage of development the class has reached in the unit. He can do most of the planning himself, but introduce some co-operative planning by having students share in decisions about specific aspects of the work, such as choosing culminating activities. He can provide alternative basic reading assignments of varying levels of reading difficulty. He can offer pupils a wide range of individual or small group projects from which each student will select one. Even with a preplanned curriculum structure, the teacher can usually make opportunity in the later part of the term for students to select one topic and organize at least a short unit of study around it.

The unit of work is always planned for a longer period of time than a single class session; for example, two weeks, a month, or even a whole term. The unit ordinarily is based on a problem, a project, or a major question or topic; for example, *Printing a class magazine, Soil-less farming, Atomic power for peaceful uses, Contemporary art, Preventing juvenile delinquency,* and *Inventions which have changed history.* Units are often planned co-operatively by students and teachers. The work on a unit ordinarily involves many different kinds of student activity, such as individual and committee research, oral and written reports, group discussions, visits, invitations to consultants to address the class, construction projects, dramatizations, laboratory experimentation, and others so numerous and varied that the mere enumeration of all of the activities that are conducted would cover many pages [12, 13]. Units of work frequently go beyond the boundaries of a single school subject; thus, the printing of a class magazine in an English class may include not only the writing and correction of student contributions to the magazine but also work in art, mathematics, and social studies.

Some units are planned in terms of subject matter within a single subject. For example, a science teacher may have a unit on the digestive system, and an arts and crafts teacher may have a unit on jewelry making. Other units may be planned in terms of subject matter that includes work in several areas. A unit of work on Africa, for example, may include the study of history, geography, economics, literature, art, and music. Still other units are based on the students' experiences rather than on definite subject matter. Such units are illustrated by the operation of the school bank or the preparation of a Latin American festival.

Units of work differ in the degree of teacher or student direction of the various activities. When the course of study is prescribed and the teacher has a given amount of material to teach during the term, the broad outlines and sometimes even the details of the units of work are likely to be selected and planned by the teacher. The science teacher, for example, who has to be sure that his students learn the functioning of the digestive system, cannot allow his students as much opportunity for co-operative planning of activities as can the teacher who is working with students who are preparing a Latin American festival.

WHAT ARE THE DIFFERENCES BETWEEN A UNIT AND A DAILY LESSON?

A unit is more than just an enlarged daily lesson. In a lesson, the teacher is usually concerned with teaching a specific skill or with developing an understanding of a specific concept. Even though the teacher may organize his lesson as part of a series of lessons that may take as long as a week in order to deal adequately with the skill or the concept he is developing, these lessons are nevertheless likely to be centered about the subject matter he is teaching.

In planning and teaching a unit, the teacher is vitally concerned with the way in which his students are being changed as a result of the activities conducted as part of the unit. Thus, the facts about the ways in which atomic energy can be used for industrial purposes can be taught in far less time by a series of lessons than by the unit method. One of the justifications for using the additional time for unit teaching is that the teacher, in addition to recognizing the importance of learning the factual material, is also concerned with developing the ability to do independent study as well as the ability to work with others in a common undertaking, and with the development of a sense of values and of interests that will persist after the unit has been completed.

Because of the limited scope of daily lessons, even when they are planned in series rather than as a sequence of self-contained periods, the activities in which students engage are also necessarily limited. Students may do independent study, but it is likely to be on a given topic that is to be taken up in class the next day rather than as part of a larger problem that has many ramifications and that calls for planning ways of attacking major problems. Time limitations alone make it difficult to incorporate within daily lessons the many kinds of learning procedures that are possible when teacher and students are free to work with larger blocks of subject matter in larger blocks of time.

The unit of work is often a more valid basis for organizing instruction than is the daily lesson plan. It is more valid logically because it enables the teacher and the students to focus their attention on major problems and it reduces subordinate questions to the proper position. It is more valid psychologically because it recognizes learning as proceeding in bigger units than daily lessons; thus, students are more interested in the major question of whether the United Nations can succeed than they are in the smaller matter of the way in which members of the Security

Council are selected. The unit plan, moreover, accepts the interrelatedness of information and skills that may have been allocated to different departments.

Since the problem is one that the students help to select and the procedure is one they help plan, the teacher becomes a partner in a common undertaking rather than the benevolent despot who must be continually convincing his subjects that he knows what is best for them. The teacher does not have to keep thinking of new ways of arousing interest for an apparently endless series of daily lessons, for the larger outline as prepared co-operatively often provides adequate intrinsic motivation for the varied activities that must be conducted if the unit is to reach the desired culmination.

Because students are more likely to see the total situation when unit procedures are employed, they learn more than they do when they see only that portion which constitutes the day's lesson. They read more; they discuss more; they do more; they learn more. Under the proper kind of direction, some of the independent study that goes into the preparation of a committee report could do credit to a college student writing a term paper. Instead of being limited to a single class text, with supplementary reading regarded as an extra assignment, students become accustomed to using all of the sources of information they can find in order to get the answers to their steadily growing list of questions.

When all of the students read the same assignment in the same book, they come to class with so nearly identical a background that classroom discussion is almost bound to be dominated by the teacher, who tries to think of questions that can prove to be controversial. Since students under the unit plan go to different sources of information and are likely to be at work on different phases of the problem, they are not so prone to prepare for class discussions by merely memorizing the assigned passages in the textbook. Class discussions themselves are ordinarily more lively and more real when the unit plan is used, for students listen in order to get the answers to questions they have asked and they report because they have something to share with their classmates.

Provision for Individual Differences

Because there is such a variety of tasks to be accomplished when the class is working on a unit, more adequate provision can be made for individual differences in ability and interest. It is unnecessary to make the fallacious assumption that all students enter each class session as equal in all respects, an assumption most teachers make when they teach an individual lesson to the class as a whole, especially when the lesson is based on a uniform assignment for the entire class. The more gifted students need not be held to the rate of progress of slower members of the class. Instead, with the teacher's guidance they can enrich their curriculum considerably as they work on individual and group projects.

The needs of the weaker student, too, can be met. Instead of being called on in class to hesitate and stumble while his quicker classmates are impatient to give the answer he cannot formulate, the slower student can investigate a simpler topic, one that he can master and that the class will listen to because it needs the information he has gathered, and he can work at other activities that are on his level of ability.

The unit plan is especially helpful in meeting the needs of students who are not as unintelligent as they may give the impression of being. Some students are slower than others, rather than less intelligent. If they are allowed to spend more time on their work and if they do not feel that only the first student to respond to the teacher's question is contributing to group progress, they may gain enough self-confidence to become accepted members of the group. The slow student, even the less able student, may have some skill or special ability he can contribute to the class if he has the self-confidence to volunteer or if the teacher and class, knowing of his interests and abilities, call on him for help. He may have just the voice quality needed in the play or the artistic ability needed for an attractive masthead for the class newspaper. These illustrations are not intended as a recommendation that the student with a beautiful voice or with unusual skill in lettering should be excused from the subject matter work in which the rest of the class is engaged. On the contrary, the recognition he gets from his special talents can bolster his ego and make him feel that he is so thoroughly accepted as a member of the group that he is more likely to participate effectively in other class activities.

Differences in interests are also easily provided for. Though the young science enthusiast does not need and should not get a secondary school education limited to science, his special interest can serve as a means of broadening his background. Having him prepare a column on recent advances in science for the class newspaper is as good a means of teaching him to write effectively as is the assignment of writing the usual letter in the English class to tell the utilities company that the last bill was in error. His preparation of a report on UNESCO and scientific progress will teach him more social studies and will probably make him a more active participant in the discussions of other committee reports than if he were allowed to assume the common attitude of prematurely specialized scientists that the social studies are just a lot of talk.

The attitudes which students form while engaged in unit work are wholesome by-products. It is sometimes more difficult for the student to be satisfied with slipshod work when he knows his classmates are depending upon him for the answer to their question. Work habits improve when students share the responsibility for planning and for seeing that the plan is carried through. The "I'd rather take a zero" attitude is less prevalent.

Habits of reading widely rather than accepting the textbook uncritically, of using the library as a source of information, of helping others and of responding to suggestions from others, of working independently and of being able to serve on committees, of using information as a basis for solving problems, of regarding the school as a place where real questions are thrashed out, of respecting those who can work with things and with people as they respect those who can work with words—these are more likely to be developed under the unit plan than under other teaching procedures that do not concern themselves so directly with the development of such traits and abilities.

Though units are more than magnified daily lessons, teachers who are limited to daily lessons can achieve some of the values of unit teaching, but with difficulty. It would be erroneous, therefore, to regard the unit and the daily lesson as being in opposition to each other, for many of the differences between these two approaches to teaching are differences of degree. There can be no opposition, moreover, because there are times during a unit when the most effective procedure is to have the teacher take time out from the unit to teach a skill or a concept that is needed for the development of the unit and that can be taught most effectively by a special lesson. Similarly, there are sometimes gaps that must be filled by daily lessons when the units which are taught do not include all that must be learned that semester.

WHAT DIFFICULTIES ARE ENCOUNTERED WHEN UNITS OF WORK ARE USED IN DEPARTMENTALIZED SECONDARY SCHOOLS?

As is to be expected, the unit plan of teaching presents difficulties to the teacher who is in a school organized in terms of separate subjects and daily periods. Although forty-one minutes may seem a long time for some classes, it is much too short for classes that must provide for committee conferences, research, committee reports to the class, and discussion and evaluation of these reports.

An inelastic course syllabus that the teacher is expected to follow is another obstacle to the universal use of the unit plan. Over a three-year period, students who are working on units that are chosen intelligently and planned carefully can cover more material than is learned in the typical junior high school or senior high school, but it is not so certain that in any one term they will cover exactly the material prescribed for the term. Old-type uniform or standardized examinations, with their emphasis on prescribed information content, tend to penalize these students. However, newer tests give greater attention to basic objectives of each course rather than to a body of information for its own sake. The tendency toward reform in test construction is found both in the nationally used examinations of the major test publishers and in the uniform examinations still administered by a few cities and states.

A major problem sometimes develops when the broad type of unit is attempted in secondary schools which continue to be highly departmentalized. There may be duplication of subject matter when the social studies teacher includes literary expression of a particular period of history or the English teacher includes social backgrounds of a literary period. Unit teaching may also result in heavy demands upon the student if each of several teachers expects extensive participation in committee activity outside of class. Sometimes the very enthusiasm with which students participate in a unit of work may create difficulties within the school organization, for students may spend so much time with their contribution to the class unit that they slight the assignments made by other teachers. Finally, procedures must be set up for appropriate correlation of subject fields and for the co-operation of the teachers concerned. For example, designing a suitable masthead for the class newspaper may seem to the English teacher to be an appropriate task for the art class. The art teacher, however, may not be willing to have this work done in his class, for his plans may call for work at this time with three dimensional objects.

Various adaptations have been made in unit plan procedures to overcome the limitations imposed by a departmentalized school organization with fixed courses of study to be followed. Thus, teachers have focused attention on units of work that are based on the prescribed work; for example, social studies teachers may substitute for separate lessons on the World Court, League of Nations, and United Nations a unit on, "How the nations of the world have developed relations with one another in order to promote world peace." Students share in planning the study to be done under this heading and set up smaller groups to probe into various aspects and report back to the class. Other teachers attempt to meet the limitations imposed by their school organization by using units of work for part of the term and then employing daily lessons as a means of teaching the other major topics in the course syllabus. Still other teachers rely on guided individual study assignments, supplemented by class discussions when needed, as their means of assuring that students will master the material in the prescribed syllabus.

Some advocates of the unit plan of teaching will object that the values of unit teaching are lost if there is too narrow a scope for the unit or too definite a teacher veto on students' planning of units on which they are to work. Accepting the validity of this objection, some teachers reply that it is only by modifying the unit plan that they can use it at all in their schools, and that these modifications make it possible to realize

much, if not all, of the value of unit teaching even when the course syllabus is used as the source of the units.

The values of the unit of work are not lost merely because the teacher
sets the major problem to be studied in terms of school requirements and
then works with the students in selecting the specific questions to be
studied and the ways of answering them. When there is a prescribed major topic that must be studied during the term, it is better for the teacher
to face that fact of life than to go through the motions of having the
class select a topic while he uses every artifice to make certain that they
choose the topic he knows has to be selected.

THE RESOURCE UNIT

Departing from the textbook or official syllabus as the source of the
curriculum requires considerable advance planning by the teacher and
the availability of varied resources for teaching and learning. The teacher
cannot invite students to participate in planning unless he has considered
carefully the objectives to be sought, unless he has himself developed a
rich background in the area to be studied, unless he can suggest a variety
of potentially effective learning activities, and unless he has examined
the availability of learning materials necessary for study and research.

Resource unit is the name given to a compilation of materials designed to help the teacher work out his own unit with his class. The
resource unit may be developed by the teacher himself; it may be published as part of the local or state course of study, or it may take the form
of a bulletin prepared by a professional association like *A Teacher's
Guide to World Trade*, published by the National Council for the Social
Studies [11]. When prepared *for* the teacher, it is normally pitched toward any one of several subject areas, and it is broad enough to comprehend a number of topics. As a result, the resource unit is likely to be
useful regardless of the direction taken in teacher-pupil planning, so long
as the major concern of the resource unit is central to the topic selected.

Resource units are built around problems or areas of interest broad
enough to require study for a week, a month, or even longer. The published resource unit will include a list of possible objectives from which
the teacher will select those which are most pertinent to the class and
to the subject. An outline of desirable information and references for further investigation are normally included for the teacher. The major part
of the resource unit is devoted to a description of possible learning activities, a listing of learning materials for the student (textbook references,
supplementary readings, articles in periodicals, audio-visual aids, and
community resources), and suggestions for evaluation to help the teacher
determine whether he has achieved the objectives initially set forth. The
published resource unit may run to seventy or eighty pages in order to

give teachers wide range of choice of objectives, learning activities, materials, and evaluative techniques. A resource unit prepared by the teacher himself is likely to be more modest since it is prepared with particular youngsters and areas of learning in mind.

NEED FOR CAREFUL PLANNING

Units of work undoubtedly create new problems for the teacher who is accustomed to having all his students working on the same task at the same time and who expects his students to be sitting quietly and listening attentively unless he has given them permission to speak. Such a teacher sees only the possibilities of confusion and disorder in a class in which he may expect to find that some students are meeting as a committee to resolve an important disagreement concerning the next step they should take, three or four students are putting the finishing touches to the exhibit case they have built, half a dozen students are trying to find pamphlets that contain the information they need, a group is working together on a large display chart for the exhibit, some students are revising the rough drafts of committee reports, other students are working in the library, and a committee is asking the teacher for his advice concerning the proper procedure to follow in making arrangements to use the auditorium for their exhibition.

The teacher's careful planning can anticipate and prevent disorder when units of work are conducted just as his careful planning anticipates and prevents disorder in more conventional classrooms. Unless the class is so large as to be unwieldy or the physical conditions of the classroom are so unsatisfactory as to constitute an insurmountable obstacle to effective teaching, no competent teacher need be afraid to conduct units of work, especially if he takes advantage of the very helpful suggestions which Burton has prepared [4]. According to Burton, the teacher who is conducting a unit of work will: *

1. Guide the group during the planning period to develop *plans which are so definite and so clear that all know what to do and how to do it.*
2. *Check with individuals and committees before they disperse* for work to see that the more detailed plans are definite and clear.
3. *Anticipate difficulties* in carrying out plans and be ready to call a group conference when the difficulty occurs and before discouragement and work stoppage can result.
4. Guide during the planning period so that *sufficient work is outlined to keep all individuals and groups busy* over a reasonably long period of time. Replanning will keep the sequence going so that lack of work does not cause disorder.

* Reprinted by permission of the publisher from William H. Burton, *The Guidance of Learning Activities*, 2nd ed. (New York, Appleton-Century-Crofts, Inc., 1952), pp. 447-448.

5. *Call for replanning conferences* as work develops unevenly. Workers may be reassigned and activities redistributed.

6. *Keep in touch with the varied activities* by moving from group to group, by participating, by asking questions, by making suggestions, thus exercising both guidance and control.

7. *Foresee certain common opportunities for disorder* and will forestall them by *developing with the pupils regular routines:*

   a. For having all materials, tools, and supplies ready before need for them arises

   b. For distributing materials, tools, supplies, books, papers, quickly and in an orderly manner

   c. For using reference materials, particularly when many pupils wish to consult an inadequate number of references

   d. For holding conferences with individual children who ask for help

   e. For using as helpers any individuals who may for any reason be unoccupied for a time

   f. For moving groups, for observing as groups, without crowding or jostling

8. *Introduce new activities to small groups directly concerned so that tryouts will be without the confusion* which might result from misunderstandings within a large group and from too many persons trying a new process without sufficient guidance.

9. Give, constantly, *direct and indirect training in the conventions and routines of group work:* taking turns, not interrupting, turning to some other aspect of one's work instead of standing around waiting for tools or materials in use elsewhere, signing in and out for tools and materials; and so forth.

10. *Develop with the pupils flexible plans for their own activities:* budgeting time, scheduling group conferences, announcing times for individual conferences.

11. Develop constantly, directly and indirectly, the understanding that *freedom carries responsibility, and that self-control and co-operation are advantageous* to the pupils themselves and are not merely something required by the school.

In practice, the value of the unit method of teaching depends to a great extent upon the teacher's ability. That the teacher is not at the front of the room directing every detail of the day's work does not lessen his responsibility nor the demands on his professional skill. Indeed, it makes even greater demands and sets a higher standard for teacher performance. If the teacher is not competent, unit work easily degenerates into the routine giving of routine reports. Little is gained when, instead of having a lecture given by a professionally trained teacher, we have four amateur lectures given by untrained student lecturers.

It is only the uninformed person who does not recognize the need for highly skilled teaching under the unit plan. If we visit a class which is working on a unit and find everything going so well that the teacher is seemingly unnecessary, it is almost certain that we are observing the work of a teacher who, far from being unnecessary, is a master of his craft.

It does not help a young teacher to master the art of unit teaching if all he discovers is that one has to be skillful to guide this type of learning activity. He wants to know exactly what the teacher does when a unit of work is being conducted. If one were to enumerate the questions that teachers do ask, the list would look something like this:

How is a unit of work initiated?
How do students and teacher plan co-operatively?
Who determines the scope of the unit?
How long should a unit of work last?
How does the teacher guide students' research work?
How does the teacher guide the activities of the various committees?
What can be done to preserve the spirit as well as the pattern of unit work?
What should be the culmination of a good unit of work?
What is the relative importance of the quality of the end product as compared with the quality of the educational process involved in the work on the unit?
How can pupil learnings be evaluated when units of work are used?

Whether prepared by or for teachers, the resource unit is intended as an instrument to assist the teacher in planning, not as a strait jacket or a blueprint which substitutes for planning on his part. Its major purpose is to give the teacher the working materials necessary for him to do an intelligent and flexible job of planning with students.

HOW IS A UNIT OF WORK CONDUCTED?

In order to indicate the teacher's role under unit teaching, we shall follow a unit from its inception to its completion. The illustration we shall use is that of a senior high school history class which developed a unit on the United Nations.

It is relatively easy to see how a unit of work can be conducted successfully under ideal conditions. What many teachers want to know is whether it can be employed in less favorable circumstances. Can it be used effectively when there is a prescribed course outline? Can a unit of work be conducted if the class period is as short as forty-one minutes? Can it be used when classes are large? How can units of work be initiated when neither the teacher nor the class has had any previous experience with such procedure? How can students who have been accustomed to daily lessons learn how to proceed under a unit plan of teaching? How can a teacher learn to solve the different classroom problems that arise when teaching is organized in terms of units of work?

The teacher who has never taught a unit of work or seen one taught in his school is ordinarily not convinced of its practicability for his own classes even after he has observed units of work being taught in other schools. Though he may be impressed by what he has observed, he may attribute the success of the procedure to the rare excellence of the teacher or the students, to the appropriateness of the curriculum, or to almost any factor other than the quality of learning that can be stimulated by the effective teaching of units of work.

For these reasons we shall illustrate the process with a unit which was conducted under relatively adverse conditions. Neither the teacher nor the class had any prior experience with the procedure. Because of this inexperience, work on the unit proceeded less efficiently, especially at the beginning, than it does when both teacher and students are familiar with units of work. If units of work can be taught even under unfavorable conditions, it is easy to understand how much more effective they can be when the curricular patterns and administrative procedures are better adapted to such work and when teacher and class have learned how to solve the problems involved in the effective conduct of units of work.

The unit of work that will be described below is not intended as an illustration of a model unit or even as an illustration of the ideal way of conducting a unit. As we shall see when we examine the unit in detail, the teacher did not make full use of all the possibilities of unit teaching. In some respects, the teacher revealed all too clearly his inexperience in conducting units of work.

Despite its inadequacies and its imperfections, the illustration has value, for it comes closer to describing the problems that confront the secondary school teacher who wishes to use units of work than would the description of a model unit conducted under ideal circumstances. Those who are accustomed to teaching by units of work sometimes forget how big is the step from the daily lesson to teaching a unit of work. Let a teacher take this step and then find that he and his class are the better for his having taken it, and he is ready for the next step and the ones thereafter. Basically, the problems which had to be faced by the teacher and the class we shall be talking about are so similar to the problems that all teachers and students have to face whenever units of work are conducted that we can gain a great deal from seeing how they began their unit, how they conducted it, and how they evaluated the results.

How Is a Unit of Work Initiated?

The class which conducted this unit of work is in a large metropolitan high school with a syllabus for each term's work in every subject. There are state-wide examinations, administered after the student has completed the year's course in American history, as well as school-wide midterm and final examinations. The thirty-six students in the class are taking the regular college preparatory course, but the teacher knows that only fifteen boys and girls have applied for entrance to a liberal arts college. Twelve other students are planning to enter junior colleges or specialized schools in order to prepare for such careers as nursing and aeronautical mechanics. The remaining students do not plan to go to another school after graduation. Some of these boys and girls know that they will go to work, while a few of the girls have indicated that they plan to stay home till they marry, meanwhile assisting at home or with a business operated by the family.

So far as the teacher knew, these students had had no previous experience in conducting units of work. From what he knew of his colleagues, it was unlikely that many of them ever used units of work in their teaching, except that they sometimes did take more than one lesson to teach a topic, but it was always the teacher and not the students who decided what was to be covered each day. The classroom furniture, by the way, was securely attached to the floor. The students' desks were arranged in six rows with seven seats to each row, except for the two rows which had only six seats in order to leave room for the teacher's desk and chair.

This class spent the first class session after the midterm examinations going over the test results. Papers were returned to the students and the class discussion centered about common weaknesses revealed by the test and about the steps they ought to take to prepare more adequately for the final examination, which was to be a state-wide test. Some indication of the students' level of achievement was given by a quick summary of the midterm examination results. The median mark for the class was 78 per cent, which was a shade lower than the median mark of all students in the school who took that examination. Three students failed to attain the passing mark of 65 per cent.

It was the following day, the second day of classes after midterm examinations, that the teacher began the day's work with the reminder that this was for them the last lap of the race; only half a term of high school remained before graduation. Knowing his students, he was ready for the applause that greeted so encouraging a remark. A moment later, he resumed. Within three months they would have their diplomas, with all of the rights, privileges, and obligations that go with the diploma. In just a few years, they would be voting citizens, free to exercise their ballot in helping to shape our nation's policies so as to banish the threat of nuclear warfare. Which problems did they think were the most serious ones now confronting the nation?

Students' participation in planning. As the students suggested problems, the teacher wrote each one on the chalkboard, commenting briefly on some of them, and, when the suggestions came more frequently, eliminating the comments in order to keep up with the questions. Within a few minutes, the board was covered with questions, some important and others trivial, but all made and received seriously. Among the questions were these:

Is another world war inevitable?
Should we have socialized medicine?
Can we eliminate racketeering in labor unions without destroying unions?
Should integration apply to private as well as public schools?

When the chalkboards were almost completely covered with questions, the teacher stepped back and said, "Let's see what we have so far."

He was expressing his opinion that these were important questions that had to be answered when one of the girls pointed out that some of the questions were duplications. The teacher suggested that all examine the questions to see whether they could be grouped under larger headings. After some discussion, the following topics were listed:

Industrial Relations
International Relations
Social and Economic Security
The Family Today
Personal Adjustment

Next to each topic, the teacher copied the questions which the students thought summarized best what they wanted to know about the topic. Some of the questions were revised in the process of discussion and it was these revised questions the teacher now wrote. Thus, *Industrial Relations* was followed by the question: "How can labor and capital work together so that the entire country can profit from our industrial capacity?" and *International Relations* was followed by the question: "Can the United Nations ever be more than just a debating society?"

"If we were to take two or three weeks together to try to find the answer to one of these big questions," asked the teacher, "which one would you like to take first?"

It was clear that the students did not agree on which one of the five questions was the most urgent, although there was relatively little support for the topic, The Family Today. Several students explained why the question they were asking was the most important of all and why the other questions could wait. Because the bell was about to ring, the teacher suggested that they postpone making the decision till the next day. In the meantime, they were asked to discuss these questions among themselves to see whether they could resolve their differences of opinion and agree on the one question they all thought most urgent.

At the beginning of the next day's class session, the teacher asked whether there was any agreement on the topic to be discussed. It was soon apparent that the members of the class had not paid much attention to the teacher's parting suggestion the previous day that they discuss the questions among themselves. It was the teacher who asked for a show of hands to indicate whether there was any greater agreement among them

now than there had been yesterday. Without further discussion, a vote
was taken, with the following results:

Industrial Relations	12
International Relations	15
Social and Economic Security	5
The Family Today	1
Personal Adjustment	2

There were only thirty-five votes because one boy was absent.

Those who had voted for International Relations interpreted the vote
as meaning victory for their side since they had more votes than any other
group, while the Industrial Relations group soon pointed out that more
students had voted for other topics than had voted for International Relations. As so often happens in a dispute, both sides were right in what they
said. Rather than see class work go off at a tangent while the two groups
of students fought it out to see which side would win—some students
were undoubtedly becoming more concerned with winning than with
choosing the best topic—the teacher suggested a compromise. What did
they think of taking International Relations first and then Industrial Relations? The class voted overwhelmingly in favor of this suggestion and they
were ready to proceed.

Teacher's role during student planning. Let's leave the lesson for
awhile and evaluate what the teacher did to get the unit started. A cynical
observer may ask whether the teacher did not waste a little more than a
period of class time in trying to get the boys and girls to agree to study
International Relations when he knew all along that this was what he was
going to have them study anyway. Why didn't he tell them at the beginning that International Relations was so important a topic that they were
going to study it together?

The teacher did not know in advance that this was the topic that
would be chosen. When he opened the discussion the first day, he knew
that he wanted to organize the class instruction in terms of a large unit,
but he did not know which unit would be chosen except that he would
use his influence to get students to think of topics that would achieve the
specific objectives set for that grade.

The expression "use his influence" is not synonymous with "manage
somehow or other to get." His opening statement illustrates the kind of influence he exerted. By referring to the total devastation that modern
warfare makes possible, he did set their minds to thinking along one line
rather than along another. Had he started another way, by commenting
lightly on the number of people who are ready to air their personal woes
on television and by asking casually whether they had any questions they
would like to have answered, the class would have responded differently.

Such questions might have been more profound than those which the history teacher elicited, or they might have been silly, but they would certainly have been different because the setting was different.

"What would have happened," inquires a curious observer, "if the vote had yielded a different result, if International Relations had received only three votes and yet had to be taught because it was in the syllabus?"

The teacher was not disturbed by this possibility since he knew that he still had two months left and could teach the topic another way if it were not selected by the class as the unit of work. One thing he did know, and that is that it would be foolish to try to force the class to choose the unit he preferred. Had he insisted on a unit of work for which only a small minority voted, it would have been a unit of work for him rather than his class.

"Wasn't the teacher lucky?" asks another observer. "Did you notice how students always said the right thing at the right time, how there were no inattentive students and no disciplinary problems?"

When anything happens consistently, it is no longer appropriate to refer to it as "luck." "Skillful" and "quick to take advantage of every opportunity" are more fitting descriptive terms. It is true that one of the girls pointed out that many of the students' questions on the chalkboard overlapped and that her comment led to the grouping of the questions under five major headings. Note, however, how quickly the teacher saw the value of her suggestion. Had this girl not made the comment, the questions would have been grouped later, either in response to a remark by another student or at the teacher's suggestion. The teacher's position is one of prestige, even under the unit plan, and he still has the right and the responsibility to make a discussion productive by asking an appropriate question or making a fruitful suggestion.

Many ways of starting a unit. "Is this how you start a unit of work?" asks the prospective teacher eager to copy into his notes all of the rules that will point the short cut to professional success.

No, this is not *the way* to start a unit, for there is no single approved way of beginning a unit of work. This is a way that one teacher used. Even he could not use exactly the same approach with another class, since the students would be different. If these students had been accustomed to organizing their activities about a unit of work, it would not have been necessary for the teacher to take so much time in introducing the procedure.

One English class began a unit of work leading up to the publication of a class magazine when a student read to the class a short story she had written.

"That story is good enough to be published," said an enthusiastic classmate.

The teacher commented that several of them had written stories that also deserved wider circulation than the classroom bulletin board afforded.

"With all the talent in this class," said the class wit, "we could fill a book."

"Why don't you?" the teacher asked, and before the period was over they had chosen an editorial board and an art staff, and were started on the magazine it took them a whole, very busy month to prepare.

When the members of an eleventh-grade senior high school class returned to school in September, they were saddened to learn that one of their most popular and gifted classmates was not coming back since the death of his father in a boating accident made it necessary for the youth to go to work to help support the family. As they spoke of the kind of job he was prepared to take, they soon realized how little thought they had themselves given to the choice of their future career. It is true that they had had some discussion of vocational guidance in their junior high school years, but they were no longer confident about the adequacy of their basis for choosing a career and they were unwilling to delay making their choice until they were halfway through college. As they spoke of the many questions to which they needed answers, they began planning the activities which they wanted to be their unit of work.

It would be unwise to get the impression that the teacher under the unit plan is an opportunist who shifts his classroom procedures in response to every chance remark made by a student. Students make many, many remarks in class. A good teacher knows which ones are best ignored and which can be used to start a worthwhile unit of work. He has to be able to judge, apparently on the spur of the moment, whether the unit of work that is about to be initiated will yield results that are worth the time it will take or whether the activity is too unimportant for this group, whether the unit of work is one they can complete or whether it is too ambitious for their limited time, resources, and ability. The teacher need be no opportunist, but he must understand his students and he must know his subject matter.

How Are Unit Activities Carried Out?

Returning to the lesson, what happens after the unit of work has been begun? The class decided to take as their major question the one dealing with international relations: Can the United Nations be more than just a debating society? What was the class to do next?

Selecting topics for study. After a few minutes of desultory discussion, the teacher suggested that they first see which questions they wanted to ask. To start the discussion, he asked a few questions which he wrote on the chalkboard.

Which nations belong to the United Nations?
How can a nation become a member?
How is the Security Council chosen?

With these questions to start them, other students suggested additional questions until once more the boards were covered with such questions as:

What can the United Nations do if a country tries to start a world war?
What power does the General Assembly have?
Why are some nations permitted to use the veto power?
Can the United Nations Charter be amended like the United States Constitution or must all the members accept the amendments?
Do we have to fight any time the United Nations tells us to?
What is the Secretariat?
Do people working for the United Nations have to pay taxes on the homes they own in the United States?
What happened to the International Labor Office and the other agencies that used to be connected with the League of Nations?
Can we arrange a trip to the United Nations?

The students were amazed at the number of questions they wanted to ask about the United Nations once they began to think about it. The teacher reminded them that the other day, when they also covered the chalkboards with their individual questions, Suzanne had suggested that many of them could be grouped under larger headings. Together they looked through the list for related questions. Some, he found; others, students found. There were such major topics as the United Nations Charter, the Security Council, the General Assembly, a Trip to the United Nations Headquarters, Agencies Working with the United Nations, and Helping the United Nations to Succeed. The questions were then rearranged under appropriate topics.

"Now all we have to do is to get the answers to all of these questions and we'll know whether the United Nations can prevent another world war," the teacher said.

"All these questions! We'll never get done—not this term, anyway," a student objected.

"Yes, it would take a long time," the teacher agreed, "if each one of you had to find the answer to each question. You can save a lot of time by dividing the work. If some of you worked on one question while the rest of you worked on other questions, you could pool your information."

"What do you mean by 'pool your information'?" was asked by one of the boys, who was, incidentally, one of the three students who had failed in the midterm examinations.

Organization of committees. Because the class had had no experience with units of work, the teacher answered the question by explaining how other classes had proceeded in similar situations, how they divided the class into committees, how the committees in turn divided the work among themselves, how the committees assembled and presented their reports, and how the class used the material gathered and presented by the various committees. If the class approved of this suggestion, and they did since they had no better procedure to offer, the next step was to create the various committees.

"What happens if too many people want to work on the same topic?" asked a girl.

"Yes, and what happens if nobody wants to work on some question?" asked another.

"Let's try choosing the topics we want to work on and see whether that works out all right," said a third student.

"If too many people want to work on the same topic, we can vote to see who should get the topic," suggested a fourth student.

To this, the student who had spoken just before her, the third student mentioned above, objected, "We can spend so much time voting on everything that we'll never do anything else. Why not try choosing our own topics first and see what happens?'"

The teacher then called on each student to indicate the topic he preferred. As each student spoke, the teacher wrote the student's name next to the topic selected. Some students did not know which of two or three topics they really wanted most, and their names were written next to these two or three topics. Four students had no preference at all— one of these was a keen and alert young man who was ready to work on all the topics because he could not decide which was the most interesting or the most important, and the other three apparently could not decide which committee choice entailed the least amount of work. Someone raised the point that one of the boys was absent, but it was soon agreed that he could probably make his choice the first day he returned to school without disturbing the others too much.

As they looked at the way in which the students had distributed themselves among the various committees, it was apparent that the method of free choice was imperfect. Some of the committees were too large—nineteen students chose the Security Council, while only two students chose Agencies Working with the United Nations and no student selected a Trip to the United Nations Headquarters.

"How large should a committee be?" asked a student.

When no answer was forthcoming from the class, the teacher told them that no definite answer could be given to this question since so much depended on the topic and on the boys and girls who were on the committee. Sometimes a topic has so many ramifications that many boys and girls are needed on the committee if all of the aspects are to be investigated. At other times, a committee that is too large becomes so cumbersome a group that the members get in each other's way. In general, he thought the committees ought to range in size from five to seven, although these numbers did not have to be adhered to in every instance. With these numbers as guides, the students were ready to re-examine their distribution of preferred topics.

"What shall we do with this question of the Trip to the Headquarters on which no one apparently wants to work? Shall we drop it?" asked the teacher.

At first, the idea of dropping the question seemed to be the best solution, but soon dissenting voices were heard.

"My mother visited the U.N. when she was in New York last year. She says anybody can get tickets to sit in on the sessions if you make arrangements in advance."

"We could hire a bus and all go together."

"What'll we use for money? Do you know how much it costs to take a trip to New York and stay at a hotel overnight?"

"I sure would like to try those earphones so you can hear in English what a speaker is saying in French."

At this point the teacher stepped into the picture with the remark, "Why don't you fellows settle it among yourselves and then come back and give us the answer?"—and a committee of four was born.

Their attention went back to the remaining six topics listed on the chalkboard. Students who had indicated more than one preference were asked to decide on the topic they wanted and, if possible, to choose the topic on which fewer students were working. This resulted in a better distribution of students among the various topics, especially since several students volunteered to join some of the smaller committees.

The largest committee was that on the United Nations and the Prevention of War, with nine members; and the smallest committee, three students, was that on Agencies Working with the United Nations. Was that committee too small to find the answer to the questions assigned to it?

"What questions do they have to answer?" a boy asked.

By this time, however, the detailed questions on this topic had been erased from the board. It would have helped, they thought, is someone had kept a record of all of the material on the board. As they reassembled the questions from memory, the class agreed that the task was larger than three students could handle. Since there were no additional volunteers for this committee, the teacher asked the Prevention of War Committee members whether any of them would consent to work on the Agencies Committee because the Prevention of War Committee probably did not need so many members. Two of these students agreed unenthusiastically to change their assignments and the committee assignments seemed all set.

Knowing that the bell would ring very soon, the teacher said, "Well, now that you have your topics and your committees settled, we can get to work. Tomorrow, we'll see how far we are able to get."

Evaluating the procedures used thus far. Now that the students have gone, we can re-examine the teaching procedures that were employed. You will note that both lessons ended vaguely. The first day the teacher asked the class to think about the various major topics and to select the one on which they wanted to work. The second day ended with the equally vague suggestion that now they could get to work. Undoubtedly some of the students were becoming enthusiastic converts to any method of teaching that for two successive days freed them from specific homework assignments.

Although class sessions should not end so inconclusively, this teacher's practice may be defended at this point, for the vagueness of the assignment was used as the means of starting the next day's work. Had this teacher used units of work before, he would have known that the students would not get far with their committee work before they met the next day. Their lack of progress may be used as the basis for the discussion of the ways in which committees should function and of the research procedures they can use. Matters of procedure mean more to students when they realize the inadequacy of their own procedures than when the teacher tries to anticipate every problem that may arise. The first day's lesson ended on a vague question because the class was so large that the discussion simply did not get far enough for a more definite conclusion to the day's work.

The way this unit of work was being conducted illustrates the difficulties of using this procedure with a large group. All will agree that this teacher's problems would have been eased if he had had twenty rather than thirty-six in his class. The size of the class undoubtedly slows the rate of progress. When there are many students, it takes longer to poll the group on their choice of assignments and more students make comments before the class can go on to the next step. The teacher has to be more alert to see that participation in the discussion is general rather than limited to the more aggressive members. Although there were times when progress was slower in this class than it might have been, the teacher did keep the class moving toward the solution of the problem.

Some teachers will object that the social studies teacher controlled the procedure too closely. "Shouldn't the class have elected a chairman to preside over the discussion, with the teacher sitting in as a member of the group?" they ask. Here, too, we do not know whether the teacher's choice of procedure was deliberate or accidental, for both types of procedures are found in unit teaching. Were the teacher challenged on this point, he could undoubtedly defend himself by arguing that since the class was so large and without previous experience with the unit plan, much time would have been lost if a student chairman had been in charge. Once students know how to proceed, the teacher's control can be less pronounced and the class as a whole can assume more of the responsibility for planning the conduct of the work.

So far, the teacher's control was more in terms of procedure than content. He did not tell the students which questions they were to include but he did help them to see how their questions could be answered. He did not tell them which major topics should be used as the basis for organizing their discussion, but he did introduce the committee procedure as a helpful way of planning their work. Students selected their own topics, with the teacher intervening only when unrestricted freedom of choice proved inadequate. Much of the teacher's effort was directed to expediting class procedure rather than to controlling the content of discussion.

When unit teaching is employed, teachers are not forced to organize committees and they need not limit their influence to procedural matters. As in all other aspects of life, there are times when committees are useful and other times when they are wasteful. Some topics are studied more effectively through assignments given to individual students or by assignments to be executed by all students. Surely, no teacher will stand by indifferently while his students fritter away their time on trivialities and ignore the basic questions on which they should be working.

Is all this voting necessary? If every procedural question that arises is to be decided by vote, it is easy to see how much time can be taken up in balloting. To be sure, there are times when it is necessary to poll the group to see just how the students stand on an important division of opinion, but working on units need not convert the classroom into an election booth. Experienced teachers do not need repeated votes in order to appraise the climate of student opinion. At times, the teacher can express the consensus, without prior balloting, and see whether it is what the students believe. The assignment of students to committees can be done in other ways than by taking a series of ballots. For example, each student can indicate in writing his first and second choices of committee assignments and the teacher, with or without the assistance of a student committee, can make the assignments. The class should be asked to vote only when the issue is important, when the exact division of student opinion must be known, and when there is no less time-consuming procedure.

Must units of work be conducted by committees? Whenever a large group is at work on a problem, there are times when division into committees is the most effective way of proceeding and there are other times when the division into committees is unnecessary. In class, committees are one of the ways of conducting a unit, but not the only one. Assignments can be given to individuals and to small groups without the formality of committee structure. Similarly, the work of committees can be made incidental to the work of the class as a whole, with the teacher retaining the responsibility for conducting the class and for incorporating the results of the work done by the committees and by individuals. Certain it is that units of work will be ineffective when committee procedure is unduly overemphasized, as though it were the goal of instruction instead of a means of furthering the learning the teacher is eager to develop.

How Does the Teacher Guide Students' Research Work?

When the class assembled for the third day of their work on the unit, the teacher asked them how much progress they had made. Enjoying the time-honored prerogative of high school seniors, these boys and girls had interpreted the vague assignment to be no assignment at all. Their other teachers had been less reluctant to make specific assignments and so these students were kept too busy doing their homework for other classes to leave time for just seeing how far they could get with the unit.

"How do you think we ought to proceed?" asked the teacher.

"Shouldn't we first elect a secretary the way we said yesterday so that we can have a record of the questions and the suggestions before the board is erased the way it was yesterday?" interrupted a student.

The class agreed that a secretary was needed. The secretary was asked to keep full notes of every class meeting and to serve as the custodian of all reports made by committees. In order to make certain that the secretary was not to be excluded from the learning that went on as students worked on a committee, the student secretary was asked to join one of the study committees.

The students also approved of a suggestion made by one of them that they needed an executive committee consisting of the secretary and two other members to plan a schedule for the presentation of the various reports and to take care of such other matters of procedure as were not worth the time of the entire class. This election, too, was held quickly.

It was encouraging, the teacher commented, to see that the class had already set up a committee to schedule the presentation of reports, but he reminded them that no committee had even begun to think of what should go into the report.

Requesting each student to think in terms of the committee of which he was a member, the teacher asked them what they needed to know before they could get to work. Within a few minutes the following questions were on the board and in the secretary's notebook:

Who is in charge of the committee, the chairman or all the members?
Should each committee elect a chairman and a secretary?
How should the committee divide the work?
How long should it take a committee to prepare a report?
What kind of report should a committee make, oral or written?
Where can we find the information we need?
Will the committees meet during class time or after school?
How can we exchange information among the committees so that they won't
    be wasting time working on the same questions?
Does the school library have the books we need?

Having learned some of the procedures of the unit approach from their first two days, they were now ready to group these isolated questions into several major questions:

How should the committee be organized and run?
How should committees plan their reports?
How can students do their research work most efficiently?

Planning committee procedures. Taking up the question of committee organization first, the class soon agreed that each committee ought to elect its own chairman, who would preside at all meetings and who would keep track of the activities of its members. Each chairman was to give the class secretary a brief daily progress report so that the entire class would know what each committee was doing. The executive committee, in consultation with the committee chairman, would assign the dates when committee reports were due. Committees would meet in class whenever reports were not being presented and could meet after school or during study periods if they thought it necessary. Closet and book· shelf space would be made available so that all could use the books and pamphlets borrowed from the library or other sources. The teacher would arrange for students to get passes to go to the library during their class period and during study periods. The teacher would also see whether the departmental office or any other room could be used in addition to the history classroom as a place for committee meetings.

The committees were assigned meeting places in the room. Committees were assigned to each of the four corners of the room. One met at the rear of the third row and another met at the front of the third row. By moving the teacher's desk as near to the front as possible, the seventh committee was able to meet around the desk. Having seven committees meeting at one time made the room noisy, but it was the noise of thirty-six boys and girls trying to convince each other.

Because the teacher was eager to have the committees get started on their work, he suggested that the class divide into committees and that they elect their chairmen. They could then use the remainder of the period to plan their own procedure. The chairmen were soon elected. Oddly enough, all the chairmen gave the same assignment to their committee members: they were to go to the school library or the public library that afternoon or evening and get whatever books, periodicals, or pamphlets they could find on their committee topic. When the bell rang, every committee was busy talking about the topic.

Using class time to evaluate progress. The fourth session of the class was held on Friday. (It will be recalled that Monday's session of the class was devoted to a discussion of the midterm examination papers.) The teacher called a joint meeting of all committees at the beginning of the period and asked whether yesterday's committee meeting had run smoothly or whether any difficulties had arisen. Two complaints were raised. First, the other committees made so much noise they could hardly hear themselves talk. Second, they were not sure they knew how to proceed with their research work in planning the committee report.

So far as the space limitations for committee meetings were concerned, the teacher had discouraging news. There were no unoccupied classrooms that period. Since the departmental office was used by several teachers who were not in class that period, the departmental office had to be considered unavailable for use by this class. Only the corridor outside the classroom was available for an additional committee meeting place. The teacher hoped that as the committees got started, some of them would be reading or writing in the school library during the period, and thus allow the other committees a little more space. In the meantime, they would have to speak very softly at committee meetings. At least they could try to speak softly. If the members of any committee were distracted by a noisy group, they could ask the group to try to quiet down. These were not ideal conditions, but he asked them to try to overcome the difficulty.

A working plan for research activity. After some preliminary discussion of the way committees should plan the research work on the reports and of the way individual students should go about getting data, the following outline was evolved:

Definition of the Problem
  What are the most important questions we have to answer?
  What other questions will the class want us to answer?

Sources of Information
  What kind of information do we need?
  What kinds of books and periodicals contain this sort of information?
  Which libraries are most useful for finding these sources of information?
  How can we find other sources of information by using library indexes?
  Are there any people or organizations we can write to or visit to gain additional information?

The Division of Work Among the Members of the Committee

Should the division of work be by questions or by source of information?

How can the members of the committee take the kind of notes that will be most helpful for the rest of the committee?

The Preparation of the Report

What form should the committee report take?

Should all members of the committee participate in the presentation of the report?

Most of the class discussion centered about sources of information. The teacher was surprised at how much these students knew about the procedures to use in gathering needed data. He made his contribution, too, and spoke of the help they could get from the Public Affairs pamphlets, the United Nations Office of Information, the Foreign Policy Association, and the publications of the State Department in Washington. Several of the students offered to bring to school some of the pamphlets and periodicals their parents had at home. The teacher was taken aback at first when one of the boys offered to bring several years' back issues of a rabidly partisan isolationist paper that had consistently been attacking the United Nations, but he raised no objection, preferring to wait to see how the students themselves would use the material and whether they would detect the way in which the editors habitually colored the news to suit their purposes.

The students then divided themselves into committees under the various committee chairmen and spent the rest of the period discussing their topics. The teacher circulated about the room, moving from committee to committee unless some boy or girl came up to ask him whether he could please come to a particular group that thought it needed him.

Teacher's role during student research. The teacher was careful, as he visited these committees the first day they were really at work, not to interfere with their discussions. In general, he said nothing unless a question or a comment was directed to him. In several instances he did not answer the questions that were asked of him. Instead, he showed them where to find the answer.

He did answer some of the more pressing factual questions, but only to expedite the work of the group. For example, in answer to the question of where they could get copies of the State Department publications, he not only told them how to order the materials but he also indicated how long it would take before they would receive the materials and suggested reading them at the central city reference library which, as a government depository, received copies of all government publications.

As the teacher moved about from group to group, he was impressed by the seriousness and the conscientiousness of most of the groups. Each student was a more important member of the group than most of them had ever been in the class as a whole.

He was gratified to note that though the more articulate boys and girls continued to be very active members of their committees, some of the more passive members of his class were much more active than he had ever thought they could be. Apparently they felt freer to talk in a small group than in a large class.

The committee chairmen varied greatly in technique. That they all ended their first session the preceding day by making the same assignment did not reflect, apparently, identical approaches to their problem or to the group situation. Two of them unintentionally became petty martinets in the way that little children who play school customarily depict the teacher's role as that of a tyrant or a shrew who is always scolding and punishing children. Three of them seemed ineffectual, allowing the discussion to go wherever the most aggressive members of the group directed it. The chairman of the United Nations Charter Committee acted as though he had been born to be a committee chairman. The teacher wanted this committee to report first so that the others could profit from its method of procedure. The seventh chairman was acceptable, but not outstanding. The teacher realized that these chairmen needed guidance in discharging their new roles more effectively.

When the bell rang, the teacher was tired, much more tired than at the end of the usual teaching period. He had been working hard all period even though he apparently was not teaching at all. It was a strain, he realized, to be alert for a full period to the needs of seven different groups and to become the person who was always being asked questions instead of asking them. He would have to learn how to budget his own time so that no group would be neglected. He was worried, too, by the fear that some of the students apparently believed all they needed to do was talk and he wondered how to get them to do the hard work of studying. He was tired, but somehow he felt that this was one of the most exhilarating class sessions he had had for some time. Perhaps it was not all fatigue, but the aftereffects of a stimulating professional experience, was the thought running through his mind when he suddenly realized he had to pack his brief case quickly in order to get to his study-hall assignment.

Committees' progress reports to the class. On Monday morning there was a brief meeting of the entire class. The secretary read the minutes of the preceding class session. For the first time, these minutes included, in addition, a brief progress report from each committee chairman. They were approved with minor corrections. Since no questions of general concern were raised, the class session was given over to the committees about five minutes after the period had started. Some of the committees were busy reading various materials and were given passes to the school library. The others sat at desks in their respective sections of the room.

The teacher called a meeting of the executive committee to evaluate the way the unit was being conducted and to plan a schedule for the committee reports. Since the members of the executive committee were members of three different class committees (the class secretary had joined the committee studying Agencies Working with the United Nations), the executive committee had a fairly clear picture of the way in which the unit was being studied. It was agreed that a meeting of the committee chairmen and the executive committee should be held later that period in order to improve the procedures which various chairmen were employing.

When they were discussing the schedule of committee reports to the class, two questions were raised. How much time will the committees need to prepare their reports? How much time will each committee need to present its report? They were convinced that each committee needed at least a week to prepare the report. One of them thought her committee could be ready within the week, if necessary. They decided tentatively to leave the rest of the week free for committee work. When they met with the committee chairmen later that period, they would see which committees could report early the following week and which would be ready later that week.

They found it more difficult to plan the schedule of committee reports because they did not know what form these reports would take. Looking at the unit as a whole, they thought it advisable to have all reports given within one week, and, if possible, to leave one period for a discussion of the topic as a whole by the entire class. This schedule meant that there would be some committees that could take a whole class period for their report, but that most of them would have to share a class period with another report. They could not prepare a more definite schedule until after they had met with the committee chairmen.

How long should a unit of work last? As this unit developed, it was planned to last for three weeks. Is this as long as a unit should take from initiation to completion? There is, of course, no definite rule governing the length of a unit, aside from the obvious generalization that it must be long enough for the unit to be completed adequately and yet not so drawn out that students lose interest or lose sight of the larger topic of which the various committee projects are only a part. There are few units in which all of the research and studying can be completed in less than two weeks, although a unit that arises as part of a larger area of interest may sometimes be completed in a short time. On the other hand, few classes can work with a unit for more than a month unless the unit is divided into smaller units. This unit on the United Nations, for example, could well be a subsidiary part of a larger unit dealing with the obligations of the United States as a world power. In a junior high school in which a science teacher and a mathematics teacher worked together on a unit on hydroponics, with the students spending an entire term in learning about soil-less gardening and in growing the produce they would exhibit at their own county fair at the end of the term, many projects were undertaken and many problems were studied during the term as work on the unit proceeded.

How Does the Teacher Guide the Activities of the Various Committees?

As had been agreed, the remainder of the week was spent working in committees. The teacher divided his time among the various committees and sometimes participated in the discussion. The committees soon discovered that a class period was not long enough for both discussion and actual research work. They decided to do their reading and writing at home and to use the class period for discussion and for drafting the committee report.

The teacher helped the committees to see the limitations imposed upon them by the decision to have all committee reports given within the span of one week. Repeatedly he presented the one question he thought they ought to keep in mind as they drafted their report: Is this the kind of report that will be most valuable for the rest of the class?

Even when students are experienced in the use of committee procedures, it is advisable for the teacher to meet with the various groups in order to guide them as they conduct their research and prepare their reports. He can help them to plan their work in terms of key questions, to select promising sources of information, and to realize that research consists of more than copying appropriate pages from many books. Left to themselves, few adolescents see anything humorous in the oft-quoted witticism, "If you copy from one book, it's plagiarism; if you copy from several books, it's research."

How effectively the committees work depends largely on the quality of the guidance they get from the teacher. He may have to remind them periodically of the major questions they are endeavoring to answer so that committee time will not be used as an opportunity for visiting and conversation. He has to see, too, that adequate materials are available so that his students do not spend period after period rehashing the three paragraphs which the textbook devotes to the topic.

In this unit it was relatively easy for the teacher to guide the activities of the various groups in the class, for all were working on the same sort of task. The guidance of unit activities is complicated when the students are engaged in a variety of activities which are at different stages of completion at any one time.

It is obvious that the teacher cannot direct every step of every activity and it is equally clear that students cannot be left entirely on their

own. As a result of the preliminary planning, the students should understand the general plan for the unit as a whole and the specific purposes
for each activity in the unit. Before any individual or committee begins
work on a special task, the teacher must meet with these students to help
them plan their procedure.

While the activities are being conducted, the teacher must be available as a consultant to whom students can go when they strike a serious
snag and he must meet with the various groups in order to see that the
work is proceeding. When necessary, the teacher will call for a conference of either the students who are working on some specific activity
or of the entire class so that they may evaluate the progress they are making and discuss changes in procedure.

It is sometimes necessary for the teacher to revive the waning interest in a unit of work which a class may have started with great enthusiasm. If the work is important, and presumably the teacher would
not have let it be started if it were not, it should not be dropped after
the first flush of excited interest has waned. The teacher may try to overcome the feeling of helplessness as boys and girls realize how large is
the task they have undertaken. Thus, he may give them the satisfaction
and the stimulation that comes from knowledge of progress toward the
goal by having individuals or groups present progress reports or even
the final reports of those who were working on smaller aspects of the
total problem. Sometimes a total group discussion of the major problem
in the light of the additional study that has been done will remind the
class of the reason for having undertaken the unit and reinforce the
interest in continuing it.

Throughout the unit, the teacher will see that students accept as
much of the responsibility for planning and conducting the unit as they
can assume, and he must develop the habit of asking rather than telling,
and of guiding rather than dominating. Under no circumstances, however, does he let the class forget that the school is concerned with the
intellectual growth of its students and that a discussion without substance is empty chitchat.

How Are Committee Reports Presented?

On Monday of the third week, the committees began presenting
their reports. After the secretary had read the minutes of the preceding
day, the class was turned over to the chairman of the committee that
was reporting. When more than one committee was to report the same
day, the class secretary acted as timekeeper and notified the chairman
when only three minutes of the committee's time remained and again
when the time was up. To emphasize the extent to which the reporting

committee was in charge of the meeting, the teacher yielded his desk to the committee chairman and took a seat as one of the members of the audience.

The first committee to report was that on the United Nations Charter. The chairman began the report by giving a brief talk on the importance of the United Nations Charter, describing briefly how it had been framed at the San Francisco Conference. He then called on one of his committee members to explain the structure of the United Nations. With the aid of a large chart prepared by the committee, this student presented the outstanding characteristics of the organization. A third student addressed himself to the question of the political, military, and financial rights and duties of the countries which belong to the United Nations. The fourth and final speaker explained how the United Nations Charter can be amended to keep it in tune with changing world conditions. During these reports, the chairman served only as the presiding officer and said nothing except for introducing the speakers before they began and thanking them after they had finished.

When these talks had been given, the chairman announced that the three other committee members who had not presented oral reports would now come to the front of the room to answer any questions that members of the class wanted to ask. He did not have to wait long for the questions to come. In answer to the question as to whether the committee considered it right that some countries should be permanent members of the Security Council, one of the girls in the class rose and suggested that the question wait till the next day when it would be taken up by her committee's report on the Security Council. Other questions were asked and answered until only the secretary's signal that it was time for the next committee to report stopped the flow of questions.

The chairman of the committee on the Trip to the United Nations took over the meeting and reported that his committee had gathered a great deal of information about a possible trip and was not ready to recommend that the class undertake an excursion this term. One of the members of the committee, the boy whose mother had spoken so enthusiastically about her visit to the U.N., spoke of the apparently insuperable obstacles to planning such a trip on short notice: the cost of chartering a bus or going by train and the other expenses of the trip, the difficulty of raising that much money on short notice, the fact that there were no more long vacations like Easter during which to make the trip, and so on. Another student spoke of the way in which they could arrange to visit the U.N. whenever they might get to New York either alone or with their families. The last member of the committee summarized what he had learned about the U.N. Headquarters and the points of interest for visitors from his interviews with several people in the community who had been there. During the discussion that followed these reports, it became clear that the class was interested in visiting the U.N. Headquarters and would try to do so some day as individuals but agreed with the committee recommendation not to plan that class excursion this term. The committee was given the added charge of preparing an itinerary which would include major points of interest and the location and function of the principal U.N. agencies.

One of the members of the executive committee presided over the last five minutes of the class period and asked for an evaluation of the reports and for suggestions that would make the remaining committee reports more helpful to the rest of the class. The comments were almost uniformly favorable. They liked the way the reports were delivered but they found that the two students who read reports were not as effective as were the others who spoke to the class rather than read to them. It was hard to understand Charles, who spoke a little too rapidly, and Marie, whose voice was too soft. Martha's report was especially easy to follow because she had taken the trouble to put a brief outline on the board before she began to speak. They thought the reports were a little hurried and wished each committee could take more time. When one boy suggested that they could save a few minutes by dispensing with the secretary's reading of the minutes, which could be posted on the class bulletin board instead of being read aloud, the suggestion was approved unanimously.

The general procedure remained unchanged for the next three days. The committee chairman took charge of the class except during the last five minutes of the period when the chairman of the executive committee led the class discussion. Some provision was made every period for members of the class to ask questions of the committee.

The reports themselves took many forms: the Security Council committee had a panel discussion on the use of the veto power; the Trip to U.N. Headquarters committee presented recommendations to the class for decision and action; the Prevention of War committee reported on some instances in which the U.N. had been able to halt or prevent hostilities and others in which the U.N. had been ineffective, with the reasons for the success or failure of the U.N. in maintaining peace; the committee on Agencies Working with the United Nations dramatized a meeting of UNESCO in order to show how a real and current problem was being met by the organization; the United Nations Charter committee based the reports on a large chart which had been prepared for display; the General Assembly report consisted of a series of short talks, with most of the time devoted to answering questions raised by the class; and the Helping the United Nations to Succeed committee had a panel discussion, led by the committee but with considerable class participation, on the ways in which American citizens can help the United Nations to be effective.

How Is a Unit of Work Brought to a Close?

On the last day of this unit, the chairman of the executive committee led the discussion on the unit as a whole. Now that they knew how the United Nations was organized and how it functioned, did they think it would be any more successful than the League of Nations in preventing another world war? The students were not overoptimistic, but they thought it important that the United Nations be made to succeed. Several students said that the U.N. had to succeed if our civilization is to survive and they wanted to continue the discussion started by one of the committees.

They asked what boys and girls could do. Some spoke of the very limited circulation of some of the excellent pamphlets they had come across in their search for material. One of the students volunteered to contribute to the school library the pamphlets he had purchased. Other students followed his lead by offering their material, too. One of the members of the executive committee suggested that copies of the various reports and of the secretary's minutes be bound and placed in the library as an aid to future classes. A student reported that he was joining the High School U.N. Council of the American Association for the United Nations and explained how others could join.

Evaluation

At about the middle of the period, the teacher asked several questions. Did they regret the way they had spent the last three weeks? The answer was an enthusiastic "No." One girl said she thought it had been the most worthwhile experience since she had been going to school. A boy said he had done more work for this unit than for any other class this term and he was confident he had learned a great deal both from his own report and from those made by other students. Another student remarked that what he appreciated most were the feeling of responsibility and the difference between this class and other classes where they were still treated as children. From the general tenor of the other comments the teacher felt safe in concluding that so far as the students were concerned, this unit of work was a success.

If they were to do such a unit again, did they have any suggestions for changes in procedure? One of the ordinarily quiet members of the class began by saying he had never thought he would be the one to make the suggestion, but he did think it would be better if class periods were a little longer. Amid general laughter, they decided it was better not to request the principal to lengthen the periods, especially when they thought of some other classes they would prefer to shorten. They were interested to hear the teacher say that many schools lengthen the period or arrange to have the class meet for two or more consecutive periods.

Other suggestions were more favorably received. Several students thought only one committee should report during a period and that the unit should have been extended three days to make this possible. One student thought they had wasted too much time at the beginning because of their lack of experience and that this time should have been used to increase the reporting time. Another student said that the committee could do much better work if they had more than a week in which to gather and to organize their material. Some students complained that the classroom was too small and one student asked whether committees could not get permission to meet in the school cafeteria, which was vacant that period.

A student asked why they could not use this procedure for the rest of the term since everybody seemed to agree it had been so valuable. Another student promptly reminded the teacher that he had promised them a unit on industrial relations after this one had been completed. The teacher explained that they had spent three weeks on this one topic and at that rate they could not study all the topics prescribed for the term.

One boy summed up student reaction by saying, "If we can spend our time in class the way we did the last three weeks, I'm sure we won't mind studying the other topics at home. You tell us what we have to study and we can have class discussions every once in awhile to see whether we understand the work we are doing at home."

In the face of such unanimity of opinion, only one course of action was open to the teacher and he announced that on Monday they would explore the possibilities of a unit on industrial relations. In the meantime, would they try to think of questions that . . . and the bell rang.

Other Culmination Procedures

In other units of work, the activities reach their culmination in ways that are quite different from this week of committee reports and class discussion. For one thing, in most units there are many culminating experiences before the work on the entire unit is completed rather than a single session or series of consecutive sessions in which all committees present the results of their work. Thus, in a junior high school unit on hydroponics, students constructed the tanks and trays they needed; they computed the cost of the materials they had to purchase and the value of the vegetables they grew; they interviewed florists and visited a botanical garden to gather information about how to grow plants; they used such books as Bromfield's *The Farm*, Wilcox's *The A.B.C. of Agrobiology*, Collins's *The Boy Chemist*, and Seymour's *The New Garden Encyclopedia*; they drew charts of the rate of growth of their plants; they saw and discussed the Encyclopedia Britannica films on *Seed Dispersal, Roots of Plants, Plant Growth,* and *Leaves;* they arranged a "county fair" in order to exhibit the produce they had grown; and they planned a program of square dances and music to be presented at the "fair." Although the "county fair" was in one sense the culmination of the term's work on their unit, each subsidiary activity reached a culmination of its own.

Throughout the term, the emphasis was placed on the use that would be made of the results of the activity rather than on ways of terminating the activity. When, for example, the first two tanks had been constructed, there was no exhibition of tanks with the youngsters explaining how these had been designed and built. Instead, the students brought their tanks to class and asked, "Are these tanks built the way we want them?" and "What do we do next?"

RELATIVE IMPORTANCE OF PRODUCT AND PROCESS IN THE UNIT OF WORK

Throughout this unit, it will be noted, the teacher's emphasis was on the educational process rather than on the tangible outcomes of the unit. He was concerned with the way the students analyzed the problem, with their methods of gathering data, with their planning of a report that would help their classmates. Little attention was given to the attractiveness of the report they later donated to the school library. Under similar conditions, other teachers would have had the students spend a great deal of time making attractive cover designs and retyping the reports for inclusion in a finished volume that would bring a commendatory note from the principal and envious or admiring comments from colleagues.

Although the preparation of an unattractive unit report is not necessarily more beneficial to the students than is the preparation of an attractively bound unit report, placing too much attention on the superficial qualities of the product rather than on the importance of process itself may lessen the value of unit work. Teachers, like students, are affected by competition. Once a school exhibits the products of unit work, teachers feel compelled to insist on products that will stand comparison. They tend, therefore, to favor the best pupils at the expense of the rest. The art teacher, for example, concentrates his attention on his star pupils whose soap carvings are beautiful and not on the mediocre students whose sculpture will never attract attention at an exhibit. Students' recognition of the importance of the work they are doing should lead to high standards of performance, but the product must not get more attention than it deserves.

In some instances the quality of the product is so important a part of the unit that it deserves a great deal of attention. A tank that is not watertight cannot be used to hold the solution in which plants are to be grown. A music class that is producing an operetta to raise funds for the Student Aid Fund must appreciate the responsibility that goes with producing a play for which an admission fee is charged. When an English class mimeographs a literary magazine, the members must see that the plot of the story rather than the spelling is original. In such instances as these, emphasis on the quality of the product is justifiable, for it develops standards of workmanship that are important outcomes of the unit.

How Do Teachers and Students Evaluate the Outcomes of a Unit of Work?

One of the ways in which the use of units of work is influencing educational procedures is in the changed attitude toward the evaluation of the results of classroom activities. When the recitation is the basic instructional pattern, it is the teacher who does the evaluating as he grades what students have said or written. With units of work, however, much of the evaluation is done co-operatively by students and teacher, even though the teacher supplements co-operative evaluation by his own interpretation and application of other evaluative criteria and procedures.

Evaluation is usually thought of as a post-mortem process. Most classroom tests, for example, are administered after a major part of the course has been completed. When units of work are conducted, evaluation tends to be a continuous process as students and teachers ask, "Is this the kind of tank we need?" and "What changes must we make in our plans if we are to discover why these plants are not flourishing?" Later, they will ask, "Did we gain enough from this unit to be worth the time and effort we put into it?" Teachers and students use the present and the future tenses as well as the past tense when they evaluate units of work, for they ask not only, "How well did we build this?" but also, "How can we build it better next time?"

A third difference between the usual evaluation practices and evaluation in schools which use units of work is the increased emphasis which the evaluation of units of work places upon the changes in the student as well as on the changes in what he knows. To be sure, we want to know how much our students have learned, but we also want to know how they learned it and how they have been changed in the process. It is in order, therefore, for teachers and students to ask such questions as, "In which ways are we working more efficiently than we did at the beginning of the term?" and "How can we make our criticism of a committee report or project more helpful to those who will present reports later?"

As teacher and class evaluate the outcomes of a unit of work, it is much too narrow for them to limit their evaluation to an analysis of the tangible outcomes. Important though it may be to know whether the operetta they produced was successful, they must ask other questions, too. Did they achieve the purposes they had in mind when they first decided to produce an operetta? Did they gain as much as they would have if they had spent their time in other ways?

There are dangers as well as opportunities when units of work are used. Unless the teacher accepts his full share of the responsibility in co-operative planning, too much time may be spent on the superficial aspects of the problem while more important questions go unanswered. Students may focus so much of their attention on their own committee work that they learn little from the work done by the others in the class. In their desire to win approval when they present their committee reports, students may spend a disproportionate amount of time rehearsing rather than researching. There can be overemphasis on what is interesting rather than on what is important. When each class selects and plans its own units, there is a strong possibility that some units will be repeated in several grades while less dramatic but more important topics are neglected. Some students, moreover, may be so useful in some of the peripheral aspects, for example, in drawing charts for the various committees or in dramatization, that they are not getting the intellectual training that is a major responsibility of the school.

Such disadvantages as these are not an inherent part of the unit of work and can be avoided if the teacher is skilled and is alert to his responsibilities for intellectual development. The unit of work is not intended as a substitute for learning basic subject matter. If it is employed effectively, students should learn much more than in a series of well-planned daily lessons. Unless they do, it is difficult to justify the repeated use of the unit as the means of teaching.

The evaluation of outcomes is related closely to the analysis of the objectives for which the unit of work was intended. Any full evaluation of the outcomes of a unit of work must, therefore, include adequate attention to determining the extent to which the unit contributed to the attainment of the ultimate goals as well as the immediate objectives of education, and to evaluating the success with which both the teacher's hopes and the students' needs were satisfied.

Making these evaluations of a unit presents far more problems than can be treated adequately in a few paragraphs. We shall, therefore, examine them later as we discuss the larger questions of evaluating the results of education.*

WHAT CAN BE DONE TO PRESERVE THE SPIRIT AS WELL AS THE PATTERN OF UNIT WORK?

The history of education can be a depressing subject, for it records the repeated story of formalism, of reaction against formalism, and then

* See Chapter 11, "Evaluating the Results of Teaching and Learning."

of this reaction itself becoming as formal and as sterile as the system it replaced. Thus, Pestalozzi's emphasis on the need for experiencing what was to be learned, instead of just talking about it, led to the formalized object lessons where students were given a piece of coal and were then asked to enumerate all of its qualities.

Will units of work suffer a similar fate? Will teachers develop model units of work with suggested questions for discussion and a list of recommended committee activities?

Requiring all teachers to teach all topics through units of work, regardless of their ability to deal with the problems involved, or of the students' readiness for an abrupt change from teacher-planned lessons to co-operatively planned units of works, or despite the practical limits imposed by an inelastic course of study and the administration of uniform examinations based on this prescribed course of study or by the practice of having the school day divided into short periods—to ignore these obstacles is to encourage teachers to be content with conducting activities that resemble units of work in every respect except substance and value.

One of the major advantages of using units of work is their flexibility, an advantage that is lost when teachers regard it as a fixed procedure that is used in exactly the same way regardless of circumstances. Thus, units of work can be utilized in schools which have no predetermined term-by-term syllabus and in those which present each teacher with a detailed list of topics to be covered each term. They can be used as the basis for teaching all of the major topics to be studied, or they can be used with one or two important topics while the others are studied in daily lessons. They can be helpful when the classes are heterogeneous in abilities and interests or when the classes are supposedly homogeneous. They are appropriate both in schools in which each department is responsible for only one subject and in the many schools in which the same person teaches two or more subjects to the same class, for example, English and social studies. These advantages of flexibility, however, are available only to the teacher who is himself flexible.

Changes in educational practice, as contrasted with changes in the words we use to describe educational practice, will come as rapidly as teachers are genuinely convinced that units of work are effective teaching procedures, that units of work can be supervised and guided by real teachers who are not the super-teachers described in books, that few units of work are perfect and that teachers need not be afraid to take a chance of spoiling a perfect method of teaching, that their school administrators will understand the difficulties experienced by teachers who are using this method for the first time, and that unit-of-work procedures must be modified to meet the limitations imposed by specific schools, specific courses, and specific classes.

In extending the use of units of work, as in so many other aspects of educational progress, it is the teachers who can best take the initiative in modifying instructional procedures.

QUESTIONS FOR STUDY AND DISCUSSION

1. In which respects would the unit of work that was described in this chapter have been conducted differently if both teacher and class had had considerable experience in using unit-of-work procedure?

2. A sophomore World History class is completing a unit on the Renaissance. A series of committee reports is in process. The first committee, reporting on Art in the Renaissance, has just given a comprehensive résumé, with each of five students recounting accomplishments in a different field of art. While the content was unexceptionable, the report took 35 minutes, and the attention of the audience began to wane visibly—and audibly, too. As the teacher, you dread the thought of the five more reports which are yet to come, if they follow the same procedure.

What can you do at this point to prevent the high interest of a week of stimulating work from being dissipated in overly long, monotonous reports?

What should have been done before the class arrived at this point?

Can you suggest a list of "rules" for committee reports?

3. A young junior high school mathematics teacher introduced the topic of insurance by discussing the social basis of insurance before presenting any of the types of problems the students were expected to learn to compute. During the discussion, one of the students said he had heard that the fire insurance rates in their town had gone down markedly because of their efficient fire department. Another student asked whether life insurance rates had also been reduced recently because of the discovery of new methods of treating diseases that had formerly been fatal. Before long, so many questions had been raised that the class was divided into groups in order to find the answers during the following week.

When the students began to look for the answers to their questions, they found that they could not understand what they were reading because they were not sufficiently familiar with the mathematical aspects of insurance.

The teacher asked some of his more experienced colleagues how he should deal with this situation.

Miss B. suggested that he take several class periods to teach them the mathematics they needed before they could proceed with their study of insurance.

Mr. L. suggested that the teacher answer their mathematical questions directly and simply, and that he delay trying to develop the mathematical skills more fully until they had completed their study of the social aspects of insurance.

Mrs. T. indicated that the teacher would regret having spent so much time on the non-mathematical aspects of insurance. She recommended that he give them the answers to the questions they had raised during their introductory discussion without taking the students' time to find the answers themselves.

Which of these three answers do you regard as most acceptable? Why?

What advice would you have given this teacher if he had consulted you?

4. One of the committees in your class is preparing a report on socialized medicine to be presented to the class. As you meet with the committee, you discover that the students are basing their research on the publications of a propaganda agency which has issued many pamphlets that are impressive in their presentation of undisputed facts but which present only those facts that

support their side of the question. The members of this committee have been so thoroughly convinced by the arguments presented by these pamphlets that they do not admit there really is another side to the question of socialized medicine.

What should the teacher do?

5. A senior high school English class after seeing several books of original stories and verse written by high school students decided that they, too, would write a book. With great enthusiasm they elected editorial committees, art committees, and a circulation committee and began to write. Their enthusiasm began to wane when they discovered that writing for publication necessitated the drudgery of rewriting and editing and more rewriting. Within a week, they were ready to drop the idea of publishing a class book.

How should the teacher deal with this situation?

6. Taking any secondary school class with which you are familiar, how would you go about conducting a specific unit of work with this group?

7. A Home Economics teacher tried to conduct a unit of work on nutrition but found that her students were so thoroughly accustomed to doing nothing more than follow specific instructions for doing an assignment made by the teacher that the girls could not accept any of the responsibility for planning activities or for working when the teacher was not there to supervise every detail.

How can this teacher develop their ability to conduct a unit of work?

BIBLIOGRAPHY

1. ALBERTY, Harold B., *Reorganizing the High School Curriculum,* rev. ed. (New York, The Macmillan Company, 1953), Ch. 6.
2. BENNE, Kenneth D., and MUNTYAN, Bozidar, *Human Relations in Curriculum Change* (New York, Holt, Rinehart and Winston, Inc., 1951), Part III, Sect. A, 4-7.
3. *Britannica Junior Units of Study Material* (Chicago, Encyclopedia Britannica).
4. BURTON, William H., *The Guidance of Learning Activities,* 2nd ed. (New York, Appleton-Century-Crofts, Inc., 1952), Chs. 12-14.
5. FAUNCE, Roland C., and BOSSING, Nelson L., *Developing the Core Curriculum,* 2nd ed. (Englewood Cliffs, N.J., Prentice-Hall, Inc., 1958), Ch. 11.
6. FRASER, Dorothy McClure, and WEST, Edith, *Social Studies in Secondary Schools: Curriculum and Methods* (New York, The Ronald Press Company, 1961), Ch. 6.
7. GILES, H. H., *Teacher-Pupil Planning* (New York, Harper and Brothers, 1941).
8. LEONARD, John Paul, *Developing the Secondary School Curriculum,* rev. ed. (New York, Holt, Rinehart and Winston, Inc., 1953), Chs. 15-17.
9. LURRY, Lucile L., and ALBERTY, Elsie J., *Developing a High School Core Program* (New York, The Macmillan Company, 1957).
10. MIEL, Alice, and associates, *Co-operative Procedures in Learning* (New York, Bureau of Publications, Teachers College, Columbia University, 1952), Part II.
11. National Council for the Social Studies, *A Teacher's Guide to World Trade* (Washington, D.C., the Association, 1953).
12. New York City Board of Education, *The Unit in Curriculum Development and Instruction,* Curriculum Research Report (New York, the Board, 1956).
13. STRATEMEYER, Florence B., and others, *Developing a Curriculum for Mod-*

ern Living, 2nd ed. (New York, Bureau of Publications, Teachers College, Columbia University, 1957), Ch. 6.
14. STRICKLAND, Ruth G., *How to Build a Unit of Work*, Bulletin No. 5 (Washington, D.C., U.S. Office of Education, 1946).
15. *Teachers' Lesson Unit Series* (New York, Bureau of Publications, Teachers College, Columbia Unversity).
16. WRIGHT, Grace S., *Core Curriculum Development, Problems and Practice*, Bulletin No. 5 (Washington, D.C., U.S. Office of Education, 1952).

Films

17. *Practicing Democracy in the Classroom* (Chicago, Encyclopedia Brittanica Films, 1953), 22 minutes.
18. *We Plan Together* (New York, Teachers College, Columbia University, 1948), 20 minutes.

CHAPTER **5**

Teaching a Class Lesson

»»»»»»»»»»»

THOUGH THE TREND in secondary education is away from exclusive reliance on the classroom recitation, a carefully prepared and ably taught classroom lesson is still an important way of teaching and learning. There are times when the class lesson is the most effective way of explaining a new concept or procedure, of clarifying misconceptions, of providing the necessary practice for mastering a skill, or of developing esthetic appreciation. In many instances topics are taught by means of class lessons, with individual study and committee projects reduced to a subsidiary or supplementary role. During work on a unit, the quality of learning is sometimes improved by having the teacher present a lesson. In some subject areas, such as mathematics, science, and foreign language, the daily lesson may be the basic method of teaching.

The same qualities which make for effective teaching of units are also important in the daily lessons. Pupils can participate in selecting the questions to be treated in a series of daily lessons just as they participate in selecting the questions to be treated in a unit of work. Daily lessons need not be independent units, isolated from each other by a twenty-four hour interval. Lessons can be planned in such a way that they are interrelated and deal with important aspects that may take as long as a week to develop. Daily lessons, moreover, can include varied kinds of activities in addition to the familiar question and answer routine and they can be adjusted to the interests and needs of the students as easily as any other classroom procedure. The procedures used in the daily lesson are sufficiently flexible to suggest a basic pattern which can be modified easily for use by members of teaching teams who deal with

148

a "class" composed of the students in two or more secondary school classes.

PREPARING TO TEACH A LESSON

How can a teacher prepare for a lesson so that he will be in the best position to guide student learning? The school bell schedule certainly limits the way in which a class conducts its activities but it should not dictate the way in which the teacher prepares for them. As he plans the work to be done in class, the teacher need not think only in terms of the lesson for the next day. It is usually better to regard the major topic rather than the daily lesson as the unit for planning, and to plan at one time all of the separate lessons dealing with this topic so that these separate lessons can be interrelated to form a unified treatment of the topic as a whole. The teacher who plans each lesson as an isolated entity, each with its own beginning, middle, and end, may have a series of lessons which, though each lesson is satisfactory, nevertheless fails to satisfy the purpose for which the major topic is included in the course of study.

Of course the teacher who is preparing to teach a lesson or a series of lessons must be certain to review the subject matter that will be discussed, but no review of the subject matter, however thorough it may be, is sufficient as the sole preparation for teaching. Many a young teacher has had the disappointing experience of staying up late the night before class cramming into his head all the information he could get on the topic he is to teach, only to find himself unable in class to get his students to be willing to share his wisdom. Dealing with incomprehensible abstractions, he searches hurriedly for the illustrations that will make vivid to his students what is so clear to him. His teaching is certain to be far more effective if his preparation includes adequate attention to planning the teaching procedures he will use as well as to organizing the material he will teach.

The teacher's preparation for a lesson must be oriented in terms of the students' as well as the teacher's role. The important consideration is not only what the teacher will do but also what the students are to do if they are to learn anything during the class session. The teacher needs to know the content that will be treated, but he must also understand how the content is related to his students' background. No effective teacher ever presents such a topic as vitamins, the Westward Migration, or Russian geography, as such. There are, instead, specific questions which the study of these topics is expected to answer, and there are specific objectives these lessons are expected to attain.

A lesson on the railroads, for example, may aim at any number of objectives. The railroads may be studied as part of the history of transportation. The lesson may be pointed toward the role the railroads have played in the development of the nation. The purpose of the lesson may be that of helping the class to understand why the railroads are subject to federal controls that do not affect other businesses and to see how these controls are exercised. The study of the railroads may be used as a way of helping adolescents to understand one of the major problems underlying many of our current labor-management conflicts today, namely, the differences in the point of view regarding what should be done for workers who are no longer needed when labor-saving machinery is introduced. For the teacher's preparation to be most useful, it should concern itself with the specific objectives the teacher is trying to achieve. It is unrealistic to assume that a "lesson on railroads" will lead inevitably to the specific points the teacher has in mind unless the lesson is planned so as to develop these points.

However flexible or inflexible the course of study may be, every teacher has the responsibility for examining the content in order to make sure that it will be presented in such a way as to be significant to these boys and girls. Whether the classroom activity be a daily lesson in a long series of daily lessons, a workshop period during which students are busy at individual tasks, or a discussion that has been planned and will be conducted by the students, the teacher must be so well prepared that these activities will fulfill the objectives they are intended to achieve.

Choosing the Topic

Few teachers realize how much leeway they have in selecting the topic of a lesson. Those who teach in schools that have a prescribed curriculum often proceed as though the term's course of study leaves them virtually no choice in planning the day's activities.

Two teachers in the same school may conscientiously teach the same material in the course of a term even though they organize the material differently and divide it into different daily lessons. For example, the sophomore English teachers in a large high school may find that they have three weeks to teach the same novel, but the teachers themselves are the ones to decide, each for his own class, just what is to be done each day. They may even teach the same subject matter the same day and yet organize it about such different questions that the lessons resemble each other only slightly. Finally, where desirable teacher-pupil planning enters the picture, it is obvious that there will be considerable differences in approach, even though students and teacher stay within the established scope of the course.

It helps the teacher to plan a more stimulating lesson if the topic is expressed in terms of a question or a problem rather than a phrase. The English class is more likely to have a good composition period if the topic is, "How can we write letters our friends will want to answer?" rather than, A Friendly Letter. A stimulating home economics period is more easily developed about the question, "How can a family which is supported by relief payments get the greatest nutritional value from the money spent for food?" than about the topic, The Relative Nutritional Value of Different Foods.

What makes a topic appropriate? The difference between a good topic and a less promising one is more than a matter of sentence structure, for it takes little imagination on the teacher's part to change a phrase into an interrogative sentence. There is an important difference, however, between a grammarian's definition of a question and an adolescent's. To the grammarian, "What are the uses of complex sentences?" is a question, but few are the adolescents who are interested in answering it. The kind of question the teacher needs as the topic is one that students ask, or would be interested in asking if they thought of it.

Some teachers who find the use of complex sentences listed as one of the topics in the syllabus resign themselves to the inevitable and present the many uses of complex sentences as just so many unrelated bits of information. Obediently, students learn that complex sentences can be used to express time, manner, reason, result, and all the other functions that grammarians enumerate. Students then examine textbook sentences until the boys and girls recognize the various uses and can give an illustration of each one. With persistent teaching, students can be taught to remember these illustrations for examination purposes and they can memorize the trick mnemonic devices by which they tell the complex from the compound sentences. Once the examination is over, the uses of complex sentences soon become so inactive a part of the students' background as to make one wonder why so much energy had been expended in teaching them.

If the teacher is determined to teach the uses of complex sentences, his first step is to see what these uses are—to an adolescent, not a grammarian. The question which the teacher must ask himself is: "If I were a fifteen-year-old sophomore, what use would I have for complex sentences?" As an obvious first step, the teacher will read his students' letters and stories to see what use they now make of complex sentences. He will probably find that they use them little, for many boys and girls have not yet outgrown the habit of joining two simple sentences with a *but* or an *and*. As he reads their written work, he will find many instances in which the meaning would be clearer and the writing more effective if the students used complex sentences, since it is only rarely that the two clauses in a sentence are truly equal. More frequently, one of the two clauses should be subordinated to the other.

What does a student mean when he writes: "We drove all day with

hardly a rest and we reached camp just in time for a swim before supper?"
As the sentence now stands, several interpretations may be made by the
reader:

1. Because we drove all day with hardly a rest, we reached camp just in time
   for a swim before supper.
2. Although we drove all day with hardly a rest, we reached camp just in
   time for a swim before supper.
3. After driving all day with hardly a rest, we were glad we reached camp
   just in time for a swim before supper.

The correct use of complex sentences does more than provide variety
in sentence structure. Complex sentences, used correctly, sharpen the
meaning so that the reader interprets a thought the way the writer intended it. At this point the teacher is ready to formulate the topic for the
lesson: "How can we improve the editorials we are writing by examining
the kinds of sentences we are using?" As the students see how they can
profit from using complex sentences, they learn more about expressing
time, manner, and the like than they would in a whole series of formal
grammar lessons that are not related closely to their expressional needs.

By looking at the lesson through students' eyes, the teacher can soon
tell which of the many forms of a topic is most challenging. If you were a
high school student, would you prefer a lesson on Common Sources of
Vitamins, or on "How can we get all the vitamins we need without buying
expensive vitamin pills?"

A good topic for a lesson, or a topic for a good lesson, is one that
makes the student an active participant. Because it invites an answer, the
question is often a good topic. Relating the question to the student is even
better, for the student is naturally more interested in questions that concern him than he is in more general questions. A question to which more
than one answer can be given is usually preferable to one which all students will answer in the same way. A question that stresses the applications of a principle will appeal to adolescents more than does a question
that appears to be abstract.

The Aims and Objectives*

In the selection of a topic for the lesson, we must think of the purposes of the lesson as well as of the appeal this topic has for the students.
Unless the teacher does have these purposes clearly in mind as he prepares
his lesson, he can easily lose sight of them as he seeks ways of appealing
to his students' obvious interests. He is more than a television master of

---

* It may be helpful at this point to recall the discussion on pp. 85-89 of the
principle that learning activities must be directed toward definite aims.

ceremonies who must keep the program going for exactly forty-one minutes and who dreads a moment of silence. The teacher wants student interest and student activity, but he must see that they are guided toward worthwhile ends.

For this reason, the aims of a classroom activity, like the topic, should be expressed in terms of students' interests and needs. When the students help to shape the development of the curriculum, the teacher must see that class activities do more than answer just the students' immediate questions. It is the teacher who must see that classroom activities fit into the larger aims of the course as a whole and that these activities make an appropriate contribution to the total educational program. When the curriculum is a prescribed one, on the other hand, the teacher has both the opportunity and the responsibility for seeing that the students' needs are not lost sight of when the various classroom activities are planned. In either case, the teacher's contribution to the formulation of the aims for a series of classroom activities is that of making certain that neither students' interests nor the course content is allowed to dominate class activities at the expense of the other.

It is only natural that students should see the immediate rather than the ultimate purposes of their activities. Concerned as the teacher is with the need for directing the activities going on in his class, he, too, may lose sight of ultimate goals. The teacher, however, has the responsibility for seeing that classroom activities are planned in terms of basic student needs and the total educational program. In an economics class, for example, the aim may be to help students understand the influence of economic factors on national and international problems. In today's lesson, concerned as it is with only one phase of this topic, the class deals specifically with the way in which high tariffs affect international trade.

The teacher must be realistic in setting the objective for the lesson. Most young teachers choose far too ambitious an objective for a single period. In their attempt to cover a large topic in one period, they tend to proceed too rapidly from step to step and to allow too little time for students to ask questions or to practice what they have learned. Experienced teachers, on the other hand, have learned to present less material each period and to use the added time for the practice which students need if they are really to learn. Rather than teach all of multiplication in algebra during a single period, it is better to teach only as much of multiplication as the students can master. Some algebra classes will be doing well if at the end of the first period they can multiply $x + 3$ by x. Other algebra classes at the end of their first lesson in multiplication can do examples of the type $(x + 3)(x - 4)$. No algebra class, however, can learn multiplication if all of the various applications and difficulties are presented in one lesson.

Planning the Approach*

The approach to a lesson is far more than merely a way of starting a lesson and it is more than just another way of arousing interest so that the students will consent to be taught. The approach that a teacher chooses in his discussion of a topic reflects his understanding of the relationship between his students and the topic. The approach influences all phases of the lesson, from the selection of the topic itself to the choice of the practice exercises.

In teaching, there are as many different approaches to a topic as there are teachers and students. The approach to the lesson may be made through a challenging question with which the teacher opens the discussion. For example, in a junior high school class the discussion of advertising was begun by the teacher's asking the students whether any store could get them to buy something they had no intention of buying.

A lesson may begin with the application of a principle as a way of introducing students to the principle. A science class may be introduced to the topic of tropism by the question, "Why do moths fly around electric lights?" The study of tropisms may also be introduced by having students plant some seeds right side up and others upside down and then having them explain why the plants nevertheless grew with their leaves in the air and their roots underground.

Presenting the new material in terms of a problem is often a useful approach, provided that the problem is on the student's level of comprehension and is so selected and so worded that it does challenge students to find the answer.

"The city of Denver, Colorado, has been called the 'mile-high' city because it is a mile above sea level. How do we know it is a mile above sea level? How can we measure the elevation of any point that is not next to the ocean?" Whether this is a problem or not depends on the ability and the background of the students in the class. To one class the procedure for measuring elevation is so familiar that the situation presented by the teacher constitutes no problem. Another class may see no problem because the students do not grasp the meaning of *elevation* or of *sea level*. To a third class, this may be a problem they want to solve because they sense the importance of measuring elevation and want to know how it can be done.

There is, of course, the time-honored approach used by so many teachers who say, "Today, we'll take the next chapter." So unimaginative an introduction ordinarily is the opening for only an equally unimaginative presentation.

* Planning the approach is one way of applying the principle discussed on pp. 78-85 that learning activities should be related to students' needs.

Organizing the Methods of Teaching

The basic pattern of the lesson must be appropriate for the students and the topic. Since there are few topics for which only one method of development can be used, the teacher usually has a wide variety of teaching procedures from which to choose the one he wishes to use for this lesson. To illustrate the many ways in which any one topic can be presented, let's examine some of the methods by which a first-year Spanish class can learn about life in South America.

The students can all be asked to study the same assignment in the textbook, with the classroom recitation used to clarify and supplement the material they have studied.

In a series of developmental lessons, the teacher can help his students to understand how people live in South America by guiding their thinking through his use of carefully formulated key questions which are asked in a planned sequence. Various groups of students can be asked to study and report on specific phases of life in South America, for example, growing coffee.

The teacher can present a series of motion pictures on the different regions of South America.

Life in South America can be studied through a series of such problems as: "Why is there so much feeling in South America against the United States? What problems does South America have to face in becoming industrialized? Why is land reform a major problem in South America? Why has the development of South America been so different from that of the United States?"

Students can participate in such projects as preparing an exhibit of articles made from South American products or preparing the exhibits for a Latin American fair.

A great deal can be learned about South American life by reading selections from the consular reports sent to Washington or by examining a copy of the cargo list of boats which travel the United States–South American route.

The problem of South America will undoubtedly be covered thoroughly if the students select The People of South America as a unit of work.

It is worthwhile for the teacher to examine the various procedures for presenting a lesson before making a detailed lesson plan because the first suggestions that come to mind may not be so good as one that comes after the lesson has been thought of from many angles. Such an exploration of different ways of teaching a topic has other values, for even a good teaching procedure loses much of its effectiveness if it is used with monotonous regularity.

Selecting and Implementing the Most Promising Methods

How can the teacher decide which of the many procedures that come to mind should be the one he finally chooses? The question can be answered only in terms of the specific situation. The teacher is in the best position for deciding which method is most appropriate for his students' abilities and interests and which is most likely to achieve the goals for the topic.

Practical considerations also enter. A busy teacher who has three classes in the same grade tries to ease his burden by selecting a recitation pattern that can be used in all three classes. When classes are small and the teaching load is relatively light, the teacher may prefer to use different procedures for each class because he will be more effective if he is not bored by the repetition of the same material. The teacher, thinking of the importance of the topic and of the amount of class time that is available, will have to select the procedure that presents the topic most effectively within appropriate time limits.

The choice of method is important, but the careful planning of the details is at least equally important. If the topic is to be taught by means of a discussion, the teacher must frame his key questions so that they will help the class to analyze the issues. If the teacher is to use the demonstration procedure, he must plan the demonstration carefully so that it will work as expected. It is embarrassing and always ineffective for the teacher to have to explain that if everything had gone right they would have seen the paper burst into flame and how would they have explained the paper's bursting into flame—that is, if it had burst into flame.

Visual aids must be selected in advance and preparation should be made for the use of such special equipment as may be necessary. It is wasteful to take time in class to decide which is the better map to use or to look through the text to find one that is suitable. The verbal illustrations the teacher will use to make the concepts clearer must also be thought through in advance. The teacher must think of the application the class can make of the principles discussed in class and must select the practice exercises that will provide sufficient graded practice to make mastery possible.

The Plan as a Guide, Not a Strait Jacket

Despite all the planning that the teacher does in advance, he must be careful not to conduct the lesson as though following his prepared plan in every detail were more important than teaching the boys and girls in his class. He must be quick to recognize student difficulties he did not anticipate and to use illustrations suggested by students' questions and comments.

How closely should the teacher follow his lesson plan once he is before his class? Since he has given his preparation so much thought, it is senseless for him to disregard it as he teaches and to rely on his memory for the wording of his key questions or for the illustrations he is to use. That he has some illustrations ready for use should not blind him, however, to the better illustrations that sometimes do come to mind while teaching, when the teacher is stimulated by his students' reactions.

The teacher should feel free to make minor adjustments in his lesson plan, but the young teacher must be wary of discarding his prepared plan too quickly. It is difficult for an inexperienced teacher to gauge student reaction quickly and accurately. Let one student ask a simple question, and the teacher may misinterpret the query as a request for a full-period explanation. If two or three students appear to be interested in going off at a tangent, the inexperienced teacher may visualize a popular demand for changing the discussion in that direction. The young teacher seldom is cynical enough to realize that some students may enjoy luring the teacher away from the topic, especially when they have not prepared the assignment for the day. Adolescents are keen enough to sense their teacher's weaknesses and are quick to take advantage of any teacher who is ready to go into a long explanation of his favorite topic if they give him even the slightest excuse.

Does this mean that the young teacher must ignore students' reactions and that he should not take advantage of the questions they raise in order to discuss a topic that an inelastic syllabus reaches later in the term? Hardly. Every question that a student asks should be acknowledged graciously and should be answered clearly—and briefly. As a matter of fact, when questions are to the point, the teacher should allow the extra time necessary to get answers from other students wherever possible.

If the question is at a tangent to the direction of the class discussion, the teacher should then try to bring the discussion back to the topic at hand. If the students' questions suggest the need for taking up an entirely different topic, the inexperienced teacher can probably lead that discussion better the next day after he has had an evening to plan the lesson.

Yet, there are times when the teacher must be ready to modify his plans drastically or even to discard them entirely. It may become apparent that the lesson is not succeeding because his students just do not understand what he is saying or they are doing. A student's question may be so important to the entire class that it is much more effective if the problem it involves is discussed immediately instead of waiting till three weeks from next Tuesday when the teacher will get to it—and the whole class will have forgotten why the question was ever raised.

Knowing when to make major changes in the plans for the day must remain a matter of the teacher's judgment and cannot be determined by a rule. If such changes are necessary frequently, it would be well for the teacher to examine his ways of preparing for class and his classroom procedure. If a lesson is well planned and skillfully taught, the teacher's lesson plan should facilitate the smooth progress of the class activity rather than set up immovable tracks along which the class must move. Just as a story which reads so smoothly that the reader thinks the author wrote the words effortlessly is in reality the result of painstaking planning, repeated rewriting and polishing, and some uninspiring drudgery, so does a good lesson proceed so naturally that the teacher's prepared plan does not attract attention to itself.

Preparing the Outline of the Subject Matter to be Covered

By preparing an outline of the subject matter that should be covered during the lesson, the teacher can make certain that he is including everything he considers important. Preliminary planning also helps the teacher to arrange the order in which the various aspects of the topic are presented so that the lesson proceeds in a series of short steps that students can take. If the lesson is one in which gradation is important, as in a bookkeeping class in which a new process is being taught, the outline should indicate the order in which the various types of situations are to be presented.

The outline should include the specific page references to any book that will be referred to during the lesson; the English teacher, for example, should not have to halt the discussion to find that passage in *The Return of the Native* which best reflects Thomas Hardy's fatalism. It is also helpful to include in the outline such factual material as the teacher may need during the lesson even though it may not be important enough for him to have memorized it.

Making Adequate Provision for Practice or Application*

If the lesson is one that develops a generalization or teaches a new process, the teacher's plan should make adequate provision for students to apply the generalization to various types of situations or to practice the new process until its correct use has become a matter of habit. It is ordinarily helpful for the teacher to plan these applications in advance lest he neglect some important ones as the lesson progresses in class. Applications that are carefully selected in advance are more likely to illustrate the most important applications than are those which are improvised.

The range and the number of applications are influenced both by the topic and by the class. Some principles are so easily grasped once they have been taught that it is unnecessary to indicate the many ways in which they are applied and a bright class will grasp the implications of a prin-

---

* The guidance of practice periods is discussed more fully on pp. 305-311.

ciple with fewer illustrations than will a less able class. The more heterogeneous the students are in ability and interests, the greater will the range
of applications have to be if student needs are to be met.

There is wide variation in the amount of practice that is needed before the teacher can be satisfied that a new process has been learned. In
some classes relatively little provision need be made for practice in class,
for the students can be relied on to get sufficient practice as they continue
with their work. In such instances only enough practice need be given in
class as will reveal whether students understand the process. With other
classes, the teacher knows that much more opportunity must be allowed
for classroom practice since the teacher has discovered that he cannot
rely on the thoroughness of work that is not done under his direct supervision.

The amount of time given to practice varies from a few minutes to
practically the entire period. In general, young teachers do not allow sufficient time for this phase of the work because they have not yet learned
that students who can follow the teacher's presentation may not be able to
use the information or skill learned in class when they are working on
their own.

The application need not come at the end of the period. It is sometimes an excellent way of beginning the lesson. A science lesson, for example, may begin with the application of the principle. After the students
have examined one or more applications, they may develop inductively a
statement of the principle that will mean more to them than it would if
the teacher began the lesson with a statement of the principle and then
followed it up by presenting illustrations. A series of demonstrations of
the uses of air pressure may thus be an effective way of presenting the
principle inductively.

Giving students an opportunity to apply what they have learned is
more than an appendage to a lesson; it is in many instances the major
justification for the lesson. When the lesson grows out of a need that students perceive, or have been helped to perceive, it is clear that they should
have ample opportunity to use the skill or to apply the generalization.
Knowledge of progress is one of the most powerful incentives to further
achievement. For this reason it is valuable to arrange for applications
which help the students to realize at the end of the period that they can
now solve the problem that seemed so pressing, and yet so insoluble, only
a half hour earlier.

Formulating the Summary of a Lesson

Most lessons are more effective when students summarize what has
been discussed than when the teacher prepares the summary, or when no
summary is made. In many discussion lessons, students get the impression

that they have been chatting and that the conversation has to be continued until the bell rings. The discussion will mean more to the students and will have a more lasting effect if they prepare a summary of the discussion which reveals how much has been accomplished that period. Similarly, the class that has been applying a principle to many different situations should summarize the conclusions it has reached concerning the way in which this principle is used.

The students' preparation of a summary may easily become a dreary affair if each lesson monotonously ends with a pupil summary. Students will soon recognize that the teacher's request for a summary means that the bell is about to ring and they will start gathering up their books and papers, while the student who has been called on is trying to summarize a discussion that may not be too clear in his mind.

The summary does not have to be requested so bluntly nor in so routine a manner. The teacher's suggestion that they now try to answer the question that puzzled them at the beginning of the period—for example, "Why did Russia first ally itself with Hitler and then fight Germany a few years later?"—may itself be an excellent summary of the discussion. If the question discussed in class is a controversial one, the students can be asked to select those arguments for each side that seem to stand up best under analysis. In a lesson that has dealt with the applications of a principle or rule—as in science, mathematics, foreign languages, or English— the teacher can ask the students to indicate the kind of situation in which knowledge of the principle or rule is most helpful.

The summary does not have to be the last step of the lesson. In most discussion lessons it is well to call for partial summaries as the lesson progresses. In a social studies class, for example, the teacher summarizes the first part of the discussion of Russia's entry into World War II by asking, "In the light of what has been said so far, how many of you feel Russia was justified in thinking she could gain more by even a temporary alliance with Hitler than by an immediate declaration of war?" and then, of course, following that question with the one word "Why?" In a lesson in which a new process is studied, as in a home nursing class, for example, the teacher may ask for a summary of the steps in the process before additional practice is given in applying the process.

In some instances, the summary is developed throughout the period as the students and teacher together construct the chalkboard outline that epitomizes the discussion. This type of continuous summary is illustrated by the home economics class that prepares an outline during the lesson on vitamins to summarize the contribution each vitamin makes to healthful living, the amount each child or adult needs daily, and the foods that should be eaten to assure an adequate supply of each vitamin.

The making of a summary can be much more than a subtle reminder that the period is about over. To be able to select the high points of a dis-

cussion, to discern the difference between a basic idea and a helpful illustration, to know what must be remembered and what can safely be forgotten—these are important aspects of learning.

Evaluation

Every lesson should carry within it at some point the kind of evaluation which reveals to student and teacher alike how much has been
learned during the day. It is this step in the process which can arm the
student to reply with something better than "Nothing," when asked by
Dad what happened at school that day.

Evaluation can take many forms. It can be a simple question at the
end of the period, "Now, what have we learned today?" or a more directive
query calling for the kind of interpretive responses included in the preceding section on summaries. In this case the evaluation is to be found *in* the
summary. The evaluation may be in the form of a brief quiz, oral or written. If prefaced by remarks indicating the purpose of the test, papers need
not be collected and graded. The evaluation may take the form of students' writing a paragraph on a provocative question which draws upon
the day's discussion and preparation.

The daily evaluation is generally brief, informal, and not necessarily
deferred till the end of the period. It is one way of putting a capstone, a
conclusion on the lesson; it gives the student a sense of progress; it underlines what has been most important in the lesson. Most important, it helps
the teacher to judge the adequacy of student achievement, for upon this
all future planning depends.

Timing the Lesson

Added to all of the problems which the teacher must face as he prepares to teach a lesson is that which is presented by the school's bell
schedule. Not only must the teacher plan a music lesson that will make
adolescent boys and girls want to hear more music by Mendelssohn, not
only must this lesson be inspiring, stimulating, and informative, but it
must also last exactly forty-one minutes or fifty-five minutes, or must be
completed early enough to leave time for supervised study. Even experienced teachers find it difficult to plan so precisely; for young teachers it is
even more difficult to know just how much they should plan to teach in
one period.

The penalty for poor timing is serious. There are few such dishearten-
ing experiences as that of the young teacher who prepares an excellent
lesson and who teaches it as well as he hoped, only to find that twenty
minutes of the period are left. When this happens, he ordinarily goes over
the highlights of the lesson and asks for student questions—and there are

still ten minutes to go. Much of the effectiveness of a good lesson evaporates as teacher and students settle down to play the game called "waiting for the bell."

Sometimes the teacher completes the day's work so rapidly because he does not appreciate how much more there is to teaching than telling and being told. Thus, the fact that one student answered the question correctly does not mean that the whole class has grasped the point and is ready for the next item. It may be necessary for the teacher to rephrase the question and ask it of other students before he can be sure that they are ready to proceed. Teaching involves much more than checking off items on a lesson plan, and there is sometimes a large gap between "covering" a topic and making certain that the students have mastered it.

When lessons are planned in terms of a sequence that will take several days to complete, the class can continue right on with the next day's work. Similarly, the teacher who knows his subject will not run out of material the way another teacher does when his knowledge includes little more than what is in the textbook plus whatever else he has read in preparation for that day's work.

On the other hand, the teacher who finds that the bell regularly rings before he is ready for it may discover that he frequently omits the most telling applications of the principle that is being discussed and that his classroom discussions end indecisively since none is ever carried to a conclusion.

There is no formula that can help the young teacher to decide how far his class will go with a given topic. In general, it is better for a young teacher to include in his plan a little more material than he is likely to use than to run short before the period is over. Only as the teacher comes to know his students better does he improve in his ability to predict how much he can safely plan for one period.

The timing of a lesson does not depend entirely on the teacher's advance preparation, since he cannot predict which unforeseen difficulties will arise. He does not know which questions students will ask in class nor how much discussion will be necessary to clarify a certain point. Sometimes a key question, one that the teacher anticipates will take some five or ten minutes to discuss, is answered so clearly and so persuasively by the first student to speak, and is so obviously understood by the rest, that nothing more need be said. On the other hand, a question which seems simple to the teacher may reveal so serious a misconception of basic principles that it may consume ten or fifteen minutes of class time.

The more active the part which students play in the development of the lesson, the more difficult it is for the teacher to prepare a precise timetable for the different parts of the lesson. For this reason, there is little to be gained by having the teacher prepare the detailed lesson plans used by some teachers whereon definite time allotments are indicated for each question and each exercise.

The teacher should keep an eye on the passage of time while the lesson is in progress. If his watch is on the desk or if he can look at his wrist watch or the hall clock without attracting too much attention, he can see whether the class will complete the activity planned for the day. When he sees that the lesson is moving rapidly, he knows that he can afford to take a little more time to illustrate the next point or that it may be possible to go on to the next topic. If the lesson is moving slowly, he has time in which to decide whether he should omit the next section of his plan or whether this topic deserves another day. The type of continuous adjustment that a teacher makes when he has almost the whole period before him is much better than that which is available to the teacher who disregards the passage of time until he looks at his watch and discovers that he has only five minutes left to bring the discussion to a climax and to introduce the new kind of assignment he has planned for the next day.

The elastic ending. Some teachers prefer to plan an elastic ending to the period, that is, the kind of ending that can be adjusted so that the lesson can end with the bell without seeming either protracted or abbreviated. The music teacher, for example, plans to end the lesson on Mendelssohn by playing excerpts from the works of other composers who wrote music resembling that of Mendelssohn. If there is time to listen to and discuss only one piece, the period ends as a rounded whole. Should there be more time, more selections can be played.

Similarly, the art teacher asks students to criticize the paintings made during the period and knows that this discussion can last two minutes or ten minutes. The English teacher has his students listen to and then suggest ways of improving the way in which different students began their short stories. The home economics teacher has her students evaluate the daily menu that is planned to provide an adequate supply of basic foods. So, too, may the teacher in other subjects think of ways of ending the period in such a way as to make the last part of the period as fruitful as the earlier parts.

The elastic ending must not be used merely as a way of filling in time. If the lesson has really been concluded earlier, the teacher should not prolong it. Instead, the remaining few minutes can be used in preparing them for the work to be done the next day, in answering questions raised by students, or in discussing some of the items the teacher wishes he had time to include in the term's work. The elastic ending can be justified not on the basis of its being elastic but as a means of using the last few minutes for work that is a legitimate part of the lesson and that does interpret and apply what has been done earlier.

WRITING A LESSON PLAN

The writing of a lesson plan has no value in itself; it is useful only to the extent that it enables the teacher to visualize the classroom situation in advance and insofar as it enables the teacher in class to profit from his advance preparation. Young teachers sometimes invest too much time in the writing of detailed lesson plans so attractively underlined in red and blue ink that they are tempted to keep them and to use them over and over again. A good lesson plan is always prepared for a specific class and a specific time and can rarely be used again in just the same form, even though it may be a useful source of suggestions for later lessons. It is for this reason that one principal suggests that his young teachers write their plans with a soft pencil—such plans can be read easily and yet will blur so soon that no teacher will bring them to class for the rest of his professional career.

Although the teacher's preparation for a lesson is a prerequisite for successful teaching, it may also interfere with effective teaching. Some teachers come to class with so detailed and so inelastic a lesson plan that they cannot adjust it readily to the class situation. They ask their questions in class almost as though they were searching for the specific words that are needed to fill in the teacher's outline. The path that the lesson is to follow is so obviously predetermined that students do not feel encouraged to interrupt the teacher's smooth presentation to ask questions which will clarify a point that is not clear to them. A teacher can be so intent on following his prepared plan that he is not sufficiently aware of student reactions to take advantage of their interest in following up some phase of the lesson more fully or to realize that they had not understood another part.

Most of these difficulties can be overcome if the teacher prepares the right kind of plan and if he uses this plan wisely. The lesson plan should not be so detailed that the teacher has his every word planned in advance. The key questions on which the whole lesson is based must be carefully prepared before class since the sequence in which these questions are asked is ordinarily better if planned ahead of time. In contrast to the way key questions are formulated, it is preferable not to phrase in advance all of the minor questions that lead up to the key question and not to memorize the comments to be made in explanation of the answers to the key questions.

What should the teacher write in his plan? The answer depends on the lesson, the teacher, and the class. The lesson plan for a biology demonstration will look different from that for an arts and crafts workshop period. The lesson plan of a recently appointed teacher will be different from that of a teacher with fifteen years' experience.

Similarly, there is no set form for the lesson plan. If the lesson plan is viewed as a functional aid to the teacher, it should take whatever form the

A SUGGESTED FORM FOR A LESSON PLAN

*Class*_____   *Date*_____

    (Many inexperienced teachers find it helpful to enumerate here the pertinent characteristics of the class for which the lesson is being planned.)

THE TOPIC:

THE AIMS—Long-range aim:

        Immediate objective:

Outline of Methods and Content

THE APPROACH:

KEY QUESTIONS:

ILLUSTRATIVE MATERIALS:

APPLICATIONS:

PRACTICE EXERCISES:

THE ASSIGNMENT:

SUMMARY OR CONCLUSION:

individual teacher finds most helpful. For example, some teachers prefer to write the key words in the plan in large capital letters so that a quick look at the plan will remind them of the point they wish to make in class. For the lesson plan to be useful in class, it should be clearly legible. It is usually better, therefore, to write it on a single, large sheet of paper than to use index cards which may get out of their proper sequence. The main point is that in both content and form the teacher should think only in terms of the class and should prepare the kind of plan he can use most effectively in class.

The outline on page 165 suggests one type of lesson plan that new teachers have found to be helpful. Obviously, it has value only as teachers feel free to adjust it to the needs of the specific class situation. The teacher will find it convenient to write in his lesson plan any reminders he may need the following day, such as "Collect laboratory books for inspection," "Ask Bob to return his copy of *Kon Tiki* to the school library," and "Election of Class Representative to the Council."

More importance is ordinarily attached to the writing of a lesson plan than it deserves as one of the phases of preparing to teach. In general, few experienced teachers write lesson plans that are as detailed as those written by student teachers. Even though an experienced teacher may prepare conscientiously, he does not have to write as much as does a novice. When a young teacher is appointed to a school and discovers that the best teachers do not write elaborate lesson plans, he concludes erroneously that good teachers do not prepare. As the young teacher gains in experience, he need write less and less, and, for some lessons, may need to write nothing at all; but he should retire from teaching before he reaches the point where teaching becomes so familiar and routine that he no longer needs to prepare.

In order to indicate how teachers modify this outline for use in class, we are reproducing the plan prepared by a junior high school teacher for the first of two lessons on combustion.*

GENERAL SCIENCE, GRADE NINE

PROBLEM: What is necessary for combustion?

TIME: Two periods (One period on heat; one period on oxygen).

OBJECTIVES: 1. To develop problem-solving skills.
2. To understand the scientific method.
3. To develop skills in using scientific apparatus, and in measurement.
4. To develop understanding of theory of combustion.
5. To learn to interpret and evaluate data.

MAJOR PROBLEM: What is necessary for combustion to take place? (Do not state problem to class, but try to develop it in approach.

* Reprinted by permission of H. Bleecker (Harold G. Campbell Junior High School, New York City).

SUBPROBLEM: Why doesn't paper burn? (one period).

APPROACH: Show class how water can be made to boil in a dish made of their loose-leaf paper, without burning the paper.

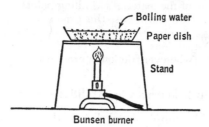

Boiling water

Paper dish

Stand

Bunsen burner

Development of Hypothesis:

This demonstration should cause the student to ask himself why the paper doesn't burn.

This is essentially our problem stated very locally.

Develop possible hypotheses:

1. Paper doesn't burn because flame is not hot.
2. Paper doesn't burn because paper has been chemically treated beforehand.
3. Paper doesn't burn because water keeps it cool.
4. Paper *does* burn, but water in dish puts flame out.

Evaluation of Hypotheses:

A. Have class discuss the hypotheses given, and see which ones they want to eliminate as being not worthy of testing.

B. Decide which hypotheses are to be tested to try to *disprove* them.

Experimentation and Controls:

Let *students suggest* methods and materials to be used in their experiments. Use pupils to perform experiments, whenever possible. Insist on a control for each experiment. Hypotheses 1, 2, and 4 can easily be disproved. Hypothesis 3 can easily be tested experimentally, with control and thermometers.

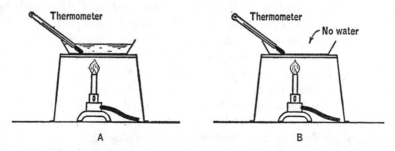

Thermometer

Thermometer

No water

A   B

Observation and Explanation:

Thermometer in A does not rise above 100°C (212°F), while thermometer in B rapidly reaches limit of thermometer. Let students check and record data on board.

Explanation to be elicited from the class is that the water in dish conducts heat away from paper so that the paper does not reach its kindling temperature.

Conclusion (From class):

1. The kindling temperature of paper is *higher* than the boiling point of water.
2. Heat is necessary for combustion, and this heat must be greater than the temperature of the material's kindling point.

Practical Application: How can we use this principle?
  A. In Fireproofing
  B. In Explosive Detonations
  C. In Engineering (wherever friction is produced)

Adjusting Teaching to Differences in Abilities and Interests

Teaching would be simple—and deadly dull—if all of the students in a class were alike in their abilities and interests. No teacher need concern himself about such a condition, for the increasing heterogeneity of the secondary school population has widened the range of differences in ability and interests in virtually every secondary school class in the country.

In the attempt to adjust instruction to these individual differences among the students in even a supposedly homogeneous class, many teachers organize their classes into smaller groups for various activities.*

There are other ways, too, in which the teacher can adjust his instruction to his students once he knows their background, their interests, and their abilities. The topic of investments, for example, is treated differently in a community in which the fluctuation on the stock market is a common dinner table topic from the way it is taught in another community in which there is never any surplus money available for buying stock.

Practically every adolescent will be subtly flattered and intellectually stimulated if the teacher shows that he thinks enough of the student to tell him about a book or an article in which the boy or girl will be interested or of an exhibit to which he should go. The teacher who takes the time to read what such a student has written and to discuss with him what the student has been doing out of class may have a profound effect.

Classroom assignments need not be uniform for the entire class and are often the easiest way of adjusting instruction to differences in abilities and interests. It is sometimes so easy to adjust the assignment to differences in interests that the teacher may deprive the student of the opportunity to broaden his interests. Even a potential nuclear physicist may profit from art experiences that have nothing to do with the color of the mushroom-shaped cloud after an atomic bomb explosion.

One of the most obvious places where the teacher should adjust instruction to individual needs is in the conduct of practice periods. Many classroom drill periods are ineffective because all students perform the same remedial exercises even though their weaknesses may be varied. By administering diagnostic tests and by using other means of diagnosing the

* See pp. 98-99 for a discussion of group teaching.

students' individual weaknesses, the teacher can assure each student the kind of help he needs.

THE ASSIGNMENT

Assignment of school work to be done outside of class is based on a belief that the school day is all too short for the important and intriguing learning experiences that the world has to offer. The short school period allows little time for values that may be achieved in out-of-school study: broader understanding, deeper analysis, practice on necessary skills, the information required for effective discussion in class, and the inspiration for further learning.

In practice, however, the assignment often falls short of achieving these values. "Homework" is all too often a routine chore assigned unimaginatively by the teacher and performed grudgingly by the pupil. Merely increasing the amount of work required of the students does not necessarily improve the quality of their education. The importance and the appeal of new learning may be obscured in a humdrum kind of activity when the students do not recognize the purpose and the teacher has not analyzed the objectives. It is necessary for the teacher to aim at objectives that are worth the students' time and effort. He must translate these objectives into specific assignments and then help students see their purpose.

Objectives of the Assignment

Two kinds of objectives may be distinguished. One relates to the general enhancement of learning—the ability to study, a desire to extend one's education independently, and the development of interest in a particular area of human endeavor. Achieving such goals depends upon a maximum of student motivation to learn and a minimum of coerced study. These purposes are best met when the student sees the "sense" of what he is doing because he has shared with the teacher in planning his out-of-school study.

A second objective, also valid, is the furthering of specific learning tasks in the curriculum. For a discussion period to be successful, students have to have a background of information and understanding—hence, the assignment to read particular sections in the text and relevant periodicals. Because understanding is so important in mathematics, the teacher may deem it a waste of time to devote a major share of the period to skills in computation which may be developed independently through the assignment. The science laboratory allows scarcely enough time for the experiment; the assignment should encourage writing up the experiment with understanding, generalizing from it, and perhaps extending the new idea with other experiments and reading.

Teachers who take this point of view see the assignment as an important part of schooling. They do not limit assignments to work that is done at home; instead, they make full use of assignments on which students work in class, in laboratories and workshops, and in the library, as well as those on which they work at home. The assignments that are used sometimes ask each student to work independently; at other times, the assignments call for the co-operative efforts of a small or a large group of students. Rather than limit assignments to the preparation for a single class lesson, teachers plan assignments in terms of the longer periods of time. Assignments should call for more than the memorization of facts or drill on skills. In some schools, the assignment offers the teacher the most promising means of enriching a stereotyped curriculum and of introducing worthwhile learning activities for which a formal school allows inadequate time.

When classroom activities are organized about units of work, with students and teacher planning the work co-operatively, the assignments, too, are planned co-operatively instead of being made by the teacher alone. As was indicated in the discussion of units of work,* planning the assignments, deciding on procedures to be followed in doing the assignments, and using and evaluating the results of the assignment are major phases of the work on a unit. Even teachers of classes which do not organize their work in terms of co-operatively planned units have found the co-operative planning of assignments to be a practicable way of reducing the gap between student and curriculum. Since we have already seen how co-operatively planned assignments can be used, we shall now examine what can be accomplished by the assignments used in school programs that are organized in terms of daily lessons taught by subject teachers.

Achieving the Purposes that Can be Served by Assignments

Providing the background for classroom activities. The most widespread use of the assignment is to provide the background for classroom activities. The typical secondary school class session is based on material previously studied by the students. When the lesson itself, however, is a stereotyped one, the assignment offers little challenge to the student. Where the class session is devoted almost entirely to the teacher's asking of detailed factual questions which the students answer by reciting the appropriate sentence from the textbook, it is natural for the student to stress the memorization of details rather than the understanding of major principles.

* See Chapter 4.

If the teacher is interested in having the assignment prepare the student for a classroom discussion, he must formulate the assignment with this end in view. Where the discussion is to center about a few pivotal questions, the students should have these questions in mind as they read. Preliminary discussion of the Westward Migration, for example, leads to raising such questions as, "What led a man to pull up his stakes and to risk the fortune and even the life of his family to move West? In what ways are these motives similar to the more prosaic reasons the student's own family had when it moved to the present residence? What new problems did this Westward Migration present to a young and growing nation?" The student who reads the chapter with these questions in mind is prepared to participate intelligently in class discussion.

Affording additional practice in applying the material studied in class. Another common use of the assignment is to afford the students additional practice in applying the material presented in class. This is the reason for the type of assignment that has English students "Take the sentences in Exercise 43 on page 83 and correct all sentences that contain misplaced modifiers."

Such assignments are inadequate for several reasons. A good teacher knows that students sometimes do not grasp fully the principles they are expected to apply. He therefore makes certain that his students understand the principle they will be applying, for he knows that applying a rule that is half-understood may lead to perpetuating misinformation. He knows, too, that students must understand the significance, as well as the meaning, of the principle before they can attack the applications in anything more than a mechanical manner. For these reasons he stresses assignments which demand more than routine application. In addition to including examples which illustrate varied applications of a basic principle, the geometry teacher thus invites his students to prepare original problems which illustrate the proposition being studied and the English teacher supplements the correction of sentences included in their textbooks by asking his students to reread their own written work in order to find instances in which they can improve a sentence by placing modifiers differently.

Adjusting class instruction to individual differences in interests and ability. Aware of the wide range of individual differences in the ability of his students, teachers modify the assignment so as to make it more appropriate for students. Some students will be excused from much of the practice material so that they may spend time with their individual study of special problems. Other students may be excused from the more difficult or the more challenging phases of the assignment so that they can concentrate on mastering the minimum essentials.

The assignment is a useful means of adjusting class instruction to the wide range of individual interests among the students. Of necessity, the teacher cannot appeal to all of his students' special interests during a single class period, but he can help satisfy these interests by the assignments he makes for individual study.

It takes time and ingenuity to adjust assignments to individual interests, but this practice has within it the possibilities of overcoming one of the most serious shortcomings of mass education. By the use of differentiated assignments, the teacher can help students to see that the study of economics is as important for the prospective engineer as for the prospective businessman, and that both housewives and businessmen must understand how the scientist explores his problems.

Supplementing the material studied in class. Assignments are useful means of supplementing the material presented in class. When controversial issues are studied, a single textbook cannot very well be the sole source of information. It is through the assignment of other reading material that the students see how the topic is treated from different points of view. Even when the topic is not controversial, students can gain a great deal from wide reading. The reading of a historical novel, for example, does much to make vivid what is discussed in the social studies class. Assignments, used effectively, can contribute much to encourage the lasting effects of material discussed in class.

*Teaching students to work and study independently.** Any program of improving the ability to study must make full use of the opportunities that are afforded by assignments. If students know how to do their assignments effectively and if they become habituated in the use of these procedures, their improvement in work habits may be as important as are the subject matter knowledge and skills they have learned from doing these assignments.

The Characteristics of a Good Assignment

The functions of the assignment as discussed also help define the characteristics of the good assignment. It must answer adequately these questions: What should be done? Why should it be done? How should it be done?

Even the most routine assignment seems to satisfy the requirement that students know what they are to do. Students are told to read the next two chapters in the novel, to solve the six problems on page 14 of their mathematics textbook, to correct the first ten sentences on page 115 of their English textbook, to study the chapter on the tariff in their history book, and the like. Superficially these assignments are definite, but students do not always understand just what they are to do. Do they know what they are to look for as they read the assigned chapters? Do they understand the principles they are applying in their mathematics and

* See Chapter 9.

English assignments? Because they understand more clearly what they must write rather than what is meant by *read* or *study,* and because written assignments are more easily checked by the teacher than are reading or study assignments, most students do all of the writing that is required and slight the rest of the assignment.

The student ordinarily receives little guidance in deciding how to proceed with his work on the assignment. The procedures are so familiar to the teacher that he assumes they are equally familiar to the student. As a result, many students work inefficiently and sometimes fail to satisfy the purposes of the assignment even though they may spend a great deal of time on it. Both teachers and students may attribute to low intelligence and inadequate preparation what is more properly explained by poor study and work habits or by the failure to grasp the purpose of the assignment and to plan a procedure that is appropriate for these purposes.

These questions, What? Why? and How?, cannot be answered fully if the assignment is given hurriedly by the teacher just before the bell is about to ring. The assignment is so important that it usually deserves about a fourth or a third of the period. Sometimes the giving of an assignment rightly consumes the whole period. For example, the secondary school social studies teacher who is introducing his class to assignments which call for a wide variety of supplementary reading can profitably spend an entire period getting students to understand the purposes to be served by supplementary reading and discussing the most effective ways of reading the kind of material they will be using.

When Should Assignments Be Given?

Ideally, the assignment should be made at that point in the lesson which leads up to the assignment most effectively. The mathematics class which has been doing various types of construction examples in class is ready for the assignment which begins, "Now that you know how to do this type of problem in class, let's see whether you can do them when you are on your own. For tomorrow . . ." Similarly, the history class that has been discussing the "Cold War" at mid-century reaches the point where the teacher says, "Before we can talk intelligently about stopping Communist aggression, we ought to examine a specific case or two. Your textbook presents the circumstances surrounding United Nations intervention in South Korea in 1950. In addition, your parents are likely to have some strong opinions concerning participation by the United States. As you read the section which begins on page 550 and as you discuss the incident with your parents, try to decide whether President Truman was right when he dispatched troops to Korea. Which questions should you keep in mind as you read? Yes, Hilda, . . ."

Although the best time to make the assignment is at the most appropriate point during the period, many teachers prefer to give the assignment at the beginning of the period. Some teachers give the assignment earlier because they are afraid that they may find that so much time is consumed by the classroom discussion that the assignment is made hurriedly or may even be forgotten. In many instances, the teacher can take care of the assignment most effectively if he announces it briefly at the beginning of the period, or has it written on the chalkboard where students can copy it as soon as they enter, and then refers to the assignment more fully at the appropriate point in the development of the day's lesson.

The teacher who announces the assignment at the beginning of the lesson must be aware of the possibility that the course of the lesson may necessitate a change in the assignment. Giving the assignment early in the period may tend to fix the lesson into a rigid pattern which discourages deviation from the original plan no matter how necessary or promising such modifications may be. Teachers who habitually announce the assignment early in the lesson must be ready to alter it should they find that the progress made in class indicates the inappropriateness of the assignment as originally given.

How Should the Students' Work Be Evaluated?

The teacher can save himself and his students considerable unnecessary work if, before he makes an assignment, he gives some thought to the way in which the class will use the assignment when it is due and to the procedures by which he can evaluate the adequacy of the students' work. Teachers frequently spend a disproportionate amount of time on the correction of assignments.

Grading all of the written assignments takes far more time than it deserves and deprives the teacher of time that he can use better in meeting with individual students, in planning more thoroughly for his work in class, in enriching his own background for teaching, and in enjoying at least a little of the leisure time which the layman associates with teaching.

If the teacher wants to know whether the students have read the assigned material, a two- or three-minute written quiz at the beginning of the period answers that question and frees all but a few minutes of class time for the kind of discussion the teacher and students prefer. This type of quiz—and it need not be given daily—has other values, for the kind of question the teacher uses will suggest to students the questions they should be thinking of as they study.

Short written assignments should ordinarily be done in notebooks. At the beginning of the period, students are asked to open their notebooks to the day's work so that the teacher may discover quickly whether all have done their work. Some students can write their work at the chalkboard while common difficulties and individual weaknesses are discussed and corrected.

More attention should be given to using the students' work than to grading it. Assignments that are properly planned by the teacher constitute an important part of the background for the work done in class. What they have read should be brought into the discussion. The answers they have written to the questions assigned in advance are read and discussed as these questions arise during the class session. That they have expressed their opinions on paper gives all students something to say when the topic is discussed in class. When students see that their preparation is essential for intelligent participation in class, they see assignments as more than just a means of filling the class marking book. The teacher who is concerned with the use that will be made of students' assignments will be less likely to make unnecessary or unproductive assignments, and he can spare his students the letdown they are sure to feel when they discover that the interesting task to which they gave so much time was, after all, only another homework assignment.

Some students will always object to doing the assignment regardless of how important it is, but all students will object to assignments that seem unnecessary or unduly burdensome. Capable teachers are always careful to avoid unnecessary assignments. They will also recognize that enthusiasm for their own subject, added to the enthusiasm of four other teachers, may result in a heavy burden for the conscientious student. The teacher must learn how long it takes his students to do their assignments for his class and must be careful not to assign more work than school regulations permit or than his own judgment recommends. Frequently, the teacher must decide not which kind of assignment will best prepare students for the class work, but how the teacher can best use that part of the students' time to which he is entitled.

QUESTIONS FOR STUDY AND DISCUSSION

1. Which of the values of the unit plan of teaching can be achieved under a daily lesson plan system of teaching?

2. A junior high school teacher made a practice of departing from his prepared lesson plan whenever the questions raised in class seemed more important than the material he had planned for the class. By chance he learned that many of the questions were asked only because the students were making a game out of seeing who would be the first to get the teacher off the topic.

What should the teacher do now?

3. How can the teacher solve the practical problems that arise as he tries to use differentiated assignments to meet the range of interests and abilities in the many classes he has each day? How can the teacher solve these problems in the area in which you are teaching or preparing to teach?

4. Of all the topics that are ordinarily included in the secondary school, select the one that you think is least worth teaching to secondary school

students today. Assuming that you had to teach this topic because of syllabus requirements, what approach to this specific topic would be most appropriate for a specific secondary school class with which you are familiar?

5. Prepare a plan for a one-period lesson that is appropriate for a specific class with which you are familiar. In which respects would this plan have to be modified if you were to teach this topic to several classes which are to be taught at the same time in a large room?

6. A teacher who has prepared his plan for a lesson with great care finds that somehow everything goes wrong as he tries to teach this lesson to his class. The questions he asks elicit little response and the illustrations he uses seem to confuse rather than clarify.

What should the teacher do?

7. Under which circumstances is the teacher justified in planning and teaching a full-period lesson while the class is engaged in a unit of work?

8. A teacher who habitually planned his lessons in great detail found that he assumed so much of the responsibility for planning class activities that his students did little more than answer the questions he asked them. When he tried to plan his lessons in terms of only broad questions, he was equally dissatisfied with the results because he found that he could not make up good questions on the spur of the moment.

What advice would you give this teacher?

9. A young teacher who spent much time preparing his lesson plans and phrasing his key questions carefully was criticized by his principal for being so dependent on his lesson plan that he had to consult it frequently during the class session. The next day the teacher resolved not to look at his lesson plan during the period, only to find that he was upset by his inability to remember the phrasing of the questions he had worded so carefully when he prepared his lesson plan.

What advice would you give this teacher?

BIBLIOGRAPHY

1. ALCORN, Marvin D., HOUSEMAN, Richard A., and SCHUNERT, Jim R., *Better Teaching in Secondary Schools* (New York, Holt, Rinehart and Winston, Inc., 1954), Chs. 4, 13, 14.

2. ALEXANDER, William M., and HALVERSON, Paul M., *Effective Teaching in Secondary Schools* (New York, Holt, Rinehart and Winston, Inc., 1956), Ch. 15.

3. BURTON, William H., *The Guidance of Learning Activities*, 2nd ed. (New York, Appleton-Century-Crofts, Inc., 1952), Ch. 11.

4. GILLILAND, Jack, and GILMAN, Robert, "Policies to Govern the Assignment of Homework in the Secondary School," *Curriculum Bulletin*, Vol. XV, No. 198 (November 10, 1959), The School of Education, University of Oregon, Eugene, Oregon.

5. GRAMBS, Jean D., IVERSON, William J., and PATTERSON, Franklin K., *Modern Methods in Secondary Education*, rev. ed. (New York, Holt, Rinehart and Winston, Inc., 1958), Ch. 6.

6. GRUHN, William T., and DOUGLASS, Harl R., *The Modern Junior High School*, 2nd ed. (New York, The Ronald Press Company, 1956), Chs. 9, 10.

7. HANSEN, Kenneth H., *High School Teaching* (Englewood Cliffs, N.J., Prentice-Hall, Inc., 1957), Ch. 7.

8. KLAUSMEIER, Herbert J., *Teaching in the Secondary School* (New York, Harper and Brothers, 1958), Chs. 6, 7.
9. MILLS, Hubert H., and DOUGLASS, Harl L., *Teaching in High School* (New York, The Ronald Press Company, 1948), Chs. 10 and 11.
10. National Education Association Research Division, *Homework* (Washington, D.C., the Association, January, 1958).
11. NOAR, Gertrude, *The Junior High School—Today and Tomorrow* (Englewood Cliffs, N.J., Prentice-Hall, Inc., 1953), Ch. 12.
12. RISK, Thomas M., *Principles and Practices of Teaching in Secondary Schools*, 3rd ed. (New York, American Book Company, 1958), Chs. 10, 12-14.
13. WIGGINS, Sam P., *Successful High School Teaching* (Boston, Houghton Mifflin Company, 1958), Ch. 10.

CHAPTER 6

Discussing as a Way of Learning

»»»»»»»»»»

THE DEMOCRATIC PROCESS sets high value on discussion as a method of identifying, analyzing, and solving problems. Democracy is a political expression of faith in the superiority of the combined intelligence of the group over the efforts of a solitary hero figure. As a result it is not surprising that we live in a culture that is saturated with meetings, committees, and conferences.

Discussion is important as a learning process because it is a way of considering various facets of a problem and also because it lays the groundwork for the many discussion situations in which young people and adults are constantly taking part. In many subjects, such as social studies and English, discussion is a basic classroom procedure; in others, like mathematics and science, it is an important adjunct to demonstration and experimentation.

Increased concern with the students' active participation in the learning process is reflected in the extent to which the word *discussion* has replaced *recitation* as the one which best describes a typical class session. Whereas *recitation* implies the acceptance and repetition of a point of view presented by the teacher or the textbook, *discussion* suggests that students themselves share in the process of learning by evaluating points of view, raising issues of their own, and seeking solutions based upon study, examination, and group analysis under the teacher's guidance.

THE NATURE OF CLASSROOM DISCUSSION

It is important, of course, that the teacher have a clear idea of what he means by *discussion*. Some teachers, unfortunately, use the term to dignify a supposedly discarded recitation procedure or even a thinly disguised lecture. At the other extreme of educational practice are those teachers who are so determined not to dominate classroom activities that a discussion in their class amounts to little more than idle conversation that rambles from topic to topic without arriving at any conclusion.

For classroom discussion to be effective, the teacher must know how to guide without dominating. He must be able to influence the trend of the discussion when he is participating as a member of the audience as well as when he is leading the discussion. He must develop his students' ability to participate in a discussion so that they will persist with a problem until it has been solved rather than be led astray by any irrelevant comment that is made. It is up to him to help the class identify itself as a group so that there will be common interest in a co-operative approach to learning problems. He must know, too, when other procedures are likely to be more effective.

What Are the Qualities of a Good Discussion?

There is an air of purposefulness about a good discussion that distinguishes it sharply from idle talk. All of the members of the class know the question or issue that is being discussed and have a basis for separating the relevant from the irrelevant. The teacher guides students' thinking by the questions he asks and by the questions he stimulates students to ask.

Good discussions rest on a foundation that is more substantial than mere talk. Ignorance is not allowed to be covered with words, even eloquent words. Both students and teachers recognize the point at which the discussion must be interrupted so that they may get the additional information that is needed before the discussion can proceed.

In a good discussion, it is the topic rather than the marking book that furnishes the incentive which leads students to participate. For widespread participation to materialize, the topic must be one which has meaning, interest, and appeal to students.

The pattern of participation reveals whether the class is operating as a group or simply as a collection of individuals responding to the teacher. In a genuine discussion, the flow is not the typical recitation pattern—teacher to student A, to teacher, to student B, to teacher, to student C, but is more "circular" in nature—teacher to student A, to student B, to student C, to teacher, to student D, and so on. Participation during a discussion rests on a social rather than on an individual basis in that students speak to each other as members of a group interested in a common problem and not as individuals reciting to the teacher.

All students are active during a good discussion period, for the discussion leader is alert to see that no small group is allowed to monopolize the discussion. Even those who do not speak are active, for they are evaluating, interpreting, and questioning what the speaker is saying. One gets the impression during a good discussion that all of the students are genuinely concerned with the topic and one is not aware of the teacher's use of devices to keep the discussion going.

The manner in which students' comments are received by teacher and class reveals the respect all have for each other's opinion. The value set upon each contribution is a function of group morale. Students who feel that they are members of a group feel responsible for pushing the discussion forward toward goals which they accept. With this sense of loyalty to the group, students are not likely to try to amuse their friends with "cute" remarks or to curry favor with the teacher. The student knows that erroneous statements will be corrected but he knows, too, that his comment will be received as having been made in good faith.

The teacher is careful not to use the discussion as a means of getting the class to accept his own opinions and evaluations uncritically. In some discussions the teacher will find no occasion to state his personal opinions. In others, the teacher will find it more helpful for the class if he abandons the colorless cloak of neutrality and expresses his opinion forthrightly, first making certain that the discussion has progressed far enough for the students to have formulated the criteria in terms of which they can evaluate his point of view rather than accept it unthinkingly. To this extent the teacher is acting as a democratic leader of the group.

When the discussion has been concluded, it should be possible to prepare a summary that includes more than a reference to the fact that some said, "Yes" and some said, "No." Even though students may arrive at different conclusions at the end of a discussion, they should have had the experience of having analyzed the issues, of having differentiated between data and interpretations of these data, of being able to define both the area of agreement and the area of disagreement, and, sometimes, of expressing the kind of conclusion which all can accept.

When Is Discussion Appropriate?

These characteristics suggest the conditions under which discussions can be conducted profitably. The topic for discussion must be one that can be developed by a meeting of minds. It is not very helpful to conduct a discussion of the methods of solving simultaneous equations, for the solution of simultaneous equations has a definite procedure that has to be taught and learned rather than discussed. Though the most effective way of teaching the solution of simultaneous equations may involve the use of inductive questions with maximum class participation, this procedure cannot properly be called a discussion lesson since it does not stress the consideration of varying points of view.

The discussion should be used only for questions that are important enough to deserve the time that discussions take. Much time is wasted if the teacher is so wary of seeming to dominate the class that everything is decided by open discussion even though the issue is so trivial that the discussion uses up time that should be spent on more important questions. Sometimes the class spends time discussing a question that is so specific and so factual that consulting the textbook or a reference book for the answer would be much more appropriate.

For the discussion method to be appropriate, it must be used for a topic on which students are sufficiently well informed or on which they can become well informed as they prepare for the discussion. If the discussion is to be used as a means of clarifying ideas, of deepening students' appreciation of the material they are studying, of extending the range of their interests, and of stimulating them to further activity, it must rest on an adequate respect for the knowledge that alone entitles one to the right to express an opinion. There is little place in the school for the kind of discussion of modern art that one is likely to get in a class in which the students know nothing more about modern art than some slogans they have heard, unless the teacher is planning to use the emptiness of the discussion as a means of getting the students to see that they really ought to know more about modern art before they can discuss it intelligently.

PLANNING A CLASSROOM DISCUSSION

How Can the Teacher Prepare for a Classroom Discussion?

The mere fact that students are talking a great deal is no assurance that learning is taking place; and a poorly planned classroom discussion may be as ineffective as a poorly planned lecture. Contrary to popular opinion, the effective conduct of a group discussion requires more preparation than does a lecture. The teacher must be so thoroughly familiar with his material that illustrations come to mind freely, and he must know his goal so well that he can help the class to keep to the point at issue. The more effective the teacher is, the more capable he is at guiding the discussion without appearing to dominate it. If the discussion is conducted well, the visitor may get the impression that the teacher is extemporizing. Few good discussions, however, are unplanned; in general, the teacher must be thoroughly prepared to make the discussion spontaneous and yet fruitful.

The teacher who knows only a little more than his students about the many social, political, and economic factors that operated at the Constitutional Convention in 1787 is in no position to lead a discussion on the framing of the United States Constitution. Because of his ignorance, he may not detect the fallacy of some of the conclusions which students will reach during the discussion, and he will be unable to ask questions or to make comments that will help his students to appreciate better the conditions under which some of the provisions of the Constitution were written. Any teacher who conducts a discussion in a field in which he is not thoroughly at home risks the embarrassment of having to admit repeatedly that he does not understand this phase or the other phase of the topic, or still more embarrassing, of having the students discover later, when they do more reading, that the impression conveyed by the teacher of the way in which a given factor operated was entirely erroneous.

Because the discussion on a topic may ramify in many directions, it is difficult for the teacher to prepare adequately on a day-by-day basis. The kind of rich background which the teacher needs cannot be secured by the teacher who reads each night only as much as he thinks he needs for the next day. More than ever, the teacher must himself be an educated person, with a scholarship that is ever fresh because it is constantly being renewed. If the teacher's background is not adequate to qualify him to lead a discussion on the topic, it may be better for him to rely on other methods of presentation and to use the discussion techniques for only those phases of the topic for which his background is adequate.

The suggestion that the teacher should be thoroughly familiar with the topic that is to be discussed need not indicate that the teacher must be the sole source of information and the sole judge of the pertinence or the validity of the comments that are made during the discussion. The most stimulating discussions are often the ones in which teacher and students explore a topic together. Nevertheless, the teacher is a more helpful guide if he has taken the time and the trouble to explore the various issues before he meets them during a discussion.

Discussion Should Center about Problems the Students Recognize as Important

As the teacher plans the discussion, he must give considerable thought to the problem about which it is to center, for a discussion is more likely to be effective if it is centered about a problem that students want to solve than if it consists of a series of unrelated questions asked by the teacher. All of the suggestions offered in the preceding chapter for the selection of a stimulating topic for a lesson plan are doubly important when the teacher is formulating the discussion problem in his own mind.

It is essential that the problem be related closely to the student if he is to accept the invitation to try to solve it. If the problem can be stated in such terms that the student is asked to make a decision, so much the better. India, for example, is a remote country for most American boys and girls. The relief of famine in India is almost equally remote, even for sensitive adolescents who hate the very idea of the existence of suffering in the world. A discussion of the causes of the periodic famines that sweep India and of the possibilities of permanently removing the fear of famine in India may, therefore, be an academic discussion rather than a way of getting students to deepen their understanding of the tragic problems that are India's.

Before students can see the seriousness of India's famine, the teacher must help them to visualize the tragedy of famine. They must realize that had they been born in certain parts of India it is they who would have been the victims of famine, regardless of their own determination not to starve. What can the boys and girls of India today do to see that the specter of famine never again haunts their country? What can be done by the Indian government? What would *they* do if they had the power?

Capitalizing on the Controversial and Dramatic

Sometimes this basic question is couched in controversial terms which invite the students to take sides and which offer a basis for organizing much of the material presented during the period. At other times, the teacher attempts to focus the discussion upon a question that makes the whole situation more personal by placing the students in the midst of the problem that is being discussed. For example, instead of discussing the railroad problem, a problem of which most secondary school students are almost completely unaware, the teacher can ask them what they would do if they were called upon to arbitrate a railway labor dispute arising from automation. The railroad says it cannot compete with planes, trucks, and buses unless it can reduce its labor costs by using automatic machines when possible and employing fewer people. The union, on the other hand, says it is unfair and unjust for the railroads to buy machinery and then fire men who have been working for the railroads for years and years and are not trained for any other job.

To deepen understanding and to stimulate discussion, the teacher may ask students to dramatize significant situations. One student, for example, may testify before an imaginary public service commission on the inadequacies and high cost of commuter service. Another may play the part of a railroad official seeking permission to raise commuter fares because of the financial problems involved in operating commuter trains, when so many people use their own cars or take a bus instead of a train. Newspaper articles, cartoons, motion pictures, filmstrips, radio and television shows may all be used as other devices to enhance interest in discussion.

Even the teacher who is sitting as a member of the group under the leadership of a student chairman has the opportunity of shaping the problem. In some instances, the teacher will exert his influence through his earlier meetings with the student chairman or with the committee that is planning the discussion. When the teacher is a member of the group, he may raise a question or make a comment that will help the class to redefine a vague question into one they can answer or to rephrase a question that is asked by a student until it encompasses the basic problem that should concern everyone.

This setting of the problem situation so that students identify themselves with the situation is no pedagogical device to arouse a superficial interest and the consequent desire to talk. It is, rather, a fundamental teaching procedure that teachers must use if students are to learn, especially when the content of the syllabus is predetermined for the teacher and the class. Students do not learn much from discussing a problem that is remote. No one learns much about any topic unless it means something to him—note how boring a young man ordinarily finds a conversation that deals with furniture and draperies and notice, too, how much greater is his interest in such a conversation a few months later and how much better he remembers the points of view that are expressed if he has been married in the meantime and is now buying furniture and accessories for his own home.

As he prepares for a discussion, the teacher should analyze the problem so that he knows the issues that are involved. From this analysis of the issues the teacher will be better prepared to frame the key questions he will ask in class in order to help his students to analyze the problem. This analysis will also help the teacher to find source and reference material he should have on hand during the discussion.

Helping Students Develop Ease and Skill in Discussion

If the ability to lead a discussion is one that must be learned by the teacher, the concomitant ability of participating in a discussion must be learned by the students. It is as unreasonable to expect students to participate effectively in a discussion when this is the first experience of the kind that they have had as it is to expect the teacher to be a stimulating guide in the first discussion he ever leads.

A class that is accustomed to having the teacher ask all the questions, with the teacher designating the student who is to reply and then himself evaluating the adequacy of the reply, is not ready to participate more actively in a freer discussion. Such students are accustomed to be silent until the teacher has called on them to recite, and they expect the teacher to evaluate what is said by another student. They are, therefore, usually unable to take the initiative during a class discussion. Since they have learned to depend on the teacher to ask the questions, they may ramble in all directions if they are suddenly asked to conduct the discussion themselves.

For these reasons, it is necessary to teach these boys and girls how to carry on a discussion. At first, it may be desirable for the teacher to plan the discussion and to act as the chairman. By his manner of asking questions and treating the responses, the teacher will indicate his readiness to have students ask the questions and to respond directly to the questions and comments of other students. The teacher will have to help the students to distinguish between the important contributions and the trivial ones, between the relevant and the irrelevant comments. By gradually giving the students more of the responsibility for conducting the discussion, the teacher can develop the ability to participate.

CONDUCTING A CLASSROOM DISCUSSION

The Teacher's Role in Discussion

Some classroom discussions are as carefully planned and as carefully directed by the teacher as is any other lesson that he teaches. Thus, the teacher who uses the discussion as a developmental lesson to teach a basic concept is careful to arrange his key questions in a planned sequence and to keep the class from wandering from the topic at hand. In other classroom discussions, such as those led by a student panel which is presenting the many sides of a controversial issue, the class will be allowed considerable leeway in asking questions and in making comments that may appear at first to be tangential. In such a discussion, the teacher participates only as a member of the audience, but he is alert to the necessity for asking the kind of questions that will bring the discussion back to relevant issues and for making the comment that will remind the students of important criteria they should be applying. In still other discussions, as may be found, for example, in an after-school club meeting, the direction may be surrendered so completely to the students that the teacher is properly reluctant to do more than make an occasional comment or ask an infrequent question.

As the composition of the group and the purposes of the discussion dictate, the leadership of the discussion will be assumed by the teacher, by a student, by a panel of students, or by an invited guest. At times, the direction and scope of the discussion will be left to the group to determine as the discussion proceeds. At other times, the teacher may have to assume active leadership of the group so that he may steer the discussion in the direction it should take if it is to be productive.

In general, the teacher's direction of a discussion must be more subtle than it is when he is teaching a class lesson. If he is leading the discussion, he will function more like a good chairman of a meeting than as the teacher of a group of immature boys and girls. When a student is serving as chairman, the teacher will be alert to the use of a skillful question or a tactful comment as a way of improving the discussion without usurping the privileges of the chairman.

How Closely Should the Teacher Guide the Discussion?

In determining how closely the teacher is to guide the discussion and how actively he himself should participate in the discussion, the teacher must be careful to avoid the extremes of domination and of indifference. The teacher who dominates the discussion, who evaluates all students' answers and decides which are correct and in which respects the others are wrong, deprives his class of much of the intellectual training they should get from learning to think a problem through to its conclusion.

On the other hand, the teacher who plays too minor a role during the discussion may be surrendering his leadership to a group that is too immature to shoulder the responsibility. In practice, this kind of teacher tends to be an ineffective discussion leader. A few aggressive students may fill the vacuum created by the teacher's ineffectiveness; unfortunately, the correlation between student aggressiveness and ability is sometimes less than perfect. Discussions in such a class tend to ramble, to go off on tangents, and to bog down in trivial difficulties that a more effective teacher would soon resolve.

Just where the teacher will find the optimum position between dominance and ineffectiveness depends on the class he is teaching and on the experience it has had in participating in discussions. The class that is unaccustomed to discussion obviously needs closer guidance than does another class that has learned the techniques of discussion. Similarly, relatively immature junior high school students can assume less of the responsibility for conducting a discussion than an older and more mature senior high school class can take.

In most instances, the teacher carries the responsibility for posing the problem and for initiating the discussion. If a student is to preside, the teacher should meet with him in order to help plan the discussion. If the participation is sufficiently widespread, the teacher can allow volunteers to do the talking. Once he realizes, however, that some students are being ignored, he must try to bring them into the discussion either by addressing a question to them or by asking them for their reaction to something which another student has said. Even the teacher who is acting as a member of the group can help bring other students into the discussion.

The teacher must try to modify the students' habit of speaking to the teacher instead of to the class. For this reason, he not only tries to seat his students in some variant of the semicircle or asks the speaker to face the class rather than the teacher if fixed seats make the semicircle an impossibility, but he also does everything he can to shift attention from himself to the speaker. He refrains, therefore, from commenting on what a student says and instead asks another student to evaluate the comment. Rather than answer the questions asked by members of the class, he tries to have the questions answered by other students.

Once the class has been brought to the point where the students are the ones who conduct the discussion, where they speak to each other as a matter of habit, and where a student's question or comment is immediately reacted to by other students without being referred to the teacher at all, the teacher can afford to become a less active participant. Even in such classes the teacher may have to step in from time to time to keep the discussion from going off at a tangent or from degenerating into quibbling, to bring other students into the discussion, and to help the students summarize the points made thus far so that they may continue the discussion.

Eager though the teacher is to have the center of the discussion shifted from himself to the class, he must not be reluctant to enter the discussion if he can get it moving forward again by his questions, his comments, his suggestion of sources of information or even his volunteering the information that is needed, or by his restatement of the problem or redefinition of the issues. Note that the teacher is ordinarily not concerned only with making certain that the discussion is being continued; to satisfy teacher and class the discussion must be kept moving forward to a conclusion.

How Can the Discussion Be Kept from Rambling?

The surest way to keep the discussion from rambling is to make certain that students know just what the problem is and that they accept the problem as being sufficiently important to deserve an answer. If the problem is expressed as a question that is written on the chalkboard, it serves as a constant visual reminder of what is pertinent and what is irrelevant.

As the discussion proceeds to an analysis of the issues, it is helpful to have these issues listed on the chalkboard. Thus, as the class which is discussing the means of preventing famine in India comes to the question *What are the causes of famine in India?* this question should be written on the board. The answers that are suggested by students are also written on the board unless these answers are challenged by other students or the teacher.

Though the chalkboard outline as it evolves during the discussion tends to confine the discussion to the topic, some irrelevant comments are almost certain to be made during a spirited discussion. Such remarks almost always do touch on one of the phases of the discussion, otherwise they would probably not have occurred to the students who made them. As long as these comments are not too lengthy or are not followed by other questions and answers along the line of thought suggested by the comment, it is better to let the student finish what he started to say. Then, tactfully, so as not to embarrass the student or to discourage others from participating, the teacher may ask a question that brings the class back to the topic at hand. Thus, a student, reacting to another student who has mentioned the floods in India as a cause of famine, may speak of the way in which Egypt has been enriched rather than impoverished by the overflowing Nile River—a comment that is not as irrelevant to the speaker as it may appear to be to the teacher. The teacher's role is to keep the discussion from wandering to Egypt by remarking, "What Henry has just said is undoubtedly true so far as Egypt is concerned. Is it equally true of India? Why are the Indian floods so disastrous to agriculture?" and the discussion is back to India where it should be if students are to solve the problem on which they are working.

Dealing with Tangential Remarks

The teacher must be alert to see that the discussion does not go off on so many tangents that nothing is accomplished. He must be equally careful, however, not to disregard the ideas which may be suggested by students but that had not occurred to the teacher. If they are relevant to the solution of the problem, they should be explored with the class, even though this means that the teacher may have to revise his remaining pivotal questions for the discussion.

The difficulty in controlling the direction of the discussion is that the tangential remark seems to be so relevant when it is introduced, just as every tangent touches the circle at one point. Thus, Henry was close to the discussion when he remarked that in Egypt the Nile floods were beneficial rather than disastrous. The discussion would wander far afield if his comment were followed, however, by the question, "Why are the Nile floods helpful?" and then by "Are the Mississippi floods helpful or harmful?" until all are engaged in a stimulating discussion of the manner in which the Tennessee Valley Authority has pointed the way to other important projects—and what other similar projects are now being considered by Congress.

Although some tangents may be far more important than the problem which the class originally prepared to discuss, few new teachers can afford to allow the discussion to go off on every tangent. If the tangential problem is important, it can be discussed better after the teacher and the class have had a chance to prepare themselves for the discussion, since they can undoubtedly discuss such problems more intelligently if they have a better background.

What can the inexperienced teacher do if he is wary about abandoning the discussion that has been progressing well and yet finds that his class, or the vocal part of it, has no such reluctance? In most instances, it is safer for the teacher to try to bring the discussion back to the topic for the day. Since the topic is a tangential one, he can follow it back to its point of contact with the day's problems and then redirect the discussion until the students can take the problem up again. In this instance he can follow a student's comment on the Tennessee Valley project with the comment that floods are a problem in many parts of the world, in the United States as well as in India, but in India the floods are more serious because they bring famine in their wake. Why don't the Indians follow the example of the Tennessee Valley Authority?

Unfortunately, it is the inexperienced teacher who is quicker to go off on a tangent than is the experienced teacher who has presented the same problem to so many classes that he discusses it with an expertness and a facility that come with repetition. Students feel freer to introduce tangential material in the class of a young teacher; in an older teacher's class they are sometimes less ready to ask questions or to make unsolicited remarks. As the teacher grows in experience, he should be more, rather than less, tolerant of student questions, even though they be tangential, because he has a better basis for organizing his material and he may be able to weave into the discussion a comment that may seem irrelevant to a less experienced teacher. It is the young teacher's problem to maintain the kind of teacher-pupil relationship that encourages students to speak freely in his class without becoming so weak a discussion leader that every remark made in class turns the discussion from its path.

How Can the Major Conclusions Be Stressed?

Because there is always someone speaking during a discussion and because so many different points of view are presented during a period, students sometimes leave a discussion with only a hazy notion of what it is that was said. They remember that two opposing points of view were expressed but they do not remember which one was later proved to be fallacious. What can be done to clarify the impressions that discussions make on students? How can the teacher make it more likely that students will remember the important points rather than some of the details?

A chalkboard outline which is developed as the discussion proceeds is a useful means of focusing attention on the most important contributions since it is obvious that the outline includes only the key thoughts and not a verbatim record of all that is said. The partial summaries that are made during the discussion also stress the important rather than the trivial. When any student contribution during a discussion is so important that it deserves added emphasis, the teacher can see that this contribution is itself discussed in class until he is certain that all students understand its importance. The teacher may ask, for example, "How many of you agree with Joe that famines in India will continue until . . . ." or "What reasons do we have for concluding that famines in India will recur unless . . . ."

If the discussion leads to a conclusion, the conclusion should be stressed. It is this conclusion that becomes the summary. In some classes, teachers find it desirable to ask students to prepare individual summaries in their notebooks where they can be referred to when necessary. In keeping with what psychologists have taught us about the greater efficacy of spaced as compared with unspaced learning, it is important that basic conclusions be referred to, when they are relevant, in other discussions held later in the term.

Students are more likely to remember the key points of the discussion if interest in the topic is not allowed to end with the terminal bell. If the discussion problem is vital and if the discussion itself is one in which students participate actively, the discussion should lead into other activities. In most discussions, there are points at which it is clear that more information is needed. Sources of information that are mentioned then should be referred to later. Similarly, references can be made to other books, including fiction, to magazines and periodicals, and to motion pictures and television programs. In some instances, the discussion should lead to the students' doing something about the conclusions reached. Students who have been discussing modern art should know how to go about getting good, inexpensive copies of some of the best examples of modern art. In the discussion of Indian famines, students should learn of organizations that are at work on the problem, organizations with which some of the students may wish to correspond or to become affiliated.

HOW CAN STUDENT PARTICIPATION IN DISCUSSION BE ENCOURAGED?

The discussion method sometimes creates the illusion of widespread student activity when actually only a relatively small part of the class may be participating and when most of the thinking is done by the teacher and not the students. It is only the teacher who can judge whether the students are active participants in the discussion, and the teacher can tell only by focusing his attention on the class as well as on the logical development of the discussion.

One of the most popular ways of stimulating greater student participation is to try to have all students speak during the discussion. Although it is usually better to have more rather than fewer students participate, trying to have every student speak every period is too artificial and too limiting a procedure. It easily degenerates into the practice of getting everyone to say something, no matter how trivial, and of impeding the discussion by silencing the student who has spoken earlier.

This practice rests on the erroneous impression that a student is active only when he is speaking and on the equally erroneous assumption that if the student speaks at least once he will be alert for the rest of the period. There are other and better ways of stimulating pupil activity in a discussion. There is more likely to be widespread participation in a discussion if the problems that are chosen for discussion are close to the students' interests and if the questions are related to their background. Students will be stimulated to contribute if the problem is a real one and not a pedagogical device for getting them to give the answer which the teacher has formulated in his own mind as the only correct one. Students will feel freer to speak if they are confident that their remarks will be welcomed rather than ridiculed. They can learn to respond to comments made by other students instead of waiting for the teacher to react to the comment before calling on a student. Getting students to participate actively in a discussion is not an isolated problem to be solved by the use of any specific procedure, for it is a basic problem to be solved only by the more effective use of discussion leadership techniques.

Ways of Stimulating Thinking

During every discussion there are usually several opportunities for calling on each student to use his judgment in weighing evidence and arriving at a decision. After one of the students has said that the Indian government is so inefficient that it is unable to tackle the problem of famine, the teacher may call for a vote by a show of hands on the question, "How many of you agree with Henry that it is the ineffectiveness of the Indian government that is chiefly responsible for the failure to prevent famine? How many of you disagree?" Lest this practice degenerate into an absent-minded raising of hands, the teacher should follow his questions with other questions, asking some students from both sides to explain the reason for their vote and the factual basis for their judgment. This question is typical of many that can be asked during a discussion to stimulate all students to think about the problem even though not all may have the opportunity to speak.

Silence, too, is an effective stimulant to thinking. In many a discussion, too much rather than too little is said. Question follows question and comment follows comment so quickly that only the fast students can keep up with the discussion. Moments of silence should not be considered as wasted if they give students a chance to formulate their own opinion before an answer is given by someone else. When a key question is asked, students should be allowed time to think of the answer. Thus, when the teacher asks, "In the light of everything we have said so far, how can the Indian farmer be educated to reduce the threat of famine in his district?" time should be allowed for the students to formulate an answer before the teacher recognizes a student who is ready to present his answer.

Securing Broader Participation

Although the number of different students who speak during the discussion is not the most telling indication of the discussion's value, it is undesirable to have the discussion carried by too small a number of students, especially if it is the same students who day after day are the only ones in the class who speak. Rather than try to curb the enthusiasm of these active students, the teacher should try to stimulate the rest of the class to take part.

When the teacher is interested in the development of a point of view and finds that contributions from the class help develop the concept in which the teacher is interested, he may not notice that these contributions come from only a few of the members of the group. In fact, the readiness with which these few students understand the problem and participate in the discussion may encourage the teacher to proceed so rapidly that most of the students are as inactive as they would be during a routine lecture. The lesson sounds like a discussion, but is actually a lecture delivered by three people instead of one. Teachers are naturally reluctant to interfere with the smooth development of an idea in order to bring into the discussion those who would slow down the rate of progress; but the rate at which new material is presented is no index to the amount of learning that takes place in the classroom.

The teacher's attitude is itself a factor that may extend or limit the degree of student participation. The teacher who welcomes all contributions and tactfully directs the re-examination of erroneous statements is more likely to have students participate than is the teacher who is sharply critical of any comments with which he disagrees. Similarly, the teacher who follows too detailed a lesson plan and is unwilling to entertain questions raised by students will find that his students soon learn not to take more active a part in the discussion than they have to.

A skillful discussion leader can do much to broaden the scope of the discussion to include more students. If he knows his students well, he knows at which point the silent members of the group can be brought into the discussion. Knowing, for example, that one of his students has an older brother who visited India, the teacher can say, "Bill, did your brother get the impression that the Indian people realized that their standard of living was much lower than ours?" and Bill, having something to say, now has an opportunity to feel the satisfaction of sharing his information with his class.

The shy student, who is reluctant to express an opinion he will have to defend, can be eased into the discussion by being asked a question calling for a factual answer that needs no elaboration. Students who do not have the background for participating in the discussion will be helped by the teacher whose assignments indicate how such a background can be developed. The student who does not participate because he has not done his work cannot participate effectively until the teacher has found how to get him to prepare.

Sometimes the teacher can get more students to speak by rephrasing the questions so that they are simpler and more easily understood. Wider participation may be encouraged by the teacher's rewording a question so that it creates a sharp cleavage in the class between those who say "Yes" and those who say "No," with the result that students take sides and are eager for the impromptu little debate that starts. Students who have lost the thread of the discussion may be brought back to it by a partial summary followed by a question put so vividly that they are active once more.

Of course the teacher is eager to have broad student participation in classroom discussions but the extent of student participation is much less important than is the quality of their participation. The discussion has little educational value if students feel that all they have to do is to say something, regardless of whether they have anything worth hearing or any basis for the comment they make. For this reason it is important that the teacher set the example of being himself well prepared for the discussion he is to lead and that he make certain that his students are also well prepared. Similarly, students who express opinions during a discussion should know the facts they can adduce in support of their opinion.

Recognizing Differences in Ability to Participate

In some classes, the range of ability is so great that a few outstandingly competent students inevitably dominate the discussion. These are the students who should be accelerated or put into a group of brighter students so that they are in a class with their peers. If such reclassification is not practicable, they can be allowed to work on individual or group research projects on their level of ability. There will thus be some class discussions in which they will participate because they have something definite to contribute. They will be excused from other class discussions so that they may do the research for their reports and so that the less gifted members of the class may participate in a discussion more actively.

Though a small group of outstandingly superior students may sometimes make a discussion more interesting than it would otherwise be, these students may also dominate the discussion to such an extent that the rest of the class is virtually ignored. Moreover, these bright students may be deprived of the stimulation that comes from working with other students of similar intellectual ability.

Widespread reluctance to speak during a discussion may not be a reflection on the nature of the questions but may suggest rather that the group is too timid to participate in a general discussion. Sometimes this reluctance is merely an indication of the fact that they have not learned how to participate in a discussion. Other students may be reluctant to speak because of the fear of censure or of inviting the teacher's sarcasm. Still others may be timid for more personal reasons. In any event, the teacher who finds that a major question goes unanswered gains nothing by appealing to his class to put their feet flat on the floor and pay attention. The teacher should try to discover the reason for the silence with which his question is greeted and then should take whatever steps may be needed to correct the causative factors.

One step that can be taken is organizational in nature. As teachers, we tend to deal with the class as a unit, perhaps because of the persisting view of teaching as presentation and the hearing of recitations. Teaching of this kind recognizes the economy of a single presentation to the class as a unit in place of repeated presentations to the class divided into three or four groups. When the method becomes one of participation through discussion, it is readily seen that division into three groups, for example, makes it possible for three students to express themselves simultaneously. The results of each group's discussion may then be reported to the whole group as suggested in the section that follows on group structure and process. The student who is reluctant to speak before thirty classmates may recognize his duty to share the load of discussion in a group of only ten. Since the teacher can be with only one group at a time, specific instructions and extremely careful statement of the discussion question are necessary. The teacher's guidance preceding group discussion and during the reporting period becomes crucial since his guidance is more limited during the discussion itself.

GROUP STRUCTURE AND PROCESS

Discussion is basically a group process in which the teacher plays the part of group leader. True, he is not a democratically chosen leader, and he is distinguished quite sharply from the other members of the group by his age, experience, and status. However, the teacher functions best as a discussion leader when he understands group structure and operation [2, Ch. 7].

How the members of a class participate in a discussion is related to the roles which they perceive for themselves in the group. People take different parts in groups, sometimes consistently, sometimes as different roles are called for; sometimes deliberately, sometimes unknowingly. Some people are always initiating the discussion of ideas or plans; they may be expected to contribute something new time and again. Others add little that is new but habitually test the new ideas of others in a crucible of critical reaction. Some serve to draw others out, continually seeking opinions and information from other members. Some contribute little that is new themselves but enjoy picking up ideas already expressed and weaving a wonderful web of elaboration around them. Some people serve a valuable function in summarizing the position of the group from time to time and keeping the group from going off on unproductive tangents. Others suggest ways of proceeding to break log jams, dissolve deadlocks, or explore possible solutions. Students can learn from practice in these roles to be more productive group members.

Not only are there the specific functions that members play in a group; there are also general attitudes expressed which support or attack group action and unity. On the positive side, some persons in a group are always encouraging others to express themselves. They are supportive of others. They try to harmonize or compromise conflicting points of view. They seek to expedite action. Basically, they are secure in themselves and in the feeling that they are established members of the group. Accordingly, they have a strong sense of commitment to the group and its effective operation and they identify their own satisfactions with group goals. While the values of this attitude are apparent, there is also a danger attendant upon it—the danger of submerging the individual personality completely in the group, with overemphasis on conformity and the consequent loss of constructive individual contributions.

On the other hand, there are those who set themselves apart from the group and express negative roles as they reject all ideas and goals which they did not think of first. This may often be a form of aggression to cover the feeling of insecurity that an individual feels in the group. This individual may continually be blocking group action, always finding obstacles in the path. Sometimes the member's own personal problems keep him from establishing a feeling of security in or belonging to the group. This failure to identify with the group may be expressed in constantly seeking recognition, in trying to dominate the group, in playing for the sympathy of the group, or in pleading special interests and grinding his own axe [6].

It is important for the student to define roles both as a self-reliant individual and as an effective contributor to group endeavor and group goals. In some schools the teacher and the program assist the students by helping them to know themselves, to recognize what they and others are doing as group members. At times submersion in the goals of the group can be unhealthy, just as excessive demands for individual recognition are not wholesome. Observation of the group in action, by setting the stage for students to share in constructive educational activities that invite genuine democratic participation, is one of the useful keys the teacher may use to identify problems in group relationships.

Group Discussion Procedures

Some techniques have become fairly common in the promotion of improved group interaction. One of these is the "buzz session," a simple device for dividing any group into smaller combinations of six, eight, or ten persons. Buzz groups are used sometimes for simultaneous exploration by smaller groups of a particular question or problem. This procedure permits freer and wider participation because in a given number of minutes the amount of expression possible is multiplied by the number of groups employed. In addition, youngsters who hesitate to express their own feelings and ideas before the total class may feel less reserved in a small group. Sometimes the buzz session is used to explore different aspects of a given problem, and often such buzz groups develop into committees that assume a more protracted effort in the direction of their chosen tasks. In some places the buzz session is referred to as *Discussion 66*, meaning six people in each group carrying on an exploratory discussion for only six minutes. Both numerical limits may have to be adapted in the light of a particular situation and issue.

One of the problems in using this technique lies in reporting effectively to the reassembled group what the constituent parts have been saying. Imaginative procedures are needed to keep the reports from becoming unnecessarily long and dull. The reporters can be allowed to present just one major point at a time. Each reporter makes his point in turn and then the process is repeated until all major ideas have been expressed. A second procedure is to use a mechanical timer which arbitrarily limits the length of each report. A third way is to allow only one full report and to ask other reporters to limit their remarks to ideas which were not included in the longer report.

Another interesting technique used to stimulate group discussion is role-playing. Some people see this technique as a contemporary response to Robert Burns' prayer:

> O wad some Power the giftie gie us
> To see oursels as ithers see us!

In role-playing, persons take the part of others, real or imagined, in order to see for themselves and to portray to others the consequences of certain ideas, attitudes, actions. Persons in a heated argument may be asked to change sides for a few minutes just to realize that one's own interpretation is not the only possibility. Students may play the part of other students who have run afoul of school regulations—or the part of the school official responsible for enforcement—to understand the issues at stake. In a problem situation, students may act out the way in which they would perform in order to solve the problem.

In some instances a "process observer" is appointed who takes notes on the productivity of a group. He notes when discussion goes off on a tangent, when the plans of individual students interfere with group goals, when there is need for summary and evaluation, and when the time has come for a "breather" so that fresh ideas or smoother tempers may enter the picture after a rest. This device serves to make the group aware of what it is doing. Overemphasis on process, however, can lead to embarrassment and inhibition of the free flow of ideas as well as being a waste of time that should be put to better use.

Group Factors in Effective Discussion

In general, the social psychologists who have been analyzing those factors which make for group productivity emphasize at the same time elements that contribute to effective discussion. A motion picture, *How to Conduct a Discussion* [10], underlines these qualities:

1. The physical setting should be attractive and comfortable.
2. There should be a good social feeling.
3. The leader should have a basic plan but be flexible in his use of it.
4. There should be direct interchange among the group members. (The leader must see that the discussion flows back and forth among the members who want to participate.)
5. The path of progress should be kept open for each individual member.
6. The experiences of the members of the group should be used to enrich the discussion.
7. All of the members should feel a responsibility for the effective conduct of the group.
8. All members of the group should understand both immediate and ultimate goals.
9. Methods and procedures should be as varied as possible. (Role-playing, films, books, outside speakers, etc.)
10. The group should base its discussion on fact and experience as well as opinion.
11. All the members of the group should try to improve the group performance.*

The ability to participate in discussions is a useful skill, not only because it accelerates the progress of school learning but also because group discussion is an important activity in a democracy. We may well be con-

* Reprinted by permission from *How to Conduct a Discussion*, Encyclopaedia Britannica Films, Inc.

tent if our students' experience at school helps them to participate in discussions conducted among equals, where all learn how to pursue the truth regardless of the biases of the members of the group. If they learn how to object to the points at issue expressed by others without being offensive, and if they learn how to modify their own point of view as a result of the arguments presented by other members of the group, they have learned to develop abilities that are significant in democratic living.

QUESTIONS FOR STUDY AND DISCUSSION

1. In a senior high school music class a few aggressive girls manage to dominate every discussion by virtue of their glibness and their readiness to speak on any topic at any time. They are not disorderly, disrespectful, or intentionally selfish. It is merely that they are so quick to respond to any question or to express their agreement or disagreement with a point of view that the other students have little chance to enter the discussion.

How can the teacher broaden the base of the discussion without destroying the interest that these girls have in the topics they are studying?

2. The teacher of a tenth-year English class is an excellent discussion leader but is disappointed to find that classroom discussions tend to be ineffective when a student chairman is in charge.

What can she do to improve the situation?

3. Four "buzz groups" are at this moment discussing, "Should our state impose a sales tax?" as part of a unit on financing state government. When you close the buzz session after ten minutes, what procedure can you suggest for reporting the discussion in each group?

4. Every time you divide the class into groups or committees for discussion, research, or study, Margaret declines to join in any group. Generally, she forms a second row all by herself behind the chairs drawn up in a circle by the other students. Margaret says she doesn't feel that committees accomplish very much. Besides, she says, she isn't likely to learn much from other students. It's really a waste of time and not so profitable as are class discussions led by the teacher who, after all, is the authority.

What further information would you like to have about Margaret before deciding what to do?

Postulate some of this information and indicate the action you would then take.

5. In which ways does a teacher have to modify the discussion procedures that are appropriate in the usual secondary school classes if he is a member of a teaching team and is conducting discussion periods with small groups of students after another teacher has presented and developed the topic with a large group of students, including those who are in these smaller discussion groups.

6. The following lesson is one of the series prepared by the Delaware State Society for Mental Hygiene as guides to teachers for lessons in Human Relations in the Classroom.* Read the material and then answer the questions that are appended.

* *Human Relations Class Outline* by H. Edmund Bullis and Emily E. O'Malley, the Delaware State Society for Mental Hygiene, Inc., 1308 Delaware Avenue, Wilmington 19, Delaware. Reprinted by permission.

LESSON 17
Losing Gracefully

Introductory Remarks by Teacher

Our last lesson showed us that to co-operate with others we must have a "team feeling." Today we are going to discuss another similar problem in getting along with others which we all have to face at times—that of losing gracefully. Many of our greatest leaders have failed repeatedly before finally achieving success. Their ability to meet failure and not let it get them down seemed to strengthen their character. You are all probably familiar with the tale of the Scottish leader, Bruce, who was very discouraged because his men had lost so many battles. As he was trying to rest, he noticed a spider spinning a web. Over and over again the spider spun a thread which broke repeatedly. Finally the spider was successful. Bruce thought that if a spider could keep on trying so could he, and he went out to lead his men—this time in a successful attack.

One of our greatest presidents, Abraham Lincoln, proved he knew how to lose gracefully for his failures only spurred him on to his eventual success. He was defeated when he first ran for the Legislature in Illinois and also when he attempted to win the nomination for Congress. He was defeated for the U.S. Senate and was unsuccessful when he ran for Vice-President. He failed in business and it took him many years to repay the debts resulting from his failure. He suffered a great personal loss when the young lady whom he had loved and to whom he had been engaged, died.

However, Lincoln never allowed himself to be discouraged by his many disappointments and failures. His ability to lose gracefully and his perserverance and determination to win made him one of the greatest leaders America has ever produced.

In our story today we have related again the familiar facts known to all Americans of his splendid speech, "The Gettysburg Address." Today many boys and girls memorize this fine speech as part of their education. Our story of it is an excerpt from "The Perfect Tribute" written by Mary Raymond Shipman Andrews.

The Story

One morning in November, 1863, a special train left Washington bound for Gettysburg. The passengers on the train included Abraham Lincoln, who was then President of the United States; Mr. Seward, the Secretary of State; Mr. Edward Everett, the most famous orator of the time; several Supreme Court Judges, and various other official dignitaries. These people were going to Gettysburg to dedicate the battlefield as a cemetery to the Civil War Dead, and Mr. Lincoln and Mr. Everett were scheduled to speak at the ceremonies of the next day.

Mr. Lincoln realized as he sat in the railroad car that he was quite unprepared and so he reached across the aisle of the car and picked up a piece of brown paper— torn from a package of books—and he began to write down his ideas for his speech.

Mr. Everett's oration was apparently all prepared, and Mr. Lincoln realized that it would probably be a brilliant one. He did not feel that he could compete with the polished delivery of Mr. Everett, but he did want the people to recognize his sincerity. He also realized that the audience would appreciate something that was brief and to the point, so he wrote and rewrote, changing a phrase here and there, rearranging a sentence or substituting one word for another, until he had achieved something that he felt was direct and strong.

At 11 o'clock on the following morning, November 19, 1863, a vast, silent multitude gathered on the battlefield at Gettysburg. They had stood entranced for two hours as Mr. Everett's fine voice delivered the speech which has since taken its rightful place in our literature. As Mr. Everett finished, the great mass of people burst into a storm of applause. They cheered him for several minutes and he accepted their enthusiastic response graciously.

As he seated himself, Mr. Lincoln rose and advanced to the edge of the platform. A ripple of laughter passed over the audience. Many of these people had seen only poor likenesses of this man who was their President. And this tall, gaunt, ungraceful man was he!

Silence settled on the crowd, and Mr. Lincoln began to speak—but his voice came in a queer falsetto, which sounded ridiculous issuing from that giant frame, and a surprised yet unmistakable titter ran through the audience and was gone. Lincoln barely paused and then his voice gathering strength and dignity began.

"Four score and seven years ago," spoke the President, "our fathers brought forth on this continent a new nation, conceived in liberty, and dedicated to the proposition that all men are created equal. Now we are engaged in a great civil war, testing whether that nation, or any nation so conceived and so dedicated, can long endure. We are met on a great battlefield of that war. We have come to dedicate a portion of that field, as a final resting place for those who here gave their lives that this nation might live. It is altogether fitting and proper that we should do this. . . ."

As he went on speaking, there was no smile on any face. The people almost seemed to stop breathing as the great words left his lips—and when he finished there was no sound—no sound at all from those thousands of people. The President stared at them a moment with gentle, resigned eyes and then he slowly crossed the platform to his seat. At that instant there began a deep sigh which ran like a ripple through rank after rank of that enormous crowd. Lincoln's heart seemed to throb with the pain of knowing that his speech had been a failure. It had been his best effort, and these his own people would not even grant him the politeness of some applause. As he sat thinking, he became aware that a choir had started singing—that his part was done and his part had failed.

When the ceremonies were over, Mr. Everett at once sought the President. "Mr. President," he began. "Your speech—" but Lincoln interrupted him by saying,

"We'll manage not to discuss my speech, Mr. Everett. This isn't the first time that I've felt my dignity should not permit me to be a public speaker."

Lincoln then went on tell Mr. Everett how splendid his oration had been—but he in turn was interrupted by Mr. Everett who said simply, "Mr. President, I should be glad if I could flatter myself that I came as near to the central idea of the occasion in two hours as you did in two minutes." But Lincoln only smiled and turned away.

It was not until a day or so had passed that he finally came to realize that his speech had been a great success—not a failure—and that the audience indeed had paid him the perfect tribute of reverent silence.

Discussion

Here again we have an example of how Lincoln could lose gracefully. He was very much upset over what he believed to have been another failure—but how did he show he could lose gracefully? (Congratulated Mr. Everett, didn't make excuses.)

When he started to speak and the audience laughed, what emotions do you think he felt? (When emotions are asked for, don't just accept the word itself. Ask why a certain emotion is named; have the student prove the emotion he is pointing out.)

Did he allow these emotions to upset him?

Many times our voices are affected by our emotions. In time of great stress, we may even lose our voice—but if we keep on talking or trying to talk as Lincoln did, we find our voice will again become normal or natural. Suppose he had not continued his speech—what might have been the result?

Have any of you had a similar experience when things did not happen as you had expected?

Did you ever have difficulty in speaking before a group? How did you feel? What did you do?

Do you know of anyone whom you feel was a good loser in sports, class, homeroom, elections, etc.? Will you tell us about it?

How many of you think you are good losers or how many have tried to be good losers? Do you remember any special time when you tried to be a good loser?

Why is it difficult for all of us to admit we have made a mistake or lost a decision or have done something wrong? (We hate to have people think less of us; we fear the punishment which may follow; we do not like to hurt people who have helped us by having them know we have done something wrong, pride.)

Why was there no applause after Lincoln had finished his address? (Crowd did not feel like cheering—they were reverent.) Yes, as one writer put it, "It would have been almost like applauding the Lord's prayer."

Several lessons ago we discussed people who had overcome handicaps. Mr. Lincoln is a splendid example of a person who overcame personal handicaps. Can anyone quickly remember one of his handicaps? Can you tell how he overcame it? (Poor family, little education, general appearance, etc.)

You may not know that Lincoln was what is called a "man's man"; he was very shy with women—but a good mixer among men. He once went so far as to eat his bread and cheese under a tree outside a tavern rather than go inside to face a woman. Did he let his shyness control his life? How do you know he did not give in to it? (He was engaged; was married, etc.)

Throughout his career, Lincoln was often swayed by his own emotions—yet he is remembered as a man with great sympathy and understanding for people who were emotionally upset.

Conclusion by Teacher

If, while you are playing games or engaging in sports, you can learn to be a graceful loser and a modest winner, if, as we said before, you can learn to play the game as well as you can regardless of score, in all probability, you will react well later on when you are playing life's game.

Many people in foreign countries as well as in our own look upon Mr. Lincoln as the greatest American who ever lived. He truly had learned how to lose gracefully and to build on life failures.

Suggested Division of Class Time

The story will take almost five minutes as will the distribution of papers and the writing of comments. The remainder of the class period is for discussion.

Caution to Teacher

Do not forget to call on those who are not actively participating in the discussions. Even a "Yes" or "No" response is considered a contribution as it may eventually lead to a volunteered response.

    a. As you think of a specific secondary class with which you are familiar, which changes would you make in the discussion plan reproduced above, as you conduct this discussion in that class?

    b. Which changes, if any, would you make in the way the discussion is initiated?

    c. Which changes, if any, would you make in the way the discussion is ended?

    d. What are the key questions in the discussion?

    e. How can you assure the maximum degree of pupil activity during the discussion?

BIBLIOGRAPHY

1. Adult Education Association of the U.S.A., Chicago, Illinois, Leadership Pamphlets: *How to Lead Discussions,* Leadership Pamphlet No. 1; *Understanding How Groups Work,* Leadership Pamphlet No. 4.
2. Association for Supervision and Curriculum Development, *Learning and Teaching,* 1959 Yearbook (Washington, D.C., the Association, 1959), Ch. 7.
3. BACK, Kurt, "Interpersonal Relations in a Discussion Group," *Journal of Social Issues,* Vol. 4, No. 2 (Spring, 1948), pp. 61-65.
4. BALES, Robert F., "In Conference," *Harvard Business Review,* Vol. 32 (1954), pp. 44-50.
5. ———, and STRODTBECK, Fred L., "Phases in Group Problem-Solving,"

Journal of Abnormal and Social Psychology, Vol. XLVI, No. 4 (October, 1951), pp. 485-495.

6. BENNE, Kenneth D., and SHEATS, Paul, "Functional Roles of Group Members," *Journal of Social Issues*, Vol. 4, No. 2 (Spring, 1948), pp. 41-49.

7. BRADEN, Waldo W., and BRANDENBURG, Earnest, *Oral Decision-Making* (New York, Harper and Brothers, 1955).

8. CORTRIGHT, Rupert L., and HINDS, George L., *Creative Discussion* (New York, The Macmillan Company, 1959).

9. DOLL, R. C., HALVERSON, P. M., LAWRENCE, R. E., and LOWE, E., "An Experiment in Training Teachers for Discussion Group Leadership," *Educational Leadership*, Vol. 10 (November, 1952), pp. 112-117.

10. Encyclopedia Britannica Films, *How to Conduct a Discussion*, 1953.

11. GRIFFITHS, Daniel E., *Human Relations in School Administration* (New York, Appleton-Century-Crofts, Inc., 1956), Chs. 8, 9, 10.

12. HAIMAN, Franklyn S., *Group Leadership and Democratic Action* (Boston, Houghton Mifflin Company, 1951).

13. HALL, Darl Meredith, *Dynamics of Group Discussion* (Danville, Ill., The Interstate Printers and Publishers, Inc., 1957).

14. HOWELL, William S., and SMITH, Donald K., *Discussion* (New York, The Macmillan Compny, 1956).

15. KELTNER, John W., *Group Discussion Processes* (New York, Longmans, Green & Co., Inc., 1957).

16. McBURNEY, James H., and HANCE, Kenneth G., *Discussion in Human Affairs* (New York, Harper and Brothers, 1950).

17. MAIER, N. R. F., *Principles of Human Relations: Applications to Management* (New York, John Wiley & Sons, Inc., 1952), Chs. 3, 7.

18. ———, and SOLEM, A. R., "The Contribution of a Discussion Leader to the Quality of Group Thinking: The Effective Use of Minority Opinion," *Human Relations*, Vol. 5, No. 3 (August, 1952), pp. 277-288.

19. TRECKER, Audrey R., and HARLEIGH, B., *How to Work with Groups* (New York, Woman's Press, 1952).

20. UTTERBACK, William E., *Group Thinking and Conference Leadership: Techniques of Discussion* (New York, Holt, Rinehart and Winston, Inc., 1950).

21. WAGNER, Russell H., and ARNOLD, Carrol C., *Handbook of Group Discussion* (Boston, Houghton Mifflin Company, 1950).

CHAPTER 7

Using the Question as an Aid to

Learning

»»»»»»»»»»

ONE OF THE major factors in getting a discussion going, in providing a sense of direction, and in maintaining interest is the nature of the questions which the teacher uses. The teacher's ability to raise thought-provoking questions is often the key to lively, informed, purposeful discussion. As students take more and more responsibility for success of the discussion, the questions are more likely to come from the students themselves—from their own desire to know. The importance of the question in discussion should not be surprising when we consider the focal part that the question plays in learning of many kinds.

One of the first indications of the young child's growing mental alertness is his fluency in asking questions. Through his insistent "Why?" and "What?" and "How?" the child gains his orientation to the world about him. Nor is the value of questions limited to early childhood. Basic to many of the curricular changes in modern elementary and secondary school education is a fuller recognition of the educational value of the questions asked by boys and girls of all ages. Whereas the curriculum formerly consisted largely of predetermined answers, with the classroom question used only as a convenient device for bringing the answers to the students' attention, the modern curriculum is based to a much greater degree on stimulating the student's intellectual curiosity so that he asks more and better questions and on guiding his intellectual development so that he can find adequate answers.

How can the teacher use questions as a stimulus to learning? Just as the question serves the child as an instrument for satisfying his curiosity, his need to know, it provides a means whereby the teacher can stimulate interest, provoke thought and discussion, and evaluate learning achievement. Because the question is such a useful tool, improvement in the asking of questions is one avenue to the improvement of teaching. The formal question-and-answer recitation is so familiar a teaching procedure in secondary schools that we sometimes forget that the question was an important aid to teaching long before the secondary school as we know it was developed. The question can be used as a means of checking inattention, as a method of discovering the adequacy of the students' preparation at home, and as a means of getting students to learn the answers the teacher wants them to remember, but it also has other and more important functions. Questions can arouse a desire to learn; they can focus attention on the most important aspects of the topic; they can sharpen the issues and bring out the areas of agreement and disagreement; and they can help the student to progress logically to the solution of a problem.

Questioning as an Art

To illustrate how the teacher can use the question most effectively, we shall examine the use to which the question was put by the greatest master of the art of questioning. Of course, we are referring here to Socrates, as we reproduce part of his famous dialogue on the nature of justice.*

"Are you willing, then," said Socrates, "that we should make a *delta* on this side, and an *alpha* on that, and then that we should put whatever seems to us to be a work of justice under the *delta,* and whatever seems to be a work of injustice under the *alpha?*"

"If you think that we need those letters," said Euthydemus, "make them."

Socrates, having made the letters as he proposed, asked, "Does falsehood then exist among mankind?"

"It does, assuredly," replied he.

"Under which head shall we place it?"

"Under injustice certainly."

"Does deceit also exist?"

"Unquestionably."

"Under which head shall we place that?"

"Evidently under injustice."

"Does mischievousness exist?"

"Undoubtedly."

"And the enslaving of men?"

"That, too, prevails."

"And shall neither of these things be placed by us under justice, Euthydemus?"

"It would be strange if they should be," said he.

"But," said Socrates, "if a man being chosen to lead an army, should reduce

* Xenophon, *Memorabilia,* Book IV, Ch. II.

to slavery an unjust and hostile people, should we say that he committed an injustice?"

"No, certainly," replied he.

"Should we not rather say that he acted justly?"

"Indisputably."

"And if in the course of the war with them he should practice deceit?"

"That also would be just," said he.

"And if he should steal and carry off their property, would he not do what was just?"

"Certainly," said Euthydemus; "but I thought at first that you asked these questions only with reference to our friends."

"Then," said Socrates, "all that we have placed under the head of injustice, we must also place under that of justice?"

"It seems so," replied Euthydemus.

"Do you agree, then," continued Socrates, "that, having so placed them, we should make a new distinction, that it is just to do such things with regard to enemies, but unjust to do them with regard to friends, and that towards his friends our general should be as guileless as possible?"

"By all means," replied Euthydemus.

"Well, then," said Socrates, "if a general, seeing his army dispirited, should tell them, inventing a falsehood, that auxiliaries were coming, and should, by that invention, check the despondency of his troops, under which head should we place such an act of deceit?"

"It appears to me," said Euthydemus, "that we must place it under justice."

"And if a father, when his son requires medicine, and refuses to take it, should deceive him, and give him the medicine as ordinary food, and, by adopting such deception, should restore him to health, under which head must we place such an act of deceit?"

"It appears to me that we must put it under the same head."

"And if a person, when his friend was in despondency, should through fear that he might kill himself, steal or take away his sword, or any other weapon, under which head must we place that act?"

"That assuredly, we must place under justice."

"You say, then," said Socrates, "that not even toward our friends must we act on all occasions without deceit?"

"We must not, indeed," said he, "for I retract what I said before, if I may be permitted to do so."

"It is indeed much better that you should be permitted," said Socrates, "than that you should not place actions on the right side. But of those who deceive their friends in order to injure them (that we may not leave even this point unconsidered) which of the two is the more unjust, he who does so intentionally or he who does so involuntarily?"

"Indeed, Socrates," said Euthydemus, "I no longer put confidence in the answers which I give; for all that I said before appears to me now to be quite different from what I then thought; however, let me venture to say that he who deceives intentionally is more unjust than he who deceives involuntarily. . . ."

Questioning as a Routine

Contrast this selection with another illustration that exemplifies the more formal use of questions in a classroom. The lesson which is reproduced below is taken from a textbook on methods of teaching published almost a hundred years ago. The children for whom this lesson was intended were approximately twelve or thirteen years old, the age at which most children today enter the junior high school.

Lesson I

ASSIGNING A LESSON. *Teacher.* You may now open your books, those of you that have books, to this picture of the Earth, and we will see if we can read Lesson I. I will read the fine print, and you may read the coarse print. All look on now, and see if I read right. [*Teacher reads.*] "What is the planet, on which we live, called?" John, you may read the coarse print.

John. [*Reads*] "It is called the Earth."

Teacher. Very well. You see that the coarse print answers the question in fine print. I will read the next question. [*Reads*] "What is the shape of the Earth?" Mary, you may read the answer.

Mary. [*Reads*] "It is very nearly round."

Teacher. Now, Samuel, you may read the next question.

Samuel. [*Reads*] "Do we live on the outside or inside of the Earth?"

Teacher. Susan, you may read the answer.

Susan. [*Reads*] "On the outside."

Teacher. Very well. Now you all see how to read this. I wish you to read over the questions and answers, so many times to yourselves, when you go to your seats, that you can give me the answers without looking on the book, when you come to me to recite tomorrow. How many of you think that you will be able to answer all the questions in Lesson I, by tomorrow morning? [*All hands rise.*] Very well. You may take your books home tonight, if you have a mind to, and study your lesson at home. I shall not be surprised if you get two lessons, but I shall only hear you recite one. You may go to your seats now, in order.

Lesson II

Teacher. How many books today? [*Hands rise. If any have not got the books, the teacher decides in his own mind, how they may be provided, and informs the scholars deficient, how it can be done.*]

RECITATION. [*The teacher, having enrolled the names of the pupils in his register, calls from the register the name of one pupil, say, Amanda. Amanda rises.*]

Teacher. [*With globe in his hand.*] What is the planet, on which we live, called?

Amanda. It is called the Earth.

Teacher. Very well. [*Amanda is excused.*] James. [*James rises.*] What is the shape of the Earth?

James. It is round. [*Hands rise.*]

Teacher. Sarah.

Sarah. It is very nearly round.

Teacher. Right, Sarah. [*James is excused. Scholars, when offering criticism or correction, do it sitting; but never without permission from the teacher.*] I will ask you all a question not in the book. Is the earth round, like a plate, or like the stove pipe, or like this ball? How many can tell? [*Hands rise.*] Maria.

Maria. It is round like a ball.

Teacher. Then it is a ball, isn't it? How deep must a hole be, to go through this globe, right through the center? [*No hands rise.*]

Teacher. Five inches. But how deep would a well have to be to go down through the Earth, right through the center? [*No hands rise.*]

Teacher. How far through did I say the Earth was, yesterday? [*Some hands rise.*] Henry.

Henry. Eight hundred miles.

Teacher. Eight thousand miles; and how long would it take to go through such a well or tunnel, if you could go in a railroad car, with the speed of thirty miles an hour? Well, it would take more than twenty days, traveling twelve hours a day. That would be a long journey, in a tunnel, wouldn't it?

[*Thus, the lesson is pursued, by proposing the questions in the book, till all the scholars have been reached, one or more times. If any scholar fail on one question, he is tried on another; and then on another, till the teacher is satisfied himself as to the amount of study the scholar has bestowed on his lesson. He is then graded, accordingly, in the register.*]

It is comforting to note that such a lesson as that on the Earth which is reproduced above is a caricature rather than a description of any teaching procedure now used in modern schools. The modern secondary school student finds it easier, however, to remember lessons that resemble that on the Earth than to recall those in which the teacher was as challenging as Socrates.

What makes the Socratic dialogue so much more stimulating a series of questions than is the lesson on the Earth? It is impossible to read the Socratic dialogue without feeling that one is in the presence of a great mind, of a mind that thinks clearly and that can help others to think clearly. Although Socrates undoubtedly never heard the expression that learning is an active process, he knew intuitively that the only way anyone can gain insight into a concept is to have the learner himself do the thinking. What Socrates did was to guide the learner by asking the questions that were needed to clarify the issues and to supply the raw material out of which the concept could be evolved. So clearly were the questions stated and so logical the sequence, that Euthydemus could not help being wiser than he would have been if he had merely memorized the textbook answers as the teacher of the lesson on the Earth would have asked him to do. Socrates opened his students' eyes so they could see, and he opened their minds so they could think. Asking them to memorize conclusions he had formulated was as unthinkable to Socrates as it should be to any modern teacher.

The ability to use questions well is an important phase of the teacher's professional equipment, but it is also a difficult one to develop. It is a fairly simple matter to present a series of rules which will help the teacher to ask questions in an approved manner and to treat the answer in accordance with the dictates of modern education. These rules, however, refer only to the superficial aspects of good questioning. They refer, almost, to the etiquette of questions. It is as though we tried to develop good character by teaching good manners. As we all know, the most polished person may still be a rogue and a scoundrel; and the teacher who observes all of the petty regulations relating to the manner in which questions are to be asked may still not be able to use the question as an intellectual challenge.

Although good manners may not lead to good character, they may help a person to get along better with his fellow-men. In the same way, the teacher's understanding of the principles which lie behind the customary rules of questioning may help him to see the significance of questions as a form of thinking, as more than a teaching device, and may thus increase the quality of his questions and improve the nature of the learning experiences in his classroom.

WHAT ARE THE CHARACTERISTICS OF A GOOD QUESTION?

What are the significant differences between good classroom questions and poor ones? There are many criteria which can be used for pointing the distinction, but we may find it helpful to confine our attention at this point to only three.

First, a Good Question Should Challenge Thinking and Invite Solution

For these ends to be attained, the question must be more than an invitation to the recitation of memorized materials and it must be more than an attempt at recreating a discussion held earlier. When the teacher phrases the question so that it presents a controversial issue, the student is stimulated to express his own point of view. Thus, an English teacher, instead of asking his class to evaluate the poem "Richard Cory," asks whether they prefer this poem to the one they read the previous day. Another teacher may tell his class that "Richard Cory" has been called both an instance of the poet's insight into human nature and an illustration of the poet's sentimentality. As they read the poem, they can decide which of these judgments expresses their point of view.

Projecting the material into the students' life is another way of increasing the stimulation received from the question. The English teacher may help his students to understand "Richard Cory" by asking them for observations about other young people they know who give the outward impression of being happy and carefree and who yet have an inward sorrow that belies the superficial attempts at gayety.

The mathematics teacher can present his material so that the class recognizes its inability to solve the problem because of inadequate information. The order of operations in an algebra class, for example, may be just another topic to be studied or it may become a challenging one, depending upon the kind of question with which the teacher initiates the discussion. Sometimes the matter-of-fact presentation of so simple an example as $2 + 5 \times 3 = ?$ may divide the class into two groups—one of them in-

A good question stimulates thought
    and encourages the students themselves to ask good questions.

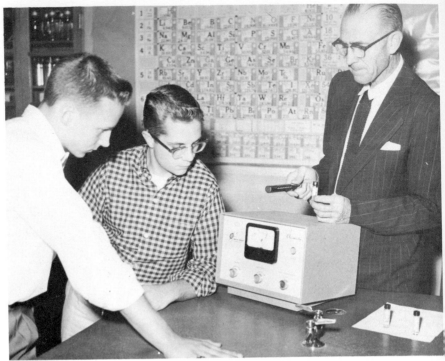

The search for the answer leads to the classroom

Buffalo Board of Education (Photo by Joseph Manch)

e library, the laboratory, and the field trip.

United States Steel Corporation

Sometimes the answer they find leads to action
and sometimes the answer suggests even larger questions
they must answer.

sisting that the answer is 21, the other being equally certain that the correct answer is 17. Out of this conflict of opinion such interest in the order of operations may be aroused that the questions that are asked are more challenging than would be the routine sequence of mathematics questions in another algebra class.

The closer the question comes to arising from the student's background rather than from the subject matter, the more likely it will be to prove stimulating. Questions should, therefore, stress the implication of the topic for the student. This principle does not apply to all questions asked in class, but rather to the pivotal ones in the discussion. So long as the basic problem is one which is vital to students, enough interest may be generated to carry the class over some of the minor questions which contribute to the major one.

Second, a Good Question Should Be Clear and Easily Understood

The student's attention should be directed to the heart of the question and not to an attempt to find out what the teacher had in mind when he asked the question. The group that is discussing the effects of the Industrial Revolution on the growth of large corporations will not be helped very much when the teacher asks, "What about the railroads?" since the student does not know what there is about the railroads that is pertinent at this time. A more specific question, such as, "Why did the federal government find it necessary to supervise the expansion of railroads?" is so much clearer that students can see the relevance to the point at issue.

Since the teacher has so many things to think about at one time, the chances are that he cannot phrase his key questions on the spur of the moment and yet have them so clear that they refer to the one point in his mind at that time. It is for this reason that experienced teachers usually prepare their key questions in advance so that they know the four or five pivotal questions on which the whole discussion hinges. Even though the trend of classroom discussion may be such that the teacher may not want to stifle discussion by presenting his five questions exactly as they were worded in advance, the very fact that he has thought about these questions with more thoroughness than is possible in the heat of an open discussion, should make it easier for him to rephrase his questions so that they appear to grow out of the comments made by his students and yet guide them along the lines of greatest value.

Third, a Good Question Should Elicit the Kind of Response that Will Contribute to the Progress of the Discussion

It is always disconcerting when a teacher asks a significant question during a classroom discussion and the students misinterpret the question so that they are all off at a tangent from which the teacher has to bring them back to the topic. The careful wording of key questions helps focus attention on the problem at hand and can reduce the tendency to wander. The teacher will have to avoid the use of such questions as, "Discuss the Industrial Revolution" or "Tell all you know about the discovery of the steam engine." Such questions as these are so vague that a student may answer them honestly without helping the progress of the lesson.

Once the teacher knows what it is that he is trying to get the group to understand, he can then ask his question in such a form that it does guide the class along a definite pattern of thought. "Discuss the Industrial Revolution" may then become a series of questions rather than a single vague one. For example, the teacher may ask, "If you had been living at the time of the Industrial Revolution, would you have known that the Industrial Revolution was in progress?" or, "In what way was the life of a seventeen-year-old boy at the time of the Industrial Revolution different from your life today?" Such questions as these start the class to thinking about that phase of the Industrial Revolution which is pertinent at the moment and reduces the likelihood of such rambling as may result from the vague request to "Tell all you know about the Industrial Revolution."

HOW SHOULD THE TEACHER ASK QUESTIONS IN CLASS?

There are, to be sure, a number of principles of procedure which govern the usual classroom use of questions as teaching procedures. One is reluctant, however, to present them as rules for fear that they will be misinterpreted by the inexperienced teacher as being commands rather than suggestions. None of the suggestions which appear below should be taken as more than the statement of a usually accepted procedure which should be followed unless the teacher's judgment indicates that his students will be served better by modifying the procedure. Objection is raised only to the person who violates the rule out of ignorance. As long as the teacher knows that he is following an unorthodox procedure and that he has good reason for departing from established custom, no serious objection should be raised by anyone.

Address Questions to the Whole Class

As an illustration of such a recommended procedure in questioning, there is the suggestion that questions should be addressed to the entire class before any student is recognized so that he may answer the question publicly. Thus, the teacher asks the whole class how the economic changes caused by the Industrial Revolution altered family life. Even though two or three students may see the point of the question immediately and be eager to offer their contribution, the teacher generally waits awhile until more of the class have had an opportunity to see the implications of the question and to begin to formulate their answer before any student answers the question orally.

The reason for addressing the question to the entire class and then inviting one student to speak, rather than following the opposite procedure of addressing the student by name and then presenting the question, is clear from an analysis of the student reaction to the two types of questions. When the teacher says, "Helen, in what way did the economic changes brought about by the Industrial Revolution modify family life?" he indicates to the entire class that only Helen need be concerned with the question, and the others can sit back just a little too comfortably while Helen does the thinking. On the other hand, if the teacher presents the question to the group as a whole and then waits half a minute or so before Helen goes on with her answer, he is more likely to encourage wider participation.

This suggestion is so clear and sensible that one may ask why it should ever be violated deliberately. There are, however, a number of instances where the teacher should make an exception to this rule. There is, for example, the lad who is so timid that the shock of being called on in class may be enough to scatter whatever ideas he has in mind. If such a student is called on suddenly and is expected to speak immediately, he may not be able to collect his wits quickly enough to respond. For such a student the mumbled response, "I don't know" is an easy way out of a painful situation; and the low mark he may receive is less unpleasant than is his discomfiture as he seeks to organize his thoughts for prompt expression. So far as this lad is concerned, it may be better for the teacher to let him know that he is to be called on. The teacher, therefore, uses such an expression as "Now, Kenneth, what would you say was the effect of the economic changes brought about by the Industrial Revolution on the way in which family life was organized?" By the time the teacher has finished speaking, the boy knows what is expected of him and he can proceed without unnecessary embarrassment.

In another situation, the teacher may find that one or two of the students have lost interest in the discussion and that a question addressed to them may be helpful in bringing them back to the problem at hand. A procedure which some teachers follow under these circumstances is to call on the student suddenly to answer the question and then to reprimand him if he is unable to answer. Technically, the teacher is within his rights when he assumes that since the question has been given publicly all students should be able to answer it. Practically, however, the procedure is a poor one. While it may bring the student's mind back to the class, it usually arouses resentment which keeps the student from participating wholeheartedly in the subsequent part of the discussion. Moreover, the teacher may even develop additional disciplinary problems when the student who has been daydreaming for a while answers the question in terms of the last thing he remembers as having been said in class. His answer may be so irrelevant as to disrupt the trend of the discussion and invite ridicule. The whole matter may be dealt with more simply if the student's name is brought into the discussion either by reference to something he has said earlier or as part of the background of a question. Thus, the teacher may say, "Now, Matthew, what would you say was the effect of the economic changes brought about by the Industrial Revolution on the way in which family life was organized?"

Do Not Repeat Questions

A second convention refers to the undesirability of repeating a question. Once the question has been given to the entire class and a student has been called on, it is not unusual for a student to stall for time by requesting the repetition of the question. If one of the purposes of addressing the question to the entire class is the encouragement of continued attention by the entire group, this value is lost if any student who is called on asks that the question be repeated for his benefit. When the teacher is careful to speak clearly enough to be heard in all parts of the room, there is no need for the repetition of the question. If there should be any sudden noise or distraction, the teacher should repeat the question for the sake of the entire class. Where a student asks for the question because he has not been paying attention, it may be well to pass on to some other student and then to return to the first student for elaboration and summary.

There is always a possibility that the student who asks frequently for the repetition of the question may be hard of hearing. In such a case, changing the student's seat and later providing for medical examination and treatment is a more adequate way of dealing with the situation than is the mere repetition of the question.

Do Not Repeat Answers

It is similarly regarded as poor form for the teacher to repeat a student's answer. Such repetition is sometimes a sign of the teacher's nervousness or lack of preparation. The teacher may get into the habit of repeating all answers automatically because he, too, has to stall for time. If an answer comes before the teacher has had a chance to think of the next question, he repeats the answer as one way of gaining a few seconds in which to collect his own thoughts.

A more serious objection to this practice of routine repetition of answers is that it detracts from the prestige of the student's contribution to the classroom discussion. Even in college classes, one finds that students tend to pay more attention to what the instructor says than to a contribution made by a student. In a large lecture hall where students are busy taking notes, one sometimes hears the click of a hundred pens being put down simultaneously. To the experienced listener this indicates that the instructor has ceased lecturing and that a student is now speaking. In a classroom discussion this indifference to the worth of the contributions made by classmates deprives the discussion of much of its value, since students learn to rely on the teacher's repeating anything of value said by a student.

There are numerous instances in which the teacher should violate this rule and should repeat the answer; but he can do so subtly. He may incorporate the most important part of the answer as part of the next question. He may ask the students to indicate whether or not they agree with the answer. His word of praise for the unusually good answer may indirectly repeat the key idea of the contribution. Where a running outline of the discussion is being developed on the chalkboard, the writing of the expression on the chalkboard serves to repeat the key idea. Under some circumstances the teacher may say that the answer was so good and so well worded that it deserves repetition, and the student may be asked to repeat it. At no time, however, should the teacher develop the habit of merely repeating everything said in class.

Make Questions Self-explanatory

It is generally considered undesirable to preface a question with an explanatory speech. Some teachers easily get into the habit of making such vague requests as, "Now, think before you answer the next question," or, "The next question is a catch question. Be careful of what you say." Although such statements as these sometimes focus attention on a key question, their use is at best only a vague and ineffective request. The good teacher may occasionally remind the class that the next question is the pivotal one which serves to summarize all of the preceding discussion; but even this procedure should not be overworked. The experienced student soon learns to ignore such a statement as, "This is the kind of question that always appears on College Entrance Board Examinations" because he knows that in that teacher's class practically every question that the teacher asks is introduced by some such supposedly attention-getting procedure.

In general, each question should be clear in itself. This makes inadvisable the use of double or triple questions. When a teacher asks a longer question consisting of two or more parts, few students will think of all parts during the ensuing discussion. When the teacher asks, "Which factors created the need for steam railways and how did the introduction of steam railways influence the development of industry?" there is little likelihood that both parts of the question will actually be answered. It is better to ask the first part of the question as a separate question and then to have the answers lead to the second question.

Design the Question to Stimulate Thinking

If the question is to be a stimulus to thinking, the teacher will have to avoid questions that look like questions but really are not. Some teachers overuse the leading question until they do all of the thinking while the class responses consist almost entirely of "Yes," "No," and "Maybe." If the teacher does use a question that can be answered by only one word, it should be followed in almost every instance with an invitation to justify the answer given. The question, "Was Lincoln justified when he issued the Emancipation Proclamation?" is hardly worth class time when it leads only to a reply of "Yes" or "No." To have value, the student should understand that such a one-word answer implies that he go on to explain the reasons for his judgment.

Plan Questions in Purposeful Order

Wherever possible, the questions should be planned in a logical sequence. If we reread the bit of Socratic dialogue reproduced earlier in this chapter, we can see how each question fits into its place in a logical pattern and how any rearrangement of the order in which the questions are asked reduces materially the effect of the entire conversation. In any well-ordered lesson plan, the sequence of questions should approach in value that employed by Socrates.

Though the question is important in virtually every kind of classroom activity, it is most important in a *developmental lesson,* that is, in a lesson in which the teacher uses a series of questions as his principal means of developing a new concept or of clarifying and correcting a misunderstanding. In the hands of an expert, a developmental lesson represents an adaptation of the Socratic dialogue for use with a group of students. Even though it's a rare teacher who aspires to being a modern Socrates, the thought-provoking quality of a good developmental lesson is achieved only when the key questions are carefully worded and the sequence in which they are asked is planned effectively. Thus, the mathematics teacher may use a developmental lesson to teach his class the law of signs and a social studies teacher can use a developmental lesson to help his students understand the problems that an underdeveloped nation faces as it makes the leap to twentieth-century industrialism.

HOW SHOULD THE STUDENTS' ANSWERS BE TREATED?

Asking questions is only one phase of the problem, for there still remains the need for deciding what the teacher can do with the answers.

No Answer

What should be done when no answer is forthcoming, when the teacher asks a question and then finds no one ready to offer an answer? In most instances this situation indicates that the question is too difficult for the students or too remote from their interests to stimulate them. Most experienced teachers will take this silence as though it were anticipated and will make such a remark as, "It is small wonder that you hesitate to answer that question without first asking another question, namely. . . ." and then the teacher substitutes for the difficult question one of its component parts. By breaking the major question into a number of smaller ones, the teacher is able to return to the major question later and to have it answered. The teacher must allow sufficient time for the students to think before he rephrases the question instead of going on, as some teachers do, to give three or four versions of a question before stopping for a response.

Unimportant Answer

What should be done when the answer is correct and relatively unimportant? Many of the answers that are offered during a classroom discussion fall into this category. When a question is asked in the course of classroom discussion, several students will express their opinions. In most instances these opinions are subjected to further discussion. Each individual's statement, however, is not sufficiently important to warrant the teacher's focusing special attention on his contribution. For example, the teacher who is interested in helping the students to evaluate the way in which automation creates additional problems for our world to solve may ask a number of minor questions which lead up to the major one. The teacher who is concerned with this major question and takes the minor contributions for granted may unintentionally give the students the impression that their efforts are being ignored. The teacher should therefore make certain that all contributions, regardless of how minor they may be, are acknowledged by a smile, a nod of the head, or the use of such an expression as "Thank you" or "That's right." If the teacher is going to develop the student's ability to participate in a discussion, he must welcome the minor offerings which help prepare the student for more intensive participation later.

Significant Answer

What should the teacher do when the answer is correct and vitally important? In every discussion period there are a few questions of pivotal importance, the answers to which summarize a considerable part of the discussion or present the issues so clearly that the subsequent discussion hinges on the answer. For example, the social studies teacher tracing the development of modern industrial life may lead up to the question, "Everything considered, what is the major contribution that the development of large corporations has made to the progress of our country?" This is clearly a more important question than one of the subsidiary queries such as "What are some of the large corporations whose products have become essential parts of our way of living?" Unless the teacher does focus attention on the answer to the key question, the students may not note its significance, and the contribution it elicits may be lost sight of during the larger discussion.

Such major answers may be stressed in any one of several ways. Various members of the class may be asked to comment on the answer, indicating their agreement or disagreement with the point of view expressed and offering supplementary bits of information. The essential part of the answer may be written on the chalkboard as part of the outline being developed in class. The teacher may occasionally comment on the answer or use the answer as the basis for the next question.

Poor or Incorrect Expression

What should be done when the answer is correct but poorly or ungrammatically expressed? It is this type of situation that often proves annoying in the classroom, for a critic can object to anything that the teacher does. If the teacher takes the point of view that his major concern is with the development of an idea or the modification of an attitude, he is going to be more concerned with the substance of a student's answer than with its form. Because the teacher fears that the freedom of the discussion may be stifled the moment he changes the student's "He don't" to "He doesn't" or indicates that it is *mu-nic'i-pal* government and not *mu-nic-i'pal government*, he may be reluctant to interrupt the student. Although his point of emphasis is a legitimate one, he will be criticized by those who feel that good speech and good English should be the concern of all teachers and not that of the English teacher alone. His critics will ask of what avail it is to set aside special periods for the teaching of good usage when the students' other teachers allow even heinous errors to pass unnoticed.

The other extreme is represented by the teacher who insists on clear and grammatical speech at all times. No serious grammatical error is ever allowed to pass unnoticed. When this teacher tries to get a group of so-phisticated adolescents to realize that idealism is not synonymous with gushy sentimentality and that qualities of self-sacrifice are not unknown even in our own world, he may find a few members of his group respond-ing to this thought. One of the students who ordinarily dismisses all in-struction in English as being unimportant may now be moved to tell of an instance of idealism and self-sacrifice that he has witnessed. The teacher, who should be pleased that this youth is beginning to participate in class-room activities, may kill the student's newborn enthusiasm by interrupt-ing him in the middle of a sentence to call attention to an error in diction or by making too pointed a correction as soon as the student has finished speaking.

No matter which of these two extremes the teacher follows, he can adduce adequate justification and be confident that his critics will produce equally valid objections. Fortunately, the classroom teacher need not go to either of these two extremes. Where the student's comment is a signifi-cant one, the teacher may accept it for the material it contributes to the classroom discussion and he may then ask the group to help rephrase the contribution so that it expresses better the point of view the student in-tended. When there is only a minor lapse from good usage, little attention need be paid to the departure from established custom. Sometimes it is enough for the teacher to correct the pronunciation of a word by using it correctly as he makes the student's contribution the basis for the next question. On the other hand, if the error is a grievous one or if it is one which a school campaign is seeking to eliminate, the teacher can direct at-tention to the correction of the error without much ado. Thus he may say, almost in passing, "You mean, 'He does'" and let the student go right on to complete the thought he was in the process of expressing.

Incorrect Answers

What should be done when the answer is partly right and partly wrong? Here the teacher should give the student the credit that is due him for the contribution he has made and then subject the incorrect part of the answer to further classroom discussion. Thus, the student who mentions two corporations as illustrating monopolies may be cor-rect as far as one of them is concerned and may be wrong in the other instance. The teacher can follow up the student's answer by asking why it is not correct to use the milk company as an illustration of a monopoly though the telephone company illustration is a good one. Certain it is that the student who has offered a contribution that is even partly right should feel the glow of satisfaction that comes to those who know that they are contributing their share to the progress of the group.

What should be done when the answer is wrong? Sometimes the

answer is not only incorrect but it may be almost wholly irrelevant to the point at issue. The teacher who sees the pattern of the discussion developing so clearly and leading inevitably to the next vital question is understandably annoyed by the student whose answer indicates that he was left far behind when the group moved on. What the teacher must recognize as the assumption that is basic in all treatment of incorrect answers is that the student who answers unwisely presents a pedagogical and not a disciplinary problem. In some classrooms, ignorance or slowness is treated as an offense to be punished rather than as a condition to be remedied. Few students deliberately answer incorrectly. In the overwhelming majority of instances, the student prefers to contribute an answer of such excellence as to elicit the teacher's praise and enthusiastic commendation. The answer that seems irrelevant to the teacher may not be irrelevant when seen from the student's point of view. To be regarded as a clown because of a contribution that is offered in good faith is to discourage this student's speaking again in the near future.

Incorrect answers must be treated tactfully. The teacher can indicate, either by asking other students to evaluate the answer or by pointing to its limitations himself, that the answer that was received was not entirely pertinent or correct. The incorrect answer, however, should never be greeted by sarcasm, censure, or ridicule.

Marks

It will be noted that no reference has been made to the use of marks as a means of acknowledging the student's contribution or of evaluating its worth. This was no oversight. In a good discussion, the marking book has no place. Students who speak should do so because they have something to say, rather than because they see a chance to get a high mark. Similarly, a student should ask a question when he needs further light and not because a good question is rewarded by a 10. Although the new teacher may find the marking book a useful disciplinary aid and a convenient way of curbing irrelevant comments, his use of the marking book should diminish as his efficiency as a discussion leader increases. One may even say that the number of times the teacher uses the marking book during a discussion varies inversely with the skill with which the discussion is being conducted.

Problems of Classroom Order*

What should be done when the class is so stimulated by the question that all seek to answer at once? The teacher who is successful in

* See Chapter 14 for a fuller discussion of the problems of maintaining effective classroom discipline.

pitching the level of his discussion at that of his students should be gratified when his students become so engrossed in the discussion that many
of them shout out the answer to a question before the teacher has recognized anyone. This condition ought not to be treated as a disciplinary
offense unless it occurs so often or to so great an extent that the progress
of the class is impeded. In most instances the students will understand
why it is necessary for someone to act as chairman of the meeting in order
that the group may continue to move forward. A brief statement expressing the teacher's satisfaction at the interest that has been aroused and
reminding the class of the way in which the group can proceed most
effectively may be enough.

Where the question presents a clear-cut "Yes" or "No" answer and
the students begin to shout out "Yes" or "No," it may be advisable for
the teacher to call for a viva-voce vote or to ask them to signify their
answer by having all who think the answer is "Yes" raise hands. At that
point he can call on some students from each side to present their point
of view.

The new teacher may sometimes find that this outburst of student
enthusiasm is less a sign of intellectual aggressiveness than of a more
annoying tendency to try out the new teacher. Some young teachers are
so fearful of stifling student participation that they exercise too little
leadership in guiding and controlling the ways in which students ask or
respond to questions. The teacher may find it helpful to control the discussion subtly at various parts of the period either by having the class
write answers to one of the questions, or by alternating periods of reading in the text or brief lectures with other periods of group discussion.

HOW CAN THE TEACHER ENCOURAGE STUDENTS TO ASK QUESTIONS?

The teacher's success, so far as the use of questions is concerned, is
indicated as much by the kinds of questions asked by the student as by
the questions the teacher himself asks. All too often, it is the wrong person
in the class who asks questions, and for the wrong reasons. Conventionally, most classroom questions are asked by the teacher, who knows the
answer, in order to see whether the student can guess the answer the
teacher has in mind. It is more effective, however, when questions are
open-ended, encouraging thoughtful response and discussion by the class.

Although there are formal procedures which will stimulate the asking of questions, these procedures become meaningless tricks unless they
reflect the teacher's genuine interest in the way the student's mind operates. The teacher who is so completely immersed in the need for "covering" subject matter that he views any question asked by his student as
being a distraction and an impediment to class progress, gains little from

setting aside a box into which students may drop questions they wish to have answered or from devoting a period a week to answering questions asked by students. By his own manner and by his reaction to the student who does raise questions, better than by any eloquent request for questions, the teacher can indicate to his class that he really does welcome the opportunity to help students to ask and then to answer their questions.

When the teacher decides in advance which questions are to be discussed in class, he has the problem of trying to arouse student interest in his questions and of maintaining group participation in the discussion. No such problem of motivation confronts the teacher whose material is vital to the students. Take, for example, the study of general science. The subject has a tremendous fascination for adolescents and seems to appeal to almost all of their fundamental psychological drives. If one were to stimulate a group of adolescents to reveal what it is they want to know about science or about any single topic in science, much of the material that now is presented in textbook and laboratory form could be presented more effectively as a way of answering the questions they want to have answered.

Discovering Questions that Concern Students

In many secondary schools it is impossible for the teacher to have so fluid a curriculum as is implied in the preceding paragraph. The teacher in even the most conventional of schools, however, can often present the most formal of topics as a series of significant questions on the students' level. The science instructor, for example, who is to teach the storage battery should not limit his preparation to listing the basic facts concerning the storage battery. He must ask himself the question, "If I were a seventeen-year-old boy or girl, what would I want to know about storage batteries?" As he thinks of this question, he will ask himself what experience such a student has with storage batteries. What difficulties have these boys and girls experienced in using them? What kinds of batteries are used by boys and girls or by members of their families? His mind will then run to portable radios, flashlights, and to automobile batteries.

As the teacher begins asking questions about these applications with which the students are familiar, he may be able to stimulate them to ask questions and to view the study of science not as the treatment of impersonal principles and supporting facts, but as the opportunity to study some of the problems of a highly industrialized and mechanized civilization. The chances are that the students will learn as much about storage batteries when the topic is presented from their point of view as they will gain from a more formal presentation of the topic; but they will gain more than knowledge if their interest in science is aroused and if they learn that the science classroom is a place where they ask questions and try to answer them.

Making the fullest use of students' questions calls for teaching of a high order. It must be sufficiently challenging that the student will be stimulated to pursue his questions until he finds the answer that satisfies him fully rather than be content with an inadequate answer which merely soothes his curiosity. The teacher must be able to distinguish between the trivial question and the one which has implications that deserve full exploration. Under the teacher's guidance the student should be helped to read widely and to observe more carefully the world about him so that he may broaden his intellectual horizon and see ever more questions that demand answers.

No teacher knows all the answers to the questions that alert and intelligent adolescents can ask, nor should he pretend to a degree of omniscience he does not possess. He must, however, be a scholarly person if he is to be able to help his students to find the answers and if he is to introduce them to challenging questions that would otherwise not occur to them. He must be a skilled group leader if his students are to distinguish between important and unimportant questions and if their search for an answer is not to be distracted every time any member of the group thinks of another question.

Our discussion of the core curriculum* indicates how the organization of the curriculum may stimulate the effective use of questions and our examination of how units of work are conducted† suggests how classroom procedures may facilitate the use of students' questions as a method of guiding learning. All other phases of teaching and of learning must also reveal such respect for the students' growing awareness of important problems that the teacher truly becomes a stimulus to his students' learning.

Years ago, psychologists used to refer to the child from three to six years of age as being in "The Questioning Age." Modern education makes such a classification inappropriate, for the questions asked by the three-year-old seem few and superficial as compared with those asked by the eight-year-old, the eighteen-year-old, and the twenty-eight-year-old. Willingness to learn and the ability to remember the answers one hears at school are important, but not as important as are the desire to ask questions and the ability to find the answers.

QUESTIONS FOR STUDY AND DISCUSSION

1. What use can a teacher make of questions if he is a member of a teaching team and is developing a topic with a group of 135 secondary school students?

* See pp. 45-52.
† See Chapter 4.

2. Among the pupils in a junior high school science class is a bright girl who answers well when she is called on but who rarely participates unless she is invited by name to speak. What can the teacher do to encourage her to volunteer questions and comments?

3. Which of the suggested procedures for asking questions did Socrates employ in his dialogue? Which of these procedures did he violate? Were his violations defensible?

4. As you examine the Socratic dialogue that is reproduced in this chapter, which questions do you think are the pivotal questions in the dialogue?

Would the dialogue be improved if you changed the order in which these questions are asked?

5. Selecting any problem that you think is suitable as a topic for a developmental lesson in a junior or senior high school class with which you are familiar, formulate the key questions to be asked during the discussion.

Are any changes needed in these questions before they meet the criteria for a good question as set forth in this chapter?

Are these questions arranged in a logical sequence?

6. A newly appointed senior high school teacher who believes that it is undesirable to grade the answers given by his students during a class lesson finds that his students are not well prepared in his class because they concentrate on studying at home for those classes in which the teacher does enter a grade in his book whenever a student's answer is incorrect.

What should he do?

7. A junior high school teacher is pleased by the way in which his students respond to his questions and by the diligence with which they carry out every assignment he gives. He is dismayed, however, to note that they rarely ask any questions of him, either in class or privately, and that they never read anything other than what he assigns.

What can he do to stimulate his students to ask questions and to read independently?

8. The teacher of a class of "slow learners" notes that while his students have been slow to learn what the school has tried to teach them, they have learned all too well that they are not bright and that teachers do not expect much of them. As a result, they are apathetic in class, almost never volunteer a question or an answer, and do not respond even to questions they can answer.

What should the teacher do?

BIBLIOGRAPHY

1. ALCORN, Marvin D., HOUSEMAN, Richard A., and SCHUNERT, Jim R., *Better Teaching in Secondary Schools* (New York, Holt, Rinehart and Winston, Inc., 1954), Ch. 13.
2. ALEXANDER, William M., and HALVERSON, Paul M., *Effective Teaching in Secondary Schools* (New York, Holt, Rinehart and Winston, Inc., 1956), Ch. 1.
3. BENNE, Kenneth D., and MUNTYAN, Bozidar, *Human Relations in Curriculum Change* (New York, Holt, Rinehart and Winston, Inc., 1951), Part III, Sects. A 2, 4-7, B 4-14.
4. BURTON, William H., *The Guidance of Learning Activities*, 2nd ed. (New York, Appleton-Century-Crofts, Inc., 1952), Ch. 17.
5. BUTLER, Frank A., *The Improvement of Teaching in Secondary Schools*, 3rd ed. (Chicago, University of Chicago Press, 1954), Ch. 11.

6. GRAMBS, Jean D., IVERSON, William J., and PATTERSON, Franklin K., *Modern Methods in Secondary Education*, rev. ed. (New York, Holt, Rinehart and Winston, Inc., 1958), Ch. 5.

7. KINNEY, Lucien, and DRESDEN, Katherine, eds., *Better Learning Through Current Materials*, rev. ed. (Stanford, Stanford University Press, 1952), Ch. 6.

8. RISK, Thomas M., *Principles and Practices of Teaching in Secondary Schools*, 3rd ed. (New York, American Book Company, 1958), Ch. 12.

9. SCHORLING, Raleigh, and BATCHELDER, Howard T., *Student Teaching in Secondary Schools*, 3rd ed. (New York, McGraw-Hill Book Co., Inc., 1956), Ch. 5.

10. STRATEMEYER, Florence, and others, *Developing a Curriculum for Modern Living*, 2nd ed. (New York, Bureau of Publications, Teachers College, Columbia University, 1957), Ch. 8.

11. UMSTATTD, James G., *Secondary School Teaching*, 3rd ed. (Boston, Ginn & Company, 1953), Ch. 11.

CHAPTER **8**

Enriching the Experiential Background

For Learning

»»»»»»»»»»

STUDENTS' BONERS are sometimes howlingly funny because of the ways in which words are misused or because of the naïve misconceptions they reveal. After we have stopped laughing, we may consider these boners rather sad. If this is what students thought they were studying, how effective was the teaching? While teachers enjoy the boners they encounter, no teacher likes to think of them as the end product of all of his efforts in the classroom.

Why do students make these boners? Of course, there are some errors that result from carelessness and from misreading or misinterpreting the question. We can hardly regard as a boner a seemingly ridiculous answer given by a student who does not hear the question correctly because of an auditory defect. For the most part, however, boners reveal that students have been using words they do not understand. In ordinary classroom activities, even alert teachers may not be aware of misconceptions because the students use the words correctly in sentences, but the sentences may mean something entirely different to the student and to the teacher.

What can be done to clarify the thinking of the adolescent who was under the impression that a newspaper which had exposed corruption in government received a *bullet surprise* when it won a *Pulitzer Prize*? If students are to deal with ideas and not with verbal misrepresentations of them, the teacher must supply a rich background of first-hand experience or some acceptable substitute.

USING AUDIO-VISUAL AIDS IN MAKING LEARNING CONCRETE

Endowing Symbols with Meaning

Everybody is familiar with the Chinese saying *One look is worth a thousand words*. Anyone who has ever tried, by words alone, to describe how a canal lock operates knows that words can be inadequate. If we could take our students to see a canal lock in operation and give them the opportunity to find the answers to the questions they would undoubtedly ask, they would soon understand canal locks better than they would have understood them if they had had to rely on extensive verbal explanations.

When obvious practical limitations make it impossible for us to take the class to see a canal in operation, we can use the motion picture film as a means of bringing the canal to the classroom. There are other ways of helping students to see how canal locks are used. We can have our students operate a miniature model of a canal and we can give them the opportunity to construct their own models of canals. Even the use of pictures, charts, and diagrams can clarify much that would otherwise be obscure. It is no accident that the expression "Now I *see* what you mean" has come to signify "Now I *understand* what you mean."

"The primary function of audio-visual materials," says a research report of the National Education Association [20, p. 6], "is to provide experience, more or less direct, whereby a child can build up his storehouse of meanings." By means of the motion picture, boys and girls can visit a coal mine one day and a wheat field the next, and by radio or television they can attend a session of a Congressional investigating committee without leaving the school. [Studies indicate that these experiences, which bridge the gap between actuality and abstraction, also facilitate the learning of facts and their retention. They go beyond the facts and can build, reinforce, or alter opinions and attitudes. The field trip or film may be used to develop interest in a topic and thereby motivate learning. Moreover, since experience is the basis of vocabulary as well as concepts, these more concrete learning activities contribute to a richer store of words and ideas.

Experiences of this type are valuable not only because they help an individual child to learn but also because they help organize learning experiences for the class as a group. How can the teacher develop similarity of background within the group as the class moves from topic to topic? The field trip, film, slide, recording, or flat picture offers an excellent path to providing common experiences for the group. Second, these procedures and materials offer a variety of approaches which can keep teaching and learning fresh. Third, economy of time in learning has been demonstrated by the armed forces and industry as well as by teachers through the use of audio-visual devices in many learning areas.

Appropriate Use of Audio-visual Aids

It is important for the teacher to be aware of the wealth of technological resources he may command to assist in learning. It is even more important that he remember that these aids are not ends in themselves; their only function is to contribute to instruction which he and his students have planned.

Can audio-visual materials be used equally effectively in any learning situation? The answer lies in the relative needs for concreteness. Belaboring with additional examples what is already grasped serves little value except possibly as review. The need for concreteness is a function of the novelty of the learning situation and also of the degree of abstractness involved.

In the early days of audio-visual aids, it was assumed that films and slides were best adapted to the needs of slow learners. Actually audio-visual materials help slow learners more with some problems and rapid learners more with others. It is not so much the nature of the group as the objective of instruction that determines the effectiveness of the materials employed. For absorption of facts alone, effectiveness of films is more marked with slow students than with bright students. Where generalization, contrast, and comparison are sought, as might be expected, films are more effective with more able youngsters [14, Ch. XII].

The assumption that audio-visual aids are best used to teach certain simple, undisputed facts has also been discarded. One of the important values of films, in particular, is their contribution to emotionalized learning. A body of research findings supports the effectiveness of motion pictures—and, by inference, television because of its similarity—in reinforcing or altering attitudes, values, and opinions. One can readily understand the emotional impact in the "You Are There!" feeling which actual events on television or filmed drama make possible.

Verbal description cannot evoke as well as does a filmed sequence the human significance of soil erosion, intergroup discrimination, or the bank closings of the Thirties. Televised proceedings put life and drama into a national political convention. Clearly and effectively, audio-visual aids can:

arouse interest;
develop a common background for new learnings;
supply a concrete basis for new vocabulary, concepts, and generalizations;
provide a feeling of actuality and reality in strange, remote, and long-ago situations;

present information and improve retention of it;
develop skills;
help form attitudes, opinions, and values.

Student Construction of Audio-visual Material

Encouraging students to construct their own audio-visual material is an important way of developing their understanding of the problems they are studying. A social studies class, for example, can prepare its own relief map with papier-mâché and construct a working model of a canal lock. Other classes can produce radio programs either for presentation over the school broadcasting facilities or for performance in classroom or auditorium. Boys and girls can make their own slides, compile individual scrapbooks, and draw their own illustrations. With adequate facilities and competent supervision, high school students have written and produced creditable motion picture films.

This use of audio-visual aids is helpful if it assures student understanding. The class that is preparing a relief map becomes much more concerned with the exact location of mountain ranges than is another class which is looking at relief maps prepared by others. Similarly, the class that is dramatizing a meeting of union representatives and factory owners in an attempt to avoid a threatened strike may see more clearly how differently the same problem appears when seen from contrasting points of view.

Because these activities are ordinarily so time-consuming, the teacher must make certain that the values are worth the time expended. In some classes students spend a great deal of time preparing detailed maps, such as a series of maps depicting the territorial growth of the United States. Students may then spend more of their time trying to trace the outline from a textbook map than they do in visualizing the almost continuous expansion of the United States from its insecure footing on the Atlantic Coast to its present position as a dominant world power.

Superficial factors sometimes get far more attention than they deserve, and students who are preparing a scrapbook may spend a disproportionate amount of time preparing attractive titles and assembling enough clippings to make a bulky volume rather than in reading extensively in order to find the most appropriate selections to be included.

The construction of audio-visual material is sometimes so helpful a means of developing understanding and skill that it may be used as the center of a unit of work. A group of students who are building a hi-fi set together learn not only a great deal about science but also a great deal about themselves, too. When curriculum prescriptions make it impossible to include such activities within the school day, they may become worthwhile projects for cocurricular activities, as an assignment to be done at home, or as suggested activities for interested students. So long as these activities are considered as part of the curriculum, whether done in class or after school, the teacher must be certain that, in his eagerness to have his students create show pieces that will be commended when exhibited, he does not overlook the more important consideration of the contribution this type of activity makes to student growth as compared with the benefit students would receive if they spent their time differently.

Teacher Preparation and the Utilization of Materials

Recalling the relative rarity with which teachers used newer materials and community resources when he was in high school, the reader may wonder at the discrepancy between potential and utilization. Novelty and the lag between the invention of new devices and the training of personnel to use them are of course one reason. In the case of community resources, the additional problem of scheduling classes in departmentalized schools also helps explain infrequent use.

So far as the use of audio-visual materials is concerned, particularly those involving the use of machines, inadequacy of teacher preparation is the major reason for infrequent use, since many teachers now in service took their undergraduate training before newer materials and equipment were common. To make new teachers better prepared to use audio-visual materials, most teacher education institutions now offer courses or units of instruction in the use of these materials and equipment. In some colleges, a voluntary practicum is set up and students are invited to take advantage, on their own initiative, of opportunities to learn to operate equipment and develop materials.

The teacher who is well equipped as a modern professional practitioner will be familiar with the selection, use, and evaluation of materials. A film is not educational simply because it is listed in the educational film index. Educational value depends upon the basis of selection and the methods with which the materials are used.

Second, the teacher needs experience in handling material and equipment so that he feels at home with a projector or tape recorder. Fortunately, the operation of most audio-visual apparatus sold for classroom use is so simple that even a person with little mechanical ability can learn to use them with just a few hours of instruction. The apparent complexity of these machines awes teachers unnecessarily; and it is regrettable that many schools have motion picture projectors and tape recorders that are utilized infrequently because teachers have not learned to handle them with ease.

The operation of these machines does require practice so that the lesson is not bungled by the teacher's lack of experience in using the machine. Every teacher who is going to use any type of projector, whether it be a film strip projector or a sound motion picture machine, should become sufficiently familiar with the machine and with the manual that explains its operation so that the lesson itself can proceed smoothly, with the projector becoming an aid to instruction rather than a major classroom problem.

Finally, the teacher will find his use of materials more effective if he has some training in the production of materials himself and enjoys the satisfaction of making some of his own slides, films, or tapes. Suggestions for developing one's own aids may be found in a number of volumes that are available on the production of classroom films, recordings, and pictures for slides and filmstrips [4, 6, 10].

The wise use of audio-visual materials and community resources can enrich teaching tremendously. It also carries possibilities for challenging experiments in creative expression by students and teacher alike.

BASIC PROCEDURES IN USING AUDIO-VISUAL MATERIALS

The principles of effective learning apply as much to the use of audio-visual materials as to other ways of teaching. Participation by the student is always important and basic to learning. A lecture given by motion pictures or television is still a lecture. Unless the materials lead students to participate in activities which point toward achievement of the desired objectives, it is difficult to justify their use. A film on the framers of the Constitution should lead to discussion of the men and their influence on the document, to further research and study in printed materials, or to checking on the accuracy of the film itself. Televised performance of a science demonstration may lead to duplication of the experiment or extension of the principles involved in laboratory work by the students, if possible.

Materials must have a direct contribution to make to the work that is being done in class. The fact that a particular program is being telecast now or that a certain film is in the school building should not normally be used to justify interference with the learning program of the class. The word *normally* is used here because events of historic significance, for example, the address which a world leader is making before the United Nations Assembly, carry their own educational justification for interrupting the planned program. In general, however, the use of materials should be governed by the teacher's careful planning.

Steps in Utilizing Instructional Materials

The use of audio-visual materials or community resources ordinarily includes certain well-defined steps. First, is the selection of materials by the teacher. Good choices depend upon the teacher's clear view of learning objectives and the reasons for using the particular medium selected. Through preview, the teacher makes a critical appraisal of available films or recordings in terms of strengths, limitations, and relationship to the objectives of the lesson or unit in process. Visiting selected community resources in advance is the counterpart of the film preview in determining the potential value of a field trip or the invitation to a visitor to come to class.

When film previews are not possible, the teacher will find the *Educational Film Guide* [26] helpful because of its description and evaluation of most films listed. Arrangement is alphabetical both by title and subject headings and follows the Dewey system of classification. Monthly and cumulative supplements keep the *Guide* current. More specific assistance may be found in guides published by city and state departments of education, which often maintain film libraries, and in the catalogs published by the film centers maintained by numerous colleges and universities. Of particular value to the teacher are booklets listing audio-visual aids in particular subject fields published by professional associations like the National Council of Teachers of English and the National Council for the Social Studies. These guides are generally available in secondary school libraries or in the office of the audio-visual co-ordinator or the principal.

After selection, the next step is preparation of the learners. The teacher who is concerned with the effectiveness of materials is not satisfied with a simple statement such as, "Today we are going to see a film on atomic energy," or, "Tomorrow we will visit a pulp and paper mill; we will all meet at the Manor plant at 2:30 in front of the main gate." Preparation in either case includes careful formulation of objectives, possible student participation in planning, and preparation of key questions to direct student observation. The teacher explains technical or unfamiliar terms in advance and provides such additional information as may be needed for an effective learning experience. He asks the students to look for particular things—to identify with certain characters in a film, to look for signs of conservation practices in a visit to a logging operation, to listen for particular themes or instruments in a recording.

The third step is conducting the experience under the most favorable circumstances possible. Optimum conditions for showing projected pictures of various types will be discussed later in the chapter. Vision and hearing problems have to be considered in the use of audio-visual materials, but even more in the case of field trips. Frequently it is necessary to divide the class into a number of small groups if each student is to see and hear in industrial plants or out in the open. If libraries or museums are to be used, appropriate arrangements have to be made in advance. When guide service is not available, the teacher has to make sure that he and the persons assisting him have the necessary background and explanatory materials. Most important, the teacher must never abdicate his leadership responsibilities to a projector whose lamp may fail, to a projectionist who doesn't appear, or to a person in the community who has something significant to share with students but does not have the teacher's know-how in the presentation of material to a group of adolescents and the stimulation of purposeful discussion.

Follow-up

The fourth phase is the follow-up activities which provide for thought, discussion, and application of what has been encountered. When audio-visual sessions or field trips are successful, they are the beginning rather than the end of the students' contact with the material. The questions that students ask after such a session should be better and more numerous than were the questions they asked during the preparatory discussions. The teacher can stimulate students to ask questions by helping them to understand the purpose of the specific activity and by assisting them to formulate the key questions to be used as a basis for guiding the students' observation during the session. The teacher's attitude toward the comments made by students is an important influence in creating an inquiring frame of mind.

The first step in the follow-up activities is to provide students with an opportunity to discuss the questions they themselves want to ask about what they have seen and heard. There are often points that they did not understand and that should be cleared up immediately. This follow-up session should also include adequate provision for discussing the key questions in order to see whether they are in a better position to answer them now than they were before the film, recording, or field trip.

Unless they do use what they learn during these sessions, little will be retained for any appreciable length of time. When these more dramatic activities are included because the students need them in connection with the work they are doing, what the students learn from these sessions should be used in subsequent class activities. Even though no specific follow-up activities be planned, students can use what they have seen and heard as they continue their study of a problem. A visit to a lumber mill, for example, may be referred to over and over again as a source of illustrations in connection with discussion on related topics.

The follow-up activities can be important in their own right rather than only as a means of assuring retention. The class that visits a sawmill may be so impressed by the many precautions taken to prevent accidents that they go on to study how accidents can be prevented in homes and in industry. In doing so, they are investigating a problem that is so important as to need no other justification. Similarly, boys and girls who admire a collection of Chinese ivory carvings in a museum exhibition and then return to school to try their hand at carving chalk and wood are using their trip as a means of stimulating artistic expression that is itself satisfying.

One of the limitations of the prescribed curriculum is that it is often too inelastic to make full use of the new interests and the unexpected questions that arise when concrete experiences are used effectively. Under these circumstances teachers may have to curtail the scope of follow-up activities or use them in a cocurricular program. If no provision at all is made for using the results of an audio-visual session once it has been concluded, one may well question the necessity for having shown a film or taken a trip.

Finally, the teacher and students have to know whether the experience has borne fruit. What has been learned? How far has the experience brought the class and individuals in it toward achievement of learning objectives? Could learning have been facilitated through other methods? How might the same method be used more successfully another time?

Too often, use of the audio-visual aid or community resource fails to meet standards of maximum efficiency. This is partially due to the lingering pattern of textbook reading, memorization, recitation, and testing as the primary teaching method. Pictures, sound transcriptions, and field trips do not fit into this mould (and there are better ways of using printed materials, too). Neglect to adapt procedures in keeping with different materials of instruction fails to capitalize on the full potential of the newer media. A parallel may be found in the original design of automobiles or horseless carriages. Use of the newer motive power made it possible to change the design of the vehicle; conversely, changed design was necessary to utilize the full potential of the gasoline engine. Proper use of newer instructional materials, also, depends on change in the design of a lesson meant originally for mastery of the limited material in a single text.

VISUAL AIDS

The Chalkboard

Some visual aids are readily accessible and can be used even by a teacher who feels completely frustrated in the presence of a machine. The chalkboard, for example, has been with us for many years, even though we find it in a number of new and pleasing variations from the old blackboard of slate or painted wood. Pastel shades have been introduced to overcome the loss of light in a room that results from use of the highly light-absorptive blackboard, to reduce glare which obstructs vision on a slate blackboard from certain angles in a room, to eliminate sharp contrast between dark and light in the room, and to improve the aesthetics of the classroom environment. Because of the reduced contrast between the chalk and the board, teachers in rooms with pastel chalkboards must be particularly careful to check visibility, from time to time, of the material on the board and to see that the board is washed frequently.

The chalkboard is the teacher's aid that has the greatest flexibility and utility. It can serve to record ideas as they are being developed; it is a convenient place for reminders to the students and for assignments; it provides a surface on which to build outlines; it is a wonderful exercise board for working through and correcting problems of written expression, mathematics, science, and almost any other subject.

Teachers often find that they can do more than write words and sentences on the chalkboard. Use of stick-figures and diagrams of various kinds helps to make an "artist" even of the teacher who firmly denies any artistic ability. In classes where the same figure is used again and again, the teacher may find it useful to make or to secure patterns of triangles, circles, test tubes, retorts, or outline maps that may be traced quickly.

There are precautions to be observed in using the chalkboard. First, visibility from all parts of the room should not be assumed without the teacher's checking it from time to time as he moves about the room. Glare from certain angles indicates the need to adjust window shades. Lack of contrast between chalk and the board suggests the need to clean the board more thoroughly, to write with a heavier stroke, or to increase the size of the characters. Second, the board should not be used to present long selections, outlines, or passages which the students spend long periods in copying. Material of this kind, if needed, should be duplicated and distributed to the class. Third, to avoid losing eye-contact with students, teachers should learn to write while facing the class or at least looking at the students. Fourth, the chalkboard is meant to be flexible space. It should not be sacrificed to permanent displays marked, "Do Not Erase." Notices and posters should be mounted on bulletin boards or other spaces in the room, with the chalkboard reserved for more spontaneous use.

Flat Pictures, Charts, and Diagrams

Flat pictures offer to the teacher a medium of illustration which is uncomplicated, easily available, and highly effective. Pictures have an advantage over other visual devices in the emphasis they give to key ideas and impressions. They are not limited to a fleeting glimpse as the projector grinds on, but they lend themselves to detailed individual study. In addition, pictures may be found to cover almost any topic.

The vertical files of the school library or community public library are often rich reservoirs of flat pictures which may be borrowed for periods up to one month. Often these pictures are simply but securely mounted and need only be fixed in place. In planning work for a new unit, the teacher should consult the school and community librarians to discover available materials. In addition, some schools and communities make available on a loan basis prints of well-known paintings which make an aesthetic contribution to the classroom environment even though not directly related to the units being studied.

That some visual aids are expensive or difficult to secure sometimes obscures the fact that other visual aids are easily accessible and just as helpful. Textbook illustrations are sometimes excellent instructional aids that are not used often or fully enough. The teacher can prepare his own file of illustrative materials by cutting pictures from books and magazines and then mounting them on cardboard so that they can be projected onto a screen by using an opaque projector. Newspaper and magazine advertisements often contain pictures that should form part of the visual aids collection available for class use. Industrial firms frequently make available single picture or poster series that deal with manufacturing processes or raw materials. For example, an excellent series on forest conservation is distributed by a large timber company.

Selection of pictures should be made on a basis of enhancing the learning process rather than simply adding a bright spot on a blank wall. First, the picture should make a specific contribution to the learning task at hand. Second, it should be large enough and clear enough to be seen and studied from a reasonable distance. Third, the picture should have artistic qualities that command interest. Fourth, the picture must be accurate both in the general impression it leaves and in the detail it includes.

Special purposes in using charts. Charts and posters used in the classroom may be employed as a means of summarizing information to which constant reference is made and also as a means of stressing a point of which the students need to be reminded. These purposes are so different that they require different kinds of charts. A chart that is designed for reference uses, such as a periodic table chart in chemistry, may contain a great deal of information, although the lettering should never be so crowded or so small as not to be readily legible. On the other hand, a chart or a poster that is being used to remind students of some one important point should have relatively little writing so that the one point to be stressed will be emphasized.

Most teachers feel that charts are not being used economically unless every inch is covered with written material. As a result, most classroom charts are so full that nothing is emphasized. The teacher can learn much about the construction of a classroom chart by examining the advertisements in newspapers and magazines. Our classroom charts resemble the kind of advertisement that appeared in magazines fifty years ago, when the advertiser filled up an entire page with closely printed material. Today, on the other hand, advertisers think nothing of paying $10,000 for a page in a magazine with nation-wide circulation on which only three or four words appear in addition to the picture of the product.

The typewriting teacher, for example, who prepares charts as guides to good typing, ordinarily lists on one chart all of the wisdom that can possibly be compressed within the few square inches that are available. It is more helpful to prepare several charts, each stressing one principle, than to incorporate all of them in a single chart.

Because anything that is seen too often becomes too familiar to be effective, charts should be changed as frequently as necessary rather than be permitted to hang until they become yellow with the dignity of age. As class needs and interests change, charts, too, should be changed.

The Bulletin Board

The classroom bulletin board should be used by teacher and students for posting pictures, clippings, and notices that are related to their present interests and activity. Using a classroom bulletin board effectively implies that more will be done with it than simply reserving space where anyone who wants to may post anything there and have it stay forever. It is advisable to have a student committee in charge of the bulletin board to see that the posted material is arranged attractively and that the bulletin board does not become so cluttered with outdated material that nothing that is posted attracts attention any longer. In even the busiest classes, students should have time to read the bulletin board material, lest it degenerate into becoming a useless piece of school equipment.

The bulletin board is far more than an exhibit case when it is used as an important way of teaching. Most city children, for example, think of agriculture in terms of the stories of farm life they read in their primary grade days. They still think of a fictional farm run by kindly grandparents, with the possible assistance of a hired hand, and on which there are some cows, chickens, and pigs. These youngsters know nothing of the agricultural revolution which introduced heavy machinery and makes liberal use of chemicals. A series of pictures showing a rig and tractor which can spread fertilizer over one hundred acres in ten hours, a mechanical cotton picker which yields a greater harvest at a fraction of the cost of hand-picked cotton, planes which spray insecticide over twenty acres on one trip, and animal dips which add pounds to each animal by ridding him of insect pests will teach city students a great deal about the magnitude of agricultural operations today and it can get boys and girls to start asking questions that will lead to greater understanding.

Projected Pictures

The opaque projector. An extension of the flat picture is the projected image. One useful device is the opaque projector into which a flat picture or page may be inserted for projection onto a screen. This machine is particularly helpful when the picture is too small to be seen by the total group without magnification, or when it is available only in a book or magazine which should not be torn apart. The opaque projector is a boon to teachers when they want the class to focus attention on a piece of work done by one of the students—a picture, a composition, a diagram, a poem. Unfortunately, the opaque projector requires total darkness and often the light control in a classroom is not adequate to permit effective utilization.

The overhead projector. The overhead projector is a most useful and little used projector, especially in mathematics and the sciences. Since the room does not have to be totally dark, the picture or chart that is being projected can be used as the basis for classroom discussion and students can take notes. It saves the time that must otherwise be spent in writing complex formulas or drawing charts on the chalkboard. Moreover, by projecting a single large image that the entire class can see at one time, the teacher can prevent or correct the misunderstandings that may arise when each student turns to the picture or diagram in his own textbook and is looking at one part of the picture while the teacher is referring to another part.

There are other advantages, too, in the overhead projector. Since the machine projects through transparent paper, the teacher can write on the paper and have the image projected for the whole class to see. Moreover, the teacher can do the writing without turning his back on his students or losing contact with them. Thus, he can draw a graph or solve an equation which all will see, and still be facing his class. The transparent paper has another advantage in that one sheet can be superimposed upon another. A social studies teacher can project a map of Africa and then superimpose another map showing how the continent was divided into colonies by the various European powers or a map indicating the transition from colonies to independent nations. Since the overhead projector reproduces all colors, it is also useful when many-colored diagrams are used as in a science class.

The slide projector. More frequently used is the slide projector, either for the older 3¼" x 4" "lantern" slide or the 2" x 2" photographic slide (35 mm.). Both of these may be used well in only partial darkness, permitting the student to take notes or write brief answers to questions while the slide is being shown. The larger slide has the advantage of being easily prepared by teachers or students. Pictures, diagrams, test questions, and literary selections can be drawn or typed on glass or cellophane and then be projected in the classroom. Clear or etched glass slides are commercially available and usable with India ink or special grease pencils of many colors. For typed or handwritten material, the teacher can secure special cellophane slides or improvise them by folding a piece of carbon paper over both sides of a piece of colorless or yellow cellophane. He then writes or types so that the carbon impression comes out on both sides of the cellophane and affixes his homemade slide to a cardboard frame 3¼" x 4" which will fit in the usual lantern slide projector.

Filmstrip. The 2" x 2" slide projector which accommodates 35 mm. slides is generally equipped with an attachment for showing filmstrips as well. Filmstrips at reasonable cost are available in every subject area. Catalogs of filmstrips in the possession of the school, school district, or film center supplying the school are usually available in the library, or in the principal's or audio-visual co-ordinator's office. In addition, the teacher can organize his own transparencies and have a strip produced at relatively low cost.

The filmstrip has the advantage of presenting a learning experience through still pictures. The teacher is free to adjust the speed of viewing to the ability and needs of the class. He can make as many or as few comments as he wishes, passing quickly over frames that are of lesser significance. He is freer to adapt the material to the learning situation than he is in the case of a motion picture whose speed, sequence, and commentary are not adaptable. Of course, the filmstrip is a series of "stills"; it cannot depict motion. Also, the sequence is fixed, and while the teacher can go back to earlier frames if he wishes, he cannot reorganize the order in which the frames are presented.

AUDITORY AIDS

Recent years have brought many new uses of sound equipment to the classroom, just as newer devices have broadened the possibilities of use. Public address systems, tape recorders, and dictating machines have added to the potential of the record player and radio.

Records have been used for some time as direct means of instruction and as inspirational devices in the study of literature, music, foreign languages, physical education, and commercial subjects. New teachers are often surprised to discover the variety of recorded poems, speeches, and drama available to them in teaching English and social studies.

Radio

A few commercial radio programs are produced especially for class listening during school time and several of the larger school systems operate their own radio or broadcast over commercial facilities. It is sometimes difficult to use the radio as a classroom aid because teachers do not have sufficient advance information of radio programs and because radio programs often occur at inconvenient times. A dramatic presention of the fight against yellow fever does not contribute much to a class discussion if presented when the students are discussing inflation. Any teacher who takes the trouble to communicate with the local radio station, however, can learn very quickly how he can get advance notice of programs in which his class is likely to be interested.

The large broadcasting chains have educational advisers who prepare material designed specifically to increase the use of radio in the classroom. Every school should receive such teaching aids and program notes as are prepared under the supervision of the educational advisers of the major radio networks and of some independent stations. Some programs can be listened to effectively with only a minor readjustment of class schedules. In other instances the teacher may find it better to use recordings of radio programs which can be played back at a time when they fit in best with the classroom needs. Some transcriptions are made available by the radio stations for purchase or rental; others, by visual and auditory aids libraries.

The Tape Recorder

The arrival on the school scene of the tape recorder has made inexpensive recording of significant programs possible right in the school. In some cases this is done through the master controls in the school public address system and played back to specific classes when requested during the day. In others it is done by the audio-visual co-ordinator at a teacher's request. This simple system of recording adds to the effectiveness of the transcription system in countering one of radio's chief limitations as an educational device—the ephemeral nature of programs which never seem to be broadcast at the right time for the right class.

The tape recorder and other dictating systems have other important values. A class discussion can be recorded and played back to help the class evaluate its pattern of discussion or to review the agreements that were reached. In correcting speech defects when learning a new language, one of the important elements is the student's hearing of his own speech. Cheap, erasable recording is again an answer. In the learning of foreign languages, the conventional record through which the student can hear over and over again the correct and authentic speech patterns of another country is supplemented by the student's taping of his own pronunciation and hearing it played back. The tape recorder is the heart of the modern language laboratory that many schools have installed to assist in the teaching of foreign languages. The tape recorder also provides a medium for making and editing committee reports which sometimes "culminate" an activity, reports which can be easily and discerningly pared down when committee members listen to their own performance and edit it carefully for presentation to the class. Revision of one's own work is one of the most difficult skills to teach. The recorder used in this way is a valuable aid in learning competence in editing, particularly when reinforced by group endeavor.

MOTION PICTURES AND TELEVISION

Motion pictures and television combine the strengths of pictured illustration and of sound to give the appearance of action, movement, and greater verisimilitude. At its best, educational television can go beyond the motion picture by giving the viewer a feeling of personal involvement, here and now.

Showing a Motion Picture

Much the same sort of questions must be considered in the preparation for a motion picture presentation as in planning for use of other visual aids. The teacher who is planning to show a motion picture film should ask himself: If I were one of my students, would I want to see this film? Which questions will be most helpful as preparation for viewing the film? How can I make certain that no untoward disciplinary difficulties will interfere with the effectiveness of the motion picture film? How can we follow-up the film so that the boys and girls will not regard it as little more than a pleasant change from more strenuous classroom activities?

To illustrate how these questions are answered we shall examine how a motion picture film on the production and distribution of milk was shown to a junior high school social studies class.*

Preparation for the showing of a film. The boys and girls in this class were studying their community and were discussing the ways in which the federal, state, and municipal governments co-operated in safeguarding the health of the people by inspecting the food supply. With the glibness of those who do not appreciate that the protection of public health is more than a matter of promulgating regulations, the boys and girls spoke of the work of federal meat inspectors and local board of health agents. Nowhere was there any indication that the students realized that these men were people and not just symbols on a chart, and that the protection of the food supply was more than another topic for class discussion.

In order to help these boys and girls to visualize the problems they

---

* How effectively a motion picture can be used as a method of teaching is indicated cleverly in a motion picture which has as its theme the question of teaching teachers how to use films. This film, *Using the Classroom Film* [24], depicts a classroom in which the pupils are studying the problems of American agriculture and shows how a motion picture film on wheat farming is presented to the class.

were discussing, the teacher asked them how many quarts of milk their families purchased daily. They soon found that the average for that class was about two quarts for each family and that their class of thirty-five accounted for some eighteen gallons of milk a day. When they were reminded of the number of classes in their school and did some rapid computation, they were impressed by the amount of milk it took to meet the needs of just those families which had children attending that one school. Thinking of their town as a whole, they estimated the daily milk needs. To these boys and girls, the number of gallons of milk consumed in their town seemed fantastically large. When the teacher read them a table of the volume of milk received daily in their town during the preceding week, they found that their estimate was not high enough because they had ignored the uses of milk in the preparation of ice cream, pastries, butter, cheese, and other milk products.

It was at this point that the teacher asked how it was possible to supply huge quantities of milk of such unquestioned purity that they never hesitated before drinking the milk set before them. They now spoke of the inspection of milk with a better understanding of the immensity and the importance of the problem. As they were discussing the various points at which lax inspection could lead to catastrophe, one of the students asked whether they could all go down to visit the local milk pasteurization and bottling plant. The class, remembering how much they had enjoyed a trip taken the preceding month, gladly accepted the suggestion of another trip.

The teacher pointed out that such a visit, although it undoubtedly would be instructive, could not tell them the whole story because it would not, for example, show how the milk supply is guarded at its source, the many dairy farms that sold the milk to the pasteurization plant. He told them of a motion picture that presented the whole story of milk and asked whether that did not seem to be a more promising source of information. Even those who had suggested the trip agreed that it would be better to see a film of the whole process than to visit a plant that performed only one or two of the operations.

Since it would take about a week to secure the film, the teacher suggested that they keep a record of the questions they wanted to ask so that they could remember these questions a week or so later when they saw the film. Each student copied the questions, which ranged from that of the testing of cows for tuberculosis to the process of homogenizing milk.

The film to which the teacher referred was one he had heard of but had never seen. Produced by a local dairy, it was distributed gratis to schools and civic organizations as indirect advertising. The film was ordered by the school for the first date on which this film and the school projector would both be available, some ten days from the date of the class discussion referred to above.

Students learn in many ways.

*Closed circuit television enables college students
to observe an elmentary school class.*

**The development of electronics has enriched
the resources the teacher has available.**

*Students using tape recorders
in a language laboratory.*

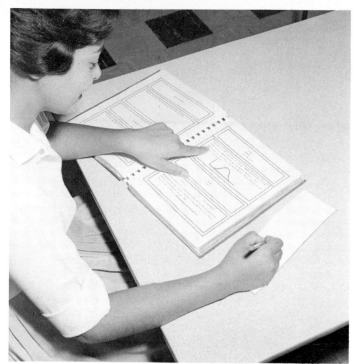

Teaching Machines, Inc.

Will the development of programmed textbooks and teaching machines broaden or narrow the scope of secondary education?

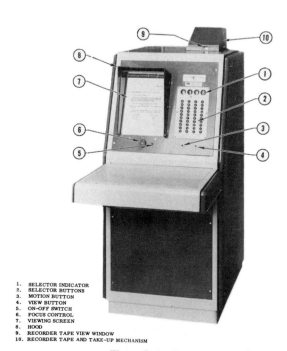

1. SELECTOR INDICATOR
2. SELECTOR BUTTONS
3. MOTION BUTTON
4. VIEW BUTTON
5. ON-OFF SWITCH
6. FOCUS CONTROL
7. VIEWING SCREEN
8. HOOD
9. RECORDER TAPE VIEW WINDOW
10. RECORDER TAPE AND TAKE-UP MECHANISM

Western Design, Division of U. S. Industries, Inc.

Learning occurs in the classroom and outside it, too.

When the film arrived at the school on the day preceding the scheduled showing, the teacher previewed it alone after school. The film was good, being both instructive and enjoyable, but it included a number of scenes that he thought might lead to unpleasant comments from some of the sophisticated boys and girls. The film itself was in good taste, but the teacher knew there would be giggling and laughter when they saw the close-up shots of the washing and drying of the cow's udders before milking began. Forewarned, he knew he could control the situation, and he went on to list the questions which he, after having seen the film, wanted to add to those the students had listed the preceding week.

Showing the film. Just before the class met on the day of the film showing, the teacher threaded the film in the machine so that as much of the class time as possible would be free for discussion. As the students entered the room, he assigned some to take care of the lights, the shades, and the portable screen.

Before the film was shown, he asked the students to consult their notebooks to review their list of key questions they hoped to have answered by the film. Grouping the questions into categories, they wanted to know how the purity of milk was safeguarded on the farm, en route to the town, in the pasteurization plant, and in the process of distribution to the consumer. Stressing the need for cleanliness and good health on the part of all who took part in the process, the teacher advised the students to see how these two factors were safeguarded at every step. He told them that there would be little sense in scrubbing the milk pails if the milking machines were filthy or if the cows themselves were dirty as they came from the pasture. Because everything had to be spotlessly clean, the cows' udders had to be washed and dried as carefully as the tank cars were cleaned.

The room was darkened and the film began. Interested though the teacher was in having his class benefit as much as possible from the film, he was careful not to interrupt by speaking. After all, a motion picture that is properly produced has a unity of its own. For the teacher to interrupt the presentation by asking a question may interfere so much with the effectiveness of the picture as to detract more than it contributes. Accordingly, the teacher said nothing during the film, not even during the brief comic relief touches when he felt tempted to use these few moments to explain the more serious part of the presentation. He was relieved to note that the emotional tone he had helped to create during the introductory discussion was a serious one and that the milking scenes were not accompanied by any untoward comments.

The follow-up activities. When the showing was concluded, the boys and girls who had taken care of the lights, shades, and screen at the beginning of the period quickly reconverted the room to a classroom again and some fifteen minutes of the period remained for a discussion that could be continued the next day if necessary. Several of the students asked questions, most of which were answered by other students or the teacher. Two of the questions called for further information. A girl volunteered to go to the library that afternoon to try to get the answer to the first question and a boy who lived near the pasteurization and bottling plant was asked to see whether he could get the answer to the second one by inquiring at the plant office.

One of the girls remarked skeptically that the film was nothing but advertising for the milk company that had produced the film and that had its name mentioned prominently several times in the commentary. They discussed this point and agreed that, though the company deserved commendation for its care in the handling of the milk, much that was shown in the film was equally true of all other milk companies in the area.

After these questions had been taken care of, the students turned to the questions they had listed before seeing the film. During the discussion they were able to answer all but two of these questions and agreed that they needed more information for these, information that could be secured by library research.

Other Classroom Uses of Films

Motion pictures are used not only to present information but also to develop attitudes and appreciation. The Orson Welles *Julius Caesar* or the Olivier *Hamlet* are not presented to review the plots of these tragedies, although they accomplish this purpose, too. Their important contribution lies in bringing these plays to life and in securing their full emotional impact. Some of this excitement and understanding comes also from recordings such as the *Mercury* Shakespeare sets, but sight added to sound has a tremendous advantage. If often takes the reading of a great actor to give meaning to the lines themselves.

In social studies, also, the movie version of a book like Edna Ferber's *Cimarron* gives reality to the opening of the west. Even the sentimentality of *The Best Years of Our Lives*, a film about World War II, gives young people a feeling for the significance to people of involvement of their country in war.

Television

The development of television has led to a great flurry of experimentation in educational television. The need for significant research in this field is such that the process of plan-trial-evaluation will continue for many years before conclusive evidence will be available. Many classroom teachers will probably be involved in one way or another in some of this research.

There are several kinds of television with which we are concerned in schools. Commercial television programs will be discussed in the section on appreciation which follows. The present section includes direct efforts at educational television through broadcast and through closed circuits. Broadcast television refers to programs that are transmitted through space either by commercial or educational channels and are available for anyone to pick up who is within range of the transmitter. Closed circuit television is transmitted by cable from a transmitter in the school building or associated facility directly to receivers in the school or vicinity. Only those sets connected by cable to the transmitter can receive the programs. Closed circuit programs may, therefore, be specifically geared to the needs of one or more classes.

Television as teaching. It is important that we recognize the distinction between *televised instruction* and *instructional television.* In televised instruction, we have a classroom teacher performing before a television camera as though he were teaching a class. In some instances, there actually is a class before the teacher as the camera telecasts the picture and the sound to other audiences. While some of these telecast lessons are extremely useful, they fail to take advantage of the facilities that television offers to the teacher. Why should the teacher act as though there were no camera present? Why should he proceed as though he were limited to the resources available to a teacher in an ordinary classroom? How can he overcome his inability to see how his students are reacting to what is being said and their inability to ask questions of him as the lesson is developed?

On the other hand, instructional television should recognize the uniqueness of television as a mode of communication and seek to make maximum use of its instructional potential without regard to older standards which are appropriate for teaching which was limited to earlier means of communication. One obvious difference lies in the fact that instruction has in the past been primarily geared to words, to verbal symbols. Television makes possible a program of instruction which is primarily visual.

Televised instruction starts off from one of two premises—that teaching may be done directly (the television program replacing the teacher in whole or in part), or that the new medium is *supplementary* to the efforts of the teacher, bringing into the classroom what could not be done otherwise, but not attempting to substitute for the teacher. Some current experimentation indicates that television may serve both purposes. Where the teaching task is seen as *presentation* and the learning task as absorption, skillful television performance by a trained actor using a wealth of instructional aids may be considered quite successful. Where teaching is viewed as eliciting *participation* by the learner, it seems that a technique which is primarily presentational is limited in its effect.

Many of the comparisons being made have to be scrutinized carefully, so that a straw man is not set up in either case. Good television has to be compared with good teaching. If the teaching is simply a lecture, reason indicates the potential superiority of a device which can marshal much greater resources than a lecturer in a classroom. But objectives have to be kept in view and the presentational superiority of television has to be compared with the participational superiority of classroom teaching when property conducted.

Television as supplementation. In terms of supplementing the teacher's efforts, there seem to be no limits to the value of television. Study of mass production can be accompanied by a television visit to a factory which overcomes problems of class scheduling, transportation, inadequate preparation or guide service, and the noise of machinery that sometimes defeats the purpose of the visit. The Security Council of the United Nations can come into the classroom. The science teacher demonstrating dissection of an animal can have tiny parts and intricate operations picked up by his closed-circuit camera and enlarged for the whole class (or several classes) to see on television screens. The small school which cannot offer advanced sciences, higher mathematics, and a variety of foreign languages may be able to tune into an educational network which can improve vastly on the correspondence courses which its students now take. The inspiration of great figures in science, literature, the arts, and political life can be brought into the classroom.

New developments with video tape also bring onto the horizon a promise of overcoming the ephemeral nature of television broadcasts similar to the contribution of tape recording in making radio programs available at the time a particular class needs it. At present the video tape recorder is still fabulously expensive (in terms of school budgets), but we have reassuring experience from the history of other great inventions that eventually production costs will be lowered. When relatively inexpensive video recording becomes possible, schools will be able to tape worthwhile presentations to be played back over television receivers on closed circuits whenever and wherever desired.

In the meantime, program materials similar to those produced by radio stations and networks are being made available to the schools by television broadcasters. Networks and program sponsors prepare advance program information, and in some cases guides to viewing, which help the teacher in selecting programs and in preparing his class for them. In addition, kinescopes (filmed records of programs to be played back through motion picture machines) are made of some programs and stocked by film libraries for loan or rental by schools. The kinescope corresponds to the radio transcription in making possible the viewing of a program from the past at a time when it is most useful in the course of a class's studies.

The arrival of television in the schools brings with it the prospect of change in the role of the teacher, in methods of teaching, in the curriculum, school administration, and the planning of school buildings. Valid principles of teaching will apply in this medium as in others, but it is inevitable that with increasing experience in educational television will come marked changes in the technique of teaching on television.

Meanwhile, certain principles seem to be valid. Teachers who have television available to them will find the suggested steps for use of any audio-visual materials meaningful: selection by the teacher, preparation of the students, viewing the program with specific purposes in mind, follow-up, and evaluation. The need to make learning an active process is great, and so is the need to avoid the assumption that seeing is learning. Questions have to be stimulated to make certain that full understanding takes place. For learning to be effective and retained, use of the concepts or skills televised must follow the presentation in short order.

Appreciation of Motion Pictures and Television

For the next decade, television will be used in most schools as radio has been in the past. Students will be asked to view particular programs at home and to use this as motivation or content in learning. This is one reason why teachers have to be concerned with development of critical appreciation of television. A second and no less important reason is the recognition that students spend so much of their lives in front of television sets and will continue to do so, though at a reduced rate, as adults.

Persons who believe that the school has a responsibility to improve use of leisure time take seriously the teaching of appreciation in the various communication media and performing arts. The English teacher has done this for generations with respect to literature and drama and, we hope, will continue to do so. In all candor, however, we have to recognize that almost all adults make greater use of television, radio, motion pictures, and newspapers than they do of books and the theater. Raising the standards of the communication and performing arts involves raising the expectations of the audience with respect to what is produced. To a great extent this is the job of English, art, and music teachers, but teachers in all fields can help students to seek and to demand motion pictures and broadcasts that have meaning and content occasionally related to their field of interest. Definition of "entertainment" as a placid, passive way of spending time can be changed to include something more dynamic and satisfying if teachers throughout the country can educate generations of students who will want to continue their science, home economic, history, and government experiences in their leisure time. To the teachers falls the challenge to create a demand for "nonfiction" in the mass media as well as in libraries.

REALIA AND COMMUNITY RESOURCES

Another type of instructional material with high potential is the world of real things. This we call *realia,* objects which students can handle or can see either in their actual environment or in special displays. One form of realia consists of the things that one may find in classroom museums and exhibits which are useful aids to learning.

Students should be encouraged to bring to school things they have at home or that they have constructed which are related to the work being done in class. The boys and girls in a French class, for example, may be able to supply a wide variety of articles that were imported from France. The teacher can supplement students' contributions by exhibiting articles that he owns or has borrowed. As a useful precaution, it is wise not to include valuable or extremely fragile articles unless there is adequate provision for safe storage and exhibition. Like the classroom bulletin board, the classroom museum should have a live collection that reflects the current activities and interests of the boys and girls in the class.

Of even greater significance is the community of which the school is a part. The community can be brought into the classroom through invitations to visitors who have special knowledge or competencies which they are willing to share with adolescents. In addition, students can go out into the community to see it at work and at play, to observe its government in operation, and to study the many social institutions which function.

The school should have a file of community resources which can serve in either capacity. In addition to this, the teacher will build his own listing of persons who have something special to contribute in his area and of places that may be visited with good results. The foreign language teacher will look for persons who are natives of countries where his language is spoken. They can help the class understand other peoples and their customs, and they can furnish a model of native speech. The science teacher will be interested in industrial, governmental, and educational laboratories in the community and in technical applications of pertinent scientific principles. Professional persons with background in science or government have much to offer for classes in science and the social studies. Newspapermen, authors, and dramatics groups can contribute to the English classes. The reader can probably extend this list much farther by thinking of persons in a normal community who will have considerable background in his subject area.

Field Trips to Community Resources

Of especial interest to students is the observation of important subjects of study in their own environment. Modern transportation facilities make it possible for the teacher to use the entire community as his laboratory. Though most teachers can only envy their colleagues in other schools who accompany their students on extensive tours of the country, few teachers take advantage of all the resources available to classes that can make only short trips by school bus or public transportation. These trips can contribute so much to the development of our boys and girls that they deserve the careful planning they need if they are to be more than pleasant excursions.

Although each visit is different from every other visit and a trip to an industrial plant is obviously different from one to a museum, there is a general pattern that underlies the preparation for all visits. As an illustration of the way in which class trips should be planned, we shall note the activities of a junior high school teacher and his class who took advantage of the fact that a dress factory some forty minutes away by bus conducted visitors on tours of the plant.

There are three major phases that the teacher must plan. For him the key questions are: What kind of preparation should be made for this visit? What should the students and I do while visiting the plant? How can we follow-up the visit to gain maximum benefit from it?

The preparation for the trip. Before the teacher can plan for a class visit to the dress factory, he must know enough about the plant to be able to exploit fully the contribution such a visit can make to the development of his students. If at all possible, the teacher should visit the plant in advance of the class visit. As the teacher makes this preliminary visit, he must ask himself such questions as: If I were one of my students, would I want to make this visit with the class? What can these boys and girls gain from a visit to this plant? Which parts of the plant will offer most to the students? Which questions will be most helpful as guides for their observation during the visit? How can I make certain that these students will conduct themselves properly on the visit? Are any administrative problems presented by the visit? How can we follow up this visit in such a way that students will consider it as more than just a pleasant way of spending an afternoon out of school?

So far as the preparation of students for the visit goes, it is important that all students know not only what they are going to see, but also why the visit is being made. For some visits, students need a better background if the visit is to be worthwhile. The teacher who has been to a plant may know the various operations in the manufacturing process. He may know something about the occupational hazards that are involved and of the specifications that must be met by the product. A class that makes a visit with a richer background will be in a better position to understand what it has seen than is another class which comes with all the openness of an empty mind.

Foreseeing problems and attending to details. The preparation for a visit consists of more than indicating the reason for the visit and the questions to be answered. There are also disciplinary and administrative matters to be considered. A teacher who takes thirty-five boys and girls on a trip through an industrial plant accepts a serious responsibility for their safety. He also has to be certain that their conduct at the plant will be such as to reflect credit on themselves and the school and to make it possible for other classes to make similar visits in the future. Like all other educative experiences, a class excursion should contribute its share toward teaching students how to meet the social need of getting along with other people.

The teacher must anticipate the difficulties that are likely to arise and he must discuss with the class the etiquette appropriate for such a visit. Adolescents are mature enough to understand that there are some questions that are asked better when they discuss the visit in class than when asked of a foreman at the plant. While the teacher is not going to ask secondary students to walk through the streets in columns of two, and to maintain silence en route, the students should understand that the very size of the group imposes limitations on the way in which they walk through the street or ride in buses. Many of the annoying situations that arise during a trip can be anticipated if the students are impressed with their share of the responsibility for self-control.

Administrative problems, too, cannot be ignored. The teacher must be certain that the plant will be open at the time of the visit. He has to know what arrangements are available for luncheon and what transportation facilities can be used. So far as the school is concerned, he will have to inform the principal of the visit, and in some instances, ask permission to take the class out of school. If the visit is to be made during school time, the teacher will have to make the necessary arrangements for having his students excused from the other classes that will be missed, as well as providing for those members of his group who cannot join the class on the trip.

Most school systems require that a parent indicate in writing that he is willing to have his son or daughter go on this specific excursion. If such a note is required by the school, the teacher should not waive this letter of consent, no matter how appealing the student or how extenuating the circumstances. Though the accident rate of school excursions is fortunately very low, even one accident in a teaching career is enough to convince any teacher that he should never take the chance of having a student accompany the class unless all the legal requirements have been met.

The trip. The second phase of the lesson is the visit itself. What should the teacher do while the class is visiting the factory? The answer depends very largely on the facilities that are available. Some institutions provide guide service so that once the class is at the plant, a special guide takes over the direction of the visit. On other visits the teacher serves as guide. Regardless of whether the teacher or a person at the plant is the guide, the value a class can gain from a visit depends on what it sees and on whether it knows what to look for.

It is more common for a class to try to see too much than too little. Once the teacher has arranged for a trip, he wants his class to see everything possible. If the visit is to be more than a sight-seeing tour, it is being conducted with specific purposes in mind, purposes that should limit the scope of the visit.

Pupil activity is important on a visit, as it is in all kinds of learning. The interrogative sentence should be used more frequently than the declarative sentence, even at the plant. Instead of pointing to so many things, it is better to ask questions that will direct students' attention to specific conditions. For example, rather than tell them that this man is cutting twenty layers of cloth at one time, it may be better to ask how he can cut so many layers of cloth at one time and yet follow the pattern created by the designer.

If a guide is available, students should be encouraged to ask questions while there is someone who can answer them correctly rather than to save these questions for class discussion later. If there are several key questions that the students are expected to keep in mind during the visit, it may be desirable for the teacher to ask these questions from time to time while they are at the plant, so that students may remember that they are interested not only in watching the machines turning rapidly but also in observing the kind of work that is done by the people who tend the machines.

Follow-up activities. The follow-up activities are the most important phase of a trip, for it is these follow-up activities that do so much to determine what lasting value the visit will have. Now that the class has been to see this factory, what use can it make of this experience? If the trip is at all worthwhile, the students will have many questions that they will want to ask. It is desirable to have these questions asked early in the classroom discussion. Some of the questions they will ask can be answered quickly by other members of the group or by the teacher; other questions will call for further research. The student who asks how the factory deals with accidental injuries when high speed machines are used may get his answer quickly. On the other hand, the student who asks how it is possible for women to differ so much in the dresses they wear when factories produce hundreds of identical dresses at once starts a line of inquiry that may require considerable study of merchandising and the problems of distribution which accompany the problems of production.

The discussion of a visit ordinarily suggests many topics that require further investigation and much material that should be read. In a discussion, students will themselves, by referring to other visits that they have made and to motion pictures they have seen or books they have read, suggest to other members of the class additional material with which they should become familiar. The discussion of the visit often suggests problems for further study, as in the case of the distribution question that was mentioned above. Many visits are sources of illustrative material that can be used in subsequent discussions to clarify material that is being presented; for example, a class that has visited a factory is in a better position to understand the implications of wages and hours laws and of other instances of labor legislation. Any visit that ends when the class leaves to go home may well be dismissed as an inadequately exploited class activity.

VERBAL ILLUSTRATIONS

All of the preceding instructional aids serve to make learning concrete by substituting sense experiences for verbal elements. These lay the basis of experience necessary for understanding the spoken or printed word, but they can never be said to replace it.

As students mature and their store of experience increases, it is possible to use these experiences as a source of illustrations without actually taking the class on trips or showing pictures. When students have the background that gives meaning to words, the words can be used as symbols of an experience. The teacher who is trying to get a science class to understand that, temperature being constant, pressure varies inversely with volume, does not get very far if he merely defines each of the words he uses or if he says, "In other words, pressure times volume equals k, a constant."

By using their experience as a source of illustrations, he can remind the students of the way the familiar bicycle tire pump works, so that when the piston is pushed down, the volume of the air is compressed until the air exerts enough pressure to force its way into the tire. He can use their experience by asking why an inflated toy balloon bursts when it is squeezed too hard.

Of all the words in the English language, the two that are probably most important for the teacher are the words, *for example*. It is the illustration that make concrete what is abstract and that makes clear what is otherwise so vague. The teacher who is trying to develop a concept can proceed much faster when he uses illustrations on the student's level of understanding so that the student applies the concept to conditions that he understands rather than to abstract words.

The words *for example* are important not only as a means of clarifying the teacher's presentation of a topic, but also as a way of making certain that students understand what they are talking about. There are many catch phrases that students pick up in the course of a school career and that they use so frequently that they think they know what the expressions mean. This use of words is illustrated not only by such expressions as *democracy* and *freedom of speech,* but also in more specific expressions, like *Amy Lowell's imagery,* and *Thomas Hardy's fatalism.* A student who refers to Amy Lowell's imagery should be able to give an illustration of what he means so that all may know that his use of the word *imagery* is merely a way of saving time by using one word instead of many, rather than a way of cloaking his lack of understanding by the use of profound-sounding terms.

In every discussion, therefore, the teacher should be free to use verbal illustrations, and both students and teachers should be ready to ask each other to give an illustration of the point that is being discussed.

Qualities of Good Illustrations

Illustrations can clarify an idea, but they can also be confusing. What marks the difference between the effective and the inadequate use of illustrations? Each illustration should be brought into the lesson for a specific reason. When the language teacher speaks of the mores of South Africa, he has to introduce illustrations so that the students understand the word *mores* and will use it in the same way that he does. When, on the other hand, he uses a term like *transportation* that all understand, it is unnecessary to take the time to give illustrations. Knowing the class, the teacher can decide when illustrations are necessary, when the class should be invited to add to the illustration he is giving, and when, on the other hand, the giving of even a single illustration will add little to the clarity of the discussion.

The illustration should be familiar to the student, lest the teacher find that he is explaining one unknown term through an illustration that may be equally foreign. The teacher who remembers the sensation he had the first time he rode in the high-speed elevator in a skyscraper may describe the sensation of a person parachuting out of a plane as an exaggeration of the sensations of those who are going down rapidly in an elevator, but boys and girls who have never parachuted from a plane and who have never ridden in a high-speed elevator may not be able to understand his explanation any better because of the illustration.

A good illustration should focus attention on the major point it is intended to clarify rather than embroider the point with unnecessary details. The long anecdotes, complete with dialect and gestures, may be amusing, but the students may be fascinated by the teacher's skill as a raconteur without being impressed by the point the teacher intended to stress, namely, that human needs are the same all over the world, despite differences in language. If the illustration is too vivid, the class may remember the anecdote rather than the principle.

Illustrations should not be more numerous than necessary. If the idea can be presented with one illustration, it is unnecessary to use two; and if two are adequate, the teacher should not use three. The economical use of illustrations can save time which will be used to better advantage in supplying illustrations for points that do need further clarification.

As with so many other phases of teaching, purposeful activity is important even during the illustration. It is inadequate for the teacher to think of the illustration, to give it, and to show its relevance. So far as possible, students should share in this process. When the class is discussing the concept of cultural lag, it is not enough for the teacher to give illustrations of cultural lag if the students, too, can present instances where customs persist even when the need for them has passed. As the teacher presents the illustration, students should be asked to make the comparison or to draw the generalization. The teacher who cites as an illustration of cultural lag the fact that urban schools still have long summer vacations even though it is not necessary for city students to leave school to help on the farm, can well ask his students to comment upon his choice of this instance as an illustration of cultural lag.

Verbal illustrations can be more than merely an auxiliary part of the lesson. They may constitute the major part of the lesson, as when the class, examining several illustrations of the same principle, attempts to evolve a statement that will explain the principle. An English class, for example, may spend much of the period criticizing the ways in which students begin the short stories they are writing. After they have evaluated and attempted to improve several of the beginnings used by students, they are in a better position to formulate the principles which should guide a young writer in starting a story.

Verbal illustrations are a useful part of the teacher's procedure because they require no special equipment and do not have to be ordered well in advance. All they demand of the teacher is an understanding of his material and his students and an imagination that is vivid enough to bring the two together. The teacher who is trying to get a junior high school class to understand what is meant by water erosion may not have the slide projector or the motion picture projector he needs at this specific moment, but if he plans this lesson carefully, making full use of instances of water erosion that they can see in their own neighborhood after a heavy rainstorm, and if he uses even so familiar an aid as a chalkboard, he can have illustrations that will help his students to understand just what water erosion really is.

THE LIBRARY

The library stores upon its shelves the many verbal illustrations that illumine and extend the generalizations of the classroom. The textbook description of life in colonial New England needs the enrichment of *The Scarlet Letter* to make Puritan values more real. Science lessons on control of disease are enriched by *Arrowsmith* and *Microbe Hunters. On the Origin of Species* is a thrill to the science enthusiast who finds still another film on evolution lacking in challenge.

Instruction in use of the library is not so simple in its purposes that it may be limited to a few routine lessons by the librarian or English teacher on the use of reference tools. If the mathematics teacher and the French teacher also believe that the library is the heart of the school, they have to find time to take their classes to the library to excite interest in library resources in their fields and to help students locate books of significance on their maturity level.

The library needs to be viewed, also, as more than a repository of books. Pamphlets, periodicals, pictures, vertical files, and research tools have to be discussed and presented by classroom teachers if maximum use of the library's accessions is to be had. In addition to the interest which the English teacher builds in literature, other teachers must seek ways to build familiarity with and interest in the nonfiction shelves, not simply to complete assignments but as a way of extending interests and the enjoyment of learning. In most secondary school subjects, teachers can find listing of supplementary readings appropriate for their students in publications of professional associations in their field. A period spent with the librarian can help to reveal specific books already on the library shelves. This conference should also lead to recommendations by the teacher for new acquisitions in his field by the library.

Secondary school teachers often feel understandably overwhelmed as they contemplate all they are expected to teach and their students are expected to learn. The enormity of the task becomes appreciably more manageable when teachers take advantage of all of the ways that are now available for making learning more concrete and thereby more effective.

TEACHING MACHINES

Among the newest additions to the devices which can be used to facilitate learning is the teaching machine (as illustrated by *AutoTutor,*

*Califone, Dyna-Slide Program Scanner, Foringer Teaching Machine)**, which has been described as not only an aid to the teacher but a substitute for the teacher. Few educational innovations have been introduced with such enthusiastic claims and such intense skepticism. It is not easy for teachers to evaluate the machine's possibilities objectively in the face of such claims and objections.

Pressey, as long ago as 1926, argued that automated teaching could free the teacher from the "routine of drill and information fixing" and thereby "make her free for those inspirational and thought-stimulating activities which are, presumably, the real function of the teacher" [16]. On the other hand, Blyth [1] points out that "the phrase 'automation of education with teaching machines' . . . represents such a summation of horrors for some people that it blocks any intelligent inquiry into the merits of teaching machines."

The devices used in automated teaching range from the relatively inexpensive "scrambled book" or the "programmed book" through fairly simple machines and up to electronic machines costing thousands of dollars. Despite the variations among them, all of them rely on similar fundamental principles. First, the learning material is carefully *programmed,* that is, arranged in advance, so that the learner can proceed without the teacher's guidance. Second, the learner is told immediately of the correctness or incorrectness of his answers to the questions set before him. Third, if his response is correct he goes on to the next step or, if his response is incorrect, he is referred back to material he should restudy or to antecedent questions he should answer.

In the "scrambled book" or the "programmed book," the authors depart from the usual textbook format in which all of the explanatory material appears in one place, the questions are grouped at the end of the chapter, and the answers appear at the end of the book, if they are printed at all. In one version of the programmed book, the page is divided into several panels. The student begins by working on the first panel of the first page, he learns from the corresponding panel on the second page whether his response was correct, and he then proceeds in order through the first panels on the remaining pages of the chapter. At this point he returns to the first page and proceeds in a similar manner with the second set of panels until he is ready to start on the third set.

How one of the teaching machines operates is indicated by the following excerpt from the manual prepared by its manufacturers:

> *The Western Design Autotutor* is basically an automatic, random-access, recording microfilm-motion picture projector. In its simplest use the *Tutor* is a

* Western Design, Division of U.S. Industries, Inc., Santa Barbara, California; Rheem Califone Corporation, Hollywood, California; Dyna-Slide Program Scanner, Dyna-Slide Company, Chicago, Illinois; Foringer and Co., Inc., Rockville, Maryland.

microfilm form of the "scrambled book," . . . with the provision for recording the sequence of choices made by the student and the time spent on each. The student finds the first unit of information on image 1 of the microfilm, along with a multiple-choice question based on that unit of information. As in the book, he selects the next image he will see by selecting an answer to the multiple-choice question. He enters the image number corresponding to his choice into the *Selector* keyboard of the *Tutor,* presses the *View* button, and the device automatically locates and projects the image corresponding to the student's choice, and the printing recorder makes a record of the image number chosen and the elapsed time since the previous choice. If the student has chosen the correct answer to the multiple-choice question, the image he (thereby) selects will contain the next unit of information and the next question. If the student chooses an incorrect answer, the image he sees next will contain material designed to correct the particular error he has committed, will explain to him how to find the right answer, and will direct him to return to the first image to try again.*

The Advantages Claimed

Since Sidney L. Pressey and B. F. Skinner, both of whom are psychologists of note, played important parts in developing teaching machines, and other recognized psychologists have also been working in this area, it is not surprising that automated teaching should seek to apply what we have learned about the psychology of learning. Thus, a response is reinforced immediately when the learner knows at once that he has made the correct response instead of waiting till the teacher has had the time to correct the students' papers and to return them. Similarly, errors can be corrected before they become habitual.

That the exercises are designed and planned by experts, with facilities for tryouts that are not available to classroom teachers, makes it more likely that the learning materials will be carefully selected and arranged in an optimum sequence.

The argument has been advanced that having the machine respond to the student's answers mechanically and completely without any emotional bias improves the motivation for learning. How can any student tell his parents that "It always picks on me. I am never called on when I know the answer and I always get the hard questions no one else can answer. Besides it never likes what I say anyway"?

Automated teaching, moreover, can provide for the full range of individual differences in learning ability, since each student starts where he is and proceeds toward a definite goal by carefully graduated steps. The amount of practice on each skill can be controlled, with fast learners allowed to proceed at their own rates while slow learners take more time.

These machines can free the teacher from the time-consuming re-

* Reprinted by permission from *Automatic Tutoring Materials and Devices,* Training Systems Department, Western Design, Division of U.S. Industries, Inc., Santa Barbara, California.

sponsibilities of explaining to the class repeatedly what each student can learn just as well by himself. They also make it unnecessary for the teacher to devote countless hours to the routine marking of routine practice exercises. Teachers should then be free to do the kind of teaching that no machine can attempt.

The machines also offer new opportunities to the educationally underprivileged, whether they be in schools that are too small to offer advanced courses or too poor to afford capable teachers.

The Doubts Raised

Despite this list of advantages, there are skeptics who remain unconvinced. What they fear is that gadget-loving America may turn to teaching machines as the panacea for all educational ills.

The devices used in automated teaching are only tools, and tools must be judged by what they accomplish and not by their inherent value. It would be as futile to attempt to evaluate the motion picture projector or the television camera as either good or bad. The same motion picture projector which shows a film that inspires and instructs can also show a film which misleads and corrupts.

The key element in the evaluation of automated teaching, whether it be done by "scrambled book" or by teaching machine, lies in the quality of the programming and in the appropriateness of programming as a way of helping students to learn. Automated teaching is limited to what can be taught verbally. Thus far, automated teaching has been used successfully to teach specific facts and processes, as in some phases of mathematics and in industrial training programs. Will automated teaching help adolescents to learn facts in such a way as to develop broad understanding, appreciation, attitudes, and the habit of using the skills they have developed? Though machines may be effective in training students to learn the answers, do they stimulate students to ask questions?

The skeptics grant that experts, with ample resources and skilled assistants, can provide better instructional materials and practice exercises than a busy teacher can. *Programming*, or arranging the materials for the machine, is so time-consuming and expensive, however, that the use of machines may result in rigid courses of study that lag behind our steadily expanding body of knowledge.

The Questions to Be Answered

Teaching machines are still so new that we really do not have enough experience with them to indicate how they can be used to best advantage. Psychologists are already reporting the results of experimentation in an attempt to evaluate the machine's effectiveness under various conditions, but we need much more evidence before we can know when they should be used or even whether they should be used. Does their effectiveness vary from subject to subject, from one type of learning to another, from age group to age group, from one level of intellectual maturity to another?

The procedures used in automated teaching underline the importance of the principles discussed in Chapter 3 as the basis for effective teaching. Will teachers examine their classroom procedures to see whether they are applying these principles? Can teachers apply to their own teaching the principles which make programming effective in a teaching machine and, in addition, retain the values that come from contact with a wise and inspiring teacher? Is the careful gradation of learning, for example, any less important when a teacher is explaining a mathematical process in class than when a student is pushing buttons or manipulating levers on a teaching machine?

Schools may be able to profit from the experience gained from the use of teaching machines in industrial training programs, provided that this experience is interpreted in the light of the differences between industrial training programs and secondary education. Certainly the aims of secondary education encompass more than do the more limited aims of industrial training programs; and adolescents, despite their impatience to be treated as adults, are not adults. Even the cash investment in the purchase or rental of the more expensive teaching machines is different for industry and schools since industry benefits from income tax reductions that do not apply to schools which purchase equipment out of tax funds and not from income.

Only rarely will the new secondary school teacher have the controlling voice in deciding whether or not teaching machines should be purchased by the school boards. Nevertheless, he must learn more about their potentialities and their weaknesses so that he can be an informed adviser and consumer.

Above all, he must be true to his professional responsibilities and evaluate them in terms of the effect upon the quality of the learning we want for our adolescents. Teachers must be objective so that they will be neither faddists who jump on any attractive bandwagon festooned with attractive slogans nor standpatters who reject anything that jars them out of complacency.

QUESTIONS FOR STUDY AND DISCUSSION

1. A high school chemistry teacher who was trying to develop an understanding of the meaning of *catalytic agent* found that somehow or other his students could not grasp the idea that the mere presence of a chemical that did

not itself enter into the equation could nevertheless affect the speed of chemical changes. Student after student tried to bring the catalytic agent into the equation even though the words and the definition they repeated so glibly indicated that the catalytic agent was not properly a part of the equation.

The teacher stopped the lesson and asked the class whether they had ever seen a group of men digging up the street to lay a new pipe. What would happen, he asked them, if a pretty girl were to drive by in a car? The worldly wise students knew immediately what would happen. Putting it prosaically, the rate of work would be lessened even though the girl did absolutely nothing to the machines the men were using.

What would happen, the teacher went on, if instead of the girl, the occupant of the car turned out to be the boss? Even though he did no more work than merely flick the ashes from a cigar with his little finger, work proceeded much more rapidly as long as his car was on the block. This boss could be moved in his car from one block to another, from one job to a second and a third, and he would be unchanged in the process, never losing and never gaining. The boss, by his very presence, accelerated the speed of the reaction.

The next day the teacher was dismayed to hear one of the boys refer, in all seriousness, to a catalyst as a "red-head who takes a man's mind off his work." In response to the teacher's further questions, the boy supplemented his answer by saying that there were other kinds of catalysts that make men work harder. So far as the teacher could gather, this lad had no understanding at all of the meaning of a catalytic agent in chemistry.

How can the teacher correct the boy's misconception of a catalytic agent?

Was the teacher wise in using these illustrations to explain the meaning of catalytic agent? How do you justify your answer?

2. Your school owns a complete set of phonograph recordings of a Shakespearian play that is being studied by one of the English classes in the school. At which point in the students' study of the play should they listen to the recordings? How can the teacher use these recordings so that the class will profit most?

3. A junior high school social studies class is watching the motion picture referred to in this chapter dealing with the ways in which the government agencies supervise the production and distribution of milk. The film is an excellent one and answers the very questions which students were asking during the preparatory discussion period. Some of the students, however, first giggle and then laugh out loud at some of the scenes they find suggestive and you sense that much of the value of the film is being lost as the mood of the students changes to that of amusement.

What would you do at this point if you were the teacher?

4. A science teacher recommends to his class that they listen to a television program on Thursday evenings that regularly presents excellent dramatizations of the fascinating story of modern scientific advances. Relatively few students listen to these programs because at the same hour another station carries the coast-to-coast broadcast of a popular comedian.

What is the science teacher's next step?

5. The company which manufactures a well-advertised breakfast cereal has sent the home economics teacher a set of attractive charts depicting the food values of cereals and the steps by which wheat is converted into bread. The charts contain no advertising matter other than that the name of the company is prominently displayed on each chart.

What use should the teacher make of these charts, which are much better than any other ones the teacher has available?

6. Instructional materials can serve as creative instruments as well as spectator devices for students. What are the learning activities in your subject area where students can develop (1) flat pictures, (2) slides or filmstrips, (3) tape recordings, (4) bulletin board displays, (5) printed material, (6) radio or television programs?

7. Your class is scheduled to go to the library as a group next Tuesday for the first time this semester. What do you want your students to see? What kinds of activities should they undertake while in the library? Prepare a plan for this kind of library period.

BIBLIOGRAPHY

1. BLYTH, John W., "Teaching Machines and Human Beings," *The Educational Record*, Vol. 41, No. 2 (April, 1960), pp. 116-125.
2. BROWN, James W., and LEWIS, Richard B., eds., *A.V. Instructional Materials Manual* (Spartan Book Store, San José State College, San José, California, 1957).
3. BUCHANAN, Andrew, *Film Making from Script to Screen* (London, Phoenix House, 1951).
4. CHILD, Eleanor D., and FINCH, Hardy R., *Producing School Movies* (Committee on Standards for Motion Pictures and Newspapers, National Council of Teachers of English, 1941).
5. DALE, Edgar, *Audio-Visual Methods in Teaching*, rev. ed. (New York, Holt, Rinehart and Winston, Inc., 1954).
6. EDWARDS, Harry L., *Simplified Film Strip Production, A Working Manual* (Bureau of Educational Research, Ohio State University, 1952).
7. FARCO, Lucile F., *The Library and the School*, 4th ed. (Chicago, American Library Association, 1947).
8. FAUNCE, Roland C., and BOSSING, Nelson L., *Developing the Core Curriculum*, 2nd ed. (Englewood Cliffs, N.J., Prentice-Hall, Inc., 1958), Ch. 10.
9. GALENTER, Eugene, ed., *Automatic Teaching: The State of the Art* (New York, John Wiley & Sons, Inc., 1960).
10. HAAS, Kenneth B., and PACKER, Harry Q., *Preparation and Use of Audio-Visual Aids*, 3rd ed. (Englewood Cliffs, N.J., Prentice-Hall, Inc., 1955).
11. KINNEY, Lucien, and DRESDEN, Katherine, *Better Learning Through Current Materials* (Stanford, Stanford University Press, 1952).
12. McKOWN, Harry C., and ROBERTS, Alvin B., *Audio-Visual Aids to Instruction*, 2nd ed. (New York, McGraw-Hill Book Co., Inc., 1949).
13. National Council for the Social Studies, *How to Make a Bulletin Board Effective* (Washington, D.C., 1945).
14. National Society for the Study of Education, *Audio-Visual Materials of Instruction*, 48th Yearbook, Part I (Chicago, University of Chicago Press, 1949).
15. ———, *Mass Media and Education*, 53rd Yearbook, Part II (Chicago, University of Chicago Press, 1954).
16. PRESSEY, Sidney L., "A Simple Apparatus Which Gives Tests and Scores and Teaches," *School and Society*, Vol. 23 (March 20, 1926), pp. 373-376.
17. Rheem Califone Corporation, *Automated Teaching Bulletin*, published quarterly (1020 North La Brea Avenue, Hollywood 38, Calif., the Corporation).
18. SKINNER, B. F., *Cumulative Record* (New York, Appleton-Century-Crofts, Inc., 1959).

19. U.S. Industries, Inc., Training Systems Department, *Automatic Tutoring: Materials and Devices* (Santa Barbara Airport, Goleta, Calif., the Company, 1959).
20. WENDT, Paul R., *Audio-Visual Instruction: What Research Says to the Teacher*, No. 14 (Washington, D.C., National Education Association, 1957).
21. WITTICH, Walter A., and SCHULLER, Charles F., *Audio-Visual Materials, Their Nature and Use*, 2nd ed. (New York, Harper and Brothers, 1957), Ch. 3.

Films

22. *Feltboard in Teaching* (Detroit, Audio-Visual Materials Consultation Bureau, Wayne University, 1951), 9 min.
23. *How to Make Handmade Lantern Slides* (Bloomington, Indiana University, 1947), 22 min.
24. *Using the Classroom Film* (Chicago, Encyclopedia Britannica Films, 1945), 21 min.
25. *The World Is at Your Door* (Brooklyn, N.Y., Brooklyn Museum, 1951), 22 min.

Source Materials

26. *Educational Film Guide* (New York, H. W. Wilson Company, 1953, 1954-58, annual supplements).
27. *Filmstrip Guide* (New York, H. W. Wilson Company, 1954, 1955-58, cumulative, plus annual supplements).
28. *Free and Inexpensive Learning Materials* (Nashville, Tenn., George Peabody College for Teachers, Division of Surveys and Field Services, various dates).
29. WITTICH, Walter A., and HANSON, Gertie L., eds., *Educator's Guide to Free Tapes, Scripts, and Transcriptions* (Randolph, Wisc., Educators Progress Service, 1960).

CHAPTER 9

Improving Work and Study Skills

»»»»»»»»»»

EVERY SECONDARY SCHOOL teacher is concerned, of course, with what his students are learning. He must concern himself also with the ability that they are developing to learn on their own—to proceed under their own steam when they are no longer in school and the teacher is no longer there to guide and stimulate learning. Are our secondary school students learning how to study? Do they know how to work independently? Has the school whetted the appetite for learning so that students want to study and know how to study effectively?

STUDY SKILLS AN IMPORTANT EDUCATIONAL GOAL

The ability to study independently is important not only for its influence on school success but also for the part it plays in the student's intellectual life after he leaves school. The student's work at school should raise his present level of interest, but it should also develop more lasting interests and give him the abilities he will need if he is to continue his studies. The value of a science course, for example, cannot be judged merely by examining the results of the final examination administered at the end of the term. If the course has been really effective, it should help the student become the kind of person whose interest in science continues into adult life, who will want to read and be able to understand articles and books that are written for intelligent adults, and who continues to grow, therefore, in his understanding of the role of science in our civilization. No small part of the value of the science course depends, therefore, on the success with which students learn to study with a decreasing degree of teacher guidance.

Schools have long been interested in teaching children how to study. For a long time, study served as an essential link in the assign-study-recite-test chain [9, Ch. 20]. In this chain, study was regarded as an out-of-class activity—to follow assignments made by the teacher and to serve as the basis for recitation in class the next day. Study was a discrete element in the procedure to be accomplished at home or in an institution optimistically named the study hall.

A Broader Concept of Study

Two developments in recent years have served to modify this concept of study and to give it greater significance. First, research in education has established the need of secondary school and college students for greater direction in study. Second, the unit concept in teaching has established a very close relationship between *study* and *learning*. Study is taken as more than the "preparation of lessons," and becomes instead the central activity in the learning experience—the working period of the unit where students seek in many ways to find the answers to their problems.

Study thus forces its way into the classroom itself, and class time becomes a working as well as a reporting (reciting) period. Because study activities and learning activities have become intertwined, the class period in many schools has been lengthened from forty-five minutes to an hour, with a corresponding reduction in the number of periods in the school day. This change in scheduling also reduces the amount of time spent in study halls, and in some schools study halls have been eliminated entirely.

Paradoxically, the ability to study has taken on greater dimensions and is more important than it was when assign-study-recite-test was the almost universal pattern of classroom procedure. What value is there in having the English student read widely if he does not understand what he reads? What does a student gain when he goes to many sources for his information instead of memorizing the material in his textbook if he does not know how to find information or how to use it?

The ability to study, to learn on one's own, is of such pivotal importance that dissatisfaction with newer curriculum practices is inevitable if students have not mastered the techniques of studying. Preparation makes the difference between a discussion which is mere conversation and one that provides for a more rigorous examination of the problem, evaluation of issues and evidence, and consideration of possible solutions. The student learns to the extent that he participates in study. He may learn little, for example, from a unit on atomic energy unless he knows how to make his full contribution to the committee that is studying the use of isotopes in medicine.

The meaning of study was narrowly circumscribed in the older recitation patterns, and too often study was synonymous with memorization, but, at least, students knew what they were to do and teachers could determine quickly whether students had done it. Today, study encompasses much more, but students are often only vaguely aware of what studying means and sometimes depressingly inept at pursuing the many activities that studying includes. As a result, we find classrooms that are in a flurry of excitement as committees report and students are evaluating, but there is little that is worth reporting. The broader concept of study must lead to greater, not to lesser, concern with developing the ability to study.

Place of the Study Hall

Schools which continue to have a study hall find that it serves many useful purposes [17]. It is, for example, a convenient room for assembling students who are not attending subject classes. Rather than have these students roam about the building and disturb classes that are at work, the school seats them in one room, supervised by a teacher who is similarly free from class obligations that period. The study hall provides seats and sometimes desks for students who wish to work on their homework assignments. In general, it contributes to the maintenance of school discipline by assuring that there will be no letdown when students are not in regular class. Yet, careful examination of study halls in general throws grave doubt upon their contribution as places where students learn how to study or where they develop good work habits.

Ordinarily, the students in a study hall at any one time constitute so heterogeneous a group that even the most conscientious and capable teacher would have difficulty in developing good study skills. An entering freshman may sit next to a senior. The boy who knows how to gather his data for a social studies report but has not yet learned how to tackle his mathematics problems may be alongside another student who, never having learned how to read for a central thought, has difficulty with his social studies problem. The room itself is often inadequate since many schools use the auditorium as a study hall, with seats that are better suited for sitting and listening than for working.

Under these circumstances, about all that a study hall can do, however efficiently it may be organized and supervised, is to provide students with a reasonably quiet room in which they may work on assignments previously made by subject matter teachers. Even a good supervised study hall is usually inadequate. Students who do not know how to work and study need guidance more than they need supervision. Guided study lessons can accomplish far more than can supervised study periods.

Need for Learning Study Skills

The word *study* has been used so widely in our schools that both teachers and students ordinarily assume that the ability to study is common. Popular belief holds that anyone who wants to can study effectively and that the student who does not work efficiently reveals only his unwillingness to apply himself. An indifferent teacher may treat such a student as a disciplinary problem and a more interested teacher may see him as a proper subject for a program of character education, but few teachers recognize his difficulties as presenting pedagogical and psychological problems.

One of the many debts we owe to educational research arises from the fact that it was through the findings of investigators that we learned how prevalent is the inability to study. Investigations conducted with elementary school pupils, with secondary school students, and with undergraduates at college reveal that inability to study effectively is a common difficulty on all three educational levels. At best, many students are inefficient; in fact, some of them use procedures which are so inadequate or inappropriate that even diligence does not compensate for poor technique.

Of course, high school and college students must have evolved some kind of study procedures, else they could not have maintained their status in school. But this kind of trial and error learning is costly. In the first place, many of these students can be helped to develop more effective procedures than they ever discover by themselves. Secondly, the degree of success these students achieve may blur the other part of the picture; namely, that students who have not evolved such procedures become the retarded and the failing students who drop out of school prematurely.

The Inadequacy of Rules

The first reaction to the realization that students did not know how to study was a wave of good advice and sound rules. When psychologists formulated rules for effective study, these suggestions were welcomed by teachers as offering the necessary remedial program. Throughout the country, copies of these rules were printed and then pasted in notebooks and textbooks. The rules were discussed in class so that students might understand their full meaning.

But advice, even excellent advice, is often disappointingly ineffective as a means of changing habits. Adolescents, like adults, listen to advice, agree that it is sound, resolve that they will follow it, and may even observe the suggestion for a short time, only to slip back into the more comfortable routine of long-established habits. Unfortunately, study rules can be understood, and even be committed to memory, without having any noticeable influence on students' attitudes and habits.

Additional complications arise from the fact that some of these rules are difficult, or even impossible, to follow. There is often a disappointing gap between the point at which a person knows what he ought to do and the point at which he actually follows that course of action. To be sure, students cannot practice the right procedure unless they know what should be done, either as a result of teaching or by intuition. But the knowledge of rules of study is far less important than is the habit of applying these rules and the desire to do so. No plan of teaching boys and girls how to study which relies solely on the presentation of rules of study and of inspirational appeals can ever do more than meet a very small part of the total problem.

Certain rules fill the student with envy. He is told to have a fixed time and place for study, to work in a well-lighted, well-ventilated, and quiet room, where he has ready access to all necessary reference material. These conditions are far from typical if one thinks of the average secondary school student who is trying to solve a problem in mathematics with one ear attuned to the conversation his older sister is having over the telephone with the young man who really did not mean to break the date he had with her yesterday, or of the other student who cannot be sure he will always get the same corner of the table on which to do his assignment while the rest of the family is busy in different parts of the room, each with his own work.

Add to these the compelling attraction of the television program that is about to start that very minute, and we can understand why a secondary school student often does his studying under such unfavorable conditions that he readily uses them as justification for not studying at all. The recommended conditions are often in such sharp contrast to the inadequate facilities the student has at home that it is easy for him to regard the other rules, too, as being unrealistic and impracticable.

A more promising approach to this matter of providing a suitable setting for studying and working is suggested by some schools which either provide appropriate facilities for students in the late afternoons and evenings or encourage community organizations to make such facilities available. Few middle-class teachers understand how near to impossible it is for even a conscientious adolescent to concentrate on an intellectual task when the home is overcrowded and the parents, if there are parents around in the evening, have little respect for intellectual activities or see little reason for providing the atmosphere for thinking and reading and writing. Rather than bemoan the indifference toward scholastic achievement so often found among culturally handicapped children, the school can do better if it works with other community agencies in helping conscientious students to develop good habits of work by making it possible for these students to work.

Encouraging the will to study. Because studying and learning are so closely interrelated, if they are not almost synonymous, anything which increases the love of learning will increase the desire to study. Thus the teacher whose enthusiasm for his subject is contagious will stimulate his students to study far more than will another teacher who routinely goes from one indifferent topic to another. Similarly, the desire to study is more likely to flourish in the classroom of a teacher where it is evident that he respects his students and is interested in their thoughts and their achievements. And of course the desire to study is influenced by the importance which the student attaches to what he is studying.

Developing work and study skills must be seen, therefore, as part of the total educational pattern rather than as an isolated problem to be attacked by itself.

Some Important Study Skills

Modern secondary school students need all of the important study skills that were needed by students of former generations plus many more that were not emphasized.

All one need do to appreciate the complexity of the many skills that are included in the one word *study* is to analyze the skills that are needed for the successful completion of even a simple school task [23, pp. 31-33]. Students must be able to use the library so that they can find the material they need and they must be able to read understandingly the references they find. They must be able to conduct experiments and to understand the reports of experiments conducted by others. They have to learn how to discover their own inadequacies in skills and the gaps in their information, and how to correct these deficiencies. They must be able to practice a skill to the point of overlearning, and they have to employ profitable methods of renewing their familiarity with material studied earlier as they use this material in the solution of new problems. They have to be able to work alone and with others, and they have to know how to evaluate the result. Since most students attach more importance to the questions they are required to answer in writing than they do to the ideas presented in the material they read, they have to learn the importance of the kind of study assignment which does not lead to written work. Students have to develop new skill in budgeting their time, for few students know how to work effectively for a long stretch of time.

Even this enumeration of basic study skills does not exhaust the number of different skills that teachers so often take for granted when they wonder why their boys and girls have not learned how to study.

What must the teacher aim at achieving if he wishes to evaluate the current progress of his students and to plan instruction where he finds it necessary?

1. Students must learn how to work effectively. They must learn how to define the task that is before them, to plan ways of accomplishing the task, to start working promptly, and to keep at the task until it has been completed. They have to learn how to concentrate on the task at hand and to minimize the effect of real and imagined distractions. They must learn to focus on the purpose they hope to achieve instead of dissipating their efforts.

We all know how long it takes an adolescent, or many an adult, to get started on a task. Before he gets much beyond rephrasing for the fourth time the title of the paper he is to write, he may sharpen many pencils and drink several glasses of water in an attempt to quench the irresistible thirst that develops so frequently when one has to start a paper. Similarly he may sit with his book open while he rereads the first few paragraphs absent-mindedly, not really attending to what he does. Can we help students learn how to begin work? Can we help them to start quickly and to take off in the right direction? Can we teach them to plan their work so that they start promptly and efficiently, without waste motion and unnecessary backtracking to repeat what has already been done?

These are skills that must be developed; they are certainly not innate. Like all skills that are to be learned, they are learned best when they are taught in accordance with the principles of effective teaching. If learning is an active process, learning how to study is also an active process and the extent to which a student learns how to study depends as much upon what he does as upon what the teacher does. Similarly, if the student must see purpose in his activity if he is to learn effectively, he must see purpose in what he is studying if he is to learn to study it better. The principles of teaching discussed in Chapter 3 and those which are included in other chapters apply as directly to teaching students how to study as to teaching them anything else.

2. Students have to improve their ability to read because reading continues to be our major means of learning. Yet, reading itself comprises many skills. Students must be able to read novels, but they must also learn how to read their textbooks, the science periodicals, and the newspapers. They must master, too, the techniques for understanding graphs, charts, tables, and maps, and for making optimum use of the table of contents and the index, the captions and the footnotes. Moreover, teachers need to help students understand the vocabulary and the concepts in their special subject areas.

Of course, teen-agers must learn to be fast readers in a society that puts more and more printed material before every one of us, but they have to learn to adjust their speed in accordance with what it is that is being read—*Kon Tiki* more quickly than *Men in White,* an encyclopedia article on space travel more slowly than a short story.

This concern with reading is a new development for secondary school teachers since they have been accustomed to regard the teaching of reading as being exclusively within the province of the elementary school. When virtually the entire elementary school population goes on to secondary education, however, it is inevitable that many secondary school students will need additional instruction in reading. Even when the elementary schools are completely successful in teaching all of their pupils the mechanics of reading, many secondary school students have to improve their reading skills if they are to keep up with the demands of secondary education. While some students may need remedial instruction in the mechanics of reading, virtually all of them will profit from developmental teaching of reading skills. The teaching of reading has become an important area for secondary school English teachers, but it must concern the other secondary school teachers as well. Moreover, because the improvement of reading skills is a complicated process, secondary school teachers will have to familiarize themselves with the procedures for teaching reading.

3. *Students have to improve their techniques of getting information.* Reading, of course, is one of these, but prior to reading itself is the problem of finding the materials to read. Hence, the teacher who is helping students find information stimulates the intelligent use of reference works —general and specialized encyclopedias, dictionaries, collections of biography, periodical index, government publications, and compilations of statistics. The teacher does not simply "leave the job to the librarian"; he helps his students make maximum use of the library and its directories as fabulous learning resources. Obviously, genuine use of the library means assignments that are not cut-and-dried, assignments that make the student dig! And much information is also to be found firsthand through resources in the community: persons with specialized information and interests, industry with a story to tell, places and things of historical interest, the natural environment, museums, and local government.

4. *Students need to be able to organize the information they have found.* To do this they need some skill in note-taking—from printed materials, talks, direct experience, and the mass media of communication like radio, television, and motion pictures. Learning how to outline and summarize is most useful. Students must learn, also, to interpret and evaluate what they have read, seen, and heard. The next step is organization and generalization, leading finally to a report, either oral or written.

5. *Students need skills in solving problems—both the problems in the mathematics and science texts and the actual problems that exist in their environment.* To prevent erosion of the new school's grounds, to

improve behavior in the school cafeteria, to reduce costs of getting adequate medical care, to gain or reduce weight—problems of this kind are real to students and carry their own motivation for study. Study in this case requires, first, that students identify the problem clearly. They must then secure preliminary information upon which they can formulate a hypothesis or plan. When they have reached this point, they are ready to gather data, later to interpret the data, and to generalize from it. Study that seeks to solve problems is different from study which aims at mastery of material in a printed source, but both types require reading, the gathering of information, and organizing new knowledge and ideas for future use.

6. *Students should know how to engage in creative activities as a form of study.* These activities include writing poems, short stories, and essays; designing a stage setting, a dress, a newspaper layout; working in the graphic arts, or composing musical pieces. But creative endeavor is also found in individual scientific experimentation, in seeking new mathematical proofs, in working out the recipe for a new cake.

7. *Finally, students have to learn to be their own judges—to evaluate for themselves what they have done.* Sometimes evaluation is easy. In mathematics, for instance, the student should develop the habit of checking his answers until the practice becomes routine. At other times, evaluation is more difficult: how does a student know whether he has really learned how antibiotics work?

How can the teacher help a student to recognize the degree to which he has done the job? Often, the standards which the teacher sets and the use that is made of the students' work have a determining influence upon the standards which students set for themselves. Why should a student bother too much if the teacher seems satisfied with any kind of work, however shoddy it may be? Why should a youth take the time to see whether he has really answered the questions if the answers are not examined critically by the class as they discuss the problem? How important is this work he does if papers are collected by the teacher and never seen again by the students?

The teacher who respects what he teaches and teaches it in such a way that students know what they are studying, and why, is in an excellent position to help his students to set correspondingly high standards for what they do. In such a class, students are less likely to be led astray by the interesting diversion of a Fall Festival, the necessity of collecting money for the Red Cross, and the bustle of rearranging chairs for a committee report. Here, too, it is clear that helping students to develop standards for evaluating their work and the habit of applying these standards are part of the basic school program and not the topic for a special lesson that can then be dismissed as having been taken care of.

PLANNING AN EFFECTIVE STUDY-SKILLS PROGRAM

In the face of such a wide variety of study skills, it seems presumptuous to speak of teaching children how to study—as though the ability to study were a single skill. A student may know how to apply a mathematical principle to new problems without knowing how to study a new principle which he does not already understand. Even if he knew how to learn the meaning of a new principle in mathematics and knew how to apply it in new situations, he might not know how to start writing an essay on the importance of this principle in modern mathematics.

Recognizing this difficulty, leaders in secondary school education have tried various approaches in attempting to meet the problem of developing a wide diversity of study skills. These include an imposing array of administrative changes. Periods have been lengthened in some schools so that the teacher will have time to include instruction in study skills as part of the regular class instruction. Class periods are sometimes divided in two, with one part devoted to teaching while the other is spent in supervised study. Special courses in how to study have been organized. In some schools the topic is included as part of an orientation course.

In general, schools which attempt to teach boys and girls how to study follow one of two procedures. In the first group are those schools which teach general study habits and then rely on the students to apply these general procedures to the various subjects. In the other schools, it is the subject matter teachers who are expected to develop in students the ability to study. The danger in the first case is that study divorced from application may degenerate into inspirational exhortation and empty practice exercises. In the second case, unnecessary repetition from class to class may result when study skills are left without co-ordination to each classroom teacher.

What is needed is a program of study activities which gives specific attention to the inculcation of wholesome attitudes and the development of effective procedures. Some combination of general instruction in study skills as well as specific attention to study skills in particular subjects is needed to take care of the problems, provided that schools interpret the ability to study as meaning much more than merely being able to do the homework assignment.

Any effective program of developing good work habits must be planned in terms of the entire school and must not be limited to the preparation of homework assignments. In the first place, it takes so long to develop these habits that a teacher whose contact with a class is limited to a single term does not get very far. Second, during any one term there are so many other teachers competing for their share of the student's time that the good study habits which one teacher may be encouraging in his class may be negated by the demands made by other teachers who are more concerned with the immediate problems of preparation for the next day than with the more basic problem of developing the ability to study independently. Third, some study procedures are so obvious that they are always taught first when any teacher decides to tackle the problem. As a result, there is no consistent and graduated attack on bad study habits unless the program is conceived of as one to be solved by the school as a whole rather than by individual teachers.

Assumptions Underlying an Adequate Program for Teaching Boys and Girls How to Work and Study Effectively

A number of assumptions underlie any adequate program for developing the ability to study.

1. *Success in study tasks depends upon the individual's background of interests and basic skills.* In the typical classroom, students exhibit a wide variation in interests and in their potential for effective study. To stimulate study the teacher should discover the particular interests of individual students as stepping stones for them as they broaden their interests. Reading ability in most junior and senior high school classes will vary by as much as six years. The teacher must keep this spread in mind when study tasks arise whose completion depends upon reading. Students differ in their ability to handle abstract ideas; they manifest differences also as they work with concrete materials in laboratories, shops, and studios. Some students like to work by themselves as individuals; others like the company of a group; still others need the constant availability of the teacher. Keeping these many differences in mind, we can see why trying to teach all students to study the same topic in the same way just does not work.

Knowing the individuals in the class and their abilities is basic to the necessary individualization of study programs. On the basis of observation, records, and consultation with parents and other teachers, the instructor is ready to direct some students to reading materials of some depth, to limit others to the texts selected for them, to encourage still others to study and express themselves through more concrete media than the printed work.

2. *For study to be effective the student must see the purpose of the work he is doing.* The boy or girl to whom schooling is a succession of tasks imposed by the teacher has little incentive for seeking ways of improving his ability to perform these tasks. To be willing to study is as important as to be able to study, for ability without the desire to use it accomplishes little. Student participation in selecting and planning study experiences helps establish the sense of purposefulness.

Not only must the curriculum be appropriate for the student, but the teaching must be of such quality as to inspire the student's respect for the worthwhileness of the work he is doing. To arouse in boys and girls a genuine interest in improving their ability to study we need more than devices to motivate them; we need the kind of inspired teaching that helps these adolescents to see meaning in the problems they are seeking to solve. The teacher who is a good craftsman can teach adolescents how to study, but it take more than craftsmanship to develop the will to study.

3. *Incidental learning alone is an ineffective way of acquiring good study habits.* Many teachers assume that students learn how to study as a by-product of the usual classroom activities. It seems reasonable that students who are taught in classes where topics are developed logically and effectively and where student participation is carefully guided should be equally logical and effective in their independent study. Yet the student may participate in a discussion, for example, without being aware of the pattern that underlies the sequence of questions. He may, therefore, be a good student in a class taught by a competent teacher without learning very much about the ability to work independently. The ineffectiveness of students' study habits is reflected in wasted time and effort and in their failure to achieve as much as should be attained by people of their ability.

4. *Study skills should be developed in a functional setting.* That it is insufficient to rely on the incidental learning of study skills should not lead the teacher to try to develop these skills in isolation. Like all other skills, the ability to study is learned better in situations in which it is used. It is important, for example, that students learn how to budget their time and how to make full use of the time spent on a given task, but it is futile to rely on special lessons in budgeting time or on special exercises in concentration. With every activity the students plan, they are getting exercise in budgeting their time; and every activity in which they engage provides an opportunity for teaching them how to work without wasting time. Much improvement in students' work habits and study abilities can be effected by teachers who recognize the importance of this improvement as an important objective of classroom activities.

5. *Efficiency in study depends not only on the student's willingness to study and on his readiness to devote the necessary time but also on his ability to use effective study procedures.* Whether a student who is collecting clippings about recent developments in science will learn anything more than how to cut and paste is influenced largely by the way he selects the articles he will clip. Similarly, a conscientious student may actually spend ten hours at his desk on Saturday, presumably reviewing his general science notes in preparation for an experiment his group will conduct, and yet be no better prepared than if he had spent half that time playing ball and then worked more effectively during the remaining time.

6. *It is inadequate to develop the ability to use effective study procedures if the student is so disturbed emotionally that he cannot work or if he is so little interested in what is going on that he will not work.*

To the extent that the teacher uses his insight into adolescent psychology as a means of understanding the pattern of adolescents' behavior, he can help them to achieve a degree of emotional adjustment that enables them to function better in many respects, including the ability to work efficiently and to carry a task through to its completion.

Studying involves abilities, but it also involves attitudes. How can we, for example, expect a boy to be able to gather his information preparatory to building a model of a Greek temple if he is so fully convinced of his inferiority that he knows, in advance, that any Greek temple he will build is bound to excite only ridicule. We must not develop the ability to study as an isolated set of skills and ignore the boy or girl in whom we are seeking to develop these skills.

7. *Study skills may be either general ones which can be applied to many school subjects or specific ones which are used only with some phases of school work.* Thus, the ability to read quickly and understandingly is a valuable aid throughout the secondary school. The ability to read a chapter and to extract the key thought may be used in many subjects but is not used so universally as is the mere ability to read quickly and well. On the other hand, the type of skill needed to master the spelling of the words used by a student may not help him to improve his vocabulary in a foreign language class or to solve problems in mathematics. While some general study abilities can be taught in a separate unit or course on how to study, the special abilities are taught more effectively in the specific subject area in which they will be used. Some of the most important study abilities, for example, the ability to organize a plan for accomplishing a task and to see the plan through to its completion, cannot be delegated to any one teacher or any one course, for these are outcomes that should concern all teachers.

8. *Study techniques must be established as habits.* Familiarizing the students with the principles of effective study is only a first step. Students must have so much practice in applying these principles that they use them habitually. This need for habituation indicates one of the weaknesses of some special units on how to study, for these units ordinarily are not long enough to establish lasting habits. It takes years and not days to develop the ability to study.

9. *The gradation of learning is as important in learning how to study as it is in all other phases of school learning.* Study abilities are so complex that one cannot teach them all at one time. Instead, they call for a graduated series of steps covering a period of years. The primary grade youngster who is learning to read silently is learning how to study just as certainly as is the junior high school student who is learning how to prepare an outline. By setting a series of goals rather than a single goal, the teacher can help the student to see the progress that is being made and can increase the likelihood of ultimate success.

If a school were to marshal its resources to develop good study procedures, what should it do? What has been said thus far indicates the kind of carefully planned school program that is needed. There must be a program for the entire school so that all teachers will know which skills are to be developed primarily by the home room teacher, which skills are the major responsibility of subject matter teachers, and which skills should be the concern of all teachers. In the case of more complex skills, like the ability to outline or to take notes, it may be advisable to indicate the goals for each term so that all teachers may know what was attempted in preceding terms. Every time the school seeks to develop a specific skill it must give adequate attention to developing the appropriate attitudes and habits, too.

With these principles in mind, let us see how these skills, attitudes, and habits can be developed. To illustrate the teaching procedures that are appropriate, we shall examine the methods of teaching both general and specific study skills.

TEACHING A BASIC STUDY SKILL

Some of the difficulty that students experience in studying is essentially a reading problem. Most secondary school students read at a convenient limit rather than at a rate that approaches their physiological limit of efficiency. A planned reading program that enables students to read more rapidly will increase markedly their efficiency in using reading as a tool.

One of the early steps in any comprehensive program of improving the ability to study should be the administration of a good standardized reading test for secondary school students, to be followed by an appropriate remedial reading program. Research conducted only recently yields convincing evidence that even high school students may not be able to read their textbooks with efficiency and understanding. English teachers have been trying to teach students to read Shakespeare's plays when these students are unable to read the editorial pages of the daily newspapers. Fortunately, current professional literature is full of suggestions for improving the reading ability of secondary school students [6, 10, 12, 22, 24].

The one word *reading* covers a variety of different skills. There is reading of the work-study type, and there is the rapid reading that is appropriate for fiction. There is reading of the scanning type when one is looking for a specific name or other bit of factual information in answer to a specific question, and there is the other type of reading when one goes through an entire book in order to get the author's basic point of view. Students must not only master the various types of reading but they must know which type is appropriate in a specific situation, lest they read a textbook as though it were a novel or read a novel as though it were a chemistry textbook. They must know how to use reference material wisely and be familiar with the use of such aids as the table of contents and the index. The effectiveness with which they use the library will depend largely on their ability to find the kind of information they need, an ability that depends in turn on their familiarity with the card index catalog, with the placement of the books in the library, and with the various reference guides that are available.

As an illustration of the way in which general study skills can be taught, we may take the procedures a social studies teacher follows in improving the students' ability to extract the basic theme from a long passage that is read, an ability which is needed by all secondary school students, regardless of the kind of school they attend. To the teacher who is interested in tracing the evolution of the emergence of the United States as a world power, it is clear that the intelligent reading of this section of their textbook will help students to understand that the Spanish-American War was part of a movement that has become increasingly important with the passing years. He therefore asks his class to study the chapter in order to see how America became a world power.

To the students, this is an ordinary assignment. Many is the time that they have been asked to study an assignment in their textbooks and so they open their books and begin to *study*. To one student, however, *study* means *read* and he begins to read the material as though it were a chapter in a novel. It is all so clear and interesting that he reads quickly and believes he understands. During the class discussion the next day he is shocked to discover how little he retains of the material he has read; he mutters that he cannot see why he understands the material so clearly at home and yet remembers so little when he is called on in class; and he is indignant if anyone questions the thoroughness of his study. A second student may begin his studying more conscientiously and may read the chapter very slowly, even word by word, and get almost nothing of the main idea underlying the entire selection. He, too, will remember little when called on during a discussion and will also be indignant if the adequacy of his preparation is questioned. A third student may supplement his reading by attempting to memorize all of the details. He may come to class prepared to answer specific factual questions but unable to participate in any discussion of fundamental issues.

Although these three students interpreted the assignment differently and used unlike procedures, all three were unprepared to use the assignment as a basis for intelligent participation in classroom activity. No mere talk by the teacher, whether it is beseeching or censuring, can do much to modify their attack on the problem of selecting the key idea in an entire chapter of a high school text. This type of assignment is an exceedingly difficult one and can be executed effectively only after the student has learned how to handle simpler assignments of the same nature. How can the teacher proceed to help these students learn how to study a chapter effectively.

Designing a Program to Improve Reading

Assuming that these students have sufficient native mentality to enable them to do their school work successfully and that they have mastered the mechanics of reading,* the teacher can initiate the program by beginning with a unit of study considerably shorter and simpler than a chapter, briefer even than a section of a chapter.

For most students, the paragraph is a convenient beginning. The teacher may present a question and ask them to find the answer in the paragraph. After they have become proficient with this type of assignment, they can be asked to read the paragraph and then to find the topic sentence, the sentence that best summarizes the thought of the entire paragraph. As a next step they can be asked to read the paragraph and to summarize it in a sentence of their own. Note how these steps are graded. The teacher does not assume at the beginning that his students can select the major thought in even a single paragraph. In his first step he asks the question first and then guides the reading. The second step calls for selective reading. It is only after the students have mastered these introductory steps that they are ready for the more difficult task of reading a paragraph and then summarizing it.

With this sequence in mind, the teacher is ready to proceed to larger reading units, for example, a two- or three-page section of a chapter. Here, too, the teacher can begin by having a question arise in the course of a discussion which can be answered by reading a section of a chapter. The teacher can write the question on the board and have the students read as much as may be necessary in order to find the answer. They may then be given an opportunity to read other small sections without the benefit of an orienting question given in advance. Later, the student is expected to find the key sentence or sentences of the section; and on subsequent days to be able to summarize the section succinctly.

Moving on to larger units and summaries. It is only after students have demonstrated that they can read a connected passage of several pages and can abstract the major thought that they are ready for the more difficult responsibility of reading an entire chapter. The gradation of steps used with the paragraph and the section should also be followed with the

---

* Because of the wide range of reading ability of secondary school students, some of the members of the class may not need the kind of program discussed in this section while others may not be able to keep up with the program unless it proceeds fairly slowly. The teacher may find it valuable to make individual assignments to students or groups of students while the rest of the class works as suggested here.

chapter as the unit of reading. Before the students are asked to read a chapter, there should be a preliminary discussion which will give them the background for understanding the material to be read. This discussion may well lead to a series of major questions which one should anticipate answering in the course of the reading. With these questions before them, the students may be asked to read the chapter and to find the answers. Later, they can be asked to read a chapter and to reconstruct the list of major captions which the author must have had in mind when he was writing. It is only then that the students are ready for the still more difficult task of reading an entire chapter in order to select the key thoughts and the substantiating evidence presented by the author.

There are several procedures which the teacher may use in order to give further exercise in summarizing a chapter. Students can be invited to edit the chapter by supplying a title for the chapter and appropriate subtitles for the various subsections. Some teachers find it helpful to ask the students to prepare the chapter for publication in a newspaper. This means that they must find the major headline, the subheadline, and also the lead paragraph which summarizes the entire chapter in a sentence or two. Both junior and senior high school students enjoy preparing appropriate headlines; and the writing of a lead paragraph is often a challenging way of preparing a summary of an entire chapter.

Other teachers use the telegram as an exercise in summarizing. The student is asked to prepare a fifteen word telegram which sums up the chapter. Occasionally, additional words may be needed, but students understand that eloquence is expensive in a telegram and that they must find a concise way of telling the whole story clearly.

Students who are asked to read the treatment of a given topic in one text and to compare it with the treatment of the same topic in another book usually find that the two accounts include the same major items but differ in their selection of the minor details. By comparing the two accounts in order to see whether any major thought presented in one was omitted from the other they get some practice not only in reading for thought but also in evaluating the relative importance of various items.

As with so many other study skills, the mere teaching of the skill is unimportant unless the students use the skill so much that it is reduced to habit. It is of little value, therefore, to have so elaborate a procedure for teaching students how to read a chapter effectively if they have no further reason to read for the central thought. It is advisable for the teacher to make certain that every study assignment is understood thoroughly by the students before they do any reading. The preliminary discussion in class should review the background that students must have before they can understand the material.

Using the assignment to direct growth in reading. If the assignment is made by the teacher, it may well include a series of guiding questions which help the students in their reading. If these questions are exclusively factual, the student will do no more than skim over the material lightly until he finds the sentence that answers the teacher's question. Instead, the kind of question that is used should call for understanding and interpretation of a larger unit. Thus, the question, "When did Commodore Perry visit Japan?'" is a poor one because it calls for little thinking, whereas the question, "Why did Commodore Perry's visit to Japan lead to increased Japanese-American trade?" may be a more helpful guide. Assignments that are planned co-operatively by teachers and students or that grow out of a classroom discussion should also be directed at finding the answers to key questions.

The discussion in class after an assignment has been prepared should stress key thoughts rather than petty details. This suggestion does not imply that all substantiating material is to be ignored but rather that the student must learn to differentiate between important material that must be grasped in order to understand the key idea and relatively insignificant details that an author includes in order to round out a presentation.

Other Study Skills

In the same way, other study skills can be developed for use in many subjects. Teachers assume that secondary school students know how to take notes even though an inspection of the notes taken by many college students often reveals little organization and little sense of the relative importance of materials read or heard. The ability to take notes independently can be developed by a series of graded steps just as the ability to read large units can be improved. The one illustration treated in detail above indicates the kind of graded approach that must be made if any other basic study skill is to be developed.

Whether such general skills should be developed as part of the home room guidance program or whether they should be developed as part of subject matter mastery is a debatable question. Because these skills are developed more effectively in a situation in which they are important than when they are taught out of context, it is often preferable to include them as part of the regular work done in the various classes. It is more natural and more effective, for example, to learn how to take notes when a class is engaged in a research project than to learn how to take notes because that is one of the learning problems allocated for discussion in ninth-year home room classes.

In a rigidly departmentalized school, it is sometimes helpful to assign specific skills to various subject areas. For example, the English department may assume the responsibility for teaching students to read efficiently, to take helpful notes, and to prepare outlines; the mathematics department can teach students how to read graphs, while the library staff teaches students how to use the library as a source of information.

The School-wide Approach to Study Skills

If there is such an allocation of responsibilities, it is essential that all of the teachers understand the program for the entire school so that there may be the necessary correlation of the work done in the various classes. It is inadequate, for example, for English teachers to develop skill in outlining, without helping students to apply this skill to their work in other subjects. Similarly, all teachers should encourage their students to use the library skills they have been developing. The Spanish teacher, for example, who has his students look for material in connection with a fiesta honoring a Latin American visitor, can use the opportunity for reviewing what they have learned from the school librarian about finding appropriate sources of information. Of course, the library has to be continuously available for research and students must be given time—either during the class period or in "free" periods—to make use of the library.

Some of these basic skills and attitudes are an integral part of any adequate program of personal orientation in home room classes. The problems attendant upon the need for budgeting one's time, for example, arise naturally in home room discussions. Students who discuss their personal plans for the future understand the purposes they can rightly expect to achieve in their present school better than do other students who have had no such opportunity to examine the school program in relation to themselves. The kind of added insight that comes from a good home room program has direct bearing on the development of the desire and the ability to study.

That many teachers must co-operate in the development of the ability to study indicates how much the success of the entire program depends on each teacher's effectiveness. No school program can succeed if each teacher neglects to use the opportunities he has because he feels certain that everybody else will stress study skills.

TEACHING A SPECIFIC STUDY SKILL

In addition to widely applicable study skills there are a number that are important only in certain subjects. For example, the student who learns how to correct his speech errors may find that this improvement in his speech study habits does not make him any more efficient when he studies a new process in his science class.

Without instruction or guidance, students sometimes develop wasteful work habits. Few students, for example, know how they should proceed when their foreign language teacher asks them to study the new words in the reading passage that has been assigned to them. Typically, the student begins by looking at the short two-column vocabulary list which ordinarily accompanies the reading material. Ordinarily his first step is to read the entire list and say to himself *La plume—the pen; le crayon—the pencil.* He goes over this list several times until he thinks he knows it. His next step is to cover the English half of the table and to supply the English equivalent of the French words. He says *La plume* and after supplying the words *the pen* he verifies his answer by uncovering the word. If he is conscientious, he will go over the list several times until he knows all of the English equivalents. He then proceeds in a similar way to cover the French part of the table while he finds the French counterparts of the English words.

Basing Study Procedures on Valid Learning Theory

The most serious objection to this student's procedure is that it rests on a fundamentally erroneous concept of the way in which one develops a speaking vocabulary in a foreign language. The student's practice of learning his French words only in terms of their English equivalents, by encouraging him to think in English and then to translate his thoughts into French, interferes with his ability to express himself directly in French. His French vocabulary will grow more rapidly if he sees these French expressions in various contexts which help him to understand the meaning rather than as an isolated set of words to be drilled.

The student's procedure of drilling on these English-French word lists is wasteful because it sets up a number of extraneous associations. Many a student who has followed this procedure has found that when he tries to think of the French word for *pencil* he has a clear picture of a list of words in the lower right hand corner of the page. He knows that the word for *pencil* is near the top of the left column and that it is right next to the translation of *pen* and alongside the translation for *paper*. While these many associations may be interesting, they all indicate the extent to which he is remembering much that he does not need to know, while he forgets the one association that is essential.

This student is spending as much time studying the expressions he understands as he does those that are difficult for him. He may know what *la plume* means; but somehow he cannot remember what *le crayon* is. Nevertheless, he spends as much time studying the meaning of *la plume* as he does that of *le crayon*. His method of study establishes serial connections which are distracting. He thinks of *le crayon* as being *the pencil* whenever he thinks of *la plume* as meaning *the pen*. In fact, many a student finds it necessary to run through the entire list before he gets the meaning of a word that is further down on the page. Thus, when he has to find the meaning of *le livre,* he says, *la plume—the pen; le crayon —the pencil; le livre—the book.* This entails a noticeable waste of time and effort before he finds the one word he needs. Moreover, he may not be able to think of the word *le livre* unless he remembers the first word in the list. All these considerations indicate how wasteful is the typical procedure for studying the vocabulary list in the foreign language book.

Developing "Know-how" for Profitable Study

The experienced foreign language teacher can readily aid the student to proceed more effectively to enlarge his vocabulary. He will help them to see that extensive reading of French material on their level of comprehension and practice in expressing themselves directly in that language are far superior to the memorization of word lists. If the teacher can make interesting French reading materials easily accessible to the student, he can develop the habit of extensive reading in French.

Students who are left without guidance may get into the habit of using study procedures that are often wasteful and sometimes positively injurious to effective learning. The junior high school mathematics teacher, for example, must help students to develop more effective ways of solving problems in arithmetic or algebra than simply trying successively to multiply, divide, add, or subtract the numbers in the problem or hunting for the one word in the problem that will offer a clue to the process to be used. The teacher must help his students to see the need for reading the problem and visualizing the situation before they reach for their pencils and start computing.

All secondary school teachers should analyze the special study procedures used in their subjects in order to help the students devise methods of studying that achieve the goal with a minimum of wasted effort. The dramatics teacher may save students untold hours by showing them how to memorize a role in a play, and the mathematics teacher may be able to show the students how to study a geometry proposition so that it is more than an exercise in rote memory.

As has been pointed out earlier, merely getting the student to understand study procedures is inadequate. The more difficult and more important step is to reduce this procedure to habit so that boys and girls will study that way even when they are not supervised.

The teacher must, therefore, make certain that students employ these procedures at all appropriate times. One way of doing this is to spend some class time on study assignments, letting the students begin their work under the teacher's watchful eye. A few minutes of classroom discussion may remind students of the procedures they are to employ. At first, this study period can be run co-operatively, with the students indicating the first step and then having the opportunity to apply that first step before they all go on to the second step. After a while, merely reminding them of the first step, second step, and so on may be sufficient and the students can go through the entire sequence themselves. Students should have the opportunity of going through the procedures on a number of different occasions, while the teacher helps those who are in difficulty.

Using Study Skills

The busy teacher in a departmentalized secondary school may well ask where he can find the time to give his students so much practice in developing needed study habits. One need not resort to the obvious question of asking whether developing the students' ability to work independently may not be as worthwhile an objective as giving them additional information about another topic in the curriculum. The teacher need not sacrifice any major phase of curricular work in order to develop the ability to study well.

Time devoted to supervised study lessons can properly come right out of time devoted to the teaching of the regular curricular material. Thus the science teacher who is planning to devote the period to explaining such terms as *geotropism* and *phototropism* may begin the period by asking the students how they would study this material if no teacher were available. After a few minutes have been spent in formulating a plan of attack, the rest of the period can be used as a directed study period so that the students gain needed practice in good study habits while covering the same material that could have been treated in a teacher-directed lesson.

The assignment for home study can be used as another means of encouraging students to study effectively. It takes more time to give a good study assignment than it takes to give a poor one, and the teacher spends additional time formulating an effective assignment. This time is invested wisely because there is marked improvement in study habits when the assignments are so well planned that students know what they are to do and how they are to do it.*

The time needed for the improvement of the ability to study can be reduced if the various departments in the school are willing to cooperate. The English department, for example, should be able to teach students to use the outline, not only as a basis for organizing a theme to be written but also as a means of taking notes effectively. The English teacher should be ready to help students use these abilities in connection with assignments that are made by other teachers. The foreign language teacher who is helping his students to learn how to conduct a self-prac-

* It may be desirable at this point to reread the discussion of the assignment (pp. 169-175) to see how it can be used to improve study and work habits.

tice period should help them to see how they can apply similar procedures in eliminating errors in English usage. If teachers knew what their colleagues were doing instead of proceeding as though each one were teaching in a one-room school, they could do much to help students to use in other classes the skills they are developing in his and to apply in his classes the skills they have learned elsewhere.

Study Value of Large Units of Work

One of the many advantages of organizing the secondary school curriculum in terms of large units is the opportunity it offers students to develop the ability to work and study independently. The reports which are made to the class by individual students and committees of students are often the result of careful research. There is no gainsaying the value accruing to the student who has learned how to analyze a problem into its major questions, who stays with a problem until it has been solved, who uses the library and other resources to find the answers to his questions, who organizes his data into a report that is helpful to his classmates, and who is ready to answer orally the questions which his classmates ask after he has presented his report. If the research is done by a class committee, the students gain the additional values of learning to work with others, of assuming and sharing responsibility, of criticizing and being criticized.

Whether these study values of unit work will be realized in practice depends very largely on the way in which the teacher guides the students' planning of the research, their preparation and giving of the report, and the group discussion that follows the report. Excessive teacher domination deprives the students of much of the value of unit work and reduces the research to little more than a series of homework assignments made by the teacher. Too little teacher direction is equally undesirable, for many students will do nothing more than copy what they regard as appropriate sections of various books. The discussion of the teaching of units of work in Chapter 4 indicates what the teacher can do to guide students as they work. If such procedures are followed, it is reasonable to expect that the students' preparation of material for class discussion should give them facility in study activities that resemble those of adult life more closely than does the conventional daily homework assignment.

THE PLACE OF WORKSHOP AND LABORATORY CLASSES IN A SCHOOL PROGRAM FOR IMPROVING WORK AND STUDY PROCEDURES

The workshop and laboratory sessions that are becoming increasingly popular in secondary schools are useful means of developing effective means of working and studying, provided that both teachers and students plan these activities carefully. Underlying the extension of workshops and laboratories into other areas than the industrial arts and science classes with which they have usually been associated is the assumption that the classroom is a place where people work on the solution of their problems rather than merely a room where people talk and listen. Whether students accomplish anything as a result of the work they do these periods depends largely on their methods of work. If the students believe in the importance of the problems on which they are working, they can see the importance of learning how to work effectively to solve these problems. These activities therefore offer a natural setting for discussing and practicing effective work and study procedures.

In workshop and laboratory sessions, it is relatively easy to get students to realize that they cannot plan their work unless they have a clear idea of their goals and an effective plan for attaining these goals. If a social studies class uses these sessions as a means of gathering data that are relevant to the solution of a problem, the boys and girls must learn to define the problem, to locate sources of information, to distinguish between pertinent and irrelevant data, to take notes that will help them to use the data when they are needed later, and to organize these data to help solve the problem.

In an English class, these sessions may be used as opportunities for students to work on the stories, the plays, and the articles they wish to include in the magazine they are writing. Here students have an opportunity for using the writing skills they have been acquiring, and they recognize readily the need for planning, for evaluating, and for editing their articles. Formulating and applying the criteria for a good short story, for example, become more than academic exercises when students are using these criteria to help them prepare a magazine of which they will be proud.

The mathematics class that uses the laboratory as an opportunity for attaining a needed degree of skill in using important mathematical practices has done more than discover a pleasant euphemism for a drill period. In a workshop period it is customary to have each student concentrate on his own weaknesses rather than to have all students do the same type of exercise regardless of their individual needs. For these sessions to be successful, each student must know his weaknesses, must know how to correct them, and must be able to see what progress he is making. Students have to learn, therefore, how to use the diagnostic tests that are found in workbooks and in the better textbooks, they must learn how to work with a minimum amount of teacher direction, and they must learn to evaluate their results.

Though each type of workshop or laboratory has its own special skills, there are some skills and attitudes that are common to all. In all workshops and laboratories it is important, for example, that students develop the habit of planning their work and of budgeting their time. If these sessions are conducted well, students may develop methods of working and attitudes toward work that may do more to develop the ability to work and study independently than is possible in more teacher-dominated class activities.

INDIVIDUAL GUIDANCE IN STUDY AND WORK HABITS

Though there are few secondary schools in which the boys and girls will not profit considerably from a good school program for improving study and work habits, even a well-planned program may be insufficient if it consists entirely of class instruction and group guidance procedures. By the time boys and girls reach adolescence, they are so heterogeneous in the habits they have developed that a group program does not make sufficient provision for individual differences. Thus, the graduates of one elementary school in the district may have had excellent guidance in the development of study and work habits while the graduates of a neighboring elementary school may present all of the extremes that result from exclusive reliance on trial-and-error formation of study and work habits.

A good school program must include, therefore, adequate provision for determining individual study needs. When classes are small, a competent teacher can know his students well enough to be able to evaluate their work habits and he can help improve undesirable ones. Interviews with students and observation of their work habits are fruitful sources of information. Individual guidance is facilitated by the core curriculum because each teacher has relatively few classes and spends enough time with each group of students to get to know them fairly well.

If classes are large and the teacher's instructional load is heavy, it is obvious that no teacher can note any but the most glaring instances of inability to study. It is unfortunate that under these unfavorable circumstances, the teacher is virtually compelled to limit his attention to the weakest members of his group and to ignore the opportunities for helping the most promising members of his group to exploit abilities that are used inefficiently.

Use of Tests and Remedial Programs

The development of published tests for measuring study procedures offers the teacher a convenient means of discovering what his students know about study procedures and, to some extent, of learning which procedures they follow habitually. Secondary school teachers should familiarize themselves with such tests as the *Iowa Every-Pupil Test of Basic Skills, Test B, Work-Study Skills, Advanced* [13], which covers map reading, use of references, use of index, use of dictionary, reading graphs, charts, and tables; and *Iowa Tests of Educational Development, Test 9, Use of Sources of Information* [14], which emphasizes selection of appropriate sources. In addition, teachers should examine student self-survey appraisals such as Traxler's *Survey of Study Habits* [26]. Because of the likelihood that new measures will be devised in this area, teachers and their students will profit if the teacher consults, periodically, such a source of information about published tests as the most recent issue of the *Mental Measurements Yearbook* [8].

If these tests are to aid the teacher in analyzing the student's study difficulties, the teacher should know the student's background, certainly his intelligence rating and his record at school, and the teacher should examine the student's various responses on the test for clues in analyzing specific needs.

Diagnosis of study needs is futile unless it is followed by a remedial program. So numerous are the possible needs that no general remedial program can be outlined. The principles and procedures discussed in this chapter suggest the ways in which study and work habits can be improved. It is up to the teacher to use these principles and to adapt the procedures to meet the many combinations of study needs he will find among his students.

Some schools choose to provide for these diverse needs through individual attention in classes of small or moderate size. Other schools provide additional help in clinics or remedial classes for students deficient in study skills, notably reading. Still other schools, in grouping boys and girls according to general ability in most classes, make the assumption that study skills will correlate highly with general ability. Although teachers and administrators feel strongly on the relative merits of these three approaches, we do not have a great weight of evidence to support any position other than one which stresses the need for persistent and specific attention to development of study skills. Even the teacher who is fortunate enough to be able to call on the services of a clinic or remedial teacher should realize that the major job of teaching children how to study is still that of the regular classroom teacher.

Study Deficiencies as a Reflection of Personal Problems

We must recognize that inability to study is not entirely a pedagogical problem. The student who has emotional difficulties cannot study effectively, regardless of the many procedures that may be recommended by the teacher. The young fellow who is in high school because his parents insist on his getting a diploma even though he would much rather go to work and earn some money does not see any reason for doing well in school. To him, a study assignment is merely a challenge to see how quickly he can dispose of it rather than an opportunity to attain the objectives set by the class and the teacher. Similarly, the student who feels that his school career is a failure because his rate of progress is slow may be so completely discouraged as to see no reason for spending time studying by one method rather than another.

For these reasons, the student whose ability to study remains unaffected by the procedures used in class should be the subject of an individual analysis made either by the teacher or by such a specialist as the guidance counselor. If the student's inability to study is the one factor which initiates such an individual case study, he may gain much more than increased efficiency in study procedures as a result of the attention given to his difficulties in studying. The guidance that follows from such an analysis may help make the student's whole school career more rewarding or it may direct his efforts to other fields which hold greater promise of helping him to become an adjusted and productive member of society.

If teaching our young people how to study makes them students in the full sense of the word, it has achieved all that we may reasonably expect of this phase of instruction.

QUESTIONS FOR STUDY AND DISCUSSION

1. What can you do if you are in charge of a typical study hall group and you wish to encourage students to use this period to develop effective study habits?

2. How can you proceed as a junior high school or senior high school teacher to discover the specific study needs of your students?

3. Although the development of good study habits is treated best when it is seen as a school problem to be solved co-operatively by teachers and administrators working together, you find that the other teachers in your school have little interest in the problem.

What can you do as an individual teacher to improve your students' ability to study?

4. How can a teacher help his students to establish good study habits when most of their studying is done at home or in the library where the teacher is not present to see which procedures they do employ?

5. How can you teach a senior high school class how to take notes on the materials they are reading in preparation for a report to the class?

6. A junior high school social studies teacher finds that many students in his seventh-grade class have never progressed beyond the stage of reading word by word so that they do not get the sense of the entire paragraph, let alone of the entire chapter.

What can he do to develop the reading skills these students need without spending so much time as to make it difficult for him to treat the social studies material he is expected to teach?

7. Which skills must a secondary school student develop before he can take helpful notes on a book he has read for your class?

8. How can a junior or senior high school teacher analyze his students'

work habits to see why a promising unit of work had to be dropped because the boys and girls were not able to work except under the teacher's close supervision?

Taking any specific work habit the analysis indicates the students have to develop, indicate how the teacher can help students to form this habit.

9. What should the school do to provide study facilities for students who live in such crowded homes that they find studying at home to be difficult, unattractive, and inefficient?

10. How can each of the principles of effective teaching and learning which were discussed in Chapter 3 be applied to improving the way students study?

BIBLIOGRAPHY

1. AIKEN, Daymond J., *You Can Learn How to Study* (New York, Holt, Rinehart and Winston, Inc., 1953).
2. ARMSTRONG, William H., *Study Is Hard Work* (New York, Harper and Brothers, 1956).
3. Association for Supervision and Curriculum Development, *Learning and the Teacher*, 1959 Yearbook (Washington, D.C., the Association, 1959), Ch. 8.
4. BIRD, Charles E., and BIRD, Dorothy M., *Learning More by Effective Study* (New York, Appleton-Century-Crofts, Inc., 1945).
5. BLAIR, Glenn M., *Diagnostic and Remedial Teaching*, rev. ed. (New York, The Macmillan Company, 1956).
6. BOND, Guy L., and TINKER, Miles A., *Reading Difficulties; Their Diagnosis and Correction* (New York, Appleton-Century-Crofts, Inc., 1957).
7. BRINK, William G., *Directing Study Activities in Secondary Schools* (Garden City, N.Y., Doubleday Doran and Company, 1937).
8. BUROS, Oscar Krisen, ed. *Mental Measurements Yearbook* (Highland Park, N.J., Gryphon Press, various dates).
9. BURTON, William H., *The Guidance of Learning Activities*, 2nd ed. (New York, Appleton-Century-Crofts, Inc., 1952), Ch. 20.
10. GRAY, Lillian, and REESE, Dora, *Teaching Children to Read*, 2nd ed. (New York, The Ronald Press Company, 1957).
11. GRAY, William S., ed., *Improving Reading in All Curriculum Areas* (Chicago, University of Chicago Press, Supplementary Educational Monographs, No. 76, 1952).
12. HARRIS, Albert J., *How to Increase Reading Ability*, rev. ed. (New York, Longmans, Green & Co., Inc., 1956).
13. *Iowa Every Pupil Test of Basic Skills, Test B, New Edition, Work-Study Skills, Advanced,* by H. F. Spitzer and others. Range: grades 6-9 (Boston, Houghton Mifflin Company, 1947).
14. *Iowa Tests of Educational Development, Test 9, Use of Sources of Information,* by E. F. Lindquist and R. V. Vaughan. Range: senior high school (Chicago, Science Research Associates, 1951).
15. KILZER, Louis R., *A Guide to Effective Supervised Study* (Laramie, Bureau of Educational Research and Service, University of Wyoming, 1948).
16. LONG, Forrest E., and HALTER, Helen, *Social Studies Skills*, rev. ed. (New York, Inor Publishing Company, 1954).
17. LONG, Watt Andrew, "The Organization and Administration of Senior High School Study Halls," *Stanford University Bulletin* (September 1, 1952).

Abstracts of Dissertations, Stanford University, 1951-1952 (Stanford University, Stanford, California, 1951-1952), pp. 632-636.
18. National Council of Teachers of English, *The English Language Arts in Secondary Schools* (New York, Appleton-Century-Crofts, Inc., 1956).
19. National Education Association, Research Division, *Homework* (Washington, D.C., the Association, January, 1958.
20. ROBINSON, Helen M., ed., *Promoting Maximal Reading Growth Among Able Learners* (Chicago, University of Chicago Press, Supplementary Educational Monographs No. 81, 1954).
21. SARTAIN, Harry, "How Children and Youth Learn to Study," *Educational Leadership* 16:155-160 (December, 1958).
22. SIMPSON, Elizabeth A., *Helping High School Students Read Better* (Chicago, Science Research Associates, 1954).
23. SMITH, Eugene K., TYLER, Ralph W., and the Evaluation Staff, "Appraising and Recording Student Progress," *Adventure in Education*, Vol. III (New York, Harper and Brothers, 1942).
24. STRANG, Ruth, and BRACKEN, Dorothy K., *Making Better Readers* (Boston, D. C. Heath and Company, 1957).
25. ———, McCULLOUCH, Constance M., and TRAXLER, Arthur E., *Problems in the Improvement of Reading*, 2nd ed. (New York, McGraw-Hill Book Co., Inc., 1955).
26. TRAXLER, Arthur E., *Survey of Study Habits, Experimental Edition*, Range: grade 8-14 (New York, Educational Records Bureau, 1944).
27. WRENN, Charles G., *Practical Study Aids*, rev. ed. (Stanford, Stanford University Press, 1946).
28. WRIGHTSTONE, J. Wayne, LEGGITT, Dorothy, and REID, Seerley, *Basic Study Skills* (New York, Holt, Rinehart and Winston, Inc., 1944).

CHAPTER 10

Improving the Permanence of Learning

»»»»»»»»»»

OUR WHOLE SYSTEM of education rests on the hope that the results of education are lasting and that the knowledge, the attitudes, the interests, the insights, and the skills which students acquire in school become part of them permanently. For us to be effective as teachers, our influence on the ways in which our students are developing must be more than ephemeral. In our concern with the boy or girl before us, we must never lose sight of the man or woman the adolescent is becoming.

"Not for just an hour, not for just a day, not for just a year, but always," may be a beautiful prediction of how long the lyricist's love will last, but it is unfortunately an inaccurate description of some of the effects of schooling. What educational psychologists prove by means of elaborate research and devastating statistics is a matter of sad experience for teachers. To us as teachers, forgetting is more than a psychological phenomenon or a disciplinary problem. It is a major pedagogical challenge that must be met if our curriculum is to do more than furnish a rich background for our students to forget.

Teachers need not resign themselves to the pessimistic view that forgetting will exact its inevitable toll no matter what they do. Instead, they must re-examine the curriculum to see how it can encourage the retention of important learnings, and they must re-examine the methods of teaching to be certain that they are not only facilitating desirable changes in student development but are also helping to make these changes permanent.

No teacher, however proud he may be of his school's curriculum, ever wishes his students to remember everything that is said or done in class.

In every curricular area there are minutiae of subject matter that need not be remembered and that will certainly be forgotten no matter what the teacher does. There are different kinds of forgetting and different degrees of forgetting. We are ready to forgive the forgetting of details if students retain the basic concepts, and we can condone the forgetting of some skills if students know how to relearn the skill should they need it later.

The degree of retention, moreover, is determined only in part by what happens in school during a given year. Will the student remember the rules involved in the correct use of indirect object pronouns in Spanish unless he continues to make use of Spanish after he has ceased studying it in school? Will his attitude toward international understanding persist if he lives in a community where family, friends, newspapers, radio, and television all feel committed to narrow nationalism?

Learning takes so many forms that we cannot speak of retention and forgetting as though all learning were alike. Some of the skills and the facts we study and some of the attitudes and interests we develop become such integral parts of us that they last a lifetime; others fade away almost at once unless used. Thus, the man who has ridden a bicycle in childhood, and then has not been on one for years, soon rides a bicycle with as much ease as he did when a boy, but probably with much more caution. Similarly, an inspiring teacher may be so effective in awakening an appreciation of the human rights of the underprivileged that some of his students will never again be smugly indifferent to those less fortunate than they, even though they may vary a great deal in the ways in which they manifest this concern.

When what a student has learned affects him deeply, it does not have to be used immediately, although retention will be greater if it is reinforced by opportunities to use or to apply what he has learned. This is the kind of learning that occurs when a topic stirs the imagination or brightens the student's eyes as he suddenly understands something that had always puzzled him. This is the learning Kilpatrick [3, p. 265] had in mind when he wrote: ". . . the child learns what he lives, *learns each response* as he sees it and feels it and *accepts* it to live by, and . . . he learns this response *in the degree that he accepts it."*

On the other hand, there is another kind of learning which may nevertheless also be important even though it does not stir the student deeply. For a mathematics student, understanding factoring need not be an emotional experience. Moreover, even after he understands the meaning and uses of factoring, he may need considerable practice with a variety of problems in order to develop such mastery as to lead to retention. While there can be no mastery of factoring without understanding of the basic processes, understanding without practice is insufficient.

Clearly the teacher who is interested in the permanence of what his students learn must know how they learn it and what he can do to help retention.

CURRICULAR FACTORS IN RETENTION

While the school cannot control all of the factors which influence retention, it can organize the curriculum and plan the teaching-learning situations so as to increase the likelihood that students will remember what is important for them to retain. Some persons assume that the way to counteract forgetting is to teach so much that students will retain part of it. What students remember should not be left to chance. Instead, teachers have to decide what to teach and how to teach it so as to influence what students will remember.

If we look at the evidence from psychological studies and at the experience of teachers, it is clear that students are more likely to retain what they learn when they feel deeply involved in what they are studying than when they see their school tasks as a series of routine chores. The more appropriate the curriculum and the more effective the teaching, the better will the students learn what the school wishes them to learn, and the greater will be their retention of what they have learned.

Everything which has been said in earlier chapters about the ways in which we should build our curricula and conduct our teaching is directly relevant to improving the quality and the extent of retention. For example, students will learn better and remember longer when what they are studying is related to their needs, including of course their intellectual needs, and to their interests, including those interests which are developed by the teacher and by the work in which they are engaged. Similarly, learning and retention are improved when students truly understand what they have been studying instead of contenting themselves with superficial ties.

Focus on Significant Learning

The curriculum must be so organized that it focuses attention on those phases of student development that we hope will be permanent. The effective teacher thinks of his course not only in terms of material to be included but also of aims and objectives. What does the English teacher hope for from the unit on contemporary American poetry? What new attitude does the social studies teacher expect as a result of the discussion of labor problems? It is these basic questions that should determine what is to be included in the material to be presented or discussed.

Once a course is viewed as being a means of attaining major goals, the teacher has a criterion in terms of which he can evaluate the subject matter of the course and he has a framework for organizing the material to be included. The English course ceases to be a series of discussions of unrelated poems, and the science course becomes more than a succession of discrete topics.

It is easy to emphasize the learning of facts and the acquisition of skills, leaving to chance the development of interests, of attitudes, and of points of view. Stress on figures of speech and the rhyme schemes of sonnets may obscure the more important aim of developing an abiding interest in poetry. Similarly, in science classes, all too often finding the correct answer takes precedence over establishing scientific methodology. The experiment which does not yield the anticipated results should lead not to "doctoring up" the end product but to analyzing the experiment to see why the forecast was not correct under the conditions prevailing.

Specific planning is necessary for the development of desired attitudes or interests. The modern curriculum, concerned with the effect that classroom and cocurricular activities have on students, rightly focuses attention on these attitudes and interests. Business courses, for example, actively seek to develop the attitudes which their graduates need as much as they do skill in typewriting or in the use of office machines. If students are to remember the attitudes they have developed in school long after they forget unused skills, the curriculum should not leave to chance the growth of these attitudes.

Many of our traditional one-year high school science courses, for example, are too brief and yet too ambitious in scope to lead to permanent changes in the way students think or in the attitudes they develop. Teachers stress the memorization of formulae that fade rapidly from memory unless they are used, and the development of laboratory skills that have little value except in the laboratory. As a result, all that many students retain is a number of fragments, such as $\frac{1}{2}gt^2$, *Boyle's Law, valence,* and *dominant trait,* often without more than a hazy recollection of why these expressions are so significant to scientists. On the other hand, those students for whom these science courses are the introduction to advanced work sometimes do not get as thorough a foundation as they need.

Organization of Curriculum

The curriculum should be so organized as to help students understand the relatedness and significance of various learning experiences. After all, the function of general education in the secondary school is to help develop well-rounded individuals for responsible participation in a democratic society. If we act on this premise, we shall tend to minimize the importance of the conventional categories of physics, chemistry, and biology which are more appropriate for the advanced courses students take later than as the basis for organizing a basic course in general education. We shall then emphasize not isolated bits of scientific knowledge but an understanding of what we mean by a scientific approach to a problem. By taking a problem and indicating how scientists prepare their hypothesis and evaluate its adequacy experimentally, the teacher can help students to develop a greater understanding of science and scientists, and may help them to use the scientist's approach to a problem as a means of solving other problems that confront them. After the students have had such an introduction to science, they will be better prepared to profit from the courses they may later take in the various sciences.

The organization of the curriculum about larger problems rather than in terms of departmentalized subject matter makes more likely the retention of school learnings. This change tends to focus the student's attention on a single problem rather than to disperse it among many unrelated areas. Yet, an integrated course as well as a highly departmentalized one is subject to the weakness of meaningless facts and overemphasis on petty details. It is nevertheless encouraging to note that current curricular procedures make it easier for the teacher to aim at emphasizing those phases of learning which are more likely to become permanent.

In the departmentalized school, the typical secondary school student pursues too many unrelated subjects simultaneously. In the same term, a student may be taking courses in English, American history, Spanish, French, and chemistry, in addition to work in the so-called minor subjects of music, art, and health education. So numerous are the demands that are made on him that he does little more than meet the minimum standards in each of his courses, since any one of his five major subjects could use his entire available time to good advantage. If he is to read all of the books recommended by his history teacher, for example, there is no time left for his other subjects. Since he scatters his energies among so many subjects as well as among his cocurricular and extra-scholastic interests, he often fails to approach the degree of mastery he is capable of achieving in even one subject area. It is small wonder that such a student retains so little of that vast store of knowledge he once inspected so casually.

The number of different subjects studied each term in secondary school contributes to the superficial familiarity that passes for knowledge in some schools. The fetish of the 65 per cent passing mark reflects the school's attitude too well. Let a student understand only two-thirds of the material set before him and the school lets him develop the idea that he has "passed," that he has discharged his obligations to that subject and can now proceed to other fields. The student expression, "I have had chemistry," has an air of finality that implies that hereafter he will make no demands of chemistry and chemistry will make none of him.

When the curriculum is organized in terms of major problems rather than major subjects, the student's activities can be so related that we may hope for a greater degree of mastery, and a more likely degree of permanence, of the basic concepts, the fundamental skills, the underlying attitudes and interests that should be developed by the thorough exploration of a major area of human concern.

The core curriculum is an obvious illustration of the way in which secondary schools are attempting to center the student's activities about major problems in the program of general education. Even so relatively minor a change as the correlation of two subjects, such as English and social studies, may also increase the permanence of the effects of schooling. For example, the time that would ordinarily be spent in an English class in developing communication skills merely as useful skills can be used to apply them to reinforcing the learnings in the social studies classes.

The novels and the plays which these students read offer another medium for developing the attitudes and the interests in which both classes are interested. Similarly the letters and the essays which students write, the discussions in which they participate, and the talks they deliver offer additional opportunities for students to develop and to express a point of view that is the concern of both teachers. Is it not likely that under these circumstances the students can carry away more than will be retained than when English and social studies classes are conducted independently of each other?

Selection of Subject Matter

Within the curriculum there is need for considerable discrimination in selecting only that which is significant from man's vast store of accumulated knowledge. Many of our courses are packed too full of material to allow for adequate emphasis on the important points. The history teacher tends to include too much history and the mathematics teacher includes too much mathematics. This overabundance of material to be taught stems partly from the tendency to include in a course everything that is relevant and important. There is so much, however, that is relevant and important that both teacher and class soon find themselves concerned chiefly with the need for "covering the material." As a result, many a class discusses in one period what merits a week of class time.

Actually, there are two problems involved. One is the problem of including too many topics so that each is dealt with superficially. The second is the problem of unending, massive, and trivial detail woven in, through, and around a topic. We find here the necessity for creating a fine balance by identifying the major concepts, topics, and skills and then elaborating these with rich, but significant, detail.

Few will object to the deletion of meaningless detail, but the expansion of knowledge has brought us to the time when even some important items have to be omitted. Comparison of American history books published recently with those of twenty years ago illustrates the point. In many new texts half of the volume is given to the twentieth century in comparison with a quarter or less in earlier editions. Events of the last generation have crowded out some material in American history whose importance can easily be argued. It is better for us to omit some material deliberately than to present a great deal and to rely on almost chance factors to determine what will be remembered.

Experienced teachers have long known that the permanence of the impression varies almost inversely with the amount of material presented. The new teacher often overwhelms the class with the extent of his erudition. The young social studies teacher is fresh from the college where he has taken course upon course in American history. He knows so much about the recent research concerning the background of the Articles of Confederation that he does not sense how little of all this will be retained by his students. Instead of focusing attention on the major points he wants to emphasize, he is likely to confuse his students by presenting too much data. As he matures in the classroom, he will find himself spending more time on fewer issues rather than attempting to compress a college course within the limits of a single class period.

METHODS OF TEACHING AND RETENTION

The classroom teacher is likely to attach too great significance to the limitations imposed by the structure of the curriculum. It is comforting for him to be able to attribute the extent of forgetting to the organization of the curriculum, for curriculum construction has been traditionally the responsibility of superintendents and principals, not classroom teachers. There is much, however, that can be done by the individual classroom teacher, even when he finds himself enmeshed in the requirements of an inflexible course of study, without waiting for a thoroughgoing revision of the course outline.

The Importance of a Sense of Purpose

Of primary importance is the element of purpose in learning. To some extent purposefulness is determined by the curriculum—the choice of learning experiences—but no learning carries its purpose automatically. The sense of purpose dwells within the student. It remains for the teacher to help the students relate the particular teaching-learning situation to their purposes, needs, interests, goals. When the students see the purpose of the learning activity, the problem of motivation evaporates. The effectiveness of learning is then limited only by each student's potential, the quality of teaching, and the availability of necessary materials.

The teacher can organize the term's work so that it stresses major concepts and basic skills. He must restrain the understandable temptation to show his students how much he knows, and think instead of his contribution to helping them to understand that which they should remember. To the extent that he shapes the curriculum by guiding classroom activities, he must seek to stress those aspects that lead to permanent changes in the students he is teaching.

Forgetting—or Ineffective Learning?

Permanence of learning depends on more than the amount or the kind of material studied in class. Since no student can remember something he has never learned, the first step in encouraging retention is to stimulate more effective learning. The experienced instructor teaches with a view to permanence, and guides classroom activities so that students will retain what they have learned.

Frequently we speak of forgetting something when it would be more accurate to say that we never really learned it. Thus we speak of our inability to remember the names of the people to whom we are introduced at a large social gathering, when it would be more appropriate to say that we never took the trouble to learn their names in the first place. Most of the devices for improving the ability to remember names are merely ways of improving the learning of these names. Thus, the memory courses that are so popular with lay people urge them to repeat the names to themselves or to try to associate the name with some characteristic— in short, to do something with the name, for we learn only as we are active in the learning process. The gains in the ability to remember names come from the increased attention and the greater activity with which these people learn the names, rather than from an improvement in memory itself.

The concept of learning as an active process is so basic to an understanding of modern educational procedures that it can hardly be treated adequately if we think of it only as a means of controlling forgetting. The need for stimulating pupil activity has entered, therefore, into the discussion of every topic we have treated thus far and will enter into the discussion of all of our remaining topics. If we are to help our students to remember, we must help them to learn. If we are to help them to learn, we must see that they are active in the process, for we learn what we use, and we remember what we continue to use.

Let a student try, in school or at home, the iodine test for starch in potatoes and in other foods, and he has a better basis for learning, and for retention, than if he is a passive spectator while the teacher performs the experiment and then describes and explains the result. There is much in science that will be learned better as students conduct their own experiments and then try to develop the generalization through inductive reasoning. Many of our newer secondary school science textbooks are rich in their array of experiments that can be conducted by students in school and at home with equipment and supplies that are inexpensive and readily available.

This is not to gainsay the effectiveness in learning of "autonomous interests"—interests which students develop as they study and which carry their own motivation apart from considerations of usefulness. An example is the student for whom mathematics weaves a web of fascination for its own sake. Here we find the makings of the scholar in the best sense, of the student who follows knowledge in and of itself. For these *rarae aves,* the word *interest* may be substituted for *usefulness.*

Merely providing opportunities for the students to use what they have been studying is inadequate unless we are certain that they understand the material or the process they are applying. Just as some people do not hear the name of the person to whom they are being introduced, many students do not have a clear understanding of what they are supposed to be learning. So long as the student regards "plus or minus" as a mystic expression which must be mumbled before giving the answer to a square root problem in algebra, and so long as he repeats mechanically that "Pressure times volume is a constant," he has nothing that is substantial enough to be worth remembering. It is all too easy for a teacher to misinterpret the students' pat repetition of the teacher's expressions as indicating real understanding and insight. By a rich choice of illustrative material, by carefully graduated steps in the explanation, and by ample opportunity for the students to use the material, the teacher must be certain that the class really understands the material before there can be any hope of retention.

Vivid Teaching and Retention

To the classroom teacher, the necessity for vivid teaching is a challenge that can help make teaching the stimulating profession it really is. The science teacher who begins his treatment of a topic by stressing its applications to the daily lives of his students or by performing an attention arresting demonstration makes a more vivid impression than does another teacher who has a stereotyped pattern of procedure. Similarly, the history teacher who makes history come alive by constant reference to contemporary affairs finds that learning is more real; and retention more marked.

The emphasis on vivid teaching may easily be reduced to an absurdity of overuse or misuse. We are not suggesting that the classroom be turned into a freak show at a carnival. The science teacher who starts fires in ten basins on the table and then shows how the type of fire extinguisher that is effective for one kind of fire is dangerous with another type may give his class an exciting period, but there is no way of predicting how much they will retain of the basic principle as compared with their clear impression of the fun they had shouting advice. The suggestions that appear in Chapter 8 with reference to the use of illustrative materials are equally effective when used here.

Let us apply this principle to a science lesson in which the teacher is seeking to develop an understanding of phototropism in plants, of their tendency to turn their leaves toward the source of light. He may begin by letting the boys and girls examine the plants in a window box in order to see how the stems bend toward the window. The students may be given an opportunity to conduct the experiment of placing a plant in a cardboard box in which only one window has been cut and then have them observe the way in which the plant adjusts itself to the single source of light. The teacher may aid the students to list the essentials that a plant must have if it is to thrive and then ask the class to see how each plant manages to supply its needs. During the discussion, but after the class has demonstrated its understanding of the principle involved, the term *phototropism* is introduced and students are helped to see how the use of this term by those who understand its meaning makes circumlocutions unnecessary. Having the students prepare a summary of the experiment is still another way of focusing attention on the expression and on the idea it represents.

This type of lesson is more likely to lead to retention than is the routine type of period in which the teacher presents a series of terms— *phototropism, geotropism, heliotropism,* and so on—and then proceeds to overwhelm the class by presenting a series of formal definitions. The class that "learns" all of the tropisms in one period may be able to get high scores on a quiz the next day, but it does not have much that it can remember in later years.

Repetition in Different Ways

One of the first lessons every newspaperman learns is that every story must be told at least three times before the reader will get the point. Here is a picture of the screen star as she alights from a plane at the local airport with a caption telling us that the current screen siren has returned home to spend a quiet week-end with her parents. Regardless of whether or not there is an accompanying picture, the story will have a headline which tells the story in all its essentials. The first paragraph of the story, the *lead,* again sums up all the important points of the news item; and, despite all this, with the second paragraph the reporter begins all over again and tells the entire story once more, this time in greater detail. Examine any newspaper article and there is telltale evidence of the reporter's having followed this rule of three: headline, lead paragraph, story.

If the reporter must tell us the story three times before adult readers will understand that a new star has come to town, how many times must a teacher convey a really important idea before it is grasped by adolescents? The reporter does not repeat the story in the same words because he knows that no reader would continue reading the article to the end. He tells it in different ways. He abbreviates the details of the story for his lead paragraph, he elaborates in the story itself, and he knows that his editor will add a headline. Even though a student is not as free to abandon a lesson as a reader is to turn to another newspaper column, the teacher cannot rely on too obvious a series of repetitions. What the teacher does is to present other instances, to call for other types of application, to use other sources for developing an idea.

Thus in Chapter 3 of this book, the discussion was centered about the principles underlying effective teaching. As the eighth question among those listed for discussion at the end of the chapter, there was a long quotation from Hilgard with its summary of the principles of learning as seen by educational psychologists. One of the reasons for including this quotation was that it was another way of presenting some of the main points included in the chapter, but without repeating them as originally given.

Spaced Learning

The psychologists' evidence is convincing that spaced learning is more effective than unspaced learning as a way of assuring retention. Applied to the schoolroom situation, this means that it is better to have the students learn a new topic, apply it, and then return to it at intervals than it is to have them explore fully one topic at a time never to return to it again. In general, a test following the close of a unit fulfills the need for the first repetition to come early, but this should be followed up at two- or three-week intervals with other repetitions. Like so many other principles developed by educational psychologists, this emphasis on spaced learning corroborates a practice of long standing among good teachers.

There are many ways in which the teacher can help the class to return to material that has been studied before. When a topic studied earlier is part of the background of a new topic to be developed in class, the discussion of the new topic affords an opportunity to continue the discussion of the older topic. Thus, the class that has studied the rise of nationalism in Italy can draw on that material when studying the rise of nationalism in Germany. Similarly, the chemistry class that has developed the concept of a reversible reaction will use that concept in much of the subsequent work.

Even the classroom test can be used as a means of periodic recall if each test that is administered includes some questions on old topics as well as questions on material studied recently. All too frequently students like to divide their subjects into separate compartments. Once they have completed the unit on labor problems they are ready to forgive and forget; they prefer not to be reminded of labor problems subsequently. It is helpful to counteract this tendency by including a question on labor problems in the test that is given following the completion of the unit on agricultural problems. By having the tests refer to material studied earlier, the teacher can stimulate the kind of cumulative relearning that helps retention. This procedure is illustrated by the inclusion of Question 10 among the questions at the close of Chapter 9, Improving Work and Study Skills. Question 10 asked the reader to see how the principles of effective teaching discussed in Chapter 3 can be applied to teaching students how to study.

So great is the pressure in our schools to include all of the material prescribed for a course that the teacher tends to focus all of his attention on the new topic discussed in class and to leave the periodic recall to the end of the term. In many classes the entire last week is devoted to what the teacher refers to as "review." Both experimental evidence and classroom experience suggest that better results follow from having these "review" lessons come during the term instead of being concentrated in the last week.

Eliminating Distractions

Returning once more to the question of why people do not remember the names of those to whom they are introduced at a gathering, we find that part of the explanation arises from the fact that there are ordinarily so many distracting stimuli at the time introductions are being made that we do not focus our attention on learning the names of the people we meet. It is easy to understand why we do not learn these names if, while the introduction is being made, we are also trying to recall the name of the very tall girl standing near the window, we are wondering whether we are dressed appropriately, we are hoping someone will open a window, and we are thinking how much happier we would be if we had gone golfing instead. To learn the names of those to whom we are introduced, we have to focus our attention on the names and ignore distracting stimuli.

Similarly, there are sometimes too many distracting stimuli in class, so much that is being said and being done at the same time, that students are not focusing their attention on the most important phases of classroom activities. Sometimes students are so preoccupied with their own concerns—personal, social, and occasional economic problems—that they find it hard to keep their minds on the classroom objective. The learning process is much more efficient when attention is concentrated on major outcomes rather than when it is dispersed among many items, some important and others trivial.

Reinforcing Key Points

Each unit of work should have a distinct contribution to make to the student's development, a contribution that he must recognize as important. The discussion during a period, or a series of periods, should lead up to a conclusion that the student recognizes as being the justification for the discussion. For this reason, one of the major contributions which the teacher makes to the conduct of classroom activities is his guidance in assisting students to recognize and to remember the culmination of a discussion or the basic principle in a lesson.

Before the teacher can focus attention on the keynote of the discussion, he himself must identify the keynote. Finding the keynote is not always a simple matter, for it may involve both careful thinking about the selection of the material to be included and the effective organization of that material. Many secondary school lessons, moreover, seemingly have no keynote to sound. Though the English teacher often has the opportunity of guiding his students to the heights from which they can see new vistas of beauty or from which they can understand what men are made of, he must often spend much time with the mundane details of spelling and grammatical usage. Even these lessons on the mechanics of English, however, must stress basic principles rather than unrelated details if they are to be effective. Many a classroom discussion that rambles on almost aimlessly can gain both force and direction from the teacher's efforts at pointing the discussion toward the solution of a major question.

What can be done with such classroom activities as the mathematics lessons that seek to give the student needed practice in applying a principle he has learned or with the metal shop lesson that provides the unexciting but essential background for the construction to be discussed later? In many instances these lessons can be made more significant to the student if they are related more closely to the key lesson, whether it be one that precedes or that is to follow the type of lesson we are now discussing. Let the students see that the mathematics problems are merely variations of a basic principle studied the day before, and a routine practice period is transformed into an effective way of emphasizing the basic principle. Similarly, if the description of a new process in working with zinc is understood as part of the background of the larger task with which they are concerned, all of the lessons are interrelated and become more understandable. A great many classroom lessons can be centered about a basic theme.

Aiming at One Target at a Time

Closely related to the preceding suggestions is the practice of aiming at one point at a time. Any teacher who has ever followed the customary practice of returning a set of test papers to the class and then skimming hurriedly over all the questions knows how futile the period is. So much has been mentioned that little has been taught. Though some students may discover what the correct answer to the fourth question is, relatively few will remember it. Here, too, the lesson will gain in effectiveness if the teacher stresses the correction of a common weakness or the development of a basic concept.

This practice of aiming at one point at a time applies to many skill subjects. The improvement of written or oral work in English is more effective if the discussion is centered on a major point, even to the exclusion of minor ones. Little is gained when the teacher tries to correct all speech errors or all grammatical errors in a single period and then has to try to correct all of these errors again in every subsequent period. The more effective teacher tends to focus the attention of the class on the correction of one common weakness even to the extent of temporarily overlooking other equally serious weaknesses. In fact, he may even refrain from using class time for the correction of some of these other errors and rely on work with the individual students who need help in those respects.

The teacher must stress one point at a time in all classroom activities, not only in those which contribute to the learning of important skills. The home economics teacher who is trying to get her class to understand the essentials of a wholesome diet must not allow herself to be distracted by the opportunity to discuss ways of setting the table or of greeting guests.

To interpret too narrowly the suggestion of stressing one point at a time may make for artificial and ineffective teaching. It is difficult, for example, to justify the development one day of the attitude that we must be considerate of our guests' feelings only to ignore it the next day as we stress that mothers must be concerned with the mental as well as the physical health of their children. On the other hand, the teacher who goes to the other extreme of including in the discussion everything that occurs to him or to any of his students is bound to be ineffective. It is up to each teacher to guide classroom activities at that intermediate point at which relevant material is included without weakening the force of the central idea about which the discussion is centered.

USING REVIEWS AS AIDS TO RETENTION

A good review is more than a mere repetition of material discussed earlier. Although a review lesson aids permanence, its major value is the contribution it makes to the student's understanding of the topic. Reviews aid retention not so much by affording an opportunity for repetition and practice as by deepening the student's insight into the problem or by increasing his appreciation of its ramifications. Truly, a re-view should be a *new* view, not a repetition. It should provide a new perspective from which to study the topic.

Posing a new problem is sometimes an effective way of reviewing. The American history class, looking back on its study of the Reconstruction Period, may be challenged to indicate how the twenty years following 1865 might have been different had Lincoln survived, or the South been victorious. Or a world history class may build a picture of Europe from 1815 to 1848 which might have eventuated from a victory by Napoleon at Waterloo. What were the events which actually took place in these two cases? How would they have been different, given a basic change in circumstances?

The English teacher guiding a review of *The Merchant of Venice* may have a committee report on Ludwig Lewisohn's more sympathetic treatment in *The Last Days of Shylock*. A common but effective device for review of a short story or novel is posing the problems of developing a movie scenario or television script and selecting a cast.

Stressing the application is still another method of reviewing. The application of principles of physics and chemistry to household appliances —the electric refrigerator, steam iron, kitchen sink—similarly makes effective review of the laws affecting gases, power and resistance, and the effect of a vacuum.

An intelligent and careful rereading of material can serve as a basis for review. Thus the instructor can ask his students to prepare a one-hour examination on the material, the questions to consist of both objective type and essay questions. The proper completion of this assignment compels the student to reread the material with a view to selecting key materials and to making worthwhile applications of the content.

Supplementary reading has long been used as a method of review. The Lewisohn parallel to *The Merchant of Venice* is an example. A Foreign Policies Association pamphlet may supplement textbook study of the United Nations; a fictionalized biography like *All the King's Men* or *The Last Hurrah* may accompany the study of government operation. The teacher then asks the class to compare the treatment in supplementary sources with that in the text. Are there significant differences? What important ideas are added to the material found in the text?

Lest we create the impression that we have exhausted the possibilities for a review, we should think of other means of review than have been suggested here. A well-planned excursion or trip sometimes enriches the students' understanding of a topic even better than will additional reading. Similarly, participation in a carefully planned forum or intelligent listening to a radio or television forum will add to understanding. By comparing or contrasting the topic under discussion with another topic discussed earlier, it is possible for a class to review both topics effectively. Even so formal an activity as the preparation of an outline or of a tabular summary may be helpful if the students bear the major responsibility for the work.

Throughout our treatment of the review runs the thought that it must be planned intelligently and executed carefully. No review can be challenging if it is merely a rehash of old material. The rare teacher may occasionally be able to think of a good review question on the spur of the moment. For most of us, however, a stimulating review lesson necessitates considerable thought and planning. Certainly neither the spirit nor the goal of a good review lesson will be produced by the routine announcement: "Review Chapter 10 for tomorrow. You may expect a ten-minute quiz."

It may be objected that these review lessons indicate how the material should have been presented in the first place. Why not use the problem approach in the first instance? Why not conduct the class on a planned visit when the material is being discussed? Should not the original discussion be based on the students' wide reading? These questions may all be answered in the affirmative without detracting from their value as review procedures. A review lesson is not a distinct type of lesson. If the material has been presented through the problem approach, it can be reviewed by using any of the other approaches. All that the review does is to enrich the student's understanding by having him relearn the topic from another point of view from that employed in his first contact.

SYSTEMATIC PRACTICE AND RETENTION

The organization of the curriculum and the teacher's effective guidance of classroom activities are important aids in the attempt to increase the permanence of much that is learned at school. Although the extent to which students remember anything they have learned is determined largely by the extent to which they continue to use it, there are some phases of schooling for which students need much more systematic practice than is ordinarily afforded. This is particularly true when there are specific subject matter skills and factual associations which must be strengthened by repeated use.

Psychologists speak of the value of overlearning as an aid to retention. In the psychological laboratory, a list of words is regarded as having been learned as soon as it can be recited without error. Any practice beyond the first successful recitation is considered as *overlearning*. Applied to a classroom situation, a mathematics student has learned how to solve simultaneous equations the first time he solves one himself. Both in the laboratory and in the classroom, the use of such a definition of learning involves the risk that students will retain little of what they have learned. If we are interested in encouraging retention rather than in plotting the learning curve, we must assure the student of ample opportunity for overlearning. Planned practice sessions are convenient and effective ways of getting that degree of overlearning which is essential for lasting retention.

A second purpose of practice periods is to reduce certain associations to the level of habit. The use of systematic practice to establish routine procedures and to make them automatic is not objectionable, provided that we do not use routinization as a substitute for reflective thinking. After the mathematics student understands that $(a+b)\,(a-b) = a^2-b^2$, he ought not to have to stop to rediscover the principle every time he is confronted by a similar situation. The principle may well be subjected to drill so that the student responds to $(c+d)\,(c-d)$ by thinking automatically of c^2-d^2 just as he thinks of 10 as soon as he sees $5+5$.

A major obstacle in the way of effective practice periods is the student's lack of interest in this type of work. Though learning a new skill may be challenging and therefore interesting, performing the practice necessary for overlearning rarely is either exciting or satisfying to the adolescent. As a result, the student goes through the motions of practice exercises almost listlessly. He may say the words given by the speech teacher and he may do the examples assigned by the mathematics teacher, but he performs these duties as chores. Work done in this spirit has little educative value.

There are two principles which are worth underlining. First, students learn to the extent that they take responsibility for their own learning. Nagging by the teacher is a poor substitute for practice which the student undertakes willingly because he recognizes and accepts the need to improve his performance. Second, the amount of teacher-planned practice or repetition which is needed varies inversely with the motivation of the student to achieve a given learning task. Do not these principles confirm experience in observing the boy who wants to make the football team as he practices with the tackling dummy?

How can the teacher arouse in his students the active interest in the systematic practice that is needed if lasting learning is to occur? From the experience of secondary school teachers, the following suggestions have evolved.

1. Eliminating All Unnecessary Practice

Some of the practice periods are unnecessary because the material is not important enough to deserve additional time; still other periods can be eliminated if more advantage is taken of opportunities for using the skills in connection with other work. Students should be led to see the need for systematic practice. They should know what it is that they are trying to make permanent and they should be aided to see the significance of the need for permanence or for automatic response.

Emphasis in practice sessions should be focused on material that demands habituation and permanence. Much of the objection to practice sessions results from their overuse and the tendency to drill on everything. Is the material sufficiently important to deserve systematic practice? The temptation to which the conscientious teacher yields is to exaggerate the importance of his material until he feels that everything is important and must be remembered. The English teacher may think that the biographical details of all the poets studied must become part of every student's background and the history teacher may believe that a great many dates and names must be remembered. If all teachers were to be severe critics of their own subject matter and were then to say that these are the few principles that must be understood, these are the major processes that must be mastered, and these are the essential facts that must be retained, the chances are that the total material that would be subjected to intensive drill would be much less than is so often the case in even the best of schools.

It is easy enough to agree in theory that all unnecessary practice should be avoided, but what can the classroom teacher do when part of the class needs practice on a specific skill? From the standpoint of classroom administration it is so much easier to have the entire class working at the same task that the teacher is likely to have uniform practice exercises for all students. Such a procedure constitutes a serious waste of time, for some students are doing work they do not need instead of performing tasks they do need. What is even worse is the effect on student morale. What interest can a student find in continuing to drill on a process he has mastered? Does it make the work seem more valuable if he realizes that he is doing the work because another student, not he, needs the practice?

2. Adapting Practice to Individual Needs

Clearly, it is necessary for the teacher to individualize practice periods in order to have each student performing the task he needs to do. If the teacher has employed diagnostic procedures wisely, it is a simple matter for him to know the areas in which each student needs additional practice. If the teacher has prepared mimeographed practice exercises, or if he has a good index of the practice material that is available in the class texts, reference books, and workbooks, each student can be assigned to specific practice material that is most necessary.

Though some students may not enjoy using practice material even when they see the need for it, the practice of individualizing practice periods does so much to increase the effectiveness of teaching and to heighten classroom morale that it should be the rule rather than the exception. It should no longer be possible for the student to feel that there is little sense in his doing his mathematics examples rapidly since that would mean only that he will be doing more examples each period. He should now know that the sooner he succeeds in attaining mastery over that process the sooner will he be able to go on to new material.

3. Knowledge of Progress

Another way of arousing interest in systematic practice is to enable the students to see their own improvement. When standardized tests are used and norms are explained simply to students, they furnish one way of helping the student to see his educational status and to note changes in his level of achievement. Individual progress charts also help him to see the improvement he is making. It is sometimes helpful to let a student retake a test he had earlier in the term or to write another paper on a topic he discussed at the beginning of the term. By comparing the earlier and the later papers he can see how much he has progressed. Where pretests are used, they can also be employed as a way of pointing to the progress that the student has made since the pretest was administered. If students can be encouraged to help diagnose their own difficulties and to select the points on which they need further drill, the gain in motivation is obvious.

4. Understanding before Practice

Experienced teachers know that systematic practice is a procedure for overlearning or for habituation, not for learning something that is not understood. Before any practice session is conducted, the teacher must be certain that the students understand the principle, the skill, or the fact that is the subject of such systematic practice. To return to the mathematics illustration used earlier, the class must understand why $(a+b)(a-b) = a^2 - b^2$ before any drill can be given to fix the connection. Practice is meaningless if the students do not understand, or if they have forgotten, the principle. The common practice of having slow students memorize rules and definitions they do not understand or of having them practice rules they do not grasp has nothing in its defense except expediency or the need for getting students to pass in examinations.

No teacher will quarrel with the Gestalt psychologists who stress the greater value of insight as compared with that of empty repetition of words or motions. A student who does not understand the principles which determine whether the adjective precedes or follows the noun in a French sentence can repeat an endless series of French sentences without understanding the principles any better. Students who are ignorant must be taught, not drilled.

5. Practice in Real Situations

Not only must students understand what they are practicing, but they must practice the skill in the setting in which it will be used. "Practice makes perfect," we are told, but this adage is applicable to classroom procedures only if students are practicing the right procedure in an appropriate setting. The English teacher who has his students read aloud a list of words which are all accented on the first syllable, such as *absolutely, applicable, lamentable,* and *positively* often finds that his students continue to mispronounce these words when they use them in their informal conversation. If the English teacher is concerned with his students' remembering to pronounce these words correctly as they speak, he must see that practice is given in context rather than in isolation.

Although a student may be able to get much more practice when the drill is specific, we must not forget that he will later have to apply that knowledge in a more general setting. The boy who thinks of $-x^2$ as soon as he sees the example $x(-x)$ may not apply the law of signs when he is actually solving an equation. Similarly, the youngster who knows where to place *not only . . . but also* in a special exercise may not use the expression correctly in his free writing or speaking. It is therefore necessary to include ample opportunity for the student to practice the material in the setting in which it will ordinarily be used. Although the speech teacher, for example, may use special word lists effectively in order to afford ample opportunity for students to practice a difficult sound, he must also give his students sufficient practice in using this sound correctly in fluent speaking. No practice program in any subject area is adequate if the practice is always performed in terms of isolated skills.

6. Economy of Time and Efficiency of Practice

In many instances, considerable time can be saved by eliminating unnecessary work and by restricting the students' responses to the one skill that is being practiced. If the English teacher, for example, is interested in having the students practice the correct placing of the correlatives *not only . . . but also* near the words modified, it is not necessary for them always to rewrite the entire sentence. They may be able to get much more practice for a unit of time if they write only the words immediately after each of these expressions. For example: *not only we . . . but also the guide; not only danced . . . but also swam.* Similarly the mathematics student who needs additional practice with the law of signs in multiplication can be spared the task of working with long examples. By using small numbers the teacher can be certain that the major part of the time will be spent with the specific skill that must be practiced. The mathematics teacher therefore finds it convenient to use such a series of multiplication examples as: $x(-x)$, $(-2)(-4)$, $(x+2)(x-3)$, and so on. Even more time can be saved if the teacher groups his class so that each student receives the practice he needs.

The teacher's good sense will have to resolve the inconsistency between the suggestion that the students' responses be limited to the one skill that is being practiced and the point made just a few paragraphs earlier that they should practice the skill in the setting in which it will be used. If all practice exercises are specific, students may not be able to transfer their training to the other situations in which this skill or this fact must be used. On the other hand, if all practice exercises consist of these larger situations, the students will spend relatively little time on the specific skill or association they need to strengthen. Both types of practice exercises are needed. The electrical wiring teacher will, therefore, see that his students get enough practice in splicing electric wires so they know how to do it correctly, but he will also see that they have opportunity to splice wires as they rewire table lamps.

7. Shortening the Practice Sessions

Short practice sessions are usually more profitable than long ones. Practice sessions are usually more effective when they are short enough to encourage intensive application rather than when they are so drawn out that students work halfheartedly. Ordinarily, six five-minute periods are more effective than a single thirty-minute period or than two fifteen-minute periods. In a short period, the teacher can be certain of more intense pupil participation than can be expected in a longer period. There is little to be gained from a practice period that is so prolonged that students lose interest in their performance.

If a practice session is to last five or ten minutes, the work must be thoroughly planned lest an undue proportion of the time be spent in getting ready for the practice or in winding up the period. This means that all practice materials should be prepared in advance. The mathematics teacher must have his examples selected, the social studies teacher must have his questions ready, and the shop teacher must have the materials and tools at hand. In a short period, the teacher cannot afford to waste time trying to phrase questions or selecting words or examples to illustrate a principle.

The use of mimeographed practice materials is often an economical procedure because it enables the teacher to assemble in advance the material that is to be presented. Mimeographed material, moreover, reduces the amount of time that is often wasted in transcribing examples and sentences when all that is really needed is that the student supply the answer. In most subject areas in which systematic practice must be provided, there

are now available excellent workbooks that provide more carefully selected practice exercises than any teacher has time to construct. The
teacher should use these materials intelligently, selecting exercises as an
individual student or the class needs them. He should not simply follow
the workbook slavishly, abdicating to the publishers his responsibility to
plan learning experiences in keeping with the needs of his students.

8. Practice as Part of Regular Work

Much of the exercise that students need may be given indirectly as they
continue with their work in that subject area rather than in special practice sessions. Thus, the speech teacher can use every period as an opportunity for giving his students exercise in correct speech. In subjects that
are cumulative, like mathematics or a foreign language, each day's work
offers an opportunity to practice skills that have been learned earlier. It is
boring and wasteful for the Spanish teacher to continue drilling his students on the correct pronunciation of Spanish vowels until each student
achieves perfection; instead, each meeting of the class can be used as an
opportunity for familiarizing the class with good oral Spanish. If the material is important, it will be used, and the practice that comes with
application of a principle to many situations is more effective than is that
which comes from formal drill periods that have been continued too long.

If we plan our curriculum wisely and teach effectively, we may yet be
able to join the chorus and sing, "not for just an hour, not for just a day,
not for just a year, but always."

QUESTIONS FOR STUDY AND DISCUSSION

1. To what extent is it likely that the organization of the secondary school
curriculum about large units of work rather than in terms of separate subjects
will improve the retention of the material that is being studied?

2. During a spirited discussion of the stand which the members of the
class should adopt concerning an important piece of legislation now being
debated in Congress, the students are more eager to present their own point
of view than to understand the points of view of their classmates. Under these
circumstances they are not likely to remember anything except what they have
themselves contributed to the discussion.

What can the teacher do to maintain the spirited quality of the discussion
and yet increase the retention of the most important points made in class?

3. During a classroom discussion it soon becomes apparent that the students seem to have forgotten completely an important concept that was developed last term but that has faded from their memory because of disuse. You
realize that if you take the time adequately to reteach the topic they studied
last term, there will be too little time to develop the topic for which your class
will be held responsible this term.

What should you do?

4. In line with the suggestion that you focus attention on key materials,

you organize class work in terms of major concepts and skills. Your school system, however, administers uniform examinations at the end of each term with questions that stress the trivial items you tend to ignore. As a result, a disproportionate number of your students fail in these examinations. What should you do?

5. Is there anything in this chapter that you would make the subject of a drill period if you were the instructor in this course?

6. Taking any chapter in a textbook you would be called upon to use if you were teaching a secondary school class, make a list of the specific items you would use for drill purposes. How can you defend the inclusion of each item on your list? How would you conduct a drill period on these items?

7. In the school to which you have been appointed it is customary to spend the week before the final examinations in a review of the term's work. Assuming that it is impossible for you to redistribute these review periods throughout the term and that you must spend the entire week in reviewing the term's work, how can you plan this week so that it will be most helpful for your students? (In order to answer this question you will have to think of the way in which a specific class spent the term.)

BIBLIOGRAPHY

1. BURTON, William H., *The Guidance of Learning Activities*, 2nd ed. (New York, Appleton-Century-Crofts, Inc., 1952), Ch. 18.

2. GRAMBS, Jean D., IVERSON, William J., and PATTERSON, Franklin K., *Modern Methods in Secondary Education*, rev. ed. (New York, Holt, Rinehart and Winston, Inc., 1958), Ch. 11.

3. KILPATRICK, William Heard, *Philosophy of Education* (New York, The Macmillan Company, 1951), p. 265.

4. MILLS, Hubert H., and DOUGLASS, Harl R., *Teaching in High School*, 2nd ed. (New York, The Ronald Press Company, 1957), Ch. 13.

5. MORT, Paul R., and VINCENT, William S., *Modern Educational Practice* (New York, McGraw-Hill Book Co., Inc., 1950), Practices 15, 18.

6. SCHORLING, Raleigh, and BATCHELDER, Howard T., *Student Teaching in Secondary Schools*, 3rd ed. (New York, McGraw-Hill Book Co., Inc., 1956), pp. 202-208.

7. STRATEMEYER, Florence B., and others, *Developing a Curriculum for Modern Living*, 2nd ed. (New York, Bureau of Publications, Teachers College, Columbia University, 1957), pp. 409-417.

8. TIEDEMAN, Herman R., "A Study in Retention of Classroom Learning," *Journal of Educational Research*, 42:516-31 (March, 1948), reprinted in REMMERS, H. H., and others, eds., *Growth, Teaching, and Learning: A Book of Readings* (New York, Harper and Brothers, 1957), pp. 110-121.

CHAPTER 11

Evaluating the Results of Teaching and Learning

»»»»»»»»»

THE SECONDARY SCHOOL curriculum is different from what it was a generation ago, but is it any better? The methods of teaching are different from what they were a generation ago, but are students learning any more or improving in their ability to use what they have learned? The teacher is concerned with the development of attitudes and the cultivation of intellectual interests, but are his students developing the attitudes and the interests he thinks he is encouraging? It is to answer such questions as these that teachers examine the evidence secured through evaluation, a process which includes two phases: the determination of values to be sought and the measurement of progress in achieving them.

When we speak of *evaluating* the effectiveness of educational procedures rather than of *measuring* their effectiveness, we are doing more than substituting the new word *evaluating* for the old word *measuring*. In the process of evaluation we are interested not only in measuring the changes that education helps bring about in boys and girls but also in judging the desirability and the adequacy of these changes. We must include in our evaluation not only the scores on tests of subject matter mastery but also the observable changes in such less easily measurable traits as the development of attitudes, the growth of interests, and the adequacy of emotional adjustment.

Evaluating the results of instruction in English, for example, by measuring the degree to which boys and girls remember the facts in the story they have read does not reflect all of the goals the teacher may have been striking to attain. If he is to evaluate his success in reaching these goals, he must find ways to measure increased interest in reading, increased understanding of character development, improved standards of literary discrimination—as evidenced in the student's actual selection and reading of books, not merely as expressed in answers to examination questions. One important aspect of evaluation, therefore, is measuring those developments which are important objectives of a learning program.

The process of evaluation is complicated by the broadened scope of educational objectives and by the reorganization of the curriculum. So long as the school day is regarded as simply a succession of periods during which students are expected to learn American history, mathematics, inorganic chemistry, English literature, and French, we can measure students' competence in these fields by using standardized achievement tests devised by experts in test construction. When we plan our curriculum in terms of larger objectives that transcend departmental lines, however, we get only a limited picture of student development if we restrict our evaluation to the use of standardized achievement tests.

Can teachers ascertain the degree to which the school meets the needs of individual boys and girls? This question presupposes that teachers know enough about these boys and girls to be able to identify their needs. To help meet the increased demand for information about students, old testing procedures have been improved and new methods of evaluating have been devised. We have learned to use anecdotal records, diagnostic techniques, standardized achievement tests, interest inventories, cumulative records, controlled observation of student behavior, and graphic rating scales, as well as a whole array of standardized tests that tell us something about the personality development and the attitudes of the boys and girls in our classes.

We are discovering how to use new techniques of measurement, but we are also finding new values in old procedures. A short story that a student writes in an English class may be graded so that it yields only one more mark to be entered in a roll book, but it may also be analyzed so that it indicates his specific needs if he is to learn to write effectively and it can help us to understand why he acts as he does. A classroom discussion is an effective means of helping students to understand the implications of a basic concept, but it also furnishes an opportunity for noting how individual boys and girls react to criticism of their points of view and for observing how ready or resistant they are to accepting suggestions from others.

EVALUATION IN TERMS OF BEHAVIORAL CHANGES

As was indicated earlier in the discussion of the objectives of secondary education, these objectives must be expressed in behavioral terms if education is to make a real difference in the lives of learners. As a corollary, the educational program has to be planned with a view to changing behavior, and evaluation must be planned so that it measures these changes.

A first step in the development of adequate teaching and evaluative procedures is the careful definition of objectives in terms that are measurable. It is clear that *developing the ability to type 40 words a minute with no more than two errors* is a more easily measured objective than the vaguer *developing skill in typing.* Can similar behavioral definitions (that is, definitions in terms of observable processes) be formulated for other objectives, for example, *appetite for learning?*

Working together, the teachers in a school can begin their formulation of a behavioral definition of appetite for learning by asking what it is that a student does when he has a well-developed appetite for learning that is different from what is done by another student with no such appetite for learning. While it would be helpful if all schools accepted this definition, such widespread acceptance is not essential since the very process of analyzing goals is bound to sharpen teaching and improve evaluation.

As the teachers look for the overt manifestations of an appetite for learning, they will enumerate such behavior as the following: the student uses classroom discussions as an opportunity for asking as well as answering questions; the student suggests topics for class discussion or personal research; the student continues to read on topics studied in class even though the class has moved on to other topics; the student engages in study activities for which he knows he will receive no extra school credit; the student reads on these topics during his leisure time at home; the books and magazines which he reads during the summer vacation include material that was referred to in class during the year. From these and other characteristics that arise during discussion, the teachers will select those which they regard as the most important manifestations of the appetite for learning they wish to develop.

Finding Evidence of Changes in Behavior

Now that the teachers know what they mean by "appetite for learning," they can evaluate the extent to which the school actually does develop this trait. In the process of evaluation many procedures will have to be used. The administration of teacher-made and of standardized tests is often helpful, though it will probably not contribute much in the instance now being discussed. Some help may come from analysis of student behavior during classroom discussion. A study of the books and magazines withdrawn from the public library during the summer months often reveals more than teachers expect from this source. An innocuous-seeming questionnaire on How Boys and Girls Spend Their Leisure Time will answer many of the teachers' questions, provided they are not put too bluntly. Conversations with parents are another source of relevant data. A classroom discussion will help teachers to evaluate the extent to which students think they have an appetite for learning, provided that the students speak freely because they regard evaluation as a co-operative process into which censure and praise do not enter.

Using Behavioral Definitions of Learning as Formulated by Experts

While the teacher's attempts at formulating his own behavioral definitions of learning are important as a means of analyzing his goals, his procedures, and the results, few teachers have the time, the facilities, or the technical training for an adequate analysis of learning. Classroom teachers should familiarize themselves, therefore, with some of the important studies in this field that have been conducted by investigators who have access to resources far beyond the teacher's reach.

Reference has been made earlier* to the work of French and others [7] in preparing behavioral definitions based on *The Purposes of Education in American Democracy.*

The Eight Year Study, which was also referred to earlier† issued a volume [1] in which the staff formulated objectives, classified them, defined them in behavioral terms, suggested situations in which the achievement of objectives is shown, and developed methods for appraisal in these situations. Similarly, the committees which studied general education in secondary schools and colleges indicated how faculties can evaluate the extent to which objectives are attained [6]. Because analysis of learning is basic to the development of sound evaluative procedures, Bloom and a committee of test experts prepared their own set of operational definitions [4].

Each of these studies is rich in its implications for good teaching and adequate evaluation.

DEFINING GOALS IN THE CLASSROOM

Though it is undeniably important to be able to measure the success with which the school is achieving the basic objectives of education, most teachers are concerned with more immediate problems of evaluation. While a unit of work is in progress, students and teacher want to know how well the activities are going, and after the unit has been completed they should examine the results to see whether they accomplished as much

* See p. 34-35.
† See page 52-55.

as they had hoped. The teacher wants to know whether his students are mastering the material they have been studying and he must be able to analyze the difficulties that are impeding progress. The teacher needs valid ways of measuring his students' growth in knowledge and understanding. He will also seek means of measuring changes in attitudes and of judging the desirability and the adequacy of the changes.

Defining the Goals in Co-operative Planning

Different educational situations necessarily present different problems of evaluation, but no teacher can evaluate intelligently unless he first has a clear idea of the trait he is evaluating and of his reason for evaluating. It is easy to challenge the value of classroom tests which are administered routinely on Fridays and at the end of a marking period, tests that often demand nothing more than the ability to recall what has been memorized. What is not so readily apparent is that many supposedly modern evaluative procedures may be equally inadequate. Before students can evaluate their own work or the work of others, they must know what they are looking for and they need criteria in terms of which they can make their judgments. Otherwise, we shall get the kind of comment illustrated by the junior high school pupil whose contribution to the evaluation of a committee report was, "Marilyn's report was very boring and it was too short."

When students and teacher plan a unit of work, some of the objectives will be equally clear to the students and to the teacher; others will be more important in the teacher's mind than in the students'. If students understand the purposes, they can formulate the criteria for evaluating the end product and for making the continuous evaluation that enables them to judge the progress they are making. Thus, the pupils in the junior high school class that spent a week at a museum studying African art knew why they were going and were able to evaluate their progress when they met for their daily group discussions. As they realized the weaknesses of some of the ways in which they spent their time that day, they were able to plan the next day's activities more effectively.

Defining the Goals When the Teacher Does the Planning

The analysis of objectives is as important in activities that are planned and conducted by the teacher as in activities that are planned co-operatively. To be sure, the analysis of objectives in terms of observable student behavior does not assure ability to evaluate student growth, but it is a necessary first step without which adequate evalution is impossible.

After purposes have been clarified and objectives defined, the next step is the selection of methods for measurement. These include formal instruments like standardized and teacher-made tests and informal measures like observation and anecdotal reporting.

THE MANY PARTICIPANTS IN AN EVALUATION PROGRAM

A comprehensive program of evaluation necessarily depends upon careful selection of objectives and upon accurate and complete measurement. Evaluation of the adequacy and effectiveness of the school's educational program is, therefore, too large an enterprise to be undertaken by individual teachers. The joint effort of test specialists and the teaching staff is needed for the job of measurement, and the selection of goals often involves the community, including parents and pupils, as well.

Each teacher needs to contribute the data he accumulates for evaluation of individual students or of the total school program. Assessing improvement in an adolescent's ability to get along with others depends in part upon the availability of information about the way he got along with others in the past. Anecdotal records submitted by previous teachers can greatly enhance this kind of evaluation. A record of the results of intelligence tests, personality inventories, and achievement tests administered by other teachers makes it unnecessary for each teacher to administer a complete battery of intelligence and other standardized tests every time he wants to know what progress is being made. Periodic evaluation of a school program must, therefore, be a co-operative venture which makes intensive use of the information contained in the student's folder or on his cumulative record card.

Because the evaluation of students and of the school is so closely related to the whole educational program, it cannot be left to the specialists in evaluation. To be sure, there are technical problems in the creation of new tests that demand the services of experts and there are some measures, for example, clinical tests of emotional adjustment, that must be administered and interpreted by specialists. In the main, however, it is the teacher who is in the best position to help the student profit from evaluation and who must, therefore, understand how to evaluate and how to interpret the results of evaluation.

Co-operation with Specialists, Parents, and Students

The teacher must be able to state his objectives, to construct adequate classroom tests, and to use standardized tests intelligently. He must know how to observe student behavior critically and how to use other procedures for learning about his students. In the planning and execution of evaluation programs, he must be able to work with guidance counselors and with psychologists, with administrators and with colleagues, with parents and with students.

The students themselves can contribute much to the evaluation of their growth. Some testing procedures, such as sociograms [9, pp. 276-287], have been devised to take advantage of the opportunities which students have for learning much about their classmates by working and playing with them. Classroom discussions, conversations with students, and requests for written comments suggest other ways of gathering the reactions to the school programs from the boys and girls who are, after all, the ones most directly affected by the program.

Guiding the student's self-evaluation is a promising development in modern secondary school practice. As the student matures, he should play an increasingly important role in the evaluation of his growth and in the analysis of his strengths and his weaknesses. Adolescents need not sit back impassively while the teacher administers tests and then informs the students of their weaknesses. Students who understand the purposes to be served by the tests they take should attach less importance to test scores than to the light these tests throw on achievements and shortcomings. Because adolescents are so often worried by their real or imagined inadequacies, it is good mental hygiene practice to teach them to evaluate their abilities objectively and to attack their shortcomings by planning and executing an appropriate remedial program and not by brooding or by flights of fantasy.

Reporting to Parents

Parents have so vital a stake in the evaluation of their children's growth that they should be called on to supplement and to assist in interpreting such data as the teacher may have. Both the parents and the school are served inadequately when parents are expected to do no more than sign the report cards that are sent home regularly.

The preparation of the conventional report card takes up a great deal of the teacher's time without being correspondingly valuable for parent or student. A major weakness of most report cards is the meagerness of the information they contain. How should the parent interpret a *C* or a grade of 75 *per cent* in mathematics? Does this grade mean that his daughter is doing as well as can be expected from a person of her ability or does it indicate that a very bright girl who can do work of outstanding ability is content with achievements of lower quality? Does a *C* grade reflect a uniform level of work or is it an average of excellent work in some aspects and barely acceptable or even unsatisfactory work in other respects? When personality traits are included on the report card, they are ordinarily couched in such vague terms as *co-operation* and *school citizenship* that a rating of *Satisfactory* or *Needs Improvement* tells the parent little about what he ought to do to help his daughter.

Although it is administratively convenient for the school when all report cards are issued on specified dates, this practice does not improve the value of the reports sent home. In classes which are working on large units, the teacher may be much more specific in a report that is submitted on October 30th, for example, than on October 15th, as required by the school calendar.

The approaching end of a marking period ordinarily presages a series of tests in almost all classes because the teacher seeks to have some "objective" basis for computing the grades he has to report. Since students often have to take so many examinations in one week, they do not have adequate time for preparation and review and are thus denied one of the values which may follow from the administration of a class test. The teacher, on the other hand, is swamped by the many papers he must read and the grades he must compute and has no time to use these tests for diagnostic purposes.

Emotional impact. Uniform marking periods are objectionable from a mental hygiene point of view, too. Little is gained when the entire school knows that on a certain day each student is taking a report card home. Sibling rivalry may be heightened when brother and sister regularly bring their report cards home for signature on the same day. The inevitable question on the school bus, "What did you get?" makes for additional overemphasis on grades and for further unnecessary comparisons.

The one value of such reports is the incentive they offer for students to work hard so that they may receive high grades. Even this value is overrated, for those students who really need the added incentive are not the ones who are stimulated. On the contrary, the slow learner who receives a low grade may be discouraged from exerting greater effort. Because school achievement depends only in part on the student's effort, it is unwise to focus so much public attention on grades. The student's innate ability, his emotional adjustment, his interests and needs, the appropriateness of the curriculum, and the effectiveness of the teaching are illustrative of factors beyond his control that will influence his grades.

What can the teacher do if he has little voice in determining the kind of report card that is used and if his school uses the conventional system that calls for grades for each student at stated times? Since the teacher knows at the very beginning of the year that he will have to report grades by a given date, he need not wait until the week when grades are due before beginning to evaluate the work of his students. By using the work of the entire marking period as the basis for grades, he will be able to lessen the tension that accompanies the administration of "the test that really counts." He certainly will do all he can to keep the report card mark from dominating the classroom activities.

Supplementing the report card. Realizing that marks tell an inadequate story of the students' work in class, the teacher can supplement them by conferences with students and parents and by individual letters. These letters can be effective without being lengthy. Brief notes commending the student who has made an important contribution, the student whose rate of improvement in some trait is outstanding, and the student who is trying hard to improve although the gain is not yet apparent, can do much to improve student morale and to lead to even greater improvement. Knowledge of success is an important incentive to learning. During a semester, every student does something that is commendable and he will be encouraged a great deal by the teacher's recognition.

The student who is not progressing satisfactorily can also be helped by a brief note home, provided that the teacher does more than merely view with alarm. The teacher must be specific and helpful. What does he expect the parent to do after receiving the letter? Parental reprimands and punishment are rarely the solution to the student's difficulties at school. The more definite the teacher is in indicating the specific nature of the student's difficulties and the more constructive he is in suggesting ways in which the parent can help the student to overcome these difficulties, the more effective will the letter be. In many instances, it is advisable to follow up the letter with a conference.

Giving fuller information. It is better to send report cards home less frequently and to make the reports more helpful than to spend much time preparing meaningless reports at brief intervals. When teachers have the time and when the arrangements are feasible, a parent-teacher conference, even twice a year, is preferable to written reports of grades and marks. Some schools have their teachers prepare individual written reports on each student, but this procedure is practicable only when classes are small, for when classes are large, the writing of individual letters is so time-consuming that teachers either resort to stereotyped notes or sacrifice time they can hardly spare. As a concession to the limitations of available teacher time, some schools use a check list which teachers fill in instead of supplying only grades, so that the parents may get a clearer picture of their children's adjustment and progress at school without requiring the teacher to do so much writing as the preparation of individual letters necessitates. These check lists, however, are often impersonal and inadequate. Other schools supplement the array of numbers on the report card with verbal comments on the student's adjustment and personality traits.

The necessity for close co-operation of home and school points to a serious inadequacy that is almost inevitable when classes are so large and the teacher's burden is so heavy that the teacher cannot find time for conferences with parents or even for the writing of personal notes. An occasional Parents' Evening is far from being an adequate solution, for no teacher in even a moderately large school can possibly deal with the situation if all the parents accept the invitation to come and discuss the problems with the teachers. Some schools devote an entire day to conferences with parents, but even a day is not enough for the kind of conference that is most fruitful. If the school believes that these teacher-parent conferences are important—and they are—provision for them should be made in the teacher's program throughout the year.

A continuous program may be maintained in those schools where a home room teacher has special responsibility for guidance or where a core program brings the teacher and students together for more than one period a day. In other schools, the guidance counselors and the administrative staff serve as the link between home and school. The many devices that have been used—not one of them being entirely satisfactory—demonstrate how important it is that the class size and the teacher's total instructional load be small enough to make for effective co-operation of parents and teachers.

USING STANDARDIZED ACHIEVEMENT TESTS

The administration of appropriate standardized achievement tests is an important phase of evaluation, largely because they enable us to compare the achievements of a specific group of boys and girls with the achievements of comparable students throughout the country.

We can interpret the scores on standardized tests more exactly than we can interpret the scores on tests constructed by teachers. Thus, a teacher in a school which administers teacher-made midterm examinations may find that his students' marks are much higher this term when he organized classroom activities about the unit of work on *Inventions That Have Changed Our Way of Living* than they were last term when he taught in terms of daily lessons. This term no student received a mark lower than 73 per cent, and the class median was 84 per cent. Last year, when the teacher presented the prescribed history by the textbook recitation method, the median mark on the midterm test was 71 per cent, and five students received marks below 65 per cent, the passing mark for the school.

How should he interpret these test results? Do they indicate that students learn more when units of work are used, or was this year's test easier than last year's? Were the weaker members of the class stimulated to work harder, or did the test happen to stress questions that were emphasized in class discussions? Is this year's class doing much better work than may be expected of typical secondary school students of its grade level, or has the teacher become so accustomed to inferior work that he no longer regards it as inferior? Does this year's class have the same, or greater, ability to profit from instruction than last year's class had? Ideally, the standardized test provides an instrument for making comparisons between the achievement of this experimental class with last year's class or with that of classes throughout the country.

Using Standardized Tests with Discrimination

We must use standardized achievement tests with caution if we are attempting to evaluate a school program that differs from the conventional secondary school program. When students are rated and teachers are judged by the results of standardized tests, we sometimes find that the indiscriminate use of standardized achievement tests perpetuates old curricular practices rather than encourages the development of new procedures to achieve newly recognized aims.

Test authors construct their items in terms of subject matter content that is commonly studied throughout the country. The test author's emphasis on topics that are generally taught runs counter to the teacher's attempt to adjust the curriculum to meet the specific needs of the individual boys and girls in his classes. The more freely the teacher adjusts the curriculum to his specific class, the more vital may school become to his students—but the lower may be their scores on a standardized test that is based on subject matter which a specific school regards as outdated.

Standardized achievement tests sometimes stress different phases of learning from those which the school is seeking to emphasize. In social studies, for example, standardized tests tend to stress factual items rather than items that measure the development of interests, the deepening of understanding, and the strengthening of the sense of personal responsibility for the solution of social problems, all of which are phases of growth that the modern teacher accepts as more telling outcomes of social studies in secondary schools.

Because the test author is working on a test that will subsequently be standardized, he wants items that will be administered, scored, and interpreted uniformly. For these reasons he may prefer objective-type questions that call for factual information, because they are more likely to have one and only one acceptable answer.

Even when the items on a standardized test are appropriate for the curriculum developed by a school, too great a respect for the norms published by the test authors may encourage a degree of complacency among teachers and administrators that keeps them from helping students to achieve as much as they should. The table of norms does not set the goals for any class, since it reflects nothing more than the average attainment of large groups of students, bright and dull, eager and apathetic, taught well and taught incompetently, in well-equipped schools and in impoverished schools. The national norms indicate what average students achieve when they attend average schools and are taught by average teachers. No teacher who is dissatisfied with mediocrity can accept norms as indicating the goals toward which he must strive. On the other hand, under less favorable conditions, use of the norms as standards may set goals far beyond anything which these boys and girls can hope to achieve.

There are times when the norms for even a good standardized test may be inappropriate for the class as a whole, let alone a single student. If a test that purports to measure critical thinking assumes that the students to whom it is administered read well, the scores obtained in a class of poor readers may reflect their reading ability rather than their ability in critical thinking.

When the standardized test is appropriate for the class and there is nothing to affect the performance of all the students—for example, no noisy football rally going on outside while the test is in progress—the scores for the class as a whole will not be affected as much by such chance factors as the effect that a family quarrel has on a student. Hence, the scores are more valid and more reliable when applied to the class than to an individual student.

Standardized tests just do not sample enough of an individual student's ability to warrant using the test results as the only basis for evaluating an individual student's achievements. It is unwise to assume that after administering a standardized test we can say that Tom, who is now starting the tenth grade, is as good in mathematics as the average high school senior, as good in English composition as the average high school junior, but is only at ninth-grade level in his social studies work. And, of course, a single administration of a standardized test does not take into account the possibilities that a student may be too disturbed by difficulties at home to concentrate on the test that day, that he may misinterpret the question, or that he may not be able to read quickly enough to complete the test within the time limit.

Using Standardized Tests to Evaluate Progress Toward Broader Goals

Standardized achievement tests ordinarily concern themselves almost exclusively with subject matter abilities. Some of the newer standardized achievement tests have been constructed in terms of current curricular concepts and are therefore much more valid measures of educational progress than are the older tests. The teacher whose concept of educational objectives includes changes in interests, in attitudes, and in the ability to think clearly is justified in broadening his selection of standardized achievement tests to include standardized tests that measure interests, attitudes, and thought patterns.

Because the teacher is usually too busy to keep up with the development of new tests as they are published and may not have the technical background in measurement to enable him to judge the various tests, he can draw upon the assistance of the school psychologist, if one is available, or he can refer to such a source as the *Mental Measurements Yearbooks* [5] which not only describe new tests but also present an expert's evaluation of them.

For the best use to be made of standardized tests, it is important that the teacher-student and teacher-principal relationships be such that standardized tests are used primarily as a means of helping to evaluate important educational procedures rather than as subtle ways of judging the teacher's conscientiousness or competence. When teachers and supervisors can sit down together to plan the testing program and, later, to interpret the test results without creating the attitude that the teacher's professional reputation is at stake, it is possible to use standardized tests to good advantage.

USING TEACHER-MADE TESTS

Even though standardized achievement tests are constructed expertly by specialists in test construction who have the time, the skill, and the facilities for making each item in the test the best possible means of measuring the specific fact or skill with which it deals and for making the test as a whole far more valid and reliable than any teacher-made test can hope to be, by far the larger share of the time spent on tests in schools is given to the administration of tests constructed by teachers.

Uses of Teacher-Made Tests

The teacher-made test is often much more useful as an aid to learning than is the standardized test because the teacher constructs his tests to meet a specific purpose with a specific class. All too often the purpose to be served seems to be only that of providing a basis for calculating the student's grade. There are other, and usually more important, uses to which the tests can be put.

Pretests. When a class studies a new topic, the teacher frequently assumes that all the members of the class need the same instruction, though some students know more about the topic before it is studied in class than other students will know at the end of the unit. The teacher who administers a pretest before a topic is studied in class is in a better position to take advantage of his students' background as a basis for enriching it instead of wasting time teaching what they already know.

Diagnosis of learning progress. As the unit proceeds, the teacher needs to know how well the group and the individuals in the group are progressing. Short tests can be given from time to time for diagnostic purposes. Such tests may disclose particular problems which interfere with learning: reading difficulties that impede reading of an essay, numerical skills which obstruct solution of problems in mathematics, misunderstanding of basic concepts of democracy necessary to understanding ideological conflicts when studying World history.

Periodic tests may be used to disclose how well students are making progress toward established goals so that the teacher may check on the efficacy of his own teaching procedures. Inadequate progress may suggest the need for changes in procedure, content, or pace.

A new view of the subject. The test situation often challenges the student to take a new view of the topic he is studying. The "original" in geometry, comparisons and interpretations in literature, and the evaluation of underlying factors in historical developments stimulate him to take a new look instead of parroting back what he has read or heard. The new view may thus serve as an effective review.

Perspective. Teachers often present a wealth of material which gives vitality to the subject being studied but which confuses students as to what is important and what is merely illustrative. The well-designed test can help the student distill what is basic from what is supportive.

Evaluation of growth. Finally, the test provides information for evaluation of growth. Testing which is confined to a variety of facts alone may be an inadequate basis for measuring learning. The teacher must make sure that the objectives he espouses in teaching do determine the content of his test instruments.

Reducing Student Tension

Teacher-made tests can be used to measure mastery without attaching so much importance to the tests that students become tense at the thought of impending tests or regard cheating as undesirable only if one is caught.

Undue emphasis on major examinations is undesirable even from the point of view of the teacher who attaches great importance to grades. The broader the base on which the grade is based, the more valid it is. Instead of reflecting what the student does on only three days during the term and ignoring the quality of his work at all other times, the student's grade should reflect the work done during the whole term.

Oddly enough, the way to reduce many of the undesirable by-products of classroom examinations, from students' tension to the teacher's burden of correction, is to give more rather than fewer tests. Tests that are frequent can be short, taking ten or fifteen minutes rather than a full period. Students are not likely to be as tense if they know that any single test is only one of many bases for grades than they are when they think that this is the one test on which so much depends. The teacher's task of correction is eased when he has short papers to correct rather than the periodically over-packed brief case full of papers. The results of short tests can be used when they are needed rather than compel teacher and class to wait for the results of the occasional long test. Since these short tests do not create much anticipatory anxiety, the teacher does not have the problem of dealing with the emotional letdown and the anti-climactic feeling that so often follow the administration of an occasional major test.

Planning the Test

If the teacher-made test is to fill its important role in modern teaching, the teacher must know how to prepare good tests [8, 11, 13, 14, 15, 17]. Since the classroom test is not designed for publication, it need not meet the exacting standards set for standardized achievement tests, but it should meet the standards for a good classroom test.

Some criteria for test construction have already been mentioned either directly or by implication. The test should serve a clearly defined purpose—for example, to diagnose difficulties, to motivate further study, to emphasize important issues, or to evaluate student progress. Test items should be consistent with the purpose for which the test is given. They should center about those aspects which have been stressed in teaching. The types of questions should be varied in order to avoid penalizing students who have particular difficulties not directly related to the learning task. For example, the student who reads slowly should not be further penalized by the kind of short answer test which requires a large amount of reading in a short time.

Some criteria will be familiar to the student who has studied educational psychology. The test must be valid—that is, it must measure that which it sets out to measure. The test must be reliable: if the test were repeated without opportunity for further learning or forgetting, the student's scores on the two administrations of the test should be consistent. The test should be as objective as possible: the examiner's subjective appraisal and attitudes should be eliminated as much as can be from the administration, marking, and interpretation of the test. Finally, the test should be relatively easy to administer and interpret.

Constructing the Tests in Terms of the Purpose to Be Served

What kind of test the teacher should construct or whether it need be constructed at all can be answered best only after the teacher knows why the test should be administered.

Classroom teachers will find it helpful to borrow one of the procedures used by those who construct standardized tests and to prepare an outline of the areas to be covered by the test before they start writing any questions. This test outline need not be elaborate or detailed, but it should include a list of the purposes of the test and of the major areas and skills to be covered, with some indication of the relative importance of each. This statement of purpose and scope is a useful guide to the selection of appropriate questions and a means of keeping the teacher from exaggerating the importance of one phase to the neglect of others.

Much of the preference that even experienced teachers have for one kind of question or another arises from inadequate understanding of test construction. Some teachers avoid using objective-type questions because they think students guess when they do not know the answer, as though students never "take a chance" when they are confronted with an essay question to which they are not sure they know the right answer. Teachers sometimes spend a great deal of time rating the answers to essay questions because they do not know that multiple-choice items can be constructed to measure judgment, reasoning, and the ability to apply information and skills in a new setting. Other teachers never use essay questions because of the difficulty of rating the answers objectively, although the teacher who prepares a detailed marking key can rate a set of essay papers with sufficient objectivity.

Using Essay Questions

For essay questions to have the values that are claimed for them, they must be carefully framed. Many essay questions that seem to call for the exercise of judgment are really nothing more than memory questions. As soon as the student sees the question, "What were the three most important weaknesses of the Articles of Confederation?" he immediately proceeds to write, "There was no strong central government. Congress didn't have the right to levy taxes. There was no . . ." as automatically as he writes "1492" in answer to the question "When did Columbus discover America?"

If the essay question is to test the ability to select and organize data, or the ability to think a problem through to its solution, the question must be designed for those purposes. Repeating a question that has been drilled on in class is clearly inadequate as a challenge to the student to do anything more than try to remember what had been said in class.

Many essay questions are worded too vaguely to indicate to the student just what is expected of him. Essay questions are sometimes so indefinite that the student learns to write as much as he can on the topic in the hope that something he says may prove to be the correct answer. What does the teacher expect when he asks a high school senior class to "Discuss the hydrogen bomb"?

It takes time to prepare a good essay question and no teacher who dashes off an essay-type test just before his class assembles can do more than write down the first draft of the first questions that come to mind. With more time, the teacher can think of the answer he wishes to elicit and then frame the question that will invite that answer.

The rating of essay questions undoubtedly is more time-consuming than is the rating of objective-type questions. If the chief factor to be considered is the demand that is made on the teacher's time in constructing a test and in rating the answers, it is better to use essay-type questions when classes are small, and to use objective-type questions when classes are large or when the test papers for all classes must be marked within a relatively short time, as when midterm examinations are conducted throughout the school at the same time and the marks are expected by the office within a few days after the examinations have been administered.

Marking the Essay Answers Objectively

The most serious objection to the use of essay questions is that the rating is ordinarily affected by such extraneous factors as the student's penmanship, the teacher's mood, and the chance factors that placed a student's paper so that it was read just after the teacher had finished rating the paper written by the best student in the class or the poorest one.

Essay papers can be rated objectively if the teacher prepares a model answer or a definite set of criteria to be followed in the rating. Before preparing a marking key, it is advisable for the teacher to read a few papers quickly to see the kinds of answers he is getting so that he may construct a guide to marking that is appropriate for rating them.

After the teacher has applied the key to the correction of a half dozen papers, he should re-examine it to see whether it is differentiating as it should between the good answers and the poor ones. An objective marking key sometimes gives so much credit for the mere mention of a topic that poor papers get higher marks than they deserve. On the other hand, the really good papers may not get all the credit they merit. For these reasons it is desirable for the teacher to try out the key on a few papers and to make such changes in the key as seem advisable. He should then proceed to mark all the papers (including those tried out) on the basis of the corrected key.

With a marking key, much time is consumed at the beginning, but the grading of the vast majority of the papers proceeds much more rapidly than when the teacher has to stop and judge each sentence of each answer separately. The teacher has the satisfaction, moreover, of knowing that he is rating all of the papers uniformly and objectively, and that he is reducing to the minimum the influence of extraneous factors that should have no bearing on the student's grade.*

A more satisfactory way of reducing the amount of time which the teacher spends on the rating of essay questions is to reduce the number of tests and the number of essay questions on a test. Many essay questions do not deserve to be treated as essay questions, for they deal with specific items that can be tested more quickly and more thoroughly by using objective-type questions that can be scored quickly. Essay questions should be reserved for major topics that deserve the time it takes to rate the answers adequately.

Using Objective-Type Questions

By this time all teachers are familiar with the virtues of the objective-type question. They know that objective-type questions are quickly, easily, and objectively scored and that their use enables the teacher to make a more valid sampling of the student's ability. Objective-type test results can be interpreted more easily by the teacher who is seeking to discover just what it is that his students do not understand. On an objective-type test the student cannot use words to cover up his ignorance or his partial understanding. On a true-false test, for example, the student cannot evade the issue by saying that "An acute angle is smaller than a right angle" and leave the teacher guessing as to whether the student really knows that an acute angle is always less than 90°. In fact, many teachers have been won over so completely to the use of the objective-type question that they overlook some of the serious weaknesses of this kind of question.

It takes so much more time to construct, let us say, the fifty multiple-choice items on a full period test than to write five or six good essay questions that the teacher often spends more time on the construction of an objective-type test than he saves by the more rapid scoring of multiple-choice questions.

Because each objective-type question deals with only one specific item, it tends to stress minutiae rather than basic concepts. Although objective-type questions do not have to be limited to memory for details, it is nevertheless true that most teacher-made objective-type tests do stress details. Test-wise students want to know whether an impending test will consist of essay questions or objective-type questions, for these students have learned that they must study the details of the course when objective-type questions are asked.

There is good reason to challenge the type of learning that is implied in most objective-type questions. Ordinarily this type of test item de-

* The procedures for preparing and using the rating guide or key with essay questions can easily be adapted for use with other types of student work, for example, for evaluating student papers and committee reports.

mands nothing more than that the student recognize the correct answer when he sees it. This is far different from the way in which the student will ever be called on to use his information except on other examinations of this type. Although the correlation between recognition and recall is high enough to justify the use of objective-type questions for marking purposes, it is unwise to use these questions so frequently that students develop the attitude that all they need learn is how to recognize the correct answer.

On objective-type questions, guessing is tolerated and even encouraged. Though students sometimes attack an essay question with more faith in their teacher's generosity than in their own knowledge, trying to guess the answer is even more tempting when all that the student need do is write the letters *A, B, C,* or *D.*

Avoiding Common Pitfalls When Writing Objective-type Questions

Every teacher who uses objective-type questions must resolve that he will include no item that deals with an unimportant point, that is ambiguous, or that hinges on the student's seeing the tiny word *not* in the item or on the student's interpreting the word *often* in the question the way the teacher does. The teacher who wishes his students to discriminate between the important and the trivial must avoid emphasizing unimportant details even though they are easily incorporated in true-false or multiple-choice questions. He must evaluate his own test items critically and should look at each item as it would appear to the student to whom the correct answer to that item means the difference between a passing and a failing grade.

No teacher deliberately writes an ambiguous question, but it is nevertheless common to find questions on an objective-type test that prove to be ambiguous to the student. An unfortunate result of the unintentional ambiguity of test items is that sometimes it is the brighter student who has difficulty in selecting the correct choice. The mediocre student, whose background on a given topic is limited to the material that was presented in class, may take the question at face value as intended. The superior student, however, who has read much more than was discussed in class, sees implications in the teacher's choice of words that render him unable to decide whether the statement is true or false.

Objective-type questions need not be limited to the memorization of unrelated facts since the questions can be framed so that they call for the ability to interpret, to judge, and to apply. A multiple-choice question, for example, may present a statement, with the student asked to select the best means of determining the truth of that statement. In order to see whether the student knows how to apply his information to a new setting, the item may present a situation different from any that was discussed in class. Several questions may be based on a single problem and thus measure many phases of the student's learning rather than just his ability to memorize.

Reducing the Amount of Time Spent in Constructing and Rating Tests

The most effective way of reducing the amount of time which teachers spend on test construction and on the correction of test papers is to reduce the number of tests that are administered, especially the number of time-consuming full-period tests. Many of the purposes that tests serve can be met fully without administering tests as often as is usually the practice.

The teacher can reduce the amount of time consumed in the construction of test items without lessening the value of these items. It is easier to construct a few items on each week's work as the semester progresses than to try to prepare an entire test at one time.

It takes less time to construct a test if the teacher uses many kinds of items than if he uses only one. Some teachers spend a great deal of time trying to find a good fourth choice for a multiple-choice item that can quickly be changed into an excellent true-false item. Similarly, teachers who have exhausted the supply of likely true-false items may find it easier to construct some multiple-choice or matching items than to keep looking for true-false items that become increasingly hard to find as the test approaches the desired length. One good essay question that will measure abilities the teacher may be ignoring in his other items may add much to the value of the test as a whole and yet reduce the total amount of time which the teacher spends in test construction and test scoring.

Having a major test consist of several types of questions—essay, multiple-choice, true-false, matching, completion—does more than simplify the task of test construction. Since each type has its own special values, such a composite test is more likely to measure the many facets of student growth than will a test that is limited to one type. A varied test, moreover, encourages more adequate student preparation for the test than does exclusive use of the essay-type question or the objective-type question.

The administration of standardized tests, when appropriate standardized tests are available, will eliminate the task of test construction and will reduce the amount of time spent in correcting the papers and in interpreting the results.

Many teachers find it helpful to follow the practice of professional test constructors of keeping a file of the test items they have used in the past. Test items can be pooled in a departmental test file, with a resultant saving in the amount of time which individual teachers spend in test construction.

It is helpful, though not essential, that the index card on which the test item appears contain a summary of the students' responses to the question and the dates when the item was used. Taking a multiple-choice item, for example, the card may indicate how many students took choice A, choice B, choice C, and choice D. The teacher can thus tell whether the item is a difficult or an easy one and whether it is necessary to re-write any part of the question. When essay questions are used, a great deal of the teacher's time can be saved by attaching the rating key to the copy of the question.

Teachers who use a pool of questions, whether it be an individual pool or a departmental one, must remember that pools become stagnant unless there is a constant source of replenishment and a constant removal of used-up material. No pool of questions should ever be regarded as complete or permanent.

When the test is viewed as an aid to learning rather than as being chiefly a basis for assigning marks, students and teachers can work together to correct papers and to use the results. If the students regard the test as a way of discovering their errors so that they may progress more rapidly, students can correct their own papers in the light of the class discussion of the correct answers and of the process that should be followed to arrive at that answer. Having the students correct their own papers is more than merely a device for easing the teacher's burden; it is, for students, a convincing demonstration that learning is a co-operative affair and that the test is an instructional aid rather than just a part of the teacher's detective kit.

DIAGNOSING LEARNING DIFFICULTIES

Test results may be used not only to indicate the student's general level of achievement but also to enable the teacher to analyze the student's achievement in detail in order to discover the specific weaknesses and to analyze the causes of these errors. The more detailed the analysis of the student's errors and the more specific the enumeration of the causes of error, the greater is the teacher's opportunity to help the student to correct these weaknesses.

To illustrate the use that can be made of diagnostic tests, let us look at a class that has just taken a standardized mathematics achievement test. It does not help a student to do better in mathematics if the teacher, during a conference with one of the slow learners, says: "Bob, your score on this test is not only one of the lowest in the class, but it is far below the level that should be reached by a boy of your mentality, and it is below the average of all the first-year mathematics students who took this test. It just goes to show that the time has come for you to stop kidding around and that you must buckle down to real work. Are you ready to get to work in earnest?"

Even though Bob is made to see the error of his ways and now has the best intentions in the world, his insight into mathematical relationships and his skill in using mathematical processes will show no marked improvement. The student who does not understand the law of signs, or who makes computational errors, needs more specific help than the exhortation to buckle down to real work.

Students can get the same algebra problems with two unknowns wrong for many different reasons: the student may not understand the situation presented in the mathematical problem he is expected to solve; he may misinterpret the problem because he does not know what some of the words mean; he may not know how to translate the problem into an algebraic equation; he may not know how to clear the equations of one of the unknowns; having determined the value of one of the unknowns he may not know how to find the value of the other unknown; he may misread the numbers in the problem and thus get the wrong answer; he may make computational errors; he may forget to change the signs when he subtracts in algebra; and so on.

This enumeration does not exhaust the array of errors that students can make in the process of solving a single mathematical problem; a determined student can make more errors than even the most experienced teacher can anticipate. Because there are so many sources of error, it is vague advice to ask the students to practice solving problems with two unknowns. He can improve much more rapidly if he attacks the source of his difficulties.

Helping the Student Identify the Causes of His Errors

Any classroom exercise can be used for diagnostic purposes if the teacher will himself analyze the specific errors made by the students. The English teacher who reads a student's composition critically can arrive at a sufficiently detailed list of individual weaknesses. The mathematics teacher will find that the careful examination of a student's test paper yields considerable information on specific weaknesses.

To discover the specific errors is important, but the teacher can do little to eliminate the error until he finds the cause. Sometimes the teacher can find the cause of the student's difficulty as soon as he locates the specific error. Thus, the mathematics teacher can often tell why the student makes the specific error of adding both numerators and denominators when he adds fractions. In other instances, it is not so easy to discover the misconception which is the cause of the error. The chemistry teacher, for example, may be unable to understand why the student wrote "Ionization is important today chiefly because of the housing shortage."

A conference with the student is often an excellent way of discovering his misconceptions and the reasons for his faulty procedures. He can be asked to solve a problem aloud so that the teacher can observe the procedures the student uses. The student can be asked to explain his answers more fully and the teacher may learn, as the chemistry teacher referred to above did, that the student confused *iron* with *ion* and thought *ionization* referred to the process of manufacturing steel from iron.

A published diagnostic test may help the teacher discover the specific source of error. The authors of a diagnostic test, after a careful analysis of the various types and causes of errors in the subject matter covered by the test, devise problems that are so carefully planned that the teacher can discover quickly the sources of student errors. Diagnostic tests have not been developed as adequately for secondary school subjects as for such elementary school subjects as arithmetic and reading. The periodicals published for secondary school teachers of the various subjects, textbooks on methods of teaching the various subjects, and the *Mental Measurements Yearbook* [5] are sources to which the teacher may go for suggested diagnostic tests.

Relating Learning Problems to the Student's Total Picture

As the year progresses, the teacher becomes better acquainted with the individual weaknesses and needs of the members of the class. It is when the year ends that the teacher knows his students best, only to find that he has to start all over again with new students. For this reason, most secondary schools keep cumulative record cards for each student. If these cumulative records contain more than a series of grades, they spare the teacher much wasted effort by making it unnecessary for each teacher to rediscover what his colleagues have already learned about a student. The cumulative record underlines the point of view that the education of each student is a school problem and not the piecemeal concern of many different teachers. It helps develop the idea that teachers are professional colleagues who can trust each other to use knowledge about a given student without being prejudiced against him.

Discovering the causes of a student's school difficulties often is more than a matter of analyzing a student's paper to see which errors he has made. The teacher who has access to the student's scores on intelligence tests may be in a position to see whether the student is being expected to deal with concepts and procedures far beyond his mental level. Another student's difficulties may be so imbedded in intellectual or emotional problems that reteaching is far from being an adequate solution.

When the student's school failures are a reflection of his personality adjustment, early psychological study and treatment should be made available, if at all possible. Any teacher who finds that the student does not respond to a carefully planned remedial program may well suspect that he is dealing with a student whose learning difficulties should be explored more fully by a psychologist or clinic.

Educational diagnosis, whether it employs standardized diagnostic tests or makes full use of the teacher's ingenuity in diagnosing without using published diagnostic tests, can do much to improve the effectiveness of instruction, but only if the results of the diagnosis are used as the basis for planning a program of remedial instruction. If the teacher's time is limited, it is better to plan a less ambitious diagnostic program—either by restricting the study to those students most in need of help or by concentrating on the most serious weaknesses—and to use these results to improve learning. There is little value in painstakingly elaborate diagnoses that are carefully recorded and filed, but never used.

EVALUATING PERSONAL AND SOCIAL ADJUSTMENT

If we are really concerned with the kind of person the student is as well as with what he knows, we must include changes in personality traits as part of the achievement we wish to measure and we must include measures of personal adjustments as being as truly achievement tests as is an arithmetic test.

Informal Measures of Personality Growth

The informality of present-day classrooms, with the many opportunities students have for participating actively, enables an alert teacher to learn much about the personality traits of the boys and girls in his class. He can observe their willingness and ability to accept responsibility, their initiative, their ability to lead others, their reaction to criticism and suggestions, the extent to which they are accepted by their colleagues, the range and intensity of their interests, and many other phases of development that are so important that they should not be ignored simply because they are not measured by the administration of standardized achievement tests.

The comments students make during discussions, their relations with the many students and adults with whom they come in contact, and the revelatory remarks that occur in their writing are other indices to their development which are sometimes much more significant than are test scores. The information we get from such sources as these indicates how much we gain when tests are used as supplements to the teacher's information and judgment rather than as substitutes for the close association of students with intelligent and sympathetic teachers.

The anecdotal record is a convenient means of preserving incidents which are sometimes revealing evidence of student attitudes and behavior.

Teachers who take the time to jot down brief accounts of specific incidents that would otherwise be forgotten soon find that they have a source of informative data that tells them much about the boys and girls they meet. If these anecdotal records are kept in individual folders in a central file which can be consulted by the other teachers, it is possible for any teacher to learn much about the boys and girls he teaches that will help him to understand them better.

Because writing anecdotal records for all the students in a large class can easily become so time-consuming a task as to be impracticable, it is essential that these accounts be brief and that they summarize the facts rather than expand the teacher's interpretation of these facts.

Even brief anecdotal accounts can be informative when they report faithfully what a student has said or done. For example, insight into Margaret's reluctance to take part in class discussion may come from reading an entry in her cumulative record envelope. Last year's English teacher jotted down a reference to a moving short story Margaret contributed to the class newspaper. The story revolved about a young man who desperately wanted to be popular but was so afraid of being rebuffed that he invented the excuse that he had to rush home from work to take care of a sick mother.

It is not surprising that teachers who have many large classes daily should know so little about some of their students, but it is not so apparent that even the teacher of a small class may also know relatively little about some of his students. After all, the teacher-pupil relationship touches only part of the adolescent's life, and the teacher may be unaware of many of the problems, the difficulties, and the hopes of his students. Yet the teacher must know more about his students if he is to help them to profit most from the experiences at school.

Using Instruments for Testing

If each teacher were a trained psychologist, well-versed in understanding the dynamics of adolescent behavior, if he had ample opportunity to be with his students in many kinds of experiences, and if he had unlimited time, we could depend on teachers to know all their students well. Under existing conditions, however, there is much that teachers can learn about their students by using available testing instruments. In most classes, for example, the teacher can learn a great deal about his students by preparing a sociogram [9] and learn it early enough in the school year to be able to use the information it yields in his relations with his students.

This is not the place to enter into a technical discussion of the problems involved in the development of personality measures but the teacher must understand some of the many problems if he is to use these measures intelligently. At the present time, measures of personality traits and of personal or social adjustment are not nearly at the same stage of development that standardized tests of school achievement have reached. It has been said that the teacher is not risking much if he administers a standardized achievement test prepared by an author whose professional standing he respects or which is issued by a reputable test publisher. No such general endorsement is possible for available personality tests, partly because these tests are still in a pioneering stage, partly because the authors of these tests have to solve some of the most complex problems of test construction, and partly because teachers have not had sufficient experience in using these tests. The teacher will find it useful to consult the most recent edition of the *Mental Measurements Yearbook* [5] for assistance in selecting the most appropriate tests to meet specific needs.

How should the teacher use these tests? He must resolve first to use no clinical test of personality unless he has had adequate clinical training and experience. It does not take long for a normally intelligent person to learn how to adjust the electrodes for recording an electrocardiogram—but an amateur reading of an electrocardiogram does the patient no good. The lay person is fascinated by the Rorschach Test and likes the idea of being able to explore another's mind by noting his interpretations of standardized ink blots. It is even easier to present the Rorschach cards to an adolescent than it is to adjust the electrodes for an electrocardiogram, but an amateur interpretation of the Rorschach Test does the adolescent as little good.

The only personality tests that classroom teachers should administer are those for which the manual of instructions clearly indicates that they are not designed exclusively for clinical use. This injunction conveys no implication of lack of appreciation of the teacher's intelligence, sound judgment, or good intentions. In this age of specialized preparation, we do not ordinarily expect clinical psychologists to be able to teach a physics lesson; we have no right to expect a science teacher to be able to administer and to interpret a clinician's test of emotional adjustment.

Uses of Group Tests for Screening

Most available group tests of personal adjustment are helpful for screening purposes. In every school there are boys and girls whose emotional problems are unrecognized by their parents and teachers because these problems are not expressed in ways that are troublesome to their elders.

When tests of personality traits are administered, a major value is served if all students with extremely unfavorable scores are referred for special study and help to the most competent people available. Because referral for special study may itself be a serious step, no student should be referred for special study merely because of a low score on a single personality test. To screen out the problem cases for individual study, it is better to use an appropriate battery of personality tests and to use the teacher's professional judgment to supplement the test results.

Even when professional psychiatric and psychological help is not available, some good may be done if these young people are brought to the attention of intelligent teachers, who are, after all, interested in the problems of youth and experienced in dealing with young people. If the administration of a battery of personality tests does nothing more than screen out a few cases who can then be helped because their problems have been detected relatively early, the testing program has been worthwhile. Not every student with an unfavorable score is actually or even potentially a seriously maladjusted person, but every extremely unfavorable score should be investigated because it may be symptomatic of emotional difficulties that may become more acute.

Aside from their usefulness in attracting attention to extreme cases, the raw scores in personality tests sometimes reveal far less than do the students' responses to specific items in the test. For example, when asked what she would ask for if she could make three wishes, one girl gave as her first wish that she could be sure that her father and her mother loved her. This response tells us much more about the girl than does her score of 69 or 79. To record the students' scores and to destroy their test papers is to save the label and throw away the package.

The Importance of Personal Understanding

The teacher has to be wary of regarding his students as a collection of test scores. There are many important traits that are not measured on any single test or battery of tests and there is much that a sympathetic and understanding teacher knows about the boys and girls he meets daily that is not elicited by tests. Personality tests supplement the teacher's knowledge of his students and they may enrich his understanding of their behavior, but they do not replace the sympathetic understanding of the really good teacher.

There is much that the teacher can gain by examining the items in a good test of personal adjustment, for these are the items that professional psychologists regard as important in the evaluation of personality traits. As the teacher examines the test, he is bound to find many questions that suggest symptoms of adjustment and maladjustment that he has been ignoring. Focusing attention as these tests do on the student's needs as an adolescent and not on the adolescent's need as a student, the test items may help the teacher, too, to see his students from another point of view.

MARKS AND GRADES

The major problem in the classroom use of marks and grades is not so much the question of how marks and grades should be computed but rather of how they should be used. There are classes which are conducted as though the mark which students receive were the most significant outcome of the day's work.

This attitude is being aggravated by increasing competition among students in large senior classes for the limited places in college. For this reason, many secondary schools are experimenting with various kinds of evaluation summaries as a better way of informing college admissions officers of the strengths and the limitations of the students who are applying for admission. The desire to go to college is and should be a powerful incentive for secondary school students but its value is largely lost when students elect only easy courses in which they can get high grades and when they attach more importance to the grade than to the quality of learning it is supposed to represent.

The overemphasis on marks can interfere seriously with the quality of the learning activities in school. The teacher who has his pencil constantly poised for making entries in his marking book can hardly encourage students to regard the classroom discussion as an opportunity to air their doubts and to seek the answers to troubling questions. When test marks are overemphasized, students tend to limit their study activities to preparing for likely questions on the test, to the neglect of other materials. Every teacher has experienced the letdown in class morale that follows the administration of so important an examination as the midterm test and knows how impossible it is in many schools to attempt to accomplish anything more once the students know that the grades for the semester have been computed.

Much of the students' overemphasis on marks is the result of parental pressure, but the students' attitude is also colored by the teacher's point of view. When students' grades are discussed publicly in class and when the teacher indicates clearly that he evaluates students in terms of their marks, it is easy to see why students attach so much importance to marks. To students, as well as to their parents, the marks that are given by the teacher are sometimes the only indication they have of how well they are doing.

Building Sounder Attitudes Toward Grades

What can the teacher do to help his students develop a saner attitude toward marks? He must first develop a more wholesome attitude himself. Recognizing that there are some classroom situations that are so unsatisfactory that the teacher must use marks and any other available incentive if students are to accomplish anything at all, the teacher must nevertheless regard the number of times that he has to resort to his marking book as a possible reflection of the inadequacy of the curriculum or the ineffectiveness of his teaching. A student's grades are a proper topic for conversation only between teacher and student or between teacher and parents; they are not appropriate topics for public discussions in class. The teacher must help his students to regard classroom tests as means of discovering weaknesses that should be corrected and not as contests between teacher and student. Each student should be able to tell how well he is progressing in class without having to wait expectantly for the test results to be announced dramatically by the teacher.

Whether the teacher wishes to or not, he must often accept the importance of the final grade submitted at the end of the term, but he need not let the final grade cast its shadow over everything that is done during the term. Final grades are important because they are used so frequently, perhaps with too much faith in them, as a basis for educational guidance and for determining whether a student is ready to go on to advanced work. In many instances, these grades determine whether the student may go to the college of his choice, or even to any college.

The final grade means so much to the student's future that it must be as accurate a measure as possible of the level of achievement he has attained. The grade should recognize all of the many ways in which students demonstrate their ability and should not be limited to the average of two or three major test marks. The reports that students make, their contributions during class discussions, the work they do in class and outside—all of these should affect their grade at the end of the term.

Setting Standards in Grading

The term grade should not reflect the teacher's opinion of the student's character or of his potentialities. The mathematics student whose demonstrated ability entitles him to the final grade of A should not have his final grade lowered to a B because he regularly was tardy in turning in homework assignments or because the teacher thinks the student is so conceited that a lower grade may have therapeutic value. Similarly, another mathematics student whose demonstrated ability entitles him to a C should not have his final grade raised to a B because the teacher knows how conscientious the student is and how faithful he is in doing every assignment made in class. There should be some other provision on the student's permanent record card for the teachers' comments on personality traits and scholastic habits that may be better bases for guidance than are the term grades, but these comments should be separated from the grades themselves.

Unless the final grades are restricted to measures of achievement, they cannot be readily interpreted by anybody other than the teacher who submitted the grade. How can we interpret the grade of B in Physics I if we do not know whether it means that the student is brilliant in physics but conceited, or that he is little better than mediocre in his mastery of the subject but is a most conscientious and personable young man?

The final grades which the teacher submits for his students should be based on standards that are set by the school rather than those set by each individual teacher. During the semester, each teacher may set whatever standards he thinks are most appropriate for his class, but when the semester ends, the grade which the student receives should indicate the same degree of mastery whether it be given by one teacher or by another. When some teachers mark generously and other teachers grade their students more severely, the student's scholastic record may be influenced as much by the teachers to whose classes he happened to have been assigned as by his own accomplishments.

When students are grouped in classes according to their ability, it is to be expected that the distribution of final grades in any one class will differ considerably from that for the school as a whole. In a class consisting of the most capable students, for example, there should be a greater concentration of high grades. On the other hand, when the slow learners or the less promising students are sectioned into special courses that lead to a special certificate, they should not be further stigmatized by being condemned to receive a succession of low grades regardless of their success in meeting the demands of their special course.

Few people know how much time and energy teachers spend in preparing and correcting tests and in computing and recording grades, but only teachers know how unpleasant these chores can be. Sensitive people are naturally hesitant to sit in judgment on fellow mortals, even though they be younger. This reluctance to rate others is heightened when one loses faith in the importance of the criteria, in the validity of the procedures that are used for rating, or in the contribution that these procedures make to improving the quality of the education our students receive.

The use which is made of evaluative procedures should be one more illustration of the way in which teachers, administrators, students, and parents can work together to attain the educational goals that alone make schooling worthwhile. Because evaluation is only a means to an end, its importance must not be exaggerated to the point where we spend more time evaluating student growth than we do in creating the conditions that encourage students to develop.

QUESTIONS FOR STUDY AND DISCUSSION

1. Construct a diagnostic test that can be administered to a class in the subject you plan to teach so that you can tell readily what each student's specific weaknesses are. Since the preparation of a diagnostic test to cover all phases of your subject is much too ambitious an undertaking, limit yourself to the analysis of one major skill; for example, balancing equations in a chemistry class, using verb forms correctly in a foreign language class, understanding collective bargaining in a social studies class, or using the correct form in writing letters in an English class.

2. As part of their apprenticeship, student teachers are expected to learn to grade examination papers and to analyze the results. Using a set of test papers written by the students in a class such as one you may be called upon to teach, analyze the papers in order to discover each pupil's major weaknesses.

3. As part of a junior high school guidance program, all teachers have been asked to administer a carefully selected battery of intelligence and achievement tests. At a teacher's meeting called to discuss the procedures to be followed when these tests are administered, one of the teachers asked what should be done if a student is caught cheating.

One teacher said he thought the student should merely be given another copy of the test and be asked to start over again, the time which the student loses in starting his test again to be regarded as a penalty for cheating.

A second teacher suggested that the teacher walk over to where the student is sitting and stand alongside him so that he would stop cheating.

A third teacher recommended that the teacher say nothing but ask the pupil to take the test over again after school.

Why is each of these three suggestions faulty?

What recommendation would you have made if you had been a member of the group?

4. One of the teachers at this school has a class of slow learners who are far below the rest of the school in intelligence, reading ability, and general school achievement. As soon as this teacher saw a copy of the group intelligence test that was to be administered as part of the test battery, she realized that her boys and girls did not read rapidly enough to do well on these tests.

Which of the following procedures is the one she should follow?

a. Familiarize her pupils with these tests by administering equivalent forms of the tests a few days before the official tests are given.

b. Paraphrase the instructions and add a few more illustrations so that the pupils will understand how to proceed.

c. Allow them slightly more time on each part of the test than other pupils will be allowed.

d. Administer the tests exactly as indicated in the manual of instructions for each test.

What is wrong with each of the suggestions you do not recommend?

5. A few years ago a newly appointed principal of a combined junior-senior high school ambitiously set out to prepare a collection of all the available standardized tests for the subjects taught in his school. After he had assembled a good collection of specimen sets (that is, a single copy of each form of the test and the manual of instructions), he found that he did not have enough money to purchase sets of the test for administration to classes.

Assuming that funds for the purchase of class sets of tests will not be available for some years, what is the best use to which his present collection can be put?

6. How can a teacher determine whether the norms as published in the manual of instructions for a nationally recognized standardized achievement test are appropriate standards for the class he is teaching?

7. A teacher who attached little importance to marks and grades succeeded in getting his senior high school science class to participate actively in the term's work without worrying about who was getting a higher grade or a lower one. During the semester each parent received a little note telling him about the work the son or daughter was doing, giving praise where commendation was merited and, where necessary, indicating the specific respects in which improvement was desirable. The examination results at the end of the semester corroborated the impression of teacher and students that they had accomplished far more than most classes had.

After the regular school report card with its array of grades for each subject was sent home at the end of the term, a parent called on the teacher to complain that his daughter's grade, although well above passing, was not high enough to help her win the scholarship without which a college education would be impossible. In the absence of percentage marks all term, the parent did not realize his daughter's work was not of A grade. Had he known, he said, he could have had his daughter work harder to get the A she needed.

What should the teacher say to this parent?

8. After you have constructed a multiple-choice, a true-false, and an essay question on this chapter, evaluate these questions as though they had been proposed for inclusion in a test on this material.

9. Which of the eight questions listed above do you regard as suitable for inclusion in a college examination for a course on methods of teaching in secondary schools? Which criteria did you use in making your selection? Which changes would you make in the remaining questions before you would be willing to accept them as suitable essay questions?

10. Examine a test prepared by a classroom teacher for administration to his class. Which changes would you recommend in the general pattern of the test, in the distribution of emphasis among the various areas tested, and in the choice of types of questions used? If you find any question on the test that you think would be better if reworded, rephrase the question so that you consider it to be more acceptable for the purposes of the test.

BIBLIOGRAPHY

1. Aikin, Wilford M., *The Story of the Eight Year Study* (New York, Harper and Brothers, 1942).
2. Association for Supervision and Curriculum Development, *Learning and the Teacher*, 1959 Yearbook (Washington, D.C., the Association, 1959), Ch. 6.
3. Blair, Glenn M., *Diagnostic and Remedial Teaching*, rev. ed. (New York, The Macmillan Company, 1956).
4. Bloom, Benjamin S., ed., *Taxonomy of Educational Objectives* (New York, Longmans, Green & Co., Inc., 1956).
5. Buros, Oscar Krisen, ed., *Mental Measurements Yearbook* (Highland Park, N.J., The Gryphon Press, various dates).
6. Dressel, Paul L., and Mayhew, Lewis B., *General Education: Explorations in Evaluation* (Washington, D.C., American Council on Education, 1954).

7. FRENCH, Will, and associates, *Behavioral Goals of General Education in High School* (New York, The Russell Sage Foundation, 1957).

8. GREENE, Harry A., JORGENSEN, Albert N., and GERBERICH, J. Raymond, *Measurement and Evaluation in the Secondary School*, 2nd ed. (New York, Longmans, Green & Co., Inc., 1954).

9. LEE, J. M., and LEE, Dorris M., *The Child and His Development* (New York, Appleton-Century-Crofts, Inc., 1958), pp. 276-287.

10. MIEL, Alice, and associates, *Cooperative Procedures in Learning* (New York, Bureau of Publications, Teachers College, Columbia University, 1952), Chs. 16, 17.

11. REMMERS, H. H. and GAGE, N. L., *Educational Measurement and Evaluation*, rev. ed. (New York, Harper and Brothers, 1955).

12. ——, and others, eds., *Growth, Teaching, and Learning: A Book of Readings* (New York, Harper and Brothers, 1957), Part III.

13. RIVLIN, Harry N., and SCHUELER, Herbert, *Encyclopedia of Modern Education* (New York, The Philosophical Library, 1943). See articles on Essay Examination, Evaluation, Graphic Methods, Measurement in Education, Objective Tests and Examinations, Rating Scales.

14. Ross, Clay Campbell, and STANLEY, Julian C., *Measurement in Today's Schools*, 3rd ed. (Englewood Cliffs, N.J., Prentice-Hall, Inc., 1954).

15. TRAVERS, Robert M. W., *How to Make Achievement Tests* (New York, The Odyssey Press, 1950).

16. VANDERPOL, Jeanette A., "Student Opinion—Sacred Cow or Booby Trap?" *The Journal of Teacher Education,* Vol. X, No. 4 (December, 1959), pp. 401-412.

17. WRIGHTSTONE, J. Wayne, JUSTMAN, Joseph, and ROBBINS, Irving, *Evaluation in Modern Education* (New York, American Book Company, 1950).

18. WRINKLE, William L., *Improving Marking and Reporting Practices in Elementary and Secondary Schools* (New York, Holt, Rinehart and Winston, Inc., 1947).

CHAPTER 12

The Cocurriculum: Bringing the

Activities Program into the

Curriculum

»»»»»»»»»»

WHEN WE REFER these days to the many student activities at a secondary school as being *cocurricular* rather than *extracurricular,* we are doing more than substituting a newer expression for a more familiar one. The change in terminology emphasizes the elevation of these activities to the status of full partner in the educational process.

It is when these activities are viewed as cocurricular that they are likely to be used most fully for students' benefit. The examination of any detailed statement of the purposes of education, such as the Educational Policies Commission statement to which we have referred several times, suggests that there are some purposes of education that can be achieved during class periods and there are others that can be furthered by effective use of students' out-of-class activities. These activities must not be used merely as a means of compensating for the neglect of students' needs during the day nor as a way of making certain that the student will spend at least one period during the week doing something he himself regards as worth doing. Instead, they must be viewed as activities that are important in their own right because of the value they have for students.

Even the secondary school with the most flexible curriculum and the most informal teachers needs a good program of cocurricular activities. The more fully the school recognizes the importance of intellectual and social development, the greater will be the importance it attaches to getting all students to participate in a program that provides school facilities and guidance for the exploration of special interests, that suggests worthy leisure time activities, that gives adolescent boys and girls a chance to work and play together, and that develops the *esprit de corps* that is the essence of school spirit.

Extra-class activities originally found their way into secondary school because of concern for the personal and social development of young people. Students found them attractive as a foil for the relatively authoritarian classroom. Club activities and other forms of participation could be centered about the social, intellectual, creative, and athletic interests of adolescents while classroom activities seemed to focus on a body of learnings selected by their teachers from the cultural heritage. The extracurriculum gave young people the opportunity to express their drive for independence from adults by permitting them to direct their own activities. In addition, the extracurricular program demonstrated the effectiveness of utilizing student interests and the value of student participation in the direction of their own learning activities.

These values are so important that many schools now recognize the nonclass activities as an important part of the school's total program. Moreover, the worth of these approaches has encouraged the trend toward more democratic procedures in the classroom itself and toward curricular modifications which put greater focus on the developmental needs of adolescents.

Despite the incorporation of some features of nonclass activities in subject classes, the cocurriculum continues to have special appeal and value to secondary school students. Free from the prescription of a fixed curriculum and from the influence of the teacher's marking book, students find in clubs an opportunity to develop their own interests and to engage in activities they consider worth doing. To many a student, it is the athletic team on which he plays, the newspaper he helps edit, the play for which he is making the scenery, the traffic squad of which he is the captain, or the Spanish Club in which he actually enjoys using the Spanish he has studied in class that gives him the sense of achievement which makes the whole day seem worthwhile.

WHAT CAN COCURRICULAR ACTIVITIES CONTRIBUTE TO THE ADOLESCENT'S DEVELOPMENT?

Do cocurricular activities deserve the important role to which they have been elevated? What are their values?

Accomplishing the Developmental Tasks of Youth

We have referred earlier to the fact that in recent years psychologists and sociologists have identified certain learning tasks of children and youth which are essential to personal and social development in our culture [8]. One of the developmental tasks is developing satisfying relationships with one's peers. Cocurricular activities, with their informal organization, provide a context in which boys and girls can work out relationships with their age mates. Sharing with others in work and in play, boys and girls observe appropriate male and female roles in our society and they grow toward their own roles as men or women. The more personal, less authoritative relationship of coach or club sponsor to students helps build more mature relationships with adults. Athletics and other physical activities lead to improved physical development. In some instances clubs contribute to the development of vocational interests which may ultimately lead to establishing economic independence, a primary goal of the maturing adult. Moreover, a set of values or a philosophy of life may be forged in the crucible of direct experience where students have responsibility, under guidance, for making their own decisions.

Developing Desirable Personality Traits

Cocurricular activities can help develop phases of the student's personality that are not emphasized during the rest of the school day. In the conduct of cocurricular activities, students can accept a degree of responsibility far greater than is possible in a class situation governed by the course of study. Any teacher who has ever worked with students preparing for an interscholastic debate, with the staff that is trying to meet the printer's deadline for the next issue of the school paper, or with the cast that is rehearsing a school play, knows how completely these students accept their share of the responsibility and how much earnest work they do voluntarily. Because they accept the responsibility for the work they are doing, the students have the opportunity to develop the traits that are so important in learning how to work with others.

Facilitating the Adolescent's Social Development

Cocurricular activities help the student's development as a social person. He needs many opportunities to make friends with others of his age and to learn to get along with many different kinds of people, and he can get these opportunities informally and naturally in cocurricular activities. The parties and the informal dances conducted by the clubs are a more important part of the adolescent's life than adults appreciate.

The recreational phases of cocurricular life are important. The generation now in school may expect with some assurance continuing reductions in the length of the workweek during their lifetime. Today's students are urgently in need of recreational outlets that will provide constructive use of leisure time both in the present and for the future. The development of sound recreational interests while the student is still in school has the double purpose of enriching the individual's life and of preventing the idle frittering away of empty hours or the antisocial use of leisure time.

Adolescents tend to become impatient with the rigorous control which parents often exert over the recreational life of younger children. It is at this point in the student's life that a constructive program of activities is more likely to be effective than preaching against improper use of leisure time. Cocurricular activities constitute such a suggestion, for the activities in which the students engage and the friendships they form do provide a basis for recreational activities that fill free time pleasantly even when school is not in session.

While cocurricular activities are necessarily directed toward current interests of boys and girls, society's concern with the large amount of free time in the average American's adult life underlines the importance of developing interests that will serve boys and girls when they are adults. Team activities, for example, serve important purposes in physical and social development but should constitute only one kind of physical activity in educating for the use of leisure time. We note, therefore, a recent emphasis on individual sports like tennis, badminton, golf, and swimming; on informal outdoor activities like camping and mountaineering; and on activities that may be conducted on a coeducational basis like skating, square and social dancing, volley ball, and some of the sports already noted.

Concern with use of leisure time leads, too, to interest in enhancing appreciation of audience-type entertainment. Group situations can be used to stimulate interest in reading, listening to music, theater going, and television viewing. The adolescent's interest in group activities may be utilized to direct attention toward creative expression in literature, music, art, drama, and broadcasting. In this way, a more permanent impression may be made on the adolescent as a discriminating consumer of the arts.

Enriching the Curriculum

School clubs often enrich the curriculum by adding activities for which the class does not seem to find enough time during the regular sessions but which mean a great deal to students. Students who are interested in creative writing find it easier to write a short story to be read at the next meeting of "The Scribblers" than to prepare the endless series of letters and themes demanded by the English teacher. The student who has just been accepted as a member of the school band may develop a more lasting interest in music than would come to him if his music classes were his only contact with music at school.

Even when the curriculum consists of vital activities of which the teacher is an effective leader, there is much that can be done in cocurricular activities. In fact, the stimulation which students receive during class sessions will develop interests which can be developed further in club work.

Let's take, for example, a school in which Spanish is taught as more than a body of grammatical rules. In their Spanish classes, the students learn to use and to understand Spanish but they also see foreign language motion pictures, they discuss current events in the countries whose language they are studying, and they visit Spanish or Latin American restaurants. What is left for a Spanish club to do? In such schools, Spanish clubs have published Spanish magazines, they have established contacts with students studying English in a South American school with whom they regularly exchange letters and small gifts, they have invited university students from South American countries who are now studying in this country to come to speak with them, they have organized Latin American fiestas and exhibits, they have organized a choir to sing Spanish songs, they have run parties at which only Spanish may be spoken and Spanish games played, and they have established record exchanges from which students may borrow Spanish records for their parties. No one need worry that alert and energetic adolescents will exhaust their idea of things to do so long as their interests are stimulated and the leadership is imaginative and helpful.

Providing for Individual Differences in Interests

Cocurricular activities supplement the provision the school makes for individual differences in interest. A small group of students interested in the construction of radio sets and in amateur broadcasting can be taken care of through a Radio Club without adding to an overburdened school curriculum. The facilities of the art rooms can be used by students who want additional opportunities for working on their own projects. Other clubs can be organized to take care of other interests.

The wide variety of cocurricular activities available to students is indicated by the fact that large secondary schools have more than a hundred clubs and teams divided into four categories: athletic, academic, service, and recreational.

Interscholastic athletic competitions are conducted in baseball, basketball, cross-country, fencing, football, golf, handball, soccer, swimming, tennis, and track. The sports in which intramural programs are most commonly conducted are basketball, handball, soccer, softball, swimming, tennis, and touch football. An active intramural program which enlists participation of all interested students can serve both to build the varsity team and to provide the opportunities for all interested students, which is the real justification for the activity.

The academic clubs, sponsored by each of the departments in the school, provide for students who are interested in creative writing, in choral work, in arts and crafts, in commercial art, and in all the other activities related to the work of the various departments. School publications include not only the school newspaper and the literary magazine but also publications issued periodically by many of the clubs.

The service activities enlist student assistance in directing traffic both within and outside the school, in supplementing library service, in coaching slow learners, in operating the mimeograph and the switchboard, and in many other ways that give students experience in working under supervision and in feeling the satisfaction that comes with knowing that they are helping to expand the school's facilities.

The recreational clubs have parties, go on hikes, or meet and discuss such hobbies as photography and collecting stamps.

Modern junior and senior high schools have so wide a variety of activities to offer that most students can easily be encouraged to participate. By providing for different levels of performance as well as by offering so many different kinds of activities, the school does something concrete about meeting individual differences.

Bringing Students Together on a Common Basis

Though cocurricular activities provide for differences among students, they also provide a basis for bringing together in the same activity many different types of students. The boy with so brilliant a scholastic record that his school program consists of Honor Class in History 5, Star English 7, Special Math 6 and the like may sing in the school chorus alongside a more mediocre fellow whom he never meets in any of his classes. The girl who spends most of her time on commercial subjects preparing to be a stenographer may dance with a boy majoring in vocational agriculture or preparing for college.

Cocurricular activities can be the most democratizing force in the school if the student's interest in the activity and his willingness to carry his share of the responsibility are the only requirements for joining. Without stressing prerequisites and marks, the school club appeals to all students who are interested in a given activity to come on in and share in the work and the fun.

Encouraging Better Teacher-Student Relationships

One of the most delightful aspects of cocurricular activities is the teacher-student relationship. There is no reason for any student to fear the faculty sponsor, for he never gives low grades, refers students to *The Office* for disciplinary action, or writes unpleasant notes to parents. Even in the most formidably formal secondary schools, the club meeting is either run by the students themselves or is planned co-operatively by students and teachers. It is here that students can see the teacher not as dictator or even as benevolent despot but as a guide and as a very useful person to turn to for help when a seemingly insoluble problem arises.

Because students usually belong to the same club for a number of semesters, they get to know the club sponsor better than they know their classroom teachers. As officers or committee members, or even as participants in a club program, they have the experience of working informally with a teacher. The club sponsor, therefore, is often the one teacher who knows the student well enough to be able to supply helpful information to the guidance counselor. To the student, the club sponsor is sometimes the only teacher he feels he knows well enough to go to for help on a personal or scholastic problem.

Serving as Laboratory for Trying Out New Curricular Activities and Procedures

Many activities that used to be regarded as extracurricular are now part of the school day. English classes prepare class magazines, produce one-act plays, conduct debates, and write short stories, even though these were all once regarded as strictly extracurricular activities. Social studies classes discuss current events instead of confining themselves to the past and relegating the present to the Current Events club.

Junior and senior high school teachers have learned that the activities formerly monopolized by the school clubs are so important a means of developing the skills, the habits, the attitudes, and the knowledge, too, that teachers wish students to have, that activities formerly tolerated only as extracurricular are now conducted in most classes, even in schools that look thoroughly old-fashioned. Cocurricular activities can continue to fill a useful function as a source of suggestions for new curricular procedures.

WHAT ARE THE CHARACTERISTICS OF A GOOD PROGRAM OF COCURRICULAR ACTIVITIES?

By implication at least, we have suggested that there are important distinctions between a good school program of cocurricular activities and an ineffective school program. What are the characteristics of a good school program of cocurricular activities?

Providing Appropriate Activities for a Varied Student Body

A good program offers an array of activities so widely varied as to attract all students, without compulsory participation in any specific activity. The school's program must be flexible, changing from time to time as circumstances and student needs vary. If schools were all to operate in this way, no school would be likely to have a cocurricular program identical with any other's. Still, competition among schools leads often to concentration on matching other schools rather than on meeting the needs of young people in each school. Small schools try to have as many athletic teams in interscholastic competition as larger schools have; and large schools sometimes have only a single team for each sport as though they were small schools. Similarly, schools try to have as many clubs as possible because of the erroneous belief that the number of clubs is an index to the effectiveness of the cocurricular program. The roster of clubs includes organizations that have been inactive for years or that are still holding on to life by electing officers and holding occasional meetings. If one school announces proudly that it has forty-two cocurricular activities, neighboring schools feel that they must equal or exceed that mark.

There is no reason why two schools should have the same array of clubs or even why any school should keep the same list of clubs over a period of years. A living organism is marked by the process of continuous birth and death—in the healthy human being, for example, old cells are dying and new cells are being born. In the same way, clubs that no longer serve a vital function should be permitted to die and to disappear and new organizations should be formed as necessary. Unless there is this process of continual change, the cocurricular program tends to become so inert that it is kept alive only by the constant prodding of principal and teachers.

In any live program of cocurricular activities there may be a long list of clubs, publications, and teams. To evaluate the adequacy of a program merely by counting the number of teams is, however, inadequate. If the building of a large number of tennis courts at a nearby state park develops such great interest in tennis that half the student body wishes to join the Tennis Club, there is no reason why they should not all be members of the Tennis Club, even though that may mean that the Badminton Club, the Chess Club, and the Ping-pong Club may have to disappear from the school scene, perhaps only temporarily. The acceptance of this point of view implies that some activities will be so popular at any given time that the school may have many clubs in the same area or many teams in the same sport, even though the deceptively small roster of different teams and clubs in the school may be much less impressive than a much longer list of moribund clubs in another school. When schools limit the number of students who may participate in a given activity in order to have enough members in other activities, students are compelled to join clubs in which they have little interest or to abstain entirely from cocurricular activities.

Stressing Student Benefit Rather Than School Publicity

Most lay people are not close enough to schools to understand what is being accomplished in classrooms by a new program of secondary education, but they can all understand a football victory over the team from a neighboring school or the band's winning first place in a state-wide competition. Illogically enough, some people in the community reason that any school which can win the county football championship and a state school band contest in the same year must be educationally sound.

Because the school needs all of the community support it can get, principals and teachers who have tasted the fruits of victory in interscholastic competition easily become greedy for more publicity. As a result, emphasis tends to be given to the development of star performers rather than to the improvement of the less talented boys and girls who may need more help. Teachers who are impatient for the acclamation given the winner tend to assume more and more of the responsibility for conducting the activity. Dramatics clubs may spend so much time rehearsing a single play for public production that there is no time to give students who are not star performers the satisfaction of hearing an audience applaud or the poise that comes from learning how to walk across the stage or from speaking to a large audience.

School publicity is a desirable by-product of cocurricular activity, but only a by-product. Any faculty that is alert to the need for school publicity can get sufficient publicity without sacrificing students' needs. If half the student body joins the Tennis Club or plays tennis in intramurals, the school is as likely to develop star performers who do well in interscholastic competition as it would if it restricted membership on the Tennis Team only to those students who had learned to play fairly well before they entered the school.

A good program of cocurricular activities usually has unexploited publicity values. One junior high school has an annual band concert in which the performers are boys and girls who did not play a musical instrument before they came to school. A senior high school recently conducted a tennis tournament limited to students who had never held a tennis racquet in their hands before they learned how to play tennis in their physical education classes. Father and son, and mother and daughter, golf tournaments make better newspaper copy than does an inter-scholastic golf match.

Guiding the Students' Choice of Cocurricular Activities

Although the program of cocurricular activities should be based on the students' voluntary choice of activities, there are many ways in which they can be helped to choose more wisely. Most students tend to join the same activities year after year, even though they can gain much from trying out new activities. Because most activities feature the performances of their best members, students are reluctant to join unless they feel they are almost up to that level of ability. Thus, a less talented student, who may find in dramatics a means of release that will help him to develop the poise he needs, may not have the nerve to join the dramatics club unless he is encouraged to do so.

We have spoken so much about the student who does not participate sufficiently in cocurricular activities that we have ignored the problem of the student who spends so much time with his cocurricular activities that he does not have enough time to do his work as a student. Some students love the excitement of interscholastic athletic competition and they do not see why teachers demand anything more of a boy who scored sixteen points in Saturday's basketball game. Other students take their editorial responsibilities so seriously they have little time for study. Still others regard their attendance at classes as the only unpleasant side of their chairmanship of the Lunch Period Dance Committee.

It seems odd that a school which regulates so carefully the number of subjects which a student takes in any one term should seem to be so indifferent to the amount of time he spends on cocurricular activities. Somewhere in the school there should be a member of the faculty who knows enough about the student's total program to be able to counsel the student who is spending too much of his time in cocurricular activities. It is this person, whether he be the principal, the dean, the guidance counselor, or the home room teacher, who should be able to guide the student's choice of cocurricular activities so that he participates in those he needs as well as in those he has already chosen.

To accomplish the purpose of participation in needed areas, permission to take part should not be employed as a reward or punishment. It is true in some cases that overindulging in activities interferes with studies. More generally, the activities promote a positive attitude toward school and better academic performance. Sometimes the student who does poorly in several school subjects finds his only recognition, achievement, and satisfaction in the social, service, or athletic components of the cocurriculum. Forbidding him to participate is not likely to improve his adjustment to more formal school work.

Making Full Use of Every Opportunity During the School Day to Accomplish the Purposes of Cocurricular Activities

Cocurricular activities need not be limited to an after-school program. Their goals often influence both the content and the procedures used in subject matter classes, and there are other ways, too, in which the influence of cocurricular activities should be reflected during the day.

Student organizations can be used to discuss and help solve some school problems. In some schools, during the election campaign for the student officers of the general organization of Student Council, the visitor sees the posters with the election promises of the various candidates, but notes ironically that regardless of which candidates are elected, the officers will have no voice in solving these problems.

Schools are often inconsistent in their selection of problems to be referred to the students or to their elected representatives. Adolescent students are ordinarily not mature enough to understand human motivation, yet Student Courts are entrusted in many schools with the responsibility for dealing with all but the most serious violations of school discipline. On the other hand, adolescents are mature enough to understand the problems that arise when the students in a large school try to eat at the same time, when all students have to use narrow stairways and corridors between periods, or when energetic and boisterous adolescents get on a bus that is already crowded with adults on their way to work. Instead of preparing new disciplinary regulations from the vantage point, and also the distance, of perspective, the principal will often find that the students themselves can understand the problems better because students are closer to these problems. Any school that maintains the outer forms of pupil self-government without giving elected student groups the opportunity to develop responsibility for *self*-government is unintentionally giving boys and girls an inadequate picture of how a democracy can operate.

Using the Lunchroom to Educational Advantage

The educational and recreational possibilities of various phases of the school day are often inadequately exploited. Many schools treat the lunch period, for example, as being an annoying interruption in the day's work. The lunch period is abbreviated as much as possible, sometimes to the point where students have to rush to the lunchroom if they are to have enough time to bolt their food after standing in a cafeteria line for ten of the thirty minutes allotted to lunch.

Adolescents, with the enormous appetites created by the needs of a growing body, enjoy a lunch period regardless of the circumstances under which it is conducted. The popularity of even unattractive lunchrooms should not lessen the school's attempt to make full use of the recreational possibilities of the happy circumstance that students eat together on the school premises.

The lunchroom in many schools is hardly the attractive room it should be if adolescents are to learn that in our culture eating is one of the social arts rather than merely a concession to physiology. The room is often crowded, noisy, poorly ventilated, insufficiently illuminated, unattractively decorated, and lacking adequate lavatory facilities if students are to wash up before eating.

The lunchroom should be as pleasant and as attractive a room as there is in the school building. For sanitary and aesthetic reasons, it should be painted more frequently than classrooms are painted, and the color scheme should be more cheering than the time-honored buff and brown. Treating the ceilings with sound-absorbing material will reduce the amount of noise so markedly that boys and girls will not have to shout to make themselves heard. Unless space limitation is too restricting, it is better to have small tables seating four or six than the long tables so often found in school lunchrooms. In short, schools must do all they can to create a lunchroom atmosphere that will lead students to think of the period as a time for eating, but also as a time for relaxation and for enjoying the opportunity for conversing with friends.

Though the physical limitations of the school plant or of the school budget may interfere with the modernization of the school cafeteria, there is no such obstacle to lengthening the lunch period, except in schools that are so badly overcrowded that students have to eat in many shifts. Aside from the fact that many students and some teachers want to get away from school as early as possible in the afternoon, there is no valid objection to lengthening the school day by half an hour in order to provide adequate time for eating and recreation at midday.

Many schools which have a sufficiently long lunch period have a planned recreational program. There are free dances in the gymnasium which can be attended by all, even by those who work after school and those who do not have the money or the clothes for parties. Concerts by the school orchestra or school band provide for other tastes. Dramatic productions in the auditorium attract an audience for students whose talents will never win them a role in the major school plays. Open forums and discussions are also popular.

After a lunch period spent in such ways as this, adolescent boys and girls return to class refreshed and relaxed so that the classes after lunch are as fresh and as stimulating as those in the morning.

ENCOURAGING WIDESPREAD AND ACTIVE PARTICIPATION IN COCURRICULAR ACTIVITIES

While many students derive considerable benefit from their co-curricular participation, it is unfortunately true that participation is sometimes far from unanimous. As Mr. Dooley once remarked, "The funny thing about money is that the poor people who need it the most are the virry ones that niver have it." Similarly, those students who need co-curricular activities the most are seldom the most active participants. Everybody admits that athletic teams attract students who already have the interest and the ability to take part in the games and do not cater to students who need all the encouragement they can get if they are to benefit from a varied recreational life.

It is not so generally recognized that this same weakness characterizes the rest of the typical cocurricular program. Which student gets the opportunity to lead others by being the captain of the team or the president of a club or the editor of a paper? Is it the retiring boy or girl who has not learned how to make friends, or is it the youth who has many friends and followers? Which boys and girls are most active in the Friday afternoon dances? Are they the students who must work such long hours after school to supplement the family income that they seldom have time to go to parties and have to stay away from school affairs that are too expensive, or are they the ones who dance well and are always having or attending parties? Do the sororities and fraternities recruit their members from among the more insecure adolescents who need the comforting sense of belonging that comes from being able to say, "We girls of Alpha Alpha Alpha always stick together"? One could go down the list of the co-curricular activities sponsored by the school and demonstrate in instance after instance that the activity could accomplish much more by changing its membership and by reassigning the duties and the responsibilities of its members.

Ideally, every student should be a voluntarily active participant in cocurricular activities. Conditions approaching the ideal can be attained if the activities conducted in the school are close to student needs and if the teachers are competent sponsors.

It is better not to gain what appears to be 100 per cent student participation in cocurricular activities by the superficially simple expedient of compelling all students to join at least one activity each term. Such a compulsory program deprives these activities of the values that come from the students' voluntary participation. Although some students who join a club only because of compulsion may later become interested and active participants, many students who join a club through compulsion rather than from choice sit at meetings almost as impassively as they would if they had to stay after school in the detention room.

Improving Club Programs

A more effective way of increasing the percentage of the student body active in cocurricular activities is to attempt to discover and to correct the causes of inadequate student participation. The faculty sponsor of a club that seems to limit its weekly meetings to variations on the theme "We need more members" should help the group to develop a program that is so alive that other students will want to join. The Naturalists' Club, for example, that does little more than care for the few exhibits in the biology room and listen to reports that other members have copied from encyclopedia articles ordinarily has little reason to expect a flood of new members. Even those students who are members will absent themselves from meetings every time they find more interesting things to do that afternoon.

An interested faculty sponsor may help the club to develop a more attractive program. Conducting afternoon and Saturday morning hikes on which members collect specimens for the school exhibits, holding joint meetings with the Naturalists' Club of a neighboring school, making "behind the scenes" visits to a museum with an opportunity to visit the rooms in which exhibits are being prepared and to talk with members of the museum staff, assuming the responsibility for maintaining the school museum and for serving as curators and guides, discussing radio and television programs that center on science and medicine, seeing motion pictures that somehow or other are not shown in class—all of these suggestions and better ones will occur to the club members and the sponsors once they stop worrying about new members and begin planning effective programs which will inevitably make the club so alive that it cannot help growing.

Participation in cocurricular activities means more than merely agreeing to join a club or team. In every secondary school there are a great many inactive club members who attend meetings often enough not to be dropped from the rolls but who gain little beyond the right to list this as one of their activities in the Senior Yearbook.

In order to encourage more students to share in the responsibility for running the activity, the faculty sponsor must use his influence to prevent any small group from monopolizing control of the club. It is ordinarily preferable to have more rather than fewer club committees, and to have the committees large enough and numerous enough so that all members feel that they are sharing in the direction of the activity.

Some schools limit students to only one key position in any one semester in order to give more students the opportunity to serve as leaders of student activities and at the same time to prevent any student from overburdening himself with cocurricular responsibilities. In these schools, a student who serves as the captain or manager of a team, the editor of a school publication, or the president of a club may hold no other cocurrilar office that semester even though he may join in other activities and participate as an ordinary member.

Discovering and Treating the Causes of Inadequate Student Participation in Cocurricular Activities

Some of the causes of inactivity may require more than the co-operation and leadership of those faculty members who are serving as club sponsors. There are students who cannot participate in cocurricular activities because they have such heavy responsibilities at home or spend so much time on part-time jobs that they cannot spare the time for club meetings. Here, it may be necessary for the principal to arrange for discussion with parents so that they may realize how much their sons and daughters are losing by being deprived of the personal contacts and the educational opportunities associated with cocurricular activities. It is possible to program many activities during the school day so that even students who have to leave promptly at the close of school to take the school bus can participate. If the principal and the teachers exert their influence to see that students' social life does not ordinarily involve spending more money than they can afford on their allowance, they may be able to reduce some of the petty part-time employment that keeps students away from more important activities.

Even after principal and teachers have done all they can to develop a varied, attractive, convenient, and helpful program of cocurricular activities, there will still be some students who will not participate. These are the instances that should be studied further by the dean, the guidance counselor, the home room teacher, or any other member of the school faculty whose job it is to see that students adjust themselves adequately to their own problems.

More than cocurricular participation may be involved. Drop-outs from high school before graduation almost universally have taken little part in activities. Some authorities conclude from this and other evidence that the incidence of drop-outs is related to lack of identification with the social life of the school. Stimulating participation in cocurricular activities may improve the nonparticipant's social adjustment and encourage him to remain in school until graduation.

Some students engage in so many activities out of school that they do not need to join the school program and they have no spare time for these activities. A girl, for example, who studies the violin and dancing with private teachers, who is a Girl Scout, and who is also an active member and chairman of the Dance Committee of the young people's group of her church, need not be urged to participate in the school's cocurricular program, even though the principal will never be able to boast of 100 per cent participation in cocurricular activities.

Other students may be reluctant to join because of previous unpleasant experiences with clubs at school or out-of-school. Very strict parents may insist that their sons and daughters come home directly after school so that school clubs will not be used as subterfuges by which these boys and girls can go elsewhere without their parents' knowledge. Sensitive adolescents who are ashamed of their shabby clothing or who feel that they are not acceptable socially in the school are wary of joining clubs or attending informal school parties. Any boy or girl who feels emotionally insecure may also be reluctant to join a school group in which he does not have the comforting feeling that he is being protected by the teacher in charge.

In every secondary school there are undoubtedly a few students who regard compulsory education laws only as a means of keeping them from getting the job and earning the money they want either so that they can spend more freely or so that they can help their family, which may need the money badly. Such students ordinarily do nothing more in school than they have to—and there is nothing in the Compulsory Education Law that compels them to join a club or team or to stay after school to rehearse for a play or to prepare articles for the school newspaper.

The diversity of the causes that may lie back of the student's failure to participate in cocurricular activities demonstrates both the impossibility of devising any procedure that will suit all cases and the necessity for investigating what may be a symptom of a condition the school should seek to correct.

Keeping All Activities Open to Any Student Who Wishes to Join

Cocurricular activities should offer the most complete illustration of equality of opportunity in the school. In cocurricular activities, unlike class activities, there are no set standards that must be met each year and, therefore, no need for setting up entrance requirements. Only students who have completed the prerequisite art courses, for example, are admitted to advanced classes in art. The Studio Club, however, need have no prerequisites other than the desire to paint in oil and the willingness to clean up before leaving. Undoubtedly some of the members will produce a finished product that will never win even honorable mention at an amateur exhibit, but they will have the satisfaction that comes from putting on canvas the picture they had in their mind.

Similarly, the Playshop need not be restricted to students who have done so well in their English or speech courses that they are ready to audition for a stellar part in the forthcoming play. There are many ways in which students who were not born to be actors and actresses may nevertheless assist in the production of the play and share in the plaudits. They need not always be behind the scenes, either, for there are plays without elaborate costuming or scenery that are produced at club meetings instead of in the auditorium.

Obviously the club and its sponsor are interested in presenting the best possible productions that they can, but clubs may do much to increase joy in creative activity for its own sake without setting up standards which are impossible except for a few students. School clubs can contribute to reducing the unnecessary perfectionism in the popular attitude toward leisure activities which results in dividing the population into two widely separated groups—the highly gifted performers and the passive spectators who will not even try to perform because they recognize their comparative lack of finesse. Somewhere in between these extremes is a considerable proportion of the public who could enjoy singing, dancing, painting, acting, writing, and playing numerous sports if they felt comfortable with admittedly nonprofessional standards.

The club sponsor will sometimes have to be careful that the wealthier members of the club do not set a financial pace with which the poorer students cannot keep step. If the school provides the equipment and supplies that are needed, there is no need for charging dues. Club trips and excursions should be inexpensive. Club parties should have such simple refreshments that price never becomes a noticeable factor.

The Secret Society Problem

There is obviously no room for snobbish secret societies in a public high school in a democratic community. All of the advantages that have been claimed for high school sororities and fraternities can be achieved through a well-planned program of school social clubs that are open to all students. Though the school may not be able to eliminate all the intolerance and the snobbishness that some students may bring to school, there is nothing to be said in behalf of a school that accepts or caters to adolescent snobbishness. Merely denying sororities and fraternities the use of school facilities is insufficient. Declaring members of sororities and fraternities to be ineligible for school office encourages perjury and gives their members the added thrill of being members of a persecuted underground organization.

A more effective way of counteracting the sorority or fraternity is to develop so varied and active a program of cocurricular activities with sufficient provision for attractive social affairs open to all students that boys and girls will see little sense in joining these exclusive organizations whose workings they have been led to understand through open discussion in school. In this, as in so many other problems of dealing with adolescents, neither the school nor the home can alone effect a solution. Parents and teachers can accomplish so much more when they work together that the problem of sororities and fraternities should be among those discussed as often as necessary at parents' meetings and in the principal's letters to parents.

THE TEACHER'S ROLE IN COCURRICULAR ACTIVITIES

That cocurricular activities need competent faculty guidance does not mean that it is the teachers who are to run the activity, possibly exerting their control a little more subtly than when they are teaching a class. So far as is possible, the responsibility for selecting, planning, and conducting the program of any cocurricular activity should be left in the students' hands. For the teacher to come to a club meeting and announce what the year's program should include is to destroy much of the distinctive value of the cocurricular activity.

Because most clubs ordinarily meet only once a week, however, there is not enough time for all of the members to suggest activities in which they can engage, to evaluate the merit of the various suggestions, to plan in detail the procedure they will follow in conducting the activity, and still have time actually to do what they have planned.

It is ordinarily more efficient to have an executive committee consisting of the elected officers and two or three other students who can receive suggestions from students at an early meeting, who accept the responsibility for studying the advisability of selecting one rather than another of these suggestions, and who then report back to the club members at a regular meeting for them to indicate their choice. The executive committee, by discussing club problems between meetings, can do much to see that the meetings themselves are planned better.

The teacher's role as an ex officio member of the executive committee is often the means by which the teacher exerts his influence over the way the activity is conducted. Never the chairman of the executive committee, and often with only a voice and not a vote in the committee, the teacher is in a position to influence rather than to dictate club policy. Participating in the discussion of club problems, he can keep boys and girls from becoming entangled in wrangles over parliamentary procedure or from bogging down in the discussion of trivial matters. More important still, the faculty sponsor may help the executive committee to recognize the existence of problems they might otherwise have ignored.

How One Teacher Worked to Maintain Democratic Operation

In one school, the members of a small clique which included some of the most active members of the club met at the home of one of the students in the group and prepared a slate which divided up the various officerships among themselves. At the next meeting of the club, the candidates selected by the clique were duly elected. During the next semester, the club operated so smoothly and accomplished so much under the leadership of this clique that the teacher, perhaps too naïvely, did not suspect the way in which the elections had been engineered.

The other club members did recognize that this clique, which already ran the school dances, had captured control of a school club. When elections were in order the following semester, those members of the club who felt excluded from the officerships also organized a slate. The teacher suddenly realized that two cliques were now fighting for control and that victory for either faction would leave the club divided. The teacher said nothing while elections were being held, for she felt that anything she said at this time might be misinterpreted as indicating her taking sides. The election resulted in a victory for the opposition, though by a narrow margin.

A few days after the election meeting, the new executive committee held its first meeting. A number of times during this meeting, questions came up that the newly-elected officers could not answer because they had not been on the committee the preceding semester. After several such instances, the teacher asked naïvely why all of the preceding officers had failed to be re-elected, especially since by school custom the secretary ordinarily was promoted to the vice-presidency and the vice-president became the new president. Did the election returns indicate general dissatisfaction with the way in which the club was run and, if so, what changes did they think desirable?

It was then that the new vice-president, after exchanging glances with the others, explained to the teacher how they had felt they had to organize a clique of their own to freeze out the clique that had excluded them. After a few minutes of discussion, it became clear that they did not like the idea of factionalism any more than the teacher did. They admitted, too, that the open forum meetings initiated last term had been successful in attracting new members and that the girl who had presided at these sessions last term was just the person they needed to keep them successful.

The executive committee had the choice, the teacher pointed out, either of ruling the fraction of the club that would remain if the other group left or of trying to win the other group over to work together for the success of the program. The program did seem more important to the executive committee, especially since they had had the pleasure of a major victory over the previously controlling clique. As victors they could afford to be generous.

The executive committee voted to recommend to the club at the next meeting that they continue the open forums on international problems so successfully conducted last semester. They recommended, too, that last semester's chairman of the forum committee be invited to serve another term in that capacity even though they appreciated that the responsibility took so much time that they hesitated to impose on her for another semester. They recommended, further, that since the forums were so important a part of the club program, that the chairman of the forum committee be elected to the executive committee. All of these recommendations were adopted by the full membership.

The teacher's problems were not over, for adolescents, like adults, gain more satisfaction from being in a clique, especially one that is in control or seems on the verge of gaining control, than they like to admit. During the term, the teacher had many opportunities to teach the lesson that a group which is so certain that international peace can come only when nations are ready to sacrifice some of their national sovereignty should be willing to subordinate loyalty to their own clique to a larger loyalty to the school. The teacher had the satisfaction of noting that there were no mass resignations from the club and that there were no distinct slates proposed for election at the end of the term. In her own way this teacher helped these students to see the hopes of democracy translated into reality, for the two student groups, as the reader may have suspected by now, came from different parts of the school district, each with its own loyalties and snobbishness. This teacher was able to use the club as a means of demonstrating that students from different levels of income and social background can be interested in the same goals and in working together to achieve them.

The Sponsor's Supervision Rather Than Direction of Cocurricular Activities

It is one thing to allow the students to assume the responsibility for running a club; the situation is different when there are large sums of money to be handled, when a school newspaper is distributed so widely that it is read by most of the students and taken home where it may be read and criticized by parents, or when a play is to be produced or a concert given with the school's reputation at stake. How much responsibility can the teacher afford to relinquish?

It may help in this connection to distinguish among types of activities. Betweeen the class and the informal club stand a group of activities where the goal is some kind of product or service which reaches the public and for which the school as a whole has to assume responsibility. These activities include many sports, publications, dramatics, and musical performances. In these cases the adviser has to walk a tightrope of tact since he is interpreting the school to the public, and the public to students participating in the activity. These situations may serve as a worthwhile opportunity to help students realize that they never work in a vacuum but in a context which includes relationships with other people. The adviser must himself be alert to his responsibility to the school and the community and must help young people recognize that their freedom of action is subject to respecting these two responsibilities.

Even under these circumstances, however, it is preferable for the teacher to supervise rather than to direct, and to advise rather than to control. The circulation manager of the school paper should have the responsibility for collecting the money paid by subscribers, and the business manager should see that advertisers pay their bills. Making the budget balance should be the concern of the entire newspaper staff.

Pointing out that they are really running a business, the faculty sponsor can emphasize the need for good accounting practices. It is unfair to boys and girls to let them handle money so carelessly that no one knows if any is pilfered. The teacher can check all financial accounts regularly without letting students feel that they are all suspected of being potential embezzlers.

The faculty sponsor of a school publication should not allow himself to be maneuvered into the position of becoming the censor who must read and approve everything to be printed in the paper. The censor's lot is an unhappy one, for the very fact that he is a censor seems to suggest that all writers must play the game of trying to outwit the censor by getting into print something that he would never knowingly approve.

The standards for deciding what kind of material should be printed and what should not appear in the school paper should be discussed at staff conferences until all writers and editors understand and accept the standards. Such matters as the need for verifying factual statements, for presenting news items without bias, and for keeping the humor columns free of questionable material should be understood by all. Provision should be made for having all articles approved by responsible editors and for consulting the faculty sponsor when important differences of opinion arise. After each issue of the paper appears, there should be a staff meeting at which the issue is discussed and evaluated by all. So far as the sponsor can make it, this should be their paper, not his. The more mature and responsible the students, the greater should be their share of the responsibility.

No teacher must allow himself to become so thoroughly identified with any public performance by a cocurricular group that it becomes his performance, not theirs. The faculty sponsor is not a director, stage manager, producer, and scenic designer. To be sure, he will help his group, but he must not reduce the students to the subordinate and uninspiring role of being his puppets. It is better to have less ambitious performances that students can give than to present elaborate plays that call for the teacher's detailed assistance on each point.*

* One high school student described the very popular faculty adviser of the dramatics club as follows: "He isn't lazy but he's the kind of fellow who says, 'If students are supposed to produce a play, it's up to the students to produce the play' and so he never offers any suggestions until after we have tried to solve the problem ourselves and have to admit we are stumped."

ASSURING COMPETENT FACULTY SPONSORSHIP AND ADEQUATE SCHOOL SUPPORT FOR COCURRICULAR ACTIVITIES

Selection of teachers for club and team sponsorship is often a clue to the school's attitude toward the cocurriculum. No school system is ready to use the teacher's experiences as a high school or college student as sufficient basis for evolving effective methods of teaching; yet many schools are content to rely on the new teacher's memory of his high school and college club experiences as an adequate basis for becoming an effective club sponsor.

The school which seeks to enhance its educational program through cocurricular activities will select those teachers who work well with boys and girls in informal situations and who have a particular interest in the activity to which they are assigned. On the other hand, the school which uses cocurricular activities for noneducational purposes will look only at the win-loss ratio in selecting coaches and will assign as many of the less popular clubs as possible to newly appointed teachers, for they are in the weakest position to refuse the assignment. So far as such schools are concerned, any Spanish teacher can direct the Latin American Club and every English teacher is a likely prospect for the faculty advisership of the school publication.

This is not a plea for modification of state certification requirements by adding another prescribed methods course in the direction of cocurricular activities, for it is questionable whether the addition of still another requirement will meet the need. It does suggest, however, the need for an in-service program of teacher education. The principal and the other supervisory officers should make their assignments in terms of the abilities and background of their teachers. Problems arising from the guidance of cocurricular activities may properly be included among the topics discussed at teachers' conferences. Provision must be made for teachers to visit other clubs in the school and in other schools so that they may see how other teachers discharge their responsibilities. Supervisors should demonstrate their willingness to help teachers with their cocurricular activities instead of conveying the common attitude that once the sponsors' assignments have been made, the supervisor is through for the year.

In addition to supplying competent faculty guidance, the school should also supply the equipment and the materials that are needed for an effective program. The faculty sponsor of a club should be as free to order a motion picture film for presentation at a club meeting as he would be to order a film for classroom use. Having each club defray its expenditures by collecting dues or other contributions from its members or by receiving a grant from a student fund is a reminder of the days when co-curricular activities were not considered an integral part of the school day. To ask the student fund to pay all club expenses is to tempt students to stress activities that will raise the most money for the fund instead of evaluating activities on the basis of their value to the participants.

Cocurricular Activities as Part of the Teacher's Program

If it is important that the school recognize that the student's participation in cocurricular activities may make such heavy demands on his time that he slights other phases of the school work, it is equally important that the school recognize how much time the teacher invests in his work as a sponsor or coach. When the direction of cocurricular activities is simply added to the program of a busy teacher who regards his school function to be primarily that of a classroom teacher, it is inevitable that he should devote as little time as possible to the club assignment.

The time which the teacher spends in the effective discharge of his cocurricular activities should be considered when his instructional program is planned for the term. Some cocurricular activities demand more time than is spent in the preparation for and teaching of a class. To ask the teacher to accept so burdensome an assignment without a corresponding reduction in the number of classes he teaches is as unreasonable as asking him to add another class to a full teaching program. If the club assignment does not warrant relieving the teacher of one of his classes, the teacher may be excused from some of the other additional assignments which teachers get, for example, the supervision of study hall periods.

That it is often the youngest and the least experienced teachers who get these heavy cocurricular assignments makes the practice particularly unfortunate, for the young teacher develops the habit of preparing for teaching and for club work as quickly rather than as thoroughly as possible.

The school that includes the sponsorship of cocurricular activities as part of the teachers' programs does more than guard against overworking its teachers. By recognizing the demands that are made on the teacher's time, the school indicates its belief that the sponsorship of cocurricular activities deserves the teacher's preparation as much as teaching does. It suggests, moreover, that the supervisory officers in the school may appropriately devote time to improving the conduct of cocurricular activities just as they attempt to improve the quality of the classroom teaching.

Faculty Morale and the Cocurriculum

The attitude which teachers take toward their sponsorship of cocurricular activities is often a revealing index of faculty morale. When teachers see themselves as respected members of the community and as members of a professional staff dedicated to their work with adolescents, there is rarely any question of their willingness to serve as club sponsors or team coaches. On the other hand, when teachers feel overworked and underpaid, they may resent the additional responsibility of working with co-curricular activities and of being compelled to stay at school after the usual dismissal time. Such expedients as subtle coercion by the principal or the payment of an additional stipend for after-school work with co-curricular activities are poor substitutes for a more basic attack on the causes of low faculty morale and a constructive attempt to correct them.

RELATING THE COCURRICULAR PROGRAM TO THE STUDENTS' OUT-OF-SCHOOL ACTIVITIES

If cocurricular activities are interpreted broadly enough to include all of the activities in which students participate when they are not in class, the school should work with the rest of the community in planning a program that encompasses evening and week-end activities. No school that is really interested in its students can afford to lock its gates in the late afternoon and remain unconcerned about what boys and girls will do until the gates are unlocked once more.

How much responsibility the school cocurriculum activities should assume for supplying wholesome recreational outlets will vary from one community to another. Where a community has a full program of youth activities, the school may not have to concern itself with the students' recreational activities. In fact, what the school has to offer may be so inferior to what students can find in their community that teachers should not waste their time or the school's resources in unnecessary competition with outside agencies. By contrast, there are other communities in which there is so little for youth to do that the school has to keep a varied cocurricular activity going into the evenings and on week-ends while it tries to prod the community into making better provision for the energies and the enthusiasms of youth.

This does not suggest that teachers should be on duty mornings, afternoons, and evenings for seven days a week, twelve months a year. Such a demand would leave teachers no time for their out-of-class professional duties and for their own cultural development and recreational interests.

It does imply, however, that the school must co-operate with other community agencies. School facilities should be made available for community use when they are not being used for school purposes. That such broader use of the school plant and equipment is becoming increasingly accepted is indicated by the fact that most of the newer secondary schools are so constructed that part of the school may be opened to the community in the evening while the rest of the building remains locked to uninvited stragglers.

School officials should meet with recreational and social work leaders in the community to help plan a comprehensive program to meet all the needs of all the adolescents. Scouting officials, directors of community centers, clergymen, public officers, social workers—all of these have so great an interest in adolescent problems that the school should join the community council of social agencies if one exists or should take the initiative in organizing such a group. Because parents see their children in so different a relationship from that of a professional worker who meets adolescents for a few hours at a time, it is desirable to invite some of the most co-operative and understanding parents to meet with the professional workers.

A broad program of cocurricular activities should have a more positive note than that of crime prevention or the preservation of good morals. It should rest on the assumption that adolescents have legitimate intellectual, social, and recreational needs that must be met. If the school does not concern itself with helping to meet these needs, it has no right to feel superior to commercially minded people who will try to do so. Just as schools do not think of conducting activities primarily for the purpose of making money, so does commercialized recreation not concern itself particularly with the educational value of its offerings. Rather than join the chorus of those who through the ages have said that youth is following a downward path, the school should join the smaller group of those who are helping provide the facilities to enable young people to enjoy their youth and to develop into adults who can enjoy their maturity.

When classroom activities are guided by a teacher who sees his major function to be that of helping boys and girls to educate themselves, many of the characteristics of the club period apply equally well to his own class sessions. It is certainly better to have the teacher try to bring the informality of the club meeting into the class session than to have the club sponsor perpetuate the artificial relations of an artificial classroom.

QUESTIONS FOR STUDY AND DISCUSSION

1. You are a new, inexperienced teacher assigned to a school where a group of enthusiastic students want to organize a photography club. They have asked you to be their adviser, explaining that the other teachers already have clubs or other assignments. They know that you have no special background but they seem to like working with you and the regulations require that they have an official sponsor.

Assuming that you are willing to help them, how would you define your role in the club?

How can you help the members develop a worthwhile program even though you know little about photography?

2. In order to encourage students to participate in cocurricular activities,

some schools require every student to join at least one club each term. To what extent are the values of cocurricular activities lost when participation is made compulsory? In your opinion, does the gain that comes from 100 per cent club membership outweigh the loss in value that comes from compulsory club membership?

3. When the members of a high school French Club heard that a theater in town planned a special three-day showing the following month of a French motion picture, the members enthusiastically agreed to organize a Saturday matinee theater party. Within a week they had sold some 125 tickets, when the teacher saw a newspaper item indicating that this film was the center of a violent controversy in New York, where it had been running for some weeks. Although the film had been modified in order to meet the censors' objections, a number of women's associations protested that it was still too immoral to be exhibited.

What should the French teacher do now that she has read the article? How should she do it?

4. As the faculty adviser of a school club, you have succeeded in developing so cordial a relationship with the members that they stay after the meeting is over just because they enjoy the informality of the conversations they have with you. During one of these after-meeting sessions, you realize that these boys and girls have accepted you so completely as a member of the group that they go right on with their gossip about the peculiarities of various teachers and the ways in which students outwit them. What should you do?

5. During the discussion of a demonstration at a First-Aid Club, of which you are the sponsor, one of the girls criticized the procedure that was being demonstrated. She quoted the home nursing teacher as having recommended a totally different procedure. Another member of the class immediately corroborated the statement that the home nursing teacher suggested the other procedure. Although you have long suspected that the home nursing teacher is old-fashioned and does not keep up with developments in her field, you never thought she would continue to recommend a procedure that had been outdated for years.

What should you do?

6. With great enthusiasm, the boys at your junior high school have organized a "Fixit" Club so that they can collect broken toys which they want to repair and repaint for presentation to a nearby children's hospital. After spending the first meeting in electing temporary officers and selecting a committee to frame a constitution and by-laws for the club, they seem content to spend all their other meetings discussing the proposed constitution and by-laws. Despite your subtle suggestions to the officers and the members, the meetings are spent in talk without there being any sign of eagerness to undertake the work for which they organized the club.

What more can you do to get them to start work without becoming the dictator rather than the adviser?

7. As a home room teacher you note that some of the boys and girls in your group rarely attend the social affairs run by the school clubs. How can you go about finding out tactfully why they do not attend?

What can you do in each of the following instances?

    a. One girl stays away because she feels she is not sufficiently attractive or interesting to be popular at such dances and she prefers not to take the chance of being outshone by the other girls.

    b. A boy has an after-school job at the drugstore which makes it necessary for him to leave promptly when school is dismissed.

c. A girl admits that she has never learned to dance because she is embarrassed when close to a boy. Besides, she thinks most of her classmates are too "fast" for her.

d. A girl explains that she goes to so many parties on Friday nights and Saturday nights that her parents insist that she come home early to do her school work on week days.

e. From what you can gather, one of your boys comes from a family that is so poor he cannot afford to buy tickets for even relatively inexpensive school dances. He stays away from free dances because he feels it would attract unfavorable attention if he were to go to the free dances and not come to those for which a fee is charged. Instead, he tells the other boys that he just doesn't care for dancing.

f. A girl tells you that she is engaged and that her fiancé does not like the idea of her going to dances without him.

g. You know that the parents of one of your students object to social dancing on religious and moral grounds. You suspect that this is the real reason for the girl's staying away from these parties even though she gives many other excuses such as her not having pretty clothes to wear or a boy friend to escort her.

BIBLIOGRAPHY

1. ALCORN, Marvin D., HOUSEMAN, Richard A., and SCHUNERT, Jim R., *Better Teaching in Secondary Schools* (New York, Holt, Rinehart and Winston, Inc., 1954), Chs. 17, 18.

2. DOUGLASS, Harl R., *Modern Administration of Secondary Schools* (Boston, Ginn and Company, 1954), Chs. 9-11.

3. FRENCH, William M., *American Secondary Education* (New York, The Odyssey Press, 1957), Ch. 17.

4. GILCHRIST, Robert S., DUTTON, Wilbur H., and WRINKLE, William L., *Secondary Education for American Democracy*, rev. ed. (New York, Holt, Rinehart and Winston, Inc., 1957), Ch. 11.

5. GRUBER, Frederick C., and BEATTY, Thomas B., *Secondary School Activities* (New York, McGraw-Hill Book Co., Inc., 1954).

6. GRUHN, William T., and DOUGLASS, Harl R., *The Modern Junior High School*, 2nd ed. (New York, The Ronald Press Company, 1956), Ch. 13.

7. HANSON, Kenneth H., *High School Teaching* (Englewood Cliffs, N.J., Prentice-Hall, Inc., 1957), Ch. 12.

8. HAVIGHURST, Robert J., *Human Development and Education* (New York, Longmans, Green & Co., Inc., 1953).

9. KILZER, Louis R., STEPHENSON, Harold H., and NORDBERG, H. Orville, *Allied Activities in the Secondary School* (New York, Harper and Brothers, 1956).

10. KIRKENDALL, Lester A., and ZERAN, Franklin R., *Student Councils in Action* (New York, Chartwell House, Inc., 1953).

11. KLAUSMEIER, Herbert J., *Teaching in the Secondary School* (New York, Harper and Brothers, 1958), Ch. 16.

12. McKOWN, Harry C., *Extracurricular Activities*, 3rd ed. (New York, The Macmillan Company, 1952).

13. *School Activities*, the extracurricular magazine. Published monthly (September–May) by School Activities Publishing Company, Topeka, Kansas.

14. THOMPSON, Nellie Z., *Your School Clubs* (New York, E. P. Dutton and Company, 1953).

15. TOMPKINS, Ellsworth D., *The Activity Period in Public High Schools* (Washington, D.C., U.S. Office of Education, 1951, Bulletin No. 19).

16. ———, *Extra-Class Activities for All Pupils* (Washington, D.C., U.S. Office of Education, 1950, Bulletin No. 4).

CHAPTER 13

Managing a Classroom

»»»»»»»»»»»

BEFORE WE START on a long motor trip, we have to
know where we are going and how we are going to get there, but we also
have to be sure our tires are all right. When tires are in good condition,
we are not even aware of their existence, but the best planned trip comes
to an abrupt stop when a tire goes flat.

In the same way, the most carefully planned classroom activity can
also come to an unpleasant halt if the classroom routines do not function
properly. In an industrial arts shop class, for example, there must be a
simple way of getting and returning tools if the students are to spend their
time using the tools rather than fighting over who is to get them. Similarly, if a class is subdivided into groups and committees, each of which
is busy with its own special tasks, the teacher must know how to keep
these groups from getting in each other's way.

Classroom Management as a Means to an End

Classroom management is only a means to an end, and never a major goal of education, but the teacher must know how to manage the
classroom if any desirable educational goals are to be reached.

Ideally, the mechanics of classroom management should operate so
smoothly and with so little attention that teacher and students are as unaware of them while concentrating on more important matters as the
driver is unaware of his tires as he decides whether or not to make a right
turn at the next intersection. Certainly we should pity the teacher and
the students when questions of classroom management become the key
determinants in planning classroom activities—when, for example, the
teacher is more concerned with where students write their name and the

date rather than with whether the short stories they write are worth reading—just as we pity the driver who has to plan his trips in terms of his tires.

Classroom Management and the New Teacher

It is at the beginning of the teacher's career that skill in class management is most important, for it is in the class of the beginner that confusion is most likely to breed misconduct and disruption of learning. Eager as a new teacher is to start his career auspiciously, he will soon discover that he may never get a chance to demonstrate his effectiveness as a teacher if his classroom is chaotic, a condition he might easily prevent by giving a little attention to the mechanics of class management.

A young teacher, who has not learned how to manage a classroom in which three or four groups of students are at work on differentiated assignments while he is working with a few students, may conclude that disorder is inherent in group teaching. Erroneously, he may reject group teaching as unworkable when it can be most productive once the teacher has mastered the mechanics of keeping several groups at work on different tasks at the same time. Recognizing his own inexperience, it would be better for him to reduce the number of groups into which he divides his class—to three groups rather than to five—instead of ignoring group instruction entirely and teaching the whole class as though all of his students were exactly alike.

Principals and superintendents often criticize teacher education institutions for not paying more attention to class management and to the teacher's role in school administration. Accustomed to working with experienced teachers, administrators are often critical of new teachers who cannot deal with several groups at once, who do not know how to take attendance and keep a record of absences, or who never order their films and their supplies on time.

Much that the teacher must know about school procedures he can learn more efficiently on the job than in advance. There is so much variation in the procedures followed in the different schools to which the graduates of a single teacher-education institution may be appointed that it would consume almost the full four years of an undergraduate program to include all of the details of all of these schools. Not only would such a procedure be tremendously time-consuming but it would also be ineffective. No prospective teacher is likely to be stimulated by a study of the many different shapes that requisition forms take nor is he likely to remember the details of school regulations until he has to follow them. Rather than swamp the prospective teacher with a mass of details he will not remember, it is better to have schools plan orientation sessions for new members of the staff and provide an experienced teacher as a mentor for the new teacher in his first semester.

What the new teacher does need is a recognition of the importance of classroom management and skill in administering his own classroom, especially in his first year, when he cannot jeopardize his control of his class. Once he has these basic skills, it is no great problem for him to adjust his procedures for use in a specific school. Thus, if he becomes a member of a teaching team, he can learn easily how class management is modified when the conventional bell schedule is altered radically and when teachers work with groups of varying sizes instead of with a standard size for all classes in the school.

IMPROVING CLASSROOM EFFICIENCY BY DEVELOPING APPROPRIATE CLASSROOM ROUTINE

The classroom is a busy place, but it need not be hectic. Although teaching is essentially a series of interactions of mind with mind, of personality with personality, and of mind with materials, the success of the whole process may be influenced by such a small factor as the ventilation of the room or the accessibility of the materials that are needed for the effective conduct of the group's activities. The teacher must, therefore, help his students to develop routines that will take care of the details of classroom administration and that will free teacher and students to concentrate on more important activities.

No activity should be routinized unless it occurs fairly frequently and under the same circumstances. To attempt to reduce to routine a procedure that comes only once in a whole year is to burden the class with the task of remembering procedures that are used too rarely for effective habit formation. The distribution of supplies, the taking of attendance, the changing of seats for group work, however, are all illustrations of procedures that may effectively be routinized.

The teacher must be wary not to thwart thinking by using routine unnecessarily. In one classroom, an English teacher routinized the procedure followed when a student read his original writing to the entire class. As the student read, the neighbor to his right listed the praiseworthy aspects of the student's contribution, while the neighbor on his left noted all of the respects in which the writing could be improved. The period was conducted with a smoothness that made effective criticism almost impossible. A student read his paper; he was followed almost immediately by the classmate who made the favorable comments; and then by the classmate who presented the suggestions for improvement. Within a single forty-minute period as many as eight or nine original contributions were treated in this way; but the whole procedure was so completely mechanized that much of the value was lost. It would have been more effective, though possibly less efficient in a purely mechanical sense, if all students had been encouraged to listen critically to an original composition and to make their own suggestions concerning the merits and the limitations of the work.

Whenever classroom instruction is routinized so that students know exactly when they will be called on and when it will be unnecessary for them to participate in class activities, the teacher is likely to be deceived by the spurious smoothness with which the class functions.

Selecting the Procedures to Be Routinized

How much routinization is necessary for efficient teaching and learning depends upon the age and maturity of the students, the physical facilities in the classroom, the nature of the activities to be conducted, and the teacher's ability to cope with classroom problems as they arise. Of course, senior high school students are treated differently from junior high school students. The collection and the distribution of materials usually require more attention in an art class than in a mathematics class.

What are some of the instances when learning will be facilitated by routinizing the details of classroom procedure? Clearly, the collection and distribution of materials should be handled in an orderly way. The departure of one class and the arrival of another one should not lead to a traffic jam at the doorway and a rush to get a seat. Students should know what they are to do when they enter a room or after they have completed an assignment earlier than the rest of the class. Controlling the lighting, temperature, and ventilation, keeping the room tidy, decorating the room appropriately with materials that are useful for instructional purposes as well as for aesthetic reasons are all important for reasons of health, orderliness, and economy of time, as well as for creating an atmosphere in which learning is encouraged.

When a class is divided into committees, each committee should have an assigned place to work so that the boys and girls do not have to start a mad rush in order to be the first ones to get to the preferred tables. The committee also needs to have a place to keep the materials they are gathering. When some of the books and pamphlets are to be used by more than one committee, some simple procedure has to be devised in order to improve efficiency and reduce the possibility of disorder.

Teaching Classroom Routine

When procedures are to be routinized, the habits have to be established by the class much as other habits are developed. It is ineffective to overwhelm the class at the beginning of the term with a long list of procedures that are to be followed in all of the various aspects of the class work. It is better to present each of these procedures separately and to make certain that the students understand the reason for the procedure as well as the exact nature of the steps to be followed. For example, if the size of the class, the immaturity of the students, or the inaccessibility of the clothing lockers necessitates the establishment of a specific routine for getting outer clothing out of the way, it is well to spend a few minutes at the beginning of the semester explaining the situation to the students and enlisting their assistance in establishing an appropriate routine.

The older and the more mature the students are, the greater should be the extent to which they assume the responsibility for the efficient conduct of classroom activities. Since it is their class, they should be able to take care of the minor problems that arise without running to the teacher for specific instructions on each point. Secondary school students should not have to ask for permission every time they think it necessary to take the unabridged dictionary to their committee table, nor should an art student pose a problem every time he needs additional water for his paints. The special complications that are introduced by the size of the class indicate the desirability of establishing sufficient routine to avoid conflict and inefficiency. Students should help plan such procedures and they should be given an increasing degree of freedom in attending to details.

Using Student Assistants

The teacher can use the chores of classroom management as a means of teaching adolescents that sharing experiences also implies the sharing of responsibilities. He can help the class to understand that working together calls for easing difficulties that would otherwise interfere with progress. Instead of appointing a few favored students to serve as his helpers, he encourages student participation in the planning of necessary routines and in carrying them out. The teacher looks to this approach as one way of helping students develop the ability to assume responsibility.

Even though all students should share in the responsibility for making the classroom an orderly and efficient place, it is helpful to have student assistants take care of specific responsibilities. Where the positions are at all important, the class should elect the student assistants or at least elect an executive committee which will meet with the teacher in allotting tasks to specific students. When assistants are used, each should have his designated task and should understand what is expected of him. It is usually helpful to rotate responsibilities so that more and more students are given individual assignments in facilitating the conduct of classroom work.

In general, new teachers tend to concentrate too many responsibilities on too few students and to be unaware of the ways in which the use of student assistants may help develop classroom *esprit de corps.* Student assistants are often chosen on the basis of their academic attainments, even though the responsibilities that are delegated to them require no great intellectual ability. On the other hand, teachers may assign such jobs to slow or retarded students in order to keep them busy while the rest of the class pursues more creative goals. To some extent, by enlisting the services of some of the less gifted members of the class, the teacher may be able to demonstrate to these students that he does recognize them as individuals. Thereby, he may lead these young people to feel that they do have a place in the group and thus stimulate them to greater participation in class and to better learning. On the whole, it is better to rotate responsibilities among all of the members of the class so that all may have the satisfaction of working for the group as a whole as well as for themselves.

THE CLASSROOM AS AN ATTRACTIVE WORKROOM

Because people are affected by their surroundings, it is important that the classroom create an atmosphere that is conducive to effective learning. It should look clean, comfortable, attractive, and lived-in, and give the impression it has always been so.

Creating Helpful and Comfortable Working Conditions

Educational psychologists are agreed that the ventilation of the classroom rarely becomes so poor that the rate of learning is seriously affected by the percentages of oxygen and carbon dioxide in the room, but it is nevertheless true that poor ventilation or poor lighting may make the class so uncomfortable as to affect the smooth progress of class work.

The major difficulty in maintaining proper ventilation and lighting is that the teacher so often remains in the same room over an extended period of time. If the early morning is a dismal one, the lights are put on and stay on even though later sunshine makes these lights unnecessary. On the other hand, if the room darkens gradually, the teacher may not realize that some parts of the room are so poorly lighted that effective work is difficult. Similarly, the teacher is not aware of the ventilation problems of the room in which he stays throughout the morning. Visitors are often shocked by the stuffiness of a room though the teacher and the students seem completely unaware of the condition. Conversely, the teacher who is wearing a heavy jacket may be comfortable in a room which has so many windows open that it seems frigid to students who have dresses or shirts with short sleeves.

The adjustment of ventilation, lighting, and heating is easily reduced to routine. The teacher can make certain to check these factors at the beginning of each period or at stated intervals during the day. Here, too, student assistance can be used to good advantage.

Secondary school students, moreover, are old enough to accept their share of the responsibility for maintaining comfortable conditions in the classroom. There is no reason why a committee should continue to work in a darkened corner when they can use a free table elsewhere in the room, nor is it necessary for a student to sit in a draft when he can move his chair to a more comfortable spot without asking that the windows be closed. Most of these adjustments can be made without attracting the attention of the class or asking for special permission. If the teacher-student relationship is satisfactory, no student will hesitate to speak to the teacher whenever he thinks that any major adjustment is necessary.

The Physical Setting

Modern school architecture has contributed to creating a desirable atmosphere for learning by making the building itself pleasant and comfortable. In many communities the school building is one of the most attractive in the neighborhood and the classroom itself has comforts and conveniences that the teacher of even twenty-five years ago never expected.

To some extent the attractiveness of the classroom is limited by factors over which the teacher has no control. Problems of school finance and rapidly increasing school populations in some communities make it necessary to continue the use of old, even dilapidated school buildings with dark, dismal, inadequately equipped classrooms which are badly in need of painting and of efficient custodial care. Environmental limitations of this kind constitute an additional handicap to effective learning, but imaginative teachers improvise as best they can to improve the situation and inspire adolescents to make even so forbidding a room into a livable place. A room in an older school which has been tastefully decorated with illustrations, student art work, and other signs of life may be preferable to a brand new room with barren, aseptic walls and shelves.

Making the classroom attractive. Except for the classic pictures of Lincoln and Washington and for stock items like the periodic table in chemistry rooms, high school classrooms often have a way of looking cheerless and untenanted. The use of pictures, models, book jackets, charts, plants, and exhibits of various kinds may serve a dual purpose. Decorations help the room express the personality of the teacher and the students using the room. They may also contribute to the learning objectives of the courses being taught there.

Certain common-sense rules are useful in displaying items. Eye-level is the most appropriate height—and this negates the desirability of using high mounting strips above the tops of chalkboards. Printed material on charts and pictures must be large enough to be seen at the distance from which students will view the item. If the chart or picture is worth posting, it is worth mentioning and discussing. In one classroom a visitor, impressed by the ingenious diagrams and pictures that were posted all about the room illustrating so many of the basic problems of modern industrial life, spoke with several of the students about the significance of one of the charts. Not a single student to whom he spoke knew the chart well enough to understand it, and several of the students revealed their complete surprise at seeing the chart in the room at all.

A room that is alive with students at work on significant activities will reflect these activities as individuals and as groups, and will place some of the interesting and stimulating materials they have gathered where all can see them. The classroom pictures, posters, and bulletin boards constitute no permanent exhibit, for they should reflect the students' interests and activities. The English class that is discussing modern poetry should reflect that interest in what is seen in the room. The clippings on the bulletin board should include items relating to modern poets and their writings. Thus, a picture of the modern assembly line in the factory may appear next to a copy of Margaret Widdemer's poem, "The Factory Girl," and a reproduction of a good portrait bust of Abraham Lincoln may be accompanied by a series of modern poems dealing with Lincoln.

Whenever the teacher finds that the classroom collection of pictures, charts, and other equipment is so good that it need not be changed at all during the term or even at the end of the term, he has either reached a peak of classroom effectiveness that few people attain or else he is learning to be satisfied with less than the ideal classroom.

Student participation. If the decoration of the classroom is to serve basic educational purposes, the teacher cannot assume sole responsibility for selecting the illustrative materials and for arranging their exhibition. By turning the problem over to the entire class or to their designated representatives, a teacher can help make the attractiveness of the room not only a goal in itself but also a means of stimulating student interest and fostering increased student participation in the learning process.

To encourage students to regard the classroom as their room, they should be encouraged to help decorate it by lending their personal material to be placed on exhibit, by helping to arrange the room, and by sharing in the responsibility of keeping it attractive. Adolescents, like adults, respond to their surroundings so that they are more likely to be careful of the appearance of an attractive room, especially of one that they have helped to make attractive, than they are of one that looks dreary.

Problems affected by departmentalization. Making the classroom attractive presents different problems to junior high school and senior high school teachers. In the junior high schools, it is more likely that a room will be used for so large a part of the day by a single class that the boys and girls think of it as their room. In the senior high school, however, the students ordinarily spend their day in so many different classes that they feel no great responsibility for the appearance of any room.

In the junior high school it is easier to have the students assume the responsibility for the appearance of their classrooms. Student committees can take care of the bulletin boards and of exhibits, and pride in their class is an effective incentive to keeping the room attractive.

In the senior high school, it is the teacher who assumes most of the responsibility for the appearance of the room although he should be quick to use student assistance when possible. The high school teacher, for example, is ready to have a student committee in each of his classes take care of the bulletin board and the exhibit case used by that class even though he may not be able to let any one committee take care of all the bulletin boards and exhibit cases. Even though the class may be only one of the many these boys and girls attend each day, they can still bring material they want to see posted on the bulletin board or placed on exhibit. Staggering the use of display space may also answer the purpose. Classes using the room in successive periods may use space for special displays in successive weeks.

Facilitating Classroom Activities by Seating the Students Appropriately

It is obvious that the way in which students are seated in the classroom should depend on the kind of activity in which they are to engage. Since many different kinds of activity go on in school, the seating arrangement must be sufficiently flexible to allow for the necessary rearrangement of students. This is why so much objection has been raised to immovable classroom furniture and why movable desks and chairs have become increasingly popular.

How should movable furniture be arranged? For most discussion lessons it is desirable to have students facing each other. Although a good teacher can conduct a stimulating discussion even when chairs are arranged in rows, the conventional seating plan hardly creates an atmosphere conducive to the give-and-take of discussion.

Arranging the students in a circle, with the teacher occupying one of the seats in the circle, appears at first to be the ideal arrangement for a discussion lesson. In practice, however, this seating plan is far from perfect. A large part of the class will have to sit facing the windows, and it is uncomfortable for anyone to have to look into the light for any great length of time. If the class is large, the seats are likely to be pushed against

the wall in order to make a sufficiently large circle or rectangle to accommodate all students. As a result, materials that may be in closets or on
tables and in bookshelves along the wall may be inaccessible. Since students will be seated along the front and side walls of the room, it is difficult to get to the chalkboard and for many students to see what is written
there. The teacher is tempted, therefore, to have everyone seated and to
rely on talk alone, when a simple chalkboard diagram may help to clarify
the question or when the chalkboard can be used to summarize the major
points developed during the discussion.

For these practical reasons it is usually better to seat students in a
semicircle, a semiellipse, a quarter of a circle, or in some other variation of the circle. When the class is large, students may be seated in two
rows of seats which run around the perimeter of the semicircle, quadrant,
or other pattern used. Such an arrangement as this brings the students,
or almost all of them, face to face and yet frees the teacher and students
to use the chalkboard and other visual aids to learning.

Adapting arrangement to purposes. For other types of activities, the
seating arrangements can be made correspondingly appropriate. When a
class is working on the development of a complex skill where the various
members have different kinds of difficulties, it may be desirable to group
students having a common difficulty so that the teacher may save time
by working with them as a group. Classes that are working on committee projects and reports can be seated in groups around tables, with each
group separated as much from the other groups as space allows. Students who are at work on individual assignments which require freedom
from distracting neighbors or ready access to reference material and supplies may be seated in rows, since that arrangement provides both pri-
vacy and freedom to move about the room without disturbing others.

Seating students in rooms with fixed furniture. Many secondary
school teachers, however, do not get a chance to worry about the arrangement of classroom furniture, for they teach in schools that have
stationary desks. Stationary furniture need not lead to stationary teaching
since it is far better to have the furniture immovable than to have an
unchangeable teacher. It is possible, for example, to remove the seats
at the rear of the room and to substitute a few tables and chairs for committee work. An undesirable seating plan may make good teaching difficult, but not impossible.

Unless the teacher has some special purpose in mind, it is just as
well to let students select their own seats, although this plan sometimes
leads to disciplinary difficulties, particularly in the younger junior high
school classes, when friends who sit near each other spend the day in
idle conversation. Teachers may as well admit that adolescents will seek
to communicate with their friends no matter where they sit. Putting them

far apart merely encourages the passing of notes and the exchange of stage whispers across the room. By allowing them to sit near each other, the teacher enables them to satisfy their natural desire to communicate with each other occasionally, with much less disturbance to the group as a whole. As one understanding and experienced high school teacher said, "Why shouldn't a fellow want to sit next to his best girl?" Rather than try to maintain good classroom discipline solely by rearranging the seating, the teacher should improve the quality and the challenge of classroom activities and develop in maturing adolescents a realization of their responsibility to the rest of the class.

Maintaining flexibility with any type of seats. The class that is not equipped with movable furniture can still enjoy some of the advantages that come from adjusting the seating plan to the classroom activity in progress. Though the seats are fixed, the students may move to other seats when necessary. In a junior high school English class, for example, the grouping during silent reading periods may be based on the special type of activities that the various sections of the class need. These same students may then be rearranged differently for the discussion of a poem written by a member of the class. The seating plan should be regarded as a flexible arrangement to be changed whenever necessary, but it should not be modified so often that students spend more time walking about the room than they do working.

Any arrangement of students in the classroom should be a natural, unforced result of the nature of the specific activity in which these boys and girls are engaged. When the members of the class form a semicircle for a discussion, the teacher should create the impression that they are gathering around to hear what Joe has learned from his correspondence with the police commissioner. It is unnecessary for the teacher to treat the rearrangement of seats for a discussion as though he were a top sergeant ordering "Execute Seating Plan B—March! Hup, two, three, four. Hup, two . . . ."

ADMINISTRATIVE RESPONSIBILITIES OF THE CLASSROOM TEACHER

While the primary responsibility of the teacher is that of guiding the learning activities of children, the classroom teacher is also an important member of the school's guidance and administrative staffs. These auxiliary functions are essential parts of the teacher's job since it is the teacher who is in daily contact with students. Duties of an administrative nature include such items as attendance, record keeping, reporting, planning of student programs, and the like.*

* See pp. 426-428 for a further discussion of the teacher's role in the guidance program.

Attendance

It would indeed be pleasant if schools could operate on the assumption that school attendance is the student's responsibility; let those who are willing to learn come, let the unwilling ones go fishing. Unfortunately, it is not possible to teach youngsters who are absent from school or those who may desire to "cut" a particular period. In addition, the school accepts legal responsibility for the child during school hours when it enrolls him. For both educational and legal reasons, therefore, it is important that the school encourage conscientious and prompt attendance and keep accurate attendance records.

Regular and punctual attendance is one of those minor virtues that loom large in the teacher's daily life. Tardiness is often distracting because a late arrival may interrupt an activity. When lack of punctuality is general, the effect on classroom morale may be so great as to interfere seriously with the likelihood that the class will achieve its goals. Despite the teacher's desire to help his students develop good work habits, he must be careful not to place so great a premium on punctuality and regularity of attendance that social pressures compel a student to come to school even though he has a bad cold and would be better off at home.

Poor attendance can be a danger sign which warns the teacher that all is not proceeding as he hopes. Students rarely stay away from the school in which the work seems either significant or interesting to them. The teacher who begins each session promptly and makes each meeting worthwhile to his students is likely to find the problem of the absentee and the straggler a small one.

Most schools have a fixed routine for taking care of absence and truancy. If the new teacher follows this procedure, he may be able to discourage the occasional lapses of even a conscientious student. These procedures, however, cannot deal adequately with the problem of truancy, for a more thoroughgoing attack on the problem necessitates the kind of individual study that is described elsewhere in our treatment of other types of disciplinary problems.* The one thing the teacher can do is to make the classroom activities so vital to students and the classroom machinery so smooth-functioning that prompt and regular attendance is taken almost for granted by both teacher and class.

Reporting and recording attendance. In most schools basic attendance reporting and recording are done by a teacher who is responsible for a home room (also called official class, roll room). This group may or may not be the same as a class assigned to the teacher for a particular subject. In some cases the home room meets for ten or fifteen minutes daily with the home room teacher, mainly for purposes of taking attend-

* The teacher's approach to such serious disciplinary problems as truancy is discussed on pp. 417-422.

ance and reading announcements. This teacher keeps the official roll for the class. He reports absentees to the office at the close of this period, and the list of absentees for the entire school is duplicated. This list serves as the check against which classroom absences are noted in order to identify students who may possibly have "cut."

It is important that the official attendance record be accurate. These records may be subpoenaed by court order to verify or refute the claim that a student was so seriously injured in an accident that he was bed-ridden at a time when the person being sued alleges that the child was well and in school. In the event of a school disaster, the class roll book is helpful in guiding the search for possible missing persons. Then, too, financial assistance from the state is generally based on average daily attendance and the roll book is the source of attendance statistics.

Of course, the teacher should recognize that many reasons may account for absence from his class—accident or a sudden illness, an errand to perform for some other teacher, a specially scheduled examination—and should suspend judgment until a student has given his explanation—documented, of course.

When the student is absent from school, prompt contact with the home is made in accordance with established procedure. Generally a form letter or printed post card is available to the home room teacher for this purpose. The home room teacher, the class teacher, and the attendance officer (or in a small school, the principal) make up an attendance team which delivers the student from temptation, assures accurate reporting, and establishes regularity and promptness which are essential for effective teaching and learning.

In some schools the home room is not conducted as a separate period, but home room responsibilities fall to teachers who have a group of students at a given time. For example, the home room may be an extension of the second period. In this case, the teacher has home room responsibilities for those students who are in his second period class, and the second period is lengthened ten or fifteen minutes to provide for routines that are essential. Schools which have core programs often assign these responsibilities to the core teacher since he has his core classes for two or three periods. A fourth variation is found in those high schools which function in the manner of a college, without home room organization. In these cases teachers simply report absences from class and the clerical staff in the attendance office use these reports to compile official attendance records.

Planning Student Programs

A second administrative function of the home room teacher is assisting students and the program committee or principal in planning student programs each semester. During the year a number of extended home room periods are provided for group guidance and administrative routines. One or more of these periods is devoted to student selection of courses for the following semester and the filling out of myriad cards and blanks that schools find necessary.

Maintaining Records and Reporting Grades

Maintaining various student records is another service which teachers normally perform. Cumulative record folders are kept in most schools. The home room teacher generally has major responsibility for these folders, for the reporting of grades at the end of the semester (and sometimes the interim report as well), and the filing of material which will be helpful in understanding the student and guiding him. In some cases this is done completely by the guidance office and clerical staff.

Teachers share in the reporting and recording of grades. In some schools subject teachers enter grades directly on permanent record forms; in others they submit lists of grades to the home room teacher, who enters them on the permanent records for students in his home room. Entries on report cards are generally copied by the home room teacher from the permanent record or from the class lists prepared by the subject teacher. In some schools report cards are marked directly by the subject teacher during class periods on the last day of the marking period. Almost every teacher, of course, serves both as a home room teacher and subject teacher. Promptness and accuracy in reporting grades eases the burdens of the other teachers in the school.

Getting Supplies

For economy of school time, every school has some kind of requisition procedure, generally limiting the number of periods during which supplies may be obtained. The new teacher should learn the way in which supplies are ordered in the school, but he must also develop forethought as to the materials he will need.

Communicating with Parents

One of the important services of the teacher is the part he plays in the communication network between the school and parents. Secondary school students are often in the process of declaring independence from their parents. Notices intended for home consumption may never even leave the school grounds unless teachers co-operate by insisting that students return responses requested from their parents. Each year it seems that innumerable notices go from school to the home, and the class or home room teacher provides one channel.

Money Matters

In addition, the teacher often finds himself serving as a financial agent. Tickets are sold for school functions, deposits are required for instructional items of various kind, locker fees may be charged, periodicals are subscribed to, books and pamphlets are sold, student organization fees must be collected. Over and above these school-connected financial transactions are the demands made by civic-minded fund raisers for worthwhile purposes as a means of awakening the community's philanthropic sentiments.

Miscellaneous Duties

Finally, there are various chores that remain to be shared by teachers in order to keep the school operating. Some seem professional, some clerical, but they all have to be done: supervising the study hall, maintaining decorum in the assembly, monitoring the lunch room and corridors, organizing book rooms and supply closets for efficient distribution, duplicating materials for use by students or teachers in the school as a whole or within a department, administering the arrangements for using audio-visual materials of instruction, planning and executing routines for school bus utilization, and there are others, too, despite the length of this list.

Lightening the Teacher's Clerical Duties

Although a case can be made for each of the many clerical duties detailed in the administrative functions just described, it is apparent that these duties can easily become onerous and an obstacle to effective teaching when they require too much of the teacher's time and energy.

Some of the burden of clerical work can be reduced by better classroom administration. Many of the reports can be reduced to routine and may even be delegated to student assistants. Once a teacher knows which reports will be expected, he can often arrange to collect the data as he goes along instead of waiting for the time when the report is due. In schools where the teacher must submit a daily record of absentees, it is easy to have a student assume the burden of preparing these reports, provided that the student's functions are carefully supervised so that no student is exposed to the temptation to omit significant material from the report. This safeguard, however, takes less of the teacher's time than does the actual job of transcribing the names on all the copies that are needed for the various school offices and does not keep any one student away from his work too long.

Clerical work is less unpleasant if the teacher understands the purposes to be served by the work that he does. Some of the drudgery of clerical work can be eliminated if teachers take the trouble to inform themselves of the use to which these reports are put. Moreover, new teachers can often save considerable time by inquiring about the short-cuts and time-saving procedures evolved by the more experienced teachers at the school.

Our conception of the function of school records has undergone a marked change in recent years. Every school record is expected to contribute toward the education of the students and is no longer a mere item of bookkeeping to be kept in permanent files. While the newer point of view does not reduce the amount of time that teachers spend in record keeping, it does reduce markedly the amount of unnecessary time that is wasted by both teachers and supervisors.

One of the complaints heard increasingly from secondary school teachers is that the burden of clerical work has increased tremendously in recent years. To be sure, some clerical work is tied up so closely with classroom teaching that it will always have to be done by teachers. Much of it, however, can be done more efficiently by clerks in the central office or by teacher-aids. School clerical staffs are ordinarily so badly under-manned, however, that clerical help cannot be spared to assist teachers. Because of this niggardly policy, teachers who are trained to work with students spend much of their time working with papers instead. Since teachers receive higher salaries than do school clerks, schools are using public funds inefficiently every time a teacher does clerical work that can be done as well or better by a school clerk. Only those who teach or are very close to teachers know how hard they work. Many are so badly overworked that they do not have time to continue their own studies or to give students the individual guidance they need. Reducing the teacher's clerical duties is an easily available means of removing a serious obstacle to effective teaching.

IMPROVING EDUCATIONAL EFFICIENCY

There is so much that secondary school students must learn and so many areas in which we must aim at mastery rather than be content with superficial acquaintance that we cannot afford waste and inefficiency. A smoothly run classroom is an important asset in improving the effectiveness of teaching and learning.

Emphasis on educational efficiency is unfortunate if it suggests the analogy of the deadening routine of the assembly line in a large factory, for in schools we are concerned as much with the process as with the product, as much with the student's personal adjustments as with his educational progress. None of these major aims can be attained in a school that worships efficiency or that is concerned only with whether teachers and students are all working at full speed throughout the day. Educational efficiency must not be achieved at the price of the tension that so often accompanies a speed-up program. Both teachers and students need periods of rest and recreation during the day, and the class sessions themselves can be productive without being tense.

Inefficiency and waste, however, have no educational value. The mere fact that a student is a slow reader does not make him a more understanding reader. The discussion that is interrupted several times by announcements over the public address system is not likely to be superior to a discussion that is allowed to proceed without distraction.

Classroom Sources of Waste

Much time is wasted through sheer lack of planning. Poorly-planned classroom discussions which ramble on without purpose and without direction are usually futile. There are classes which never start punctually, with much time consumed merely in getting under way. If the teacher has his material planned in advance, it is easy for him to get into the habit of starting with the bell so that students learn to be ready at the very beginning of the session. Lest the more capable students get into the habit of working lackadaisically by having the pace set by the slower members of the group, the teacher should indicate what students should turn to next after they have completed the task on which they are working.

When students are working on their own or in committees, they should have a clear idea of what they should do and how they should do it—and then get started at once doing it. Unless committee assignments are clear and the students have become accustomed to working efficiently, a tremendous amount of time can be wasted as committees fumble about for something to do and as students use committee time for visiting and chatting. Individual and committee work must be guided by the teacher and the needed materials of instruction must be available if we are to avoid the inefficiency and the demoralization caused by floundering.

The various phases of the classroom session should be so carefully planned that there is no delay between one type of activity and the next. For example, the physics teacher who plans a demonstration must select in advance the student laboratory exercises he wishes to use as follow-up activity. Materials needed and instructions for the exercise must be at hand for distribution.

The efficient teacher also selects the best materials and procedures for a given learning situation. He makes use of duplicating machines to avoid time-consuming dictation of endless notes or copying by students of materials which he has laboriously written on the chalkboard. In addition to saving time for more effective learning devices, the teacher prevents the frequent errors which students make in copying materials in so routine a manner.

Closely related to the unnecessary copying of notes is the unnecessary writing that uses up so much of the time of practice periods. There is little justification for asking students to recopy sentences from their English textbooks when all that the teacher wants is the correction of the spelling of a single word. In most other practice periods, the amount of time given to practice can be increased while the length of the period is reduced if the teacher eliminates unnecessary writing.

Still another source of wasted time is the administration of unnecessary tests. As we saw when we discussed evaluation procedures, classroom examinations have many purposes and should be used only when one or more of the purposes will be attained through the administration of the test. The teacher often finds that his evaluation of his students' work in class yields as much information as he can get by administering special tests. Moreover, by designing his tests more carefully, he may be able to discover as much through a short test as he would through a series of long tests.

In some respects simultaneous instruction of the whole class is bound to be less efficient than individualized instruction, but wise planning can reduce some of the waste of time. In general, teachers do not make adequate provision for individual differences in ability and knowledge. With almost any topic taught in school, some students know more at the beginning of the year than other students will know after the unit has been completed. When pretests are used wisely, the teacher has an inventory of his students' understanding and errors and can use this information as a basis for adjusting instruction to meet individual needs. Students who have mastered a topic or skill may thus be freed to go on to other problems on which they should be working. The individualization of drill periods saves considerable time by keeping students from wasting time on material they know thoroughly.

Every procedure we discussed earlier in this book that makes teaching more effective also makes education more efficient. Poor teaching from which students learn little of importance is unjustifiably wasteful. Similarly, the teacher who does not make full use of the many audio-visual aids to learning may work hard at preparation and at teaching without getting results commensurate with his efforts.

Administrative Sources of Waste

Other sources of waste are beyond the teacher's control. To limit our concern with the elimination of wasteful practices to an examination of classroom procedures is to ignore other and more serious sources of inefficiency. Some can be eliminated quickly by intelligent school administrators; others will persist until our changing educational philosophy is reflected in changed educational procedures.

One of the petty nuisances of teaching arises from the frequency with which the teacher and students are interrupted by announcements on the public address system or messengers from the office who bring requests that can just as well wait till the end of the day. To be sure, there are emergencies when a principal must reach a student immediately or when he must get in touch with some or all teachers without delay. Genuine emergencies, however, occur rarely. Because every announcement and every messenger interrupt a train of thought, these interruptions must be reduced to a minimum. Teachers and principals must have so much respect for class work that they will not disturb a class session. Notices should be typed and mimeographed for distribution to teachers at the end of the day or before school begins, and students should be called to the office only when they are not in class.

Few people realize how much time during the school year is spent on organization and administration rather than on teaching. In most American schools, the last two weeks of the semester are devoted almost entirely to testing and to the clerical work attendant upon the end of the semester's work. Even when classes are held during the last two weeks of the term, little is accomplished since both teachers and students treat class sessions after final examinations as being unimportant. When uniform examinations are conducted, there is an additional loss of time if teachers spend much time coaching students on details that are important only for obtaining higher grades on these tests.

Teachers should be free to teach. Every time we use a teacher as a clerk, as a lunch room supervisor, as a collector of funds for various purposes, or for the countless nonteaching chores or building assignments teachers are being called upon in increasing measure to assume, we are making inefficient use of the professional abilities teachers have so carefully developed. Even though teachers can get to know their students better by seeing them in a nonclassroom setting, as in a fund drive office, the lunch room, the study hall, or the corridors, these nonteaching assignments consume too much of the teacher's time and energy that should be devoted to teaching and to preparation for teaching.

Wasteful Curricular Practices

There are curricular sources of waste that cannot be removed easily by making minor adjustments in class or school administration. Though we can save days by modifying class administration and we can save weeks by improving school administration, we can save months or years by modernizing the curriculum. How much time is wasted by having boys and girls study topics that mean nothing to them at the time and that they will never use? The increasing attention to curricular reorganization, by making full use of the varied backgrounds of the members of the school faculty to meet the needs of boys and girls and by stimulating adolescents to participate actively in their own education, may help the secondary school to become far more effective than some of our schools now are.

Students become accustomed to working at a level far below their ability if they are given assignments they can master even when they exert less than maximum effort. There are students who can complete the normal elementary and secondary school program in less than the traditional twelve years or who can pursue advanced studies for college credit. The year or two they save in their earlier schooling can be used to hasten the collegiate or professional education they should have. Under present conditions, we tend to delay the young man's and the young woman's entrance into adult life far beyond the optimum point.

We can increase the effectiveness of our schools by attracting into teaching young people of the caliber our students deserve. Communities that pay inadequate salaries get inadequate teachers; and inadequate teachers, however conscientious they may be, can hardly be expected to raise students above their own level of mediocrity.

It is customary to measure efficiency in terms of dollars or man-hours saved. It is possible to startle the lay person by estimating the staggering sum of money or the number of miles of express highways that could be built with the man-hours wasted by inefficient teaching or by the inefficient use of the teacher's time.

But dollars and man-hours are inappropriate and inadequate units for measuring educational efficiency. How shall we measure the improvement in the emotional climate of the school and in student morale when the curriculum is so appropriate for the students that teachers do not have to fight student resistance to learning? How shall we measure the improvement in the teacher himself when efficient class management makes it so much easier for him to live with adolescents that he can be the calm person adolescents need? How shall we evaluate the gains when a better use of our school year yields additional time that can be used to develop the abilities and the knowledge our students must have? How can we measure the social benefit that will follow if we can enrich the background of all young people by giving them the equivalent of a junior college education without prolonging their period of schooling?

It is such tangible and intangible outcomes that should lead us to make our schools as effective, and that means as efficient, as ingenuity and study can make them.

QUESTIONS FOR STUDY AND DISCUSSION

1. The students in your home room class spend only one period a day in their home room. Under these circumstances what can you do to increase their concern with the attractiveness of that room?

2. Because of the crowded conditions in a school, it is necessary to use each room every period, even though it often happens that a room that is equipped for one type of class is being used by another. Assuming that you are a teacher of art, what can you do to overcome the handicap of having to use an ordinary classroom for one of your art classes?

3. On the second day of the term, the students of a high school home room class decided by vote who were to be the chairmen of various class committees. Elizabeth M., one of the girls who happened to be absent from school on the day the vote was taken, was elected Chairman of the House-keeping Committee, which attends to the details of keeping the room neat and attractive.

When Elizabeth returned to school the next day and was informed by her classmates of her election to this committee chairmanship, she immediately went up to the teacher and indignantly announced that she would not accept this assignment. Elizabeth was so wrought up over her election that the teacher entered into a prolonged conversation with her, partly to calm the girl down and partly to discover the cause for so emotional a reaction to a routine assignment of tasks.

As the story came out during the conversation, Elizabeth was upset because she felt the other students elected her to be class housekeeper because they did not consider her to be their social equal. Her father is the superintendent of an apartment house in which some of these girls live and her mother has served as laundress for some of these girls' families. In Elizabeth's words, "I'm not going to be anybody's slave. I'm not going to pick up the papers they're too proud to pick up themselves."

How should the teacher handle this situation?

4. A teacher in a woodworking shop had a display case in the corridor near the main entrance to the school in which he exhibited samples of the work done by the students in his classes. One day, while the principal was visiting the class, the teacher announced that he was ready to change the exhibit then on display and asked each student to choose his best piece of work for inclusion in the exhibit.

During a conference with the teacher later in the day, the principal indicated his disapproval of the teacher's plan to exhibit the work of all students, including those who were doing inferior work. The principal suggested that the teacher arrange an exhibit shelf in his classroom on which all students would see their work on exhibit but that the more prominent corridor display case should exhibit only work of such quality as would impress visitors.

Do you favor the teacher's or the principal's point of view? Why?

5. A junior high school teacher finds that his students apparently have

been accustomed to such close supervision that they accomplish little when they are on their own. Thus, if he is working with one group of students, the other students work only half-heartedly at their tasks, even when their assignments are clear and specific.

How can the teacher correct this situation?

6. Because the school library facilities are so limited, the students have developed the habit of rushing to the library as soon as work starts on a major unit of work and withdrawing all of the books and pamphlets the members of a committee think they may need. As a result, the library shelves are so depleted that other students are denied access to books that are being kept in storage by various committees. When the teacher suggested that no books be withdrawn from the library except for immediate use, the students protested that a great deal of time is wasted if they have to keep borrowing and returning books to the library and if they have to keep changing their plans because the specific materials they need are not available at that time.

What procedures can the teachers and students develop to deal with the library situation?

7. As preparation for a discussion of the effect that population movements are having on the school neighborhood, the members of a high school class have prepared a number of charts for class use. Because there were so many charts, the students came to school early that morning and mounted them before going to their first-period class. By the time these students returned to this room in the early afternoon, several other classes had used the room. The committee which had worked so hard preparing the charts and mounting them were dismayed to see that some of the charts were torn either accidentally as students brushed by them in entering or leaving the classroom, or possibly out of mischief.

What can the teacher do to prevent similar destruction in the future when he is not in this classroom during the morning and the room is shared with many teachers and a great many students?

BIBLIOGRAPHY

1. ALCORN, Marvin D., HOUSEMAN, Richard A., and SCHUNERT, Jim R., *Better Teaching in Secondary Schools* (New York, Holt, Rinehart and Winston, Inc., 1954), Ch. 6.
2. ALEXANDER, William M., and HALVERSON, Paul M., *Effective Teaching in Secondary Schools* (New York, Holt, Rinehart and Winston, Inc., 1956), Chs. 3, 5.
3. BURTON, William H., *The Guidance of Learning Activities*, 2nd ed. (New York, Appleton-Century-Crofts, Inc., 1952), Ch. 22.
4. GRAMBS, Jean D., IVERSON, William J., and PATTERSON, Franklin K., *Modern Methods in Secondary Education*, rev. ed. (New York, Holt, Rinehart and Winston, Inc., 1958), Ch. 12.
5. HANSEN, Kenneth H., *High School Teaching* (Englewood Cliffs, N.J., Prentice-Hall, Inc., 1957), Chs. 4, 11.
6. MILLS, Hubert H., and DOUGLASS, Harl R., *Teaching in High School*, 2nd ed. (New York, The Ronald Press Company, 1957), Ch. 26.
7. NOAR, Gertrude, *The Junior High School—Today and Tomorrow* (Englewood Cliffs, N.J., Prentice-Hall, Inc., 1953), Ch. 13.
8. RISK, Thomas M., *Principles and Practices of Teaching in Secondary Schools*, 3rd ed. (New York, American Book Company, 1958), Ch. 20.

9. Schorling, Raleigh, and Batchelder, Howard T., *Student Teaching in Secondary Schools,* 3rd ed. (New York, McGraw-Hill Book Co., Inc., 1956), Ch. 5.
10. Wiggins, Sam P., *Successful High School Teaching* (Boston, Houghton Mifflin Company, 1958), Ch. 7.

CHAPTER **14**

Contributing to the Adolescent's
Personal and Social Adjustment

»»»»»»»»»»»

THERE ARE FEW TIMES when people are more naïve with respect to secondary education than when they speak of classroom discipline. People are always looking for tricks of the trade that will make anyone, however ineffective he may be as a person or unskilled as a teacher, almost miraculously effective as a leader of adolescents once the students are enrolled in a class of which he is the teacher.

Effective discipline cannot be achieved by tricks. Basically, it is a reflection of the teacher's understanding of people and of his ability to work with them. There are conditions and procedures which are almost certain to lead to poor discipline, but there are no conditions and no procedures which are equally certain to lead to good discipline. When a classroom is chaotic, disciplinary problems are likely to multiply and flourish. On the other hand, improving the teacher's efficiency in managing a classroom will not eliminate the threat of poor discipline if the curriculum is inappropriate or if there are some seriously disturbed adolescents in his class.

Discipline has to be viewed in two aspects: partly as the maintenance of classroom order, morale, and productivity; partly as the development of *self*-direction by the student. The latter aspect is truly the ultimate aim of all education; the former represents environmental conditions in which self-discipline can develop and learning take place.

Discipline, whether viewed as classroom management or as increasing self-direction, depends upon the adolescent's personal development and adjustment and on his adaptation to the new social situations in which he finds himself on the threshold of adulthood. For this reason, classroom discipline cannot be considered intelligently without studying the personal and social needs of the individual and the nature of group relationships in the classroom—the problems of the individual and the problems of the group.

UNDERSTANDING ADOLESCENTS

Among the important mainsprings motivating behavior, good or ill, are the emotional needs that are common to all of us. A basic need is the construction of a healthy self-concept [3], the painting of a self-portrait which gives satisfaction to the person as an individual and as a human being who interacts with other people. The person who looks upon himself as an individual of some worth and substance is likely to do those things which enhance the handsome self-portrait he is painting. On the other hand, the person who feels that he is inadequate in most situations, that other people don't like him, that he is guilty of sundry moral and social lapses, is likely to act in conformity with the grotesque creation that he carries around in his mind.

Satisfaction of basic emotional needs improves the self-concept; failure to fulfill such needs makes the picture grayer. The young person looks for affection from his family and for acceptance, at least, by his teachers. He wants to feel that he "belongs" in the informal society of his peers. He needs to believe that he is *achieving*, that he is doing worthwhile things and doing them well—learning, earning, getting along well with others, performing in sports and recreational activities.

It would be unusual if the adolescent's personal problems were not reflected in his behavior at school. Important and exciting as is a first love affair, it is not the only strong emotional experience an adolescent has. The girl who sees herself being excluded from parties to which everybody else seems to be going, the boy who worries about the senselessness of studying Ricardo's theory of rent when his own family has many economic problems that are much more pressing; the adolescent who thinks he is an adult and is treated like a child—how can these young people be interested in a discussion that deals with topics that are as remote from their pressing problems as the question of which girl a young man should invite to the Junior Prom is remote from the problems of their work-a-day and practical parents?

Not All "Storm and Strife"

Such considerations as these are partly responsible for the common belief that adolescence is a state of development marked by acute emotional stress. It is amusing to hear adolescense discussed by college classes as though it were a pathological condition, a sort of children's disease that comes later than measles and whooping cough. Of course adolescence is a period of emotional conflicts and problems, for all periods of life have their emotional conflicts and problems.

In our concern with helping the adolescent to face his problems realistically and to solve them intelligently, we must be careful not to exaggerate their seriousness. Nor should we forget that most of the problems are the normal ones of normal people. To be sure, the adolescent can be aided a great deal by a wise and sympathetic teacher who can help him to see his problems from a better vantage point and in whose presence he can think of solutions that would not otherwise come to mind. He can be helped immeasurably by a teacher who sees him as an individual and not merely as a sophomore English student who has failed in the mid-term examination. But he will be helped little by the teacher who comes to the class as to a mental clinic and who sees his students as being but the first pages of long case histories.

Every teacher wants to help every one of his students, and the teacher is understandably depressed when he sees the magnitude of the emotional burdens shouldered by some of his students. Yet there are limits to the amount of help which a teacher can give to the adolescent in dealing with personal problems. In most instances, the teacher has little control over the factors that are complicating the child's life. He may help most by making the school phase of the adolescent's life as satisfying as possible. There is no reason for the teacher to feel a sense of guilt or inadequacy because he cannot take the place of the clinician whose services are not always available, unfortunately, to all who need them.

SOURCES OF THE ADOLESCENT'S PROBLEMS

Family Sources

The differences between the child's and his parents' sense of values may be quite marked at adolescence. These differences are only variations of the basic one, namely, the parental difficulty in appreciating the growing sense of independence and self-reliance that is, and should be, an important characteristic of growing into adulthood and maturity. Where parents are wise, this process of maturing, of accepting more and more responsibility, is initiated in early childhood and is increased gradually and steadily. Such parents seek to develop a degree of mutual respect and confidence which makes it possible for the adolescent to discuss his problems at home, knowing that he will be understood and not ridiculed.

Changes in the American family have had some profound effects upon all aspects of the adolescent's life, including his life at school. Thus, the increasing extent to which mothers go to work outside the home has meant that adolescents have had to do without family supervision of recreational activities formerly taken for granted when mothers were home as their children returned from school. The freedom with which adolescents have access to the family car and the ease with which they can thereby get away from neighborhood supervision of recreational activities are also significant. American families have tolerated changes in dating practices and allow their boys and girls much more freedom than their parents ever had. With a curious lack of logic, families which have relaxed their control over their young people are ready to blame the school for all of the excesses that are committed by boys and girls who are incapable of dealing with their new freedom.

The ambition which families have for their children is the mainspring for parental sacrifices which enable boys and girls to go on for further education in order to reach a level of achievement never attained by the parents. There may well be a serious conflict, however, between the parents' hopes for their children and the children's abilities and ambitions. In such instances, parental ambitions may present hazards to adjustment rather than assets. One high school student, for example, after listening to an inspiring talk on honesty and the desirability of being able to live with one's self remarked, "It's easier to cheat and live with myself than to get a low mark and live with my father."

Coming from a family of distinguished and successful people may be a handicap to the youngster who does not share his parents' interests and talents. Such a child may sometimes resent the derogatory comparison he imagines when he is introduced as Mrs. Brown's son or Janice Brown's younger brother. The son of a prosperous family may feel just as hostile toward the adult world as does the son of a lesser known family, and may turn delinquent for the same psychological reasons. That he is better dressed, his parents better known, and the police more tolerant may help explain why his delinquency is sometimes dismissed as youthful exuberance to be ignored rather than as criminal tendencies that need institutional treatment.

By contrast, the adolescent who comes from a culturally handicapped family sometimes finds little encouragement in his home or community for the life of a young scholar. Living in a crowded room in a congested home in a blighted area, he has none of the facilities or the inducements for studying that many teachers take for granted. He may run into difficulty at school because of the attitude he may have developed of suspecting everyone in a position of authority as a potential threat and because of his readiness to fight any boy or girl who gets in his way.

Social Sources

Some of the roots of adolescent behavior in school are to be found in the world in which the adolescent lives. A society which worships material possessions has little reason to wonder why boys and girls do not put love of learning high in their scale of values and sometimes seem to have little interest in academic achievements. After all, when a teen-ager hears his parents discussing how much certain people are worth, he knows they are talking about *worth* in terms of wealth and not knowledge or contribution to the progress of mankind. Isn't it only natural that such an adolescent should approach his teacher and his school work with a different attitude from that of another boy who from childhood has heard his family sing the folk song of his people which paints so attractive a picture of the world that is opened to the child who learns to read?

Like everybody else, adolescents are affected by social and economic factors. Adolescents have little motivation for studying when they see their schooling as ending in a blind alley for them because they know the jobs they will be able to get when they leave school will have nothing to do with what they are studying in school. Wars, depression, inflation, and unemployment are bound to affect adolescents both directly and by the effect on their families. Students who bring to school the bigotry they have learned outside its walls may be unwilling to work with some of their classmates. Adolescents can be seriously disturbed when they see their way to social and vocational adjustment blocked by their family's economic or social status. The variety of these instances of social sources of adolescent problems—and there are many more that can be cited—points to the importance of the teacher's understanding not only his students but also their families and their communities if he is to be successful in modifying the attitudes and the behavior of the boys and girls in his classes.

Personal Sources

Although the home is a factor in many adolescent problems, there are other difficulties in adjustment in which the home is not the sole, or even the major, factor. The adolescent's physical condition, for example, sometimes helps to explain his behavior. Sensory deficiencies like poor hearing or vision are obvious handicaps at school. The youth whose height or weight varies markedly from the class average may be sensitive on that score. Blemishes, such as those caused by acne, scars, and any type of physical impairment either real or fancied, may make him so sensitive that his adjustment difficulties are increased. The adolescent boy with his changing voice and the adolescent girl with her changing bodily proportions may be self-conscious and unwilling to participate in any activity which brings them into the limelight.

Both the person whose mentality is markedly above the mean of the class and the one whose native equipment is seriously below the class average may be expected to find it uncomfortable to adjust to a level of instruction that is geared to the average student's ability. The classroom activities may be similarly inappropriate for the student whose interests differ markedly from those of his classmates.

The adolescent who wants more attention than he gets—and his desire for attention may itself be the result of many factors—may become the show-off who disrupts group activities. On the other hand, the adolescent's desire to be identified with "the crowd" and to act and think as *they* do, may present a classroom problem when the school's views and standards do not coincide with the "crowd's."

These many factors illustrate, but do not exhaust, the varied emotional forces that may underlie the disciplinary situation the teacher wishes so hard to correct. Small wonder it is that these problems do not disappear even after the teacher has given two inspirational talks, one reprimand, and three detention slips.

School Sources

In his zeal for discovering the causes of adolescent problems, the teacher should not ignore the factors to be found within his own room. Even so prosaic a detail as poor ventilation or poor lighting may be the source of classroom difficulties. Classroom organization may be so poor that confusion is great enough to induce, and conceal, poor adjustment to the work done in school. Where the curriculum is inappropriate and the methods of teaching are dull, it is understandable that students turn to more immediate and more interesting activities. If the teacher's standards are inflexible and the student's sense of progress and achievement gives way to the conviction that there is no use in trying to come up to those standards, the demoralization may be expressed in misconduct.

Unpleasant though the thought is, the teacher's own personality may interfere with his students' development. Adolescents rarely respect a teacher who is weak and vacillating, who makes threats and ignores them, who makes an announcement and keeps changing it as students protest. On the other hand, the petty tyrant who is little more than a grown-up bully will find students bold enough to challenge his authority. The teacher who is tense and who charges the room with an air of nervous tension seldom understands that class disturbances are means by which healthy adolescents escape from tension. Similarly, the teacher who shouts incessantly and who usually speaks too loudly has a class that also speaks more loudly than necessary. The neurotic teacher who uses the classroom situation as an outlet for his own unsolved emotional problems creates serious difficulties and soon discovers how cruel adolescents can be.

The young teacher may be an ineffective leader of adolescents because his very youth may encourage students to take advantage of him. Moreover, he may not have had enough experience in dealing with adolescents to base his appeals on levels to which they respond. Thus, a young teacher may try to achieve popularity by treating his students almost as though he were a contemporary of theirs and then be dismayed to find that they, in turn, treat him with a breezy informality he considers disrespectful.

The teacher's personality enters into the disciplinary picture in still another way. Misconduct may easily be interpreted by the teacher as a threat to his own ego. To many a teacher, it is humiliating to have disciplinary difficulties because they seem to emphasize his own inadequacy. If a student does not learn French or mathematics, the teacher can absolve himself from a feeling of guilt by attributing the failure to the student's inferior mentality. When the student is defiant or unruly, however, the teacher is likely to blame himself for being unable to control his class. These feelings of guilt and inadequacy hamper the teacher in his work with the class because he cannot view the problems objectively.

The teacher plays a role which has in it some of the qualities of the scholar, the actor, the parent, and the top-sergeant. With experience, the skillful teacher leaves behind the chrysalis of reserve which characterizes the scholar and develops the necessary out-going qualities of a leader. The way in which the teacher relates to people is important; but some simple characteristics like personal vigor and dynamic speech are also significant.

The conscientious teacher may well ask what he can do to improve his student's adjustment if the student has so many different kinds of justification for being maladjusted. He may even wonder why so many students nevertheless act like decent people, generous and co-operative in their relations with their classmates and their teacher. How can he ever hope to correct any instance of serious maladjustment if his treatment has to await the completion of an individual analysis that must take considerable time, especially if he is to discharge his responsibilities to the other students at the same time?

The situation is not as hopeless as it seems. The teacher can help create a classroom atmosphere in which adolescents function with ease and he can help correct some of the minor manifestations of emotional difficulties before they become serious.

SOCIAL FACTORS IN PERSONAL DEVELOPMENT AND CLASS-ROOM DISCIPLINE

The school is an excellent laboratory for developing the ability to live in a democratic community, for the school constitutes an environment in which maturing students can be given increasing responsibility for solving the problems that arise when people live and work together.

The adolescent is influenced in many ways by the actions and attitudes of the group with which he identifies himself. Because the individual tends to strive for that which the group prizes, group attitudes are an important source of motivation and affect his level of aspiration. As a result, a teacher will never succeed in group or individual discipline if he seeks for causation only in the individual and his problems and fails to inquire into the over-all group morale, group interests, and the interrelationships in group structure.

Classroom discipline is dependent in large measure upon the group attitude toward school. These attitudes tend to typify the particular culture of the school's service area but, within the larger school and community culture, each classroom group develops a personality of its own. Every teacher will recognize differences between one class and another despite the fact that the same subject, the same grade level, and students of similar ability are involved. Thus, English 2 in the first period seems to be more responsive, more orderly, and brighter (or less responsive, less orderly, and slower) than English 2 in the fifth period.

Understanding Group Process as a Way of Making Teaching More Effective

Learning is an individual process in the sense that each student has to learn for himself. Yet learning in a school situation is always accomplished in a group context.

The importance of the group in individual learning and in social adjustment indicates the necessity to understand the structure and behavior of groups of adolescents. The teacher can employ such understanding to improve his own effectiveness in working with secondary school students. He can also help the students themselves to understand how the group operates so that they may become better group members and leaders. "Better," in this case, must be defined in terms of both enhanced personal fulfillment and improved group productivity. The teacher can help a class develop the feeling that it is a group with common goals and interests [24].

When a sense of group solidarity is established, *group reinforcement* takes place, and the motivation and efforts of each student are supported by parallel interests and strivings of others. At the opposite pole, a teacher may concentrate simply on the learners as individuals. This focus leads to ignoring the friendship groups and cliques which exist or develop, but these groupings nevertheless often keep the class from operating as a unified group. In such a case, the teacher is hard put to it to analyze individual behavior which has its origin in small group interests and attitudes. Finally, by ignoring the personal interactions of a classroom and the concerns of the students, the teacher may succeed in arraying the whole class against him. This result represents the development of a group with negative attitudes.

Key Questions in Evaluating Disciplinary Procedures

The new teacher is interested in group attitudes and performances for two important reasons—because the group is an important part of the learning environment, and because order and discipline in the group represent a *sine qua non* for the teaching-learning process. Sheviakov and Redl [23] present three important questions to the teacher in their thoughtful pamphlet on discipline. First, they point to a recurring need on the part of the teacher of choosing between the individual's well-being and the group morale. What is the effect on the group of administering or withholding punishment in the case of a single individual? Jim, for example, may be suspicious of all teachers because of many negative experiences in the past (most of them, unfortunately, warranted). Just as the teacher is bringing Jim around to accept him as a person more interested in Jim than in the inexorable laws of crime and punishment, Jim does something which is normally punishable in a way that all can see. Should the teacher punish Jim as the class expects, or should the teacher risk group resentment in his effort to show Jim that he will stand by the boy even if Jim does something wrong?

A second question is important for the teacher because it may serve as a criterion in judging his own operation. Does specific action taken constitute "managerial manipulation" or does it lead to genuine change in attitude? In the face of individual or group misbehavior, the teacher is required to salvage the situation in some way. The teacher has to assess his action in terms of what takes place. Has he merely manipulated the situation to restore order or has he used the situation to promote lasting changes in the way in which students look at the issue that was involved?

Third, the teacher must ask himself: *How* does he know that his particular approach "works"? What is the evidence one looks for? Quiet? Order? Friendly group relations? Respect for the teacher as the responsible leader of the class? Co-operation with other students to achieve the goals of instruction? Feelings of guilt and unworthiness on the part of the student? An injured or an enhanced self-concept? Fear of authority? Self-reliance?

The Teacher's Concept of Discipline as a Reflection of His Educational Values

What a teacher regards as a well-disciplined class is often a revealing index of his educational values. The teacher who tells you proudly how he finally succeeded in convincing his class that he is to be the unchallenged master of the situation has a markedly different interpretation of educational goals from that of another teacher who speaks with much satisfaction of the way his students made certain that two new students who came from poor families felt thoroughly at ease at the first school party they attended.

From the classroom teacher's point of view, the goal of good discipline is to develop those habits of student behavior and to inculcate those attitudes which best enable the class to conduct the activities in which the group is engaged. Viewed practically, discipline is a means to an end. The teacher wants neither silence nor active participation in discussion for its own sake. Silence is needed when students who are at work should not be distracted by bits of conversation; active participation in discussion is valuable if students are to profit from the exchange of ideas and points of view. Student co-operation should rest on an understanding of the need for co-operation rather than on fear of arousing the teacher's ire by not co-operating. The teacher regards a student as well-disciplined if the student habitually is co-operative, even when he is left unsupervised and has to decide for himself what is the right thing to do.

Like teachers of all times, the modern teacher wants his students to behave in socially acceptable ways, but he wants this behavior to rest on understanding and self-discipline rather than on fear of detection and punishment. It is small wonder that good discipline and effective teaching are so highly correlated, for both demand insight into adolescent psychology and the ability to get along well with students.

The Place of Classroom Regulations

When schools are small and the class size is also small, life is so simple that few school regulations are necessary. It makes little difference, for example, where cars are parked if only a few cars are brought to school each day. In a large high school, by contrast, where a hundred cars or more are parked near the school on a typical morning, some plan must be worked out so that these cars will not present a traffic problem and a fire hazard. Similarly, the library in a small school can be run more informally than is the library in a large school.

The various regulations which schools develop as guides to conduct must be seen as ways of coping with problems arising from the necessity of having people work together smoothly. Because some conditions are found in all schools, procedures for dealing with these problems must be developed in all schools. Compulsory education laws, for example, often dictate the age at which children must begin their schooling and the minimum age they must attain before they can leave. In other respects, schools vary so much that regulations also vary. In one school, for example, it may be necessary to have detailed procedures for regulating corridor traffic, while other schools can get along with few or no special procedures for guiding the path students follow as they go from one class to another.

Ideally, this pattern of behavior should be developed together by students and teachers rather than be imposed on students by a higher authority, whether it be the teacher, the principal, or the board of education. In most phases of classroom life, we can achieve this ideal of co-operative development of behavior standards. Much of desirable classroom behavior is merely a classroom application of the general principle of respecting the rights and the feelings of others. What is discourteous or inconsiderate outside of school is equally discourteous and inconsiderate in school.

Student Role in Making Rules

Sometimes, convention and unwritten law are not adequate bases for solving specific problems that arise. In one class, for example, the students supplemented available library facilities by contributing the newspapers and magazines they received at home. When they were preparing their reports, later in the term, some students began cutting out pictures and articles from their newspapers, believing that since they were giving this material to the class they could cut out anything they wanted to from their own newspapers. Other students protested that these newspapers and magazines were donations to the class library and should not be cut up by anybody.

Under these circumstances, it would have been a simple matter for the teacher to decide the issue himself and to promulgate an appropriate set of regulations. For the teacher to have done so, however, would have deprived the class of an excellent opportunity for seeing how they could resolve a problem in human relations in which, as in most social problems, there are no right side and wrong side, but rather two sides each of which, from its standpoint, is right.

This illustration may be misinterpreted as implying that the teacher submit for class discussion all questions of classroom procedure. Such a suggestion is hardly practicable, for the class may spend so much time on procedural and organizational details that no time is available for anything else. Some questions are too petty to deserve so much attention and time. Others may not be within the area in which students are free to decide how they will act. If fire laws, for example, prohibit smoking in the school building, it is futile to ask students to discuss the question of whether smoking should be permitted at evening dances in the gymnasium. Group discussions should be reserved for procedures where choice is possible and where the implications for adolescent development are so rich that they deserve class time that could be devoted to other matters.

Having Students Understand the Reasons Behind the Rules

Adolescents understand the necessity for some degree of regulation, even when they have not formulated the rules. They accept the rules of basketball when they are playing in the gymnasium and they are ready to follow parliamentary procedure at a club meeting. They are not likely, however, to accept regulations that seem arbitrary or unnecessary. Any attempt by the teacher to enforce such a rule may be interpreted by the adolescent as a personal challenge to devise ways of violating the rule without being detected.

To understand and accept the social basis for classroom regulations, students must grasp not only the meaning of the rule that is proposed but they must appreciate its background and justification. Instead of merely laying down the law that henceforth all library books must be returned before nine o'clock, the teacher must aid the students to understand the difficulties that confront an undermanned and overburdened library staff. Adolescents can understand that the members of the library staff can plan their own day more efficiently and be of greater service to the student body if they can allocate some activities to specific parts of the day. The proposed regulation now ceases to be merely another bit of school ritual and becomes a needed modification if the school is to function effectively.

Before the student can accept the principle that discipline is a social problem, it is clear that the teacher himself must also accept and apply the social basis for classroom organization and control. Whenever the teacher finds the members of the class to be consistently ignoring or violating one of the procedures recommended by him, he ought to see whether the procedure is necessary. He may find that his students are sufficiently mature that there is less need for rules and more may be left to the students' initiative and discretion. The adolescent wants to believe that he is an adult and he chafes under the restrictions of regulations that seem petty or childish. The fewer and the simpler the rules, the greater the degree of responsibility that is assumed by the students, the better will be the spirit of the class and consequently the discipline.

DEVELOPING WHOLESOME AND EFFECTIVE CLASSROOM ADJUSTMENT

In the classroom the teacher has a two-fold interest in the way his students behave. He is interested in helping these young people to mature emotionally and socially, but he is also interested in achieving the other goals of education. Some instances of adolescent misconduct may be normal as seen by the psychologist and yet be extremely disconcerting to a mathematics teacher who has only a limited amount of time to get his students to understand that tangents to a circle from a given point outside the circle are equal. If classroom work is to be effective, the teacher must make certain that it is not interrupted by misconduct, however understandable the misconduct may be.

The most effective way of dealing with disciplinary problems in the classroom is to see that they do not arise and that they are nipped in the bud when they do develop. This comment is not as silly or as vague as it seems at first to be. If the teacher can develop a classroom climate in which disciplinary problems do not flourish, he is much better off than if he tries to devise procedures for dealing with misconduct.

What kind of classroom is conducive to the development of desirable social behavior? It is one in which the teacher understands adolescents and knows how to get along with them. It is a classroom where the curriculum is appropriate for the students and in which the teacher is a skillful technician. It is a classroom in which the teacher knows the difference between petty infractions of rules that can be dealt with quickly and the more serious violations which may call for major psychological services and even possible removal from a school that is not designed to deal with seriously disturbed adolescents.

Oddly enough, one of the best ways of developing effective classroom discipline is for the teacher to plan his work as though he were taking good discipline for granted as a natural phase of good education. The teacher who is convinced of the worthwhileness of the activities in which the class is engaged approaches his tasks in a workmanlike manner that encourages his students to view them the same way. He is ready, for example, to start work promptly and there is something in the way he begins that indicates that this is not the place for horseplay.

Many schools find that it pays to insist on the students' being dressed appropriately and that they behave with decorum—without going in for uniforms or for elaborate codes dealing with dress—because of the subtle suggestion that the school is an important place and not an adjunct of the playground. Under these circumstances, it is relatively simple to indicate that there are limits to freedom that are necessary for efficient and smooth operation. Many students find it much more reassuring to be in such a school than in one in which extreme permissiveness leads to chaos and tension.

The Effect of Good Teaching

Many a teacher has found that discipline improved as his teaching improved. It is axiomatic that there will be more disciplinary problems in a dull period than in one that is interesting and challenging.

Whenever a teacher finds that his classes are habitually inattentive or unruly, he should examine his approach to the curriculum and his own classroom procedures. There are many ways of bridging the gap between the learner and the subject matter, even when the subject matter seems far removed from the natural interests of adolescents. When the teacher plans classroom activities so that they are understandable, interesting, and challenging to adolescents, the discipline in the class will improve more rapidly than it will from a whole series of public or private reprimands. In some instances, widespread inattention or misconduct should be considered by the teacher as virtually a vote of censure.

The Use of Positive Rather Than Negative Appeals

The influence of methods of teaching on discipline is only one application of the general principle that the teacher should rely on positive rather than negative means of maintaining good discipline. Both students and teachers should be concerned with what they should do rather than with what they should not do. As a corollary it follows that the teacher should be as quick in recognizing and rewarding good behavior as he is in detecting and censuring undesirable conduct. Teachers are often so busy correcting undesirable manifestations that they tend to ignore, or to take for granted, the good work that is done.

The judicious use of praise is a powerful stimulant. When the student who is usually inattentive does say something in a discussion, the teacher must not be too preoccupied to acknowledge the contribution. The young teacher who returns to secondary school as a teacher immediately after his own career at college and graduate school may be accustomed to standards far above those of the secondary school. He may not appreciate the thought and effort which a girl puts into her first imperfect sonnet. As the years go by and he understands his students better, he will cherish these adolescent attempts at originality. No teacher can afford to reserve his recognition for work of a quality that merited praise in his own college class.

Adolescents are sufficiently sophisticated to know the difference between merited praise and flattery. They do not expect to be praised all the time, but they want to feel that the teacher accepts and respects them. If they err, they want the criticism directed against what they have done rather than against themselves as individuals. Many adolescents are too unsure of themselves and of their status as members of the group to be able to work well when they think the teacher has little use for them or what they have done. When they regard the teacher as one who is always nagging or scolding, they develop a sort of protective shell that keeps them from hearing or responding to almost anything the teacher says.

The Effect of Smooth Classroom Management

Smoothly functioning classroom machinery is an important factor in developing a well-disciplined group. The details we spoke of in the preceding chapter as we discussed the management of a classroom are important because they set the stage for effective learning and eliminate the confusion that may lead to disorder and misconduct.

Classroom machinery should be kept simple, with as few regulations as possible. Regulations should be eased by the teacher and greater degrees of responsibility should be assumed by the students as the semester progresses. At the beginning of the year, for example, the teacher of a large class may find it necessary to require students to obtain his consent before going to the reference shelves. As the students develop the habit of using reference materials well, it should no longer be necessary to require them to ask for permission to go to the shelves.

Closely related to the smooth functioning of classroom machinery is the suggestion that the class activities be planned so carefully that all students know just what they are to do. Class work should start promptly and there should be no lag between one type of activity and the next. The teacher must make suitable provision for the student who works so rapidly that he has nothing to do while he waits for the others to complete the task. Sophisticated adolescents are usually unimpressed by such vague requests as that they take out their books and get to work or that they go over their work once more. They have to be taught how to use their free time constructively or the teacher will have to indicate definitely the kind of activity they are to turn to as soon as they complete the work they are doing.

It is often possible to vary the assignment on which the class is working so that all students will be ready to resume the discussion at about the same time. The teacher must be careful not to make the abler or the faster students feel that they are being given additional work merely to keep them busy while their slower classmates plod through the assignment. He must also be certain to arrange the order of the exercises or questions so that the basic ones come at the beginning for all students to do and that the more difficult and more challenging questions come later, when only the better students will have time to work on them. This procedure is illustrated by the science teacher who listed on the chalkboard several problems arising from the application of the principle they were discussing. The discussion led to the students' taking the time to formulate their solution to the problems. While all students had enough time to complete their work on some of the problems, the ablest students were able to try their hand at solving all of them. The class then resumed the discussion of these problems as applications of a basic principle in physics.

When students are sitting around idly, there is of course greater like-hood of poor discipline than when they are at work on an important task. For example, inattention and irrelevant conversation may become annoying when a group discussion has become a monologue or a dialogue. The teacher must therefore be able to lead a classroom discussion so that all students are involved in it, even when they are silent participants. Similarly, he may be inviting disorder if there is nothing for active boys and girls to do while he walks about the room inspecting their written assignments. Instead, he may use their assignments as the basis for a class discussion and delay his inspection until his students are at work on another task.

Because continued strain may lead to tension, objection may be raised to the teacher who starts work promptly and keeps all of his students working at full speed throughout the entire day. There is no reason why students should be tense merely because the school day is so well planned that it is full of challenging and worthwhile activities. The class is more likely to be tense when a harassed teacher has to resort to the constant use of punishment in a desperate attempt at keeping the students under control.

Being Alert to Early Signs of Trouble

To prevent serious disciplinary problems, the teacher must be alert to the early symptoms of disorder. The teacher who discovers that a few ir-relevant comments called out by the class wit have destroyed the mood he has been trying to create for the discussion of a serious problem can re-gain control by introducing a brief period of written work growing di-rectly out of the discussion and not presented as a punitive measure, or he can use some other means of shifting from the type of activity that is lead-ing to difficulty. The brief use of the lecture method of presentation, silent reading, and reference to the textbook or other materials are other ways in which the teacher can prevent a classroom discussion from getting com-pletely out of hand.

There are telltale signs of incipient difficulty that no experienced teacher ignores. It is such a short step from inattention to disorder that the teacher must be alert to signs of inattention and must try to bring wander-ing minds back to the task at hand. Sometimes all that is needed is a ref-erence to something a student has said or done, with mention of his name, for we all tend to perk up whenever we hear our name. If inattention is more general, it may be necessary for the teacher on the spur of the mo-ment to change the manner of presentation or to think of a question, an illustration, or an application that will enliven the discussion. When it is a student report or a committee report that is demonstrating that pupils can bore their classmates as well as a teacher can, the teacher, as a member of the audience, can ask a tactful question or two to good effect.

It is almost always unpleasant and sometimes difficult to deal adequately with a serious disciplinary problem. Moreover, it is usually unnecessary to face such a situation if the teacher corrects minor problems before they grow into serious ones. The teacher who makes home study asignments an integral part of class work instead of an unrelated chore and who regularly checks to see that all students do the required work will not be called on to deal with the situation where most of the students are unprepared for the day's work. A quarrel between two students can be stopped before it becomes an open fight.

This need for noting early symptoms of disorder should not lead the teacher to be so watchful that he exaggerates the importance of petty matters that are best ignored. Many a young teacher sees and hears too much; each minor lapse from decorum then becomes an offense that must be punished. Each teacher must determine for himself the difference between a minor misdemeanor that should be ignored and the type of misbehavior that must be corrected at once lest it lead to greater difficulties later.

Threats and Promises

The use of threats and promises as a device for curbing an uncooperative or unruly class is one that occurs regularly to inexperienced teachers. The initial success of the use of a threat or a promise invites repetition until the teacher finds that his constant use of them leaves his class unmoved.

Experienced teachers avoid the use of threats and promises. In the first place, they commit the teacher in advance to a specific way of reacting to a future occurrence. How can the teacher predict, for example, that the next student who comes to class unprepared will do so under circumstances that will justify the teacher's excluding him from class? Secondly, the teacher is most likely to resort to threats when he is excited or upset, and threats made under such circumstances may not reflect the teacher's sober judgment. Many threats, moreover, are empty; and some are downright silly. To tell an adolescent that he will live to regret his act is to be so vague as to be meaningless and ineffective. On the other hand, to announce in all seriousness that the teacher is not going to stand for any nonsense from this point on is to confess that he has been ineffective in controlling nonsense up to now.

Special mention must be made of the threat, and even the practice, of excluding students from class and of sending them to the dean's or the principal's office. Many schools frown on this procedure because it refers to the principal some problems which the teacher should be able to solve.

Some schools regard the number of problem students referred to the office as an index of the teacher's ineffectiveness. Students, too, may interpret the teacher's action as indicative of weakness. There are times, of course, when these considerations should not deter the teacher from asking his superiors to remove a boy or girl from the class. There is, for example, the case of the student whose misconduct is so serious that it is an immoral influence on the others.

In most instances in which students are sent to the office because of misconduct, the situation can be dealt with more effectively by having the teacher discuss the problem in the student's absence with a supervisor or with an experienced teacher in the school. By virtue of their experience and greater familiarity with the students, they may be able to suggest plans of treatment that would not otherwise occur to the teacher. This type of conference should add to the teacher's professional standing rather than detract from his stature as a teacher, for he comes not as the perplexed teacher at his wits' end who needs emergency assistance, but as a young member of a profession who consults the expert for aid in solving a professional problem. If the teacher views referral to the office in this light, there is clearly no need for warning the student that the teacher is planning to take this step.

Sensitivity to Student's Feelings

The influence of the teacher's understanding of adolescent psychology is illustrated by the way an experienced teacher avoids challenging an adolescent to take issue with him. Having the respect of his peer group is a strong adolescent need. The teacher therefore tries to prevent a situation from arising in which the adolescent boy or girl must choose between his peers and the teacher. Adolescent tempers flare up quickly, and, let alone, die down almost as fast. The teacher who forces the issue while the student is stubborn finds that the student dares not do what the teacher asks, lest the class think him a coward.

The emotionally adjusted teacher does not need to bolster his ego by demonstrating that he can break the adolescent's will, and the wise teacher knows that he must not allow misconduct to masquerade as heroism. The teacher who demands a public apology from the boy who muttered something to himself as he sat down after returning from the chalkboard is almost certain to be rebuffed. If at all possible, is it not better to pretend not to have noticed the muttering and then to speak to the boy privately a few minutes later after the boy has had a chance to cool off? What might have been an unpleasant or even a disastrous incident can now be used as a way of modifying the boy's attitude.

The better the teacher knows his students the more successful is he likely to be in his relations with them. The teacher who knows that a particular girl is extremely sensitive to criticism will be careful not to put her in a situation in which she is exposed to criticism from all parts of the room. The boy who is keenly disappointed because he was not admitted to the school honor society can be given some extra praise for the way he has gone about collecting data for a report delivered in class.

There is so much the teacher can do for his students when he knows them well that it is distressing to see how many schools there are that give the teacher so many and such large classes that the teacher-student relationship is almost impersonal. In fact, some teachers meet so many different students each day that it is a feat to learn their names, but learn their names quickly the teacher must, lest the students feel that the teacher is indifferent to them.

We all like to be called by our right names. If we do anything praiseworthy, we want the praise to go to us as individuals, not to the "fellow sitting in the seat behind Mary." On the other hand, it is easier to preserve good discipline when the teacher removes the protective cloak of anonymity and speaks with Bill Robinson rather than to "you, with the green sweater." The new teacher or the teacher of large classes finds it convenient, therefore, to prepare a seating plan the first day he meets his students so that he may learn to call them by name almost immediately.

DEALING WITH CLASSROOM MISCONDUCT

Although the teacher should view his methods of discipline first from the positive point of view of developing his students' ability to adjust themselves to the needs of working together, he must also be prepared to help correct the type of student that obstructs the group's progress. The redirection of unsatisfactory patterns of behavior is no minor matter to be dismissed casually by the routine administration of punishment. Before the teacher can hope to correct a serious disciplinary difficulty, he must know the background of the problem.

That the teacher must have sufficient knowledge of the adolescent's background and behavior patterns as a basis for the correction of unwholesome reactions rests on no superficial acceptance of the belief that students are always right and that misconduct is a reflection only of the teacher's lack of ability. Merely punishing the student who cuts classes will not touch the difficulties that may be at the root of the truancy. Before the teacher can lead the student to attend classes regularly, and to be there mentally and emotionally as well as physically, he must know the factors that led the student to absent himself.

Dealing with Minor Classroom Misconduct

Teachers can overdo this probing into the roots of disciplinary difficulties until they have no time for teaching. Many instances of minor classroom misconduct present no grave problems that require psychological analysis or expert treatment. No teacher can afford to make a detailed study of the psychological motivation of every minor lapse from classroom decorum, although he can undoubtedly profit from studying the causes of minor infractions that occur too frequently.

Fortunately, most of the petty misconduct that may disturb the class and the teacher does not arise from deep emotional conflicts. It is unnecessary, for example, to dig deep for hidden explanations if a student enters a class late because he stopped to talk with a friend in the corridor.

Because these minor infractions of classroom etiquette ordinarily do not reflect serious emotional disturbance, they can be dealt with easily. In most instances all that the teacher need do is to speak to the student. Sometimes, even that is unnecessary. If two students are conversing during a class discussion, the teacher can bring them back to the discussion by addressing a question to them. When it is clear that they could not have been following the discussion because of their conversation, it is unnecessary to embarrass them and to distract the class by waiting for them to think of something to say in answer to the teacher's question. It is usually preferable for the teacher to pass over the incident lightly, calling on another student, instead, with such a comment as "Well, what would you say, Gertrude?"

Dealing in this way with two students who have been conversing with each other rather than paying attention to the class discussion illustrates several principles which should guide the teacher in dealing with classroom misconduct. First, the teacher must be insistent that misconduct is not tolerated and should be alert to the early manifestations of misconduct. Second, the teacher should not embarrass a student by rebuking or humiliating him in public. Third, the teacher should not exaggerate the seriousness of the offense. If it can be corrected quickly and mildly, the teacher need not resort to drastic punishment, or even to any kind of punishment. Fourth, the teacher must be ready to forget the incident as soon as it has ended. If a student who was inattentive is now participating in classroom activities, the teacher need make no sarcastic comment about how glad he is that "Brighton has decided to pitch in and help us."

To be sure, there are causes for minor misconduct as well as there are causes for serious misconduct, but these causes are more likely to be corrected easily by any teacher who is ready to evaluate and to modify his classroom procedures. Though even a minor instance of misconduct may sometimes have deep psychological significance and suggest the desirability of studying the student further, the chances are that such a student's emotional difficulties will also attract the teacher's attention in other ways.

Dealing with Serious or Chronic Misconduct

There is no reason why we should expect the secondary school teacher to be able to deal with all of the disciplinary problems to be found in our schools, for there are students who are there because of our compulsory education laws, even when the schools have no appropriate program for such adolescents and no facilities for caring for them. There are communities, for example, that are so inadequately prepared for dealing with juvenile delinquents that children who are arrested for having committed serious offenses are returned to the schools while the courts consider what disposition is to be made of the case. The presence of such seriously disturbed adolescents can disrupt an entire school, let alone a class, regardless of how capable or devoted the teacher is. It is unfair and unwise to expect the teacher, singlehandedly, to solve a problem that is too complex for all of organized society to handle.

What can the teacher do when he has to deal with the serious problems of discipline he encounters in his own class? Often there is a dramatic classroom crisis that the teacher must attend to at once, without any opportunity for reflection before starting a well-considered rehabilitation program. When a student is cheating flagrantly during a test, this is no time for the teacher to ask, "Do you and your parents agree on what you should do when you are graduated from high school?"

What action should the teacher take immediately after discovering serious or chronic misconduct? He must see that this instance of misconduct is stopped at once and that repetition is discouraged. Students who are quarreling may be separated and then assigned to activities that will take these two students to different parts of the room. The class that is turning into a farce what is intended as the dramatic reading of the climactic scene of a play may be asked to study the next scene silently in order to plan for a classroom dramatization of that scene.

What the teacher will do on the spur of the moment depends very largely on the circumstances, the personalities of the students concerned, and the teacher's own personality. Within limits, almost any form that the reactions of an intelligent, well-adjusted teacher may take will be appropriate. Such a teacher will not lose control of himself at this time and he will not use the incident for an emotional outburst or as the excuse for vindictive action. The temporary expedient that is employed should not commit the teacher to a program of action he will have to follow after he has studied the problem further and has learned more about the causes.

Seeking to correct basic causes. The more important phase of dealing with the serious offender relates to what the teacher can do to correct the basic causes of the student's action. Many teachers seem to believe that all they need do is to talk to the student. Sermons can sometimes be effective, but no clergyman has ever preached so powerful a sermon that he did not have to preach another sermon the very next week. There are times when talking to a student is useful because he just does not realize how serious his misconduct is, but more often he needs more than a "talking to."

If the teacher has enough psychological skill to handle interview techniques successfully, talking *with* the student is useful. In such a conversation, the teacher can learn more when he is silent than when speaking. His questions should not be a form of cross-examination, for most teachers are inept as prosecuting attorneys. Instead, what the teacher does is to ask questions which will get the student to talk so that the teacher may get to understand the background of the child's behavior. Ideally, the teacher's questions should help the student to understand his behavior and to see the need for change. Such change is more likely to come if the student is helped to think his problems through than if the teacher does all of the thinking and the talking.

It is impossible to conduct such a conversation in an atmosphere of tension. For this reason, it cannot take place immediately after the offense. Neither teacher nor student is likely to be reasonable while emotions are still aroused. Striking while the iron is hot may be excellent advice for a blacksmith, but it does not point the way to modification of adolescent behavior.

The teacher's attitude toward those who violate the classroom social code should be one of firmness, but not anger. The teacher should not treat misconduct as a personal affront to himself and, under no circumstances, should the student get the impression that the teacher is trying to "get even" with the student for what had been done.

On the other hand, the teacher must not be weak, or seem to be weak, in his treatment of misconduct. He does not have to apologize for insisting that his students conduct themselves properly and he should not enter into any bargains with them in an attempt to purchase good conduct. Whenever the teacher learns that he is being unwise or unfair in his demands on his class, he should modify his procedure, but this change should not be granted as a concession in an attempt to purchase improved behavior.

The teacher has to be alert to the possibility that in his zeal for helping a student in difficulty he may be unfair to the others in the class. There should be no special privileges available only to the unruly. Thus, it is poor practice to permit such students to drop an unpopular subject and substitute another one unless such permission is also available to all other students.

Looking for further help. What can a teacher do when a student's conduct does not improve as a result of such a conversation or series of conversations? Ordinarily, such failure means that the teacher needs more information about the student. The teacher may find helpful clues by consulting the student's cumulative record, by speaking with some of his other teachers, by consulting the guidance counselor or other school specialists, or by discussing the problem with one of the school's administrators.

It is sometimes advisable for the teacher to meet with the student's parents, although there are some secondary schools in which all parent conferences are conducted by an administrator or by a guidance counselor. When the teacher meets with the parent, the approach should be that of a teacher who is asking for parental assistance in helping an adolescent in whom both school and home are interested and not that of a teacher who is tattling about what one of his students did, and what is the parent going to do about it?

There are many instances in which a teacher is fully capable of dealing with misconduct without any outside assistance, but there are also instances in which the problems go beyond the classroom and, therefore, beyond the teacher's control. For example, it may be that the causes of the difficulty are to be found in the fact that the student is enrolled in a curriculum for which he is ill-suited and that he should be transferred to another program. At another time, it may be necessary to get medical help for a student or to have his family referred to a social service agency. In such instances as these, the principal or his designated representative must be brought into the picture.

The teacher's interest in studying the background of his problem cases is unpardonable if it leads him to use amateur psychiatry in a case where expert care is needed. The new teacher should be especially willing to consult his principal or the guidance counselor for information about available clinical facilities and for suggestions about the best way of enlisting their services. Fortunately, most students do not need such specialized assistance and can gain a great deal from contact with a wise and sympathetic teacher who can see the adolescent's problem through adolescent eyes, but with the insight and the experience of the mature adult.

The teacher is a busy person who usually does not have unlimited time to spend on intensive psychological study and guidance. Even a competent teacher, moreover, may not have the special abilities and training that such counseling demands and he does not have at his disposal the facilities that a good child guidance clinic takes for granted. He will usually be limited to the information at his disposal, the data summarized on the cumulative records in the office, his own contacts with the student and the parents, and the light that can be shed by other teachers who know the student.

Working with a student as an individual. Much of the information the teacher needs is readily available. With only a little effort he can learn enough about the student and the nature of the offense to be able to embark on a remedial program. In order to demonstrate how even a busy teacher can proceed with his study of the individual student, we shall take the instance of a health education teacher who found that one of his students cut his gymnasium period frequently.

Before the teacher spoke with the boy or took any action in the matter, he went to the office and examined the boy's cumulative record card. Nothing that he saw there gave him a clue to the excessive absence from health education classes. The general picture he got was of a normal, healthy adolescent boy with a mentality a little above that of the median student in that school and with a school record that was correspondingly favorable. From all he could learn, the home situation was a favorable one. His teachers regarded him as a well-adjusted lad who got along satisfactorily with his classmates and the faculty. During conversations with other teachers who knew the boy, including the lad's previous health education teacher, all the health education teacher could discover was general agreement that this was a modest, likable chap who had never been in trouble before.

Once the dean of boys learned that the lad had been cutting classes, the usual administrative machinery was put to work and the boy had to report to the dean daily with a card signed by the health education teacher indicating that the boy had come to class.

Dutifully the boy reported daily to this teacher immediately after school was dismissed to have his attendance card signed. He was always greeted cordially as indicating that the teacher was willing to let bygones be bygones. In class, the teacher treated him as just another member of the class but he made sure to pat the boy on the back and say "Nice shot" when the basketball went into the basket.

One day, when the boy came in with the card to be signed, the teacher asked him whether he intended to try out for the school basketball team. The lad replied that he did not care enough for basketball to want to play on the school team and spoke of the time he tried to be the catcher on the school baseball team and of his disappointment when he was not accepted even as a substitute.

Eliciting the student's explanation of his behavior. It was at this point in the conversation that the teacher referred to the difficulty he had in understanding why so active a chap should cut health education classes. At last, thought the boy, the reprimand was coming, but there wasn't any. Instead, the teacher went on to explain that his experience had taught him that boys usually had a reason for what they did and that he was curious about the reasons for the truancy. Now that the lad was coming to class regularly, the teacher was willing to forgive the former truancy, but he would like to know the reason in order to help other fellows. The lad's casual answer, "It was just a crazy idea I had," did not convince the teacher.

With a litle more prodding and joshing, the story came out. One day, while the boys were undressing to go down to the swimming pool, there was quite a bit of horseplay in the locker room. Someone teased him by referring to him as a child. He then realized what he had long suspected: he was not as well developed as the other boys were. He disliked the idea of exposing himself to unflattering remarks about his immaturity and he therefore absented himself whenever he expected swimming to be part of the day's activities. Now that he was compelled to come to class regularly, he managed to be a little slow in taking his shoes and socks off so that the others would be out of the locker room before he completed his undressing. No, he had not spoken to his father, because Dad would probably have laughed at him. He had not discussed this with any teacher, either, because you just don't talk to teachers about things like this.

It was then the teacher's turn to do most of the talking, with the boy interrupting frequently to ask questions or to make comments. He spoke of the tremendous range of individual differences in the rate of development and explained that these variations were normal. Without saying so in so many words, he indicated that the boy was not underdeveloped or even abnormally slow in attaining maturity. He sympathized with the boy's sensitiveness but pointed out that the age of pubescence has little effect on the youth's later development.

They then went on to discuss the inadequacy of worry, brooding, and seclusiveness as ways of solving a personal problem. Why didn't he go to see the school physician when he was worried about his physical development? Such a visit could still be arranged, although it probably was not necessary since the regular medical examination did not indicate any need for concern. They talked on until the lad was obviously reassured and relieved. The boy's expressions of gratitude and the cordiality with which he greeted the teacher the next day were repayment enough for the interest the teacher had shown and the time he had spent.

Concern for Students' Adjustment as More Than Interest in Discipline

Psychologists often point to the serious emotional conflicts that may not be discovered by the teacher when the boy's or girl's emotional outlet takes the form of meek, submissive behavior rather than the more aggressive reactions of the student who becomes a disciplinary problem. The shy student who never volunteers in class; the girl who resents criticism, however mild; the boy who eats his lunch alone and seems to have no friends—all may need help as much as does the youth who quarrels with the corridor patrol.

It is unquestionably true that this approach to problem behavior does take time, but it is time well spent if it aids the adolescent to solve his own problems more effectively than he had been doing. The time spent with these students may not amount to more than the time the teacher would otherwise be devoting to the regular round of after-school meetings with his disciplinary cases. There may even be a saving of time if the intensive treatment of the serious cases keeps them from becoming foci of infection that turn an entire class into one large, hopeless disciplinary problem. The insight into adolescent psychology which a young teacher can get from the intensive study of even a few students should enrich his understanding of all his students and should make him a wiser and a better teacher.

THE PLACE OF PUNISHMENT IN THE IMPROVEMENT OF ADOLESCENT ADJUSTMENT

Punishment is an inadequate means of improving adolescents' adjustments or even of preventing classroom misconduct. Punishment alone cannot prevent a repetition of the offense by other students, for fear of punishment may lead only to craftiness in escaping detection. Thus, the teacher can reduce the amount of obvious inattention during a classroom discussion by punishing those he finds inattentive, but he may be deceived by the appearance of attention and never learn how to conduct a class session that really is stimulating. At best, punishment is a sort of emergency first-aid treatment; rarely is it a solution to the problems the teacher faces, and frequently it complicates rather than eases these problems.

Under existing conditions we can understand why a group of junior high school students who were unruly when the last motion picture was shown in the auditorium is not permitted to see the next one, why the defiant student is excluded from class activities, and why the chronically tardy ones are asked to sacrifice an afternoon to stay in the detention room after school. Our understanding of the teacher's reason for administering punishment under these circumstances does not imply, however, approval of the use of punishment as a substitute for the correction of the conditions that lead to misconduct.

Adjusting the Punishment to the Individual

If punishment aims chiefly at correction, the punishment should be influenced more by the student's personality than by the nature of the offense. Although preparing a sort of minor penal code that lists the punishments to be inflicted for various offenses may give the teacher the appearance of being impartial, such a predetermined list ignores completely the individualities of the students concerned. Two students may commit the same offense, but for reasons that are so different that a uniform system of punishments may be unjust and ineffective for both of them.

To avoid giving the student the impression that inflicting punishment is the teacher's means of getting even with someone who has offended him, the teacher must be certain to keep his own feelings out of it. Punishment should never be used at a time when the teacher is so angry that any punishment he metes out, regardless of how just or wise it may be, will be misinterpreted as being part of the teacher's emotional outburst. Similarly, the teacher does not refer to *his* class or *his* reputation. He is concerned with *our* class and *our* reputation. Punishment should be inflicted on behalf of the class. For example, if the boys and girls have to work so hard to arrange this trip, it is unfair to them to let one person spoil the trip for all the others.

The purpose of punishment influences both the nature of the punishment and the spirit in which it is administered. Since the teacher is interested in improving the student's ability to adjust to a group situation, he must be wary of using any form of punishment that jeopardizes that adjustment. A public rebuke or reprimand, or any comment that humiliates the student, may cause him to lose status in the group and may thus increase his difficulties in getting along with his fellows. Sarcasm may do so much harm by destroying the adolescent's faith in himself or his regard for the teacher as to outweigh the temporary improvement of behavior it effects.

Punishment may sometimes aggravate instead of relieve classroom problems. It is sometimes unwise to bar a student who has been disorderly in class from going on a trip with the class or from attending a motion picture presentation the others are going to see, for the trip or the motion picture may improve his classroom conduct by arousing his interest in the problem the class is studying. Punishment that is too severe or unjust, from the students' point of view, may lead to resentment rather than to a desire to mend one's ways.

Avoiding the Pitfalls of Inexperience

Inexperienced teachers tend to use more severe and more frequent punishments than are necessary and, having exhausted all of the forms of punishments they know, to keep searching for that one new punishment that will bring order out of chaos and that will change insolence to co-operation. In a school where referral to the office is regarded as so serious a step that an experienced teacher resorts to it only rarely, a new teacher may use this procedure so often that it becomes too commonplace to attract much notice. The teacher who uses low marks as a form

of punishment may discourage the student who sees no reason for working when inevitable failure for the quarter or for the semester lies ahead.

The young teacher may not know when punishments should be
avoided or discontinued and he may not use trifling punishments so effectively that more serious punishments are unnecessary. As soon as the
student shows any indication of wishing to return to the good graces of
the class and the teacher, that desire should be encouraged by commending him for the improvement rather than be frustrated by the teachers's
continued harping on former misdeeds.

Some of the inexperienced teacher's difficulties arise from his own
feeling of insecurity in the classroom and from the attendant desire to
assert his authority. He is reluctant, therefore, to use so subtle a punishment that the class does not realize the student is being punished. When
a young teacher finds that he has lost control of a spirited discussion, he
should change to another kind of classroom activity that he can control
better as though the other activity were a planned part of the day's work.
He should not expose his own failure by stressing the point that he is
abbreviating the discussion because of his students' unsatisfactory behavior.

No experienced teacher will ever let the class regard a legitimate
class activity as a form of punishment, but the young teacher thinks nothing of assigning the writing of a report or the reading of a book as a form
of penance. The competent teacher rarely punishes an entire class for the
misdeeds of a few, but the inexperienced teacher or the incompetent one,
finding the search for the causes of disorder to be too difficult, takes the
easier path of punishing the entire class. Not only may the teacher thus
develop general resentment on the part of co-operative students who
should be his first disciples, but he may get these students to feel and act
like disciplinary problems, while the real offenders regard the teacher as
weak and ineffective and are encouraged to continue stirring up trouble
because they are treated no worse than the others.

WHAT CAN THE TEACHER DO TO HELP A MALADJUSTED ADOLESCENT?

There is a great deal the teacher can do to help his students. At the
very least, he can understand the adolescent. Once the teacher learns
more about the young fellow who is so uninterested in class and who is
often so irritable that his classmates avoid him, he may sympathize with
the boy who has to stay up late helping his parents behind the counter of
the corner candy shop and who then goes to sleep in a room that is so
crowded and noisy that he has never known the kind of restful night's
sleep that teachers take for granted all students get. It is true that the
teacher cannot raise the family income to the point where it can afford to

engage additional paid assistance and that he cannot rent a larger apartment for them that is farther away from the all-night bus terminal. Nevertheless, he can do much for the boy by realizing that failure to read extensively does not indicate indifference and that drowsiness in class is not meant as discourtesy. If the parents are sympathetic and co-operative, they may help by rearranging the working schedule so that the boy does not make too great a sacrifice. Even if the teacher can point to no specific change to which his insight into the student's problem has led him, he can avoid aggravating the problem by seeing emotional problems where there are none. And let no one underestimate the comfort and the encouragement a harassed adolescent may gain from the sympathetic understanding of an intelligent teacher.

Understanding the Student and Helping Him Understand Himself

In other instances, the student may understand himself better, may see his own problems more clearly, and may face them more realistically and more confidently after a number of informal conversations with his teachers. These conversations must not be confused with the familiar after-school "hearings" during which the teacher calls on the student to explain his misconduct and then warns him against a recurrence of the offense. What we have in mind here is the chat that fills in the silences while teacher and student are working on a common chore after school, such as rearranging the supplies in a closet, or that takes place as both of them walk to the bus stop and wait for the bus.

Sometimes what the teacher learns will be translated into modifications of classroom procedure. The student who feels shunned may be entrusted with additional responsibilities that make him see himself as an important member of the group. The shy youth may be led into small group activities and then into participation with larger groups. Guided participation in cocurricular activities may be a stimulating means of providing additional outlets for adolescent interests and energies and may prove useful avenues of self-expression. A change in the student's program may help make his school career more appropriate for his needs and his abilities. There may be, in addition, a number of specific changes in the teacher's own procedures as a result of the information gleaned from the study of individual students. Many a teacher who recognizes fully the cruelty of sarcasm and who conscientiously avoid belittling students may nevertheless discover that some of his mannerisms or habitual expressions achieve the same effect.

In some instances the best procedure for the teacher to follow is to refer the case to the experts and to attempt no therapeutic work himself. How often the teacher can do this depends on the seriousness of the problem, and, of course, upon the facilities that are available. With the growing recognition of the value of guidance work with adolescents, more and more secondary schools are developing guidance offices manned either by specialists or by classroom teachers who have special training and other qualifications for this work and who combine a curtailed program of classroom teaching with some time spent in the guidance office.

The teacher who takes advantage of the services of the school psychologist or guidance counsellor, or of the facilities made available by outside agencies, must know the procedures followed in his school for getting help. In general, the teacher should make it a rule not to refer any case to any outside agency without first discussing the matter with his supervisors. Not only may the supervisor be able to help the teacher select the most suitable agency to be used, but he may sometimes know enough about the student to make referral for special study unnecessary.

THE TEACHER'S ROLE IN GUIDANCE

What we have been discussing indicates how large a part the teacher plays in guidance of the boys and girls he teaches. The teacher is expected to assume this role, not only incidentally, as an adult friend might, but in several specific ways. Today, most schools have specialists who are assigned to guidance work, but no guidance program can succeed without the sympathetic co-operation and the active assistance of the teachers on the school faculty.

To be sure, there are some student personnel problems that can be solved better by specially trained people who have the necessary training, facilities, and time. Guiding the readjustment of a seriously disturbed adolescent is no job for a sympathetic layman, for such a student needs professional assistance in addition to sympathy. Similarly, a professionally trained guidance counselor can do more than most classroom teachers to help young people explore their vocational interests and abilities so that they will not have the disillusioning experience of shifting from job to job after graduation until they happen to find one they can keep. The timely assistance of a competent psychologist may help uncover the causes of a slow learner's inability to progress in school and may suggest remedial procedures that will make this student's school career more than a series of visits to the dean's office.

There is so much that competent guidance workers can do for our boys and girls that all teachers should be enthusiastic rooters for adequate guidance service, especially for a guidance service that is more concerned with helping boys and girls than with preparing attractive profile graphs or fascinating case studies. The school's guidance counselors must supplement rather than supplant the teacher's guidance service, for it is the teacher who is in daily contact with all students. Unless each teacher treats every boy and every girl with understanding and consideration, no guidance office can undo the harm, no matter how fully it is staffed.

The classroom teacher, because of his close contacts with his students, is in a position not only to detect students who need professional psychological assistance but also to create a wholesome emotional climate in which boys and girls can develop. The teacher's attitude often decides whether the adolescent regards himself as a potential failure or as a young person who has potentialities that should be developed.

The Home Room Teacher

The home room is ordinarily inadequately exploited in a school guidance program. One may indeed wonder who attached the name *Home Room* to the room where boys and girls hang up their coats, call out "I'm here," and then rush out to more interesting rooms. Perhaps he was a visionary who hoped that by calling it the *Home Room* both teachers and students would try to make it live up to its name.

Before a home room can deserve that name, several changes ought to be made, some of them beyond the province of the individual teacher. Until the home room period is extended sufficiently, it can never be anything more than a sort of waiting room. Many schools allot about ten or fifteen minutes to the home room. After the attendance has been checked, notes collected from those who were absent the preceding day, and official notices read to the class, there is too little time for the students to do anything but talk to each other or try to copy from another student the homework that should have been done the preceding evening.

The method of assigning home room teachers also needs change, especially in large schools. Teachers, even those who are concerned with their influence on individual students, seldom realize how much less personal the secondary school seems to most students than were the elementary schools from which they came. Instead of having one teacher for the entire day, the secondary school student may meet as many as eight different teachers, each of whom in turn meets so many students that the teacher-pupil relationship is much less intimate in the secondary schools than in elementary schools. At the end of the semester, when students and teachers do get to know each other fairly well, everything is reshuffled all over again.

The home room teacher can supply a needed degree of continuity to offset this semiannual reassignment of teachers and students. For this reason, more and more schools do not change home room teachers each semester. Each student thus knows at least one teacher well enough to be able to approach him for help, and each teacher knows one group of students in terms of more than their achievement in his class. The fact that the home room teacher may not be teaching any of these students may be an asset, for their relationship will not be affected by the factor of grading and being graded. If the home room teacher does teach these students, he can use the insight he gains in class to improve his understanding of the boy or girl in their guidance relationship.

More than mechanical routines. In some secondary schools the home room teacher does little more than check attendance and collect money for the student activity fund and the Red Cross. A much different concept is needed when a full period is provided at least once a week for home room activities. When time is made available in this manner, there is ordinarily a definite program of activities for the various school grades. During the first semester of both the junior and the senior high schools, attention is given to helping the student to orient himself to the new school and for becoming acquainted with the school's facilities, with the various curricular programs that are offered, with the cocurricular program, and with school regulations and traditions. Similarly, there are basic themes for other terms: selecting a career, choosing a college, learning how to get along with others.

As we saw when we were discussing how to teach students the techniques of effective study, the home room can be used to help teach those general study habits that are common to all subjects and that are taught better in the home room than in any subject classroom. Since secondary school students take such different combinations of subjects, only a study program that is centered about the home room can assure all students a graded and continued series of activities designed to develop good study habits.

The home room teacher can become a valued personal counselor since he is the first member of the faculty to get reports on the student's progress in his various classes. Subject matter teachers, on the other hand, sometimes have so many students that they cannot be expected to examine each student's record to see whether he is doing as well as should be expected.

The home room teacher is the logical person to try to develop the kind of relationship with the student's family that seems so natural in the elementary school and so unattainable in the secondary school. Parents' Nights at secondary schools, particularly in senior high schools, often fall short of being effective because parents try to speak to so many teachers and teachers meet so many parents. A home room teacher can meet the parents and, by knowing enough about the students' total record at school, be able to ask more pertinent questions and to make more helpful replies to the parents' questions than can the subject teachers.

Clearly, there are many ways in which secondary school teachers can help their students. Improving the personal adjustment of adolescents requires intelligence, insight, and skill, but the rewards are so great as to make the goal worth attaining.

QUESTIONS FOR STUDY AND DISCUSSION

1. A recently appointed junior high school mathematics teacher finds that although there have been no serious disciplinary difficulties in his class, there is a steady buzz of conversation throughout the period. The teacher is certain that the conversations do not interfere with the progress of class activities but the principal has indicated that visitors get the impression that, at any one time, about half of the students are engaged in conversation rather than in work.

What would you do if you were the teacher?

2. A senior high school English class prepared an anthology of original verse written by members of the class. An elected editorial committee was assigned the responsibility of recommending the poetry to be included, the final selection to be made by vote of the entire class.

The editors were disappointed at first by the slowness with which acceptable contributions came. After repeated appeals for students to submit their poetry, they were encouraged when five poems were submitted the same day, three of them by one of the best English students. In order to encourage other students to contribute, the editorial committee arranged to have these poems read aloud.

After the poems had been read to the class, students and teacher joined in evaluating the poetry. The three poems submitted by the same student were particularly commendable because of the richness of the imagery and the appropriateness of words and meter.

That week-end, the teacher relaxed at home by reading a contemporary magazine and came across the poem she had been praising a few days earlier as the original work of this star student. When she compared the student's work with the published poem on Monday, she found that the two poems were identical except for a minor change in wording.

How should the teacher handle this situation?

3. An experienced teacher of twelfth-grade students explained that she never had any serious disciplinary difficulties in her class because she made it clear that she would stand for no nonsense. The first time any student came unprepared he had to do a triple assignment for the next day. If he came unprepared again, he had to stay after school every day for a week. Misconduct was punished by lowering the student's final grade. Those who know this teacher say her classes always run smoothly and that her students regularly do well on college entrance examinations.

What can you say in defense of this teacher's procedures?

What are the most telling criticisms of her procedures?

4. At a faculty forum on adolescent problems, one of the teachers commented that although it was undoubtedly interesting to discuss the students' psychological problems there was little the teacher can or need do about them. Speaking for himself, said he, he was too busy teaching to have any time left for trying to guess why boys and girls behaved as they did. Besides, he added, you don't have to be a psychologist to understand why students will cheat on tests if you don't watch them or why they'd rather fool around in class than do their work. Moreover, he'd rather resign from teaching than condone insolence or inattention in class simply because a student had an unsympathetic mother or a domineering father.

To what extent was this teacher right in what he said?

What are the most serious objections to his statement?

5. In a school in which most classes are conducted in a formal question-and-answer manner, a teacher is succeeding in getting his students to participate actively in group discussions. Although the teacher is gratified by the rapid progress his students are making in the use of discussion procedures, he is disturbed by a growing tendency among students to call out questions and answers without waiting to be recognized by the chairman and by the increasing number of irrelevant comments that are made by students who are trying to be funny.

The teacher has spoken to the class twice about the way in which flippancy interferes with effective discussion, and on the second occasion reprimanded the class mildly for their inability to conduct a mature discussion. For a day or two, the discussions improved slightly, but the students soon resumed their flippant attitude.

What should the teacher do now?

6. A junior high school has an auditorium which can accommodate about half of its total student body at one time. For this reason the school program of assembly meetings is planned in two parts, with one half of the school attending assembly exercises on Mondays while the other half goes to the auditorium on Wednesday mornings. Those students who do not attend the auditorium exercises spend the period in their home room classes. As a result, each class has one long home room period a week in addition to the brief period each morning.

How would you plan to spend this home room period if you had a class of seventh graders?

What changes would you make in your plans if your home room class consisted of eighth graders?

What changes would you make in your plan if your home room consisted of ninth graders?

7. A health education teacher noticed that one of the girls in her class is so aggressive in protecting her own interests that she is disliked intensely by her classmates. This girl is such a cheat that the other girls try to freeze her out of participation in their games whenever possible. The girl is bright, attractive, and not without a degree of personal charm that would make her popular enough if she did not work so hard to make herself unpopular.

In order to help the girl overcome the personality handicap, the teacher had a number of long conversations with her. In the course of one of these talks the girl said that her mother had repeatedly told her not to let anyone take advantage of her. The teacher indicated that there were better and more positive guides to behavior than merely seeing that no one ever put anything over on you.

The next day, the teacher was visited by the girl's mother, a determined woman, who wanted to know why any teacher dared to meddle in the relationship of mother and daughter. The mother indicated that she and her husband had gone far in the world by taking good care of their interests and they would stand for no teacher's telling their daughter to do otherwise.

What should the teacher say to this parent?

8. At a recent meeting of the board of education a resolution was passed prohibiting girls from wearing slacks or shorts to school and requiring boys to wear sweaters or jackets over their shirts. Students were not to be admitted to class if they violated these regulations. The resolution provided further that students should be informed of this regulation by having all teachers read the resolution to their home room classes the next day.

When one of the teachers read this notice to his class of sixteen- and seventeen-year-olds, student reaction was violent. The students wanted to know by what right the board of education interfered with so personal a question as the way one dressed. Some students said it was their duty to defy so arbitrary a rule. Others objected that they were being treated like little children. One of the boys reminded his classmates sarcastically that the principal always referred at assembly meetings to their growing maturity, to their ability to govern themselves, and to the principal's policy of explaining the basis for any school order he had to issue.

At this point in the discussion, one of the students turned to the teacher and asked him point blank what he thought of the board's action.

What stand should the teacher take?

9. On the first day of the term, Miss Williams, an attractive young teacher, succeeded in establishing excellent rapport with all her classes except one group of high school seniors who were almost as old as she was and treated her as though she were one of their classmates.

Thinking that her own breezy manner may have contributed to the laxity of class discipline, Miss Williams decided to be more formal for a while in her relations with this group.

The next time she met this class she busied herself at her desk as her students trooped into the room so that there would be no opportunity for an exchange of banter with them. When the bell rang, Miss Williams rose from her seat, took the attendance, and asked them to open their books to the chart they had been asked to prepare at home. The first student she called on to explain how he had drawn his chart answered cheerily that he had been too busy to do the work. The laughter that greeted this comment was cut short when the teacher curtly remarked that she was sorry he was unprepared and made an entry in her marking book.

Miss Williams called on another student and the lesson proceeded smoothly. A few minutes later one of the students said to his neighbor, in a tone that was clearly audible throughout the room, "Gee, she's sore today."

At this point, the teacher said, "We'll accomplish much more if there are fewer irrelevant remarks."

One of the older boys in the class then called out, "Aw, quit acting, Miss Williams. We know you. You're not really so mean."

Do you approve of what Miss Williams did this period? On what basis do you justify your answer?

Which changes, if any, would you have recommended in the teacher's procedure?

What should Miss Williams say and do now?

BIBLIOGRAPHY

1. Association for Supervision and Curriculum Development, *Guidance in the Curriculum*, 1955 Yearbook (Washington, D.C., the Association, 1955).
2. BOND, Jesse A., "Analysis of Observed Traits of Teachers Who Were Rated Superior in School Discipline," *Journal of Educational Research*, 45:507-516 (March, 1952).
3. COMBS, Arthur W., and SNYGG, Donald, *Individual Behavior: A Perceptual Approach to Behavior*, rev. ed. (New York, Harper and Brothers, 1959).
4. CUNNINGHAM, Ruth, and associates, *Understanding Group Behavior of Boys and Girls* (New York, Bureau of Publications, Teachers College, Columbia University, 1951), Chs. 2. 4-6.

5. GESELL, Arnold, ILG, Frances L., and AMES, Louise B., *Youth—the Years from Ten to Sixteen* (New York, Harper and Brothers, 1956).
6. HAVIGHURST, Robert J., *Human Development and Education* (New York, Longmans, Green and Co., Inc., 1953).
7. HYMES, James L., *Behavior and Misbehavior: A Teacher's Guide to Action* (Englewood Cliffs, N.J., Prentice-Hall, Inc., 1955).
8. JENKINS, Gladys G., BAUER, W. W., and SCHACHTER, Helen S., *Guide Book for Teen-Agers* (Chicago, Scott, Foresman and Company, 1955).
9. KVARACEUS, W. C., *Juvenile Delinquency: What Research Says to the Teacher,* No. 15 (Washington, D.C., National Education Association, Department of Classroom Teachers, 1958).
10. LANGDON, Grace, and STOUT, Irving W., *The Discipline of Well-Adjusted Children* (New York, John Day Company, 1952).
11. LINDGREN, Henry C., *Mental Health in Education* (New York, Holt, Rinehart and Winston, Inc., 1954).
12. LLOYD-JONES, Esther, and SMITH, Margaret R., eds., *Student Personnel Work as Deeper Teaching* (New York, Harper and Brothers, 1954).
13. MATHEWSON, Robert H., *Guidance Policy and Practice,* rev. ed. (New York, Harper and Brothers, 1955).
14. MOORE, Bernice M., *Juvenile Delinquency: Research, Theory and Comments* (Washington, D.C., Association for Supervision and Curriculum Development, 1958).
15. OHLSEN, Merle M., *Guidance: An Introduction* (New York, Harcourt, Brace and Company, 1955).
16. OLIVA, Peter F., "High School Discipline in American Society," *Bulletin of National Association of Secondary School Principals,* 40:1-103 (January, 1956).
17. PATOUILLET, Raymond, "Homeroom Guidance," *Teachers College Record,* Vol. 54, No. 3 (December, 1952), pp. 150-153.
18. RATHS, Louis E., *An Application to Education of the Needs Theory* (Bronxville, N.Y., Modern Education Service, 1949).
19. Research Division, National Education Association, *Schools Help Prevent Delinquency* (Washington, D.C., the Association), Research Bulletin, Vol. 31, No. 3 (October, 1953).
20. ROTHNEY, John W. M., *The High School Student: A Book of Cases* (New York, Holt, Rinehart and Winston, Inc., 1953).
21. SALISBURY, Harrison E., *The Shook-up Generation* (New York, Harper and Brothers, 1958).
22. SEGAL, David, *Frustration in Adolescent Youth* (Washington, D.C., U.S. Office of Education, 1951 Bulletin, No. 1).
23. SHEVIAKOV, George V., and REDL, Fritz, *Discipline for Today's Children and Youth,* new revision by Sybil K. Richardson (Washington, D.C., Association for Supervision and Curriculum, National Education Association, 1956).
24. THELAN, Herbert A., and TYLER, Ralph W., "Implications for Improving Instruction in the High School," National Society for the Study of Education, Forty-Ninth Yearbook, Part I, *Learning and Instruction,* Chapter XII (Chicago, University of Chicago Press, 1950).

CHAPTER 15

As One Teacher to Another

»»»»»»»»»»»

WILL YOU FORGIVE ME if I write a letter instead of preparing another chapter? Writing a book is difficult for a teacher, for he is accustomed to speaking with a small group of young men and women. A book, on the other hand, is addressed to the wide world. As you know, a letter addressed "To whom it may concern" is seldom as worth writing as one that starts "Dear Dick," or "Dear Paula."

When you are teaching a college class, you don't have to choose your words nearly so carefully as when you are writing. If you make too sweeping a generalization, your students bring you to earth quickly with their question, "For example?" If you become unrealistic in your description of educational procedures, they soon ask, "How can you do that at George Washington High School?" As you help them to see the potentialities as well as the limitations of that school, all of you are the better for thinking of a specific situation rather than of an abstractly unreal school. Readers, however, don't ask questions.

It is when you sit at a desk alone trying to put down one word after another that you realize how much you need your students. The ancients were wise when they said: "One learns much from his teachers, more from his colleagues, and most from his students." Writing this book at all is possible only because I have come in close contact with so many of you that, in my imagination, some of you are sitting close by my desk right now. I know, too, that my preparing the second edition was facilitated no end by the comments I have received from the students and teachers who were good enough to communicate their reactions to me.

You have to know how to read a book on education if you are going to profit most from it. You have to be able to distinguish between statements of fact and expressions of opinion; between educational principles

433

that are so important that they form the basis of all teaching, and specific applications of these principles that vary from situation to situation. No textbook on methods can give you all the help you need to become a good teacher. If the treatment stresses only general principles, it is usually too vague to tell you just what to do with the specific class you are teaching. A treatment that is too detailed, on the other hand, is equally inadequate, for you have no general principles on which to rely if your class is different from that described in the text.

BECOMING AN EFFECTIVE TEACHER

Every class is different from every other class; every student of yours is different from all other students; and you are different from every other teacher. It is unusual, therefore, for you to be able to apply anything exactly as you read it, or for you to be able to imitate in every detail a lesson or a procedure that you saw used so effectively by another teacher with another class.

Part of the teacher's art is that of being able to modify procedures and techniques to meet the needs of a specific group of students until it seems as though the procedure or technique were devised solely with these students in mind. It is as useless for a new teacher to imitate what another does, rather than the spirit in which it is done, as it is to try to ride a bicycle along the track left on a wet road by another bicycle. This was a lesson that was impressed upon me early in my teaching career.

My first term out of college was spent teaching an admittedly difficult class in a difficult school in a community that had more than its quota of crime, vice, and poverty. Taking advantage of a local school holiday, I spent the day visiting classes in a demonstration school operated by a neighboring teachers college. Every young teacher will appreciate my eagerness to pick up suggestions I could use.

On my visit, I saw teaching of the quality ordinarily encountered only in the pages of textbooks on methods of teaching. As I sat there admiring the teacher's skill and personality, I was impressed by the informality of the relationship between students and teacher and by the ease with which they discussed the poem they were reading together. The group burst into spontaneous laughter when one of the girls read aloud the lines she liked best, but read it with such over-prolonged dramatic pauses and such exaggerated inflections of her voice that she seemed to be burlesquing the teacher's reading of poetry. The teacher ignored the outburst and continued the discussion, only to find that part of the group was more interested in clowning than in poetry.

After spending a few minutes in a fruitless attempt to recapture the earlier mood, the teacher turned to her class and said, "Since you are apparently no longer interested in what this poet has to say, there is no sense in our continuing with the discussion at this time. You may go on with anything you want to do, and I shall do my own work."

It seemed as though an invisible cold wet blanket had suddenly descended on each student. All of the students were solemn and depressed. The teacher took out a set of papers and began to grade them. Soon, one boy came up and spoke to the teacher and, after leaving the teacher, walked over to one of the girls and conferred quietly with her. A minute or so later both went back to the teacher's desk and spoke to her. The teacher put her papers away, looked up, and said aloud, "Now that I understand what happened and why it happened, I feel better. Let's go back to the poem we were reading together." And she smiled! Her smile lifted the gloom more quickly than the hot summer sun evaporates the morning dew on the lawn. I was impressed at the beginning of the lesson; now I was completely awed.

I returned to my difficult class the next morning armed with a new pedagogical device. Waiting for my first chance—and I didn't have to wait long—I stood just as the other teacher had stood and, imitating her manner as best I could, said, "Since you are apparently no longer interested in what this book has to say, there is little sense in our continuing with the discussion at this time. You may go on with anything you want to do, and I shall do my own work."

I, too, took out some papers and began to grade them, but no student came up to confer with me. It was apparent, very soon, that the class didn't care whether we ever went back to our discussion. Realizing that there was no use in continuing this procedure any longer, I made some face-saving excuse and resumed my struggle with the class.

I had found no magic formula for achieving a good lesson, but I did learn an important truth. One cannot appropriate another teacher's procedure any more than one can appropriate another's coat. Try wearing someone else's clothing and you soon discover that what fitted the other so perfectly is too big or too tight for you. Teaching procedures are even more difficult to copy, for they must be appropriate for you, for your class, and for your subject. Only rarely can one copy successfully the specific details of another teacher's procedure. Adaptation is usually more successful than adoption.

Because the first year is often a difficult one, it is sometimes over-emphasized both by the teacher himself and by the institution that has helped prepare him for teaching. The new teacher who used to be so annoyed by the fact that his master teacher sat at the rear of the room when he was doing his student teaching soon appreciates how big is the gap between the minor problems he encountered as a student teacher and the full-fledged problems he faces when he carries the complete responsibility for all of the class activities. Discouraged because his class does not respond as he would like it to, he does not realize that the difficulty is largely the result of his own inexperience.

The new teacher must remember that he is still a novice and cannot expect to reach the status of an expert in a matter of days or weeks. It may take a new salesgirl at a five-and-ten-cent store only a relatively short time before she is as good as her most experienced co-worker, but it takes a recent medical school graduate many years before he is as skilled a surgeon as his chief of staff. The art of teaching cannot be learned while one is an undergraduate at college; it cannot be mastered even in the first year of teaching. If teaching is the profession we say it is, the teacher should be better at the end of the first year than he was at the beginning; he should be much better five years later, and still better fifteen years later.

Important though it is that you succeed during your first year, it is even more important that you keep on improving as you go on teaching. If you really are interested in the subject you are teaching, you will continue your own reading and study after you have met all of the requirements for all of the degrees you will ever receive. One of the peculiarities about your intellectual backgound is that it cannot remain static; as soon as you stop adding to it, it begins to deteriorate. Living on one's capital is always an uneasy way of life; when it is one's intellectual capital that is being consumed without being replenished, the result is disastrous for the teacher.

The longer you teach, the better should be your insight into adolescent psychology and the greater should be the ease with which you get along with the boys and girls in your classes. With greater experience in teaching should come a richer understanding of the meaning your subject has for your boys and girls. Some young teachers do not realize that the difference between a twenty-year-old college woman and a sixteen-year-old high school girl is greater than the four years' difference in their ages. A high school class may be unnmoved by your rendition of the lectures on *Romeo and Juliet* that led every senior class at your college regularly to accord your English professor the distinction of being voted the best teacher on the campus. The closer your contact with adolescents, the better will you be able to read *Romeo and Juliet* through their eyes; and the greater will be the success with which you can get them to see the play through your eyes.

I feel confident that almost all of you can become fairly effective teachers who are as good as the average teacher, but I hope you are appalled by the thought of spending your professional life on the level of mediocrity. No young teacher ever begins by wanting to be mediocre. If you can keep the dismal picture of a stagnant mental life before you as a warning, if you want to enjoy the thrill that teaching continues to have so long as you keep on trying to be a better teacher, the chances are very good that you will eventually become the teacher you want your students to have.

Your students can help you reach that goal. After all, students are in the best position to observe a teacher. They see him day after day, when there is no possibility of his staging a special performance to impress a visiting supervisor. They are with him when he is fresh and when he is tired; when he is teaching the topic he obviously enjoys and when he is paying tribute to the dead hand of time-worn curricular practices. They know when he is stimulating and when he is dull. They note mannerisms and personality traits that are annoying even though the teacher may be unaware of them. They appreciate the teacher who treats them as people worthy of consideration, but they are quick to sense the indifference, the partiality, or the sarcasm of an unsympathetic teacher. Students cannot give you the technical appraisal or the constructive suggestions you can get from a competent supervisor, but only they can give you a picture of yourself as you appear to your class.

How can you get this help from them? Certainly, you are not going to invite them to discuss you publicly. To the observant teacher, the way students react in his classes provides rich material for an evaluation of his own teaching procedures. The very expressions on students' faces are revealing. It is easy to sense that occasional moment when the class is moved by a teacher's question or comment and to see the difference between such a reaction and that of a class listening politely while the teacher goes on earning a living for his family.

The teacher ought to spend some time after school reviewing what happened during the day. What did he do that made his fourth period so stimulating? Why did that same approach fall flat the sixth period? Why hasn't he been able to establish rapport with the three boys who sit near the window in his freshman class? These questions suggest no period of brooding or moody introspection. If he is thinking rather than daydreaming, he should be able to determine that some procedures and attitudes should be continued and that others should be modified.

Some teachers find it helpful to ask their students for their reactions, being careful to avoid making the inquiry too pointed or too personal. One teacher, for example, at the end of the year asks his students to answer three questions about the course, not about the teacher: *Since this course is to be taught again next year, which features of this course as you had it would you keep? What would you change? Are there any other comments about this course that you want to make?* In order to avoid embarrassment and to encourage frankness, students are asked not to sign their comments.

I must admit that I have used some variation of these questions myself. Putting the questions in terms of the course rather than the teacher makes it seem less like a bid for verbal bouquets. For me, these comments have been invaluable. Though I have used this procedure with elementary school, secondary school, college, and university classes, there hasn't been a class that did not respond to the questions with all the seriousness I could have wished. There hasn't been a year in which I have not found suggestions I could employ the succeeding year. Asking students to indicate the features they wanted retained was as helpful as asking them to indicate the changes they thought should be introduced, for it enabled me to evaluate how widely a specific change was wanted. One reassuring aspect of these comments is that students never asked that the course be made easier or pleasanter. They did not mind working hard, provided that they saw that the work was important for achieving a goal they recognized as worth reaching.

It is unfair to demand that students be specific and constructive in their comments. If the students tell you that they find their textbook too confusing, you should not expect them to be able to analyze the author's style in order to indicate how it can be made clearer to adolescents, nor should you expect them to be so familiar with the literature in your subject that they can suggest a better textbook for you to use. They are being helpful enough if they get you to look for a more appropriate book or to find better means of teaching them how to use the book that is prescribed by the school authorities.

I have found students' written comments to be an excellent means of supplementing the oral comments made in class or in conversation. Most students are too easily embarrassed to tell you directly anything that is too damning or too flattering. When a student does say something to you, you have no way of knowing whether he is reflecting only his personal point of view or one that is widely held. It is well worth the few minutes it takes to get the reactions of all students.

I am sure you will respect the opinions expressed by your students, otherwise you would not ask for them, but you must not attach so much importance to them that you accept every suggestion uncritically. Some of their criticisms may be petty, and others may relieve minor problems only to create more serious ones. It is better to treat their suggestions as raising questions you should consider, not as commands to be obeyed unhesitatingly.

To a teacher, this kind of student reaction is so beneficial that I wish it were possible to get the same kind of assistance from readers. As I sit down to write, I have an outline of the points I wish to stress and of the illustrations and applications I shall use. No matter how carefully I plan nor how conscientiously I edit what I have written, I cannot be sure that my method of organization, my choice of illustrations, and my manner of writing give you the help you want and need. Just as the revision of a book might be much better if readers and author planned it together, so would learning activities improve if they were planned co-operatively.

THE TEACHER-STUDENT RELATIONSHIP

It is essential that a teacher have a good memory. I am not referring here to the ability to remember names, faces, and dates, though that ability is also useful. What I have in mind as being even more important is the ability to remember what he felt like when he himself was a student, to recall vividly the qualities of those teachers who made him feel that going to school was worthwhile, and to keep him from ever becoming the dull, uninspired, frustrated teacher he hopes never to be.

There have been numerous investigations which have tried to summarize the qualities of a successful teacher. Investigators have queried college students, high school students, and even elementary school pupils in an attempt to discover the traits that distinguish the teachers whom students regard as the best ones they have ever had from the teachers whom students dislike just as intensely. This going to the students for guidance represents no attempt to make the teacher's popularity synonymous with his effectiveness. It rests rather on the sound assumption that the students are in a key position to judge teachers.

I intended to summarize these studies for you because I thought you would want to know what your students would like you to be. After many attempts at such a summary, I have given up because there is so little there that you do not know. If you will only recall your own days as a student, you can prepare a list of your own that will mean more to you than any list prepared by others.

As you think of your own teachers, the chances are that you will enumerate personality traits more frequently than teaching procedures. You think of Mr. Alfred's genuine enthusiasm for biology and of the way in which the boys and girls were fascinated as he spoke of the world revealed by a microscope. You think of Miss Crown's smile and of how she made you all feel that she liked having you around. It's hard to forget how calmly Mr. Frane accepted the fact that some students find mathematics difficult and how easy it was to ask him questions about the points you didn't understand.

Merely thinking about these men and women who have done so much for you puts you in a pleasant frame of mind, but not so pleasant that it makes you forget how Miss K., soured by a life of struggle, treated her students as though having to be in contact with them were part of her daily sorrow. You remember Mr. P., who knew so little about physics and about adolescents that he had fits of temper and shouted and banged on his desk in an attempt to make up in fury for what he lacked in insight.

One thing that stands out in every evaluation of teachers is how modest are the standards which students set for teachers. They do not expect their teachers to be world famous scientists or concert violinists or Broadway actors, but they do want men and women who are themselves so well adjusted that they do not have to become petty tyrants in order to compensate for emotional maladjustments. They can ignore an occasional lapse in teaching procedures, but they do not forgive so readily the teacher who is sarcastic, who is rude, or who is partial to some of the members of the class.

They expect the teacher to be older, wiser, and more learned than they are, and they are ready to have him use his background and skill in order to make them wiser and more learned than they are; but they are intolerant of the teacher who acts as though he is so far above them that he can hardly take any interest in their immature efforts. They know they should be corrected when they make errors, but they do not see why they should be humiliated or ridiculed for having made errors.

Students are entitled to teachers who know what they are to teach and how to teach it, but they are also entitled to teachers who recognize each child's right to develop self-confidence and self-reliance. Students are in a better position to learn when teachers have helped them build a concept of themselves as persons who are worthy of respect and affection in school and out. This does not mean that everything the adolescent does must be accepted as wise and correct—even the student himself does not think he is always right in what he does. It does mean, however, that the student must always be treated as courteously and as considerately as the teacher would treat his own colleagues. Because the adolescent may have serious doubts about his ability and about his likelihood of succeeding in life, it is important that the teacher-student relationship build up the adolescent's respect for himself.

No young teacher can expect to be a master teacher when he enters his profession; he cannot expect to know so much about his subject or his students that he has the answer to every question he is asked; but he need yield to no one in his respect for the boys and girls he teaches. The moment he ceases to respect them and they cease to respect him, his period of maximum usefulness as a teacher has ended, even though he may still be classified for payroll purposes as a teacher.

Though teaching has its skills, it is more than a trade. Any college graduate who is willing to make the effort can learn enough about teaching procedures to earn some money by meeting his classes regularly. Teaching, however, is more than meeting classes regularly or even coaching students to get high scores on College Entrance Board Examinations. When a class is fortunate enough to be taught by a genuine teacher, every boy and girl is different at the end of the year from what he was at the beginning. They know more, but they also understand more and they appreciate more. To them mathematics is more than a way of manipulating numbers and letters to find how much the grocer should charge for a pound of tea or how fast is the river current; mathematics to them, is a way of thinking. To such a class, poetry is more than a way of saying in rhyme and meter something that is difficult to understand in the first place; for the study of poetry opens their eyes to the world in which they live, its beauties and its problems, and they see in poetry the expression of hopes and sentiments that most of us are too dull to sense or too inarticulate to express. To the class that has been introduced to social studies under the guidance of a real teacher, history is far more than dead facts about dead people. Seeing the historical background of our present problems enables them to face the future with the confidence that knowledge brings, and with the humility that comes with the realization that we are a small part of something bigger than any of us.

No alert and ambitious young college graduate need worry that teaching will ever become so monotonous as to be devoid of intellectual challenge. As long as the teacher is alert to the problem presented by his attempt to broaden the vision, deepen the understanding, and enlarge the interests of growing boys and girls, he need never lack for challenges to all his skill and all his intellect. It is only the unimaginative or the overworked teacher who finds teaching dull.

MEETING THE TEACHER'S MANIFOLD RESPONSIBILITIES

True it is that the teacher's burdens have become increasingly heavy, and I seem to be suggesting that they become even heavier. Instead of asking the teacher to supervise the kind of study hall where he can do his clerical work once he has taken the attendance and quieted the students down, we ask him to teach his students how to study. We ask him to prepare for his responsibilities as a club sponsor and to use his home room as a guidance period. We even take from him the comforting assurance that he can dig himself a rut and teach the same lessons year after year. Is there no limit to what people will expect of a classroom teacher? Can he be a psychologist, a club leader, a guidance specialist, a counselor in human relations, and still have any energy left to teach?

The problem is a real one, but the remedy is not to be found in neglecting any of the many major responsibilities that have been assigned to the teacher in the modern school. Nor can the problem be solved merely by adding more specialists to the school staff unless we are willing to divide the boy or girl into so many different parts that we lose sight of the fact that Mary Williams is a real person and not a reading problem plus a health problem plus an educational guidance problem.

To a large extent, the problem is a financial one. We have kept adding to the teacher's responsibilities without making a corresponding reduction in the number of students with whom the teacher comes in contact. Any teacher can take care of classes of forty to fifty students if the lecture method is to be the main method of teaching. An experienced teacher can have classes of thirty-five to forty if he uses the traditional recitation testing procedure based on a single textbook.

It is impossible, however, for a teacher to have five classes daily with thirty-five to forty students in each class and still accomplish all he is expected to do these days. Such a teacher cannot diagnose the causes of every student's difficulty and then plan appropriate individual remedial programs. He does not have the time for the reading he must do if his background for teaching is to be kept up-to-date by reading more than the class textbook. There isn't enough energy for the teacher to work so hard with his classes and to spend his afternoons and evenings meeting parents, preparing for class, correcting students' work, and constructing the carefully planned tests we expect of him, and still be an enthusiastic club sponsor and a sympathetic and understanding guidance counselor.

The situation is made even worse in many places by inadequate salaries. Many teachers, especially those with several dependents, must supplement their income by accepting additional jobs and thus reduce still further the time and energy that should be used for their students and themselves. If our adolescents are to get good teachers, teaching should be so much more highly paid a profession that it will attract young people of the caliber we need. In all too many schools, teaching seems to have become a part time job as teachers dash out of schools to rush to their second job as insurance salesmen or run home to get the evening meal started for the family. The salary must be sufficient to enable the teacher to maintain the standard of living of a professional person and to give his sons and daughters the opportunities that are open to the children of other professional people, without making it necessary for him to take additional employment.

The changing concept of the teacher's function should be accompanied by appropriate modification in the size of the class, lest we find that the changing concept is reflected only in books and not in classroom practices. The question for a community or the local board of education to answer is not: Can we afford to hire more teachers and have smaller classes? The question is: Can we afford to have large classes?

There is more to this plea for smaller classes and higher salaries than the common desire to get more money for less work. Those who are interested in seeing that adolescents get the stimulation and the guidance they need cannot help being dismayed at the sight of eager college graduates being reduced to overworked, tired, uninspired, and uninspiring teachers. Few communities have the right to be disappointed that some of their teachers fall short of expectations. It is rather an unrecognized tribute to the professional attitude of teachers that they are so concerned with the welfare of their students that they subsidize the education of youth by their own sacrifice. While we are all grateful to these teachers, one cannot base a system of free education for free people on the voluntary sacrifices of teachers.

I hope you will forgive my having wandered for a few minutes from the topic at hand to talk of the need for increased support of education. I feel a little like the teacher who reprimands those students who have come to class for the fact that a few others are playing truant that day. You are not the ones who have to be won over to the idea that classes should be smaller and teachers' checks, larger. The message is so important, however, that we must keep pleading it on every occasion until it wins general acceptance.

Yours is a more immediate question: How can you accomplish all you are expected to do if you are appointed to a school with large classes and heavy teaching loads? Under the circumstances, I think the best thing for you to do is to concentrate on one or two phases of your work each semester, doing the other tasks as well as you can with a minimum of additional preparation.

Let's begin with the assumption that the teacher's time is so limited that it is impossible to prepare adequately for everything every semester. The teacher who regularly attempts everything rarely has the time to do anything well. By concentrating on a few things each semester, the teacher will become progressively better as time goes on and will be studying such different phases of his work in succeeding years that he will avoid the boredom that accompanies the continued repetition of the same activities.

In your first semester of teaching you will have enough to do if you prepare thoroughly to teach your classes. Concentrate on that, even though it means you will be a mediocre club sponsor. The next semester you may be able to concentrate on one of your classes by reading a great deal in the subject matter of the field, meanwhile drawing on your present background for your other classes. You can spend some of your remaining preparation time with your cocurricular activity. During your third semester, you can select another class as the center of your personal study program and also study how you may best meet your guidance responsibilities. By the fourth semester, you are ready to resume studying for the first class.

In this way you always have a central problem about which to organize your reading. Every two or three semesters you make a fairly exhaustive study of recent advances in the field covered by each course. The intervening semester need not be dull times for the class that is not getting the benefit of this intensive preparation. Ideas that you get as you prepare for one course can also add to the effectiveness of other courses. Certainly the teacher who brings his knowledge in any one field up-to-date every year and a half is better equipped for teaching than is another teacher who divides his time so impartially among all his classes that he never has time to read more than the textbook for any course.

The teacher who assembles or constructs diagnostic tests and plans remedial programs for each major weakness for a single course each semester will have a better diagnostic and remedial program at the end of a few years than will other teachers who are so appalled at the enormity of the task of preparing such material for all classes that they do it for none.

There is a valuable by-product of this spiral system of teacher preparation. Because the teacher is apportioning his time in terms of years rather than days, he will not have the harried look of those who attempt the impossible and are consequently depressed by the thought of all the work that is still to be done. Constant study, though with a new problem or center each semester, will whet his own appetite for learning without which no teacher can hope to stimulate his students' appetite. At the opposite pole is absorption in the routine work of the classroom which paralyzes interest in further study and blurs concern for the boys and girls entrusted to the teacher's care. A sense of continuing stimulation and progress helps the teacher to keep the trees and the forest in proper perspective.

THE TEACHER'S RELATIONSHIP WITH OTHER PROFESSIONAL COLLEAGUES

So far, I have been stressing the teacher's relationship with his students because I think, and I hope you will agree with me, that that is the most important relationship in the school organization. There are other relationships, too, that are also important for the teacher's success. I refer to the teacher's relationship with other teachers, specialists, and the principal, and to his relationship with parents and the rest of the community. The classroom is an important part of the school, but it can be made even more important if the teacher knows how to work with the rest of the school and with the community.

The teacher must learn how to get along well with his fellow teachers for both personal and professional reasons. Because the school constitutes a little community of its own, the teacher's life is a happier one if he is treated as an accepted member of the community. In terms of the students' welfare, teachers who work well together can accomplish far more for their students than the same teachers can if each is suspicious of the others.

From what I know of the many young teachers with whom I have worked, I am certain that you want to be accepted by your colleagues as well as by your students. Yet we all know of young teachers who unintentionally make themselves unpopular with the other teachers. Each faculty has its own mores, and your colleagues are not more tolerant of newcomers who violate these customs than you are of the newcomer in your circle of friends who regularly does things that shock you.

Keep one eye on the way in which your colleagues act as a guide to the way in which you should act. If you are in a school where the teachers dress simply because they cannot afford to spend much money on clothes, it is in bad taste for you to show off your own elaborate wardrobe. You can dress well and simply rather than go to either the extreme of setting a standard that puts the others to shame or of looking like a candidate for admission to the county home. If the other teachers do not smoke in the teachers' lunchroom or in the rest room, you should not be the first one to fill it with smoke. If the teachers' room is the place where teachers have been going when they want a quiet room in which to read or work, you should not engage in such loud conversation as to disturb the others.

The lunchroom may not serve food that is as elaborate in variety or as dainty in appearance as that of your favorite restaurant, but it does not help matters any if you pick at your food with ill-concealed distaste. Even your choice of a seat in the lunchroom or teachers' room may be irritating if you blandly appropriate a place that custom has regularly allocated to another.

These illustrations are not the product of my overactive imagination as though I were trying to think of ways in which some new teachers may conceivably annoy others. Every one of these instances is based on unpleasant situations created by recent college graduates who were thoughtless rather than rude.

These illustrations do not mean that teachers may not dress as they please, smoke as they please, eat as they please—and vote as they please. We must all be alert to the necessity for defending the teacher's right as an American citizen to enjoy all the freedoms of other citizens. There is nothing in the Bill of Rights or in our unwritten law, however, that says teachers must smoke in school corridors or that the mathematics teacher should dress as though she were going to a cocktail dance instead of a sophomore mathematics class.

The simplest rule for the teacher to follow is that of being considerate of the feelings of his colleagues, which is what any well-bred young man and woman would do anyway. This suggestion implies a genuine respect for the right of the other teachers to maintain their own set of values. If you cherish the right to vote as you please, you must respect their right to vote as they please. When you get to know your colleagues better, you will recognize which of them are so set in their beliefs that it is futile for you to try to discuss contemporary problems with them, and which teachers will enjoy such discussions as much as you do. You will be a more effective influence on your colleagues if you do not rush matters by trying to convert everybody to your way of thinking as soon as you join a school faculty.

The very fact that you are young and fresh from college presents many advantages, and many problems, too. Although you may find many colleagues who are such good teachers that they fill you with envy and make you despair of ever reaching their level of effectiveness, you may also find other teachers who seem determined to ignore every principle of education enunciated later than 1940.

You may be tempted to show them how much more you know of educational psychology than they do and to give free lectures at lunch on how they really ought to teach. Don't! To them you are only a novice who, despite the fact that he has not yet had the experience he needs to become a model teacher, is ready to criticize those who have been teaching for more years than he has been alive.

Unfortunately, few schools give the young teacher so light a program that he can visit the classrooms of his more experienced colleagues. In most schools, he is likely to have only one period a day during which he has no classroom or building assignment. Even so, you should try to take advantage of every opportunity to visit the classes of those teachers who invite you to come or who accept your first hint that you think you can learn much from visiting other teachers—but don't force yourself on teachers who are embarrassed by visitors. As you leave the class or when you meet the teacher later in the day, thank him for having extended the privilege of visiting and indicate how helpful it is for a new teacher to see how experienced teachers meet various classroom problems and guide learning. Avoid making the not uncommon mistake of acting as though you could, with very little coaxing, tell them what they really should have done.

They may even ask for advice with a disarming introduction: surely, you should have some suggestions for improvement arising from your very recent study of modern teaching methods. Remember that few people who ask for advice really want advice; what they are usually eager for is confirmation that they are right in what they are doing. Teachers will respect you the more for your modesty in recognizing that there is much you have to learn about teaching before you can tell other teachers how to teach. Helping to improve teachers-in-service is itself a major task for which principals and superintendents are relatively well paid. Don't take away their livelihood by offering your services gratis.

It is poor taste to criticize another teacher face to face, but it is unethical to criticize other teachers in your conversations with students or parents. I know that you will welcome your informal relations with students who stay in to help you after school and that you will enjoy their anecdotes about other teachers. Their confidence will make you feel that at last you have established rapport with them and have made them realize how different you are from other teachers. Even at the risk of maintaining some of the barriers between teachers and students, I hope you will find some way of changing the topic of conversation tactfully when your students start to discuss their other teachers. After all, how would you like to learn that one of your colleagues regularly met some of your students after school for a discussion of what happened in your class?

Similarly, you should not criticize any other teacher adversely in your conversations with parents. Any boy or girl who tells his parents of a difference of opinion he had with a teacher is bound to tell the story from his own point of view. The story you hear from the parent is a second- or third-hand version of an account that was prejudiced from the beginning. It should be beneath you to court favor with parents by joining in condemnation of a teacher who is not there to present his side of the story. Without antagonizing the parent by contradicting him or by questioning the accuracy of his statements, you can explain how difficult it is to judge a teacher by listening to a student's account without knowing the particular circumstances that led to the teacher's action. I hope you will have enough respect for teaching and for teachers not to believe every bit of gossip you hear.

There is one type of teacher against whose influence you should be warned. I am thinking of the cynical and disillusioned teacher who long ago gave up trying to teach and who urges you to "forget everything you learned at college and go in there and. . . ." It is easy to forget everything you learned at college, and it is easy to give up the struggle to be the stimulating teacher you wished to have when you were a student. It takes more than intelligence to become a good teacher; it takes persistence, courage, and a conviction of the importance of good education. I hope, your students hope, and I think you, too, hope, that you will accept the challenge to make what you learned at college function in your own classes. The kind of advice this teacher is giving you makes teaching nothing more than a job; and as a job, teaching is dull and monotonous. How happy is the teacher who offers this advice? Would you like to become his kind of teacher?

In a modern school you will have other colleagues besides teachers. You may find yourself coming in contact with people in some or all of the following categories: clerks, psychologists, psychiatrists, social workers, guidance counselors, grade advisers, deans, nurses, doctors, and attendance officers. Each of these men and women has a distinct contribution to make to the improvement of the educational process. I hope you will not accept the fallacy so common to teachers of assuming that anyone who is not teaching a class has a soft job and should be given a class in order to reduce the instructional load carried by classroom teachers.

Even for purely selfish reasons, you should be grateful that you have available the assistance that can be given by your nonteaching colleagues. For example, every time a psychologist diagnoses the learning difficulties of one of your slow learners he reduces by one the number of students whose difficulties you have to analyze. Because the psychologist is better trained for this work and because he is more familiar with procedures and instruments that can be used, he can help you to teach your students better than you could without his services.

Because each of these people has his own job to do, you have to co-operate with him if he is to be as effective as he can be. Ordinarily, each of them is expected to do so much more than he can possibly accomplish that he should not have to waste time making two or three requests for information that could easily have been supplied in answer to a first request.

Most schools have a definite procedure for channeling the teacher's requests for special assistance so that no one of these people will be swamped by requests for help from all the teachers at once. Learn what the procedure is in your school for getting clerical assistance in preparing a mimeographed stencil of material you want to distribute to your classes or for getting a psychological examination for one of your students. You will ordinarily get better service if you follow the procedure set by the school.

When you have a difference of opinion with one of these people—for example, if you do not see the sense of a recommendation made by the school psychologist—try to arrange for a conference with him to discuss the problem instead of saving your reactions as choice bits of gossip in the teachers' room. As you talk to the psychologist, try making the assumption that he had a reason for his recommendation and that you are going there for help—at least, you can begin with that assumption until it is proved wrong—instead of walking in with the air of one who has determined that it is about time the psychologist learned a thing or two. In general, the more co-operative and tactful you are as you begin your conference, the better off will your students be.

With the growing use of team teaching and the spreading practice of employing teacher aides, co-operation in teaching has taken on added dimensions. In a sense, team teaching is not a radically new idea because the departmentalized secondary school has long had groups of teachers working with the same pupils. Yet, team teaching does differ markedly from departmentalized teaching, for the team of teachers consists not of teachers of equal rank who co-operate as peers but of teachers with varying degrees of preparation, of expertness, and of responsibility.

For team teaching to be effective, the teachers must learn how to plan their work co-operatively, with clear definitions of each teacher's responsibilities and with equally clear provision for working together. Teachers have to cede some of the autonomy they have always had in dealing with their own classes and to accept leadership. On the other hand the team leaders have to be able to assume the chairmanship of the group without depriving the other teachers of the feeling of personal responsibility for the students' growth.

The most important justification for team teaching is not economy, but the possibilities it offers for improving the quality of education. Schools have demonstrated that they can use team teaching effectively if they have the subsidy needed to prepare teachers for team teaching and to employ first-rate people as members of the team, for example, when the master teachers they use as team leaders are really masters at teaching and at leading a group of colleagues. There is much that teachers have to learn about co-operative teaching before team teaching can be successful as standard operating procedure. School systems will also have much learning to do, lest team teaching degenerate into merely a device for using unprepared and substandard teachers instead of fully prepared and expert teachers.

Similarly, teacher aides can improve secondary school education, but only if they are used wisely. Why do we need a teacher with years of study and experience for collecting milk money, for grading routine papers, and for sending post cards to the parents of absentees? Yet each of these chores can be more than drudgery. The teacher who grades students' papers, for example, knows more about the misconceptions that have developed and of the students' progress than if he never looked at their papers. Similarly, working individually with the slow pupil or the gifted one is more than a chore to be passed on to a subordinate. While teacher aides can relieve the teacher of some of the school's drudgery and thereby free him to use his talents as a professional person, the teacher must be wary of thinking of himself as being so highly trained a specialist that he teaches without knowing the boys and girls he is teaching.

Schools have principals and superintendents, too. This is more than a custom: it is a necessity. After you have visited or taught in many schools, you will be able to recognize the influence of the principal and the superintendent, even though they may be seen only seldom. This is not the place to discuss principles of school administration and the supervision of instruction, but the relationship of the teacher to the administrator is relevant at this point.

The school administrator is more than an employer; he is a professional colleague who can help you because of his greater experience and prestige. He should not be used as a bogey-man to whose office you send every student who annoys you. When the teacher-administrator relationship is a wholesome one, you should feel free to go to him for guidance in the solution of professional problems in which you need help. Instead of sending students to the office for disciplinary action, try going there yourself in order to discuss what you as the teacher should do to deal with the problems presented by these students.

Because the school can function best only when teachers and principals accept the same educational philosophy, education cannot proceed effectively when teachers and principals are pulling in opposite directions,

The trend in educational administration has been increasingly in the direction of giving the teacher a greater voice in determining school policies. When a new policy is under discussion, each teacher has the responsibility for contributing his ideas for the improvement of school services.

Once a policy has been adopted, even though it may not be the one you prefer, all teachers should try to make that principle succeed. It is not fair to the students to have some teachers try to sabotage some feature of the school program just because these teachers do not like it. More than loyalty to the principal is involved; it is a matter of loyalty to the students as compared with pique at being on the losing side of a debate. If the difference of opinion is a serious one, if the policy is one that the teacher cannot accept without violating principles that he regards as all important, the teacher should consider the possibilities of joining another faculty whose philosophy of education he can accept wholeheartedly.

THE TEACHER AND THE COMMUNITY

In contemporary American education there is an increasingly close relationship between the school and the rest of the community. So far as the teacher is concerned, this means both that he can use the resources in the community and that he is expected to be an active member of his community.

Since it is the parent group in the community that is closest to the school, it is natural that the school should try to make the parent-school relationship as close and as cordial as possible. The Parent-Teacher Association is more than a group of benevolent citizens who can be depended on to buy new curtains for the auditorium stage and to pay for the dental treatment of needy students. Because the parents have even more vital a stake in the education of their children than the teachers have, the parents should be treated as partners in a common enterprise. Parents' meetings offer a natural forum for the discussion of major changes that are being contemplated in school procedures. In general, the better informed the parents are about the school program, the more fully they feel that they are not regarded as intruders by the principal and teachers, the more likely it is that parents will work with the principal and teachers to make their school one of which they can all be proud.

Some school people are less enthusiastic about parents' associations than they profess to be, and it is only fair to admit that many parents' associations are far from ideal partners. In many communities the parents association is not representative of all parents but is dominated by a small clique that is using the organization as a way of furthering their personal social ambitions or of advancing their political program. Some parents' associations are dominated by a small group of "better citizens" who seem determined not to let the "wrong parents" take too active a part. There are

others that are run by local busybodies who keep meddling in school affairs and who act as though the birth certificate issued by the local board
of health were roughly the equivalent of a Ph.D. in Educational Psychology.

Without attempting to dominate the parents' association, the principal and teachers can nevertheless help the organization to be more
effective. It is perfectly proper for the school to urge all parents to join
their association and it is just as proper for the principal and teachers to
volunteer their services in making the program a co-operative one. When
the occasion arises, the principal and teachers must be careful to help the
parents see that there are areas of school administration and classroom administration that must be reserved to the school authorities, even though
parents are entitled to know the principles underlying these administrative procedures.

As a teacher you will have your own part to play in developing good
home-school relationships. When you attend a parents' meeting, try not to
act in a condescending manner toward parents as though you thought
your kindness in coming to the meeting were enough of a concession for
you to make to the parents' interest in their children. You, who reject the
older view that children should be seen and not heard, should not accept
the equally outmoded view that parents shouldn't even be seen. I hope
you will not be the snob who is less patient and less considerate because
he is speaking with a parent who has had less formal education than the
teacher.

As you speak to parents, deal with them in such a manner as to indicate your respect for their interest in their children's welfare. If you want
to discuss a problem with them, present it as a problem in which you are
both concerned, rather than as one more instance where it is necessary for
you to tell the parents what they must do to mend the errors of their ways.
Tell them about some of the pleasant things you know about their sons
and daughters so that parents will know that you, too, see these boys and
girls as individuals, with their little virtues and their faults, rather than as
being only problem cases. Be a good listener and give their point of view
the considerate reception you would like them to give your point of view.
Above all, treat the parent as a welcome guest and not as an intruder to be
disposed of as quickly as possible. Some of your best friends are parents;
and some of the parents can become your best friends.

Working with other members of the community also has its compensations. You do not want to become so absorbed in your teaching that you
forget there are other relationships in the community than the teacher-
student relationship. You ought to take the intelligent interest in community affairs you would have the other members of the community take.
Although organizations like the Boy or Girl Scouts, churches, and community centers will be eager for your assistance in leading their youth groups,

you should not restrict your activities to those closely related to teaching. It is only through active participation in many types of community activities that you can develop many-sided interests. The more you know about the community your students live in, the better will you be able to help them live a full and satisfying life in their world. As a matter of fact, the greater your participation in community life, the richer is your life likely to be both as a teacher and as a person.

Despite your eagerness to serve the community in which you teach, you may sometimes find it necessary to guard yourself against being exploited by various agencies that regard school faculties as excellent sources of unpaid skilled workers. Community participation can be effective without making excessive demands on the teachers' time and energy.

Your relations with the community are not entirely a matter of your giving your service; there are many services which the community can give you. There are resources in the community you can use in your teaching: places to visit; people who can visit your class or be interviewed by members of your class; public and family libraries that can supplement your school resources; families that will lend you material for demonstration or exhibit purposes; agencies that can help you solve some of the personal problems of your pupils; and other forms of assistance that vary with the community.

Making full use of community resources not only improves your teaching but also brings you and your community closer together. People are often more sympathetic toward those they help than to others to whom they feel indebted for favors received. The police captain who is invited to tell a social studies class how the local department co-operates with state and federal law enforcement agencies; the president of the P.T.A. who is invited to bring her collection of Spanish records to a language class; the insurance man who is asked to explain to a mathematics class how fire insurance rates are computed for various types of buildings—all of these people feel closer to the school because they have been appreciated enough to be asked to help.

By this time you should be convinced that teaching has so many phases and problems that it can be strenuous, but it is never dull or monotonous unless the teacher is determined to make it so, or unless he is so badly overworked that he can never rise above the routine aspects of teaching.

STARTING A CAREER IN TEACHING

The enthusiastic new teacher often views his first teaching position as an opportunity to conduct a one-man educational revolution, as his one chance of giving expression to his own interpretation of educational philosophy. Freed from critic teachers and master teachers, he can now demonstrate how a class should be taught. Although this point of view is a stimulating one, it may create additional difficulties for you, especially if you introduce innovations at too rapid a pace, or without adequate student preparation for the impending changes.

Despite popular belief, the adolescent is a conservative person, especially in his attitude toward educational procedures. He is ready to follow the educational pattern with which he is familiar as though that were the only possible procedure. Accepting a new teacher involves a readjustment; accepting a new teacher with an entirely different point of view from that with which he is familiar and with a strikingly new type of classroom procedure, may require a greater adjustment than he can make easily. In the universal custom of trying out the new teacher, the student may conclude that the new teacher isn't any good and that his ideas are impracticable.

You, too, have an adjustment to make. It is difficult enough for a new teacher to adjust himself to a new role in a strange school with students who are still unknown to him, but it is even more difficult to try to make the adjustment while he is introducing marked changes in the educational pattern. Because his own and his students' difficulties jeopardize the likelihood of his plan's succeeding, the new teacher often goes through the trying experience of introducing a new point of view, only to have to abandon it within a few weeks. Erroneously, he may conclude that his plan of procedure or his point of view was poor, when all that was really at fault was his own impatience in introducing the changes without preparing the class for accepting his point of view.

No small part of the conservatism of many older teachers may be traced to early unfortunate experiences with hastily conceived and inadequately planned departures from accepted practice. It is difficult to convince the teacher who has had a rebuff early in his professional career that the same ideas may be practicable if he tries them again when he is more mature and more experienced.

The new teacher with an original point of view will be more likely to see his ideas translated into reality if he introduces them slowly than if he tries to introduce, during his first week of teaching, everything of which he has ever thought. You will find that it is far better for you to begin the semester as students expect you to. This is one reason why you must be so familiar with the point of view of the school to which you are going. You can introduce changes gradually as you become better acquainted with your students, the school, and the community. If there are any changes that are initiated more easily at the beginning of the semester than during the semester, you may do better by delaying these till the beginning of your second semester or second year.

These suggestions are not a plea for smugness and unvarying observance of established educational customs. On the contrary, they are intended to facilitate the introduction of new ideas and procedures and the development of an individualized educational philosophy that gives meaning to one's professional life.

The teacher must prepare for his first day of teaching by assuring himself of his mastery of his subject matter. Even the teacher who has just been graduated from college where he may have taken innumerable courses in his area of specialization and been graduated with honors may not be adequately prepared for secondary school teaching. As a college student, you were answering the questions of college professors; now you must answer the questions of adolescents—and adolescents ask questions which are different from those that occur to college professors.

Adolescents are interested in applications and implications rather than in names and theories. They turn to theory readily enough, but only when they see in the theory a means of finding the answer to the persistent Why? and How? The recently graduated college physics major knows much about alternating and direct current in electricity, about the uses of each type, and of the ways of transforming direct current into alternating current. Learned in physics though he is, he may not know what to tell a boy who asks what happens when an American tourist tries to use his electric razor in a European hotel which operates on direct current. The boy wants to know whether the razor will be ruined, whether it will stop and go intermittently, or whether it simply will not work at all.

Of one thing the new teacher can be certain: all students like to leave the first meeting of a class feeling that something has been accomplished, that they have started on a year that promises to make its full contribution to the satisfaction of important needs. To regard the first meeting as only a "get acquainted" period may be merely a euphemistic way of indicating that the teacher is unprepared to make that first day a fruitful one. After all, one can get acquainted with others while working together on a significant task. The new teacher who thinks blithely that he can spend the first few days with his class in "exploring the field" must learn the difference between exploring and aimless wandering.

The atmosphere of a good first lesson is the atmosphere of any good classroom activity, whether it comes at the beginning of the year or the end. The first day should be a good sample of what is to come. Ideally, it should lead to a good second day, then to a good third day, and so right through to the end of the year. It should present the teacher for what he is, namely, as one who is vital and dynamic, interested in his students and convinced of the worthwhileness of the activities in which they are all to participate. If the preparation for the first day does this, it may accomplish more than introducing the student to the work of the semester—it may help the teacher to form the habit of planning his work from the point of view of its significance to the student.

The inexperienced teacher sometimes finds that the procedures used by more experienced teachers are not effective when he employs them. Boys and girls who are co-operative and considerate elsewhere in the school may be boisterous in his class and those who respond to courteous requests from other teachers may ignore his equally courteous requests. The disciplinary difficulties of the young teacher arise from many sources. Because of his inexperience, he may not be as skilled a teacher as are his more experienced colleagues. His explanations may not be as clear nor the discussions as stimulating as they are in other classes. His classroom procedure may not yet be smooth enough to invite effective co-operation and he may create difficulties by clumsy class administration.

Since you are probably not much older than your students, they may not treat you with the respect they have for their other teachers. Adolescents may also enjoy trying you out to see how flustered you get when they feign ignorance of the request you made so clearly yesterday. Many a young teacher has discovered that the students find trying to understand the structure of the atom is less interesting than watching the teacher try to locate the source of the quacking noise that convulses the class as soon as his back is turned.

As a young teacher, you may have to exert a firmer degree of class control than is necessary for a more experienced teacher. This does not mean that you are to be a martinet, that you are to stride into the class announcing that you are the boss, ready to meet the challenge of all who dare defy you. Even if such a tyrannical pose were not objectionable from every point of view, it would still be a stupid attitude for you to take, for anyone who understands adolescents knows that they will soon accept so tempting a challenge. The young teacher has to be pleasant without being flippant, just as he has to be firm without being domineering. Although you may be young enough to be mistaken for a fellow-student, you must carry yourself with the dignity of one who is there as a leader.

No teacher, especially not the young teacher, can afford to lose his temper in class. The teacher who becomes excited because some girl accidentally dropped her handbag, spilling its contents all over the floor, while he was reading aloud the most dramatic passage in the play the class is studying, may find that some of his students deliberately drop things while he is reading aloud just to tease him. You will need all your wits at all times, and you cannot be in full control of the situation when you lose your temper. What you say and do under such circumstances may remain to create additional difficulties after you have recovered your calm.

One of the reasons students misbehave in a new teacher's class is that they feel safe in the general confusion that cloaks individual responsibility for misdeeds. The sooner the teacher indicates that he knows the identity of his students, the quicker will he be able to correct one of the weaknesses of his own position.

You may find it helpful to prepare a blank seating plan in advance of the first class session and to fill in the students' names during the very first period. Some teachers accomplish this by assigning some sort of written work the first period and then going about the room copying the students' names from their papers. Other teachers try to learn a few names the first period and then call on these students by name as though they knew the names of all the students. Many teachers memorize the names of their students in their first evening at home after meeting the class. At any rate, you must know the names of most, if not all, of the students before the class reconvenes the next day and thus eliminate much of the disciplinary difficulty the new teacher faces.

These first few days you will have to plan the classroom activities so carefully that students will not have to sit idly while you try to think of what they should do next. Much of the disciplinary difficulty that new teachers encounter arises in those intervals when all or some of the students are idle. Such intervals of inactivity often are found at the beginning of the period before work gets under way, near the end of the period when the teacher runs out of material, and between phases of the lesson when the teacher and class are waiting for the slow students to finish what they are doing so that all may proceed together to the next phase. With more thorough planning, the teacher can eliminate these periods of idleness with their invitation to energetic adolescents to think of pleasant ways of spending the time.

As you plan classroom work, keep a watchful eye on the possibility of misconduct. You should be wary, for example, of using illustrative materials that may lead to difficulties. Thus, a squeaking model of a steam engine may give the young wits an opportunity to show off their abilities as mimics. Exhibiting pictures that are too small to be seen clearly by all members of his group may be another invitation to the kind of disorder that a new teacher should seek to avoid. You may well decide to minimize the amount of student movement about the room the first day or two; it may be better not to plan to send large groups of students to the chalkboards at one time and not to conduct several group discussions in different parts of the room. Since the collection and distribution of materials may present disciplinary pitfalls at the beginning, these, too, should be reduced to a minimum.

Disciplinary considerations must not be allowed to become the prime factor in determining which classroom activities should be conducted. All that the new teacher need do is to examine his proposed procedures in the light of the difficulties that may arise and then to modify his plan so as to reduce the possibility of trouble. It is thus a good idea to include some written work in each of the first two or three class sessions. A class that is restless or disorderly may be brought to order fairly quickly by the distribution of paper. This type of work may be brief, lasting no more than five or ten minutes, and yet be an effective sedative for an over-excited class. For example, when the discussion in the hygiene class begins to lag or to show signs of passing out of the teacher's control, it may be advisable for you to give them all a chance to answer the next question on paper. Having some of the students read from their papers is an easy transition to continuing with the original discussion.

It may seem at first that these repeated references to the ways in which the new teacher must avoid disorder represent a retrogressive step to the days when strict order was considered as the major goal for the teacher to attain. I intend no such conclusion. The new teacher is in a difficult position because he does not know his students and they do not know him. Under these circumstances, many adolescents regard the teacher as fair game and try to see how far they can go. The first few weeks often furnish a modern version of the medieval "trial by ordeal" and the teacher must survive these first few weeks if he is to continue his professional career.

It is as narrow to regard these first weeks as setting the pattern for your later procedures as it is unrealistic to assume that the pattern of behavior followed by an experienced teacher can be followed by a young teacher in a strange school. An experienced teacher, for example, may use humor as an excellent way of introducing that easy and informal classroom atmosphere we all desire in a modern class. On the other hand, you can tell a number of very funny stories the first day and start such gales of laughter as easily lead to boisterous and unruly conduct. If I suggest, then, that you curb your sense of humor and that you be pleasant rather than witty, it is with no thought that your sense of humor may not later become one of your most valuable teaching assets.

Some teachers are fortunate in that they begin their careers under such favorable circumstances and with such superb personal and professional equipment that they can dismiss this concern with the problems that so often beset the beginning teacher. Most new teachers are not so fortunate. Indeed, many a new teacher is likely to be discouraged by the gap between his anticipated picture of himself as a teacher and the disappointing realization that even his best efforts are inadequate for solving the problems he faces. It is at that despairing moment that you need to understand that the first semester is so often a difficult one. It may even be a disastrous one if it leads you to abandon your education philosophy and to abandon your professional hopes for the routine job of routine teaching.

During the first year, the teacher is the student, and the students are the teachers. What the new teacher must learn is to translate principles into practices, and hopes into realities. Your first year is a successful one if it enables you to face your second year with greater confidence, with richer insight, with more effective classroom procedures, but with the same or even greater enthusiasm for the significance of the teacher's role in a program of modern, democratic, public education.

George Bernard Shaw once observed that it is unfortunate that youth is wasted on young people. It would be too bad if only the inexperienced teacher could enjoy the thrill of being a new teacher. Some teachers are always young teachers, no matter how long they have taught. Other teachers are always inexperienced, for they spend their entire professional career repeating the procedures they used in their first year. The ideal teacher is the one who can retain the freshness, the enthusiasm, and the ambition of the young teacher and still gain the insight and the skill that come with experience.

Whether you will mature, or merely age, as you go on teaching is so important that it should be a major concern for you, for your colleagues on the faculty, and for your principal and superintendent. It is difficult for the teacher to continue his professional development if his supervisors are unsympathetic, if his instructional load is so heavy that he cannot do more than go through the motions of teaching, or if the school's equipment is so inadequate that he cannot enjoy the sense of satisfaction that comes with the feeling of achievement.

To some extent the teacher's attitude is the determining factor in his professional development. A friend once asked a famous actor who was starring in a play that had been running on Broadway for a year how he could stand the monotony of playing the same role night after night. The actor replied that it was far from monotonous because each night he had a different audience to win over. What a difference there is between this actor and the one who does nothing more than say the same words and make the same gestures night after night and twice on Wednesdays and Saturdays.

Teaching can be an endless succession of first years for you, if you prepare for each class as for the first one, and if you regard each new group of students as young people whom you must get to know so that you can influence their development.

WHY TEACH?

I don't think I'd blame you if you were to ask why anyone should become a teacher when there are so many other fields open these days to young men and women who have the intellectual ability, the prolonged education, and the personality traits required for successful teaching. If you don't like boys and girls well enough to want to be with them every day or if you find the teacher's work distasteful, this is a good time to drop the idea of teaching. There are no people who are so miserable as those teachers who should have entered another field. You cannot be a halfhearted teacher and enjoy your life, because adolescent boys and girls are too alive to allow you to treat them with indifference. A restaurant cashier can stay at her desk all day even though she despises making change, but a teacher cannot go through the day despising his students. Don't enter teaching because of the summer vacation, for ten months of mental torture will rob the vacation of whatever joys it may have.

For those of you who enjoy teaching, there are many compensations. It is pleasant and stimulating to work with adolescents, for they are alert and growing, and being with them makes you, too, feel alert and growing. You have these boys and girls at a time when you can help influence their hopes and their attitudes, their sense of values and their senseless prejudices. It is empty to talk of what Education can do for Youth. Think, instead, of what you and I can do for our own students. You and I as teachers with our students—that's what Education is. In our own classrooms we are in a position to do our mite toward helping to create the kind of world in which we want to live. This responsibility is both the major challenge and the biggest source of satisfaction in teaching.

Adolescents are so appreciative that it is satisfying to work with them. Ask any English teacher how he feels when, after reading aloud from a play his class is studying, he overhears one student whisper to another, "He should've been an actor." Ask any social studies teacher to describe the facial expression of his students when their eyes light up with the feeling that now they understand why we entered two world wars. Ask any music teacher to tell you about the boy who confessed one day as he was leaving class, "You know, some of these records sound swell. How much does an album like the one you played today cost?" Ask any teacher how he feels when he finds that students at the end of the term have accepted so completely a point of view he has labored to develop that they speak as though the point of view were theirs rather than his.

If you are interested in your subject, teaching offers you a means of continuing your interest in the area. In effect the English teacher is subsidized by the community to continue becoming better acquainted with literature, the art teacher is subsidized for sharing his interests in art with young people, and the science teacher can continue his study without worrying about whether his piece of research has commercial possibilities.

As a teacher, you will be working with as pleasant a group of people as you are likely to find in any field. Your colleagues will be people with similar interests and similar goals. In most schools, teachers get along so well with each other—and you don't have to have much to do with the one or two you dislike—that teachers are reluctant to leave one school to go to another. Your principal is a different kind of employer, for tenure removes the threat of being fired as a factor in the relationship. Your students will sometimes be irritating and sometimes exasperating, but, by and large, you will enjoy so respected a position that you will have to be careful not to grow too conceited and smug.

Even the problems you face in teaching are problems you can respect. You aren't worried about how much you can charge for a pound of butter without losing customers. Instead, you puzzle over how you can help Mary Jane to be more sure of herself so that she will not have to be such an annoying show-off. You try to find a better way of broadening the vision of your students so they understand that other peoples have other cultures which should be respected and that the word *native* has no disparaging connotations for non-natives. You worry with Michael Jackson about what career he should follow so that he can use his undoubted gift for numbers. In teaching, you are never trying to outsmart other people, and there is genuine satisfaction in knowing that in instance after instance your students are better off because of you.

At your age you are undoubtedly so confident about the future that economic and social security seem trivial considerations. Later on you will appreciate the freedom that teaching will give you to live as you want to without worrying about whether the boss has a nephew whose eye is on your job or whether a recent graduate is ready to take your job at half your salary.

There are two important decisions you have to make. I hope that as you look back on your life ten, twenty, or forty years from today you will be able to say, "If I had my life to live over again, there are some things I'd do differently, but two things I'd do again, I'd marry the same person and I'd enter the same profession."

QUESTIONS FOR STUDY AND DISCUSSION

1. Miss D., a young teacher of English and social studies, was heartened by the cordiality of her new colleagues and by their evident desire to do everything possible to help her succeed. Mrs. B., the teacher in the adjoining room, was particularly cordial and dropped in to visit Miss D.'s class several times during the first day of the term to see how she was getting along.

After school, both teachers went to Mrs. B.'s apartment for some tea and a chat. Mrs. B. wanted to hear all about her new colleague's problems and made very definite suggestions as to the way in which these problems should be solved. Since she had taught most of these students last year, she explained that she knew exactly how these boys and girls should be treated.

The next afternoon, Mrs. B. walked home with Miss D. and asked how the day had gone. Not one to be satisfied easily with a vague answer, Mrs. B. questioned in detail the way in which her suggestions of the previous afternoon had been carried out. Before many days had gone by, Miss D. began to dislike these prolonged conversations. Miss D. wanted the opportunity to solve her problems in her own way. Although she appreciated Mrs. B.'s maternal interest in her, she preferred to be regarded as a regular teacher rather than as a little girl. What made the situation more difficult was that the two teachers were more than a generation apart in educational philosophy and the younger teacher did not approve of many of the suggestions which her senior colleague apparently expected her to accept unquestioningly.

What should Miss D. do?

2. A mathematics teacher in a senior high school invited his class at the end of the term to submit anonymously their frank evaluation of the work done in class that term. About half of the class responded to the invitation. Two of the students praised the clarity of the teacher's explanations and the friendliness of his manner. The comments made by the other students can be summarized best by the following excerpts which, in various forms, were repeated by many students: "Cut out the homework assignments you give." "Don't be such a tough marker." "Stop kidding yourself. We don't think this stuff is worth bothering with no matter how you teach it."

How can the teacher use these comments?

3. When the superintendent of schools learned that a music teacher was retiring in June, he engaged a recent college graduate to fill the vacancy. The prospective teacher spent several days with the present music teacher in order to be better informed about the kind of music program he could plan for the following year.

From this visit, the new teacher concluded that the present music program was limited almost entirely to prescribed music classes in which most of the time was spent singing songs and listening to a few well-worn records.

During an interview with the superintendent, the new teacher spoke of the much richer program he thought the school ought to have, although he was careful not to make any belittling comments about the veteran teacher who was retiring. He recommended that there be at least one advanced course in music for students who wanted more than the prescribed music courses. He suggested that the music teacher could do much to enrich the instruction in other classes. He spoke of the desirability of organizing a glee club, a school band, and an orchestra. In answer to the question of where he would find enough student musicians for both a band and an orchestra, he replied that he would be glad to give instrumental instruction to the boys and girls. The superintendent was pleased by the young man's enthusiasm and promised to co-operate fully.

After spending a busy summer getting materials ready, the teacher began his work with confidence and was pleased by the way in which his colleagues and his students responded to the new music program. He was busy the first week of the term and his days became even busier and more hectic as the weeks went by. At the end of his first month he realized that he was completely swamped and that he had planned much more than any single teacher could accomplish.

What should he do?

4. What was gained and what was lost by the teacher who regularly destroyed all his lesson plans at the end of each term so that he would not be tempted to get into the habit of teaching the same lessons year after year?

5. To what extent can a young teacher, who is starting his teaching career in an extremely conservative secondary school, plan to introduce any major educational innovations during his first year at that school?

6. To what extent can the teacher make any preparation in advance if he knows he is to be the seventh-grade teacher in a school that emphasizes the student planning and execution of units of work?

7. Assuming that you are to begin your teaching career this September in a specific secondary school with which you are familiar, how would you plan to spend your first day with your classes?

8. A young college graduate accepted an appointment to fill a vacancy created by the unexpected resignation of one of the teachers at the end of January. When he met his classes for the first time early in February, he was unable to account for the sullenness he sensed in most of his classes.

While having lunch with the other teachers that first day, the new teacher learned that the teacher who resigned had been extremely popular with his students and that his resignation had been requested by the superintendent who objected to the way this teacher sided with the students in their protests against various regulations promulgated by the superintendent when he assumed office a few months earlier. When the students heard that the teacher had been asked to resign, some of them began organizing a strike in his behalf and called off the strike only because he pleaded with them not to make it difficult for him to get another teaching position by giving him the reputation of being a troublemaker.

Now that the new teacher understands the background of his students' sullenness, what can he do about it?

BIBLIOGRAPHY

1. CANTOR, Nathaniel, *The Dynamics of Learning* (Buffalo, N.Y., Foster and Stewart, 1950).
2. CHASE, Mary Ellen, *A Goodly Fellowship* (New York, The Macmillan Company, 1939).
3. COHEN, Morris R., *A Dreamer's Journey* (Glencoe, Ill., The Free Press, 1949).
4. COVELLO, Leonard, *The Heart Is the Teacher* (New York, McGraw-Hill Book Co., Inc., 1958).
5. DAVIS, Billie, "I Was a Hobo Kid," *Saturday Evening Post*, Vol. 225, No. 24 (December 13, 1952), pp. 25, 107-108.
6. EGGLESTON, Edward, *The Hoosier Schoolmaster*, new and rev. ed. (New York, Orange Judd Co., 1902).
7. HIGHET, Gilbert, *The Art of Teaching* (New York, Alfred A. Knopf, Inc., 1950).
8. HILTON, James, *Goodbye, Mr. Chips* (Boston, Little, Brown and Co., 1934).
9. JERSILD, Arthur T., *When Teachers Face Themselves* (New York, Bureau of Publications, Teachers College, Columbia University, 1955).
10. LIEBERMAN, Myron, *Education as a Profession* (Englewood Cliffs, N.J., Prentice-Hall, Inc., 1956).
11. MEARNS, Hughes, *Creative Youth* (Garden City, Doubleday, Page, 1925).
12. PAGE, Walter H., *The School that Built a Town* (New York, Harper and Brothers, 1952).
13. PERRY, Bliss, *And Gladly Teach* (Boston, Houghton Mifflin Company, 1935).
14. PETERSON, Houston, *Great Teachers* (New Brunswick, Rutgers University Press, 1946).
15. SMILEY, Marjorie B., and DIECKOFF, John S., *Prologue to Teaching* (New York, Oxford University Press, 1959), pp. 3-123.
16. STUART, Jesse, *The Thread that Runs So True* (New York, Charles Scribner's Sons, 1949).
17. WEBER, Julia, *My Country School Diary* (New York, Harper and Brothers, 1946).
18. WELLS, H. G., *The Story of a Great Schoolmaster* (F. W. Sanderson), (New York, The Macmillan Company, 1924).

19. WILLIAMS, Emlyn, *The Corn Is Green* (New York, Random House, Inc., 1941).

Film

20. *Passion for Life* (New York, Brandon Films, 1952). In French, with English subtitles, 1 hr., 25 min.

APPENDIX

IN ORDER TO ILLUSTRATE the extent to which the improvement of secondary education concerns all countries, not only ours, we are reproducing below a recommendation which was adopted by the representatives of sixty-six nations at the Twenty-third International Conference on Public Education (Geneva, Switzerland, July 6–15, 1960) which was convened jointly by the United Nations Educational, Scientific, and Cultural Organization and the International Bureau of Education.

Teachers and administrators will be interested in noting both the resemblances between our problems of secondary education and those of the other nations, as well as the differences between their problems and ours.

RECOMMENDATION No. 50
TO THE MINISTRIES OF EDUCATION
concerning the
PREPARATION AND ISSUING
OF GENERAL SECONDARY SCHOOL CURRICULA*

The International Conference on Public Education,

Convened in Geneva by the United Nations Educational, Scientific and Cultural Organization and the International Bureau of Education, having assembled on the sixth of July, nineteen hundred and sixty, for its twenty-third

* Reprinted by permission of the International Bureau of Education, Geneva, Switzerland.

465

session, adopts on the fourteenth of July, nineteen hundred and sixty, the following Recommendation:

The Conference,

Considering the interest shown in the problem of school syllabuses by international bodies of an educational nature, and in particular by the International Advisory Committee on the School Curriculum set up by the United Nations Educational, Scientific and Cultural Organization,

Considering Recommendation No. 46 to the Ministries of Education on the preparation and issuing of the primary school curriculum, adopted on the fifteenth of July, nineteen hundred and fifty-eight, by the International Conference on Public Education at its twenty-first session,

Considering that the present intensive development of education at secondary level entails not only structural changes but also the readjustment of school curricula and syllabuses in the light of a great variety of national and international needs,

Considering that the reports submitted to the Conference by the Ministries of Education show that more than half the countries are at present working on the preparation or revision of secondary level curricula,

Considering that general secondary education, which was formerly the privilege of a minority, is now becoming available to an increasingly large number of children whose intellectual ability, social background and future occupation may be very varied,

Considering that the extension of secondary education to a wider range of children should not lead to a lower level of education and culture,

Considering that general secondary education should not be limited to the intellectual, moral, physical and aesthetic fields but should also prepare young people for life and for socially useful work,

Considering that the rapid progress of science and technology calls for broader modes of thought and new modes of action,

Considering that the total sum of human knowledge has increased, and is still increasing at an ever quickening pace, in the fields of science, literature and art,

Considering that the most widely accepted concept of general secondary education is based on a proper balance between the humanities and the sciences,

Considering that a recommendation of universal import cannot cover the many diverse theoretical aspects of the problem of general secondary school curricula, and that such a recommendation, to be effective, should be confined to the statement of concrete practicable measures,

Considering that, in spite of similar aspirations, countries in very different positions must reach varied solutions of the problem of the preparation and issuing of general secondary school curricula,

Submits to the Ministries of Education of the different countries the following Recommendation:

General Principles Governing the Preparation of Curricula

(1) When drawing up general secondary school curricula, the following points must be taken into consideration: (a) the various aims assigned to this type of education; (b) its structure, whether uniform in character or organized in stages and divisions; (c) the relative importance to be given to each subject or group of subjects; (d) the environment in which the pupils live and receive their education; (e) the pupils' capacity for assimilation and the needs and interests of their ages and sex.

(2) In the absence of absolute principles which may be accepted and profitably applied in all countries, it is nevertheless recommended that a proper balance should be maintained in the relative importance given in curricula and syllabuses to such things as the pupils' intellectual, moral, social, manual, physical and aesthetic education, in order to ensure the complete and harmonious development of the individual child.

(3) In order to achieve this balance, it is desirable to bear in mind when drawing up curricula the varied contribution which each subject can make not only to the pupil's store of factual knowledge, but also to the development of his personality and to his attitude to the world around him.

(4) It is important to give moral education the emphasis demanded by present-day conditions and to ask all teachers to stress the moral and social implications of what they teach and of the situations with which pupils may be confronted within and without the school community.

(5) The dual tendency to give more room in general secondary education to work and knowledge of a practical and vocational nature and to intensify the study of general subjects in secondary technical and vocational establishments should be encouraged.

(6) It is important when drawing up syllabuses to stress, though without adding a new subject to the curriculum, the contribution which the teaching of some subjects can make to good relations, peace and understanding between nations and races.

(7) General secondary school syllabuses should be considered as the natural sequel to those used in the primary school; it is therefore desirable that at the beginning of general secondary education and upon entrance to the upper stage, where one exists, allowance should be made in the curriculum for transition, in order that pupils may be spared excessive strain in readjusting themselves, which is a source of discouragement and failure.

(8) When preparing general secondary school curricula it is advisable to take into account, as far as possible without detriment to the normal educational development of the majority of pupils, the requirements of post-secondary establishments.

Principles Relating to the Structure of Education

(9) In countries where secondary studies cover two stages, curricula should take into account the aims allotted to each of these stages, the first

being more general in character and constituting the logical continuation and expansion of primary education, while the second provides an opportunity of giving prominence to some particular category of subjects and may act to some extent as a preparation for further education.

(10) In countries where the first stage of secondary education, either wholly or in part, is a period of general culture and guidance common to all the pupils—a solution which deserves to become more widespread—, the content and arrangement of the curriculum should allow for the pupils' choice of course and for selection by the teachers or specialists responsible for it.

(11) In countries where secondary studies comprise several divisions, and where the syllabuses used take into account the particular aims of each of these divisions, it is important to remember the more general aims of secondary education as a whole; in the same way, in countries where the curriculum provides a choice of subjects in order to take into account the pupils' needs, interests and abilities, it should be ensured that this differentiation does not take place to the detriment of subjects which are indispensable to the pupils' wider education.

(12) In countries where general secondary education does not comprise divisions and is therefore more uniform in character, it is desirable to allow for the greatest possible adaptation of the curriculum to the pupils' needs, interests and abilities.

(13) Courses should be so designed that at various points during their secondary schooling pupils may pass from one division to another, or from general to specialized education and vice versa.

Principles Relating to the Content of Syllabuses

(14) Syllabuses should be divided up into years of study, taking into account the appropriate objectives for each grade, the abilities, achievements and interests of pupils of various ages, and the actual time available for instruction.

(15) In order to be effective, general secondary school syllabuses should be within the capacity of the pupils in the classes for which they are intended.

(16) The content of the syllabus for any given subject should be in line with the particular aims pursued in the teaching of this subject and with the general aims of the stage or division in which it is taught.

(17) Fixing the relative importance to be given to each subject is a vital aspect of the preparation of curricula, and the allotments made should be periodically re-examined in the light of changing local conditions and the findings of recent educational research.

(18) It is clear that in the different divisions of general secondary education the subjects which constitute the core of the division must take the largest place, but this should not prevent other subjects from receiving the attention due to them, even when the secondary course terminates in a highly specialized examination.

(19) It is desirable to ensure that the syllabuses for the different sub-

jects are not separated into water-tight compartments, but that full use is made of the close relations which may exist between different subjects and of the opportunities they offer for supplementing each other, always providing that any unnecessary overlapping and repetition are avoided.

(20) The fairly common tendency to overload curricula and syllabuses, either by the introduction of new subjects or by expanding the content of each separate subject, presents a real danger; to avoid this, the introduction of new subject matter into the curriculum should be offset by the removal of other matter which has become of less importance, and syllabuses should offer a selection of essential topics rather than an accumulation of material.

Drafting Procedure

(21) Whichever authority is responsible for general secondary education, the preparation of curricula for this type of education should be the work of specialized bodies on which teachers should always be represented.

(22) It is essential that the preparation and revision of the syllabuses for each of the subjects taught at secondary level should be carried out mainly by specialists in the subjects concerned, with the reservation that in lower secondary education it may be preferable for several related subjects to be taught by the same person.

(23) When syllabuses are prepared by groups of specialists, it is desirable to ensure the coordination of these different groups, which should base their work on common principles and should consider themselves as constituent parts of the same whole.

(24) Work on the preparation of syllabuses should be coordinated not only as regards the different subjects in the general secondary school curriculum, but also in relation to preceding education, subsequent education and parallel types of secondary education; to achieve this coordination, it is essential to call in teachers from other branches (primary education, teacher training, technical and vocational education, higher education).

(25) It is important that the authorities responsible for the preparation of curricula should be able to call upon the advice of specialists in didactics and in the psychology of the adolescent.

(26) In order to link the school more closely with its cultural, social and economic environment, it is advisable that the parents and representatives of the different bodies which for various reasons are interested in general secondary education should have the opportunity of expressing their views on the curriculum.

(27) In view of the importance of psycho-pedagogical research in the preparation and revision of secondary school syllabuses, it is desirable that such research should be encouraged in suitably equipped centres, with the cooperation, as far as possible, of teachers who are interested in this type of work.

(28) Authorities responsible for the preparation of curricula should allow for a preliminary period of investigation, bearing, among other things, on:

(a) children's characteristics and rate of development at an age affected by the problems of adolescence; (b) significant scientific progress in the various fields covered by the subjects taught; (c) up to date information provided by both general and special didactics; (d) the scientific and educational training of the teachers involved; (e) current trends in the cultural, social and economic fields; (f) comparative studies of the syllabuses used in other countries; (g) the result of experiments carried out in this connection either within the country or abroad.

(29) Before curricula are finally accepted, they should if possible be tried out under expert supervision either in experimental schools or in carefully selected ordinary schools; in any case they should be introduced gradually, in order to facilitate such modification as may prove necessary.

Issuing Procedure

(30) In countries where curricula are issued by a central authority it is desirable that sufficient latitude should be given for their adaptation to regional or local requirements.

(31) In countries with a decentralized educational system it is advisable to encourage the various authorities responsible for issuing syllabuses to co-operate among themselves with a view to eliminating all unnecessary differences in the syllabuses for the various regions and thus to minimize the disadvantages arising from pupils' change of domicile.

(32) Although there are disadvantages in revising syllabuses at too close or too distant intervals, it should not be forgotten that the scientific progress achieved in some branches of knowledge requires that the corresponding syllabuses should be brought up to date more frequently than the syllabuses of other subjects.

Application

(33) In order to stress the close connection between method and content, it is desirable for curricula to include a brief account of the basic conception of the teaching of each subject and suggestions for teaching it based on the work done in the fields of educational psychology and experimental education.

(34) The issuing of new curricula should be the occasion of courses, lectures, pedagogical meetings, study groups, articles in the press, etc., so that teachers may be informed of the principles underlying the proposed changes.

(35) The pedagogical training of secondary school teachers should include both theoretical and practical familiarity with the syllabuses they will be called upon to use.

(36) It is desirable that syllabuses should be considered as a guide and a concrete aid rather than as a rigid set of regulations excluding due adaptation and reasonable liberty for the teacher.

(37) All suitable steps should be taken to ensure that textbooks should

correspond as far as possible to the new curricula, though without ignoring the expense which this involves.

(38) It is desirable to see that when curricula are changed the schools have at their disposal the special accommodation, equipment and the various teaching aids (laboratory apparatus, audio-visual aids, etc.) required for the application of the new curricula.

(39) In the application of the syllabus for any particular subject, it is important to remember the needs of those pupils whose rate of progress is slower or faster than that of the average; this objective can be achieved in a variety of ways including both special attention inside the classroom and extra activities outside school.

International Aspects of the Problem

(40) The increasing amount of movement from one country to another accentuates the problem of the equivalence of secondary level studies and qualifications; although no standardization of curricula is envisaged, an attempt should be made to achieve sufficient uniformity to facilitate the recognition of secondary studies pursued abroad.

(41) Contacts aimed at achieving greater uniformity in the terminology used to designate the subjects taught, or at enabling the preparation of comparative studies on the basic resemblances and differences between the curricula used in the different countries, should help to solve the problem of the equivalence of studies.

(42) As in the case of school textbook collections, international collections of curricula would be of prime interest not only to specialists in the preparation of curricula but also to education authorities and teachers; national, regional or international educational documentation centres should therefore be enabled to keep collections of this kind up to date.

(43) In plans for technical assistance, either national or international, it is desirable to include, for countries requesting such aid, the appointment of specialists who would play an active part in the preparation of curricula

INDEX